SOUL TO SISTERHOOD

*Sharing our Stories,
Sharing our Love*

Jamie Day

BALBOA.PRESS
A DIVISION OF HAY HOUSE

Copyright © 2021 Jamie Day.

All rights reserved. No part of this book may be used or reproduced by any means, graphic, electronic, or mechanical, including photocopying, recording, taping or by any information storage retrieval system without the written permission of the author except in the case of brief quotations embodied in critical articles and reviews.

Balboa Press books may be ordered through booksellers or by contacting:

Balboa Press
A Division of Hay House
1663 Liberty Drive
Bloomington, IN 47403
www.balboapress.com
844-682-1282

Because of the dynamic nature of the Internet, any web addresses or links contained in this book may have changed since publication and may no longer be valid. The views expressed in this work are solely those of the author and do not necessarily reflect the views of the publisher, and the publisher hereby disclaims any responsibility for them.

The author of this book does not dispense medical advice or prescribe the use of any technique as a form of treatment for physical, emotional, or medical problems without the advice of a physician, either directly or indirectly. The intent of the author is only to offer information of a general nature to help you in your quest for emotional and spiritual well-being. In the event you use any of the information in this book for yourself, which is your constitutional right, the author and the publisher assume no responsibility for your actions.

Any people depicted in stock imagery provided by Getty Images are models,
and such images are being used for illustrative purposes only.
Certain stock imagery © Getty Images.

Interior Graphics/Art Credit: Kristine Casart

ISBN: 978-1-9822-7273-9 (sc)
ISBN: 978-1-9822-7274-6 (e)

Print information available on the last page.

Balboa Press rev. date: 12/30/2021

Presents

Sharing Our Stories
Sharing Our Love

Written by:
Jamie Day

Transformed by:
_____

I am you.
You are me.
We are her.
She is we.
We are one.
The women in this book are you.
The resilience, strength, love, and wisdom in their stories is yours.
We feel it and recognize it within ourselves so that we can in turn share it and offer it to others.
Take the spark.
Grab it.
Embrace the flame of your own brilliance and light the way for me
so that I can remember mine, too.
We are Oracles.
We are Priestesses.
We truly do deserve all of the time, attention, and love that we give to everyone
and everything else.
Connect into the deepest recesses of your inner knowing and love yourself.
Do that!
With no explanations and no apologies.
Heal within so that you, Medicine Woman,
- and yes, Dear Sister, I am talking to *you* -
can heal all of the spaces and places in between.
Thank you.
I love you.

~Written and Conceived by **Jamie Day**~
~Photographs by **Kristine Casart**~
~Edited by **Misty Ross**~
~Oracle Card Art by **Connie Buckler**~
~Cover Art by **Paige Ramsay**~

Dear Sister,

Thank you for picking up and opening this book. Before we begin, please pause, close your eyes, and take a deep breath. Imagine that this book has a warm golden light surrounding it. As you hold it in your hands, feel the energy from each page spinning and weaving to create a connection with your heart. Feel that connection and visualize what it looks like. What information does it have for you? Take another deep breath and open your intuition even wider. Witness the golden thread now connecting your heart to the heart and Soul of every woman who has ever lived. Breathe deeply once again and, with what you *sense* about this book, *know* your intentions for working with it. Allow your truth to come forward as you gently and courageously claim what your heart is telling you.

What is this book all about? Great question. And go *you* for going for it and setting your intentions without really knowing what you are getting into! You are trusting your gut and that is something that we are going to be doing a lot of together. This is not a typical book. *Soul-to-Sisterhood* is a Love Letter to you and to all women everywhere throughout all time and space. This book isn't a story, although there are 36 stories of humanity told through the context of womanhood. This book isn't filled with epic prose designed to make your heart sing and your mind journey, although your mind and your heart will open. This book is a testament. An opportunity. A sort of *workbook* conceived with the intentions of providing assistance, support, and comfort as you transform, replenish, regenerate, and fall totally in love with yourself.

Each page reiterates the timeless, very true, yet often forgotten message: **You are never alone.** Finding ways to see yourself in every Story, Theme, and Sacred Play Suggestion is a high vibratory offering of collaboration and co-creation… almost like a sacred circle of encouragement for birthing your own unique map of self-compassion, self-dedication, self-loyalty, self-assuredness, and self-love.

This book is a lot and it can seem overwhelming. 180 Sacred Play Suggestions… 108 Themes… 36 Stories… 36 Crystals… 36 Book Titles for Suggested Reading… I know! I get it! I have danced with all of this for over two years. However, please don't approach this relationship with expectations, limitations, self-imposed timelines, guidelines, or responsibilities. Those things don't exist here. What exists between you and this book is now Sacred Space. From this moment forward, within this bubble of Divinely Feminine dedication, devotion, and love, let's agree to trust the process together. When you are ready, once again ground your intentions and finish the statement below.

My intentions for working with this book are:

_____

_____

_____

_____

OK, you've now got a very basic idea of what this book is about. If you are ready, jump in and go for it. If you want some more information, listen to your intuition and keep reading. That is how this entire project has come into being. With daily trust in Soul's guidance, I have been a Soul-led devotee of my Higher Self through every step of the book's creation. The number of Chapters, the layout, the Crystal Love, the Oracle

Cards... all of it has come to fruition and been incorporated without question. I offer this as support as you create your own personal practice with the text. It isn't homework. There aren't rules or regulations. The only direction I offer is to let this be an intuitively led creation process for personal empowerment, peace, and bliss. Don't feel like you have to read this book cover to cover. Don't feel like you have to start at the beginning. This is about you and your Greatest and Highest Good and the offerings here are meant to provide support for years to come.

Let's try it. Visualize that golden thread again and see it connecting you to this book and to all women everywhere throughout all time and space. Take a deep breath and let the book fall open on your lap. Let that page be a guide to whatever is there - Story, Theme, Sacred Play Suggestion, Crystal Love, Suggested Reading, or Glossary Word. Trust that whatever has come forward has presented itself - bespoke for you - at this moment, at this time, from your Soul for your Greatest and Highest Good.

That feels pretty juicy, doesn't it? Try it again. What do you notice? Are connections being made and needs being met by your own understanding of and relationship to your Higher Self? Hope so! Keep going and allow this pleasurable playfulness to fill your cup.

Now, if you *do* want to read this book cover to cover and do every activity in a certain amount of time, go for it! You do you. Plain and simple. You are the most important part of this entire equation. You, your needs, your processes, and your desires deserve to be honored, respected, valued, and met. Do this for yourself. However it looks and feels to honor and value your needs and desires... do it! Do it often and don't stop. In fact, do it now. What do you need and desire at this moment? Is it to keep reading this introduction or is it to let a Chapter find you? Whatever your answer, jump around, play, and have fun.

~Honesty~

Not every Story will resonate with you each time you open this book. The Themes may or may not strike your fancy on any given day. You might love some of the Sacred Play Suggestions and others you may not. Follow your heart. Only do what feels right *when* it feels right to do so. You may feel different tomorrow.

Some Stories and Chapters are shorter, and some are longer. This is intentional. You may have five minutes to work with the book, you may have an hour. Trust that what you need will make itself available to you within the timeframe you have. While they vary in length, all of the Stories and Chapters have been created with the same intentions and attention to detail.

Some Sacred Play Suggestions may seem similar and there are many that deal with relationships. Although all are unique, the similarities you sense in the activities are there to help you deepen the excavation process. Relationships, *especially* the crunchy ones, are our greatest teachers. The many Sacred Play Suggestions which focus on conflict resolution, empathy, and release are designed to offer comfort, support, and peace through the oftentimes complex and sometimes unpleasant journey. I know that we can receive completely new wisdom and guidance from something that we have read over and over depending on where we are at any given moment. My hope is that this experience translates and these activities offer you exactly what you need at exactly the right time, no matter if they feel familiar or not.

The Stories, Themes, and Sacred Play Suggestions are all created to a) remind you that you are never alone, b) remind you that you are loved and that this world is lucky to have you, and c) bring things to the surface for processing and transformation. Some things in this book will require more of your attention than others. That is the goal. If you find yourself needing additional support during your experience with *Soul-to-Sisterhood*, please, please find someone qualified to talk with. As a formerly licensed mental health clinician, I cannot say enough good things about therapy. I love therapy, I have a therapist, and I feel honored to have been a licensed therapist. Processing with another person as a neutral support system offers too many benefits to list here. Do your research, trust your heart, and love yourself enough to go deep - in a safe way - by securing additional assistance for reassurance and encouragement.

OK, final thing. While the women featured in this book are diverse in many ways, the lack of racial diversity is something that I have struggled with for a very long time. One Black Sister Goddess, three Latina Sister Goddesses, one Brazilian Sister Goddess, and two Swedish Sister Goddesses - among all the other White, American Sister Goddesses - doesn't really fill the pool of potential for Feminine perspectives… and I am right there with you. By calling this book *Soul-to-Sisterhood*, am I in any way insinuating that if you don't look like the women featured on these pages that you aren't part of 'The Sisterhood?' *Hell*-to-the-**no**! That couldn't be further from the truth. For me, Sisterhood transcends everything - color, race, creed, religion, politics, motherhood, ethnicity, etc. That does not mean that I don't see diversity, respect it, understand it, and honor it. I do and I want to learn more. I am a humble student and know that I need to experience more. However, for this book, by the very nature that we are women, we are connected. No, there is not a lot of colorful diversity in this book. That is the truth. But there ***is*** a lot of colorful and diverse life experience and that connects us all regardless of our differences. Have you ever lost someone and grieved so much you were sure your heartache had caused your heart to actually break? If so, your reflection is here on the pages of this book. Have you ever struggled with addiction, depression, anxiety, or suicidal thoughts? If so, you are here, Mama. Have you ever questioned that there must be more to intimacy, sex, authenticity, and female empowerment? If so, welcome Sister. Have you ever cried yourself to sleep at night, battling with the demands, restrictions, and punishments of living in a Patriarchal world? Aunt, Grandmother, Cousin… thank you for being here.

If you feel ire for me about the lack of diversity, I welcome it. Bring it to me and together let's dance a dance of co-creation and collaboration to rebirth a new understanding of Sisterhood. If you find yourself feeling angry and want to turn away from any potential opportunities for healing and transformation that this book may offer, turn-in. Let's find one another and, with a connection made Soul-to-Soul, conceive a new understanding of what *true* Sisterhood can look and feel like.

~Reasons~

The idea for this book came from a woman who shared with me that a marketing and promotional tool might be helpful for understanding my work. For her, Divine Mommy (the name I had given my women's groups) was a bit confusing and sort of a turn off because she thought I was doing a mommy-and-me type of playgroup. Once she learned about all that we did and explored in Divine Mommy, she suggested that a book of personal stories from participants would be a great way to explain what the groups actually were. As you can see, this idea has grown, and grown, and grown!

The women on these pages have all agreed to be a part of this very intimate, very authentic project and they are all way-showers in their own right. The energy of connection between myself and each S2S Sister Goddess is its own unique dynamic. I know these women. I love them. I respect them. I am inspired by them. Their stories remind me that I am a powerful, valuable, Medicine Woman as well. That is why they are here: to hold up the mirror for all of us and reflect the message that their strength *is* our strength. However, I felt that I couldn't maintain the energetic and spiritual integrity of this project if, during its creation, I sought out women to be a part of it with the motivation of ticking a box to be politically correct. These are my personal feelings and you might disagree. That is OK. Listen, I've already sort of mentioned that our Souls - yours and mine - *know* each other regardless of if we actually *know* each other. We are Sisters, right? Yet, being in this book - a physical, third dimension process which required a Sister hanging out her truth (*in written word*!) for all the world to see… I felt like we needed to know each other in the face-to-face kind of way for me to ask that. But our circle is by no means complete. We need you. All of you. These Stories of triumph - of extraordinary, everyday women triumphing over extraordinary things every day - they are just a tiny spark in the bright flame of Divine Feminine energy. An energy that each one of us possesses. We need each other and we need to come together for that spark to burn brighter, bigger, and higher. To me, that need is a primal, cellularly-held ancestral conviction of women supporting women, lifetime after lifetime after lifetime, no matter what. Will you join us?

I woke up from a long nap on my fortieth birthday. I had been sleeping the sleep of toxic femininity and I didn't even know. I was exhausted, brittle, and very close to not liking anything about myself when I was guided - pushed really - to go on a silent retreat for four days. That experience inspired me to start Divine Mommy. I came out of that silence knowing I knew something - not exactly quite sure what the *something* was - but feeling the invisible pull to create an opportunity for women to fall back into love and appreciation with themselves.

A year and a half later, I read *Shakti Woman: Feeling Our Fire, Healing Our World, The New Female Shamanism* by Vicki Noble and my soul cracked open. I was reading on an international flight, and as I devoured the book, I wept. The whole eight hours, I cried, snotted, and snorted. I was being filled with information that felt like a hot, familiar lava flowing through my veins. Yes, I had been awakened from the sleep, but I was still walking and talking through the filters of repression, denigration, and the silent - yet culpable - acceptance of the Feminine being inferior to the Masculine. It was a total 'holy-what-the-fucking-shit' moment.

I got home and shifted gears. I found Vicki and went to study with her. I consumed countless other books and works by Female Shamans, Feminine way-showers, and teachers of the Divine Feminine. I began to craft a new type of curriculum to share what I was learning, and I started this book. For the last five years, I have walked the walk and talked the talk to share this information. I haven't stopped, and I won't. For one more day I cannot live within the walls of a life that casually calls people a "pussy" when they aren't being brave, cool, or strong. I refuse to honor a way of being that silently or otherwise tells boys, girls, men, and women "You run like a girl… throw like a girl… fight like a girl… etc." as a pejorative explanation for doing something that is considered less-than. I reject any more flippantly voiced comments about how surprising it is when a woman becomes successful. Never again will I stand for the shaming and double standards around Feminine sensuality and sexuality. No way no how will I ever again feel the need to hide my beautiful and powerful menstrual cycle. And never, never, never again will I be a mean girl. I vow to burn the fields of gossip, back-biting, and tearing another Sister down for anything done for any reason - conscious or otherwise - to relieve my pain, gain approval, or improve my status. That bullshit has been going on for way too long. It has gotten us here. It has to stop.

That is why I tell you that I love you and that I am grateful for you at the end of every Sacred Play Suggestion. All 180 of them! If you do nothing else with this text, flip through and read the last few sentences of each Chapter's Sacred Play Suggestions. If nothing resonates with you about this book, you at least have many,

many reminders of how loved and valuable you are. I had a friend that used to challenge me when I told people that I loved them. He would ask, "How can you love everybody? That isn't possible." I respectfully disagree. I am an energetic being, as are you and every living thing. My goal is to live in love-consciousness. For me, that means identifying gratitude and expressing love energy all. the. time. in *every* way. Am I consistently successful in doing this? No. I'm still working on it. But for me, being open and honest about how I value you, your time, and your interaction with this book is important. Like I said, even though we may not *know* each other, our Souls recognize and understand the mutual importance and significance of one another; for that I want to reiterate the message that I do love you and I am very grateful for you. If you weren't you and I wasn't me - no matter how we engage on the physical plane - we wouldn't be here working together to love, heal, and transform ourselves so that we may go forth and compassionately love, heal, and transform our worlds. We've got big work to do together, Sister. You might as well hear that you are valued and loved over and over. Let it be a sweet reminder to keep your self-love and self-care cup as full as possible.

Now, does all of this mean that I don't like men or the Masculine? I'll quote myself for the answer: *Hell*-to-the-**no**! I love men! I love the Masculine. I love both the Masculine and Feminine energies inherent and alive within every living thing. Although for me, looking to find fault and assign blame isn't what I am focused on. Yes, I do think it is wildly empowering and beneficial to understand how we got here, and the writers featured in this book are a great place to begin your own discovery process of *Our*story. Reading and studying the perspectives of Feminist Herstorians dedicated to the authentic research and history of the Matriarchal Societies from which most of our earliest ancestors originated has been invaluable in my healing from the wounding of a Patriarchal world and *his*tory. With first-hand experience of what it feels like to be a girl and woman raised and living in the Western World, I can definitely speak to the liberation and transformation I felt when discovering the Divine Feminine. However, this does not make me feel like fighting men, because I see our existence today as one of every living thing being deeply wounded by the denigration of the Feminine. Yes, from what I understand, since the Bronze Age, the men have traditionally been the ones in power, and that power has violently brutalized the Feminine. Yet, I don't see this from the context of men against women. I know I speak from the luxury of not having been burned or tortured in this lifetime merely for being a woman. I do. But for this work, I see us all as Souls embodying our own unique footprint of both the Masculine and Feminine. I also *feel us* as *Souls* - and that includes everyone - crying out for healing and balance. Yes, the Feminine has been deeply and viciously wounded. So has the Masculine. The closest and perhaps most devastating place to witness this is within the dynamic of the family. Have we gotten this right yet? I know there are many great families out there, and this is by no means a blanket swath of judgment. But the breakdown of the lives of our children, those little beings that eventually turn into adults and get to either save or destroy the world one day… let's shift this so that we can make their lives better. Let's heal ourselves for our future. Let's do the work of recalibrating, rebalancing, revaluing, and regenerating all of the aspects of the Divine Feminine and Divine Masculine. Let's create a better world within so that we can create a better world for all.

As a woman, I know our power, ladies. The more I study and experience, I see, feel, witness, and believe in our abilities to fully embody our Inner Goddesses. Damn, we are so beautiful, creative, psychic, talented, fertile, connected, and wise! We are Priestesses. We are Oracles. We are Medicine Women. We are Crone, Maiden, Mother, and Enchantress all in one. We are the life-givers, sustainers, nurturers, and comforters. We are strong, resilient, and cyclical beings. We must remember this. We must step into this empowerment. We must give birth to this new way of being - this new paradigm of love - because as women it is our birthright… and we need each other! We are so much stronger together, and that is why we have been systematically - with surgical-like precision - cut away from one another. That has to stop. If you are reading this, you are here, and you are ready. Our Divine Purposes may not be exact replicas of one another's, but they are intersecting now. I ask again with the utmost humility and respect – please join us. Join us in creating a new world. A world that honors, embodies, actualizes, and expresses our very good and very loving *humanness* simultaneously through our differences and similarities… through our Feminine and Masculine… through our authenticity and compassion… through our needs and desires… through our hopes and dreams. How we got to where we are is no one's fault, but Sisters, this is our opportunity to shift it. Through our capacity for stepping into our Inner Divinity as women, as light bearers, as ceremonialists, as way-showers, as Mothers giving birth to this new way of being, we can heal the Feminine within ourselves so that we can unquestionably, unequivocally, undeniably, and unconditionally ask the Masculine to join us. It is in this space *together* that we will heal our family, our entire Human Family, our entire Earth Family, and beyond.

Phew! OK, if you decide to put the book down now, thank you. If you are still with me and choose to keep reading, thanks to you, too. Both are acts that honor *you*, and that is where we start… honoring our needs, intuition, and instincts. Alright, let's talk structure. I've already mentioned that the only way to go about creating a working relationship with this material is to create your own way. Take a moment and define this for yourself. On the first page of the introduction, you wrote your intentions for working with this book. Let's do that again and add to it how you feel called to make this book your own personal Sacred Object. Just like Crystals, Oracle and Tarot Card Decks, Journals, etc., this book is now yours and ready to continue the energetic bonding process to deepen your connection. The pages of this book have been created to host and hold your transformation through your journaling and artwork. What do you feel called to create as an invitation for all of this to enter into your consciousness? How can you facilitate a Soul-to-Soul connection between yourself and this book? Take a moment to explore this by finishing the sentence below.

My Intentions and Ideas for Creating a Soul-to-Soul Connection with this Book are…

_____

_____

_____

_____

_____

~Process~

Wow! Thank you for taking the time to get clear about this. Let's head into some particulars about how the Stories came into being. Like I said before, not every Story will resonate with you every time. These came about from a recorded interview process in which each Sister Goddess and I had a conversation that lasted anywhere from 45 minutes to two hours. After the photo shoot and interview, I transcribed the conversation and came up with around eight to twelve pages of text. Then, I sat at my computer, Aligned and Attuned with each woman Soul-to-Soul, and asked to be led as to how best to craft their Story. Since we seldom talk and share in an order that is chronological (we skip around, tangent, and circle back on topics and points of interest), I never changed the intention of what someone said, but I shifted content around for a flow that followed a storytelling format of beginning, middle, and ending. After I had a first draft, I would call each Sister Goddess and read their Story to them. At that time, we made revisions together. My promise to each woman has been that they lead this process in order to feel authentically represented in both their truth and their participation in the project. After the first round, some Sisters were fine with their Stories, while others had multiple revisions. Some rewrote their Stories entirely, and some we rewrote together. After all of that, they picked their picture, the piece was edited for grammar, and then a final proofread was done for any remaining typos.

There are 36 Chapters because three plus six equals nine, which is a very sacred number to me and to many others. Nine is a number of Divine Perfection, completion, the final number of our base 10 numerical system, and is composed of three trinities: 3 + 3 + 3 = 9. It is also the number which is represented in the Sacred Mantra Practice of chanting 108 times (1 + 0 + 8 = 9) around the Mala. I did this chanting practice many times while studying with my teacher, Vicki Noble. This practice has remained very special to me, not only because of my respect and love for Vicki, but also because of the balance and empowerment I feel when chanting. I was also super excited to learn that the number 36 has special meanings in the Jewish Tradition. A very generous and loving man - who is a Drama Therapy Association Board Certified Trainer and was my mentor to becoming a Registered Drama Therapist - agreed to read over the Sacred Play Suggestions in the book that are Drama Therapy based. He asked about my decision to have 36 Chapters and shared with me that the Jewish people have a custom of assigning a numerical value to each letter of the Hebrew alphabet. Sometimes this custom also assigns meaning to these numbers. According to him, the word Chai (not the word for Indian tea, but pronounced with the guttural *ch*) is spelled חי, means "life," and is represented by the number eighteen. For many Jewish people, it is customary to give monetary gifts in multiples of eighteen for birthdays, Bar or Bat Mitzvahs, weddings, or other special occasions, to add extra meaning to the gift. Therefore, giving gifts of $36 (*twice* Chai) symbolizes a wish for the person to have a "double life." Even more exciting is the belief outlined in the Talmud as to Lamed Vav Tzadikim, which translates to "36 righteous ones." This is said to be a notion rooted in more mystical Judaism and is understood to mean that there are 36 special people in our world at all times. If these "just souls" are not present - meaning that if even one of them was missing - the world as we know it would come to an end. Every generation has these 36 special people who "greet the Shechinah," otherwise known as the Divine Presence or the Divine Feminine.

I mean… wow! I didn't *know* all of this, but I *knew* it in my bones that this book had to feature 36 Chapters. I even had a good friend pull out of the project at the final hour. I was devastated. The whole yucky situation was devastating, and it threw me into a pretty sad state for quite a while. During this low period, I vacillated back and forth on keeping the book at the 35 Chapters. I did not have the energy or heart space to ask one more Sister, to do one more interview, to compose one more Story, to come up with three more Themes and five more Sacred play Suggestions. That is, until I *did* have the energy. Around this time, I reconnected with a friend. While walking together on the beach I told her about the project, explained what had happened, and asked her to be the 36th Goddess. Without a hitch, she said yes, and it was pure perfection. She is an amazing addition and I got back to my sacred number. Woot-Woot!

I've already mentioned about the 108 Themes, which also gets us to the magickal number of 9, and the 180 Sacred Play Suggestions which - you guessed it - bring us to 9 as well. I wasn't even thinking of this when I was listening to my Higher Self help me to craft the structure of the 'Making This Story Your Own' sections in the book. My internal monologue was more like, "Seriously… this is gonna take fo-evah!" But I did it, and I am so glad that I did because the magickal energy of Soul's Guidance is all over this work.

On that note, let's address the whole magic with a 'k' situation. A good friend of mine said it best when she explained how 'magick' offers a more esteemed connotation to honor the beautiful, organic, orgasmic, and mysterious aspects of the Feminine. As opposed to the word *magic* - a term used to describe slight of hand tricks - *magick* invites us into the inexplicable, mercurial, and powerful world of femininity and the Divine Feminine. Alternately light and dark, regenerative and destructive, wild and nurturing, soft and empowered, the magick of the Feminine is intoxicating, sensual, brilliant, unmatched, and the most sought-after energy throughout all of time. That is why, when referring to us and our gifts, I spell the word *magic**k***.

So, what happens when you open the book and then close it again because you don't even know where to start? Let me see if I can help. I shared three of the Sacred Play Suggestions with a woman who had spoken to me about some things she was dealing with in her life. I mentioned that the self-directed activities in the book might be helpful. She was eager to give them a try and I told her to let me know when she had worked through them so that we could do some additional processing together. A little over a week went by and I heard nothing. By this time, I was wondering what could have happened. Did she hate them? Did her dog eat them? Had she won the lottery and bounced to Fiji? Finally, she expressed feeling resistant to the material and didn't really know why. Ah crap… bad feedback. A year or six months ago this might have sent me into a negative spiral. But not now. Not today. Nope. I was ecstatic! Resistance was wonderful! It was a land of opportunity and offered us a chance to dig deeper. If we could dance with resistance a little bit, I knew we were going to mine some gold. She was able to share with me that looking over the activities put her right back into the role of feeling like the kid in school who just couldn't cut the mustard. She was overwhelmed with thoughts and feelings that she needed to make her work something *more* - more meaningful, more spiritual, more deep - and that left her feeling like a student who couldn't finish her homework.

There is that word again - homework. Only, hey girl, *haaay,* newsflash reminder: this material isn't homework. This is an entertaining, experiential, and interactive invitation to fall in love with yourself. There is no right or wrong way to do that. There is only **your** way. If you only feel called to crack open one chapter and read one Story, you get a gold star. If you are sort of *'eh'* about the whole thing and find a few Themes that are helpful, you get a gold star. If you love every piece of this book and work your way through all of the Stories, Themes, and Sacred Play Suggestions… yep, you get a gold star, too. If this book only sits on your bookshelf until you decide to sell it at your garage sale in a few years, boom! Gold star for you! Follow your heart and let this book serve you in whatever way feels best.

~Resistance~

There, now with that off of our chests, let's get back to business. Resistance is totally normal and natural. Who has the time to work through all of this stuff? There are a million really good reasons why this book is too much. It's too deep. It's too heavy. There's too many questions. There's too many steps. It's too time consuming. It's too weird. It's too different. Honey, I've been told my entire life that I am *too much*. As a kid I needed too much attention and I asked too many questions. As I got older, I was too bold. As I became socially aware, I realized that I was too pretty, too smart, or too strong to fit in. When I started working professionally as an actor - *puh-lease* - where to start? I was too sexy, too loud, too old, too young, too blonde, too curvy, too tall. The list could go on. And if I am too much of something, I am *not* enough of something else. That doesn't fit for me anymore. So, babe, if you've ever been told that you are too much or not enough, let's meet in the middle and Goldilocks our 'just right' together. That goes for your work on the page, too. The woman I mentioned above told me all of her initial answers felt too simple. She was holding these crazy expectations over her head to be something *else*, something other than her natural, sweet, quirky, and intuitive self. Shit, honey… *that* is what we don't have time for! If you are feeling this way at all, quickly turn to **Pearle's Chapter** and do **Sacred Play Suggestion #5:** *Dance Time* on page 202. Get your groove on and shake that *too-much-not-enough-ness* out!

OK, better? Good. From this moment forward, the journaling, art, musings, and processing on these pages are yours. No matter what comes up and out, ***all*** of it is worthy, brilliant, deep, meaningful, needed, valuable, cool, amazing, and awesome. Trust that these things are coming in from your Higher Self and that they are presenting themselves for your Greatest and Highest Good. Go fast through the material or go slow. Take whatever time feels right to you. If resistance comes up, good. What is your resistance telling you? Is it yours, or is that someone else's voice in your head? If resistance is there and you feel in your heart that this material isn't for you full stop, way to go, Sister! Congrats on living your truth. If resistance is present and yet there is also just the tiniest of tugs at your consciousness to keep going for whatever reason, keep going! Trust yourself. Trust your Higher Self. Trust the process. Your resistance could be there so that when you don't feel it anymore, you have a more compelling story regarding the efficacy of the work. And, you just might feel inspired to share.

Yes. That is one of my main visions for all of this. My prayer is that this book becomes a transitive inspirational tool for connection. If a Story, Theme, or Sacred Play Suggestion resonates with you, chances are you know someone else for whom it might resonate as well. Call them up and share it with them. Invite them over and go through the material together. My editor came up with the idea of shifting around the concept of 'Game Night' and hosting a 'Soul Night' where she invites a circle of girlfriends over to work through a section of the book. Can you imagine how connected your 'Ladies Night Out' might be if you all read through and discussed a Theme together before leaving the house? If you have ever felt called to start a women's group but didn't feel like you had enough material, now you've got 180 reasons to lead! Take this work and make it yours. Mold it… fashion it… redesign it… and most important - **use it**. Most everything in here can translate to group work and couples work and some Sacred Play Suggestions are just downright fun to do with the fam. Trust your gut and go for it!

~Layout~

FYI… additional information on the words that look like this in each chapter can be found in the juicy Glossary at the back of the text. As I say back there, these definitions fit with *my* usage of the word, term, or concept. They may not line up with your definition or what you have been taught is the meaning of these things. That's OK. I'm not trying to change your mind; I'm just trying to give you a better idea of where I am coming from.

There are also places at the end of some Chapters where there is an extra page for journaling and going through the Sacred Play Suggestions a second, third, or twentieth time. Use this space as you need. It is there for you and doesn't have to go with any particular chapter. And truthfully, that extra space is the serendipitous byproduct of formatting. Go figure, huh?

Several of the Sacred Play Suggestions are meditative. Since I'm not there hanging out so that we can do these meditations together, ask yourself what you need in the moment to better facilitate your experience. You can read the guided meditations either silently or out loud and actively experience them as you read and speak. You can record yourself reading them and play them back. You could even do them with a friend and take turns facilitating. Option number three is my fav because I like thinking about you and your girls getting together to vibe one another up!

In loads of places in this book, I say 'The Greatest and Highest Good.' When I write this, I really do mean, what is the Greatest and Highest Good that can come about for you and for every living thing? The only catch is, the Greatest and Highest Good isn't about what our Ego wants; it is about what our Soul needs. It is channeled in from our Divinely Feminine intuition and instinct. This is about what our Higher Self directs us toward in order to express our truth, authenticity, and self-love so fiercely that we inspire others to do the same. Give it a whirl. Remember, let it (whatever *it* is) flow easily without judgment or criticism. Breathe, put your pen to the paper, and let your Higher Self do the talking.

What is My Greatest and Highest Good at this moment at this time?

_____

_____

_____

_____

_____

~Crystal Love~

Last two orders of business before giving you a rundown of ideas for when to use the 180 Sacred Play Suggestions (SPS). Let's chat about the Crystal Love sections and the Soul-to-Sisterhood Oracle Cards. Like everything in this book, the guidance for each Chapter to be connected to the medicine of a Crystal presented itself and I obliged without question. However, the process of pairing the Chapters and the Crystals started way before the Crystal Love sections were even a conscious thing. At home I have a big bowl of Crystals that I incorporate into my work. Even though I know them all and have knowledge of their healing powers, over a year ago I was guided to create a written document of each Crystal's beneficial properties. I actually fussed and crabbed my way through the entire thing. It took forever because I have about 150 Crystals in that bowl, and for the life of me I couldn't figure out why I was being called to shift my focus away from writing the book to create a personalized document on the specific healing powers of the Crystals. That is, until I *did* figure it out. When the clear message came in to offer a Crystal Love section correlating the wisdom - or *medicine* - of each woman's journey to that of the healing medicine of the Crystals, I was totally prepared. I Aligned and Attuned with each woman, (to get a better idea of this process, turn to **Kialey and Kristin's Chapter** and read through **Sacred Play Suggestion #1:** *Higher Self to Higher Self* on page 442) and then sat with my hand in the bowl of Crystals. Eyes closed, I asked for the Crystal Wisdom to present itself for the Greatest and Highest Good. When given the nudge that the time was right, still with eyes closed, I would pull a Crystal from the bowl and trust that it was the right one for that Chapter. I let each woman know the Crystal that had chosen her story, and then gifted her that Crystal from my bowl.

For right now, since the book is printed in black and white, I've opted to keep pictures and other information about the Crystals on the website. If you want a little more visual stimulation, head on over to www.soul-to-sisterhood.com and click on 'The Cards and Crystals' tab.

~S2S Oracle Card Deck~

As for the Soul-to-Sisterhood Oracle Card Deck, I am so excited about these cards that I can hardly stand it. If you aren't already familiar with this companion product, get ready to have some p-l-e-a-s-u-r-e! Each of the 36 Stories is being turned into a juicy and gorgeous work of supportive and empowered art. With wisdom taken directly from the women featured in the book, you can play and journey with these Oracle Cards in whatever ways that strike your fancy. In addition to the 36 Cards representing the Stories, there are also Cards to represent the four archetypes of the Divine Feminine: Crone, Maiden, Mother, and Enchantress, and four cards to represent the archetypes of the Divine Masculine: King, Warrior, Lover, and Magician. Anybody counting? That gets us to 44 cards, which is a beautiful number… but wait, there is a 45th Card! The Rose Quartz Card of Unconditional Love. You know what that gets us, right? $4 + 5 = \_\_\_\_$? Yep, we are in the lovelight of number 9.

When you have the deck, play with it in any way that you want. Thinking about how to connect the two - the Book and the Cards - I came up with an idea that you might like. Shuffle your Cards and connect your energy to their energy. As you do this, imagine the wisdom of Sisterhood being washed over you in a comforting, warm glow. When you are ready, pick your first Card and place it face up. This is your first port of entry into the experience. If you have chosen a Sister Goddess, go to her Chapter and read her Story. If you pull a Divine Feminine or Divine Masculine Card, look at the list of Divine Feminine and Divine Masculine Sacred Play Suggestions highlighted in the SPS Site Map on page 20 and choose to do the first one that jumps out at you. If you pull the Rose Quartz Card, let the book fall open and read that Chapter's Crystal Love section. After reading about the Crystal, if you'd like to dig deeper, turn to **Jamie's Chapter** and do **Sacred Play Suggestion #4:** *Crystal Force Field* on page 561.

Now, if you have the time, keep going and pull three more Cards. In the order that you chose them, place them in a second row underneath the first. This second tier of Goddess Energy is to direct you to the wisdom of the 108 Themes. If you have pulled one of the Divine Feminine or Divine Masculine Cards, or the Rose Quartz Card, repeat the instructions from the paragraph above. However, if you have pulled a Sister Goddess Card as the first Card, go to her Chapter and read her first Theme. For the second Card, if you've pulled a Sister Goddess Card, go to her Chapter and read the second Theme. Same thing for the third Card. Whatever Cards you pull, know that this wisdom is from your Higher Self and offers an opportunity for perspective and guidance at this particular moment. Trust that this is coming in *for* your Greatest and Highest Good so that you can *bring about* the Greatest and Highest Good. Capische?

Alrighty Aphrodite, ready for row three? This time pull 5 Cards and get ready for some SPS (Sacred Play Suggestion) love to come your way. In the order that you pulled them, place your Cards face up below the second row. Same thing as above if you've pulled a Divine Feminine, Divine Masculine, or the Rose Quartz Card. If you've pulled a Sister Goddess Card for any of the five Cards, the Sacred Play Suggestions of that particular Sister's Chapter are calling you. For the first Card of this third row, if you have pulled the 'Jacki Card,' go to Jacki's chapter and do the *first* **Sacred Play Suggestion:** *Heart to Heart*. If you pulled the 'Stella Card' for your *second* Card, go to Stella's Chapter and do **Sacred Play Suggestion #2:** *Kintsugi*. If for your *third* Card, you've pulled the 'DeWanda Card,' go to DeWanda's Chapter and do the third **Sacred Play Suggestion:** *Wasband*. Same thing for Cards four and five. (*BTW*…it is beyond exhilarating to put this all together in this way! Thanks for being here with me, Sister. Love you!)

Finally, pull one last Card and place it face up beneath row three. Whichever Card you pull, know your Higher Self is going to guide you in the process. If it is a Sister Goddess Card, read her Story and reflect on the Themes. If you have a Divine Feminine or Divine Masculine Card, go to the Glossary, read the definition of that Archetype, and jot down whatever comes to mind. If you have pulled the Rose Quartz Card, take a moment and journal about how you are going to show yourself Unconditional Love.

As always, working with the cards in this way is just a gentle suggestion. Work with them in whatever way you want. Just the wisdom presented on each one of them through the words and the beautiful imagery is plenty! I only offer the above as an option. However, please, please, please create your own way of energizing, working with, relating to, and connecting the Cards to the Book... and of course that includes your own unique brand of magick for connecting the Cards and the Book to *you*!

Thank you. I can't express my gratitude enough. Please don't hesitate to get in touch if you need anything. You can email me at: jamie@divine-mommy.com or find us on our website: www.soul-to-sisterhood.com. Feedback and constructive criticism are always welcome. Meanness and destructive assholism, not so much. If you fall into that second category, go to **Mary Lu's Chapter** and do **Sacred Play Suggestion #3: *Higher Self Support*** on page 187 to transform that bad juju into something more productive.

OK Sister, with the intentions of peace, love, and more blissful orgasms, I say goodbye for now....

Love you.

Love,
-jamie

☺ *Suggestions* for Sacred Play Suggestions (SPS) ☺

Body Movement and Wisdom

*Feel the love from your cells in **SPS #2:** *Cellular Town Hall* in Lynn's Chapter, p. 8
*Get cozy and clear with **SPS #5:** *Skin-to-Skin* in Shelby's Chapter, p. 86
*Hear your hands in **SPS #4:** *Hands* in Jamie's and Kery's Chapter, p. p. 140
*Draw where you feel, know, hide, and show in **SPS #4:** *Body Wisdom* in Pearle's Chapter, p. 201
*Birth magick today with **SPS #1:** *Idea Children* in Jennifer's Chapter, p. 230
*Up your energy with **SPS #2:** *Thymus Thump* in Emilie's Chapter, p. 245
*Open and transform with **SPS #4:** *Soft Belly* in Kim's Chapter, p. 316
*You ask and your body answers in **SPS #1:** *Body Talk* in Matilda's Chapter, p. 389
*Get into your body with **SPS #3:** *Intentional Movement* in Kei's Chapter, p. 155
*Receive hope and inspiration in **SPS #2:** *5-Pointed Star* in Elizabeth's Chapter, p. 210

Chakra Balance and Sacred Chants

*Meet a major Minor in **SPS #3:** *Alta Balance* in Sarah's Chapter, p. 96
*Activate your Heart Chakra with **SPS #4:** *I AM Love* in Connie's Chapter, p. 258
*Sing out and sing free with **SPS #2:** *Mantra* in Pat's Chapter, p. 106
*Spiral around your Energy Centers in **SPS #3:** *Kundalini Rising* in Kristin's Chapter, p. 344
*Open your heart with **SPS #4:** *New Love Mantra* in Kristin's Chapter, p. 346
*Breathe, chant, and birth in **SPS #4:** *Breath of Fire* in Matilda's Chapter, p. 392
*Rebirth your Superpowers with **SPS #2:** *Sacral Chakra* in Mindy's Chapter, p. 462
*Anchor and Align in **SPS #4:** *Earth Star Chakras* in Monika's Chapter, p. 488
*Attune your Centers in **SPS #4:** *Equal Energy* in Stella's Chapter, p. 542

Creativity Connection

*Get you inner poet laureate on with **SPS #5:** *Black Out Poetry* in Lynn's Chapter, p. 17
*Draw from both sides in **SPS #2:** *Heart Art* in Shelby's Chapter, p. 82
*Wear the rainbow in **SPS #3:** *Color Gift* in Jacqui's Chapter, p. 171
*Try out your magick wand in **SPS #1:** *Heart Healing* in Pearle's Chapter, p. 197
*Fire up your awareness with **SPS #3:** *Creative Goddess* in Elizabeth's Chapter, p. 212
*Super charge your heart with **SPS #2:** *Love Heals* in Connie's Chapter, p. 255
*Step into your younger self with **SPS #3:** *Fairy Tale* in Allison's Chapter, p. 269
*Give and receive in **SPS #3:** *Compliments* in Monika's Chapter, p. 486
*Celebrate your perfect imperfection with **SPS #2:** *Kintsugi* in Stella's Chapter, p. 540

Dramatic Purge

*Create relief for father energy in **SPS #4:** *Stepping-In* in Lynn's Chapter, p. 15
*Rewrite your roles in **SPS #3:** *Role Change* in Pat's Chapter, p. 108
*Know the unknown in **SPS #1:** *Tele* in Kei's Chapter, p. 150
*Reveal your true self with **SPS #4:** *Inside-Outside* in Allison's Chapter, p. 271
*Open to endless possibilities in **SPS #3:** *Yes, And…* in Michelle's Chapter, p. 284
*Recast guilt and blame in **SPS #1:** *Extraordinary Life* in Nisla's Chapter, p. 293
*Set the stage in **SPS #4:** *Really Talk, Really Listen* in Kialey's and Kristin's Chapter, p. 446
*Become your own best influencer in **SPS #1:** *Four Corners* in Mindy's Chapter, p. 458

Elevate your Environment

*Create your Sacred Space with **SPS #1:** *Temple of Goodness* in **Krissy's Chapter**, p. 52
*Honor your living space in **SPS #3:** *Sweet and Sacred Objects* in **Shelby's Chapter**, p. 84
*Get some fab Feng Shui with **SPS #1:** *Five Elements* in **Jacqui's Chapter**, p. 167
*Promote daily prayer opportunities with **SPS #5:** *Prayer Basket* in **Kristin's Chapter**, p. 347
*Construct a Divine Design in **SPS #3:** *Mandantra* in **Jaana's Chapter**, p. 357
*Spruce up your space with **SPS #2:** *Gratitude Tree* in **Kialey's and Kristin's Chapter**, p. 444
*Purify and illuminate in **SPS #4:** *Fire* in **Mindy's Chapter**, p. 468
*Speak and infuse your valuable prayers in **SPS #5:** *Seven Directions* in **Stella's Chapter**, p. 544

Energy is Everything!

*Gauge your emotional energy with **SPS #4:** *Bliss-Bundle-Scale* in **Jacqui's Chapter**, p. 174
*Embrace your Inner Guru with **SPS #3:** *Higher Self Support* in **Mary Lu's Chapter**, p. 187
*Raise your daily energy with **SPS #5:** *Intentions* in **Mary Lu's Chapter**, p. 191
*Shift what you say, hear, and think in **SPS #1:** *Positive Thoughts* in **Emilie's Chapter**, p. 244
*Create a new habit with **SPS #1:** *Prayer Power* in **Connie's Chapter**, p. 253
*Receive messages from the Spirit World in **SPS #5:** *Spirit Messages* in **Michelle's Chapter**, p. 288
*Swing your support efforts with **SPS #4:** *Sympath-Empath* in **Elizabeth D.'s Chapter**, p. 432
*Get things moving with **SPS #5:** *Chi* in **Kialey's and Kristin's Chapter**, p. 450
*Plentifully realize in **SPS #5:** *Money Mantras* in **Monika's Chapter**, p. 493
*Embody your pure potential with **SPS #4:** *Crystal Force Field* in **Jamie's Chapter**, p. 561

Friendships and Feelings

*Go big and bold with **SPS #4:** *Feelings* in **Shelby's Chapter**, p. 85
*Try out life-sized authenticity in **SPS #2:** *Authentic Self* in **DeWanda's Chapter**, p. 122
*Shift feeling into a chosen way of being with **SPS #4:** *Embodied Action* in **Kei's Chapter**, p. 156
*Honor your emotions in **SPS #1:** *Authentic Feelings* in **Kim's Chapter**, p. 311
*Amp up your spice in **SPS #4:** *Ghost Pepper* in **Misty's Chapter**, p. 410
*What's beneath the question? Find out in **SPS #3:** *Are you OK* in **Elizabeth D.'s Chapter**, p. 430
*Slow down in **SPS #3:** *Duh* in **Kialey's and Kristin's Chapter**, p. 445
*Authentically share your feelings in **SPS #5:** *BFF Letter* in **Liz's Chapter**, p. 46
*Dream big in **SPS #1:** *Perfect Best Friend* in **Jamie's and Kery's Chapter**, p. 134
*Nothing is personal in **SPS #1:** *Heart to Heart* in **Jacki's Chapter**, p. 519

Plants, Animals, and Pure Sass

*Rewire the Plant Family connection with **SPS #3:** *Plant Realm Guidance* in **Maria's Chapter**, p. 27
*Engage your Spirit Animal in **SPS #4:** *Animal Spirits* in **Krissy's Chapter**, p. 56
*Embody an ethical practice with **SPS #1:** *Honorable Harvest* in **Jaana's Chapter**, p. 352
*Re-narrate problems into possibilities in **SPS #3:** *Wasband* in **DeWanda's Chapter**, p. 123
*Try out some flirtatious fun in **SPS #5:** *Maiden Flirt* in **Kei's Chapter**, p. 161
*Imperially declare yourself with **SPS #2:** *Silly Selfies* in **Pearle's Chapter**, p. 198
*Move and groove with **SPS #5:** *Dance Time* in **Pearle's Chapter**, p. 202
*Fashion your own tune to croon in **SPS #5:** *Verse and Chorus* in **Jaana's Chapter**, p. 359
*Set your soul ablaze with **SPS #1:** *Goals* in **Monika's Chapter**, p. 477
*Run wild and free with **SPS #1:** *Epona Goddess* in **Stella's Chapter**, p. 538
*Indulge with **SPS #5:** *Ascetic Hedonism* in **Jamie's Chapter**, p. 565

Recalibrate

*To-do lists go from hohum to humdandy with **SPS #5:** *Get To-Have To* in **Maria's Chapter**, p. 29
*No really does mean NO in **SPS #2:** *NO* in **Krissy's Chapter**, p. 53
*Hold tight for a reset in **SPS #2:** *Long Hug* in **Sarah's Chapter**, p. 96
*Connect to your ground in **SPS #5:** *Land Love* in **Pat's Chapter**, p. 112
*Release the wounded-healer with **SPS #5:** *Be Yourself, Be the Change* in **Jacqui's Chapter**, p. 176
*Love your past with **SPS #2:** *I Like Myself* in **Jennifer's Chapter**, p. p. 231
*Discover your connectedness with **SPS #4:** *Sacred Circles* in **Nisla's Chapter**, p. 304
*Govern your own standards with **SPS #4:** *Boundaries* in **Katia's Chapter**, p. 376
*Own your Leadership Role in **SPS #1:** *Interdependent* in **Elizabeth D.'s Chapter**, p. 425
*Energize and visualize through your dreams in **SPS #5:** *Dreamscape* in **Mindy's Chapter**, p. 469
*Summarize and solidify your values with **SPS #1:** *Mission Statement* in **Kristine's Chapter**, p. 501
*Sharpen your shingle with **SPS #1:** *Your Sign* in **Jamie's Chapter**, p. 552

Reconnect

*Reestablish your love of Time with **SPS #1:** *Time Talk* in **Maria's Chapter**, p. 23
*Put down the device in **SPS #1:** *Tech-Free* in **Gabby's Chapter**, p. 65
*Ask someone to join you in **SPS #5:** *Inclusion Love Loop* in **Gabby's Chapter**, p. 71
*Reach out and touch someone in **SPS #5:** *Connection Opportunity* in **Sarah's Chapter**, p. 99
*Nothing is concrete with **SPS #3:** *Playfully Bonded* in **Jennifer's Chapter**, p. 232
*Unite and bond with **SPS #5:** *Visible Connections* in **Allison's Chapter**, p. 273
*Grow your community with **SPS #2:** *Reaching Out* in **Nisla's Chapter**, p. 298
*Express empowered equality with **SPS #5:** *OurStory Logo* in **Matilda's Chapter**, p. 394
*Allow it ALL in with **SPS #5:** *Both, And* in **Elizabeth D.'s Chapter**, p. 433
*Find out what IS going right in **SPS #5:** *Positive Good* in **Jacki's Chapter**, p. 528

Reflect and Release

*Order up forgiveness in **SPS #3:** *The Gift of Forgiveness* in **Lynn's Chapter**, p. 13
*Send it onward and upward with **SPS #1:** *Cutting Cords* in **Liz's Chapter**, p. 35
*Re-tell the story YOUR way in **SPS #3:** *Re-Storying* in **Krissy's Chapter**, p. 54
*Connect and release in **SPS #4:** *Surrender and Acceptance* in **Mary Lu's Chapter**, p. 188
*Gently replace rigidity in **SPS #4:** *Rules* in **Elizabeth's Chapter**, p. 213
*Cultivate peace with **SPS #4:** *Neutrality* in **Michelle's Chapter**, p. 286
*Reframe survival mode in **SPS #1:** *Thrival Mode* in **Kristin's Chapter**, p. 341
*Let go of that which no longer serves you with **SPS #2:** *Labels* in **Kristin's Chapter**, p. 342
*Self-Reflect, grow, and transform with **SPS #2:** *Stereotypes* in **Matilda's Chapter**, p. 390
*Deepen understandings in **SPS #3:** *Why* in **Jacki's Chapter**, p. 523

Relationships

*Soften the angles of confusion with **SPS #1:** *Life-Angles* in **Lynn's Chapter**, p. 6
*Finish unfinished business with **SPS #2:** *Talking Stick* in **Jamie's and Kery's Chapter**, p. 136
*Grow up gracefully with **SPS #5:** *Adult Currency* in **Jamie's and Kery's Chapter**, p. 141
*Really see and hear the younger you with **SPS #2:** *Inner Child* in **Kim's Chapter**, p. 313
*It's time to talk to her in **SPS #2:** *Clitoris Conversation* in **Nancy's Chapter**, p. 328
*Direct the conversation in **SPS #4:** *Family Circle* in **Jaana's Chapter**, p. 358

*Change your perspective on your perspective in **SPS #3: *Soulmates*** in **Misty's Chapter**, p. 407
*Understand why you do what you do with **SPS #2: *Security Circle*** in **Elizabeth D.'s Chapter**, p. 428
*Vibe Higher in **SPS #1: *Higher Self to Higher Self*** in **Kialey's and Kristin's Chapter**, p. 442
*Become the perfect partner for yourself in **SPS #2: *Perfectly You*** in **Jacki's Chapter**, p. 521

Self-Love and Sensory Bliss

*Manifest beautifully in **SPS #2: *Magickal Senses*** in **Michelle's Chapter**, p. 282
*Invite your Soul to stay and play in **SPS #3: *I Know This is True*** in **Nisla's Chapter**, p. 300
*Welcome your Divine Purpose with **SPS #1: *Pleasure*** in **Nancy's Chapter**, p. 326
*Rub-a-dub for the Best and Highest with **SPS #2: *Abhyanga Massage*** in **Maria's Chapter**, p. 25
*Gaze at a beautiful sight with **SPS #2: *Picture Love*** in **Liz's Chapter**, p. 39
*Reclaim the basics with **SPS #4: *What Do You Need*** in **Liz's Chapter**, p. 44
*Play naked in **SPS #1: *Love Bath*** in **DeWanda's Chapter**, p. 117
*Time to create that dating profile in **SPS #1: *First Date*** in **Elizabeth's Chapter**, p. 208
*Practice makes perfect in **SPS #5: *Self-Care Practice*** in **Nisla's Chapter**, p. 305

Source Wisdom and Soul's Guidance

*Walk the high road with **SPS #4: *Higher Self Help*** in **DeWanda's Chapter**, p. 125
*Delight yourself with **SPS #5: *Core Sense of Joy*** in **Connie's Chapter**, p. 259
*Weave your own Divinity in **SPS #1: *Answering Your Own Prayer*** in **Allison's Chapter**, p. 266
*YOU are the Altar in **SPS #5: *Radiance*** in **Katia's Chapter**, p. 381
*See your story from Source's perspective in **SPS #5: *Source's Story*** in **Krissy's Chapter**, p. 58
*Follow your heart to Source in **SPS #3: *Drawing God*** in **Pearle's Chapter**, p. 199
*You are enough in **SPS #5: *To Minister*** in **Emilie's Chapter**, p. 248
*Become a Sacred Site in **SPS #4: *Temple of You*** in **Nancy's Chapter**, p. 332
*Expand and ascend into bliss-filled love in **SPS #5: *Sacred Sex*** in **Kristine's Chapter**, p. 511
*Choose your connection in **SPS #4: *Ego and Soul*** in **Jacki's Chapter**, p. 526
*Stop, be, and trust in **SPS #2: *No Pushing*** in **Jamie's Chapter**, p. 558

The Divine Feminine and The Divine Masculine

*Step-In to the Cycle with **SPS #3: *Archetypal Wisdom*** in **Liz's Chapter**, p. 40
*Gain new perspectives with **SPS #3: *Gift Economy*** in **Gabby's Chapter**, p. 67
*Revalue your first menstrual cycle with **SPS #4: *Menarche Meditation*** in **Gabby's Chapter**, p. 69
*See yourself as Sacred in **SPS #1: *Divine Feminine Altar*** in **Pat's Chapter**, p. 105
*Balance the input and output with **SPS #2: *Mother-Crone*** in **Jacqui's Chapter**, p. 169
*Step into your clarity and empowerment with **SPS #3: *Enchantress*** in **Nancy's Chapter**, p. 330
*It's a marvelous night in **SPS #5: *Moon-Bath*** in **Misty's Chapter**, p. 412
*Learn and love through the **SPS #1: *Divine Masculine*** in **Shelby's Chapter**, p. 77
*Own your consistent centeredness with **SPS #4: *The King*** in **Emilie's Chapter**, p. 247
*Support your sensuality with **SPS #5: *Inner Lover*** in **Nancy's Chapter**, p. 334
*Value ALL of you in **SPS #2: *Masculine-Feminine*** in **Katia's Chapter**, p. 372
*Share your talents with **SPS #3: *The Magician*** in **Kristine's Chapter**, p. 507
*Hydrate your Soul with **SPS #4: *Water*** in **Kristine's Chapter**, p. 510

Shifts and Transformations

*Embody your Inner Activist with **SPS #4:** *Social Change* in Maria's Chapter, p. 28
*Notice the gifts with **SPS #2:** *Biggest Blessing* in Gabby's Chapter, p. 67
*Meet and greet your needs in **SPS #1:** *Spectrogram* in Sarah's Chapter, p. 93
*No more "I'm fine…" in SPS #3: *Not OK and Not Fine* in Jamie's and Kery's Chapter, p. 138
*Don't worry… be happy with **SPS #1:** *I AM Now* in Mary Lu's Chapter, p. 183
*Create the good to happen for you in **SPS #5:** *Good Karma* in Jennifer's Chapter, p. 236
*Grow and know with **SPS #3:** *Creating Compassion* in Connie's Chapter, p. 256
*Relate to overwhelm differently in **SPS #1:** *Compassion Fatigue* in Misty's Chapter, p. 401
*Release and fly and with **SPS #2:** *Transformation* in Kei's Chapter, p. 153
*Love through the windows of your soul in **SPS #2:** *Mirroring* in Mary Lu's Chapter, p. 186
*Transmute responses in **SPS #5:** *Peacefully-Remaining-Connected* in Elizabeth's Chapter, p. 219
*Dare to discuss with **SPS #4:** *Courage Conversation* in Jennifer's Chapter, p. p. 235
*Simmer it down in **SPS #3:** *One Year Left* in Kim's Chapter, p. 315
*Pencil in perfection in **SPS #2:** *Failure on Purpose* in Misty's Chapter, p. 405
*Receive, feel, know, see and hear with **SPS #3:** *Blessings Bag* in Stella's Chapter, p. 540
*Molds are for cheese with **SPS #3:** *Moldy Molds* in Jamie's Chapter, p. 558

You, Glorious YOU

*Shift the shit with **SPS #4:** *I Matter* in Sarah's Chapter, p. 98
*Meet HER in **SPS #4:** *Ultimate YOU* in Pat's Chapter, p. 110
*Own your organic goodness in **SPS #5:** *Natural Virtue* in DeWanda's Chapter, p. 128
*Claim it all in **SPS #3:** *The 'I've Done' List* in Emilie's Chapter, p. 246
*Take flight with **SPS #2:** *Angel Wings* in Allison's Chapter, p. 268
*Honor and treasure all sides of you in **SPS #1:** *The Whole You* in Michelle's Chapter, p. 280
*Excavate new pathways for beauty with **SPS #5:** *You Are Beautiful* in Kim's Chapter, p. 318
*Breathe in a new habit with **SPS #2:** *Cherish Yourself* in Jaana's Chapter, p. 355
*You are all of that… *and* a bag of chips in **SPS #1:** *Who Am I* in Katia's Chapter, p. 371
*Hone your handle with **SPS #3:** *Names and Nicknames* in Katia's Chapter, p. 374
*Shine your light in **SPS #3:** *You Are Amazing* in Matilda's Chapter, p. 391
*Love yourself, love the world in **SPS #3:** *Self-Love* in Mindy's Chapter, p. 465
*Send love to every version of you in **SPS #2:** *Love Yourself* in Monika's Chapter, p. 483
*Get to the core with **SPS #2:** *Who Are You* in Kristine's Chapter, p. 503

~WELL DESERVED GRATITUDE~

Right out of the gate, I'm going to say "thank you" to everyone and everything throughout all time and space. I couldn't have done it without you. Seriously. If I have ever - or have never - met you, it doesn't matter. This book and all of its contents has been inspired by you. We are all connected, and you deserve the credit. Thank you.

The biggest hugs of gratitude go to the Goddesses in this book. Your trust, patience and love kept me going. Thank you, ladies. I love you.

The second biggest hug goes to my creative team. These Sisters are Goddess-sent! Kristine, Connie, Misty, Amanda, and Paige… Thank you. I love you.

While working on this book, three dear ones transitioned from the Earth Plane. Frank, Lydia, and John, we love you and look forward to seeing you again soon!

Extra special gratitude and love goes to my daily support system- Phil, Pearle, Ozzie, Delilah and Cookie.

Also, I have to thank the fam. Mom, Dad, and Sis… I love you. Dave, Jessie, and Craig… love you too! Eje, Ev, and Emsie, love you kiddos, as well!

Special hugs also go to Doc Fedder, Sandra N., and Carla J. for reading through all of the Sacred Play Suggestions and giving their blessings for Drama Therapy, Esoteric Healing, and Trauma Informed Care accuracy, ethics, and acumen.

A huge thank you to my teachers! Vicki Noble, you are my inspiration. Brooke Medicine Eagle, your teachings and friendship have kept me grounded and energized. Kaia Ra, the *Sophia Code* has and will continue to change my life for the *good* for*ever*. Bern Bloom, thank you for being my Esoteric Healing teacher. The energy from my heart to yours knows no time nor distance.

For all of my friends who have generously gifted me their time to read through different iterations of the book, thank you. Christina, Kristine, Erin, Kim, Mena, Victoria, Mindy, Jacki, Shelby, Elizabeth, Christine, Jane, Anna, Claire, Deborah, Dave, Nancy, and Kery… thank you, dear ones. Your heartfelt opinions mean the world to me.

Thank you to my dear friend, Trista Hendren, for helping me obtain permission for the poems and quotes used in the 'Pearle' chapter.

Thank you to the best acting teacher in the world, Steven Williford. Your lessons have lasted the test of time as proven by all of the Sacred Play Suggestions inspired by you and your wonderful acting classes.

Thank you to the 36 authors listed in the 'Suggested Reading' sections of each chapter. Your work is needed, valuable, supportive, transformative, and timeless.

Thank you to the Crystalline Realm for offering your wisdom and support for each chapter. The book *Love Is in The Earth- A Kaleidoscope of Crystals*, by Melody was a priceless resource for each chapter's 'Crystal

Love,' section. Thank you, Melody! Also, a big thank you to my friend, Kristy, for suggesting this book to me. And finally, a thank you to my friend Susan Moen of The Crystal Cave for letting me take pictures and videos of her beautiful crystals.

Thank you to the authors, therapists, facilitators, healers, publications, friends, family members, and teachers who inspired the 180 Sacred Play Suggestions. Thank you to Robert Moore, Douglas Gillette, Viana Stibal, Vick Noble, Kaia Ra, Linda Kohanov, Stephen Levine, Olivier Clerc, Don Miguel Ruiz, Deepak Chopra, Stephen Schwartz, *Light of Consciousness: Journal of Spiritual Awakening*, John Maxwell Taylor, Georg Fuerstein, Stephen A. Schwartz, Julie Wells, Mary Ann Bodnar, Kathleen Horne, Carl Jung, Marion Woodman, Merlin Stone, Carol P. Christ, Riane Eisler, Bruce Robertson, Bernadette Bloom, Steven Williford, Dale Allen, Anne Hearon Rambo, Elizabeth Locey, Dr. Dan Siegel, Bessel van der Kolk, MD, *The 40 Carrots Family Center*, Carla Johanns, Christina Rodrigues, Doc Fedder, Dr. David Spangler, Dr. Cynthia Andreas, Brooke Medicine Eagle, Susan Moen, Angelika Werkstetter, Jacqui Albert Pepper, Genevieve Vaughan, Lara Owen, Kim Scott, Miranda Gray, Shelley E. Taylor, Erica Boucher, Sherry Crelin, Andrea Patterson, Jenny Lee Stern, Betsy Craft, Magenta Pixie, Maria Luera, Starhawk, Marija Gimbutas, Regena Thomashauer, Massimilla Harris, Ph.D, Bud Harris, Ph.D., Shelley K. Green, Joseph Moreno, Dr. Bruce Sogolow, Murry Bowen, MD, Sherry Ruth Anderson, Patricia Hopkins, Shel Silverstein, Sue Monk Kidd, Linda Reuther, Trista Hendren, Lisa Powers Tricomi, *Deliver the Dream*, Charmain S. Borda, Dr. Debra Harris Nixon, Regena Dewitt, Kery Helmer, Linda Condon, Karen Drucker, Robyn Posin, Katie Player, Chris Friday, Adam Ratner, Christina Rodrigues, Kate Alexander, Will Luera, Richard Hopkins, *The Florida Studio Theatre*, Elise Rodriguez, Kathryn Parks, Jason Cannon, Rebecca Hopkins, Jason Henley, Carolyn Myss, Michael A. Singer, Betty McCormack, Csongor Daniel, Robin Wall Kimmerer, The Dalai Lama, Dr. Patrick Nave, Glenn Cooper, Kent Hoffman, Bert Powell, Dr. Neil Burris, Dr. Harriet Kiviat, Illa Bonnell, Marjorie Day, Peter Levine, Terri Marks, Aunt Jan, Aunt Mary, Lori Wallace, and Lydia.

Thank you to my Sisters who said "no." By owning your truth, you firmly rooted me to mine.

With total transparency, I give complete credit to the Microsoft Word Thesaurus for being my quiet, creative, supportive, and brilliant co-writer.

Thank you to all of the plants in my house and garden for their consistent guidance, comfort, and support.

Thank you to all of my Spirit Guides, Ancestors, Ascended Masters (Isis, Hathor, Green Tara, Mother Mary, Mary Magdalene, Quan Yin, and White Buffalo Woman), Angelic Guides and Supporters, Animal Spirits-especially Mother and Sister Hawk, Mahla, Mahsa, and Xelha.

And, finally, thank you to all of the wise, empowered, inspiring, loving, and dedicated women who have participated in the Divine Mommy Groups, Divine Mommy University, Divine Mommy Workshops, Divine Badass Workshops, and the Divine Badass Retreat Weekends. All of you, every single one of you, are part of this entire project. I love you and I am forever grateful to you.

Contents

Lynn 3

"My addiction really is my blessing.
Today, my business and my life reflect this."

~Themes~
Sobriety of the Soul
Expectations and Resentments
Living Happy, Joyous, and Free - No Matter What

~Sacred Play Suggestions~
* Life-Angles * Cellular Town Hall * The Gift of Forgiveness
* Stepping-In * Black Out Poetry *

~Crystal Love~
Pink Tourmaline

Maria 21

"Have compassion for yourself and others.
It is all about seeing things from
someone else's level of consciousness."

~Themes~
Oneness
Things Will Always Improve
Walking the Talk

~Sacred Play Suggestions~
* Time Talk * Abhyanga Massage * Plant Realm Guidance
* Social Change * Get To - Have To *

~Crystal Love~
Rainbow Fluorite

Liz 33

"I feel more content now with what is…
and that means being more content with it all-
the good, the bad, and the ugly."

~Themes~
Being Your Own Best Friend
Trusting Those Who are Trustworthy
Trusting Yourself

~Sacred Play Suggestions~
* Cutting Cords * Picture Love * Archetype Wisdom
* What Do You Need * BFF Letter *

~Crystal Love~
Mookaite

Krissy 49

"Sharing my grief helped me to realize
that this whole thing was something that happened to me,
but isn't actually happening anymore."

~Themes~
Following Your Own Timeline
Releasing Blame and Guilt
Finding the Helpers

~Sacred Play Suggestions~
* Temple of Goodness * NO * Re-Storying
* Animal Spirits * Source's Story *

~Crystal Love~
Quantum Quattro

Gabby 63

"I am the kind of person to do anything and everything
I possibly can to help our planet
and the creatures living on it."

~Themes~
We Can All Make a Difference
Believe in Yourself
Talk it Out

~Sacred Play Suggestions~
* Tech-Free * Biggest Blessing * Gift Economy
* Menarche Meditation * Inclusion Love Loop *

~Crystal Love~
Smoky Quartz

Shelby 75

"Our emotions are our ultimate currency."

~Themes~
Honoring Emotions
Healing Dysfunctional Family Cycles
Living Your Authenticity

~Sacred Play Suggestions~
* Divine Masculine * Heart Art * Sweet and Sacred Objects
* Feelings * Skin-to-Skin *

~Crystal Love~
Vesuvianite

Sarah 91

"It is so important to connect and support each other
and to figure out how we can navigate this world together."

~Themes~
Being Open and Being Vulnerable
Feeling Overwhelmed
Trusting Your Inner Wisdom

~Sacred Play Suggestions~
* Spectrogram * Long Hug * Alta Balance * I Matter
* Connection Opportunity *

~Crystal Love~
Onyx

Pat 103

"As a mother, educator, and grandmother,
I too can stand up for what I know is right."

~Themes~
Connecting to Your Matrilineal Ancestors
Finding Balance
Continued Education

~Sacred Play Suggestions~
* Divine Feminine Altar * Mantra * Role Change
* Ultimate YOU * Land Love *

~Crystal Love~
Chrysocolla

DeWanda 115

"I can now see spaces, places, and pieces of me that I want to explore
and connect to that I didn't even know existed."

~Themes~
Love the Skin You Are In
Be Big, Be Bold, Be You
Living Happy, Healthy, and Whole

~Sacred Play Suggestions~
* Love Bath * Authentic Self * Wasband
* Higher Self Help * Natural Virtue *

~Crystal Love~
Carnelian

Kery and Jamie 131

"We don't have to walk away and pretend something never happened because there is a conflict or a crunchy time."

~Themes~
Feeling Insecure
Pretending Everything Is OK
Friendships Change and Grow

~Sacred Play Suggestions~
* Perfect Best Friend * Talking Stick * Not OK and Not Fine
* Hands * Adult Currency *

~Crystal Love~
Amazonite

Kei 147

"I have no idea where I am in the healing process. Maybe I haven't even started."

~Themes~
Your Mother is a Person, too…
Isolation
Letting the Light Shine Through

~Sacred Play Suggestions~
* Tele * Transformation * Intentional Movement
* Embodied Action * Maiden Flirt *

~Crystal Love~
Apache Tear

Jacqui 165

"Be the change first. You can help others second. Heal yourself. Heal the world."

~Themes~
Responsible *To,* Not For
Putting Yourself First
Heal Yourself, Heal the World

~Sacred Play Suggestions~
* Five Elements * Mother-Crone * Color Gift
* Bliss-Bundle-Scale * Be Yourself, Be the Change *

~Crystal Love~
Labradorite

Mary Lu 181

"I know that losing my dad
has made me the woman I am today...
and I wouldn't change her for anything."

~Themes~
Having the Courage to Leave
Forgiving the Unforgiveable
Being OK with Right Now

~Sacred Play Suggestions~
* I AM Now * Mirroring * Higher Self Support
* Surender and Acceptance * Intentions *

~Crystal Love~
Black Tourmaline

Pearle 195

"As long as you keep having fun
and as long as you are kind,
people will want to play with you."

~Themes~
Being Silly
Saying STOP
Kindness

~Sacred Play Suggestions~
* Heart Healing * Silly Selfies * Drawing God * Body Wisdom
* Dance Time *

~Crystal Love~
Tiger's Eye

Elizabeth 205

"My life lesson has been to change course
when something isn't working.
For me, pain is usually a sign to reevaluate."

~Themes~
Breaking Your Own Rules
No Need for Justification
Liberation from Passion

~Sacred Play Suggestions~
* First Date * 5-Pointed Star * Creative Goddess * Rules
* Peacefully - Remaining - Connected *

~Crystal Love~
Chrysoprase

Jennifer 227

"Me being who I am has created the possibility
for my children to fully become
who they are meant to be."

~Themes~
Honoring Yourself, Your Sensitivity, and Your Sobriety
You Are Never Alone
Finding Your Life's Purpose

~Sacred Play Suggestions~
* Idea Children * I Like Myself * Playfully Bonded
* Courage Conversation * Good Karma *

~Crystal Love~
Amethyst

Emilie 241

"I feel more love and I am more aware of love
than I have ever been in my entire life."

~Themes~
Unexpected Life Changes
Unconditional Love
Faith

~Sacred Play Suggestions~
* Positive Thoughts * Thymus Thump * The 'I've Done' List
* The King * To Minister *

~Crystal Love~
Rose Quartz

Connie 251

"Do you want your Soul to grow
or do you want to compress it?
Answer that and then do it."

~Themes~
Taking Responsibility
Relationships
Love is the Most Important Thing

~Sacred Play Suggestions~
* Prayer Power * Love Heals * Creating Compassion * I AM Love
* Core Sense of Joy *

~Crystal Love~
Selenite

Allison 263

"Because of what I have been through, I am dedicated to parents being honest - in age appropriate ways - with their children."

~Themes~
The Toughest Gratitude
Loving What is Lost
Teachable Moments

~Sacred Play Suggestions~
* Answering Your Own Prayer * Angel Wings * Fairy Tale
* Inside - Outside * Visible Connections *

~Crystal Love~
Angel Aura Quartz

Michelle 277

"We have a lot more power than we give ourselves credit for."

~Themes~
Our Minds Are Powerful
Honoring Gifts
Living the Best Life

~Sacred Play Suggestions~
* The Whole You * Magickal Senses * Yes, And… * Neutrality
* Spirit Messages *

~Crystal Love~
Hawk's Eye

Nisla 291

"My story of motherhood has shaped and transformed me."

~Themes~
We Are in This Together
Breaking Negative Cycles
Look to Your Resources

~Sacred Play Suggestions~
* Extraordinary Life * Reaching Out * I Know This is True
* Sacred Circles * Self-Care Practice *

~Crystal Love~
Unakite

Kim 309

"I believe we come forth
with all the knowing
we could ever need in this life."

~Themes~
Connecting to Your Inner Child
Letting Go of Limiting Belief Systems
Owning Your Beauty

~Sacred Play Suggestions~
* Authentic Feelings * Inner Child * One Year Left * Soft Belly
* You Are Beautiful *

~Crystal Love~
Rhodochrosite

Nancy 323

"It finally clicked for me that
I was indeed a beautiful,
fiery, passionate being."

~Themes~
There is Fire Within You
Asking for What You Desire
Sacred Sexuality

~Sacred Play Suggestions~
* Pleasure * Clitoris Conversation * Enchantress * Temple of You
* Inner Lover *

~Crystal Love~
Dragon's Eye

Kristin 339

"Becoming a mother gave me the strength
to know that I wanted to be my own person.
That I wanted to find my own power."

~Themes~
Letting Things Be
Surviving Survival Mode
You Are Powerful

~Sacred Play Suggestions~
* Thrival Mode * Labels * Kundalini Rising * New Love Mantra
* Prayer Basket *

~Crystal Love~
Malachite

Jaana 349

"Children come to us.
It doesn't matter how.
That is how I see it."

~Themes~
Resilience
The Parent You Want to Be
Making Choices Out of Love

~Sacred Play Suggestions~
* Honorable Harvest * Cherish Yourself * Mandantra * Family Circle
* Verse and Chorus *

~Crystal Love~
Jade

Katia 369

"I took my power back the moment
I started being true to myself."

~Themes~
Success
Social and Cultural Boundaries
Self-Care

~Sacred Play Suggestions~
* Who Am I * Masculine - Feminine * Names and Nicknames
* Boundaries * Radiance *

~Crystal Love~
Cinnabar

Matilda 387

"Everyone can make bad decisions
and it isn't worth it getting
all worked up about it."

~Themes~
Everyone Makes Mistakes
Living Your Truth
Don't Give Up

~Sacred Play Suggestions~
* Body Talk * Stereotypes * You are Amazing * Breath of Fire
* *Our*Story Logo *

~Crystal Love~
Andalusite

Misty 399

"I have learned to slow down,
enjoy the little things, and live in the moment."

~Themes~
Releasing the Pain
Be Kind, Patient, and Loving Toward Yourself
We are Hurt and Healed in Relationship

~Sacred Play Suggestions~
* Compassion Fatigue * Failure on Purpose * Soulmates
* Ghost Pepper * Moon-Bath *

~Crystal Love~
Red Jasper

Elizabeth D. 421

"I know that the words I say really matter.
If I want something enduring, it has to be based on trust."

~Themes~
What I Say Matters
Don't Leave Angry
Women in Leadership

~Sacred Play Suggestions~
* Interdependent * Security Circle * Are You OK
* Sympath - Empath * Both, And *

~Crystal Love~
Snowflake Obsidian

Kialey and Kristin 437

"For this type of friendship, you have to work on it.
You have to open up and talk about the hard stuff."

~Themes~
Giving and Receiving Love
Second Chances
Discovering Your Spiritual Self

~Sacred Play Suggestions~
* Higher Self to Higher Self * Gratitude Tree * Duh
* Really Talk, Really Listen * Chi *

~Crystal Love~
Peach Moonstone

Mindy 455

"My healing took time. But I got through it
and I know we all can get through
these really tough situations."

~Themes~
Perseverance
Releasing Other's Advice, Opinions, and Expertise
Trusting in a Higher Power

~Sacred Play Suggestions~
* Four Corners * Sacral Chakra * Self-Love * Fire * Dreamscape *

~Crystal Love~
Howlite

Monika 475

"We must believe in ourselves,
our education, and our experience."

~Themes~
Doing Things for You
Trust in Yourself, Your Education, and Your Experience
Plan for Your Future

~Sacred Play Suggestions~
* Goals * Love Yourself * Compliments * Earth Star Chakras
* Money Mantras *

~Crystal Love~
Pyrite

Kristine 499

"For me, veganism and motherhood
go hand in hand. They are both about
compassion and doing the right thing"

~Themes~
Becoming Who You Are
Trusting in Your Body
Letting Love be Your Guide

~Sacred Play Suggestions~
* Mission Statement * Who Are You * The Magician * Water
* Sacred Sex *

~Crystal Love~
Garnet

Jacki 517

"We've all got the potential to awaken to the beauty
available to us in this life."

~Themes~
Living in Beauty
Releasing Toxicity
Focus on What You Want

~Sacred Play Suggestions~
* Heart to Heart * Perfectly You * Why * Ego and Soul
* Positive Good *

~Crystal Love~
Aquamarine

Stella 535

"I don't have to earn love...
I just have to receive it."

~Themes~
Choosing the Gifts
The Universe has a Plan
Stepping into the Light

~Sacred Play Suggestions~
* Epona Goddess * Kintsugi * Blessings Bag * Equal Energy
* Seven Directions *

~Crystal Love~
Bloodstone

Jamie 549

"We are all unique, Divine, perfectly imperfect works of art.
We've been through what we've been through to make
us *us,* and the world needs us just as we are"

~Themes~
Grace
Your Past is Past
Tapestry of You

~Sacred Play Suggestions~
* Your Sign * No Pushing * Moldy Molds * Crystal Force Field
* Ascetic Hedonism *

~Crystal Love~
Astrophyllite

Soul-to-Sisterhood __Namaste__

From My Highs to My Lows
From My Bliss to My Shame
When I Am in That Place in Me
And You Are in That Place in You
Which is Every Moment of Every Day
We Are One
We are Never Alone

Namaste
I Love You

Lynn

Sobriety is always a big part of my empowerment because by getting sober, I learned how to live. Sobriety is how I've learned to navigate in this world, and by God's grace, I have just celebrated 21 years of sobriety. To take it back to where it all started, I have to mention that I was raised by a single mom. We lived in apartments and my sister and I were often left unsupervised. Not because my mom didn't care. She was working all the time, trying to make ends meet. I remember hanging out with kids of other single moms in our apartment buildings, bored, picking up cigarette butts off the street, and just looking for something to do. I was probably eight years old at the time, and my sister - who was four years older than me - was leading the way. That progressed to smoking pot and drinking beers. With my mom being gone so much, I was left to my own devices, and it all just kind of happened. As I got older, I was getting along in the world. I was popular in high school. I was the homecoming Queen. Everything was sort of going my way, despite my own self. My goal was to become a cheerleader was really the first thing that sparked a desire in me. Thankfully, from ages 10-25 I cheered, and this led me to college on a full ride athletic scholarship for dance. When you grow up in Tennessee, you know that the Memphis State Pom-Pom Girls are the best in the nation. Getting on that squad was my ultimate goal, and I got it. I traveled around, performing for the NBA, and that really helped me stay sober. When I was dancing, I didn't feel like I needed drinking or drugs. Oh, the party was always there and always at my house because there was seldom a parent at home. But when I was cheering or dancing, I could stay focused. My father had been out of the picture since I was a baby. When I was very young, my first boyfriend - who was eighteen when I was fourteen - stepped into that protector role. Even with all of that, until I was about 25 I was able to maintain because I could stay motivated by my dream to cheer and dance. After college, I was touring as a dancer with a well-known rock band. Then the NBA hired me to go and cheer in Europe. When they offered to send me to Spain, I thought I had hit the big time. I initially went for two weeks and ended up staying for two years. I thought I had it made! Only, this is where my lack of life-skills really started showing up. I was all alone in Spain and I got really lonely. I didn't know how to cope. I started eating to fill the void. I gained weight. When my boss started to get on me about my appearance, my only reference point for fixing it was remembering what the girls in college did: take laxatives and throw up. I didn't even think to go on a diet. I didn't think to ask for help. I didn't tell anyone. I just became bulimic. I've learned that with addiction, you go through the same preoccupations, obsessions, and attempts to control the uncontrollable with whatever 'it' is that you use: men, gambling, food, sex, drugs, it doesn't really matter.... Looking back, the bulimia was the first time I knew that something was wrong with me. I felt alone in the world. As much as I had going for me on the outside, I was *really* struggling on the inside. My mom and I weren't close. My dad was gone. I think a lot about that lonely version of me. I know that I was just doing the best I could do. After the contract in Spain was finished, I moved to California to work with a friend of mine who had a dance company. That quickly ended and I found myself in Los Angeles at a crossroads. I didn't want to go home. I had no plan. So, I stayed. I got a job at a trendy nightclub as a cocktail waitress. It was a blast! All the hottest celebrities were there. There was always a line out the door, and tips were given in cocaine. At this point, the drugs were working for me. I was having fun with the cocaine and without any real consequences. I kept using and using. Soon I was using more and more and I realized I couldn't stop. I had a problem. I finally told my boyfriend, who was a bartender at the night club, that I thought I had a problem with cocaine. In that moment, he was great. He just told me not to worry and that we wouldn't do it anymore. I was so relieved! I felt so supported! Like this was going to be so easy! We just wouldn't do it anymore. Done. I called him the next night, while he was at work, and he was super excited to tell me that he had just dropped two tabs of ecstasy. He was shitfaced. I remember, at that moment, feeling this gut punch because I realized how alone I was. Shame and guilt also started to kick in. I kept comparing myself to my friends, who seemed to be able to start and stop using whenever they wanted. The lying and hiding came next, which fueled me to use even more. It took about seven months until I was living on the streets, having seizures, weighing less than 100lbs, and completely sick. I called my dad. I had no relationship with him, other than a phone call on my birthday or the holidays, but I called him and asked him to come and get me. He wasn't going to, but my older sister got on the phone and told him to get his ass on the plane. He did. He actually came twice. The first time he showed up, I was so consumed with guilt and shame I ran away from him. The second time, I went with him. I didn't have on any shoes or any of my belongings… I just got on the plane and went to a treatment center. I'd gone to other treatments and detoxes before, but it was always because other people wanted me to go. I had tried treatment a few times before, but this was the first time that I really wanted to get clean. After the 90 Day program, I decided to live with my dad. I had so many expectations. I thought that he would be ready to give me the love and attention I didn't get as a child. It didn't turn out that way at all. He just went to work. It was another day for him. I was devastated. When my 'friends' in California called and told me they missed me, I went back without a second thought. The disease of addiction is progressive, so when I relapsed, it was worse. It was like I had never stopped. I went into full-fledged paranoia. At that time, an angel who was really just a guy that I had known from my using days, literally picked me up by the back of my shirt and took me to the airport. Again, with no shoes… he just bought me a ticket and threw me on a plane. Somehow, he saved me at the time when I was ready to learn the lesson that expectations are just premeditated resentments. I knew I had to forgive my dad. I had to find a way to let it all go. I went to another treatment center and stayed for a year. This was when the first true healing occurred for me. I started to realize that I was worth something and that I could forgive while also setting boundaries of what I knew I needed and deserved. I decided to stop talking to my dad. I stood in my power to not participate in a relationship that wasn't meeting my needs. I didn't have to judge or be mad. I could stand in my authority to say, "No thanks, I'd rather have nothing than crumbs." After about a year and a half of no contact, my dad finally reached out me. He called me and told me he loved me and that I was important to him. He said all of the things I had wanted to hear since I was a little girl. That year, I went to his house for Thanksgiving. In the middle of the night, we both ended up in the kitchen, from opposite ends of the house. We had a beautiful healing moment. We hugged each other. He apologized. I apologized. We made a vow then and there that we would be the best father and daughter that we knew how to be. From that moment forward, we did. My dad died a year later, nine days after my daughter was born. He got diagnosed with Pancreatic Cancer when I was pregnant. I'm so glad that he got to see me sober. I went back and forth to Nashville when my dad was sick, and we spent a lot of time together. I got to experience with him all of the unmet relationship stuff in the last year of his life. I am forever grateful for that. Now as a parent, I see that I am almost living a repeat of my mother's life. I'm a single mom raising two daughters, with my ex-husband raising someone else's children right down the street… although I am doing it differently. I am healing this by modeling for my daughters that it is possible to live life happy, joyous, and free regardless of anything. That is the most important thing I can give them. My mom had a lot of pain and she couldn't give me that message growing up. She struggled. Her life was hard. She didn't have the luxury of going to 6 treatment centers and talking about healing and forgiveness every day for months. In this sense, my addiction really has been my blessing. Today my business and my life reflect this. They also reflect my values of sobriety, clean living, supporting my local community, and the spiritual principles of doing things with integrity, honesty, and beauty. All super simple. This is what I am passing on to my children. I focus on what I want, instead of what is going wrong. I have an amazing tool kit today and I couldn't have done any of it without God. If it can happen for me, it can happen for anyone. Back then, I couldn't stay sober for five minutes. Now I've got over two decades. Never give up. Keep trying. Be honest with yourself. Ask for help. When I think of everything that I've been through, I never thought that I would be a successful business owner but really, anyone can do it. Remember, the good and the bad are all changing *all* the time. The double life of addiction, of fear, of trying to control what everybody thinks, and of isolation… it can pass too. When you get down to root cause of changing your heart with the power of forgiveness, the circumstances are irrelevant. I believe that we can only keep what we have by giving it away. When I give away my time, my love, my strength, my joy, my story, that is when they are truly mine.

Making This Story Your Own:

Lynn's story gives value to Soul-centered sobriety.
Take a moment, breathe, and reflect.
What stands out for you when you read her words?
Is there a situation in your life that is similar to Lynn's?
Perhaps part of her story feels connected to your own.
How can you relate her experiences to your past, present, and future?

- *My Connection to Lynn's Story* _____

  _____

  _____

  _____

  _____

  _____

Knowing that you aren't alone, let's gently explore some other themes from Lynn's story together:

- **Sobriety of the Soul**
  - When you think of the word *sobriety*, what comes up? Do you reflect on the sobriety of the physical body as it relates to mind altering substances? What about a more philosophical approach? If sobriety is a state of clarity, what would happen if you sobered up to your true feelings? What would change if you got sober about your thoughts? How different would your life be today if you regarded your authentic hopes and desires with a sober commitment? Can a reevaluation of mental, emotional, and spiritual sobriety hold more appeal than the illusion of an un-sober existence?

- **Expectations and Resentments**
  - What are your expectations? Can you identify the expectations you have for yourself, your relationships, and your life? How are your expectations different today than they were five years ago? One year ago? If they are different, can you explain why? Has the amount of expectations increased? Have they become more rigid? Or have they softened and decreased? Thinking about your expectations in this way, what feelings come up? Are these feelings positive or negative and do they serve your highest good? If so, how? If they are not serving your highest good, can you shift or release your expectations to be more in alignment with what you do want?

- ***Living Happy, Joyous, and Free - No Matter What!***
  - Do you live happy? Do you live joyous? Do you live free? If yes, how? If no, why not? What is holding you back? Are these things truly responsible? Perhaps *you* are holding *yourself* back from happiness, joy, and freedom? Can you sit with your answer without attributing fault or blame? Where did you learn about living happy, joyous, and free? Did you have a good role model? If you didn't have a good model, how can you hold yourself accountable? Maybe living this way seems unrealistic because you haven't had enough practice? Perhaps the '*No Matter What*' that Lynn talks about is really self-love? With compassion, patience, and understanding, how can you - no matter what - find ways to create happiness, joyfulness, and freedom within your life?

Sacred Play Suggestions:

~ SPS #1: ~
* Life-Angles *

A triangle is considered the strongest of the shapes. Would you believe that our subconscious mind already knows this information and utilizes it quite frequently? Sometimes this is for the greater good. Other times, this is done to relieve anxiety with the distraction of involving a third party. The best example of this is gossip. How often have you or have you witnessed someone else attempting to resolve their feelings by talking unkindly about another person? Take this very simplified example for instance: Julie gets mad at Barbara because Barbara cancels plans last minute. This hurts Julie's feelings, but instead of addressing this directly with Barbara, Julie calls Tammy and complains to her. Julie labels Barbara as a flake and she and Tammy commiserate about Barbara being unreliable. Tammy even shares another story from a different friend to corroborate the accusations against Barbara. Julie and Tammy are now bonded at the expense of Barbara, yet Julie's feelings are only temporarily alleviated. In a nutshell, Tammy is now complicit in this hurtful exchange, Barbara would be very upset if she found out what was said behind her back, and the whole situation is a big, toxic, energy drain with no resolution and no relief. This is just one of a plethora of examples that well-known Psychiatrist and theorist of human behavior, Murray Bowen, MD, termed as triangulation. No surprise that the word sounds so much like strangulation. These types of triangular relationship dynamics can come in many different forms and they don't always have to involve three people. These triangles can also involve substances, addictions, behaviors, choices, etc. Traditionally, these triangles bond two entities together through a misguided attempt to relieve tension. When this happens, the initial relationship where the tension was created is forced to the periphery. However, this initial relationship remains energetically central for all involved because no authentic resolution has taken place. Looking at relationships in this way, where have you brought in a third party to alleviate tension without addressing the situation directly? Take a read through a few more generalized examples and see if anything else resonates.

1. A woman is unhappy in her marriage and she bonds with her best friend by consistently complaining. The complaints put her husband in a negative position and the friends create a strong partnership in opposition of him. The woman's feelings are not resolved. The best friend is not a replacement for the husband. The marital dynamic remains unhappy.

- **1. Wife + 2. Husband + 3. Best Friend =** *Triangulation*

2. A man feels consistently disrespected by his boss. He does not have the courage to ask his boss for better treatment and drinks alcohol every night to cope with his feelings of disrespect. The man's feelings are never addressed and therefore do not change. He drinks more and more over time trying to relieve his negative feelings, but it does not work. His relationship to alcohol remains dysfunctional.

- **1. Man + 2. Boss + 3. Drinking Alcohol =** *Triangulation*

3. A mom feels left out of her oldest son's life after he has gone away to college. The mom complains to the daughter still living in the home about her feelings of disappointment. The daughter feels stuck between her mom and her brother, but since her brother is gone, feels forced to side with her mom. The son comes home for school break. Mom and daughter are both cold to him due to mom's unresolved feelings and sister's loyalty to mom. Hurt, the son feels left out and doesn't understand why. The issue continues unaddressed. During the next visit home, the mom and daughter present as an impenetrable duo. Slowly, the son stops coming home from school entirely.

- **1. Mom + 2. Son + 3. Daughter =** *Triangulation*

4. A dad doesn't quite understand his teenage daughter. He feels unconfident next to her growing social calendar and convinces himself that she doesn't want to spend time with him anymore. The dad begins working on his classic car in the garage to ease his complex feelings regarding his daughter growing up. The daughter is hurt by her dad's absence and spends even more time with her friends. The classic car wins awards and dad has to travel to car shows on the weekends. Dad is around even less, and daughter perceives that he loves his car more than he loves her. The relationship becomes more and more estranged.

- **1. Dad + 2. Daughter + 3. Working on Classic Car =** *Triangulation*

In the squares below, draw some triangles. As you identify the places in your life where you are triangulating relationships to relieve tension, label one corner of each triangle with your name and the other corners with the names of the substances, behaviors, people, choices, etc., involved. As you draw, take note if any aspects of your triangles overlap. Now, grab a darker pen or marker, and turn all of those triangles into circles and spirals. As you draw, let your pen or marker go around the curves as many times as needed. While you do this, quietly allow guidance to come forward to inform you how to shift these relationships to more authentically reflect your feelings and needs.

When you are finished, journal or silently contemplate this new step in your honest and integral expression.

I Will Authentically *Relate* to My Relationships by…

_____

_____

_____

_____

See what other shapes come to mind as you begin to relate to your relationships with this new awareness. The shape of the spiral is a well-known symbol of the Feminine. Shifting, turning, and coiling around itself, the spiral reminds us that we are fluid, non-linear, cyclical, and never-ending. The spiral can also remind us that death is not an end of life, but only one part of an infinite cycle. Our energy is absolute and regenerates itself through the unlimited processes of birth, life, death, and renewal. Our relationships carry our energy and they too can be conceptualized through this lens. Thank you for dedicating your time to this activity. Getting clear on our conscious and unconscious patterns in our relationships can be very empowering. This awareness is not ever meant to make you feel bad, guilty, or ashamed. This awareness is only intended for freedom, release, and bliss. You can't unknow what you know, Sis. I know that I love you and I am grateful for you. You are a light bearer. Takes one to know one. ☺

~ SPS #2: ~
* Cellular Town Hall *

Did you know that every cell of your body loves you? They do! In his book, *The Mastery of Love: A Practical Guide to the Art of Relationships: A Toltec Wisdom Book*, Don Miguel Ruiz writes that the cells in our bodies are totally and completely loyal to us. Think about it. They work in harmony. They at least *try* to give it their best shot - *every time* - to meet our *every* request. Don Miguel Ruiz even says that they pray to us… that we are their God! Wowza! What a concept, right? Cells are really smart! They are powerhouses of information, wisdom, energy, efficiency, and dedication. Cells are filled with good stuff that is directly created *for* and given to **YOU**. God or Goddess - they depend on *you* - and they offer much in return. What if you were to ask them what *they* needed or wanted as a sort of 'thank you' for all of this unconditional devotion? Let's have a Cellular Town Hall! According to the integrative form of energetic work based on the writings of Alice Bailey called Esoteric Healing, every part of our anatomy and physiology has a psychological contribution. With that in mind, this is going to be a multi-disciplinary exercise. In your imagination, create a space for the Town Hall to take place. Take some deep breaths and acquaint yourself with this environment. With an awareness of your physical body, invite the different parts of you to join. Below is a general guide for understanding which parts of the anatomy bring what - psychologically speaking - based upon my studies of the Esoteric Healing Work.

- **Heart:** Processes Heart Aches and Hurts
- **Stomach:** Processes Emotions and Thoughts
- **Breasts:** Nurtures and Offers Sustenance for Self and Others
- **Liver:** Holds and Processes Anger

- **Spleen:** Brings Spiritual Energy Down into the Physical Body
- **Pancreas:** Processes Issues of Dependence, Independence, and Unmanaged Stress
- **Ovaries:** Hold the Seeds for New Life, New Ideas, and New Creations
- **Womb/Uterus:** Magickal Spot for New Life to Grow and Develop
- **Adrenal Glands:** Responsible for Rapid Physiological Responses to Stress
- **Kidneys:** Filters Fear and Stress
- **Spine:** Metaphysical Support System
- **Eyes:** Seeing Intuition
- **Ears:** Hearing Intuition

In your imagination, ask the cells from each body part to come forward individually. When you are ready, you can follow the prompts and questions on the following pages or create your own. Be sure to name the cells specifically when you address them.

**"Cells from my <u>Heart</u>, I honor your complete loyalty.
Thank you for your hard work, dedication, and love."**

- What do you need or want from me at this moment at this time? _____
  _____

- What would you like me to know? _____
  _____

- What can I do to help you do your job even better? _____
  _____

**"Cells from my <u>Stomach</u>, I honor your complete loyalty.
Thank you for your hard work, dedication, and love."**

- What do you need or want from me at this moment at this time? _____
  _____

- What would you like me to know? _____
  _____

- What can I do to help you do your job even better? _____
  _____

**"Cells from my Breasts, I honor your complete loyalty.
Thank you for your hard work, dedication, and love."**

- What do you need or want from me at this moment at this time? _____
  _____

- What would you like me to know? _____
  _____

- What can I do to help you do your job even better? _____
  _____

**"Cells from my Liver, I honor your complete loyalty.
Thank you for your hard work, dedication, and love."**

- What do you need or want from me at this moment at this time? _____
  _____

- What would you like me to know? _____
  _____

- What can I do to help you do your job even better? _____
  _____

**"Cells from my Spleen, I honor your complete loyalty.
Thank you for your hard work, dedication, and love."**

- What do you need or want from me at this moment at this time? _____
  _____

- What would you like me to know? _____
  _____

- What can I do to help you do your job even better? _____
  _____

**"Cells from my Pancreas, I honor your complete loyalty.
Thank you for your hard work, dedication, and love."**

- What do you need or want from me at this moment at this time? _____
  _____

- What would you like me to know? _____
  _____

- What can I do to help you do your job even better? _____
  _____

**"Cells from my Ovaries, I honor your complete loyalty.
Thank you for your hard work, dedication, and love."**

- What do you need or want from me at this moment at this time? _____
  _____

- What would you like me to know? _____
  _____

- What can I do to help you do your job even better? _____
  _____

**"Cells from my Womb, I honor your complete loyalty.
Thank you for your hard work, dedication, and love."**

- What do you need or want from me at this moment at this time? _____
  _____

- What would you like me to know? _____
  _____

- What can I do to help you do your job even better? _____
  _____

**"Cells from my <u>Adrenal Glands</u>, I honor your complete loyalty.
Thank you for your hard work, dedication, and love."**

- What do you need or want from me at this moment at this time? _____
  _____

- What would you like me to know? _____
  _____

- What can I do to help you do your job even better? _____
  _____

**"Cells from my <u>Kidneys</u>, I honor your complete loyalty.
Thank you for your hard work, dedication, and love."**

- What do you need or want from me at this moment at this time? _____
  _____

- What would you like me to know? _____
  _____

- What can I do to help you do your job even better? _____
  _____

**"Cells from my <u>Spine</u>, I honor your complete loyalty.
Thank you for your hard work, dedication, and love."**

- What do you need or want from me at this moment at this time? _____
  _____

- What would you like me to know? _____
  _____

- What can I do to help you do your job even better? _____
  _____

**"Cells from my Eyes, I honor your complete loyalty.
Thank you for your hard work, dedication, and love."**

- What do you need or want from me at this moment at this time? _____

_____

- What would you like me to know? _____

_____

- What can I do to help you do your job even better? _____

_____

**"Cells from my Ears, I honor your complete loyalty.
Thank you for your hard work, dedication, and love."**

- What do you need or want from me at this moment at this time? _____

_____

- What would you like me to know? _____

_____

- What can I do to help you do your job even better? _____

_____

Have as much fun as you can with this! Envision what those sweet little beings are wearing. Hear their unique voices. *Really* listen to their requests. As silly as this may feel, don't diminish the power of what you have just accomplished. With the potency of intentional thought, you've just created a new, mutually reciprocal, and loving relationship with your body. Wow! Thank you! Love you!

~ SPS #3: ~
* The Gift of Forgiveness *

In his book, *The Gift of Forgiveness: A Magical Encounter with Don Miguel Ruiz*, Olivier Clerc posits an idea for forgiveness that turns our typical equation of forgiveness on its head. Whether we realize it or not, when someone hurts us or does us wrong, a sort of currency gets established. This becomes the currency of: you did me wrong, you owe me something… therefore, I will sit and wait in my state of hurt until you make it right. When we think of it in this way, this approach to forgiveness can leave us doubly wounded. One, we've been hurt. Two, we will stay in our hurt or the hurt will go unresolved until someone else takes the initiative for action towards resolution. This is not only doubly wounding, it is completely disempowering. How often have you been able to *make* someone else do something? Sure, there are examples of people doing this in our lives when they are under duress or they feel obligated. Yet, this is forgiveness we are talking about here. For you to truly feel that the other person is taking responsibility for something, it cannot be forced, coerced, half-assed, or done with an agenda. If it is in any way, we are going to sense it and it won't be an authentic resolution. In his book, Clerc makes the suggestion that to take our power back, we must create space within our hearts to shift the equation and ask for forgiveness from the people who have hurt us. *What the - what the...!?! **I know**!* It is so different than what we are used to, but give it a think through: we take our power **back** by ***asking** for forgiveness*. According to Clerc, this changes our mental script from self-righteousness and judgment to humility and peace. If it still sounds wonky, that is OK. This is the complete opposite of what we have been taught. But think about it; when we sit around hurt and angry, waiting for someone else to '*make things right*' - whatever *that* may be and however *fleeting* - we are actually hurting ourselves. We are closing off our hearts and using the hurt and anger as justification. Yet, when we take matters into our own hands and ask for forgiveness from those who have done us wrong, we release pride and move toward accepting love. Therefore, this *"Gift of Forgiveness"* practice isn't about anyone other than us. Asking for forgiveness from someone who has hurt *us* pardons, absolves, and exonerates *us* from the bondage of self-judgment, self-criticism, and self-loathing. The feelings we hold in our hearts that restrict our capacities for love, especially our love of self, are holographically mirrored in the amounts of love we allow ourselves to give and receive. Let me break that down: what we feel internally will be expressed externally. Holding onto hate and resentment hurts us. So why not change it? We have the power... and guess what? This forgiveness request happens within the meditative space of own consciousness. No phone calls or emails. No weird coffee dates. Only our own hearts and Souls need to show up at this party. Deep thoughts, huh? Ready to give *"The Gift of Forgiveness"* a try? In his book, Clerc has his own methodology and verbiage. The following is my interpretation of his work.

- Find a quiet space and get relaxed.
    - Unplug from what is going on around you and take some deep breaths. Allow a feeling of comfort to support your Physical, Emotional, Mental, Soul, and Spiritual bodies. Ask the energies of humility and grace to be present. Use your imagination and intuition to create space and openness within your heart.

- Ask for forgiveness from others.
    - When you are ready, imagine a door at the opposite end of the space you've created within your heart. In no particular order, allow the people you would like to ask for forgiveness from to come through the door. These are the people you have been waiting to receive an apology from. Only now, by asking them for forgiveness, you receive freedom from the tensions, conflicts, and judgements. One-by-one, allow them to stand before you, look them in the eye and ask, "Please forgive me." Ask as many times as you need. When you feel a shift that something has unlocked, opened, or changed within you, move on to the next person.

- Ask for forgiveness from yourself.
    - The last person who walks through the door is you. When you are standing face-to-face with yourself, imagine a bright love-light surrounding you. Connect to yourself and align your breath. Intentionally honor the part of you that is your Higher Self. Intentionally honor the part of you that is your Wounded Self. In this space, as you gaze upon the imperfect perfection that is you say, "Please forgive me." Allow the guilt and shame to fall off of your body. Release the criticisms and judgements. Tell this version of you how you feel and listen with an open heart as she in turn shares her feelings. Hug her deeper and harder than you've ever hugged anyone before. Fill her with love and as her body melts into yours, become aware of this new way of being.

- Express Gratitude.
  - Feel a deep well of thanks within your consciousness. Allow all of the things in your life that you are grateful for to bubble up to the surface. Express your gratitude for life, love, for the people whom you've just asked for forgiveness, and for yourself. With each expression of "Thank you," allow your heart to open wider. Become aware of the innocence that is you. This is the deepest and purest part of you that knows, without a doubt, how loving your heart is. Breathe into this inner-wisdom, and with your hands on your Heart Chakra, honor yourself for the deep and courageous work you have done.

Wow, wow, wow! Deep thoughts. Deep work. Deep potential for freedom and transformation. Deep opportunities for release. Deep initiations for self-love. Honey, you deserve it. All of this and more. I love you. I am in awe of you and your strength. Thank you. Thank you for being here - *right here* - right now!

~ SPS #4: ~
* Stepping-In *

In undergrad I studied acting with a magnificent teacher. As we worked through scenes and monologues, my teacher would talk about the techniques of stepping-in and as if. These are well known techniques that many in the industry have crafted and utilized over the years, but this ability to step-in to another person's reality - whether it be a character in a play or a person in our lives - has always struck me as a powerful way to access empathy, compassion, and understanding. Many of us in our adult lives have come to realize that we didn't have perfect parents. We laugh at this notion because our rational minds know such a thing doesn't exist. Yet, subconsciously, a lot of us still navigate life *'as if'* this *should* have been true. Lynn talks about the freedom she felt being able to release her father from unmet expectations. Perhaps we can apply these acting techniques to our relationships with our parents and experience a bit of the same. Pick a parent, or someone who was like a parent to you, to be your partner in this exercise. Don't worry, this person doesn't actually need to be here with you because we are going to work with imagination and intuition. Once you have chosen your scene partner, find two to three items of clothing around your house for each of you. These are your costumes and they should be easy to take on and off. Some examples are: coats, hats, scarves, sweaters, jewelry, etc. Now it is time to design the set. Choose where you would like this scene to take place, making sure there are chairs for both of you to sit. Place the costume pieces on their respective chairs with one chair representing you and the other your parent. Next, pen the script outline below. To do this, take a moment and reflect on this relationship. What are some thoughts and questions that you have for this person and where would you appreciate compassion, empathy, clarity, and understanding?

Questions and Thoughts for Compassion, Empathy, Clarity, and Understanding

1._____

2._____

3._____

4._____

5._____

When your script outline is written, place it on the chair representing you. With the items on the chair representing your parent, get into *costume*. Put on the clothing pieces you have chosen for them and sit in their chair. In this way, you are literally '*stepping-in*' to the scene, '*as if*'' you are them. Take a moment and get into character. To assist in this process, take into consideration the *given circumstances*. These are the things that you know about your parent's age, family dynamics, social experiences, marital status, physical health, emotional health, educational experience, occupation, etc. This attention to the backstory can help put things into the character's perspective. It can also create compassion, empathy, clarity, and understanding before you even start the scene. From this informed place, *in character* as your parent, read the first line of the script outline. From your character's point of view (remember, you are now playing them just like you would a *role* in a play) begin to address the thoughts and questions with clear explanations, accountability, and when applicable, conscientious efforts to take responsibility. This response is delivered directly to the opposite chair and the items representing you, '*as if*' your scene partner is talking directly to you. As you speak from your parent's perspective, take note of the information coming up that could - through compassion, empathy, clarity and understanding - potentially inspire release, resolution, and acceptance. Do this for each of the five things listed above and allow for anything else that needs to come forward to be discussed, processed, and transformed. Use the space below to record any information coming through to help you remember specifics when the scene is finished.

Important information for release, resolution, and acceptance regarding Question #1 _____

_____

_____

Important information for release, resolution, and acceptance regarding Question #2 _____

_____

_____

Important information for release, resolution, and acceptance regarding Question #3 _____

_____

_____

Important information for release, resolution, and acceptance regarding Question #4 _____

_____

_____

Important information for release, resolution, and acceptance regarding Question #5 _____

_____

_____

Additional information for release, resolution, and acceptance _____
_____
_____

When this part of the conversation feels complete, take off the costume for your parent and lay the items on the chair. As a final step, put on the items chosen to represent *you* and sit in *your* chair. Now, you are playing yourself. Say any additional things you would like to say. This is your chance to respond, clear the air, and get anything else off of your chest. When the dialogue feels finished for now, thank your parent for their participation and end the scene. If you feel there is still unfinished business, leave your set and costumes in place for another run-through. Rehearse, revise, and rewrite this play as many times as you need. When you feel ready for closing night, strike the set by putting the chairs and costumes away. Journal or reflect on the following to solidify the shifts, insights, and awareness that came forward as a result of doing this activity.

- Now, this relationship is _____
  _____

- I feel differently about _____
  _____

- I can release _____
  _____

- My expectations are _____
  _____

- In the future, I want to _____
  _____

Thank you for playing. Engaging in this work can initially feel strange to our adult sensibilities. However, if we can relax and intuitively interact in ways that consistently offer opportunities for insight, release, and rebirth, it does get easier. I promise. Love you! Thank you for doing this.

~ SPS #5: ~
* Black Out Poetry *

Sometimes the beauty in life can come from the most unexpected of places. Take Black Out Poetry for instance. Not only does it reduce, reuse, and recycle, but by blacking out certain chosen words on a page of text in a book, it can simultaneously create a poem and a visual work of art - for free! Chances are, you've got some old books, newspapers, or magazines lying around. Once you have randomly let the page choose you (meaning, you let the book fall open and trust that this page was meant for you), scan the page and see if any words jump out. People that teach this form of art suggest finding an anchor word or phrase that helps you create a theme for your poem. As you continue to scan the page, start to circle or outline words that relate back to your anchor word or phrase. Go through the text a second time and try to put your poem together with the outlined words, adding in any new words or phrases needed to make your poem flow. Now that you have a basic first draft, use a dark marker or pen and begin to black out the words and phrases that are *not* part of your poem. You will probably have lots to black out. This is where the element of visual art can come in. As you are blacking out the words not needed, you can create a work of visual art to surround your black out poem with different colors and designs. This page is now a priceless expression of you and your creativity. Hang it up or keep it in a special place to remind you of the quiet moments when you created beauty. Thank you, beautiful! I love you.

Crystal Love: Lynn's Crystal is the heart-healer extraordinaire, Pink Tourmaline (*tour*-muh-leen). This crystal, which attracts love energy to us in the physical and spiritual realms, can creatively re-inspire and re-heal our hearts to trust in love again. Pink Tourmaline can also promote the peace and relaxation needed to alchemize destructive feelings, thereby supporting us to restore our beliefs in kindness, joy, happiness, and beauty. If you are needing some extra self-love encouragement, play with placing a piece of Pink Tourmaline over the Heart Chakra to disperse emotional pain and increase receptivity to pleasure. Additionally, if you are feeling the aches of spiritual growth and ascension, allow this stone to share and reconfirm the commitment of the Universal forces of unconditional love and oneness. When you are ready, use Pink Tourmaline as an endorsement towards enlightenment, fusing all aspects of love together with its pink light of compassion, tenderness, healing, and harmony.

Suggested Reading for Beautiful and Pragmatic Soul-Informed Sobriety, *The Untethered Soul: The Journey Beyond Yourself* by Michael A. Singer.

Additional Journaling and SPS Space

Maria

I moved to the United States from Brazil in 2004 to pursue my dream of learning more about American Musical Theatre. I auditioned and was accepted into the American Musical and Dramatic Academy in New York City. For two years, I studied in an intensive conservatory program. I learned the English Language and American Culture through Musicals. I feel grateful - and at the same time can identify - that this training program was almost like a military academy for Broadway. Their whole way was to prepare you for the 'real world' by crushing you. I think I made it through 'un-crushed' because I already had such a strong sense of self. After graduation, I moved to Boston and went to Graduate School. It was in this program that I discovered 'Theatre of the Oppressed,' which is a model for Social Justice theatre. This model was created by a Brazilian Director. I remember feeling really upset that I didn't know about this type of theatre even though it was created by a Brazilian. Soon, I started focusing more on this type of theatre for social change and I began working with immigrants. At this time, I felt very privileged to be in the United States, speaking the language, and involved in the Arts. I was not here to get multiple jobs and send money home, like a lot of the immigrants that I worked with. I also became aware of being a 'white' immigrant. Even when my accent was much stronger, I was never questioned about my legality in the States. I feel that this is because my skin is very light. I look white. There is no other explanation. It was not fair, and I wanted my work with Social Justice theatre to highlight this injustice. It was doing theatre, in Spanish and English, that I met my husband. He is Latino and from Mexico, and as we got to know each other more, we had so much to talk about. We could identify similarities in our backgrounds as well as our love for theatre and traveling. Even my mom noticed it. One time, when my parents came to visit, she said, "Oh my gosh, you two talk so much, you have so much to say to each other." I feel like that has always been the case with us and now, we are going on eleven years of marriage, with two beautiful daughters. Six years ago, we made the decision to move our family out of Boston and down to Florida. It has been one of the best decisions. It has allowed us to slow down. The 'American Way of Life' - one of rushing all the time - is very difficult. It is even in the language, 'time is money,' and 'hurry up and wait.' In Brazil, I worked 40 hours a week and still had so much extra time for friends, my family, and myself. Here in the States, I was constantly asking, "How can I work the same hours and feel like I have time for nothing else?" Moving allowed us to step off of that treadmill. I feel more in touch with nature and with myself now. I feel so connected to the world around me. I notice the sweet encounters and have become way more attuned to my needs for self-care. I grew up with a mother who didn't practice a lot of self-care. She was very giving and everything she did, and still does to this day, is for others. I didn't feel that I had to live my life that way. I realized that I could not take care of anybody else unless I took care of myself. More than anything, I wanted to model this for my girls. This way, when they are adults, they know that they can voice their needs and put themselves first. Every time I say, "I need this for me… this is important to me," they are learning how important it is to dedicate time for self-care. I decided a few years ago to give myself a birthday gift and I went for a three-day meditation retreat at the Chopra Center in California. I learned about Primordial Sound Meditation. As a musical person, it resonated for me because it is about mantra, sound, and vibration. I also learned about Ayurveda, the 'Science of Life.' These two philosophies helped me to get even more in tune with the oneness of all things. They also helped me become more connected with my own culture and my ancestors. When I like something, I cannot just read a book about it, I cannot just study, I have to learn enough about it to teach. When I left that retreat, I made the decision that I was going to become a meditation teacher and I signed up for the teacher training. I also decided that I wanted to teach Ayurveda, so I have signed up to become certified through a local Ayurvedic school. I want to do this for myself, for my kids, and for my lifestyle. I also want to be able to share this and incorporate it all with my Social Justice theatre background. Studying these two philosophies has helped me become more aware of the various 'roles' that we all play in our lives. I play the roles of mother, sister, daughter, wife, teacher, and so many more throughout a day. We all do. We have the language and the costumes we need to step into these different roles, and just like actors on the stage we play the roles; but we are not confined by these roles. I have struggled with this. Now that I am in my forties, I am just making sense of this as my children become more independent. As a result, I feel younger and stronger than I did when I was in my twenties. I know that I can model this for my daughters and let them see that life doesn't always have to be about restrictions and reactions. This process for me has been about letting go and unlearning behaviors. All of my training has led me to believe that no matter what, I have to do what is for my highest good. I have to walk the talk. In a way, I've had to mother myself through these processes of learning how to get more in touch with myself, learning how to say no, and allowing myself to be in the present moment. My culture has also taught me many things. Yes, Brazil has a 'machista' culture, which gives the message that 'women should be seen and not heard,' and that definitely does not work for me, but I have learned to speak my truth around that. My culture has also gifted me with a sense of optimism and hope. Facing the many problems of a military dictatorship, a very corrupt government, and two impeachments (just in my lifetime!), the Brazilian spirit seems to always believe that things *will* improve, that tomorrow *will* be a better day, and that there is nothing we cannot solve… and if we cannot solve it, there is nothing to worry about. I say, "If there is a problem and there is nothing you can do, don't worry about it." I also say, "If there is a problem and you can do something, don't worry about that either, because you will do what needs to be done." As part of growing up, there was always music and celebrating, no matter what. I try to incorporate all of that, all of my roles, and balance them with a passion for life-long learning and joy. It is funny, but it seems that when most people want a life change, they either quit their jobs or go to California. I've recently done both. With all that I am studying and teaching, I just want women to know: smile more, be silent more, and trust that we are all just doing our best. Have compassion for yourself and others. It is all about seeing things from someone else's level of consciousness. For me, it is meditation, Ayurveda, and theatre. I want to know… what is yours?

Making This Story Your Own:

Maria's story reminds us to slow down and get clear on what we want and need.
Take a moment, breathe, and reflect.
What stands out for you when you read her words?
Is there a situation in your life that is similar to Maria's?
Perhaps part of her story feels connected to your own.
How can you relate her experiences to your past, present, and future?

- *My Connection to Maria's Story* _____

_____

_____

_____

_____

Knowing that you aren't alone, let's gently explore some other themes from Maria's story together:

- ***Oneness***
  - When you look around, what do you see? Do you make sense of the world by categorizing people and things as *other* or *not part of you?* If you shifted your thinking and embraced everything as part of you, what would be different? Plants, animals, trees, other people - even inanimate objects - if you thought about them as being connected to you, what would change? Would there be more respect and responsibility? Maybe more love and acceptance? More connection and tenderness? What if this concept of oneness was reciprocal? What if everything you came into contact with felt the same way about *you*... mutually giving and receiving respect, responsibility, love, acceptance, connection and tenderness? What would be different then? Could or would incorporating the concept of oneness into your life be helpful? Why or why not? If so, what are a few small shifts you can make?

- ***Things Will Always Improve***
  - What is your initial reaction when you think about being positive or optimistic? How about when other people act this way? If others maintain a positive outlook, even if you feel the circumstances don't warrant it, how do you react? When this happens are you open and free of judgement? Are you critical and negative? What *do* you believe about life's gifts and challenges? What would you *like* to believe when it comes to life's gifts and challenges? How different are the two answers? How do you feel about the statement: *things will always improve*? Do you agree or disagree? Could adopting this philosophy more, or in a different way, be beneficial?

- ***Walking the Talk***
  - Are your words and actions in alignment? Another way to say it could be, do you *walk your walk and talk your talk*? If so, how have you learned to do this? If not, what is preventing you? How generous are you with others when you perceive them as not being authentic in word and deed? How generous are you with yourself when you realize you have done the same? Are these answers close or equal? What are a few, easily identifiable things you can do to create a more authentic lifestyle?

Sacred Play Suggestions:

~ SPS #1: ~
* Time Talk *

What if we could change our relationship to time so that we didn't always feel rushed, or in a race against the clock? Being on the perpetual treadmill that Maria talks about is not only exhausting, it can leave us feeling powerless. Yet, many physicists and astronomers talk about time as a concept - or construct - meaning that humans have created this idea. We know that time travels at different speeds depending on where you are in the Universe and how fast you are going. Our minds, when combined with the powers of our hearts and souls, are the biggest, most efficient super conductor-computers around. Why don't we try to create a new construct around time? One that empowers us and allows us to feel like we are captaining the ship of our daily to-do lists instead of the other way around. In her book, *Seven Planes of Existence: The Philosophy of the Theta Healing Technique*, Vianna Stibal talks about time as a Universal Law which resides in the Sixth Plane of Existence, or the Sixth Plane of our Consciousness. With imagination, intuition, and a little ingenuity, let's hop on an elevator and go have a conversation with **Time**. Get comfy and let your big brain do its magick by reading through the following guided visualization.

Take a few deep breaths and become aware of the physical world that you are in.
Acquaint your senses with your current environment.
Gauge what you see, hear, smell, taste, feel on your skin, and feel in your body.
Begin to align your awareness with your imagination on each inhale.
Give yourself permission to have an experience on each exhale.
Slightly close your eyes and visualize a hallway with an elevator.
As you walk towards the elevator doors, you take in the environment of the hallway.
You get in the elevator and press the number 6.
Notice which direction your elevator goes and the speed.
When you arrive at number 6, the elevator doors open to reveal a completely unusual world.
You step out and everything is different.
The air is different than anything you've ever breathed before. The scenery is different than anything you've ever seen before. The sounds are different than anything you've ever heard before.
You walk into this special place and explore.
All of a sudden, you look up and a being is standing in front of you.
*This being is **Time**.*
Time introduces themself and is very happy to see you.
From Time, you instantly feel love and appreciation.
Time offers you a seat.
You agree and sit down.
As you get comfortable, Time opens the dialogue by saying, "I've been hoping you would come."
You feel in your heart this is a safe space, so you continue the conversation....

In any way that feels right, talk with Time. Below are a few suggestions for this conversation. Use them or come up with your own ideas. The objective is to create a new, loving, empowered, and mutually respectful exchange with Time.

- Apologize for being angry with Time.
- Take responsibility for your participation in the race against Time.
- Ask what you can do for Time.
- Request a new relationship with Time.
- Ask Time how to maintain this new relationship.

When your conversation feels complete, thank Time and say goodbye.
Walk back through the world of Time and enter the elevator.
Press the number 3 to return to our world, the Third Dimension.
When you arrive, the elevator doors open, and you walk back into the present moment.
Feel the cleansing energy of Mother Earth coming up into your body on each inhale.
Solidify your connection to the ground on each exhale.
Continue aligning your awareness to the present moment.
Slowly open your eyes.
Once again, acquaint your senses with your environment.
Gauge what you see, hear, smell, taste, feel on your skin, and feel in your body.

When you are ready, journal or reflect on your experience with Time.

- The world of **Time** looked like _____

  _____

- **Time** appeared to me as _____

  _____

- When talking with **Time**, I felt _____

  _____

- The most important thing I said to **Time** was _____

  _____

- The most important thing **Time** said to me was _____

  _____

- My new understanding of **Time** is _____

  _____

- My new relationship with **Time** will be _____

  _____

Recalibrating our relationship with Time can offer much relaxation and liberation. Although the clock will never stop, by creating a reciprocal relationship with Time that is rooted in respect, we can cultivate a partnership with Time that feels empowering. I like that idea. I like it a lot. I also love you. Thank you for doing this activity. The less of us there are rushing around trying to *beat* time, the more of us there are slowing down to *be **in** the moment*. Stop and smell the flowers, babe. You've got all the time in the world.

~ SPS #2: ~
* Abhyanga Massage *

In Ayurveda, the traditional system of Hindu medicine that Maria teaches, there is a well-known and regularly practiced self-care ritual known as Abhyanga (A-bee-*yang*-a). This ritual is an Ayurvedic Oil Massage done with the intention of enhancing energetic flow while being attentive and loving to the body. Daily devotees of this practice share that Abhyanga can provide comfort and strength as well as feelings of being deeply loved. You can do this massage all over your body, or if you prefer, you can keep it localized to hands or feet. This ritual is traditionally done in the early morning to aide in the removal of toxins accumulated during the night, yet since we can use self-love at any time of the day, practice Abhyanga when it best fits your schedule. If you've got them, use natural, organic, cold-pressed oils for your massage. Sesame oil and sunflower oil are great options. If not, since this is about fitting self-care in whenever and however you can, use whatever lotion or oil you've got handy. Start by brushing a dry washcloth gently over your skin to remove the dead skin cells. Next take a few deep breaths, and with your hands on your heart, ask what it is that you need right now. Write down what comes up.

What do I need right now?

_____

_____

_____

_____

Taking what you have written, turn what you need into a shortened **I AM** phrase or Mantra. For example, if something that you need right now is *peace*, your **I AM** Mantra will be: **I AM** *Peace*. Allow the Mantra to reflect your abilities to provide what you need for yourself by claiming it. Some examples are:

- **I AM** Loved
- **I AM** Connected
- **I AM** Safe
- **I AM** Abundant
- **I AM** Grounded

    ○ **My I AM Mantra** _____

Warm your hands by rubbing them together as you speak your Abhyanga Mantra. When you are ready, begin applying the oil. With loving touch, guided by your intuition, send your Mantra into your body over and over as you massage. Your Mantra might shift as you move around and that is fine. Listen to your body and love yourself in exactly the way you need. Apply more oil as needed and spend as much time as you can loving yourself with this dedicated practice of well-deserved self-care. When finished, take a few moments to journal around what came through for you during this Abhyanga Ritual.

- Abhyanga Wisdom for my **Body** _____

    _____

- Abhyanga Wisdom for my **Heart** _____

    _____

- Abhyanga Wisdom for my **Mind** _____

    _____

- Abhyanga Wisdom for my **Soul** _____

    _____

Once again repeat your **I AM** Abhyanga Mantra and finish with your hands on your heart. Bask in your love and feel some of mine in there, too. I love you. Thank you for this self-care. When you take care of you, I can feel it... and it feels fab!

~ SPS #3: ~
* Plant Realm Guidance *

Have you ever talked to a plant? As silly as the question sounds, we know they listen. There are countless social media posts out there with pictures of plants that have been verbally loved versus verbally abused and the differences are remarkable. Maybe when you were a little girl, you used to climb trees? In their book, *The Feminine Face of God: The Unfolding of the Sacred in Women*, Sherry Ruth Anderson and Patricia Hopkins interview several women who talk about being mothered and loved by trees. Why do we forget about this when we grow up? Not only do plants feed us, they give us shelter, medicine, clothing, beauty - and if that wasn't enough - they also provide us a nice place to sit while we enjoy their generosity. How do we return the favor? Maybe it really is like Shel Silverstein's book, *The Giving Tree*. The only reciprocation needed is love and gratitude. We know that everything has an energetic footprint. You don't even have to dust off your 'Tree Hugger' t-shirt to remember from science class that plants, just like us, convert food to a useable source of energy for sustenance, growth, and reproduction. Based on the example above, plants, like humans, react when either positive or negative energy is coming at them. Lastly, we know that they communicate in far more elegant and sophisticated ways than we can currently decipher. With Suspension of Disbelief - a theatrical term that basically means, 'I am going to temporarily accept what I would usually disregard as unrealistic so that I may enjoy what is happening in this moment' - let's see if we can talk to the Trees, sing with the Snapdragons, and dance with the Dill... the herb, *not* the pickle. Find your foliage: grass, house plants, garden plants, trees, weeds... everyone counts, and **every** *one* is important. If getting a plant in front of you IRL (*in real life*) isn't happening at this moment, no worries! Energy follows thought, and your energy is powerful! Think back to a time spent in nature and connect into the Plant Realm that way. When you are ready, get comfortable and get quiet. Take a few deep, cleansing breaths. Connect your energy into the Earth. Connect your energy into Source. Become aware of every cell of your body and set the intention to ***lighten your touch*** as you connect and commune with Plant Consciousness. Vianna Stibal, mentioned above in Maria's Sacred Play Suggestion #1, also suggests in another of her books, *Theta Healing: Introducing an Extraordinary Energy-Healing Modality*, to go in "as light as a feather when you connect to plants." This is because human energetic patterns are much denser than that of plants and we want to be respectful and cautious of overwhelming them and potentially causing them harm. As lightly as you can, intentionally connect into your chosen plant. Ask permission to enter into their space. When permission is granted, visualize going into the consciousness of the plant. Clearly express your gratitude for this adventure and conversate in whatever way you feel called. Some examples of things to inquire about and address could be:

- Ask for wisdom related to grounding and anchoring or giving and receiving.
- Ask to be shown the wisdom of oneness from the plant's perspective.
- Ask how to be more in touch with nature.
- Ask how to be more in touch with yourself.
- Take responsibility for your relationship with the Plant Realm up until now.
- Create a Sacred Contract with the Plant Realm for mutual respect, love, and gratitude, from this day forward.

When your conversation feels complete, again express gratitude, say goodbye, and begin to gently pull your energy back into yourself. Reacquaint with your human sensibilities and assess your senses. Take long, deep breaths and continue recalibrating your energy back into the Human Realm. When you are ready, journal or reflect on this experience and the guidance gifted from the Realm of Plants.

My Guidance from the Plant Realm

How do you feel? Ready to change your name to Lily or Rose… maybe even Nightshade? Seriously though, the Plant Realm is beyond dedicated to us. When we can open our awareness to the wisdom and love pouring forth from them, it feels amazing. It is also a great reminder that we are capable of receiving and reciprocating that same kind of dedicated love. You can start now and receive my love. I love you. Thank you for doing this!

~ SPS #4: ~
* Social Change *

Creating social change can feel daunting. Yet making a difference is actually easier than we've been led to believe. In the article "The Eight Laws of Change" by Stephen A. Schwartz, which was featured in the Spring 2016 Volume of the *Light of Consciousness: Journal of Spiritual Awakening,* he writes that small simple choices, made individually within the collective are really all that it takes. Schwartz goes on to share that, counter to what we have been taught, social change isn't dependent on money, political power, or violence. Lasting social change is brought about by small, daily choices made in compassionate and life-affirming ways. This means that each one of us can make considerable waves in the Ocean of human consciousness with just our attitudes, opinions, and day-to-day lifestyle choices. Pretty empowering! What do you see in our world today that you would like to change? Maria talks about social injustice and highlights the pervasive reality of white privilege. Her chosen compassionate and life-affirming action is rooted in a form of Social Justice theatre called the Theatre of the Oppressed. In the box on the next page, write down five things that you would like to change in the left column. Next, for each of the five things you've identified, connect them to five small, daily lifestyle choices that you can easily make and write those in the middle column. Finally - and employ your imagination a little here - visualize five things that will be affected and changed by your small dedicated choices and write those in the right column.

Changes I Want to See	Choices I Will Make	Ways I'll Make a Difference
1.	1.	1.
2.	2.	2.
3.	3.	3.
4.	4.	4.
5.	5.	5.

See what happens when you commit to these choices for 5 days. If it feels right, make another commitment to find 5 people, or 5 groups, who share in your passion for change. Schwartz wraps up his article with the inspirational message that this concept is not mere "utopian fantasy." As individuals we can make big differences just with our choices, attitudes, and intentions. He also goes on to suggest that when we actively join with others and work towards the common goals of increased wellness and happiness, we truly can create a better, more sustainable, connected, and loving world. If we take a look throughout our human experience, lasting social change has been accomplished by those who have made love and peace their mission. They did it and so can we! It will come as no surprise that - according to numerology - the number 555 carries with it the spiritual significance of freedom, exploration, travel, and change. Love you! Thanks for doing this activity!

~ SPS #5: ~
* Get To – Have To *

Have you ever listed everything that you do in your life on a Get To/Have To list? One of my teachers, Kaia Ra, author of *The Sophia Code: A Living Transmission from the Sophia Dragon Tribe*, talks in her programs about the notion of 'get-to' versus 'have-to'. Below, there are two columns. The left side is the **Get To** column and the right is the **Have To** column. Begin making a mental list of all the things you regularly do. This list includes the physical responsibilities of your daily schedule, as well as any emotional, mental, and spiritual responsibilities. Cover the gamut of everything you do for yourself and everything you do for everyone (and everything) else. As you create this list, write each thing in either column based upon how you feel about it… meaning does this thing feel like you *have* to do it, or does it feel like you *get* to do it?

Get To	Have To

Now, take a look at your lists. Is one column longer than the other? Is it surprising that you put certain things in the **Get To** column? Is it surprising that you put other things in the **Have To** column? Here is a thought… what if you could transform the *have-tos* into *get-tos*? Give it a try. Pick five items in the **Have To** column and play with your perspective. How can you change the energy of these particular responsibilities? How can you take ownership of these five things so that they are empowering? Keep transforming the **Have To** column into the **Get To** column and work through your entire list. Answers and solutions aren't necessarily the goals. If they come up, great! However, we know from Maria's Sacred Play Suggestion #4 that small daily choices made from a place of compassion can create big change. Apply that same theory here. Look to identify small and simple things that can change your relationship to your daily responsibilities and activities. How can something shift from being an energy drain to an energy boost? Life can be much sweeter when the to-do list becomes a gift for ourselves and others. The way we look at it really is up to us. Thanks for doing this. Your energy around all of your new *get-tos* will be motivational and inspirational! I love you. As a final step, support this transformation in the future by clarifying your process.

I change my *Have To* list into a *Get To* list by…

_____

_____

_____

Crystal Love: Maria's crystal, Rainbow Fluorite (**floor-***ahyt*), is known to many as a stone of discernment and aptitude. Due to its wondrous combination of purple, blue, green, clear, and yellow Fluorite, this Rainbow variety is a powerful healing stone that can offer many gifts. Oftentimes used for issues with concentration, this stone's mental support is bar none. Try using Rainbow Fluorite to ease chaos, disruption, and disorganization of the mind. The calm, stabilizing, and cleansing energy of this Crystal can provide protection from negativity in social situations, balance intuition with rationale, bring freshness to stagnant situations, offer sequentialization for our thought processes, organize the input of external information, and defend against narrow mindedness. Can you say, "wowza!" Well, it doesn't stop there. This stone can promote physical and spiritual peace during meditation by opening our consciousness to Divine Timing and it also works beautifully with our Chakras. Try placing a piece over the Ajna for quick thinking or over the Heart Chakra to stimulate nourishment of the physical body. To melt away rigidity when it comes to ideas and behaviors, try placing a piece over the Throat Chakra. Get a piece on the Solar Plexus Chakra for calm reasoning and objectivity. To shield against the stress created by our relationship to our devices, try placing a piece over the Sacral Chakra. And, finally, try placing a piece over the Basic Chakra to ground forward movement and momentum in your life. The most important thing when working with Rainbow Fluorite? Have fun, follow your intuition, and allow the possibilities to be endless.

Suggested Reading for More Smiles, More Silence, and More Connection to the Natural, Sweet Wonders of Life, *Buffalo Woman Comes Singing* by Brooke Medicine Eagle.

Additional Journaling and SPS Space

Liz

I'm happier now than I've been in a long time. I guess I feel more content now with what *is*, and that means being more content with it *all*: the good, the bad, and the ugly. I have a toolbox of many things to help me with this, but the most recent thing I've been using is: treating myself like I would treat a friend. Running everything through that filter allows me to stop the crazy and regroup. It helps, and I've been feeling really good since doing that. In the last few years, for sure, I have developed some behaviors towards myself that aren't great. I can look back and see that all of this began during an abusive relationship. The relationship was really damaging while I was in it, but it was also especially damaging after I got out of it. It's been a real journey to honestly evaluate how I talk to myself. I sort of picked up where my relationship left off and started speaking negatively to myself about my behavior, my looks, my achievements. As I continued to do this dirty work, that negative voice morphed into consistent self-shaming, and I kept it all a secret. The truth is, I would never hold anyone else to those same standards. I'm a yoga instructor, a pretty healthy person, I try to build others up, and here I was living out this dirty little secret of doing the exact opposite to myself. It made me feel like a total hack. When I say I kept this a secret, I really mean that. I was so ashamed. I wasn't even open with the people closest to me. It hasn't been easy to be honest about this toxic behavior towards myself, when I have done so much 'self-help' type of work. So, I've started small and shared with a few good friends. In doing this, in trusting in those who are trustworthy, I've discovered that there is nothing to be embarrassed about. Yes, others feel the way I feel; but I've also realized that if a friend came to me and told me she was feeling the way I have been feeling there would be no judgment and I would never make her feel badly about it. Sharing with people who are capable of hearing and supporting me has lightened the load. Finding those people isn't always easy. For me, time has helped identify these special people in my life. Over the years, I have been lucky to cultivate friendships with people that I have been able to see in many different life situations. Watching and observing from this perspective has helped me discern whom I can trust with this type of sensitive, personal information. Getting to this place of realization has been a slow burn. A lot like how the seed of self-doubt, planted when I was in the abusive relationship, was a slow burn. I watered that seed and it grew, little by little. Slowly the self-loathing would build, and then the shame would come. Next followed the internal verbal abuse. If I embarrassed myself - or did something that I thought might be embarrassing - I would beat myself up about it and then act like everything was fine. I had this big secret that I was holding in, and I never let myself up for fresh air. This went on for years. It still creeps in. It is very sneaky. If I think I have handled it in one area of my life, it will sneak into another area and it's like, "Oh wow! That is new… I didn't realize I would find a way to give myself a hard time about *that*…" When I think of how this pattern has creeped into my relationships, that has also been a huge light bulb. Somehow I had bought into the idea that I couldn't trust myself. I began to defer to the other person, convincing myself that they were a little bit smarter than me, or that they would have a better understanding of what was 'right.' Whether it was a friend or a romantic partner, I had this underlying feeling of, "Well, they probably know better." Of course, everybody has an inner voice. Everybody has thoughts. I always teach this as a yoga instructor: you are your most important teacher. In my relationships, I was teaching myself to constantly defer to the other person. After a while, it began to ring false because a weird sort of inequality showed up. I began feeling resentful towards my partner in any given situation for taking charge; yet this was a dynamic that I had created. Oftentimes, I was so angry because I didn't feel powerful enough to speak up and share what I knew to be true about what I wanted and needed. That resentment caused a lot of other sneaky things to manifest. I started not feeling good, getting sick, drinking too much, not being able to sleep…. just not feeling right, and not being able to pinpoint why. What I realize now is that all of those symptoms were coming from not trusting myself. I would wake up every morning with a sense of dread. I had been feeling like this for years. The scariest part is, I didn't even know it. I thought that I was going to feel this way forever. I started having really strong reactions about having my picture taken. I avoided cameras and situations where that might happen. If someone did snap my photo, I wouldn't look at it. When given the chance, I spent some time with this reaction. It became clear to me that I didn't want my picture taken *because* I was feeling so badly about myself. I even started to avoid looking in the mirror. In my heart, I felt that I was faking it and having to look at myself would be proof. Finally I thought, "What if I did look at myself? What if I did look at these pictures?" So I did, and nothing happened. It sounds so simple, but it was so difficult to come to this realization. I looked at these pictures of myself and I applied the same filter: What if I was looking at a picture of my best friend? Would I judge her like I was judging myself, or would I automatically see her beauty with no critique? Definitely the second answer. So, I started to approach my own image with the love and care that I would give someone else. If a critical thought came in I would ask, "Could I say this to someone, or something, I cared about?" If the answer was "no," I stopped. If anyone else is feeling this way, start small, and share how you are feeling. The first friend I talked to about all of this… she sent me an email the next day and said, "When I was listening to you, I kept getting the feeling that this is BIG." It was BIG because it was true. The truth is important. The intimacy and vulnerability of my truth was what she was recognizing. Then I talked to another friend, and we processed it together in a different way. Each time I shared it all got a little bit lighter. Now I can face it. I'm no longer embarrassed. I am sad about it all, but through this awareness I can move forward and feel good. I've learned there are safe places to share things. There are friends who can help. We are not alone. There is always someone who will be able to understand and who will want to help. No matter who you are, how strong you are, how much of a perfectionist you are, or what you've done… nothing is ever too big or too small to matter to someone. Start with your pet. That is a good way of feeling safe. When I was deep in that space of always judging and questioning myself, I didn't even trust in my abilities to figure out who was safe to share this with and who wasn't. I was always convincing myself that someone knew better about what was right for me. Like I said, that wasn't a conscious seed, but it was planted, and somehow, I came to believe it. I watered it. I fertilized that question of whether I was trustworthy or not. It is hard to come back from that, yet you can. It takes time. Nurture yourself through. If you are tired, rest. If you are hungry, eat. If you are thirsty, drink. If you need to move, walk. These simple things are the easiest concepts to forget when you get compromised. They snowball. When you feel like turning inward, reach out. Ask yourself, "What do I really need right now?" Listen to that and do it. Keep it small. This is a great way to remember how to trust in yourself again. One hour stacks onto the next, and before you know it, you will start to build the confidence that you know what you need better than anyone else.

Making This Story Your Own:

Liz's story points out several common topics that a lot of us struggle with.
Take a moment, breathe, and reflect.
What stands out for you when you read her words?
Is there a situation in your life that is similar to Liz's?
Perhaps part of her story feels connected to your own.
How can you relate her experiences to your past, present, and future?

- *My Connection to Liz's Story* _____

_____

_____

_____

_____

Knowing that you aren't alone, let's gently explore some other themes from Liz's story together:

- *Being Your Own Best Friend*
    - How do you talk to yourself? If your inner voice was loud enough for others to hear, would you talk to yourself in a different way? Why, or why not? What *do* you say to yourself and *how* do you say it? What do you say regarding your looks, achievements, and choices? If a close friend told you she was saying these things to herself, what would you tell her? How is this different from your conscientiousness around your own self-talk? Based on how you treat yourself, would you even want to be your own best friend? Why, or why not and how can this shift? How can you work towards relating to yourself with more kindness, love, and compassion?

- *Trusting Those Who are Trustworthy*
    - Do you have people in your life who are capable of being genuinely supportive? How do you know this and how have these people proven themselves to be trustworthy? How do you determine whether or not to trust someone? Do you take your time and discern through observation? Do you give your trust quickly and freely? Has either approach offered welcome relief, frustrating disappointment, or both? How can your process of establishing trusting relationships work better for you? For the relationships that have proven themselves genuine, how can you create more trust and allow them to support you in other ways? What are a few small steps you can take today to begin initiating and developing these reliable and trustworthy connections?

- *Trusting Yourself*
    - Do you trust yourself? When you feel a certain way about something do you rely on your own counsel above all others? If you do, why? If you don't, why? When did the relationship to trusting yourself in this way begin? Would you like to trust yourself more? Do you speak up and share what you know? Do you silence your voice and your wisdom? Do you experience a mixture of both? What feels *most* right to you? Do you know? What would it be like if you trusted yourself above everyone and everything else? What would change? Which relationships would need to shift to accommodate this new level of empowerment? How can you begin trusting yourself in this way?

Sacred Play Suggestions:

~ SPS #1: ~
* Cutting Cords *

Positive or negative, our experiences and relationships can behave like glue. Adhering to the very core of our being when this glue dries, it is invisible… always there, always tethering, but virtually undetectable. This glue of life can keep us stuck to the good and the bad. It acts like long elastic bungee cords, letting us go out just so far before snapping us back. From this perspective, these cords hinder our freedom. When we aren't free, how can we grow? We can get an intuitive feeling about these cords and how they connect us to everything. Give it a try. Think of two relationships in your life… one positive and one that could use some work. *Feel* what kind of cord connects you to both and record your findings.

Positive Relationship Cord

- What is the relationship? _____
- What makes this relationship positive? _____
    - Close your eyes and visualize your connection as a cord.
        - Where does the cord connect to your body? _____
        - What are the characteristics of the cord? (size, width, color, texture, etc.) _____
        _____
        - How does the cord feel? _____
        _____
        - Does the energy of the cord flow freely in both directions? _____
        - Does this cord align with your highest good? _____
        - Do you want to keep this cord? _____

Negative Relationship Cord

- What is the relationship? _____
- What makes this relationship negative? _____
    - Close your eyes and visualize your connection as a cord.
        - Where does the cord connect to your body? _____
        - What are the characteristics of the cord? (size, width, color, texture, etc.) _____
        _____
        - How does the cord feel? _____
        _____
        - Does the energy of the cord flow freely in both directions? _____
        - Does this cord align with your highest good? _____
        - Do you want to keep this cord? _____

When you think about the energy exchange and the potential for energy pollution within relationships, who and what we gift our time to becomes a very important decision. Even the smallest of interactions can create big ugly cords and the most divine collaborations can create co-dependent dynamics which leave us feeling like we must give up our power to receive love and acceptance. The thing is, these cords are our own creation. They are constructed out of our wounding patterns and dysfunctional cycles. They are not our fault. No fault exists here. But they are our responsibility to change. We know that our minds are powerful and, within the realms of visualization and imagination, much can be released and regenerated. Let's begin this liberation process by *cutting* the cords that no longer serve us. First, identify what can be cut.

What cords are no longer serving me?

- List all people, relationships, feelings, experiences, behaviors, thoughts, patterns, and places that you would like to release.

_____

_____

_____

_____

Once you have your list, take a moment to breathe and relax. Prepare yourself for this step-by-step visualization process by getting physically comfortable. When you are ready, begin.

Step 1:

Imagine your physical body gently floating in space. The light is soft, but you can see clearly. Time has slowed and any moment from the past, present, or future may be easily accessed. In this etheric location, see the cords connecting you to every person, place, or thing that you have ever come into contact with. Continue to breathe deeply and record any notes, information, or guidance below.

_____

_____

_____

Step 2:

See where the cords are connecting to your body. Clearly witness the location of the connection and how they are connected. Continue to breathe deeply and record any notes, information, or guidance below.

_____

_____

_____

Step 3:
Let your instincts begin to define the cords with characteristics. See their size, width, color, and texture. Let the characteristics offer you information for these cords that span all time and distance. Continue to breathe deeply as the defining traits become clearer. Record any notes, information, or guidance below.

_____

_____

_____

Step 4:
Gauge how the cords feel for you in this moment. Look within them and discern if the energy is receptive and reciprocal. With trust in your inner wisdom, see which cords can be cut for your Greatest and Highest Good. Continue to breathe and honor your feelings at this moment. Cutting some cords may feel scary. Cutting others may feel sad. The release of others may bring joy and bliss. All feelings are valued and valid. Record any notes, information, or guidance below.

_____

_____

_____

Step 5:
In your imagination, a beautiful pair of very large and very sharp golden scissors is gently placed in your hand. When you are ready, begin to cut the cords no longer serving you. As you cut each cord, pay close attention to the sensations manifesting for you physically, emotionally, mentally, and spiritually. Continue to breathe deeply as you record any notes, information, or guidance below.

_____

_____

_____

Step 6:
As the final step, once the cord is cut, send it out to the Universal energy field for transformation. As you witness the cord traveling onward, offer a send-off of gratitude by saying, "Thank you, you are no longer serving me." Continue to breathe deeply as you witness where the cord travels and what the transformation process for each one looks and feels like. Record any notes, information, or guidance below.

_____

_____

_____

Wow! Thank you for doing this. Sometimes this kind of work isn't easy and other times it can feel downright weird. Cutting cords to situations that aren't in alignment with our Greatest and Highest Good can offer a freedom that we didn't even know we were craving. As you continue this process of release, know that I am very grateful for you and that I love you.

~ SPS #2: ~

* Picture Love *

Quickly locate five pictures of yourself. If they are on your phone, use the first 5 you come across. If they are actual photos, use the first five that you see. No censoring. Next close your eyes and say your name out loud in the following ways.

- Say your name as if you are accepting an award.
  - What does it feel like to say your name this way? _____
  _____

- Say your name like you would hear it said when you were younger and in *big* trouble.
  - What does it feel like to say your name this way? _____
  _____

- Say your name as if you are going to introduce yourself to a room of professional colleagues.
  - What does it feel like to say your name this way? _____
  _____

- Say your name how you hear it when someone is repeatedly trying to get your attention.
  - What does it feel like to say your name this way? _____
  _____

- Say your name the way someone who loves you unconditionally would say it.
  - What does it feel like to say your name this way? _____
  _____

Close your eyes once again and step fully into this last person's awareness in your imagination. When you open your eyes, you are going to look at these five pictures through the eyes of a being who loves you totally and completely. How does this filter of unconditional love look to you and how do *you* look through it? From this perspective, find two absolutely loving and lovable things about each picture and write them down.

Picture #1

1. _____

2. _____

Picture #2

1. _____

2. _____

Picture #3

1. _____

2. _____

Picture #4

1. _____

2. _____

Picture #5

1. _____

2. _____

Look at your pictures together and read aloud the ten loving statements from above. Gaze at your beautiful and divine self as you reclaim this unconditional love for your own. I see you Sister… and *dah*-ling, you look *mah*-velous! I love you! Thank you for doing this!

~ SPS #3: ~
* Archetypal Wisdom *

As we gaze up at the night sky, we are invited to be sacred spectators of Mother Moon's transformational wisdom. Before the advent of electric lighting, we followed her in many ways that supported and improved the quality of our lives. Planting and harvesting, communal gatherings, and tribal council were just a few things that the cyclical nature of Mother Moon fostered. We women even tended to cycle right along with her! The different phases of her Lunar Cycle have influenced the different layers of our Feminine consciousness throughout all of time. From Dark, to Waxing, to Full, to Waning, our bodies, minds, hearts, and souls have instinctually reacted and responded. These reactions and responses correlate to our Menstrual Cycles as our bodies shift from Bleeding, to Pre-Ovulatory, to Ovulation, to the Luteal Phase (more commonly known as PMS). The Lunar and the Menstrual cycles also blend and balance with the seasons of Mother Earth as we flow from Winter, to Spring, to Summer, to Fall. Finally, the cycles are also associated with the

Archetypes of Womanhood which pour forth as Crone, Maiden, Mother, and Enchantress. Each aspect of the cycles - Moon, Menstrual, Seasonal, and Archetype - have much wisdom, guidance, and energy for us. Below is a chart depicting how they relate.

Moon	Menstrual Cycle	Season	Archetype	Energetic Influence
Dark	Menstruation	Winter	Crone	Time to pull in, rest, purge, and release. Deep psychic wisdom is present for intuitive processes to take over.
Waxing	Pre-Ovulatory	Spring	Maiden	Upbeat and playful energy abounds. Time to plant the seeds of new life.
Full	Ovulation	Summer	Mother	Very nurturing and fertile time holding deep femininity and powers for collaboration.
Waning	Luteal (PMS)	Fall	Enchantress	Dramatic and powerful time of expression and emotion. Sexuality is intense and primal.

If you are no longer experiencing a Menstrual Cycle you will still feel these energies and you just might cycle right alongside Mother Moon and follow her timeline. Or you might feel more aligned with a longer cycle and follow the seasons of Mother Earth. If you are still cycling, you might not exactly line up with the moon phases. That is OK! Just knowing that we are connected with and inspired by these larger forces can be empowering. In addition, allowing our Feminine psyches to relax into the wisdom of these correlating energies can offer much support, comfort, and guidance. Let's play a little and see if we can rouse some cyclical wisdom with writing and drawing. Knowing the season is usually a given. You can find out the Lunar Phase by checking online. Sometimes figuring out our Menstrual Cycles can be a bit more challenging. If you can, remember when you were last bleeding. Count the days from that day to today. Each menstrual cycle lasts approximately a week. Estimate where you are by equally dividing the days as follows: Day 1-7 *Crone*, Day 7-14 *Maiden*, Day 14-21 *Mother*, and Day 21-28 *Enchantress*. The Archetypes may already evoke potent connotations in us from personal experience as well as mythology, common folklore, stories, and fairytales. Allow whatever wants to come up to come up as you play with these energies.

What feelings does the Season of <u>Winter</u> conjure up within me?

_____

How does the *Dark Moon* make me feel emotionally and mentally?

_____

When I hear the word *Crone*, which part of my intuition awakens?

_____

Where do my energies flow - inward, outward, or both - when I am *Menstruating*?

_____

Now draw whatever shapes, images, or textures come to mind. Let this artistic expression flow from you without thinking. Take a deep breath and go!

My Dark, Winter, Crone, Menstrual Wisdom

What feelings does the Season of *Spring* conjure up within me?

_____

How does the *Growing Moon* make me feel emotionally and mentally?

_____

When I hear the word *Maiden*, which part of my intuition awakens?

_____

Where do my energies flow - inward, outward, or both - when I am *Pre-Ovulatory*?

_____

Now draw whatever shapes, images, or textures come to mind. Let this artistic expression flow from you without thinking. Take a deep breath and go!

My Growing, Spring, Maiden, Pre-Ovulatory Wisdom

What feelings does the Season of <u>*Summer*</u> conjure up within me?

___

How does the *Full Moon* make me feel emotionally and mentally?

___

When I hear the word *Mother*, which part of my intuition awakens?

___

Where do my energies flow - inward, outward, or both - when I am *Ovulating*?

___

Now draw whatever shapes, images, or textures come to mind. Let this artistic expression flow from you without thinking. Take a deep breath and go!

<u>My Full, Summer, Mother, Ovulation Wisdom</u>

What feelings does the Season of <u>*Fall*</u> conjure up within me?

___

How does the *Waning Moon* make me feel emotionally and mentally?

___

When I hear the word *Enchantress*, which part of my intuition awakens?

___

Where do my energies flow - inward, outward, or both - when I am in my *Luteal Phase*?

___

Now draw whatever shapes, images, or textures come to mind. Let this artistic expression flow from you without thinking. Take a deep breath and go!

My Waning, Fall, Enchantress, Luteal Wisdom

Our connection to the natural world is a Superpower. So what are you going to do with all of this wisdom and magick? Complete this timeless activity by finishing the following statement.

With My Intuitive, Instinctual, and Cyclical Wisdom I will...

_____

_____

_____

Look at you! You are glowing and it isn't just the moonlight. Sharing our divine and profound connection to the natural world through our cyclical wisdom and Feminine intuition is one of my very favorite things. Thank you! I love you.

~ SPS #4: ~
* What Do You Need *

What do you need right now? Take a moment. Place your hands on your heart, ask the question, and provide the answer. "I don't know" is totally acceptable.

What do I need right now?

_____

_____

_____

Check in with the basics, too. Just like Liz so wisely reminds us in her story, no one knows better than you what you need. With some empowered and dedicated nurturing, we can rebuild the self-confidence and self-assuredness necessary to meet our own needs.

- Are you tired? _____

~If so, **Rest**.~

- Are you hungry? _____

~If so, **Eat**.~

- Are you thirsty? _____

~If so, **Drink**.~

- Are you bored? _____

~If so, **Move**.~

Liz's wisdom is simple and elegant. Yet, how often do you let these seemingly insignificant things slide because something else surfaces that appears to be more important? Start small… meet your basic needs… trust yourself again. Wow. Try doing this for one week and take note of what is different. Record your findings below.

Day 1: Meeting My Needs I Notice _____

_____

Day 2: Meeting My Needs I Notice _____

_____

Day 3: Meeting My Needs I Notice _____

_____

Day 4: Meeting My Needs I Notice _____

_____

Day 5: Meeting My Needs I Notice _____

_____

Day 6: Meeting My Needs I Notice _____

_____

Day 7: Meeting My Needs I Notice _____
_____

As a final step, place your hands on your heart and once again ask, "What do I need right now?" Really listen to your answer and meet your own needs.

What do I need right now?

_____
_____
_____

Your needs are important. Every single one. From the basics to the more complex, they are valuable and worth meeting. When we do this, we become teachers and way-showers for others to meet their needs too. What a gift! *You* are a gift! You *are*! I'm serious! I love you. Thank you!

<u>~ SPS #5: ~</u>
<u>* BFF Letter *</u>

Write your best friend a letter. If you don't have a best friend, make one up! In this letter, tell your best friend everything that is going on in your life. Let's give it a try and create an outline for this marvelous missive. Remember, maybe you are at a place in life where you don't feel as if you have a BFF. Perhaps you have several best friends and you can't decide which one to write to. For this activity, you can either make one up and envision this potentially perfect friend, blend a few friends together, or write to your ultimate best friend - your Higher Self. The most important part of this activity is that you authentically share what is going on for you at this moment.

- Who is your best friend? _____
- What makes them your BFF? _____
  _____

OK, this is your best friend and they love you beyond all time and space. They are worthy of hearing your truth and you are worthy of sharing it. There is no need to censor anything because in this letter, everything about your feelings, needs, wants, and desires is valued and valuable. Create your outline below and trust that everything you say will be honored, held, and responded to with love and respect.

<u>Tell your Best Friend…</u>	
What is making me **happy** right now…	What is making me **sad** right now…

What is making me **stressed** right now…	What is making me **relaxed** right now…
What is making me **worried** right now…	What is making me feel **blessed** right now…

OK, ready to write? Grab a piece of paper and put it all together. If you don't have time to write, no worries! Voice-to-text it or take a video of yourself speaking the letter out loud. When you are done, if you have written it, fold your letter and stash it somewhere safe. If it is on your phone, save your work and close out of the program. Now, change your energy. If you were inside, go outside. If you were sitting, stand up and stretch. If it was quiet, put on some music. Take enough time for your body, heart, and mind to relax and shift focus. This might be five minutes, an hour, a week, or a month. You are in charge, so you decide when you feel different. After the shift, go back and reread or listen to your letter. Wait… there is a curve ball. As you read through your letter, pretend that your BFF wrote it to *you*. I know! Plot twist!!! Now… answer her. Write a return letter (or, voice text or video a reply) and support her with all of the love, compassion, understanding, knowledge, and wisdom that you possess. When you are finished, keep both. Let the letter and the response serve as reminders that you are a dynamic being. Sometimes you will have the answers. Sometimes you won't. Sometimes your energy will feel supportive. Sometimes your energy will feel receptive. All aspects of you are allowed and all are needed. No matter how you are feeling at any given moment, nothing changes the fact that you are a loving, compassionate, and wise woman. Don't ever forget; you are an amazing best friend and this world is lucky to have you! Thank you! I Love you!

Crystal Love: Liz's Crystal is Mookaite (**moo**-*kayht*). This Australian Jasper is known as an Aboriginal Mother Earth Stone. Use this Crystal to tap into the Archetypal Mothering Energies and allow it to reawaken self-worth and self-confidence, support emotional regulation, promote willingness to accept change, balance your inner and outer experiences, and fortify your immune system. Connected to the Solar Plexus Chakra, this stone is highly restorative, stabilizing, empowering, revitalizing, and purifying. One of the biggest gifts Mookaite gives us is perspective. With this in mind, use Mookaite for a Soul-based outlook when it comes to setting goals, integrating new things into your life, versatility in your relationships, and seeing all sides of a situation. When you need a little more oomph to connect your physical energies to your instinctual energies, use Mookaite to get that life-force flowing without procrastination.

Suggested Reading to Soulfully Reboot your Mind, Body, Spirit Connection, *Showing Up Naked: Peeling Back the Layers to Your Authentic Self* by Erica Boucher.

Krissy

I always wanted to be a mom. When I was little, I wanted to have six kids. That changed when I was pregnant with my first. It was a tough pregnancy. I threw up every day for seven months, on the train, as I commuted into New York City from Connecticut. Being sick and pregnant in Manhattan is no fun. I got pregnant with my second child when my son was three months old. It was somewhat planned. I had so much trouble getting pregnant the first time, my husband and I thought we would just go for it since we were already in baby-land. A few years later, with two healthy boys, we got pregnant again. We were trying for a girl. I was ten weeks pregnant when I lost the baby. The miscarriage was so traumatic. I went through the labor at home. There wasn't anything I could do. There was so much blood and so much pain. My doctor tried to tell me what to expect, but I don't know if anything can prepare you for that. I couldn't believe how much was inside of me at ten weeks. When I got pregnant again just a few months later, my husband and I were ecstatic. We felt like we were given a second chance. For one of the ultrasound appointments early on, I remember that the nurse couldn't find the baby's heartbeat. She wasn't alarmed at all and made a joke that sometimes her machine didn't work very well. Finally, she found a heartbeat. I didn't feel too sure about it. I thought she was just picking up my heartbeat, but she was so confident that I let myself believe everything was OK. I was being so careful, too. I wasn't taking any medications. I was watching everything so closely. I didn't want to do anything to compromise the baby. At another early appointment, we got to see the baby on the screen. He was like a little soccer player in there, bouncing, jumping, turning, and spinning. We named him Jack. My boys were four and five at this point and they were so excited to have a little brother. They would hug my belly and say over and over, "We love you, Jack!" Right before my twenty-week screening, I started to sense something wasn't quite right. I was out with a girlfriend the night before and I said to her, "I think something is wrong with the baby." The energy wasn't there. The next day was the ultrasound. As I lay on the table, looking at the screen, I saw this round ball. The picture looked kind of blank. I kept looking for that bouncing baby boy in there. The technician turned off the screen and told me that she was sorry, but that she couldn't find a heartbeat. Time stopped. I was immediately overtaken with gut wrenching sobs. My husband was crying, too. I kept thinking, "Not again. Please not again." My first thought was that I had done something. That this was my fault. It didn't feel normal for a baby to just die. My head started filling with questions. Was it my work? I got a chair massage one time, was that it? We had done everything we were supposed to do. We had waited to tell people until the first trimester was over. His picture from the ultrasound was on all of the announcement cards. I just wanted to know why this had happened. No one could give me an answer. The doctor shrugged and said, "It's bad luck." All of a sudden, my body started to react, and I felt like I had to get the baby out. It felt like I was going into labor right there. The office staff told me that it doesn't really work that way, and that I had to make an appointment to have the baby surgically removed. I remember saying to them, "No, this baby has to come out now." I called around and we ended up going to our small-town local hospital. When my husband and I got there, it felt like we were the only patients in the whole place. It felt like a church; quiet and peaceful, so unlike a hospital. Everyone was so kind. The nurses would come up to me and say, "We are so sorry that you are here for this." They even asked me if I wanted to hold him. At that point, I was so emotional, I declined. I didn't think I could do it. I was given the option to be induced and deliver vaginally or to have a surgical procedure to remove him from my body. In the state that I was in, I just wanted the baby out. Being induced and delivering him felt like a whole additional layer of psychological trauma that I just couldn't handle. I was at the bottom of my energy. I remember being given the drugs to put me out. It was all so surreal. I woke up, foggy, not really clear on what I was doing there or what had just happened. I felt the most loving presence on my left side. She was holding my hand. I don't know what she was saying to me, but it was gentle and comforting. I don't even know if she was real. As I continued to wake up, I began asking everyone if they had seen my baby. All I could focus on was if anyone had seen him and if anyone could tell me what he looked like. I felt so guilty that I hadn't taken the opportunity to hold him, look at him... *see* him. I wanted so badly to know him. To know my baby. To be able to remember what he looked like. Waking up in the hospital in the aftermath of it all was the beginning of the grief process. It was *a lot* to deal with. When my husband and I told our boys, they reacted so differently. We told them that baby Jack's heart had stopped beating. My oldest looked at us and said, "I get it, Mom." My youngest didn't say much. He sunk into a depression. The whole thing, making sense of it all, has affected them more than we could have ever realized. To them, losing their little brother was something profound. It was my youngest son's birthday party the very next day. Trying to keep life as normal as possible, we decided not to cancel. It was awful. People sprang to help - which was great - but they didn't know what to say. It quickly felt like I was being told to move on... to be thankful for the two children I *did* have... to get over it. That didn't help. For so long afterwards, I had flashbacks of the moment when I was told there was no heartbeat. It would hit me at random times and the feeling of panic would overtake me. I would sit frozen and haunted. Feeling helpless and powerless, thinking over and over that this somehow was my fault. I just wanted an answer. Why had this happened? If I could have an answer, then I could know what to blame. One night, I had a dream about a baby in the womb with these things sticking from the fingers into the placenta. The picture was so vivid. I looked it up online and found that this is actually something that can happen in utero. The picture from my dream was right there on my computer screen. A baby can grow into the placenta and it can cause a miscarriage. Finally, something made sense. I found some peace with this, like Jack had come to give me an answer. Getting back to regular life was hard. Two young kids had to be taken care of. They had to go to school. They needed a mom. I was a zombie. I felt like all I could do was sit on the couch and watch news shows. I felt so heavy, like I was weighted down. I couldn't stop thinking about the baby being ripped from my body. I couldn't let go of the hopes and dreams that I had for him... for all of us. This went on for about six months: then I suddenly went into action mode. I decided to move. I needed to move. To get away from where this had all happened. I told my husband, "I am moving. I am taking the kids. You can come if you want." Everyone tried to talk us out of it. They told us we were running away and that we didn't have the money to move. For me, there was no other option. I wasn't running away from anything - I was running *to* something. I wanted to create a fresh start for my family with new air to breathe, new support, and new comfort. I followed my heart and I am so glad that I did. Moving offered me what I needed. I was finally able to start working through the grief. I found the Divine Mommy Group. As I witnessed other women sharing from their hearts and souls, I was inspired to let my sadness out. Until that moment, I didn't even realize how depressed I was. It sounds so obvious, but when it is you, sometimes it is so hard to see what is going on. I kept thinking that maybe I needed to exercise more or eat better food. What I needed was to share my story. There was one particular day in Group when I finally felt ready to let it out. I wept and told the other women about Jack. I talked about how badly my heart ached for my baby. I shared that I still felt hollow, like something inside me was missing. Someone was holding my hand and I knew- **I just *knew*-** that I was safe and supported. I hadn't felt that way since that presence was sitting next to me in the hospital. At that moment, I felt like I had permission to go on... like I could begin to move forward without the guilt. Sharing my grief helped me to realize that this whole thing was something that happened to me, but it isn't actually happening anymore. I used to feel like I was reliving it every day. Slowly, after that day of sharing in Divine Mommy, I was able to feel a comfortable distance from everything. Like the pain wasn't so deep. Like the pain had been transformed. That very afternoon, I got this crazy feeling to go and get another dog. It just popped into my head. Trust me when I say that this was not something we had even talked about in my household, but the feeling was so strong, I couldn't ignore it. The boys and I went to an animal shelter and we were in the waiting room when a woman walked in with a small black dog in a crate and said to everyone,

"This is Jack. He isn't feeling well. I am going to take him home and bring him back next week." I froze. My oldest son perked up and whispered to me with tears in his eyes, "Mommy, it's Jack!" Right at that moment, this sign behind the front desk started flashing with the words, 'Thank you, thank you, thank you,' over and over. I went into action. I stopped the woman holding the dog and told everyone in that room my story. I told them about my Jack. I told them about what had happened to me… to us… I even told them we would trade in our cat for this dog, which they didn't find too funny, but nothing was going to stop me from getting that puppy. The staff at the shelter was so professional. They told me I had to come back next week and that it was first-come, first-served. We were the first ones there the following week, and we got him. We got Jack… this crazy little puppy who is so like that wild little soccer player I met all those months ago on the ultrasound screen. Jack reminds me every day of how lucky I am. Now I can fully understand the depth of what I have gone through. I know that everyone's process is different. That is OK. I also know that I don't ever have to get over it. What happened to me is a part of me. It is my connection to my child. Why would I ever want to get over that? Thinking about my baby and remembering him helps me to see the good that has come out of this situation. He helps me notice all of the helpers that have come forward to show kindness, comfort, and love. He teaches me not to second guess myself. To trust that I do know what I need. He inspires me toward inspired action. I still miss him, cry, and grieve the lost hope. Yet, one of the scariest things imaginable has happened to me and I have lived through it. I am still here. The pain has been worth the lesson. Day by day, I am listening to my heart and I am teaching my children to do the same. Maybe that was Jack's lesson, to teach us all that there are people here to help. Just like that wise woman who held my hand after the surgery, Jack reminds me that angels really do exist, and that this world really is a good place.

Making This Story Your Own:

Krissy's story takes us on a journey of Motherhood, Sisterhood, and Womanhood.
Take a moment, breathe, and reflect.
What stands out for you when you read her words?
Is there a situation in your life that is similar to Krissy's?
Perhaps part of her story feels connected to your own.
How can you relate her experiences to your past, present, and future?

- *My Connection to Krissy's Story* _____

_____

_____

_____

_____

_____

Knowing that you aren't alone, let's gently explore some other themes from Krissy's story together:

- ***Following Your Own Timeline***
    - Have you ever felt influenced or pressured when it comes to your way of processing the events of your life? Have there been times when you weren't true to your needs for comfort and support

after experiencing something painful? If so, why did this happen, where did this response come from, and would you like it to change in the future? How do you feel when witnessing others process the events of their lives? What happens when you observe someone else feeling big feelings? Is the commonly heard advice to "*just get over it*" and "*be thankful for what you **do** have*" present when either you or someone else is trying to heal? Does this way of thinking work for you? If not, is there a way to allow for more time and space around your healing process?

- ***Releasing Blame and Guilt***
  - When something goes wrong, do you hold yourself responsible? What is your first reaction when you make a mistake? Is it easy for you to find ways to blame and admonish yourself? Do you search for *why* something happened and repeatedly question your motives, decisions, and actions? Do you feel like somehow you deserve what happens to you? Whose voice is in your head during those painful moments? Is there a way in which the guilt and shame help you feel insulated or protected? Is it easier to hold yourself accountable than to ask someone or something else to take responsibility? Does it feel more fitting to blame yourself than to accept that sometimes things just cannot be explained? If so, in what ways are these responses helpful? Would it be beneficial to shift them? If so, how can you begin this process?

- ***Finding the Helpers***
  - Do you allow others to support you during times of need? If you do, would you like to open yourself to receive more support? If allowing others to support you is not something you currently do, would you like this to change? What prevents you from asking for and accepting help when you need it? Do you believe that the world is a good place? Does this answer influence why you do - or do not - seek support from others? Do you believe that people are inherently good? Does this answer influence why you do - or do not - seek support from others? What would it take to feel safe enough to seek out and receive the support you need? What will be different when this happens and what about your life might change?

Sacred Play Suggestions:

~ SPS #1: ~
* Temple of Goodness *

Do you have a special spot in your home that is dedicated only to you? This is a space filled with *your* things, infused with *your* energy, and capable of holding *your* intentions. This is **not** a workspace. This is **not** the communal spot where everyone tends to gather. This is YOUR space to recharge, refresh, and restore. This is your very own 'Temple of Goodness' and you are the worshipped deity. It doesn't have to be big and lavish. It just has to be yours and it has to be sacred. Maybe you already have a spot and some rededication energy is being called for or maybe you are starting fresh with this 'Temple of Goodness'…. Regardless of where you are in the process, some things to keep in mind are: 1.) You are the most important person in the Temple & 2.) The Temple and the things within the Temple only have to be special for you. So, where is this Temple going to be? If you have a room to dedicate, wonderful! If not, get creative. You can use a closet, a corner, a shelf, a cabinet, or a place in the yard. If you use your car, use the passenger seat or a backseat to ensure that you aren't where you would normally be sitting. Now you get to decide what will be on your temple gates. This is a statement that will announce the Temple's importance, affirm the Temple's purpose, and honor the

Temple's Goddess - aka YOU. Take a few minutes to journal around the following. When you are finished writing, simmer down what comes up and out into your Temple's Divine Declaration.

- This Temple's Importance is_____

- This Temple's Purpose is _____

- This Temple will Honor its Goddess by _____

_____

Divine Declaration for My Temple of Goodness

_____

_____

Next, decorate this beautiful Temple with anything that you want. Fill it with charms and pictures. Arrange figurines and Crystals. Or leave it clear and empty. Let this Temple honor and reflect where you have been, where you are now, and where you want to go in the future. Once your Temple is decorated, take it all in with a few quiet moments of gratitude. This is sacred space, created *by* you *for **you***. When you come here, be reminded that you are *you* and that is *enough*. In this place, you are glorious perfection. In your Temple, you are the priority. You can trust yourself, and you can create your own peace. Your temple is stunning and so are you! Love you! Thank you for doing this!

~ SPS #2: ~
* NO *

Owning our "no" is powerful. Yet, how often do we really give ourselves permission to do it? This concept has been talked about a lot recently and suggestions for saying "no" can be found in everything from books to social media memes. A friend recently said to me, "Remember Jamie, the answer of "no" *is* an option." It was so simple, but her comment got me thinking. "No" really is an option. It always has been, and it always will be. When was the last time you said "no" and how did it feel? What was going on that created the opportunity for you to choose "no"? Take a few minutes to journal and reflect.

The Last Time I Chose ~"No"~ as an Option

Alright, now let's look underneath "no" and discover what fuels it and if that fuel is working for us.

- The last time you said "no," did you feel any *negativity* towards the situation or people involved?
  _____

- The last time you said "no," did you feel any *judgment* regarding the situation, or the people involved?
  _____

- The last time you said "no," did you feel a need to *justify* your answer to yourself or others?
  _____

- The last time you said "no," did the negativity or judgement provide that *justification*?
  _____

- The last time you said "no," did you feel any negativity or judgement towards *yourself*?
  _____

Sometimes saying "no" is easier when judgement or negativity is present… sometimes, we actually create the judgement and negativity as the justification. What if we could easily and freely say "no" without the baggage? Negative feelings and negative judgements are always going to be present in life, but do we need them - or better yet - do we need to *create* them in order to say "no." If this is our pattern, our "no" option can become habitually related to needing a negative reason for justification. How much time and energy might we save if our "no" didn't involve scrutinizing someone or something else? Take a few minutes and discover a new fuel for your "no." Find fuel that is empowered and energized and doesn't need any justification, only a respectful relationship to your intuition and instincts. When you are ready, write a statement affirming your new "no."

My New Empowered and Energized "No."

_____

_____

Sometimes "no" really is the most loving answer for everyone involved. With your hands on your heart, practice saying "no" out loud. Infuse your "no" with love and see what happens. Your dedication to explore your "no" gives me the energy I need to explore mine. Thank you. I love you!

~ SPS #3: ~
* Re-Storying *

Remember making up stories when you were younger? Daydreaming and fantasizing were beneficial for us then and they still are now. Not only does this type of imaginative wandering give our brains a chance to rest and relax, it can also provide opportunities to try out new things and ideas. This can be especially true for the unresolved feelings that accompany the disempowering situations and events of life. Krissy shares some powerful wisdom with her realization that "what she went through happened to her but isn't actually happening anymore." Oftentimes when we experience something disempowering, hurtful, or traumatic, we relive certain aspects of the story over and over. Our thoughts can feel like they are stuck in a loop. We can't change what happened, but we can change our *relationship* to what happened by tapping into our powers of imagination and visualization. We've already lived through it, and because of that we have feelings attached to it. By re-storying the experience with an outcome that is more preferable to us, the unsettled feelings can begin to shift and fade. Think of an event or situation in your life where you still have unresolved feelings. Don't try to relive what happened, you've done that enough already. This time tell the story to yourself in a way that has an ending or resolution of your choice. As you create this new story, pay attention to what is happening for you physically, emotionally, and mentally.

Step #1

In your imagination, retell yourself this story with a **new** ending of your choice.

- As I create this new story, my **body** feels _____

- As I create this new story, my **feelings** are _____

- As I create this new story, my **thoughts** are _____

Step #2

Tell the new story to yourself again and this time, **shorten** the events of what happened by quickly going through the details. Then **stretch out** and elongate the parts of your more preferable ending. Continue to pay close attention to what is happening for you physically, emotionally, and mentally.

- As I create this new story again, my **body** feels _____

- As I create this new story again, my **feelings** are _____

- As I create this new story again, my **thoughts** are _____

Step #3

This time **compress** the events of the story into photographs and turn the movie in your mind into a series of static images. After 5-10 images, switch back to video and continue on with your new ending. Stretch this awesome ending out and **add** in additional information. Let your imagination go wild! As always, continue to pay close attention to what is happening for you physically, emotionally, and mentally.

- As I continue to shift this story, I notice my **body** _____

- As I continue to shift this story, I notice my **feelings** _____

- As I continue to shift this story, I notice my **thoughts** _____

Step #4

Repeat Step #3 as many times as you need, each time **reducing** the effort and energy around the first part of the story until you are down to a single photograph. As a final step, solidify your new relationship to this story by clarifying what new feelings are present.

- As I continue to create and recreate my relationship to what happened, I notice _____

This new story is fresh and energized! Stay connected to it and see if anything else continues to shift. Thank you. This is important work and you did it. I love you!

~ SPS #4: ~
* Animal Spirits *

Animals are all around us. We see them, love them, dream about them, draw pictures of them, and read stories about them. No matter if the animals are real or fantasy, our connection to them is strong and timeless. In different alternative and healing modalities, animals are connected to the Feminine Side of our consciousness and can be very powerful guides and healers. Because animals don't communicate with a verbal language that is easily decipherable, sometimes their guidance remains unknown. But what messages do they have for us? Although our abilities to understand may vary, communicating with Animal Spirits can happen for anyone. Take a moment and think of at least two animals that you have felt a deep connection with. These can be animals that you have always loved, or animals that you feel attached to. Even if you don't have particularly warm and fuzzy feelings about them, include the animals that you repeatedly see or are regularly conscious of. In your imagination, visualize at least two of these animals sitting before you.

One last thing to keep in mind while you communicate with your Animal Spirits is to allow your chosen animals to embody and represent the energy of their *entire* species. When you are ready, close your eyes and ask the following questions of both. Allow their answers to percolate up from any place in your body or consciousness. Trust your first impressions and rely on your intuition. Talking to Animal Spirits in your head may feel a bit wonky at first. That is OK! Keep on going and just allow yourself to have an experience.

- **My Animal Spirit #1 is** _____
    - What is our connection? _____
    _____
    - What would you like me to know? _____
    _____
    _____
    - How can I be more open to your guidance? _____
    _____
    _____

- **My Animal Spirit #2 is** _____
    - What is our connection? _____
    _____
    - What would you like me to know? _____
    _____
    _____
    - How can I be more open to your guidance? _____
    _____
    _____

Your Animal Spirits will show themselves to you in a variety of ways. Be open, remain curious, and stay aware of your five senses. You may receive messages by sound, sight, smell, taste, or touch. Keep having fun with this as you continue opening your awareness to these Animal Spirits. Their love is unconditional, and their wisdom is, too! Love you! Thank you for taking the time to do this activity.

~ SPS #5: ~
* Source's Story *

When we experience something traumatic, the right and left sides of our brains can stop communicating. Logic and emotion become individual entities and their much-needed collaboration can get compromised. As discussed above, when the memories of the trauma become chronic, we can experience feelings and sensations similar to those we felt during the original event over and over. As this continues, our brains start to believe that these feelings are the norm and this can become a permanent state of being. Once this occurs, because our brains love us so much, we will unconsciously create situations to provoke similar feelings - literally erring on the side of familiar - regardless of how uncomfortable or painful they may be. This is definitely a space where logic and emotion would really benefit one another - and us! One way to get our systems calm enough for the right brain to start talking to the left brain again is writing. Writing our stories out can be like a pouring big bottle of glue on our brains. This is because writing transfers emotional energy into the cognitive space of logical and linear functioning. Writing lets us dribble the ball back and forth between both sides, picking up and collecting on the benefits of having a brain that communicates in a balanced way. Once the event can be held on both sides, a new level of processing what has happened can begin. Write out the story of something that has happened where you feel the right and left sides of your brain stopped communicating.

My Story

_____

_____

_____

_____

_____

_____

_____

_____

_____

Now, deeply connect to your understanding of Source energy. This is whatever - or whoever - Source is for you. Through you, allow Source to write the story once more, sharing from Source's perspective what happened. Notice if any new information comes forward. Also, attune your awareness to this different viewpoint and see if a new relationship between logic and emotion can be forged.

Source's Story

_____
_____
_____
_____
_____
_____
_____
_____
_____
_____
_____

Read through the two stories again. Are there any new understandings around what you have experienced? Can Source's perspective offer comfort or support? In your mind, try layering the two stories over one another. What happens when they are blended and told simultaneously? Finish the following statement as a final step to this activity.

When I Connect to Source, I also Connect…

_____
_____
_____

Great job working with these different levels of understanding and processing! In her story, Krissy offers us another opportunity for transformation. That day in group when she felt safe and supported, she shared her story. She courageously allowed her Sisters to support her and the burden of what happened no longer felt so heavy. *You* are sharing on the pages of this book. You are sharing with your Higher Self, your Angels, your Heart, your Soul, and so many more energies and beings that love you. Include me on that list. I may not be right there in the room holding your hand in the physical realm, but I am right there with you holding you in spirit. I love you. Thank you for taking the time to do this activity.

Crystal Love: Krissy's Crystal is Quantum Quattro (**kwon**-tuhm **kwot**-roh). This rare and unique stone is a combination of several Crystals and depending on where you are in the world, its recipe differs. Quantum Quattro is sometimes comprised of: Shattuckite (**sha**-tuh-kahyt), Malachite (**mal**-uh-kahyt), Chrysocolla (kris-uh-**kol**-uh), and Dioptase (**dahy**-op-tays), in a Smoky Quartz (kwarts) matrix. Other times it is thought to be comprised of: Ajoite (a-**ho**-ahyt), Shattuckie, Crysocolla, and Quartz. Regardless of its ingredients, this stone reminds us that the whole is stronger and higher in vibration than the sum of its parts. If you need grounding and protecting, consider it done. If a balance of body, mind, and spirit is in order, check that off the list, too, as Quantum Quattro's healing abilities are truly wonderful. Use this stone to bring about peaceful, loving energies while you release emotional blockages and realign your inner strength with your inner truth. Keep a piece close by to clear attachments so that you may fully claim your spiritual maturity and become a gateway of Divine Healing Light. When used with sincere prayer, this stone can also release cellularly held traumas sending them down into Mother Earth for transformation and transmutation. Depending on the formula, the Dioptase will clear your entire Chakra System, the Shattuckite will release stuck energies from past lives, the Chrysocolla will provide calm acceptance, the Malachite will liberate old habits and thought patterns, the Smoky Quartz will offer grounding and protection, the Ajoite will connect you to the Divine Feminine, and the Quartz will act like a super-charged battery pack. If that wasn't enough, this Crystal continues to shower us with love by building our immune systems and releasing judgment.

Suggested Reading for Healing Trauma, *The Body Keeps the Score: Brain, Mind, and Body in the Healing of Trauma* by Bessel Van Der Kolk, M.D.

Additional Journaling and SPS Space

Gabby

I am eleven, almost twelve and I am very passionate about the Earth and about animals. I want people to know that animals matter. That their lives are important. I also want to share with people what is really going on with our Earth. To share how we all can make a difference. It is important for me to be able to teach children because we are the next generation. Kids today, we can get used to not using plastic. We can get used to the changes needed to fix what has been going wrong. We are open to listening and loving in a different way. Sometimes, when it comes to doing something like standing up for the environment, we can say, "I can't do anything." But you can always do something. I want people to realize this, especially kids. We can change our society. We can make changes that others will notice. Even in small ways, it all makes a difference. This is one of the main reasons I am in favor of more online schools. Less paper is used that way. For this reason, I hope that parents can find a better way to balance screen time. I know too much screen time is not a good thing. It definitely affects you. I'm a kid and I love technology, but I also know that screens suck you in and you don't realize how much time you spend on them. We are all doing this. When we are on our screens so much, we can't love the natural world around us. When we rely on technology so much, we just start to believe that whatever we want will always be there. Technology becomes this distraction to get away from life. When we do that, we forget to live in the world. We just stay at home and order everything online. That is so sad. We aren't getting out and creating relationships with nature. When we don't have a relationship with something, we can't be compassionate. I can be compassionate with nature because I spend so much time outside. I feel connected to plants and animals like they are my brothers and sisters. A squirrel can run up a branch and look at me and I can understand that they are telling me, "Please give me space. Don't hurt me. I am your friend." When people are mistreating the environment or animals, I say something. If I see someone kicking a tree, I stand up for the tree. If I see someone being mean, I say, "Please don't step on that bug. Please don't kill that bee." I try to explain to people that we shouldn't mistreat this planet that we live on. This is our home. This is our Mother Earth. When you hurt her, you are hurting yourself. It is awful when someone goes ahead and does something mean just because you told them not to. When that happens, I get mad. I have a temper. I try to deal with situations like this with words and kindness, but it is hard. I was just learning in class about the differences between being passive, assertive, and aggressive. Being assertive is empowering. Something I would like to get better at is being assertive when solving problems. This relates to what I am going through in Middle School. To be a young woman today is interesting and hard. When I was younger, it seemed like everyone was happy and everyone was friends with everyone else. In Elementary School, the focus was on where to play and how to have the most fun. In Middle School, your brain is way more focused on what other people think, what is popular, what to wear, and how to make people like you. This is the weirdest time of my life. I am going through so many changes. My body is developing and, honestly, I am really scared. It already feels so different. I remember one day I was a little girl and now I know I'm not anymore. It is all so confusing. All of these transitions feel so randomly emotional. One second, I feel super happy and the next, I feel super upset. I deal with it by talking it out. I sit with my mom and talk it out until I feel better. Talking is a very good way to help with all of this. When you are feeling big feelings, you really need to tell somebody. Share what you are going through and when you feel like you can't really deal with things, take a break. I wish girls my age didn't worry so much about what other people think. People tell me all the time to just let it go. I have a hard time doing that but loving myself makes it easier. I journal. I take a piece of paper and write down everything that is going on in my life: then, I focus on what is going right. If we do something that reminds us of what we do have, it helps. Other things help too, like including others. There was this kid in my old school who used to be really mean to me. The other day, I saw him sitting by himself at lunch. I kept looking over at him and it made me feel really bad. So, I got up and went over to him and asked him how it was going. He said that things weren't going so great. We ended up talking for a bit and had a good conversation. It was a lot of fun! Now we are friends and it is like a fresh start. Helping others and reaching out to people all ties back to my love of the Earth and my love for animals. Both of those things, as I am trying to figure out who the heck I am supposed to be, remind me of who I actually am. I know I am the kind of person who will do anything and everything I possibly can to help our planet and the creatures living on it. I also know that Human Beings, as a species, can improve. We need to do better. We can do better. We have the privilege of being born on this planet. If we just keep taking things - before we know it - we will have taken too much and will wish we had done things differently. People seem so worried about the past and the future that they can't enjoy the present moment. This takes us away from being able to love. Just like how kids are so focused on growing up so fast. I don't want to become an adult and think, "I wish I would have been a kid when I had the chance." I don't want to grow up and have regrets. I have faith that we can do this. I have faith that kids today can find a new way of living. We can all take more assertive action. Humans, animals, and plants can live together as equals. Let's reduce the waste and be grateful for what we have. Let's share and give instead of throwing stuff away just to buy more. When we are grateful for what we've got, we do a better job of taking care of everything. When we stay in the present moment and when we focus on what is going right, we know who we are. As a kid, with my relationship to nature, I know I have what I need, I know how to advocate for what I believe in, and I know how to preserve this world that we are so lucky to have.

Making This Story Your Own:

Gabby's story is inspiring and insightful.
Take a moment, breathe, and reflect.
What stands out for you when you read her words?
Is there a situation in your life that is similar to Gabby's?
Perhaps part of her story feels connected to your own.
How can you relate her experiences to your past, present, and future?

- *My Connection to Gabby's Story* _____

_____

_____

_____

_____

Knowing that you aren't alone, let's gently explore some other themes from Gabby's story together:

- ***We Can All Make a Difference***
    - What are you passionate about? What would you like to change in the world? What would you like to heal? If we all can do *something*, what is the *something* that you can do? What inspires you? What do you inspire in others? What do you do when you feel called to make a difference? Why do you do this? Is there *more* that you can do? What are your values? Are they in alignment with your choices? If so, how do you manage this? If your values don't feel aligned, what shifts can you make? How can you continue to lead by example? How can you continue to create the change you would like to see?

- *Believe in Yourself*
    - Who are you? What kind of a person are you? When people ask you these questions, how do you answer? What about when you ask them of yourself... do the answers differ? If so, why? Do you truly feel that you know yourself? What are your strengths? What are your gifts? What are your principles, standards, and ethics? When you really believe in something, what happens? What do others notice? When you really believe in yourself, what happens? What do you notice?

- *Talk it Out*
    - How do you get support when going through a challenging situation? Do you believe that talking about your struggles will help? Do you try to figure things out on your own? Where did you learn these coping skills? Are they still working for you? Would you like to try something different? If so, what might feel comforting to you the next time you need support? Who or what can offer this type of support and how can you create these types of supportive relationships? How might opening up in different ways and talking more about the things going on in your life be beneficial?

Sacred Play Suggestions:

~ SPS #1: ~
* Tech-Free *

Gabby shares some potent wisdom regarding the extent of our technology use. Have you had a technology-free meal, event, or day lately? Can you remember what it was like when we didn't have technology? If you added them up, how many minutes per day do you spend on your phone, computer, or tablet? What would you be doing differently with that time if you weren't on those devices? A five-minute social media scroll before bed adds up week by week. Let's make use of those precious moments. Make a list of five simple technology-free activities that you can incorporate into your day.

1. _____

2. _____

3. _____

4. _____

5. _____

For the next five days, pick one activity to do each day.

Day 1:

Go technology free during the activity.

- What do you notice about the *world* around you? _____
_____
_____

Day 2:

Go technology free for at least **three minutes** before the activity, during the activity, and **three minutes** after the activity.

- What do you notice about *yourself*? _____
_____
_____

Day 3:

Go technology free for at least **five minutes** before the activity, during the activity, and **five minutes** after the activity.

- What do you notice about your *feelings*? _____
_____
_____

Day 4:

Go technology free for at least **ten minutes** before the activity, during the activity, and **ten minutes** after the activity.

- What do you notice about your *thoughts*? _____
_____
_____

Day 5:

Go technology free for at least **fifteen minutes** before the activity, during the activity, and **fifteen minutes** after the activity

- What do you notice about your *imagination*? _____
_____
_____

Reflecting on this five-day activity, do you feel a different level of awareness and mindfulness around technology, your relationship to it, and how it affects your relationship to yourself and others?

_____
_____
_____

Five days! You just dedicated five days' worth of awareness and energy to yourself! Way to go, Sister! How do you feel? You deserve this. You deserve **500** days! **5,000**… and ***more***! Your thoughts, feelings, and imagination are so special and so needed. Connecting into them is a gift for yourself and for the rest of us. When you feel good, you think good thoughts, and your imagination creates amazing things. I'm getting excited just thinking about what you are going to come up with to make this world a better place. Thank you for being you! Love you!

<u>~ SPS #2: ~</u>
<u>* Biggest Blessing *</u>

What is going right in your life? What wouldn't you change? Why does it sometimes seem so difficult to focus on the good when the going gets tough? The positive things happening in our lives are often forgotten when we feel compromised by big situations and big emotions. It is OK. Training our brains to recognize, remember, and highlight the positive is like training for a marathon, only this marathon never ends! We may not need to *train* as much as we get better with positive recall, but this is a life-long commitment. An idea to help us with this is a 'Gratitude' or 'Blessings' Jar. If you have one, great! Use it. If you don't - no worries - you can use any jar or bowl you already have around the house. Get a few pieces of scrap paper, cut them into two-inch strips, and set them by your jar with a pen. As often as you can, intentionally write down on these strips of paper what is going *right* in your day. These are the *positives*. These are the things that you do NOT want to change. When you are finished, fold the strip of paper up so that you can no longer see the words and put the folded piece of paper in your jar. At the end of each day, pull out the pieces of paper and read them aloud to yourself. Record a week's worth of your biggest blessings.

- **<u>Day 1</u>**: My Biggest Blessing _____

- **<u>Day 2</u>**: My Biggest Blessing _____

- **<u>Day 3</u>**: My Biggest Blessing _____

- **<u>Day 4</u>**: My Biggest Blessing _____

- **<u>Day 5</u>**: My Biggest Blessing _____

- **<u>Day 6</u>:** My Biggest Blessing _____

- **<u>Day 7</u>**: My Biggest Blessing _____

Wow! Seeing seven big blessings can really highlight what is going *right*. Keep going for seven more days. As you fill your jar, don't forget to take credit. You are vibing in these blessings and you deserve just as much gratitude as you are giving! Some is coming at you now… I am grateful for you and I love you.

<u>~ SPS #3: ~</u>
<u>* Gift Economy *</u>

Mother Earth is the ultimate gift-giver and her *economy* is one of rich generosity. We receive food, water, air, shelter, beauty, and much more with almost nothing required in return. This type of economy is known as a Gift Economy, and that term has been coined by the brilliant writer, activist, feminist, song writer, and internationally known speaker, Genevieve Vaughan. The "Gift Economy" is based on the mutually beneficial standards of *relationship* which include: well-being, emotional resonance, balance, harmony, mutual respect, and secure attachment. This is the Economy of *The Mother* and is similar to the relationship between a mother and child. In the relationship of mothering, the value is in the enjoyment received from both parties when the beneficial feelings of connection and happiness are present and reciprocal. Take a look at the words below. Based on a Gift Economy Paradigm, how can you gift these things with no expectation of goods, services, or money in return? This is **not** about sacrifice. This is about the loving generosity in your heart and the rich compensation experienced when joy is shared.

• Love	• Empathy	• Clarity	• Wisdom
• Understanding	• Stillness	• Compassion	• Energy
• Peace	• Mercy	• Safety	• Generosity
• Connection	• Comfort	• Concern	• Gratitude
• Support	• Joy	• Forgiveness	• Kindness
• Softness	• Freedom	• Sisterhood	• Friendship
• Care	• Laughter	• Depth	• Relationship
• Nurturance	• Interest	• Honesty	• Pleasure
• Reassurance	• Encouragement	• Inspiration	• Cheer

What happens when you gift these qualities to **yourself**? _____

_____

What happens when you gift these qualities to **others**? _____

_____

What happens when you gift these qualities to **Mother Earth**? _____

_____

How can you incorporate more of the Gift Economy Paradigm within your **relationships**? _____

_____

As a final step, once again consider the collective value of the "Gift Economy" and its needed relational qualities. Journal and reflect on this final question.

**Based upon your understanding of the Gift Economy Paradigm,
do you value your Feminine gifts of *mothering* differently?**

_____

_____

_____

There are 36 opportunities on the previous page to *gift*. Divide them up and for the next week or two play with gifting them to yourself and others. Pay attention to what happens when you make gifting a practice. The transitive nature of *gifting* is reflected in the conscious and unconscious desire to pay it forward. You may not get to see how your gifts travel, but that doesn't negate their potency. Keep it up darling, and together we will pour love into this world. Here is some right now… I love ***you!*** Thank you!

~ SPS #4: ~
* Menarche Meditation *

For many, many years - and in some indigenous cultures still today - when a girl has her first menstrual cycle, she is celebrated. This sacred time, known as menarche *(mi-**nar**-kee = beginning month),* is rejoiced for several very important reasons. During these ceremonies, which some identify as the most cherished of all of their tribal rituals, a girl is honored for this blessed transition into womanhood. Community members celebrate her ability to create new life for her people during these special times. She is also honored because - through this holy transformation of menstruation - her abilities for oracular visioning are *turned on.* The girl is now a woman. For most of the tribes that celebrate menarche with festivals, parties, rituals, initiations, and celebrations, her psychic gifts of menstruation are henceforth recognized as essential for the tribe's abundance, longevity, and success. Imagine for a moment if this had been your experience and your first period was welcomed with no secrets, fears, embarrassment, or seclusion. What could have been different if a wonderful and meaningful celebration had been created in your honor upon your first bleeding time? A celebration attended by all of your friends and loved ones where your powers, gifts, and talents were publicly cherished, respected, and valued because you were now a woman, and becoming a woman is one of the greatest gifts imaginable. We no longer have ceremonies in our Western culture that honor and value the physical transformation from girlhood to womanhood. In fact, instead of being celebrated, our menstrual cycles have been denigrated and medicalized. No longer considered sacred, the Divine Feminine Power of our Blood Magick now resides in the realm of secrets. What used to be celebrated is not talked about… or if it is talked about, typically it is discussed with feelings that range from irritation to regret to shame to disgust. This magickal time of immense energetic power, psychic visioning, and physical, emotional, and mental cleansing - which we are gifted with *once per **month*** - has been stolen right out from under our noses and it is happening over and over and over. For those of us who did not have a ritual welcome into our Bleeding Time, or have the precious opportunity to welcome someone else into hers, let's begin reclaiming menarche. Take a moment and let your mind travel back to the time of your first menstrual cycle. If you don't remember it exactly, that is OK. Some of us have experienced extreme trauma around our menarche and the specific memories aren't easy to recall. If this is the case, connect into your younger self when you were on the cusp of womanhood. As your mind journeys, allow your body to relax and your breathing to slow. Visualize this younger version of yourself standing before you. Hear her say "hello" as she reminds you of her exact age and shares with you what was happening in your life at this moment. Look at her and from your adult sensibilities ask if you can recreate the experience of menarche together. With your younger self, decide what words you would like to hear and what treatment you would like to receive in honor of your first bleeding time. Take a moment and record these below.

- What would I like to hear? _____

_____

- How would I like to be honored? _____

_____

Read through the following.

*As your younger self basks in this precious validation of her being and becoming, her ethereal figure holds out her hand with an invitation. You grasp her hand in acceptance, and your consciousness begins to blend with hers. Looking down at your body, you realize that you have momentarily stepped into this younger version of yourself. As your mind acclimates to hers, so does your heart and Soul. You are now her. Your senses fill with the smells of lavender and roses, and in the corner of the room you see a wonderfully elegant white bed. Curiously, you walk over and lie down. Your body is caressed by a softness that you have never before experienced. Touching your hands to your heart in thanks, you discover that you are wearing a beautiful white robe made of the finest cloth. Following your body's natural line from your heart to your belly, you gently move your hands downward and let them rest over your womb. A tender rhythm begins. The tempo is smooth, and you instinctually know that this is your body's natural wisdom pulsing through your skin. You can feel the messages from your womb telling you that today is a new day. Today is a new beginning. Today you are a woman… and like the sacred cycles of Mother Moon and Mother Earth, your body will reflect the light and the growth of the natural world. From this moment forward, your intuition will reflect a deep inner knowing of that which cannot be seen but which can be **known**. You feel a deep love welling up from your heart as you honor yourself and this sacred lifecycle. You breathe in gratitude for this rich opportunity to accept your Divine inheritance. Slowly, you begin to sense that others have entered this sacred space. You open your eyes to smiling faces of all ages. All of the women of your tribe have come forth to witness your transformation with warm welcome and emboldened joy. A beautiful wise-woman steps forward. A look of fond tenderness is in her eyes. As she gazes at you, a feeling of being treasured washes over your awareness. She gently holds out her hand and offers you a gift. Upon her outstretched palm is a talisman of your womanhood. You take the item, thank her, and stand up to meet her gaze. She embraces you as if she has waited a very long time to hold you close. You align your breath with hers, and as you pull back you hold the item she has given you close to your heart. Looking directly into your eyes she says, "Welcome, daughter. Welcome sister. You now hold the power of life." You smile broadly in acceptance. The whole room cheers and erupts into an exultant song to celebrate you, your acceptance, and your transformation. You listen happily and then join in the serenade… trusting that for the rest of your life you will be respected, valued, and cherished.*

When you are ready, begin to reacquaint yourself with your physical body and the present moment. Slowly wiggle your fingers and your toes. Roll your shoulders and smile. Open your eyes and take another moment or two to remember your precious Talisman of Womanhood.

- Describe the wise woman in your vision. _____
  _____

- Who is the wise woman? _____
  _____

- Describe your Talisman of Womanhood. _____
  _____

- What is particularly meaningful about this gift? _____

_____

Thank you for doing this activity. Our bodies and our cycles are deserving of the highest honors. Reclaiming our Feminine Divinity by celebrating menarche is a gift that is ours for the taking. Breathe deep into this powerful work. By doing it, you are healing the women who have come before you, the women who walk the Earth with you, and all of the women who will come after you. I can feel it and I am forever grateful. I love you.

~ SPS #5: ~
* Inclusion Love Loop *

We've all been that kid sitting alone in the lunchroom. Pulling our energy in to project the message, "Hey, I *want* to be alone. This is my *choice*. I am *totally* cool with it." All while inwardly wishing, hoping, and praying that someone - *anyone* - comes to sit with us, ending our misery and letting the rest of the jerks in the cafeteria know that we are indeed wanted after all. So there! Maybe the cafeteria scenario doesn't resonate, but we have all experienced what it feels like to be publicly left out and it sucks. In school, most of us either didn't know or couldn't embrace the wisdom of 'you get what you give,' but we are definitely experienced and mature enough to employ that wisdom now. In the next twenty-four hours, find a way to include someone that you wouldn't normally include in something that you are doing. Let your intuition be your guide. This is the perfect opportunity to shift the lunchroom energy and invite the person sitting alone over to your table… but that is just one idea in a sea of potentials. Send a group text and include a new friend, create an online meeting and invite an old friend to participate and give input, ask a neighbor that you haven't had a chance to connect with to go on a walk, invite the family you just met at the park over for a playdate, or ask a colleague to join you for a workout. The thing is, this is way more about you than it is about them. This is about you opening your heart to give love so that you can open your heart to receive love. Pay close attention to how you feel while doing this. Witness your own process as you witness the process of the person you have invited. During the beginning, middle, and end of this experience, take note of what is going on for you.

- Deciding who to invite, I felt _____

_____

- While inviting the person, I was _____

_____

- During the activity, I felt _____

_____

- During the activity, I noticed the person I invited was _____

_____

- Right after the activity, I noticed _____

  _____

- Doing this I have learned _____

  _____

Don't let this extroverted love loop die on the vine! Keep going! Do it again and again and again. Put yourself out there and connect. Before you know it, you will be getting loads of what you are giving… some prime, grade-A, capitol: L-O-V-E! In fact, get ready to receive right now. I am sending you love and lots of it! Gratitude, too!

Crystal Love: Gabby's Crystal is the mysterious and beautiful Smoky Quartz (kwawrts). Grounding, stabilizing, anchoring, and protecting are this stone's superpowers. Known to be a good balancer of opposites, this Crystal can soften negative energies, clear mental channels, alleviate worry, and help us to detoxify our bodies, minds, and spirits. Smoky Quartz is also a powerful connector to Mother Earth. Similar to Mother Earth's "Gift Economy" this stone gifts humanity with enhanced abilities for communication and cooperation. When you want to inspire others to be concerned for our environment and to respect all living things, try wearing a piece of Smoky Quartz. Play with having a piece in your pocket to relieve stress and anxiety so that the joy of life and belief in your abilities is amplified. Additionally, use Smoky Quartz when you need a boost in the 'loving your body' department. With Smoky Quartz, you can feel an increased attraction to yourself which will lead to a surplus of vitality and passion for the world around you.

Suggested Reading to Reclaim Your Transformational and Cyclical Wisdom, *Her Blood is Gold* by Lara Owen.

Additional Journaling and SPS Space

Shelby

I am a child of many parents. That is one of the unique things about me. I have two mothers, a dad who raised me, and a birth father. I'm actually named after my birth father, Shelby, as was his father. That feels closely interlinked. It also feels interesting to me in the context of breaking generational patterns. My birth father left when I was small, and that was really hard. I was so little and it was all so confusing. The one memory I have of my parents being together was hearing them fight over who was going to go get Santa cookies. I don't really know why my father left. Every year, for most of my childhood, he would promise to come and get me and my brother, and every year he would break it. That was awful. It gave me the message that I wasn't important. That I wasn't valued. I remember having a lot of anxiety as a kid and I didn't have much emotional support. My nickname was 'Nelly Drama,' and people were always saying to me, "Shelby, stop being so sensitive." I had all of this anger and no outlet to process or understand it. My mom was very stressed and dealt with a lot of anxiety, too. Looking back, I can see that my mom was in a place where she couldn't be honest about who she really was. She had to hide her feelings. As a result, we all lived under this 'suck it up buttercup' kind of mentality. My childhood was sort of a hot mess. Things just didn't make sense. Kind of like how it is hard to believe that a caterpillar can turn into a butterfly. Somehow, in the hot soupy mess of the cocoon, it just happens. That was me. I was in that dark soupiness for a long time. Things shifted when my mom came out as a lesbian my sophomore year of high school. That started the process for both of our transformations. It wasn't necessarily a safe space back then to be open about your sexuality. This was only twenty years ago, but in our small rural area my mom had to hide who she was. I'm positive that if she had never come out, I would not be the strong woman I am today. I found out that my mom was a lesbian when I returned home from a two-and-a-half-month missionary trip in Europe. The morning after I flew home, jet-lagged and exhausted, my mom came into my room sobbing. I was sure someone had died. While I was gone on the trip, I had really bought into organized religion. I was lost and it was a perfect fit. There were rules to follow. There was community and connection. The first thing I said to my mom after she told me was, "Are you going to be able to come to heaven with me?" I don't even know how that came out of my mouth. I was numb. I didn't know what to think. Because I had been gone for so long and because we lived in such a small town, all of my friends already knew about my mom. I couldn't even call someone to share my secret. I ended up calling the Youth Pastor of my church and he told me that I had to choose between the church and my mom. He said that if I continued living with her, I was going to hell. I didn't know what to do. I moved in with my dad, my mom's second husband, the man who raised me. I loved being with him, but I hated being away from my brother and sister. It just felt wrong. I tried going back home for a bit and that didn't work. I ended up at my best friend's house. Her father was a mentor to me. If I had to describe a true embodiment of the Divine Masculine, it was him. He loved everything strongly and comfortably and his motto was, "Love them anyway." He looked at me one day and said, "God wouldn't have made your mother the way she is if he didn't love her." A lightning bolt hit me, and something just clicked. It was like, "Of course!" All of the other stuff holding me back from accepting my mom and her partner just seemed ridiculous from that moment forward. Love them *anyway* and in **any** way. I moved back home and got one of the biggest gifts of my life: witnessing what true romantic and reciprocal love looked like. I got to see these two women in true partnership loving, living, and sharing their lives together. I did not know that this kind of love existed until I saw them together. My mom and her partner taught me what a balanced and loving relationship could be. That love and that connection gave me the strength to begin to heal my heart, which I then opened to love when I met my husband. It was in Citizenship Class. As he was packing up his red backpack, I heard this voice in my head say, "There you go, that is your guy." My first reaction was, "*Really*?" But as I looked at him more, I began to think he was pretty great. I slowly fell in love with him and was able to access more empathy. As the years progressed, this led to my birth father and I developing a relationship. He was sort of like a distant uncle that I talked to every once in a while. When I had my children, I started to sense the cycle of broken promises starting again. This time the hurt was there, and it hurt a lot, but there was also an awakening. I sat with my feelings. I let the sadness come out and recognized something within myself: I was not going to let the pattern continue. As an adult, I could understand the trauma that my father had been through. I could identify that he didn't have the tools or support he needed to become a parent. The instinct might have been there, but he had been hurt so badly, he panicked. I was going to break this generational pattern. I went to the beach and, as I cried, I wrote him a letter. I told him that I was not mad at him and that I loved him. I also listed all of the things that I did have in my life because of his decision to leave. I listed my father, my sister, that whole side of my family, my mom's partner, my husband and my children. All of the things, the ripples of positivity from his absence, that I was so grateful to have in my life. At the end of the letter, I asked him to make a decision. I told him that I would not hold it against him either way, no matter what he decided. I told him I would never stop loving him and I asked him to decide if he was going to be all in or all out as a grandparent. I told him that I could not have him in and out of my children's lives. That I could not and would not stand for it to happen again. I sent that letter with love and with peace and I never got a response. It is OK. I can acknowledge that this pattern hasn't been and isn't perfect. I'm not perfect. Neither is he. Maybe this is just what we need right now. I support him and love him from afar. I take a lot of strength in believing that he is proud of me because **I** am proud of me. This wisdom comes from honoring my emotions. By doing that, I feel like I heal the child within. Now my emotions are my superpowers. I feel my feelings, sit with them, and walk through them. This makes me so much more aware as a parent, wife, and businesswoman. Raising my daughter is like looking into a mirror on a daily basis. Because of what I have gone through I acknowledge her feelings. I let her wrestle with them. I explore them with her. As I do this, she is learning how to do it for herself. In my marriage, I apply the same principles. When I honor myself and my feelings, I'm determined, I don't rush into decisions, and I am better able to love through tough situations. I also try to be the one who listens. Sometimes I over listen and convince myself that I hear what is not being said. But, another side of my emotional intelligence is that I listen to listen, not just to respond. This is key in all of my relationships. When I do this, I am really hearing the people around me. I am really listening for what is being communicated. To me this is an act of true love because I am honoring their feelings. It is no secret that feelings get a bad rap in business. A really bad rap. What we don't acknowledge is that feelings are the ultimate currency in everything and in all relationships. That is what business is: relationships. People say it is all about networking. Well, what is networking? Networking is creating relationships. Everything we do boils down to feelings. How does someone or something make us feel? I take so much wisdom from my childhood experiences as I approach life in this way. Sometimes when I can't make sense of how I feel, I write it out. Nothing more. I write, walk away, come back, reread, and there they are: the nuggets of goodness. I highlight my own good advice. I pay attention to my own wisdom. I know exactly how I feel. We can all do this. We can all put our emotional intelligence over our intellectual intelligence. If we just sit and listen to ourselves, we will find out that we really are brilliant people.

Making This Story Your Own:

Shelby's story invites us to think about how our past informs our present.
Take a moment, breathe, and reflect.
What stands out for you when you read her words?
Is there a situation in your life that is similar to Shelby's?
Perhaps part of her story feels connected to your own.
How can you relate her experiences to your past, present, and future?

- *My Connection to Shelby's Story* _____
  _____
  _____

Knowing that you aren't alone, let's gently explore some other themes from Shelby's story together:

- **Honoring Emotions**
  - Do you push your feelings to the side? Why, or why not? How often do you stuff or stop your feelings so that you can follow through with daily responsibilities? When did you begin putting your feelings below a *to-do* list? Did you learn this behavior from anyone? Was this behavior forced on you? Is there someone in your life whose feelings seem to take precedence over your own? Are you sometimes too exhausted to even deal with your feelings? Do you engage in other activities to silence your feelings or to distract yourself from honestly feeling them? What would it look like if you were to begin genuinely feeling your feelings? What would it take to feel safe enough to explore and honor all of your emotions?

- **Healing Dysfunctional Family Cycles**
  - Can you identify negative traits from your family of origin that are being repeated in the present moment? Can you trace these qualities or behaviors back through the generations? If so, how are these cycles being played out in your current relationships? Thinking about generational patterns, what comes up for you? How do you feel about these people? What would it be like if you put yourself in their shoes? What would it take to create the possibility for compassion? How can you access understanding for their choices? What about forgiveness for their mistakes? Can you take a moment and gift yourself the same amounts of compassion, understanding, and forgiveness for either consciously or unconsciously repeating these family cycles?

- **Living Your Authenticity**
  - Is there an authentic part of you that is kept hidden? If so, which part and why? Are you choosing this out of shame, guilt, or fear? Would your life be better, easier, and more joyful if you were able to fully express this aspect of yourself? What else would be different about your life if this was not a secret? What is the **worst** thing that would happen if this part of you was free to be fully and authentically expressed? Who and what else would be affected? What is the **best** thing that could happen if this part of you was free to be fully and authentically expressed? Who and or what else would benefit? Is there a way to safely explore living more authentically? Is it helpful to shift your thinking and relate to this as a mystery versus a secret?

Sacred Play Suggestions:

~ SPS #1: ~
* Divine Masculine *

In her story, Shelby mentions that her best friend's father was a true mentor of the Divine Masculine for her. What does Divine Masculine mean to you?

My Understanding of The Divine Masculine

My understanding of the Divine Masculine is that it is the Archetypal Energy of the Fully Expressed, or Fully Actualized Masculine within every living thing regardless of gender. This energy is full of selfless protection, calm and compassionate clarity, and kind and generative support. When this energy is compromised or not allowed to be fully expressed within the human experience, we can encounter the destruction, violence, abandonment, force, and vengeance of the what is known as the Wounded Masculine. Take a moment and connect into your Masculine Side. Below are a few general qualities attributed to the Masculine Energy or Archetype. Knowing that these qualities have nothing to do with gender but are expressions of the Masculine within each of us, give them a read and take notice of what initial thoughts and feelings come up. Add any other general Masculine qualities that come to mind in the additional spaces.

~ General Qualities of the Masculine ~

Success	Personal Achievement	Productivity	Independence	Rationale	Linear Thinking	Efficiency

Next, think about the following questions in regard to how these qualities are present within your relationships and daily interactions. Use the space at the bottom to answer the last question and for additional journaling.

<u>Success</u>
• Is this quality in balance for me? _____
• How has this quality supported me? _____   _____
• Do I *over*-identify with this aspect of the Masculine? _____
• Do I *under*-identify with this aspect of the Masculine? _____
• How has either over- or under- identification affected me and my relationships?

Personal Achievement

- Is this quality in balance for me? _____

- How has this quality supported me? _____
  _____

- Do I *over*-identify with this aspect of the Masculine? _____

- Do I *under*-identify with this aspect of the Masculine? _____

- How has either over- or under- identification affected me and my relationships?

Productivity

- Is this quality in balance for me? _____

- How has this quality supported me? _____
  _____

- Do I *over*-identify with this aspect of the Masculine? _____

- Do I *under*-identify with this aspect of the Masculine? _____

- How has either over- or under- identification affected me and my relationships?

Independence

- Is this quality in balance for me? _____

- How has this quality supported me? _____
  _____

- Do I *over*-identify with this aspect of the Masculine? _____

- Do I *under*-identify with this aspect of the Masculine? _____

- How has either over- or under- identification affected me and my relationships?

Rationale

- Is this quality in balance for me? _____
- How has this quality supported me? _____
  _____
- Do I *over*-identify with this aspect of the Masculine? _____
- Do I *under*-identify with this aspect of the Masculine? _____
- How has either over- or under- identification affected me and my relationships?

Linear Thinking

- Is this quality in balance for me? _____
- How has this quality supported me? _____
  _____
- Do I *over*-identify with this aspect of the Masculine? _____
- Do I *under*-identify with this aspect of the Masculine? _____
- How has either over- or under- identification affected me and my relationships?

Efficiency

- Is this quality in balance for me? _____
- How has this quality supported me? _____
  _____
- Do I *over*-identify with this aspect of the Masculine? _____
- Do I *under*-identify with this aspect of the Masculine? _____
- How has either over- or under- identification affected me and my relationships?

Now, take a look below at some general qualities often attributed to the **Divine Masculine**. Again, these have nothing to do with gender. Take note of what thoughts and feelings come up in the empty box.

~ Qualities of the Divine Masculine ~

Selfless Protection	Centered	Compassionate	Kind	Generative	Supportive	Experienced

Finally, with the questions on the following page think about how these Divine Masculine qualities can be actively present and balanced with the general qualities of the Masculine discussed above.

How can I incorporate the following Divine Masculine qualities to more authentically understand and express my Masculine Side?

~ How can I balance **Success** with the **Selfless Protection** of myself and others? ~

_____

_____

~ How can I balance **Personal Achievement** while maintaining **Centeredness**? ~

_____

_____

~ How can I balance **Productivity** with **Unconditional Compassion**? ~

_____

_____

~ How can I balance **Independence** with **Unwavering Kindness**? ~

_____

_____

~ How can I balance **Rationale** with **Generative** and **Life Sustaining Choices**? ~

_____

_____

~ How can I balance **Linear Thinking** with **Steadfast Support** of myself and others? ~

_____

_____

~ How can I balance **Efficiency** by always **Acting from Experience**? ~

_____

_____

After completing this activity, see how it feels to stay aware of your Masculine Side. As you actively engage and balance your Masculine aspects with your understanding of the Divine Masculine, see what happens. Just being mindful of how these things play out within our lives and relationships can make a big difference! Thank you for doing this activity. Your understanding, compassion, and conscious embodiment of the Masculine is needed and valuable. I love you!

~ SPS #2: ~
* Heart Art *

When you imagine your heart, what comes to mind? Do you think of an organ? Do you think of a feeling or an energy? When you lead from your heart, what part of your body goes first? When you connect into your heart, does the left or the right side of your body feel more energized? Grab a few markers, crayons, and other art supplies and find a quiet place. In the empty box below, draw your heart and divide it into two halves. Have fun with color, line, and texture, and as you create your design, allow both sides to inform your work. Incorporate symbols and words as they come to mind and take your time to fully decorate your _Heart Art_ creation. When you are finished, take a look at your piece and write down the first four or five words that come to mind on the line below. This is the title for your beautiful work of art.

_____

My Heart Art

Now, observe your artwork once more and this time look through a lens which highlights the right side of the heart as your Masculine Side and the left side of the heart as your Feminine Side. You may already be familiar with this concept. In many modalities of energy work, body work, and mental health support, the right hemispheres of our brains and the left sides of our bodies are known to represent the Feminine, and the left hemispheres of our brains and the right sides of our bodies are known to represent the Masculine. When you are finished contemplating your beautiful creation, take a few moments and answer the following questions.

- Looking at your *Heart Art* from the perspective that the left is the Feminine and the right is the Masculine, what do you notice? _____

- Is there anything you would like to add? _____

- Is there anything you would like to change? _____

- How do you interpret your work of *Heart Art*? _____
_____

- What wisdom does each side have to offer? _____
_____
_____

- What wisdom does your whole *Heart Art* offer? _____
_____
_____

As a final step, take your art supplies and connect the two sides of your heart. This will signify an awareness to the loving, respectful, and peaceful balance between your Masculine and Feminine Sides. When you are finished, once again answer the questions from the beginning of the activity. Your *Heart Art* is beautiful… just like you. Love you!

When you imagine your heart, what comes to mind?

_____

When you lead from your heart, what part of your body goes first?

_____

When you connect to your heart, do you feel it more on one side or the other of your body?

_____

~ SPS #3: ~
* Sweet and Sacred Objects *

We fill our living spaces with some of the most precious and interesting things. Look around where you are sitting and observe the non-essential items. Artwork, trinkets, decorations, books, antiques, and furniture are probably just a few of the things you notice. This *collector-gene* seems to be a pretty universal human trait. Throughout time, humanity has created and collected special items, sacred objects, and artwork in the attempts to make life sweeter, more understandable, and more meaningful. Stay in the room where you are or get up and take a walk around your home. Let your intuition guide you to something and, when you have found it, take some time for a multi-sensory observation. If you can, touch the item. If not, simply being near it is enough.

- Open your **eyes** to fully experience and observe this object. Answer:
    - What do I **see**? _____
    - What do I feel in my body? _____
    - What is my **connection**? _____

- Open your **ears** fully experience and observe this object. Answer:
    - What do I **hear**? _____
    - What melody plays? _____
    - What **memories** come up? _____

- Open your **nose** to fully experience and observe this object. Answer:
    - What do I **smell**? _____
    - What am I reminded of? _____
    - What **person** comes to mind? _____

- Open your **mouth** to fully experience and observe this object. Answer:
    - What do I **taste**? _____
    - What food craving is present? _____
    - What meal do I **remember**? _____

- Open your **skin's awareness** to fully experience and observe this object. Answer:
    - What do I **feel** on my body? _____

- ○ What other information is there? _____
- ○ What **wisdom** comes forward? _____

Paying close attention to the information and guidance coming forward from the sacred objects in our environments can be a daily reminder of where we have been, where we are, and where we would like to go. As a final step, journal or reflect on the question below.

**What can I begin doing in honor of myself and my living space to make
life sweeter, more understandable, and more meaningful?**

_____

_____

_____

Thinking about you loving yourself through your living space is inspiring! Thank you! Love you!

~ SPS #4: ~
* Feelings *

Shelby offers potent wisdom with her statement, "Feelings are the ultimate currency." What does that statement mean to you? Have you ever thought about your feelings in this way? The term *currency* is often used in regard to money, or trade. In our modern world, money - used for the exchange of goods and services - is given much importance. Some may say money is valued over everything else. Connecting money to feelings can seem a bit strange, but we do it all the time. There is a reason why most of us can still hum "Can't Buy Me Love" by The Beatles. Sure, the tune is catchy, but it goes deeper than that. We still want to believe that the power of love can transcend the power of money. Like Shelby says in her story, "everything we do, it all boils down to feelings." If we can remember that, perhaps we can also remember how *powerful* and *valuable* our feelings really are. Read through the following lists of feeling words.

Sorry	Weepy	Drifty	Nervous	Embarrassed
Special	Bored	Hurt	Overwhelmed	Shy
Angry	Lonely	Confused	Sore	Energetic
Loving	Beautiful	Clumsy	Relaxed	At Ease
Sexual	Sad	Peaceful	Playful	Teary
Joyful	Weird	Comfortable	Sensual	Rejected
Proud	Dreamy	Frustrated	Funny	Friendly
Confident	Loved	Tense	Mad	Thankful
Hungry	Full	Irritated	Happy	Annoyed
Hangry	Vibrant	Unloved	Inspired	Refreshed
Purified	Sacred	Purified	Strong	Creative
In Pain	Devoted	Selfless	Authentic	Powerful

Choose a few of the following options to honor your feelings as the "ultimate currency."

- Circle all of the feelings you have felt in the last 24-48 hours.
- Write a letter to your feelings.
- Put on a piece of music that reminds you of one of the feelings above. Dance and move your body in ways that honor the feeling.
- Call someone and ask them the last time they felt one of the feelings above. Share your story of the last time you felt this way too.
- While in the car, hit the scan button on the radio. For whatever song comes on, finish this sentence: This song makes me feel_____ because_____.
- Choose ten or more of the feelings above and give them a color and a texture.
- Create a Feelings Flow Chart. Start with one feeling and identify how this feeling flows into other feelings creating either a functional or a dysfunctional pattern.
- Come up with your own unique way to honor the 'ultimate currency' of your feelings.

Spending time with our feelings can reboot our brains to revalue our emotions. When we begin to value them in this way, others do, too. Your emotional currency is priceless and you are the ultimate intuitive translator of this empowered, instinctual wisdom. Go, momma, go! I love you and I love watching you do your thing! Especially the dancing! ☺ Thank you for doing this activity!

~ SPS #5: ~
* Skin-to-Skin *

Find a quiet spot and connect to your breath. For the next three inhales and exhales, focus on receiving whatever you are meant to receive during the inbreath and giving whatever you are meant to give during the outbreath. There is no specific direction on how or what to give and receive. Just create an awareness around the two states of being. If it helps, try placing your finger on the prompts below for the three breaths.

Breath 1: Breathe in - *Receive*…. Breathe Out - *Give*
Breath 2: Breathe in - *Receive*…. Breathe Out - *Give*
Breath 3: Breathe in - *Receive*…. Breathe Out - *Give*

Allow your breathing to return to normal and bring your awareness to your body. Place your hands on your body and feel the warmth of skin-to-skin connection. As the gentle heat moves downward from the top layer of your skin and seeps in deeper, create a Sacred Contract between you and your body for giving and receiving **love**. As you connect from your feet to your crown, alternately send love *to* and receive love *from* your body. Since love is our true state of being, living *in* love ***is*** living in authenticity. How about channeling in some more of that sweetness? Move from place to place around your body and follow the reciprocal exchange of love with an inquiry. Ask the different places, "What could I be doing to live more authentically?" Record your answers below.

- **Your Feet:**
  - Give and receive **love** to your **feet.**

  - Ask: What could I be doing to live more authentically? _____
  _____

- **Your Legs:**
  - Give and receive **love** to your **legs.**
  - Ask: What could I be doing to live more authentically? _____
  _____

- **Your Hips:**
  - Give and receive **love** to your **hips.**
  - Ask: What could I be doing to live more authentically? _____
  _____

- **Your Vagina:**
  - Give and receive **love** to your **vagina.**
  - Ask: What could I be doing to live more authentically? _____
  _____

- **Your Back:**
  - Give and receive **love** to your **back.**
  - Ask: What could I be doing to live more authentically? _____
  _____

- **Your Belly:**
  - Give and receive **love** to your **belly.**
  - Ask: What could I be doing to live more authentically? _____
  _____

- **Your Breasts:**
  - Give and receive **love** to your **breasts.**
  - Ask: What could I be doing to live more authentically? _____
  _____

- **Your Shoulders:**
  - Give and receive **love** to your **shoulders.**
  - Ask: What could I be doing to live more authentically? _____
  _____

- **Your Neck:**
  - Give and receive **love** to your **neck**.
  - Ask: What could I be doing to live more authentically? _____

  _____

- **Your Face:**
  - Give and receive **love** to your **face**.
  - Ask: What could I be doing to live more authentically? _____

  _____

- **Your Crown:**
  - Give and receive **love** to the **crown** of your head.
  - Ask: What could I be doing to live more authentically? _____

  _____

As a final step, place your hands on your heart and envision wrapping your body in a golden light of love and gratitude. Throw in some love and gratitude from me, too! I love you and I am so thankful for you. Finish with three easy breaths and go love the world *"anyway in **any** way."* You know… *like we do*!

Crystal Love: Shelby's Crystal is Vesuvianite (vuh-*soo*-vee-uh-nahyt), or sometimes known as Idocrase (*ahy*-duh-kreys). This stone is connected to our Heart Chakra and represents loyalty, cooperation, and our relationship to the intuitive and creative inner realms of the psyche. Vesuvianite also supports us as we process and heal, releasing anger and dissolving fear so that we may open our minds and hearts to more purely connect with our Souls. If you want a deeper awareness of your feelings, get a piece of Vesuvianite and ask it to help you allot more attention toward your emotional intelligence and emotional maturity. Also known to aid in the processes of spiritual ascension, this Crystal can clear our minds from negative thought patterns while offering us the perspective to notice what is needed by our higher selves versus what is wanted by our egos. Additionally, this stone is said to increase our sense of smell - a powerful trigger for recollection - allowing access to important memories. Finally, because of Vesuvianite's interesting olfactory superpowers - which lead to increased levels of awareness and retention - try using it when you want to create a new memory. Play with holding a piece close to your body as you visualize a balanced version of yourself living your fully expressed authenticity.

Suggested Reading to Fully Understand, Actualize, Express, and Embody Your Divinely Masculine Qualities, *King, Warrior, Magician, Lover: Discovering the Archetypes of the Mature Masculine* by Robert Moore and Douglas Gillette.

Additional Journaling and SPS Space

Sarah

My journey is one that continues every day, all day. It is a journey to remind myself that I matter, to speak my truth, and to empower myself and my family. There are days when I am taking care of a lot. So much more than just the surface things. My daughter is on the Autism Spectrum. Over the past few years, I've had to push, I've had to fight, and I've had to scrap to get her the services she needed and deserved. I've called so many different places, read tons of information, and have become an expert in Sensory Processing Disorder, Autism, and Anxiety. It hasn't been easy, and it hasn't always worked. But a lot of support has come because I've been vulnerable enough to reach out. To connect. To get to know strangers. For instance, I found a neurologist because I was talking to a friend at lunch one day and the waitress overheard me. She came over and said, "I heard what you said, and my daughter is on the spectrum, too. I think this could be a helpful resource for you." I only found that out because I was open enough to share my world with another woman. I shared my struggles. Yet a lot of us aren't vulnerable enough to do that. We seem to keep it all locked in until it's too late. There comes a point where it's just too much to bear and it oozes over. If you can open up and connect with people, so much good can come from that. Last summer was really hard… it was one of the hardest summers that I've ever had. My daughter was really struggling. She was having a really, really rough time transitioning to her new baby brother. Her sensory stuff went off the charts and we ended up being a shut-in family for a few months. I was feeling completely overwhelmed and exhausted. I had a newborn baby and a little girl that ate all her meals in a teepee. She was terrified of cars driving past our house, the washing machine, and the vacuum cleaner. Even the sound of her brother's cries would set her off. I found myself in a new place where I didn't have the tools to help her. She was having a lot of fight or flight moments and we were trying to figure out how to support her. There were some days where I couldn't reach her. She was off in orbit and the only way I could connect was by stepping into her fantasy play. So, we played. We played a lot! I wanted to find a way for her to understand where she fits in the world and how she can relate. I also wanted her to feel safe and surrounded by love. Mission accomplished! But by the time school started, I was feeling completely overwhelmed and exhausted. I started talking to friends and I am so glad that I did, because they encouraged me to find someone to talk to about how I was feeling. I needed a moment to stop and think of how I fit in. Not only in my family, but in the world. I found out about the Divine Mommy group. I signed up and I learned so much! I learned things that I'd never been exposed to before… like the chakras and ideas about interconnection. The love and support that we found within each other was just amazing and exactly what my raw little 'Mommy-heart' desperately needed. It was like a sisterhood of women who could connect on so many different planes while having different backgrounds and personalities. One of the things that I've actively tried to do since being in the group is to not ever judge another mom. I just send her love, support, and hope. As a result, I've made so many great friends. I've found a tribe of women that I connect with on different levels - all different kinds of moms, all sharing similar struggles, and all amazing. This is what has meant the most to me after participating in the group. It is so important to connect with each other, to support each other, and to figure how we can navigate and share this world together. I trust myself now. Before, I never fully felt like I could trust myself. I felt like I wasn't fully enough. Then I realized, that is garbage. I am enough. I am the person that my daughter needs. I am teaching my children to be amazing humans. I am empowered to stand up for myself and to trust myself. That has changed everything. It has changed my family's world. It has even changed my relationship with my husband. There have been some growing pains as I have started to claim things back for myself. We're still working on it as a couple, but the sense of empowerment and the innate trust that I've developed has been transformative. So, don't wait to put yourself in the mix. It is just like the airplane oxygen mask. You have to put your mask on first before you can help other people. That is so hard for a lot of moms because we're always taught that you have to put everybody else first and then you get the leftover scraps. This message has got to change. You've got to think about yourself in that mix. And if you're completely empty, there's no way you can ever fill anybody else up. Don't wait. You deserve it. We all have to put ourselves in the mix. When you do, you never know what kind of magic can happen.

Making This Story Your Own:

Sarah's story shines a light on things that a lot of us deal with.
Take a moment, breathe, and reflect.
What stands out for you when you read her words?
Is there a situation in your life that is similar to Sarah's?
Perhaps part of her story feels connected to your own.
How can you relate her experiences to your past, present, and future?

- *My Connection to Sarah's Story* _____

_____

_____

_____

_____

Knowing that you aren't alone, let's gently explore some other themes from Sarah's story together:

- **Being Open and Being Vulnerable**
    - How open are you? Does the phrase 'letting your guard down' resonate? Why, or why not? Do you do things for everyone else, but push your own feelings and needs down and tell yourself they aren't as important? If so, why do you do this? Are you of the mindset that it is easier to just keep everything inside? Do you ever wonder what might happen if you let your feelings out or let your guard down? If so, when did this begin? How old were you? When did the pattern of pushing down feelings and vulnerabilities become a habit, and are you even aware of it anymore?

- **Feeling Overwhelmed**
    - Do you identify with the words overwhelmed and exhausted? Can you remember a time when you weren't tired? Does the routine of your life sometimes feel like a comfort and a prison at the same time? Does adding in one more thing to the daily grind, even if that thing is your self-care, feel like just too much? When did you start feeling this way? Was there someone in your life whom you learned this way-of-being from? Does feeling chronically exhausted keep you distracted from some other deeper feelings? If so, what would it take to feel rested enough to begin processing these deep feelings?

- **Trusting Your Inner Wisdom**
    - How often do you listen to your inner voice? Do you hear her at all? Do you listen to her and then make excuses for knowing what you know? Does not being able to explain **how** you know what you know make you feel frustrated? Do you follow her guidance? How often? How often has

she been right? How often has she been wrong? What keeps you from trusting her? Along the way, have you been taught that the things found in books - or the things that can be 'proven by science' - are more reputable and reliable than your instincts and intuition? Has this perspective worked for or against you in the past? Does it work for or against you now? What would you like to change when it comes to honoring your intuition?

Sacred Play Suggestions:

~ SPS #1: ~
* Spectrogram *

Sometimes we don't realize how much our needs are not being met. In our personal and professional lives we get bombarded by other people's needs, wants, desires, and expectations. In doing our best to meet these various requests our own cups can get drained down below the empty line. So subtle is this process that - day after day - our empty cups begin to feel completely and utterly *normal*. Most of the time we don't recognize this until something else in our lives literally screams for our attention. Our bodies get sick. Our relationships suffer. Our spirits deflate. Our hearts get sad. We experience these symptoms as problematic because so often they do cause problems.... But what if these symptoms have deeper meanings? Perhaps they are here to tell us that running on empty is no good. There is a great Drama Therapy exercise called the Spectrogram. The Spectrogram is a simple and effective way to bring new perspectives and insights to habitual thoughts and behavior patterns. Let's give it a try. Look at the line below. The left end of the line represents 0% and the right end of the line represents 100% and every place in between has a value.

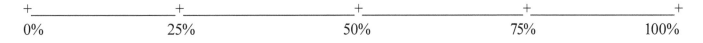

0%   25%   50%   75%   100%

To get the hang of it, answer the following silly questions by drawing a mark on the line to represent your answer.

- How often do you wear socks?
    - *If you wear socks about 35% of the time, draw a mark on the line at 35%.*
- How often do you dress up for Halloween?
    - *Repeat the same process. If you dress up for Halloween once every five years or so, put your mark between 15-20%.*
- When you are out, how often do you stop and pet cute dogs?
    - *Do you? Well, you should... Pet therapy is real! Put your mark on the line to represent how often you stop and love on cute pupper dogs.*

Spectrograms help to get us out of the 'always' and 'never' response patterns. By making us answer with specific percentages, we realize that seldom do we do something 0% or 100% of the time. Spectrograms also make us think about our behaviors and choices. It doesn't hurt that they are also a fun way to tie in awareness around the thoughts and feelings underneath those habituated behaviors and choices. Before this next round of questions, stand up and take a lap around the room. This way the energy of your body will be allowed to flow and participate. In addition to the mind, allowing the body's natural wisdom to be part of the process is helpful. Answer the following questions on the percentage lines provided and journal or reflect on the additional questions below.

1. How much time per day do I need for myself? (*answer on the line*)
2. How often do I take the time that I need? (*answer on the line*)

+_____+_____+_____+_____+
0%   25%   50%   75%   100%

What comes up when you look at both of your answers? _____
_____

Would you like either percentage to change? _____

How would you like them to change? _____

What can you do to shift each so that they are 1% closer to being in alignment with your needs? _____
_____

What would it take to bring them 5% closer to being in alignment with your needs? _____
_____

What would it take to bring them 20% closer? _____
_____

1. How much time do I devote to caring for others?
2. How much time do I devote to caring for *myself*?

+_____+_____+_____+_____+
0%   25%   50%   75%   100%

What comes up when you look at both of your answers? _____
_____

Would you like either percentage to change? _____

How would you like them to change? _____

What can you do to shift each so that they are 1% closer to being in alignment with your needs? _____
_____

What would it take to bring them 5% closer to being in alignment with your needs? _____
_____

What would it take to bring them 20% closer? _____

_____

1. How often do I help others when asked?
2. How often do *I* ask for help when I need it?

+_____+_____+_____+_____+
0%   25%   50%   75%   100%

What comes up when you look at both of your answers? _____

_____

Would you like either percentage to change? _____

How would you like them to change? _____

What can you do to shift each so that they are 1% closer to being in alignment with your needs?_____

_____

What would it take to bring them 5% closer to being in alignment with your needs? _____

_____

What would it take to bring them 20% closer? _____

_____

Take a look at your answers. Go back, reread them, and see if you can identify the thoughts and feelings underneath the behaviors and choices. Having this awareness is great, but don't be hard on yourself if the percentages aren't matching up in ways that you want. In fact, go easy on yourself. Stand up and take another walk around the room to get your body involved once again. When you feel ready, ask your body to help you come up with the answer to the following question.

How can I love myself enough to put my needs first?

_____

_____

_____

Your needs are important. **You** are important. Creating time for ourselves, caring for ourselves, and asking for help when we need it is hard. Think of these things as if they were the tiniest muscles that need the most attention in the gym. The more you put yourself first, the stronger those little muscles will become. Self-care is not selfish. It's a necessity! Thank you for taking the time to do this activity. I love you. I can't wait to see the loving things that you are going to do for yourself… starting *now*!

~ SPS #2: ~
* Long Hug *

Did you know that consistent and gentle touch and compression can help calm our Nervous Systems? It can and it doesn't take a great deal of time. In fact, 25 seconds of doing so can bring about big shifts. Let's give it a whirl. Grab your phone or watch and set the timer to 25 seconds. Now, wrap your arms around your shoulders and squeeze. Gently compress down until the pressure feels just right. Once you get this embrace exactly the way you want it, intentionally send love into your body. As you breathe in, snuggle into yourself, and on the out breath, drop your shoulders. Try repeating this self-hug a few times and see what you notice. If you have someone close by who is willing to be your partner, or if someone you love could use a reset and they are cool with a 25 second hug, try this with another person. Be sure to hug for a minimum of 25 seconds. When the hug is complete say "thank you" to yourself and your partner, if you have one. Keep this tool in your toolkit for the next time you feel anxious or stressed. You can also play with massaging your hands, arms, and shoulders after the hug. This small act of self-love can help you create your perfect reset button. Thanks for doing this activity. Love you!

~ SPS #3: ~
* Alta Balance *

Our bodies are amazing! We have organs, bones, muscles, tissues, skin, and different physiological systems. Most of our physical body is so elegant and so complex that modern science is still studying it to learn more. In addition to the physical body, which we can see and touch, we have an etheric body which we can sense and feel. This etheric body is known as an energetic body. Our energetic bodies are comprised of different systems that work together with both the etheric and the physical anatomy. This beautiful connection creates our daily experiences with all of our reactions and responses, and these interactions can be felt on the physical, emotional, mental, and spiritual levels of our consciousness. The Chakras, known as the Major Energy Centers of the etheric body, are located on the midline of the physical body. There are seven of them from the base of the spine to the crown of the head. Since they are on the etheric plane, they cannot be seen and touched, but they can be sensed and felt. This may sound a bit odd, but the wisdom of the etheric body is hidden in plain sight. Our language and universal physical reactions can prove it. When our feelings get hurt, we might say "My heart is broken." When we say this, is our heart organ broken? Not really. But the energy center at our hearts, the Heart Chakra - which deals with our abilities to unconditionally give and receive love - is definitely compromised and can *feel* broken. How about when we get really, really upset? A typical response is, "I am just sick about it!" Did our stomach organs randomly decide to produce more acid and give us a sour tummy for no reason? No. It was the responsive relationship between the energy center at our navels, the Solar Plexus Chakra - which is the seat of our emotional body - and the corresponding anatomical and physiological systems of the digestive tract, which all come together to process the big feelings. Thinking of them in these terms, the Major Chakra Centers are truly *major*. They rest on the center of the body where 23 lines of concentric energy cross. In addition to the seven Major Chakras Centers, there are also 70 Minor Centers where 14 lines of concentric energy cross. For right now, we are going to focus on a minor center known as the Alta. The Alta is located at the back of the head and this Minor Center is important in a *major* way. According to the energy work that I study, a modality called Esoteric Healing, the Alta is the circuit board for the Nervous System. If all of this is about as clear as mud, that's OK. Within the energy medicine fields of practice and study, there is a belief that 'energy follows thought.' Simply put, this is kind of like the concept from the movie *Field of Dreams:* "If you build it, they will come." If you can give yourself permission to just have the experience, you can experience the etheric body without really being able to explain it. Give it a try. Without touching your body, hold your hands behind your head about four to six inches away from your skin. See if you can feel the energy. It may feel like a shift in density or heat. A friend of mine said he knew he was tapped into the energetic field when it felt like there was cotton candy between his fingers. If you feel something, great. If not, don't give up. Remember: *energy follows thought*. If you are having trouble feeling the energy, set your intention to do the work first and you will sense the energy second. It might take some time and it might take a few tries and that is totally OK! Now back to the Alta. If you like visuals, you can imagine a yellow butterfly at the back of your head representing the outside of the Alta Minor. Let's see what information our Altas have for us. Follow the six-step practical below.

1. Physically and energetically connect to your Alta Minor by holding your hands about 4-6 inches from the back of your head.

- What do you feel or notice? _____

2. Maintain this connection and take a deep breath in.

- What do you feel or notice? _____

3. Still maintaining the connection, exhale.

- What do you feel or notice? _____

4. In your imagination, draw or intuit a line connecting your Alta Minor to a Source, or Universal Energy.

- What do you feel or notice? _____

5. In your imagination, draw or intuit a line connecting your Alta Minor down into the Center of Mother Earth.

- What do you feel or notice? _____

6. In this place of being anchored to Source and grounded to Center, ask for balance to come to your Alta.

- What do you feel or notice? _____

Once you feel any sort of shift or release in your Alta Minor, take a few more deep breaths and let your hands drop. One of my favorite things about energy work is that there is no right or wrong way to do it. As long as we have ourselves, our breath, and our intuition, the ability to shift, balance, and move the energy through our physical and etheric bodies is at our fingertips. Now *that* is empowering! Keep trying this activity and notice the different sensations, information, and guidance coming through. As with most energy work, there are energetic boundaries to maintain when it comes to facilitating on other people. If you feel called to share the work with others, please make sure you have their permission to balance their Alta Minor. Thank you for taking this time to do this activity. Isn't energy work fun? Great job connecting to and balancing your Alta! Love you!

~ SPS #4: ~
* I Matter *

Sarah offers much grace and wisdom in her story. Daily life and the challenges of parenting, partnering, working, and running a household can leave anyone feeling exhausted and overwhelmed. Forgetting to take care of ourselves in the mix of meltdowns, meals, phone calls, bills, and other responsibilities is extremely easy to do. Yet, our families need us to stay empowered, and so do we! When we get down and forget our own needs, we can begin to feel utterly discouraged. Captaining a ship from a place of near collapse *sucks*. The facts are we *DO* matter and our truth *IS* important. Read Sarah's courageous words and take note of any feelings that come up.

- **I matter. I speak my truth. I empower my family.**

Try writing the sentence three times.

- _____.

- _____.

- _____.

How does it feel when you write Sarah's words? Do the words flow? Do you feel rooted in the present moment? Are you thinking of the grocery list? Let's turn these words into a Mantra and say them out loud. A Mantra is a Sanskrit word that translates to '*mind tool*,' or '*mind liberator*.' Say Sarah's words out loud three times and see what comes up.

- **I matter. I speak my truth. I empower my family.**
- **I matter. I speak my truth. I empower my family.**
- **I matter. I speak my truth. I empower my family.**
    - What do you notice? _____
    _____

Next, sing the words three times. Don't worry, there is no judgment. Sing only for yourself, in any rhythm and melody, and claim these words for your own.

- **I matter. I speak my truth. I empower my family.**
- **I matter. I speak my truth. I empower my family.**
- **I matter. I speak my truth. I empower my family.**
    - What do you notice? _____
    _____

Speak the words again and pick a feeling to embody underneath them such as *bold, strong, stalwart, steadfast, powerful, assured, embodied, inspired, energized*, etc.

- I matter. I speak my truth. I empower my family.
- I matter. I speak my truth. I empower my family.
- I matter. I speak my truth. I empower my family.
  - What do you notice? _____
  _____

Try engaging with these words a few more times in whatever ways you feel called and gauge what additional feelings come up. Finally, write these words on a separate piece of paper and put them in your pocket. Carry this paper with you as a reminder. Thank you for doing this activity. Love you!

You **DO** matter. You **DO** speak your truth. You **DO** empower your family.

~ SPS #5: ~
* Connection Opportunity *

Ready for a fun self-love mission? Your mission, should you choose to accept it, is to find one daily task and turn it into an opportunity for either a new or deeper connection. Over the phone, on the computer, or in person, try to genuinely connect with at least one person today. With eye contact, if applicable, and genuine curiosity, step out of your comfort zone and start a different type of conversation. Ask the cashier at the grocery store where they are from. Hail your mail carrier and ask what the best part of their day was. The next time you encounter a service industry professional, inquire how they got their name. Nothing is too silly, simple, or mundane. The only rule is - this is not a monologue; this is a dialogue - which means that you continue the conversation by sharing your answer to the same question. Take notice of the following.

- How did I feel before making the connection? _____
  _____

- What was it like listening to someone share? _____
  _____

- How did I feel before sharing? _____
  _____

- How did I feel after sharing? _____
  _____

- What did I notice and learn about myself? _____
  _____

- What did I notice and learn about others? _____

  _____

- What did I notice and learn from the entire exchange? _____

  _____

Connecting like this can be silly, zany, and fun. It can also shift energy. Chances are you can sense how your energy is shifted, but don't underestimate your ability to shift someone else's. Pause for a moment and with a deep breath, honor your loving and powerful commitment to connect and make this world a better place. No matter how simple, every act of kindness to self and others counts. Way to go, Sister. Thank you for doing this. I love you!

Crystal Love: Sarah's Crystal is the subtle and strong Onyx (**on**-iks). This stone is great for the self-control and self-mastery needed to make wise decisions. Put those qualities together with Onyx's abilities to increase feelings of self-confidence, stamina, and courage, and you just may notice more happiness and good fortune manifesting into your life. Use this stone to alleviate the fears and worries associated with difficult times and life stress. Try holding a piece of Onyx to help you understand all sides of a situation. Increasing the connection to our instincts, Onyx can also fast track our capacities for seeing, hearing, and intuiting guidance. When you feel alone on your path, use this Crystal to bolster trust in your personal strengths as it can gift you the courage to take your own counsel above all others. As you more firmly center and align with your Higher Powers, employ another wonderful gift of Onyx and use this stone to transmute and ground any seemingly negative by-products of your transformation process.

Suggested Reading to Play with Your Inner Intuitive Goddess, *The Magic Path to Intuition* by Florence Scovel Shinn

Additional Journaling and SPS Space

Pat

I grew up in Saline County, at the old Bonnell Homeplace, in Cottage Grove, Illinois. The home I grew up in was built by my grandfather for my grandmother as a wedding present. My father was an only child, so when he and my mother married they moved in with Grandma and Grandpa. My mom and dad had eight children over a span of 27 years, and I am number seven. It is kind of interesting, my parents had me when they were in their forties, which people didn't really do back then. Even though our town was small, my parents owned a general store that my mom ran while my dad was out working construction. They sold blasting powder and gasoline, and the store even had an old post office. I remember fun times playing in that old store building with my younger sister when we were little. My mom was an amazingly strong woman. She was one of six and her father was a coal miner. She was only five-foot tall, wore a size 12 girl's shoe, and because she had a fiery temper was nicknamed 'Piss Ant.' She was a mother beyond belief. She lived for her children. I remember we had a big garden and she would can things all night long to keep our cellar full. It was her job to keep us all fed and she did that in wonderful style. I always remember her working from the time the sun came up till we all went to bed. I grew up with this strong work ethic and a strong, innate sense of caregiving modeled by my mother. Things changed when I was twelve. It was Christmas Eve and we were waiting for my father to come home from work. We heard an unexpected knock on the door. I saw police officers and I remember my mother crying and saying out loud, "How am I going to raise these two little girls?" My father had been killed in a car accident. Since my mom didn't drive, and we lived way out in the country, we moved into town and lived with my Granny Pearlie. This experience became one of my biggest motivators to become an educator. After my father was killed, no one at school even asked me how I was doing. In 1961, things were different, we didn't know about counseling services. People didn't know what to say and tragedies weren't openly talked about. My mother was so stoic. She would say, "I don't know why this has happened, but we are going to be fine. You girls are going to go on to school and you are going to make something out of yourselves." My Granny was the same. In the year that we lived with her before she passed away, she talked to me a lot and inspired me to go on and get my education so that I could make a living for myself. Both of these amazing women, along with my older sister, were my cheerleaders. They were really responsible for making me the woman I am today. All of these early experiences taught me that, as we go through life, we really have to embrace it all and *'go with the flow.'* That saying from the seventies so perfectly describes what you really have to do in life. I feel so blessed to have had such a great childhood. Although I lost my mother at the age of 33, I owe my strong sense of self to her and my Granny. Although they weren't 'strong' by today's standards - they didn't drive, they weren't educated, they didn't work outside of the home - these two women were the strongest and most ethically sound human beings that I have ever met. They passed those qualities on to their children and grandchildren. Because of their influence - as a mother, educator, and grandmother – I, too, can stand up for what I ethically know is right. I believe we all know right from wrong, but we don't always walk it. These women walked the walk and talked the talk. I truly think they were born with it… that strong sense of motherhood and womanhood. My mother was born in 1908, and although she was a whole generation older than my peers' mothers, she kept up with the trends and fashions. She was an avid reader and a great listener. I've tried to pass this strength and dedication on to my own daughters…. not only to be avid readers, but to see what it is like to pursue a Doctor of Education at the age of 60. My mother had six of her eight children at home. I can remember her telling me stories that as soon as she would get done birthing a baby, the other children would be right there on the bed saying, "Mommy, tie my shoe" or "Mommy, I'm hungry." She would care give because she had to, getting up to fix supper just hours after birthing a baby. It was expected of her. Yes, times were different, but somehow she was able to find this internal well of strength. My Granny Pearlie used to talk to me as a child and say, "Get your education and have a career so that you don't have to depend on anyone for money." My mother agreed. You see, they knew. They had worked their whole lives, expected to work night and day and never be paid for their efforts. They knew what it was like to be so dependent. They didn't want that for me. In the 1950s and 1960s both of these women were such progressive thinkers. My mother would shake her little hand at me and say over and over, "You get that education so that you have power." She also instilled in me a strong sense of love for myself. She taught me that I could always count on myself. That I was capable. That I could do it. I've always tried to live up to that and I think I have. Although I have experienced the loss of divorce, the grief of losing a child, and the pain of losing a spouse, even though those events were devastating, I never stopped hearing my mother's words telling me, "This is a journey.... You are walking a journey... and you can do it." She also taught me that even during the darkest of times, I can find a way to enjoy every day. I can see the power in what she taught me and also the fallibility. Being a woman with a career, I know the hardships of trying to balance working outside of the home with my children and grandchildren. Back in 1975 when I had my first child, I had both my education and a career to support myself. I also felt alone and isolated. Intellectually, I knew how to do the jobs - the mothering and the working - but I didn't know how to balance the two. It was really difficult being a wife, mother, daughter, teacher, sister, and friend. I didn't have a model for how to do it and often times felt extremely inadequate. I also had a hard time being honest with my mother about my struggles and vulnerability because she looked at my life with such a sense of freedom. I didn't even try to help her understand my reality of jumping in and out of roles - feeling spread so thin - because I didn't want to make her feel bad. At that time, there was still no division of labor between the husband and wife. I was expected to work and make money and also carry all of the responsibilities of child rearing and homemaking. I worked all day at a job and then came home and worked all evening in my house. I would come home and think I was going crazy. I was working so many hours and I was so exhausted. At that time, there weren't any support groups around for women. We were all expected to be silently grateful that we *could* work and get an education while having the honor of maintaining the home. I started exercising. I started running and working out at the local YMCA, which was a big help: but there was no one to really talk to. We had fought so hard to earn these 'rights' that we were all afraid to complain. We were afraid to speak up and say, "Yes, we can do the job, but we need some help, too." Thank goodness we've come a long way since then. It was the way of the times and it has been quite a ride living through the 1960s and 1970s, fighting for civil rights for everyone, but also fighting for women's rights, too. It's made me tough and it's been a journey, but I wouldn't change a thing. My hope is that younger women today can take the time to really assess their feelings, desires, and passions. To really follow their hearts. So much of the work we did thirty and forty years ago was so that women today could comfortably find other women and soul sisters for deep connection and support. When you can, connect into your mothers, grandmothers, aunts, and ancestors. Let those women who share your bloodlines give you strength. Remember that they were finding their own balance, too, just like you. Get to know who those women were. Open lines of communication where you can so that you can connect into your roots. That way you can begin to really know who you are. Thinking back to my mother and my grandmother, who they were, where they were from, the land that they lived on, it gives me a sense of deep peace and strength. Stay in touch with that feeling. Stay positive. Stay connected. And never quit learning.

Making This Story Your Own:

Pat's story reminds us that by connecting to our ancestors we can reconnect to our empowerment.
Take a moment, breathe, and reflect.
What stands out for you when you read her words?
Is there a situation in your life that is similar to Pat's?
Perhaps part of her story feels connected to your own.
How can you relate her experiences to your past, present, and future?

- *My Connection to Pat's Story* _____
_____
_____
_____
_____

Knowing that you aren't alone, let's gently explore some other themes from Pat's story together:

- **Connecting to your** Matrilineal Ancestors
    - Do you know your female ancestors? When you think of them, what comes to mind? Do you recall names and faces? Do you remember stories and legends? Have these memories influenced you in anyway? If so, how? If not, why? Would connecting to your ancestors or connecting to them in different ways be beneficial? When those who come after you reflect on having you as an ancestor, what kind of legacy would you like to leave?

- **Finding Balance**
    - How many different roles do you play in a day? What about in a week? A month? A year? Are the different roles easy to identify? Why, or why not? What is the balance like between your professional and your personal roles? When these roles are out of balance, what happens? Which roles do you freely show and share? Which ones do you keep hidden? Do some of the roles you play feel like they aren't right? If they are no longer a fit, is there a way to change or release them? What about a new role that you would like to step into? Is there something preventing you from doing this? How would changing the roles you currently play be helpful for you and your relationships?

- **Continued Education**
    - How do you define the difference between wisdom and intellect? Where do you rank yourself in regard to both? Is this personal assessment based on what *you* feel to be true, or has it been influenced by an outside entity? What are your thoughts on education, continued education, and higher education? Where did these thoughts and values come from? How do you feel about your own education? Could your feelings be more positive? What is the reason for either seeking or not seeking additional opportunities for your education? Are there relationships in your life that are directly inspiring or inhibiting your desires for continued growth and learning?

Sacred Play Suggestions:

~ SPS #1: ~
* Divine Feminine Altar *

When you think about an Altar, what comes to mind? Human beings have been creating Altars - significant places of prayer, devotion, and reverence - since our early primitive times. For us today, an Altar can be any space or place that we intentionally and energetically recognize as sacred. Altars can be permanent or temporary, large or small, complex or simple. The only requirement for an Altar to become an Altar is an acknowledgment that the space and the objects placed there are important. For this activity, we are going to create an Altar to honor our Feminine Side. How this Altar honors your Feminine Side is completely up to you. Some ideas for Altar creation are:

- Your Divine Feminine Energy
- Your Female Relationships
- Your Feminine Ancestors
- Your Female Reproductive Organs
- Your Inner Goddess(es)
- Anyone, Anything, and Everything That You Want!

Once you have decided what your Altar is honoring, next you get to decide where your Altar will be placed. There are no rules for Altar placement. Just follow your intuition and have fun. Take a moment to walk around your house and see what areas call out to be your Altar. Allow corners, tabletops, shelves, cabinets, drawers, and any other special nooks and crannies to catch your attention. When you have found the perfect location, it's time to gather your sacred items. You probably already have loads of things to use for the creation of this Altar. Candles, flowers, pictures, crystals, scarves, jewelry, books, and rocks are all wonderful ideas. As you gather these items, feel their energy and pay tribute to their importance. Now you get to experience the happy joy of creating this special space. Take time with the placement of each item, asking *it* where *it* would like to be placed. Gently and lovingly lay out the cloths and scarves. Get each piece just right, paying close attention to the design elements of height, color, texture, and energy. When your Altar is complete, take a few precious moments and sit quietly in front of this dedicated space. From your heart, send an intentional thread of energy into every chosen item, wrapping the entire space in love. This is your Sacred Space. This is your Altar. Come back here regularly to rejuvenate and replenish. Ground your work by taking a few minutes to journal around the following.

- My Altar is dedicated to_____

- My intention for this Altar is_____
  _____

- The meanings of my Sacred Items are_____
  _____

Although I can't see your altar, I can feel it. It is beautiful! Just like you. Doing this inspires me to create Altars everywhere! Let's do it! We can create a *'Random Acts of Altars'* Movement! Who knows what might happen if we did? Special Sacred Spaces from rest stops to restaurants… from board rooms to beaches… I enjoy thinking about that. I also enjoy thinking about *you* at *your* Sacred Space, enjoying *yourself.* Thank you for taking the time. Love you!

~ SPS #2: ~
* Mantra *

Mantras are a great way to calm our minds and set intentions. The word Mantra is a combination of two Sanskrit words: ***manas*** and ***tra***. When those root words are combined, the word **Mantra** translates to mean:

'mind tool' or *'mind liberator.'* Many things can become Mantras. Words, phrases, song lyrics, and social media memes are all worthy contenders. All that matters is that the words or sounds, when sung repetitively, are meaningful to the singer. Yep. I said it. The words *sung* and *singer* are the operative ones in that previous sentence. Before you give up on the idea of singing Mantras, think about this…. A Mantra is an open invitation into the transformative world of music and this invitation has no expectations and no prerequisites. Anyone at any time with any skill level is invited to sing Mantras. As an added bonus, when we sing - especially when we sing with other voices - our brains release hormones that help us relax and make us want to bond. It is a total win-win! Below are some options of Mantras to try. *Sing* them as many times as you would like. A traditional Mantra, sung around Sacred Mala Beads or Sacred Prayer Beads, is sung 108 times. This is to signify you as the number 1, the never-ending relationship you have with your Higher Power is the circle or 0, and the infinite nature of that relationship is represented by 8 (which just happens to be an infinity sign on its side). However, if you don't have the time or the inclination to sing a Mantra 108 times… no worries. This is your Mantra Practice. Sing as many times as you want. Make up your own melodies and rhythms. Play with alternatively singing your Mantra in your head and then singing it out loud. Everything counts here because this is about YOUR relationship to YOURSELF and no one is an authority over that except YOU.

Mantras to Try:

- **OM**- Calls in a state of Supreme Consciousness; believed to be the sound of the Universe and the original vibration of all life.
- **Maaaaaa-** Calls in the Spirit of the Great Mother.
- **OM Shanti, Shanti, Shanti**- Sanskrit mantra that symbolizes peace of body, mind, and spirit.
- **I Am Exactly Where I Need to Be**- Empowers us to be in the Present.
- **I AM Enough-** Because you ARE!
- **I AM perfectly imperfect-** Helps us release expectations.
- **Make up your own-** It will be perfect, I promise!

Once you have created a Mantra Practice, take notice of what works. After singing, fill in the following:

- Today, I sang the Mantra_____
- I sang _____ times.
- I felt_____
- I noticed_____
- I shifted _____
- Tomorrow, I will sing the Mantra _____

I stopped myself from writing 'and the day after that,' 'and the day after the day *after* tomorrow,' 'and that day after the day after *that…*' 'Sing, baby, *sing*' will have to suffice. The world needs your voice. *I* need your voice. Invite others to join. If no one else is there, ask your pets and plants to chant along. Your divine chorus offers infinite reasons to celebrate *you*. Hey, that makes *me* want to celebrate! Whoo-hoo! Thank you! I love you.

~ SPS #3: ~
* Role Change *

Pat's story offers us much to consider regarding balance, especially when it comes to the roles we play in life. When you think about it, how many different roles do you play throughout a day, a week, a month, or a year and what do your costumes look like? A teacher of mine once told a story about a harrowing court case she had to participate in. She specifically chose a red power suit for the trial because she wanted to embody the role of *'Strength.'* After the trial, she reflected many times that her red suit gave her a sense of empowerment during a very difficult time. I tend to wear workout gear most days. After realizing this and taking notice of how this costume facilitates my daily responsibilities, I named my costume the *'mom-i-form.'* Sometimes we are in costume without even knowing it, and the roles we play physically define us without our conscious participation. Sort of like when we experience our own version of the well-known recurring dream where – boom - *surprise!...* right in the middle of the dream we are plopped naked at a public event. Even though we are dreaming, we wake up, baffled and questioning, "What could that *mean*?" We feel thrust by our subconscious into the roles of *'Helpless,' 'Embarrassed,'* and *'Defenseless.'* The only fun part about that dream is telling people about it afterwards. Let's make our own fun and try our hand at some intentional costume design. Go to your closet. Even though it is hard, try not to clean, organize, or hang anything up.

This is <u>Step #1</u> and this is important:
Randomly choose five items of clothing.

Now, set those five pieces of clothing to the side and shift gears. Think of all that you have done since you woke up this morning. Below there are twenty spaces, fill them in, and add more if you need.

THINGS...	I...	HAVE...	DONE...	TODAY...

Great job! Looking at all of your accomplishments, see if you can identify at least five different roles that you have filled today. This is all about what pops into your head. Be as general or as specific as you want. For example, a general *'Mom'* may be one of your roles. Or you can get more specific and indicate which version of *Mom* by specifying: **Stressed** *Mom*, **Patient** *Mom*, **Wild** *Mom*, or **Crabby** *Mom*. Maybe *Taxi-Driver* or *Lunch Maker* feels more appropriate. Don't forget about *Judge, Therapist, Babysitter,* or *Supportive Friend*. These Roles are versions of *you* that you step into multiple times a day to make your life work.

Role #1	Role #2	Role #3	Role #4	Role #5

Now, with your five different Roles, assign each one an item of clothing from <u>Step #1</u>.

For example:

- *Stressed Mom* gets the red scarf.
- *Taxi-Driver* gets the black hat.
- *Supportive Friend* gets the old white jean jacket.
- *Judge* gets the green cardigan.
- *Patient Mom* gets the pink blouse.

These items of clothing are now your costumes to represent each of your five roles. OK, it's showtime! Go ahead and get into costume. You can put on all of the pieces at once, or you can put them on one at a time… your choice. As you are putting on the costumes for this very deep and well-crafted character (a.k.a. YOU) take note of each costume's color, texture, and fabric. Finally, let's put it all together by journaling and reflecting on the following questions.

- How do the costumes feel? _____
    - What information do you get from the colors, textures, and fabrics? _____
    _____
    _____

- Does each costume fit the role? _____

- Does each costume fit your body? _____

- Are they comfortable and how is their comfort level important to the Role? _____
_____

- Do you like the costumes? _____

- What feelings come up when you wear them? _____
_____

- Would you like to change the costumes? _____

- Why and how would you change them? _____

- Do the costumes bring up thoughts, memories, or sensations? _____
_____

- Are there certain costumes that you would like to wear more often? _____
_____

- Are there costumes that you would like to get rid of? _____
_____

As you journal and reflect, let the guidance come from both the costume and the role. Through this process, gauge which roles are working for you and which roles are not. When you are finished, take the costumes off. As you remove each piece, ask:

- What changes can I make today so that my roles feel **comfortable**? _____
_____

- What changes can I make today so that my roles feel **enjoyable**? _____
_____

- What changes can I make today so that my roles feel **empowered**? _____
_____

- What changes can I make today so that my roles feel **inspired**? _____
_____

Wow! So. Much. Information! Have fun with this. Wear your costumes often and see if anyone begins to notice. We are going to transition in and out of various roles for the rest of our lives. We might as well enjoy them as much as possible. When you see me wearing my *mom-i-form*, come and give me a hug. I will probably need it. Love you! Thank you!

~ SPS #4: ~

* Ultimate YOU *

When you have a few quiet moments, imagine having achieved everything in your life that you want to achieve. Big thing to think about, right? Try breathing into this possibility a few times. As your imagination bubbles and percolates, allow your awareness to stay in the big picture energy of the achievements happening rather than the smaller picture energy of questioning *how* they happen. All that you want to achieve may not be clear or easy to visualize. If this is the case, lucky you! So much opportunity lies in the unknown. We become different iterations of ourselves from moment to moment based on what life throws at us. What we want today may change tomorrow and that is OK. For this activity, the '*what*' and the '*how*' aren't nearly as important as the '*who*' because the who is *you*. To rephrase the opening sentence: imagine what **you** will look like when you have achieved everything that you want to achieve. At the risk of sounding like a Rodgers and Hammerstein lyric from *The Sound of Music*, this version of you has climbed every mountain, dreamed every dream, followed every rainbow, and left no rock of life unturned. Absolutely anything and everything you could wish for… this version of you has worked her magick and made it happen. Let's meet her!

Connect into your breath and as you deeply inhale and exhale… gently close your eyes.
Envision a long Temple hallway stretching out before you.

You stand in the inner most chamber of this Sacred Temple, the holiest of holy places.
From where you are, you can see directly to the gates.
Gazing down this beautifully adorned passageway, the path is clear.
Suddenly, the Temple gates open. Someone enters and begins walking toward you.
You can tell right away that this being is stunning, strong, and wise...
completely in possession of her body, mind, and spirit.
As she continues to come closer, much about her is familiar.
Step-by-step, she gets nearer.
You sense her powerful energy.
You see her beautiful form.
You recognize her unconditional love.
She looks at you directly in the eye and your awareness floods with knowing.
*She is **YOU**.*
You are staring directly into your own eyes.
A huge smile spreads across both of your faces.
Pure devotion, dedication, loyalty, and tenderness flows between you.
She says, "I am here for you."
*You exhale the breath that you've been holding in anticipation, and a **conversation** begins.*
As you talk, all questions are asked, and all answers are given.
Stay in this loving place with yourself for as long as you need.

When your conversation feels complete, take a few additional minutes to note the following observations about this version of you. Use the following questions or come up with your own.

- What do you look like? _____

    o What is your age? _____

    o How is your hair? _____

    o What type of clothing are you wearing? _____

    o What do you notice about your body? _____

    o What do your hands tell you? _____

    o What do you see in your eyes? _____
    _____

    o What do you feel in your heart? _____
    _____

    o What do you sense from your spirit? _____
    _____

- What wisdom came forth? _____
  _____

- What guidance can you begin implementing today? _____
  _____

This all-knowing version of you is inside of you at all times. You may not feel like it, but she is there. When you need her, ask for her. She can come forward through the powers of your imagination with offerings of wisdom, support, comfort, and clarity. She is here for you. Trust in her and trust in yourself. I do. I trust in you. I see your inner wisdom. I see your inner strength. Thank you for dedicating the time to connect into *you*! Love you!

~ SPS #5: ~

* Land Love *

Pat shares about her deep ancestral connection to the land where she came from. This is the land where her ancestors lived and loved. This is where her roots are. Where is your land? Not just the land you *own*, but the land you *love*. This can be a place from any time or dimension. You may have visited this land. Perhaps you have read about it in books. Maybe this land is from your dreams. This is the land that inspires you. It is where you feel at home, connected, loved, and *at one* with all living things. Yes, this place is beautiful, but it is more than that…. This land is *alive*. It breathes and has a heart that beats. This land receives just as much life-force from you as you do from it. This land has memories and it is wise. If this land is accessible and if you can get there, get your feet on the Earth for this activity. If not, that is OK. In your imagination, visualize being there and consciously connect your physical body to the ground. Allow roots to grow from the bottoms of your feet, dancing and spiraling down into the soil. Once grounded, grow branches and leaves up from the crown of your head to touch the sky. Now, as you are anchored and aligned with this sacred place, open your consciousness to receive. Allow the land to share its wisdom with you.

You Ask the Land

- What wisdom do you have for my **Physical** Body? _____
  _____

- What wisdom do you have for my **Emotional** Body? _____
  _____

- What wisdom do you have for my **Mental** Body? _____
  _____

- What wisdom do you have for my **Spiritual** Body? _____
  _____

Invite the land to share its guidance, feelings, and sensations with you. As this information comes in, pay attention to your thoughts and feelings. Ask any questions you may have and patiently wait for the answers. Once you have received all that you need, maintain your intentional connection and prepare to reciprocate. This relationship between you and the land is a mutual exchange of love, dedication, and wisdom. You have much to give this wizened land and the land is now patiently waiting to receive your gifts. Let your intuition be your guide. Reciprocate by allowing the land to receive your care, connection, and appreciation. In your imagination, hear the land asking you the following questions. With ease and clarity, acknowledge and share the answers coming forth.

The Land Asks You

- What wisdom do you have for my **Physical** Body? _____
  _____

- What wisdom do you have for my **Emotional** Body? _____
  _____

- What wisdom do you have for my **Mental** Body? _____
  _____

- What wisdom do you have for my **Spiritual** Body? _____
  _____

When the exchange is complete, gently say goodbye and commit to another visit. As you return to the time and space of the present moment, take a few deep breaths. Feel your feet on the floor and place your hands over your heart. With gratitude for where you have been, reconnect to where you are now. Acquaint your senses with your current environment and notice what you see, hear, smell, taste, and feel. As a final step, give thanks for your relationship to this sacred land. Thank you for connecting into this deep, natural wisdom. Reconnect into your land whenever you need. It is just a thought away. Love you!

Crystal Love: Pat's Crystal is the beautiful blue green Chrysocolla (*kris*-uh-**kol**-uh*)*. This re-energizing and revitalizing stone is pure love for all of our Energy Centers. With its stunning palette and amazing hues, connecting to Chrysocolla is like connecting our consciousness to the consciousness of our Great Mother Earth. Just like the Divine Feminine energies which hold and nurture humanity, Chrysocolla can ease emotional heartache and allow us access to the strength, balance, and understanding needed for healing and harmony. When life starts to feel out of control, ask this stone to support you in speaking your truth. When your voice starts to feel frozen, try placing a piece of Chrysocolla on your body to open your Throat Chakra. When negativity and fear prevent you from vulnerably sharing your needs for closeness and connection, request the wisdom of Chrysocolla for support. Once supported, this stone can additionally remind us of our capacities for love, dedication, and loyalty. Truly a well-rounded healer stone, Chrysocolla can show us that authentically walking and talking our truth not only raises the vibration of our character but can build a strong inner sense of self-confidence and self-acceptance.

Suggested Reading to Connect into the Powerful Ancestral Wisdom from the Divine Feminine, *If Women Rose Rooted* by Sharon Blackie.

DeWanda

I'm practicing. I'm dragging myself through vulnerability. I never really got it before. I would say, "Oh, I'm going to be a little more vulnerable" - but not until I really started speaking my truth, literally stating what is going on for me in the moment, did it sink in. As a child, I was very active and very emotive. I was often admonished for my behavior: fidgeting, being too boisterous, too theatrical. I grew up in the South and went to a segregated school. I was a dark-skinned black girl born to a light skinned black woman. Interracial colorism - the hierarchy of light skin versus dark skin between people of the same race - really exists, and was highly prevalent during the times I grew up in. My mother would scrub my skin relentlessly in the bathtub, trying to lessen the darkness. Sometimes she scrubbed so hard that I couldn't let my elbows or knees touch the sheets in bed because my skin was so tender. Very early on I started asking the question, "What is wrong with me?" In my house, because of my dark skin, I had to be better at everything to be taken seriously. My language had to be more eloquent, my education more perfect, my manners more spotless. I learned to take in my environment and adjust accordingly. I would take on a role to see what to do and not to do to be accepted. That morphed into my personal relationships. I would figure out the role they wanted me to play and I would fill it. I became the ultimate people pleaser. So much so, that when someone would ask me about how I was feeling, I couldn't answer. I had no idea. I never thought about how I felt. I spent almost thirty years of my life in two marriages only thinking about how my husbands felt. I've spent almost three decades in the role of pleaser. I've got more time behind me now than I do in front of me, and I am committed to not having another shitty relationship. I've spent 28 years trying to turn donkeys into stallions. I ask myself, "Could I have been OK with the donkey? Could I have been OK with doing the work for both of us?" The answer is always no. The whole issue of looking outside of myself and relying on others to feel happy, healthy, and whole is something I can't do anymore. I have to put myself first. I've been doing an open mic, and at the start of my routine my jokes are about my two marriages. During my first divorce, I was very distraught. I got married young - before my 21st birthday - and had two daughters before I was thirty. When we split up, I was devastated and cried and begged him to come back for weeks. I never wanted to be a single mom. For my second marriage, it was a very different scenario. I contemplated the divorce, made my decision, took off work early on Friday, went to see an attorney, scheduled an appointment with a therapist, and was home that afternoon sitting by the pool looking at dating sites. It was this experience that gave birth to my ideas of creating 'wasbandLife.' The Urban Dictionary defines the term as, 'a person that you were married to and you are now divorced from.' Wasband is a term that I started using as my second ex-husband's moniker. A term that definitely beats 'asshole' when referring to an ex. Wasband has become a whole way of life for me. I want to share this lifestyle with other women who, like me, have gone through the painstaking process of divorce and want to come out on the other side healthy, happy, and whole. Divorce is not the end of life as you know it. Your sex life doesn't have to end. You don't have to become rigid or angry and resentful. You can co-parent in a positive, functional way. I now see spaces and places and pieces of me that I want to explore and connect to that I didn't even know existed. My world had gotten so small in my unhappy relationships. Today I am expanding, and **I** am my top priority. Exercise is my medicine. It keeps me going. I walk twenty miles a week, 'rucking' with a 25-pound backpack. I meditate. I take time when I get out of the shower and massage oil into my skin, sending love into every part of my body. I have *'Naked Days'* where I literally walk around in the nude all day. It has helped me realize that I like my body better naked than with clothes on. Yes, I have nights when I cry myself to sleep with loneliness. I lay in my big California Queen bed and think, "If I could just have a pair of hands… not even a whole body… but just to have some hands on me would be enough!" But I'll tell you, more mornings than not after I've cried myself to sleep, I wake up and stretch across that big old bed, and I think, "I'm ready. I'm ready to start another day." I put my tennis shoes on and I'm out the door doing my thing. As a 59-year-old mother of three and a grandmother of five, I'm OK with being me. I don't have a recipe for exactly how to do it or not to do it, but I'm working every day to learn these lessons. I'm aligning myself with my values. I want to understand how and why I feel what I feel. I'm living and sharing my motto, my lifestyle, and my dedication to being Happy, Healthy, and Whole.

Making This Story Your Own:

DeWanda's story takes us on a journey of self-acceptance and self-love.
Take a moment, breathe, and reflect.
What stands out for you when you read her words?
Is there a situation in your life that is similar to DeWanda's?
Perhaps part of her story feels connected to your own.
How can you relate her experiences to your past, present, and future?

- My Connection to DeWanda's Story

_____

_____

_____

_____

_____

Knowing that you aren't alone, let's gently explore some other themes from DeWanda's story together:

- ***Love the Skin You Are In***
    - What do you feel when you look in the mirror? When you try on clothes, what is your first reaction? When you look at your hands, what comes to mind? What about your feet? Your legs? Your belly? Your chest? Your face? As you observe your skin, muscles, and bones, where are your thoughts? Are they in a place that is grounded in kindness, love, and support or not? Why and when did this begin? Is this someone else's critical voice that you hear or is it your own? Perhaps it is a blending of perspectives from the past, present, and future? How does this internal voice influence your relationship to yourself? Is this influence OK with you? Would you like it to shift? If so, what are a few small things you can do right now to begin *loving the skin you are in*?

- ***Be Big, Be Bold, Be You***
    - How often do you freely voice your thoughts and ideas? Where and when do you openly share wisdom, expertise, and intelligence? Do you ever censor or stop yourself from doing this? Is there certain company in which you can't be as big, bold, and YOU as you'd like to be? Do you ever attempt to be quieter, softer, or more pleasant and if so, why? How does it feel? Is it authentic? If you were *always* as big and bold as you wanted, what might happen? Would the outcome be different for different relationships? Are there relationships where you can't be your big, bold self? If so, are those relationships necessary? How can they shift to allow your fully authentic self to shine through?

- ***Living Happy, Healthy, and Whole***
    - What makes you happy? What makes you healthy? What makes you whole? When you think about these questions, are your answers based in the future? If they are, what keeps them from being answered with your present circumstances? Have you thought about this? How about what is making you happy, healthy, and whole *right now*? Do these answers come easy? How much value do you place on these things and where did that value system come from? Is it still valid, or would you like to spend more time and energy on this? If so, what can you do today to begin living this way?

Sacred Play Suggestions:

~ SPS #1: ~
* Love Bath *

DeWanda provides us with beautiful imagery to ponder when she shares about her '*Naked Days*.' I know this woman well and she is always stunning… inside and out! Thinking about her being free, unencumbered, and totally naked for a full day causes my heart to speed up a little. It *sounds* so wild and liberating! It *feels* so natural and open. It *is* so beautiful and inspiring. I can't even imagine walking around for a *whole* day **naked**… But I want to! I want a whole day of witnessing my own beauty, sensuality, sensitivity, and lack of restriction from both my clothing and my thoughts. Don't you? I'm guessing I might know what you are thinking because underneath all of the wild and free talk, I'm thinking it, too, and it sounds something like, "Awesome idea, never gonna happen." I get it. People in and out of our space all day. Spouses, kids, animals, air conditioner repair people, a package delivery needs a signature, your online book club… the list goes on and on as the reasons pile up for why you can't spend a whole day loving on your naked body. I know! And really, that is only part of it. A whole day… **naked**? What? A whole day of scrutinizing this or that about our bodies? A whole day of not being able to cover ourselves up and temporarily forget about what we don't like? A whole day of our inner critic running on a loop with things like, "You should have kept up with that diet… you should have gone to that spin class… you should do a forty-day yoga challenge… you shoulda… you shoulda… you shoulda…" AHHHHHHHH! OK, breathe. We are just talking here. Let's simmer this idea down into bite-sized chunks. You get naked for baths and showers, right? The next time you do this, tack on an extra five to ten minutes. Finish washing your body and then give yourself a '*Love Bath*' where you intentionally direct love energy into every part of your body. In her book *Showing Up Naked: Peeling Away the Layers to Your Authentic Self*, Erica Boucher talks about this and I say, let's do it! The next time you shower or bathe, make a commitment to yourself for a Love Bath. First off, make sure your space is comfortable, private, and warm enough. As you touch the various parts of your beautiful body, listen for guidance as to how they want to be touched, paying close attention to their desires for warmth, pressure, and movement. Also be aware and open to any feelings coming up. When feelings from your body do present themselves, allow them to fully be seen and heard. Don't try to change them or talk yourself out of them. With genuine awareness and curiosity, give your feelings permission to be here, thank them, and wrap them in love. When you are ready, put your hands on your bare feet. With a skin-to-skin connection, start intentionally sending them love. There are places below to record messages, guidance, and information. Love on your body where you feel called. You don't have to give a Love Bath to every spot suggested here. Follow your intuition and just do what you can. You can always return to this activity when you have more time.

My Feet
As I send love into my naked feet, they tell me…
~How they want to be touched, held, and caressed~

_____

~How they feel~

_____

From my heart and Soul, I once again direct love energy into them.
I honor their feelings. I thank them for being here.
They respond with the messages…

_____

My Legs, Thighs, and Hips
As I send love into my naked legs, thighs, and hips, they tell me…
~How they want to be touched, held, and caressed~

_____

~How they feel~

_____

From my heart and Soul, I once again direct love energy into them.
I honor their feelings. I thank them for being here.
They respond with the messages…

_____

My Belly and Sides
As I send love into my naked belly and sides, they tell me…
~How they want to be touched, held, and caressed~

_____

~How they feel~

_____

From my heart and Soul, I once again direct love energy into them.
I honor their feelings. I thank them for being here.
They respond with the messages…

_____

_____

My Vagina
As I send love into my naked vagina, it tells me…
~How it wants to be touched, held, and caressed~

_____

_____

~How it feels~

_____

From my heart and Soul, I once again direct love energy into my vagina.
I honor its feelings. I thank it for being here.
It responds with the messages…

_____

_____

My Back and Shoulders
As I send love into my naked back and shoulders, they tell me…
~How they want to be touched, held, and caressed~

_____

_____

~How they feel~

_____

From my heart and Soul, I once again direct love energy into them.
I honor their feelings. I thank them for being here.
They respond with the messages…

_____

_____

My Breasts
As I send love into my naked breasts, they tell me…
~How they want to be touched, held, and caressed~

~How they feel~

From my heart and Soul, I once again direct love energy into them.
I honor their feelings. I thank them for being here.
They respond with the messages…

My Arms and Hands
As I send love into my naked arms and hands, they tell me…
~How they want to be touched, held, and caressed~

~How they feel~

From my heart and Soul, I once again direct love energy into them.
I honor their feelings. I thank them for being here.
They respond with the messages…

My Face, Neck, Head, and Hair
As I send love into my naked face, neck, head, and hair, they tell me…
~How they want to be touched, held, and caressed~

~How they feel~

From my heart and Soul, I once again direct love energy into them.
I honor their feelings. I thank them for being here.
They respond with the messages…

_____

_____

As you travel around your glorious physical body, feel the love energy present everywhere you have touched, creating a force field from the tips of your toes to the crown of your head. Now, as a final step, we are going to go rogue and journey within. Let's send love into our Egos and Souls and see what happens. Get as naked as you can with these two aspects of yourself and let it all - the good, bad, and ugly - hang out. No hiding or censoring is needed here because this is a love zone.

My Ego
As I send love into my naked Ego, it tells me…
~How it wants to be touched, held, and caressed~

_____

~How it feels~

_____

From my heart and Soul, I once again direct love energy into my Ego.
I honor its feelings. I thank it for being here.
My Ego responds with the messages…

_____

_____

My Soul
As I send love into my naked Soul, it tells me…
~How it wants to be touched, held, and caressed~

_____

~How it feels~

_____

From my heart and Soul, I once again direct love energy into my Soul.
I honor its feelings. I thank it for being here.
My Soul responds with the messages…

_____

_____

Thank you for taking this dedicated time for self-love and self-care. I see you, Sister. I know it isn't always easy to fit these things in, but you did it! Thank you! I love you! When everything feels complete, take a few minutes to bask in the power of your own love.

~ SPS #2: ~
* Authentic Self *

Do you ever have a quote that just sticks with you? I do. I have lots. I love books that have loads of other writer's quotes in them, too. I guess it makes it feel like more of a group effort. I found the following quote by Jungian Analyst, Marion Woodman, in one of my favorite books, *Into the Heart of the Feminine*, by Massimilla Harris, Ph.D. and Bud Harris, Ph.D.

> "Take time to recognize that there are things going on within you that need to be felt, or said, or lived, or grieved. Pay attention to these things both within yourself and within the people in your life. Pay attention to the Authentic Self."

The idea that my Authentic Self needs my attention to feel, live, say, or grieve the things going on within me and my relationships struck a chord. How much goes unsaid, unfelt, unlived, and ungrieved in our lifetimes? Where does all of that stuff go? We know the answer. We might not know it consciously, but the deeper layers and levels of our consciousness definitely feel it. That unexpressed *stuff* comes back around as dis-ease and dysfunction. Not easy to live with but easy to identify when our relationships and bodies break down. What would happen if we found another outlet? What might transpire if - from this moment forward - we said what we needed to say, felt what we needed to feel, lived how we needed to live, and grieved what we needed to grieve? Think about the bigger systemic effects…. Who would witness us living this way and be inspired to do the same? What relationships might shift from dysfunctional to functional? What connections would feel richer and more authentic? How would this change the way we value, love, and relate to ourselves… and how might *that* change the world? I get excited thinking about the possibilities! Below are four empty columns. Go through and begin to fill them in with the stuff from your past, present, and future that needs to be felt, said, lived, and grieved. List all of the people (*including you*), places, things, and situations in your life that could benefit from your Authentic Selves' attention and energy. Take your time to fill in these columns. Wait until the very last minute to put the big-ticket items on there if that feels easier. Starting small and safe can be a great warm-up.

Stuff to be Felt…	**Stuff to be Said…**	**Stuff to be Lived…**	**Stuff to be Grieved…**

When the columns are filled in, go through and circle one thing under each that will be the easiest to do. Now, create a simple plan in your mind for how to authenticate these four aspects of your life. Once the plan is complete, keep going. Circle the second easiest thing to do in each column and continue on with four more plans. Keep going as long as you need to feel prepared. When you are ready, put plan into action – and, as Marion Woodman posits, "pay attention" by actually *doing* it. One thing to keep in mind as we authenticate… it might not always feel good at first. Our genuine wants and needs and their subsequent boundaries - no matter how loving we feel them to be - might be met with resistance. Change can be big and scary. When we shift, everybody around us has to shift, too. This might take some patience and faith, but you are worth it! You can do it! Love you! Thank you!

~ SPS #3: ~
* Wasband *

Can we talk 'Wasband?' How amazing is that word? How empowering is it to rename something we feel negatively about and create a new positive - or at least somewhat rascally - relationship to it? This is actually similar to an intervention used in a model of psychotherapy called Narrative Therapy. This model is amazing, and I totally suggest finding out more about it. One helpful step employed in a Narrative Therapy session is to take whatever is bothering us or whatever the *problem* is out of our bodies and out of our relationships and put it on a shelf with a brand-new name. Basically, what DeWanda so insightfully did with "Wasband." She didn't like the feelings around what the relationship with her ex-husband could potentially turn into - so she switched them, and created a whole new narrative. When we do this, we create a new way of being *in relationship* to something. Wasband makes us giggle, but more is there, too. We instantly get a feeling from the word. It is playful. It makes us curious. It feels spontaneous. We know something deeper is present, but somehow it helps us make the subject approachable. Much different than the other option DeWanda gives us which is: "asshole." Think of the difference! If you just met someone and they said, "Ugh, my ex is such an asshole!" versus "Ugh, my ex is such a Wasband!" What would your reaction be to those two statements? Asshole is negative, definitive, and keeps us rooted in a place of blame. Hey, the ex may very well be an asshole of gargantuan proportions, but how does continually referring to them as that help anyone? A term such as Wasband is like a gift to the giver. The person who uses Wasband isn't staying mired in the negative. They are opening themselves up to the possibility of things getting better. They are also creating a *new* relationship to the *whole* relationship that is more receptive, constructive, and generally more fun. Let's try it. What are some relationships in your life that feel negative or have negative components? These are the relationships that are a total drag. They feel yucky. They make you want to grab your blankie and hide. They can be to anything, not just people, and they pretty much suck the life force out of us. Let's start with four. In the boxes on the next page, doodle and draw what these four relationships represent for you. Then, on those little lines in the smallest writing possible that can still be legible, write the name of each relationship under its respective drawing. Remember these relationships can be *to* anything… an ex, as DeWanda demonstrates, is a great example. But don't forget the other relationships in your life. What about your relationship to your weight, the aging process, or your job? How about the compulsive behaviors we engage in like shopping, gambling, eating, using drugs or alcohol, etc.? Also think about life choices like remaining in an unhappy relationship, giving away your power, or being unkind to yourself or someone else. All of those relationships count and they all can be transformed into a new narrative. Ready?

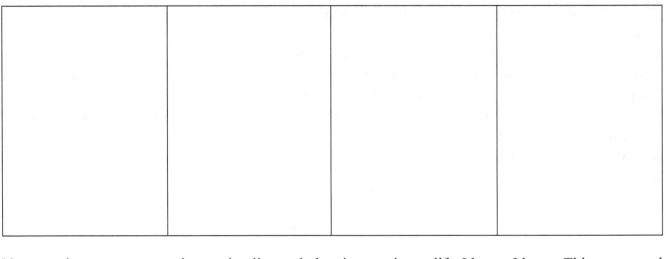

Now, one-by-one, you are going to visualize each drawing coming to life. I know, I know. This may sound weird, but this is *us*… we've done lots of weird stuff together already and we will do lots more. In your imagination, let these relationships materialize into something tangible inspired by your drawings. OK, now - poof! - by your side are four containers. Think Aladdin's magic lamp… or those little ceramic containers with the big corks that you can find at roadside restaurants with words like 'Hugs,' or 'Old Farts' etched on them. Anything that can be a secure holding place will do. Now, just like the All-Powerful Genie, you are going to magically vaporize each of these relationships. Put them in their jars and screw the lids on tight. OK, another - poof! - happens and miraculously, there is a shelf right in front of you. Magically float all of those jars over to that shelf and line them up. As you look at them, take a moment and breathe. Breathe into the new space you have just created within your life. Breathe into the new opportunities. Breathe into the new stories. Breathe into the new you! Alrighty, guess what time it is? It's Wasband time! Time to create the labels for your jars. What is going to make you giggle, throw your hands up, shake your head, and want to share more about your chosen monikers? What are the new names for these relationships that will give you more reasons to smile, connect, play, and be spontaneous? Draw your four jars with their new labels below.

Woo-hoo! How does that feel? I feel rascally just thinking about all of the fun you are going to have with these new relationship titles. If you choose to share them, who will be the first to know? List them on the next page. Also think of one thing that is going to shift for you in regard to each of these relationships based on their new names. Love you! Your sense of humor is on point, Sister. Thank you for doing this activity. Keep going and help someone else do it, too!

Who Gets the Funny First?	**What Will Shift for Me Right Now?**
1.	1.
2.	2.
3.	3.
4.	4.

~ SPS #4: ~

* Higher Self Help *

Sometimes just putting something on paper can make it easier for us to understand and implement. I really try to live from my Higher Self. This is the part of me that is my *Soul*. It is unconditional love and compassion. It knows exactly what I need, and it is tirelessly working to help me be happy, healthy, and whole. Am I able to maintain this way of being? *Most* of the time, maybe… *a lot* of the time, possibly… but all of the time? Not a chance. I want to. I *really* do! But *wanting to* is only part of it. Living this way has to be based in faith. I am not talking about religious faith here, although sometimes that helps. This is a faith in me and my Higher Self. This is the unshakable faith that I know what is best for me at all times and that means walking the high road of what is *right* versus what is *easy* **every** time. This faith is a grounded trust in myself, my empowerment, my wisdom, and my love. It has to be unshakable. It has to be strong and steady. And even when the shittiest of the proverbial shit is hitting the fan, it has to be the **only** choice. I say this after coming off a multi-day fight with my husband. A fight that has come after many others in recent months and one that is making us both question our marriage. As I sit and write, I have no idea what is going to happen. I am raw. I am sad. I am scared. And although I know the power that my Higher Self has to guide me, I want nothing to do with her. At least my lower self doesn't. I *want* to stay angry. I *want* to fight. I *want* him to say he is sorry. But you know what, I have already gotten those things - vindication, validation, and apologies - about a million times and I am still here, embroiled in this ugly pattern. So that tells me this is up to me to shift within **myself**. If everything stays the same, then everything stays the same. I know I don't want that. I also know that I don't know what is going to happen. I feel very exhausted, overwhelmed, and terrified… but if I want things to be different, then **I** have to be different. Try this with me, write the first five words or short phrases that come to mind when you think of your Higher Self without editing or censoring what comes up.

My Higher Self

1._____

2._____

3._____

4._____

5._____

Next, write the first five words or short phrases that come to mind when you think about what makes you feel most connected to your Higher Self.

I am MOST connected to my Higher Self when…

1. _____
2. _____
3. _____
4. _____
5. _____

That feels good, huh? It does for me as well. I'm getting some ideas on new ways to express myself from this perspective in the effort of being heard and seen in a different way. Now, on to five things we can easily identify that splinter us away from our Higher Selves. For me, and for most of us, this is triggered in our relationships. When things get pressurized, my lower self takes over and wants to fight and protect. This is totally understandable, right? But again, fighting is what has gotten me here… feeling like my life partner is my worst enemy and I don't want that anymore.

I feel the LEAST connected to my Higher Self when…

1. _____
2. _____
3. _____
4. _____
5. _____

How can we combine this Higher Self awareness so that we solidify our connection to her instead of disconnecting when we need her most? I was hoping you had an idea…. ☺ Just kidding, I have an idea. Let's step-in and reattach these levels of our consciousness. How, you ask? I have some ideas for that, too. Get comfortable and close your eyes. Take a few deep breaths and ask to connect to her. Nothing too fancy. No wordy guided mediations or visualizations. Only your faith that your Higher Self is present and ready to talk. Take another deep breath and allow her to materialize in your imagination. Give her a big hug, if you want to and don't let go. This can all be done in an embrace. I could use a hug, that is for sure! While held in her arms, ask her the first question that pops into your head. Record this question and answer below.

- **Question #1**_____

    ○ **Answer #1**_____

    _____

Next, create your own question regarding how to stay connected to her when you feel disconnected. Remember, she is going to answer in ways that are clear, authentic, and completely in alignment with your highest good. As much as we say we might welcome this style of communication, sometimes it doesn't always feel warm and fuzzy. It is OK to have reactions that feel scared, put off, or resistant to what she offers. Allow your feelings to come to the surface. Honor and love them and tell them "Thank you." Breathe, close your eyes, and keep going.

How to Stay Connected?

- Question #2- _____
    - Answer #2 _____
      _____

Alrighty, final question for this activity, but please feel free to keep this conversation going as long as you need. Find out from her what you need to know at this time - regarding anything. This is the soup-du-jour of the convo… so ask what you need to know *right now*. I want some guidance on how to compassionately **not** stay the same so that I can maintain being healthy, happy, and whole. What about you?

What I need to know?

- Question #3- _____
    - Answer #3 _____
      _____

Way to go! Let's put it all together and combine the three answers to create a love letter from our Higher Selves. This is our love letter to remind us that we are never alone, that we always can trust our inner wisdom, guidance, and intuition, and that we can always, *always* make the **right** choice when we lead from love. And, hey, I love you. Remember that! I do. I am so darned grateful for you my human consciousness can hardly stand it! Fill in the blanks below and reread this sweet testament as often as you need.

Dear _____

(What does she call you? Have fun with this.
Is it Sweetheart, Sister, She of the Wild Women, My Love, Darling of the Most High…?
*We are **all** Regal Queens of our Destinies. We might as well have a cool title to match!)*

(Answer #1) _____
_____

(Answer #2) _____
_____

(Answer #3) _____

_____

I Love you.

_____

(Anything else she wants to add...)

_____

(Sign her name above. Ooooh, this is super fun, too! What do you call her? I'm not even going to give suggestions. Let your creativity run wild!)

~ SPS #5: ~
* Natural Virtue *

Take a moment to reflect and journal around the following questions.

When and where am I *pushing*? When and where am I *allowing*?

_____

_____

_____

Next, free write whatever comes up around the following.

Bold Courage and Prideful Arrogance

_____

_____

Meek Humility and Weak Righteousness

_____

_____

Just Truth and Unjust Deceit

_____

_____

All of the words above either fall into the category of virtues or vices and are sometimes understood as general human qualities. Yet, seldom are we ever *totally* one or the other. The Universal experience of life usually gifts us opportunities to experience varying degrees of both… and if we are lucky, we learn, incorporate, and grow. Courage, humility, justice, and truth are just a few virtues that we often hear about. Ancient Greek philosopher, Aristotle had twelve and his list included wit and friendliness! It is thought that virtues release our energy and vices degrade our energy. From that perspective, our pure essence and our pure being is the physical embodiment of virtue. These good things are *our nature*! Not the other way around! When we are courageous and truthful - or any other virtue - we are authentically releasing our human spirit. We are *allowing* the truth of our light to be fully present. When we are arrogant and unjust - or any other vice - we are unwittingly degrading our human spirit. We are *pushing* the light away and moving further away from our natural state of being. Isn't that just beautiful to think about? *You* are beautiful, Sister. So am I. OK, last step, I promise… reflect for a time and finish these final three statements. Thank you for doing this! Remember, the more you shine your light, the more I can shine mine. I love you!

- When I allow my pure state of being to shine, I experience my **bold courage** as _____
  _____

- When I allow my pure state of being to shine, I experience my **meek humility** as _____
  _____

- When I allow my pure state of being to shine, I experience my **just truth** as _____
  _____

Crystal Love: DeWanda's Crystal is Carnelian (kahr-**neel**-ee-yuhn), a very protective and stabilizing stone that can ground us in the present moment, stimulate our analytical precision, sharpen concentration, and dispel lethargy. Carnelian is a huge support to the Sacral Chakra and gifts us with strong, yet tender, energy as we explore our relationship to sexuality, creativity, security, and acceptance for the never-ending cycles of life. Along with this support, Carnelian can awaken us to our gifts and talents, increase our receptivity to love energy, motivate our innate curiosity, and insulate us against envy, rage, and sorrow. Put all of this together, and we have a stone of action that imparts the physical and spiritual energy needed to get us moving towards activities, perspectives, and belief systems that revitalize our life force. Worn on the body, or kept close to other stones, Carnelian can also purify negative conditioning so that we learn to trust ourselves and our potential.

Suggested Reading for Timeless Perspectives on Empowered and Transformational Self-Love, *Sacred Woman: A Guide to Healing the Feminine Body, Mind, and Spirit* by Queen Afua.

Kery and Jamie

Kery: We met six years ago. My husband told me that Jamie was my soul sister and that I had to meet her. I didn't believe him.

Jamie: He had been telling me about Kery, too, for a few years, and I finally met her when she showed up at my 38th birthday party.

Kery: When I first met Jamie, I thought, there is no way she can be as cool and as nice as my husband says she is looking the way she looks.

Jamie: When I first met Kery, I knew that the future of our friendship was dependent on this first connection. I didn't feel like I was 'auditioning' exactly, but I knew that this moment was important.

Kery: I quickly realized that Jamie was a person who yes, was beautiful on the outside, but could also get her feet in the mud, talk dirty, and be fun and down to Earth all at the same time.

Jamie: One time a few months later, Kery and her family were over at our house, and my husband and I were at odds over something silly. I overheard my husband say something totally innocent like, "Jamie put out some glasses for you guys." Maybe Kery picked up something in his voice, because she responded, "That girl is quickly becoming my best friend." She didn't know I could hear her, but I remember thinking to myself, "Wow, I feel so blessed! I'm Kery's best friend!"

Kery: When I finally opened up and admitted that Jamie was someone I wanted in my inner sanctum, I didn't want to let go for a second. Watching Jamie be so open and loving with people, her acceptance, and her ability to be a place for connection inspired me not to be so sharp and closed off.

Jamie: For me, as we spent more time together, I would watch Kery hold space for people and be amazed at her level of patience and understanding. She would tell me about situations, and I would get fired up, already attached to an outcome of what I thought was 'right,' but Kery would always show me that I wasn't responsible for anyone rising to any occasion.

> We really learned *from* each other and *with* each other for these first few years.
> We had a blast! Then, we decided to collaborate. The sky was the limit.
> We dreamed of buying property and having horses and hosting retreats for women. We
> were on fire! We did a couple of great workshops. We were really going for it.

Kery: Then, I started to feel insecure. I was dealing with a toxic situation at home and that was taking the life-force out of me…. but I felt like I couldn't match Jamie in her level of study and research and the capacity in which she shows up and delivers. I thought, "I am way out of my league here, I'm not enough to handle all of this." I started to go down the rabbit hole of darkness. I pulled into my little Cancer Crab shell and hid.

> But we didn't talk about it.
> We just kept pushing forward because we had the pressure of producing more and more events.

Jamie: As I felt Kery retreat, I came on even stronger. I was feeling resentful and feeling abandoned. Instead of being able to say what was going on, I faked it and acted like everything was great. I never told Kery how much I was hurting because I was too afraid to be honest, as if being vulnerable and open with her would somehow make me lose her. Ironically, that is exactly what happened.

With no big event or no big fight, we completely fizzled out.
We went from being together multiple times a week and communicating
multiple times a day for four years, to almost nothing for six months.

Jamie: I was heartbroken because I felt like I had lost not only our partnership, but I had lost Kery.

Kery: I was so mad at myself because I was feeling jealous of Jamie, but I knew it was my own self-sabotage.

That is when the emotional roller coaster started for both of us.
We were both angry and sad that we couldn't fix what had happened.
We were happy for each other, but we were also feeling extremely competitive when either one of us would accomplish something. The worst part was, we were trying to make sense of all of this crap on our own because we didn't have our closest friend to talk to. It was awful!

Jamie: Then, after a few months, we started texting and emailing back and forth trying to make sense of what the hell had happened. I felt like I had to get ugly and gritty with Kery about how I was feeling. I also was struggling with the feeling of, 'why can't I just let it go?' I realized that stuffing my real feelings to be considered *nice* or *easy* was just a bullshit way to stay inauthentic and safe.

Kery: For me, when Jamie brought up old wounds that needed to be healed, I also got really inspired to investigate my part in all of this. I realized that, when I was younger, I had to fight to get recognition. Growing up, there was only ever room for one - one president of the class… one homecoming queen - and that was me because I fought for it. Working with Jamie, I convinced myself that I didn't have what it takes to fight for it anymore. It wasn't true, but that was the lie I kept telling myself.

Jamie: This situation, and coming through the other side with Kery, has taught me that I am not good at recovering. Once I get hurt, I have trouble finding my way out of that space. I have to be really honest and say that, although I want to fix things with Kery so badly, I still don't feel completely safe. Kery has shown me, through her ability to be vulnerable and transparent, that it is time to heal this part of myself.

Kery: I told Jamie, when we were really cracking this conflict open wide, that when I really care about somebody, I don't fucking give up. Jamie knows this about me. She has seen me dig my heels in. Whatever time this friendship needs to become what it is meant to become, I am here, because we are not 'done' by any stretch of the imagination.

Jamie: It is my hope that women can read about us and know that friendships, especially the ones between women, are allowed to grow and shift. Sometimes that growth process is really difficult. It hurts and it is painful. But it doesn't have to be an ending just because it becomes uncomfortable. When shit gets real with someone you love, that can be a pivot point for a new beginning. We don't have to walk away and pretend something never happened because there was a conflict or a crunchy time. The conflicts and crunchiness provide us a different choice for healing.

Kery: I love Jamie. I'm 'showing up naked' with her now more than ever before. Jamie and I have owned this… we have moved in it… danced around in it and gotten our feet dirty. Things are so much better on the other side. This whole situation has taught me that friendships need to be nurtured, tended, and cultivated. It has inspired me to reach out to some old friends that I might have taken for granted. Friendships that, today, I am proud to say I have responsibly recreated. In doing this, I have fully shown up for the people in my life that I care about. This has also helped me because these relationships have fed me and fed my soul. I know we can inspire other women to heal their female friendships and to heal these parts of themselves.

We are like the Lotus flower blooming in the mud and muck.
The gorgeous, pure, fresh flower blooms to perfection because it has the mud.
It doesn't change or camouflage the mud.
It needs the mud… and so do we.

Making This Story Your Own:

Kery's and Jamie's story speaks to the heart of female friendships.
Take a moment, breathe, and reflect.
What stands out for you when you read their words?
Is there a situation in your life that is similar to Jamie's and Kery's?
Perhaps part of their story feels connected to your own.
How can you relate their experiences to your past, present, and future?

- *My Connection to Kery's and Jamie's Story* _____

_____

_____

_____

_____

Knowing that you aren't alone, let's gently explore some other themes from Kery's and Jamie's story together:

- **Feeling Insecure**
    - Where can you identify insecurities in your personal and professional relationships? Where did these feelings come from and how have they impacted you? Do you talk about them? If so, do you talk about them with the people involved, or do you talk about these feelings with people who are *not* involved? Does this help? What relationships in your life are secure? How have you created this security? When you think about feeling secure and insecure in your relationships, is there a way to initiate more balance and would it be beneficial? Why, or why not?

- **Pretending Everything is OK**
    - How often do you say "I'm fine" when you aren't? Are there times when you don't express how you feel because you just want to keep the peace? When something is bothering you, do you stay silent out of fear? If yes, can you remember when this started? If you don't stay silent, how did you begin to express yourself in this way? When you do pretend that everything is OK - even

when it is not - what happens? How is pretending that *'everything is OK'* beneficial for you and your relationships? How is it not beneficial? When it comes to communicating your feelings, would you like to be doing it differently? If so, what are a few small shifts you can make in order for this new communication style to feel more natural?

- ***Friendships Change and Grow***
  - When the reliable patterns of friendships begin to change and things no longer feel comfortable in the same ways, what happens? How do you react? Is this reaction viable for maintaining these friendships? Is it viable for sustaining growth? When you think of your closest friendships, how healthy and sustainable have they been in the short and long term? Thinking of your friendships in this way, is there anything you would you like to change? If so, what you would like to change and how would you like to change it? If there are no changes to make, can you identify how these relationships are fulfilling and how they can remain fulfilling in the future?

Sacred Play Suggestions:

~ SPS #1: ~
* Perfect Best Friend *

Book stores today are filled with titles meant to assist us in manifesting the perfect romantic partner. At some time, you've probably even written a list of qualities that this amazing person might possess. What if we shifted that a little and started to put the same type of energy towards manifesting a perfect best friend? It can't be all that different. What qualities would you want in a BFF (Best Friend Forever)? Go ahead and list them below.

MY Perfect BFF

1. _____
2. _____
3. _____
4. _____
5. _____
6. _____
7. _____
8. _____
9. _____
10. _____

11. _____

12. _____

13. _____

14. _____

15. _____

Next, think of a song that is going to be you and your besties newly appointed theme song. Journal or reflect and get clear as to why you chose this song.

- BFF Theme Song _____

- Why is this the *Perfect* BFF Song? _____
_____

Next, pick a color for you and your bestie. Think about why this color is the color of your new friendship.

- BFF Color _____

- Why is this the *Perfect* BFF Color? _____
_____

Next, dream big and think of three to four things that you and your bestie are going to do together. This partnership is about what will fill your heart and feed your Soul… and *everything* is allowed.

Together, My BFF and I Will…

_____

_____

_____

_____

_____

When this *BFF Manifesto* feels complete, sit quietly with it for a few minutes. Take some deep breaths and ask yourself the following questions.

- Is there anyone in my life that already meets my needs in these ways? _____
_____

- Am I currently - or have I previously - prevented anyone from meeting my needs in these ways? If so, *how* and *why* and what can I do differently in the future?

  _____

  _____

- Based on what I would like in a best friend, how can I be more like this for the people in my life?

  _____

  _____

- How can I become more like this kind of best friend for myself? _____

  _____

Best friends are amazing! These friendships can be the juicy and connective waters of mental, emotional, and spiritual intimacy. However, don't fret or punish yourself if you don't have a best friend. Like all relationships, friendships shift, change, and grow. Start by treating yourself as a BFF and you may find that this relationship is all you need. At any rate, creating space within your consciousness around self-love, self-kindness, and self-dedication is a great start! Thank you for doing this! Love you!

~ SPS #2: ~
* Talking Stick *

Unfinished business can grow into a big ugly monster. When words go unsaid and hurts go unaddressed in relationships, things can quickly get out of hand. Before we know it, what once felt indestructible and solid can become brittle, broken, and feel completely beyond repair. Best friends and lovers alike experience this dynamic and are oftentimes left with no idea of how to go about 'righting' the 'wrongs.' These beautiful relationships sort of just dangle in the ether, withering away, but never truly *going* away because the hurt, confusion, and desire for repair still remain. Sometimes a spark of inventiveness can offer a light in even the darkest of places. You might not think so but infusing an object with intentions can help redirect ***your*** energy towards repair, resolution, and reconnection. The concept of a talking stick is well known. This indigenous empowerment tool was often used in ceremony and was permeated with different intentions for effective communication. Today talking sticks are regularly used in all kinds of formats from couple's therapy to corporate meetings. The idea is that when you hold the stick you talk, and when someone else holds the stick, you listen. I have seen talking sticks decorated with gems and jewels and I have seen them plucked right off a tree. The important thing for us - and for this activity - is the *energy* of the talking stick… specifically, what energy the talking stick will possess and how we will trust and honor that energy with our intentions. Before making a list of relationships for potential repair, locate your talking stick. Take a walk and find the perfect one for you. You probably have something in your house right now that could work. This stick, or stick-like object, needs to be easy to hold in your hand and pass from person to person. Once you have your stick, decorate it if you would like and begin to infuse it with your chosen intentions for effective communication. Some intentions to play with are: loving communication, honesty, peace, connection, intimacy, repair, awareness, unconditional love, courage, healing, the highest good, etc. A simple way to infuse your talking stick is to tie a piece of ribbon or yarn around your stick to represent each intention. Go for three at first so that you can easily remember which intention goes with which piece of ribbon. Write down your three intentions below.

Talking Stick Intentions

1. _____
2. _____
3. _____

Once you have the ribbons tied around your talking stick, hold the stick close to your heart and continue to share your energy with this sacred object. When you feel ready, envision a relationship in your life that could use some repair and resolution. Visualize this person sitting in front of you and with your talking stick in your hand, claim the energy that you would like this exchange to possess and state your three intentions for talking.

- With the energy of _____
- I *talk* with these three intentions _____
  _____

In your imagination, say all that you need to say. Take responsibility where you feel it is right to do so. Ask them to take responsibility where you feel it is right for them to do so. Stay aware of how your energy and intentions affect your ability to effectively communicate.

- My energy and intentions helped me communicate more effectively by_____
  _____
  _____

Now, prepare to pass the stick. This is happening in your imagination, so place the stick where you have visualized the other person to be sitting. Once again, claim the energy that you would like this exchange to possess and restate your three intentions, this time for *listening*.

- With the energy of _____
- I *listen* with these three intentions _____
  _____

In your imagination, allow this person to say all they need to say. Let them take responsibility for their part in the situation and allow them to ask you to take responsibility as well. Stay aware of how your energy and intentions affect your ability to effectively *listen*.

- My energy and intentions helped me listen more effectively by_____
  _____
  _____

When this conversation feels complete, take a few minutes to reflect about the insights that came forward. Sometimes, for various reasons, these reparative conversations can only happen via the inner realms of the imagination. Does that mean that this type of visualization and the energy of your talking stick aren't valid? No way! This is all about creating opportunities for *you* to feel resolution, connection, and repair in any way that offers comfort, support, and release. If this conversation can translate from the realm of the imagination into a face-to-face exchange and you feel ready and prepared, that is wonderful. Utilize your talking stick as much as you choose. It is yours and it is a great reminder of your empowerment, energy, and intention. It is also a token of love. Keep it close and know that you *are love* and you *are loved.* I can be a reminder of that right now... I love you! Thank you for doing this reparative and connective work. The more we *heal*, the **more** we heal. Solidify this work by journaling and reflecting on the following.

- My talking stick, my energy, and my intentions will continue to support me by _____
_____
_____

~ SPS #3: ~
* Not OK and Not Fine *

I got to work with an amazing woman who has a tattoo on her arm that struck me deeply. When looking at her arm from my perspective, the tattoo reads 'I'm Fine.' Yet, when she turns her arm upside down, those same words read 'Save Me.' Wow, right? How often do we say "I'm fine" when someone asks us if we are OK... even when we aren't? When asked if anything is wrong, how many times have you responded "Nothing," when 'nothing' couldn't be further from the truth? What we say and what we mean are oftentimes two totally different things. That tattoo got me thinking about *subtext*. In acting, there is a technique whereby you uncover the character's subtext - the truth of what is *really* being communicated - underneath the written text of the script. We do this in real life all the time. Sometimes we are aware of our subtext and sometimes we are not. Think of your token response. Are you more of an "I'm fine" or a "Nothing" kind of gal? Perhaps both resonate and they become a blend of "Nothing, I'm fine." Let's play with subtext a little bit. Pay close attention to how familiar it feels to say these words with these particular feelings.

- Try saying "I'm fine..." with the subtext of **anger**.
    - What do you notice? _____

- Try saying "Nothing..." with the subtext of **sadness**.
    - What do you notice? _____

- Put it together and try "Nothing, I'm fine..." with the subtext of **loneliness**.
    - What do you notice? _____

- Try all three- "Nothing." "I'm fine," and, "Nothing, I'm fine..." with the subtext of **frustration**.
    - What do you notice? _____

Building on this is another acting technique that combines using a particular *subtext* with an intended *action*. This technique is done to provoke an emotional response in the other actors on stage. This technique mirrors yet another '*in real life*' occurrence. How often to do you say things in certain ways to provoke specific feelings and responses? Sometimes we are conscious of doing this and sometimes we are not. We really can communicate so much by saying very little. Try it! Imagine you are on stage with someone in your life. This time use your chosen subtext and pair it with an action to incite a particular feeling in your scene partner.

- Say "Nothing..." with the subtext of ***friskiness*** and the intended action of ***playfully engaging*** your scene partner.

    o What do you notice? _____

- Say "I'm fine..." with the subtext of ***rage*** and the intended action of ***belittling*** your scene partner.

    o What do you notice? _____

- Say "Nothing, I'm fine..." with the subtext of ***unhappiness*** and the intended action of ***confusing*** your scene partner.

    o What do you notice? _____

Below are a few more suggestions for subtext and action. Play with any words or phrases that you know you often use or that come to mind, and couple them with the options below.

Subtext	**Action**
- Rage	- To Anger
- Annoyance	- To Annoy
- Peace	- To Calm
- Fear	- To Scare
- Enthusiasm	- To Enthuse
- Love	- To Energize
- Upset	- To Distract
- Insulted	- To Offend
- Serenity	- To Quiet
- Anxiety	- To Panic

- Phrase or Word "_____"

    o Subtext _____

    o Action _____

        ▪ What do you notice? _____

- Phrase or Word "_____"

    o Subtext _____

- ○ Action_____
    - ■ What do you notice? _____
- Phrase or Word "_____"
    - ○ Subtext_____
    - ○ Action_____
        - ■ What do you notice? _____

There are countless emotions that we use as subtext and countless actions that we use to provoke feelings and responses. Becoming aware of *how* we are saying what we are saying and *why* we are saying it can be really beneficial. Understanding our feelings can help us get to know ourselves better. Identifying how we attempt to get others to feel things, without necessarily being clear or authentic, can offer much personal insight and awareness around our relationships. How can you, from this moment forward, give responses akin to "I'm fine" or "Nothing" with no contradictory subtext and no intended actions? What would more truthful replies sound like? Come up with a few and give those a whirl. See how they feel. Practice does make it easier.... I promise! Thank you for taking this time for self-awareness. Your authenticity is inspiring! Love you!

~ SPS #4: ~
* Hands *

Either with a partner or alone, look at your hands. Really look at them. See your skin, knuckles, nails, cuticles, and palms. Are there rings or other jewelry? What story do your hands tell? What information do they offer? If you are with a partner, switch and look at each other's hands. Let your awareness stay focused and notice any other thoughts and feelings coming up. For the following three to five minutes, close your eyes. Use a blindfold if it will help. Without the sense of visual sight, hold and caress your hands. Massage, rub, and touch each finger and nail. Explore your palms, wrists, and the backs of your hands. Feel the temperature, texture, softness, and hardness. With your finger, trace the indentations of the lines and follow the ridges of bone and tendon. Stop and feel your pulse in your veins. Let your mind wander and allow any information and guidance to come forward. When the three to five minutes is over, if you are working with a partner, switch and explore each other's hands. When finished, journal and reflect about what came up for you during this exercise.

- What was it like touching your hands? _____
_____

- What information did your hands share? _____
_____

- What did you learn about yourself? _____
_____

- How did you feel having your eyes closed? _____

  _____

- How did it feel receiving intentional, inquisitive touch? _____

  _____

- How does this exercise relate to your life? _____

  _____

- How does this exercise relate to your relationships? _____

  _____

Stay holding your hands for a moment or two after you are finished writing. Take a few deep breaths and send love into these exquisite appendages. We do so much with our hands, and they do so much for us. Let them direct your next move. What do your hands want to do? Mine want to grab you and give you a big hug. Thank you for doing this! Love you!

~ SPS #5: ~
* Adult Currency *

A very wise man, our couple's therapist, has talked to myself and my husband at length about the currency of adult relationships versus the currency of parent-child relationships. In a parent-child relationship, when the child is 20 and under - give or take a few years - the expectation for the parent to meet the child's needs without the child clearly asking for their needs to be met is OK. However, the currency of adult relationships is different. It is not OK, in adult relationships, to expect our partners to step into this parental role. In our adult relationships - and this includes romantic partners as well as friends - we must be clear about our needs, we must clearly ask our partner in the relationship to meet our needs, and we must find a way to be OK if our partners decline to do so. Maybe a little harsh in light of our desires for romance and connection, but so practical for sustainability, longevity, and I'm gonna say the 'I' word: *intimacy*. In theory and in life this does make sense. Yet, how often do we want our needs to be met instantly, spontaneously, and without a boring old conversation clearly outlining exactly what it is that we want? We have been led to believe that intimacy - platonic and otherwise - is an exciting rush of a soulmate reading our minds, matching our desires with their own, and therefore knowing us *so* well that they are able to telepathically meet our needs because our needs are the very *same* as theirs. As an adult, I don't have a long-term friendship that works like this and I know my marriage sure doesn't. Think about it, are you clearly asking for what you need from the people in your life and if not, why not? Once you get your mind wrapped around that - clearly asking for your needs to be met - can you be OK with the third part of the adult relationship equation? Can you or will you be OK when your partner says, "I can't do that." What happens then? This is where your boundaries can come into play. Can you manage if your partner does not, cannot, or will not meet your needs? And, what does this type of *managing* look like? Is it at your own expense? Does it mean that the relationship needs to shift in some way? Perhaps the relationship ends? What are your boundaries around *not* having your needs met? Maybe it is OK sometimes, maybe it is not. These are tough questions to think about. Writing may help with clarity. Pick a few of your closest relationships and journal around the following questions, circling your most preferred answer when choices are given.

Relationship #1

- With _____, I ***always/ sometimes/ never*** ask for my needs to be met.

- This is because _____
  _____

- My needs in this relationship are _____
  _____

- When I do ask for my needs to be met by _____ and they decline to meet them, I feel OK managing my own discomfort ***never/ sometimes/ all the time***.

- To get my needs met, I can shift my part in this relationship by _____
  _____
  _____

- To meet my own needs, my boundaries around this relationship must _____
  _____
  _____

Relationship #2

- With _____, I ***always/ sometimes/ never*** ask for my needs to be met.

- This is because _____
  _____

- My needs in this relationship are _____
  _____

- When I do ask for my needs to be met by _____ and they decline to meet them, I feel OK managing my own discomfort ***never/ sometimes/ all the time***.

- To get my needs met, I can shift my part in this relationship by _____
  _____

- To meet my own needs, my boundaries around this relationship must _____
_____
_____

Relationship #3

- With _____, I *always*/ *sometimes*/ *never* ask for my needs to be met.

- This is because _____
_____

- My needs in this relationship are _____
_____

- When I do ask for my needs to be met by_____
and they decline to meet them, I feel OK managing my own discomfort *never*/ *sometimes*/ *all the time*.

- To get my needs met, I can shift my part in this relationship by _____
_____
_____

- To meet my own needs, my boundaries around this relationship must _____
_____
_____

Great job! The currency of adult relationships is challenging, especially if we weren't given the opportunity to experience a functional parent-child currency. Give yourself time, grace, and love around this. Asking for our needs to be met can be hard and scary. This is a really vulnerable thing to do. But you deserve it! So does your inner-child and so does the woman that you are about to become. When it gets tough to keep these loving boundaries around your needs, step into the parent-child currency with yourself and mother your own needs into being. No conversation needed. Just an intuitive connection and an unconditional dedication to **you.** Now, that is *really* some excitement and romance! Love you! Thank you for doing this!

Crystal Love: Jamie's and Kery's Crystal is Amazonite (**am**-uh-*zuhn*-ahyt). Known for its powers of resolution, we can use Amazonite like a magickal calming wand to soothe our nerves, emotions, Chakras, brains, and nervous systems. A communication enhancer and reliever of worry and fear, this stone gifts us the ability to see both sides of an issue while respecting and understanding multi-dimensional points of view. Because of this, Amazonite creates an energy of Sisterhood and wraps us in the Universally felt love of tight friendship so that we can speak the words that need to be spoken without creating explosive situations. A great balancer of Masculine and Feminine energies, Amazonite brings forth clarity for the body, mind, ego, and Soul. When feeling a bit irritable, try using this Crystal to dispel aggravation and negative energy. Combining the wisdom of the Heart Chakra and the Throat Chakra, Amazonite rejuvenates our abilities to give and receive love while releasing negatively held belief systems that keep us stuck in dysfunctional patterns of unhappiness and disempowerment. With all of Amazonite's talents, this stone is a great support system as we process the layers and levels of Spiritual Consciousness.

Suggested Reading for Healing and Empowering Female Friendships, *Rise Sister Rise: A Guide to Unleashing the Wise, Wild Woman Within* by Rebecca Campbell.

Additional Journaling and SPS Space

Kei

My daughter, Allison, is forever twenty-six years young. When she transitioned from her life here on Earth to wherever she is now, she had just had her birthday. She had a very common malady. A urinary tract infection. It was like the perfect storm of everything going wrong. She had just finished her coursework for a master's degree in counseling, she had just quit her job, she had moved apartments, and she was trying to finalize plans for her internship to become a licensed counselor. All of that was great, but she had been dealing with this infection on and off for about two months, and she didn't stop to take care of herself. It was in the middle of the night on May 31st, 2010, that she finally went to the Emergency Room. Her boyfriend told me that when they got the hospital, Allison was in such pain that she was speechless. She couldn't even talk and tell the doctors what was wrong. They ended up diagnosing her with Mononucleosis. She called me to tell me all of this when they were leaving the hospital. I wanted to go up right away, but she told me to stay put. I think I brought anxiety into Allison's world. We had a history of ups and downs. Not that our love ever wavered - there was never any lack of the mother-daughter love - but because of the unique family dynamics that we had, I had lived in conflict for many years and I feel that she paid the price. In the few months leading up to all of this, we had finally made some great strides. She was older, more mature, and able to see me in a different light. I think she was beginning to accept me as a person, as a unique individual apart from being her mother. She was able to see me in a broader context than just the woman who raised her, disciplined her, and took her to school. Being seen as a person unto myself felt like such a gift for both of us. It wasn't until the next day that she called me again. She was breathing funny. I have a really hard time accepting my own reaction here because I thought she was being dramatic. She was wheezing and puffing, gasping for air. She told me that she needed me. Of course, I was on my way immediately. I got a call from Allison's boyfriend that they were going to the clinic and to meet them there. He was so worried. He told me her lips were blue because she was having such trouble breathing and yet, she called me. When I got to the clinic, I went right to Allison. I walked up to the end of the bed where she was lying. She was sitting up and she looked completely ashen. She looked at me and said, "Mom." I said, "Allison." Right then, the medical staff leaned over her and put on an oxygen mask. That was the last time I saw her face with no machines or devices. The last time I saw her eyes. Her last word to me was, "Mom" and my last word to her, the last word that I know she could hear me saying, was her name. That was it. They transferred her to a different hospital shortly after I arrived. I was so morbidly in denial. I asked to ride in the ambulance. They said no. When we got to the ER, I was taken to a private waiting room. I should have known something at that point, but I was just following along. After about an hour, a doctor came to talk to me and said, "I want you to know we are doing everything we can to save your daughter." I said, "What the hell does that mean?" I just didn't understand. I was in such a fog. I could not comprehend that my daughter was dying. In spite of everything that was in front of me, it was the furthest thing from my mind. They put her into a medical coma. The doctors were jovial and cracking jokes. They told me that this process sometimes takes a few weeks. I kept thinking, "This is just a medical coma, they are going to treat her and bring her out of it." Nowhere in my mind did I imagine that anything other than that was going to happen. I kept finding all of these reasons to believe that everything was going to be OK. Over the next week, I called some of Allison's friends and told them to come and see her. I said, "She is in a coma, but she will know you are here." I bunked out in the ICU for days. My life took on a kind of routine. Then, one night during shift change, things seemed to get busier. I asked what was going on and I was told that the extra nurses were just checking the monitors. Then they started to pack Allison's bed up to take her out of the room. I asked about that and they told me that they were just taking her for some tests. I had been there for a week at this point and I had never seen anything like this. I felt like something wasn't right, but I was still so foggy, I kept convincing myself everything was

OK. What did I know? Maybe after one week they do this? When the staff brought Allison back into the room I asked if everything was OK. The doctor called a bit later and said to me, "The prognosis doesn't look good." I said, "What does that mean?" He repeated himself to me again. It was like nobody could actually speak the words and tell me what was going on. I said, "She's not gone?" He replied, "Yes." Allison was there, right next to me. I was looking at her as the doctor was telling me this. The doctor finally said, "The machines are breathing for her. Her brain is not functioning anymore." I didn't know what else to say. I couldn't formulate questions. It was the middle of the night and I was being told by phone that my daughter was gone. The doctor said that he would be in to talk with me the next day and he hung up. I was given the opportunity to call people and let them come to see Allison before they turned off the machines. I called everyone in Allison's address book this time. I told people what was going on and let them know if they wanted to come and say goodbye, they could. People came in droves. From all walks of life. Allison had this way of becoming friends with everybody. There were all shapes, sizes, and colors. It was the most diverse looking collection of people that you could imagine. I didn't know most of them. I looked at someone and commented, "I don't know who most of these people are." They replied back, "They are here for you." That was the best answer. When the doctor walked into the room, I could tell he was shocked to see such a motley looking crew. He said, "This is only for family." I spoke up and said, "This **IS** Allison's family." All of these people, so many of whom I didn't even know their names, wanted to know what was going on with Allison. The doctor said a lot of medical stuff, a lot of which I didn't understand, and then he finally confirmed that she was indeed gone. Allison remained hooked up to the machines for the entire day. People kept coming in and out to say goodbye. By about seven o'clock, everyone cleared out, and it was just me and my sister. It probably took about ten minutes or so for the nurses to turn everything off. As they disconnected her, Allison faded quickly. I watched her lose her color. I watched her body move for the last time. It is still such a very vivid memory. I can still feel her. I wrapped my arms around her, and I sobbed. I still don't know today if I've really made sense of everything. After Allison died, I went to her apartment and stayed there. I didn't want to leave. I didn't want to go home. We had two memorial services for her. At the second service, we had an eighty-member choir. It was like a funeral for a Princess. After that, I quit teaching. Most of my students for piano and voice were either younger children, or young adults, and my teaching style was almost like music therapy. These kids would come in with their hearts on their sleeves, and I knew that I could not be the person interacting with them. In the space that I was in, I wouldn't be helping them and they wouldn't be helping me. So, I quit and I just stayed at home. I had always wanted a solitary life. I had ended an off-again-on-again romantic relationship several months before Allison died and I still haven't established any romantic relationships since then. I think for me, Allison was just about the only person that I've ever really loved. She was a person who embodied her creativity. She was all heart, all brain, and multi-talented. She loved to laugh, and she was crazy funny. She would tell me all the time, "Mom, you are hilarious!" She had these funny faces that she would make, and she had no problem getting on the floor to wrestle with her friends. She was so animated. So smart. So insightful. She always wanted to bring help to people in need. She had big struggles, too. But she was working on them. I have a little fantasy. I don't believe that when people move on, they look down from heaven. I don't believe that they turn into butterflies or that they inhabit the bodies of other living things. What I believe is that in her new ethereal life, Allison is very, very busy. I believe that she is being called to places in need and that she is hovering over them, wings high, helping and healing, and bringing all the powers of life. I want to follow her lead in that way. When she was a child, I followed her lead. I didn't do everything right and there are still questions and feelings of guilt. I wish I had done things differently. I wish that she hadn't been a latch-key kid. I wish that I hadn't worked so much. That I hadn't been a single mom. But, despite all of that, she knew I was fiercely on her side. She knew that I honored her feelings. That I valued her experiences. That I consistently and authentically attended to what she needed. I don't have words for what my experience is like with Allison today. I have no idea where I am in the healing process. Maybe I haven't even started. I do love to think about her. I love to remember her stories. I like it when I hear other people say her name. I have her things around me all the time. I wear her jewelry. I drive her car. I spray her perfume. I light her candles. I miss her so much. I wish that I had more time with her. None of these feelings are complete because she isn't here to feel them with me. Allison taught me many lessons. She taught me about accepting people. She was always prepared to listen. She wasn't judgmental. I'm not angry at God for taking her. I know I am a better person for having had her in my life. It was a miracle that I got to have her for as long as I did. She got to live long enough for us to see eye-to-eye about a lot of things. We got there. We did. Then she was gone so quickly. I am grateful to God for letting me have her for twenty-six years. That was twenty-six precious years of my life that could not have been fuller. I mean, she was the kid who had me teach her Beethoven's "Moonlight Sonata" in the middle of the night when she was only thirteen. "No music theory," she demanded, "Just show me where to put my fingers!" As I taught her how to play this piece by rote she exclaimed, "Oh my gosh! I am playing Beethoven!" I know she wants that same kind of joy for me. If I could hear her voice today, she would be on me for living the way I live. For isolating myself. She would say to me, "Mom, get your ass out of the house and start being with people." I think she is right.

Making This Story Your Own:

Kei's story touches a place deep in our Feminine psyche.
Take a moment, breathe, and reflect.
What stands out for you when you read her words?
Is there a situation in your life that is similar to Kei's?
Perhaps part of her story feels connected to your own.
How can you relate her experiences to your past, present, and future?

- *My Connection to Kei's Story* _____

_____

_____

_____

_____

Knowing that you aren't alone, let's gently explore some other themes from Kei's story together:

- ***Your Mother is a Person, too…***
    - When you think about your mother, what feelings come up? Do you recall past memories and images? Do present day interactions come forward? Are the feelings around these memories and interactions fulfilling, unfulfilling, or perhaps a mixture of both? Do you think you may remember some things as better or worse than they actually were? Is there a good reason why your recollections would either glorify or negativize these life experiences? Can you picture your mother as an individual? Can you envision her as a woman experiencing her own unique reality of fears, wounds, hopes, and joys? When you see her as merely human, does this help

you connect to her in a different way? When seeing her as more than just the role of *mother*, does this offer you a new understanding of her experiences and choices? Is there more empathy and compassion? Is there gratitude and release? If yes, why are these feelings present and how are they beneficial?

- ***Isolation***
  - When you are feeling big feelings, do you isolate or reach out and connect to those around you for support? If you isolate, can you identify the benefits? If you connect, can you identify the benefits of doing this? Is either response - isolation or connection - one hundred percent in alignment with your authentic needs? If so, how is this response in alignment? If not, how can your responses shift in order to be in alignment with what you truly want and need?

- ***Letting the Light Shine Through***
  - When things get hard and life seems unbearable, what happens? How do you respond? Are you the type of person that goes deeper into the darkness? Are you the type of person that forges ahead towards the light? How are these responses either beneficial or not beneficial for you and the way that you deal with hardship, pain, and grief? When you stay in the darkness, what do you notice? What happens to your mindset, relationships, and beliefs? When you forge toward the light, what do you notice? Does this allow the time and space needed to process your feelings? Could there be a different way to balance the light and the dark as you navigate through difficult situations and challenging times? If so, what would this look like for you?

Sacred Play Suggestions:

~ SPS #1: ~
* Tele *

Joseph Moreno is the creator of Psychodrama, an experiential form of psychotherapy. In his work, Moreno utilized the concept of tele. Tele can be described as the *unknown knowing*. It is the awareness - or *knowing* - with which we evaluate our world through feelings, observations, and perceptions. The concept of tele is closely related to instincts and intuition, two wonderful qualities of the Divine Feminine. Although many still feel that the *unknown* is potentially negative… when it comes to honoring the Feminine Side of our consciousness, the unknown is a very good thing. The unknown keeps us rooted in our instincts and intuition to prevent us from jumping too quickly into the world of analytic rationale. This allows both sides of our awareness to work in tandem - blending feeling with logic - and creating a more balanced and functional approach to life. In this way, tele is a very powerful transformational tool because it combines our imagination and intuition with logic and detail in order to generate new insights and understandings that can be realistically applied to all aspects of life. In her story, Kei shares about how healing it was for their relationship when her daughter, Allison, began relating to her as both a woman and a person in addition to relating to her as a mother. Let's see if we can apply this type of energy to the relationship we have with our mothers. Take a moment and think about your mother, the person you identify as your mother, or a mother-figure in your life. In your imagination, visualize a younger version of her. Now, with your understanding of tele, begin to create her story. This isn't about fact finding. This is about using the powers of tele to *know* the *unknown*. Let the specifics come from both sides of your awareness, employing imagination, intuition, memory, and history as you answer the questions below. For the time it takes, allow your mother to be human… just a person with her own unique fears, wounds, hopes, and joys. In your mind, as she is standing before you, let her come to life.

- What were her hopes and dreams? _____
  _____

- Who supported her? _____

- Who abandoned her? _____

- Who loved her? _____

- Who did she love? _____

- Who broke her heart? _____

- What brought her joy and freedom? _____
  _____

- What brought her sadness and doubt? _____
  _____

- What were her struggles? _____
  _____

- What were her successes? _____
  _____

- Did she feel liked and accepted? _____
  _____

- Did she feel loved? _____
  _____

- How did her family of origin affect her? _____
  _____

- How did her religious upbringing affect her? _____
  _____

- How did her race and ethnicity affect her? _____
  _____

- Did she feel financially secure? _____
  _____

- How did her socio-economic status affect her? _____
  _____

- What was her relationship with her mother like? _____

- What was her relationship with her father like? _____

- Did she get to pursue her education? _____

- Did she get to pursue a career? _____

- Was she lonely? _____

- What was her fondest memory? _____
  _____

- What would she change about her life? _____
  _____

- How would she describe herself? _____
  _____

- What kind of mother does she want to be? _____
  _____

- What dreams does she have for you? _____
  _____

When you are finished, take a moment for yourself to integrate all of the information that has come forward. As a final step, reflect or journal around the following questions.

- What are you most aware of after doing this exercise? _____
  _____

- What was it like to relate to your mother in this way? _____
_____

- Were there any correlations to your life and experiences? _____
_____

- Did any new understandings or compassion come forward? _____
_____

- What insights will offer additional support for your relationship to your mother? _____
_____

- Is there a way this exercise can be supportive and helpful in relation to your own motherhood journey? _____
_____

Sometimes seeing our mothers as human beings can be helpful and sometimes it can be heart breaking. Allow this exercise to gently support you as you continue to make sense of this complex and powerful relationship. Breathe deeply and ground your energy back into your own consciousness. When you are ready, reflect on the following question, and as you write, know that you are loved… by me and so many others. Thank you for doing this. Love you!

How can I become the best Mother for myself?

_____
_____
_____

~ SPS #2: ~
* Transformation *

In her story, Kei offers us lovely images to envision. One of them is Allison as a powerful angelic force offering healing and hope to those most in need. This visualization is one of transformation, a very prevalent power of the Divine Feminine. Although we witness it all of the time, transformation in any shape or form can feel impossible when life gets challenging. No matter what the event(s), when things become a chronic struggle, we can forget that options other than survival exist. Isolation, whether it be physical, mental, emotional, or spiritual, can come next. Most times, we don't even realize it. Just like butterflies, we, too, can benefit from being in a cocoon. But as the natural world teaches us… just like them, we, too, must remember our abilities for reemergence. Draw a self-portrait in the following box. You don't have to be an artist. Set the intention to draw yourself and go for it!

[Empty box for drawing]

Once your drawing is complete, let the word **transformation** begin to float in your consciousness. Say it out loud a few times. In your imagination, see it written on a blackboard. Write it on your portrait. Break it down, syllable by syllable: trans-for-ma-tion. As you continue to see, speak, and hear this word, start to think of all the places in your life where you would welcome transformation. Now, write these things on your portrait. Everything in your physical, mental, emotional, or spiritual life that could use a makeover… write it down and claim it. OK, now it is time to identify what is holding up the process. What is preventing this transformative energy from coming in and offering new opportunities for growth, fulfilling dreams, creating happiness, manifesting pleasure, and living in bliss? Get your mind and heart thinking together on this one and don't censor. This isn't about being nice. This is about being honest. Below, create the list of what is blocking you. Use as many of the spaces as you need.

What is Holding Me Back?	
1.	12.
2.	13.
3.	14.
4.	15.
5.	16.
6.	17.
7.	18.
8.	19.
9.	20.
10.	21.
11.	22.

I left space for 22 options because I love that number and when you add 2 + 2 you get 4. The number four is known to be a number of practicalities, willpower, loyalty, and determination. We are going to utilize all of those qualities to ground this transformation for a total cocoon conversion. Ready to reemerge? Wherever you happen to be right now, look around and start to gather small items to represent each blockage listed above. Get creative and have fun! Use little rocks, shells, bingo chips, crackers, leaves, twigs, hair ties… anything that is close by and convenient. You can even get specific and have certain items represent certain blocks. When you have enough, put the entire pile on your self-portrait. Now, stand up and look at yourself buried underneath all of that *stuff*. What comes to mind? When you are ready, choose one item on your portrait and decide: what is one small shift I can make to begin transforming this thing from an obstruction to an opportunity? No facts are needed. No big solutions are required. Let your intuition be your guide as you employ the four gifts of *practicality, determination, loyalty,* and *willpower.* As you remove each item piece by piece, write and reclaim your revitalization process below.

Transforming Obstruction to Opportunity	
1.	12.
2.	13.
3.	14.
4.	15.
5.	16.
6.	17.
7.	18.
8.	19.
9.	20.
10.	21.
11.	22.

Keep going, item by item, until everything is removed. When you are all clear, look at that beautiful face and tell her you love her. Tell her that I love her, too. As a final step, add any finishing touches to your self-portrait to reflect the work you have just done. Big hugs, Sister. Big, *big* hugs of gratitude coming your way! Thank you for doing this.

~ SPS #3: ~
* Intentional Movement *

Another component of Psychodrama is physical movement. Oftentimes in a psychodrama group, the facilitator will get participants up - walking and talking at the same time - to process feelings. The idea is: stuck body = stuck everything. Whereas with movement, an active body can equal a more engaged mind-body-spirit connection. Let's try it. Think of something that you've been trying to figure out or something that has been weighing on your heart and write it down below.

Now, hold what you've just written in your mind and let your body begin to process it. Stand up, and as you inhale bring your arms up towards the sky while gently bending your knees. At the top of your inhale, with your arms fully extended, count to three. Now, reverse and as you exhale bring your arms back down and straighten your legs. When the exhale feels complete, hold and count to three again. Repeat the breathing and movement five to ten times. When you are finished, think about the situation again and write what comes to mind.

Is anything different? Did any new ideas, thoughts, or perspectives come forward? Repeat the breath and movement cycle a third time and take notice of how your thoughts and feelings continue to shift.

Three rounds of intentional breath and movement will energize even the most sluggish of systems. That is wonderful, however, what happened to the original situation? Or, better question, what happened in regard to your *relationship* to the original situation? Connecting our very wise and beautiful bodies to our minds, hearts, and Souls can create infinite opportunities for new perspectives, thoughts, and feelings. As a final step, take a moment and solidify this connection by journaling or reflecting on the following statement. Thanks for doing this. Love you!

When I connect to my body's natural wisdom, I...

_____

_____

_____

~ SPS #4: ~
* Embodied Action *

We may not be aware of it, but each feeling that we experience manifests somewhere in our physical body. Think of joy. Can you identify where you feel joy? Think about sadness. Do you feel it in the same place, or do you feel it somewhere else? What about sorrow? When we are feeling things like happiness, joy, and love... we want those feelings to last. However, when experiencing the other side of the spectrum with feelings like rage, loneliness, or gloom... recognizing and honoring the feelings is a beneficial step, but then what?

When those feelings stick around, they can leave us chronically exhausted and consistently overwhelmed. How do we go about transforming them so that we don't keep feeling them? According to Bessel van der Kolk, M.D., in his book, *The Body Keeps the Score: Brain, Mind, and Body in the Healing of Trauma*, we go about transforming the feelings via a process of intentional and purposeful embodied action. When we do this, he says, we can create new relationships *to* the feelings and new experiences *of* the feelings which in turn can reteach our brains how to handle the feelings in more functional ways. He also adds that this process can be comprehensive when we add in an element of physical play. So, let's break it down. These big heady feelings that demand so much mental and emotional real estate are actually asking us to be more playful and childlike in order to process and transform them? I love it! Let's try it. Put on some music and start to move in whatever way feels comfortable. Let your awareness float around a bit and when you are ready, start to play with different emotions. Embody the feeling of happiness. What do you notice? How do your muscles and bones feel? How is your body positioned? How would someone know you are happy just by looking at you? Next, try sadness. Notice how your body is different. Also, notice your thoughts. Do they begin to mirror your movements in anyway? Let's keep this playful energy going. Below are suggestions for embodiment and transformation. As you play, express with your movements while remaining attentive to your thoughts and feelings. Be patient and gentle with yourself as this may take a few tries.

Transforming helpless to empowered.

- Embody feeling **helpless.**

    - What do you notice about your *body*? _____
    _____

    - What do you notice about your *thoughts*? _____
    _____

    - What do you notice about your *feelings*? _____
    _____

- With movement and play, physically transform **helpless** to **empowered** and repeat the process two or three times.

    - What do you notice about your *body* now? _____
    _____

    - What do you notice about your *thoughts* now? _____
    _____

    - What do you notice about your *feelings* now? _____
    _____

- Is your *experience* of these two feelings different in any way? _____
  _____

- Is your *relationship* to these two feelings different in any way? _____
  _____

Transforming rage to bliss.

- Embody feeling **rage.**

  - What do you notice about your *body*? _____
    _____

  - What do you notice about your *thoughts*? _____
    _____

  - What do you notice about your *feelings*? _____
    _____

- With movement and play, physically transform **rage** to **bliss** and repeat the process two or three times.

  - What do you notice about your *body* now? _____
    _____

  - What do you notice about your *thoughts* now? _____
    _____

  - What do you notice about your *feelings* now? _____
    _____

    - Is your *experience* of these two feelings different in any way? _____
      _____

    - Is your *relationship* to these two feelings different in any way? _____
      _____

Transforming frozen or stuck to capable and able.

- Embody feeling **frozen and stuck.**

    - What do you notice about your *body?* _____
    _____

    - What do you notice about your *thoughts?* _____
    _____

    - What do you notice about your *feelings?* _____
    _____

- With movement and play, physically transform **frozen and stuck** to **capable and able** and repeat the process two or three times.

    - What do you notice about your *body* now? _____
    _____

    - What do you notice about your *thoughts* now? _____
    _____

    - What do you notice about your *feelings* now? _____
    _____

        - Is your *experience* of these feelings different in any way? _____
        _____

        - Is your *relationship* to these feelings different in any way? _____
        _____

Transforming frazzled to relaxed.

- Embody feeling **frazzled.**

    - What do you notice about your *body?* _____
    _____

- What do you notice about your *thoughts*? _____
  _____

- What do you notice about your *feelings*? _____
  _____

• With movement and play, physically transform **frazzled** to **relaxed** and repeat the process two or three times.

  - What do you notice about your *body* now? _____
    _____

  - What do you notice about your *thoughts* now? _____
    _____

  - What do you notice about your *feelings* now? _____
    _____

    ▪ Is your ***experience*** of these two feelings different in any way? _____
      _____

    ▪ Is your ***relationship*** to these two feelings different in any way? _____
      _____

Transforming brittle to playful.

• Embody feeling **brittle.**

  - What do you notice about your *body*? _____
    _____

  - What do you notice about your *thoughts*? _____
    _____

  - What do you notice about your *feelings*? _____
    _____

- With movement and play, physically transform **brittle** to **playful** and repeat the process two or three times.

    o What do you notice about your *body* now? _____
    _____

    o What do you notice about your *thoughts* now? _____
    _____

    o What do you notice about your *feelings* now? _____
    _____

        ▪ Is your ***experience*** of these two feelings different in any way? _____
        _____

        ▪ Is your ***relationship*** to these two feelings different in any way? _____
        _____

Wow! Great job moving your body. Knowing that these powers of transformation are at your disposal, how can intentional and purposeful *embodied action* be beneficial in other areas of life? Alright, now sit down and relax. Thanks for doing this activity. It was quite a workout! Love you!

~ SPS #5: ~
* Maiden Flirt *

Of the four Archetypes of the Sacred Feminine - Crone, Maiden, Mother, and Enchantress - the wisdom of the Maiden brings us the energy of rebirth. The Maiden correlates to the Waxing Phase of the Lunar Cycle, the season of Spring, the Pre-Ovulatory Phase of the Menstrual Cycle, and the color White. The Maiden is also known to bring in the dynamic and inspirational influences of rejuvenation and renewal. Pair this along with her upbeat energy, playful confidence, and productive ambition… and you've got one power-packed Archetype! No matter our chronological age, all women are influenced by the Maiden's vibrancy, enthusiasm, and joyful radiance. "Who me?" you question. "Joyful, radiant, vibrant, and enthusiastic…. Yeah, *right*!" It is understandable. There are probably plenty of reasons why you don't feel these things at will, but you can! In honor of the Maiden, gaze at the open, white space below for a minute or two.

Now, think about your first hot and heavy crush. Really think about how you felt - the butterflies in your stomach… the not knowing what to say… the strange giggling episodes taking over your body at random… and from right here in this midst of this visualization, fantasize about flirting! Flirt with your first crush, if it isn't too weird, since this crush was probably in Middle School. If it is too weird, just shuffle in another crush. Take that butterflies-in-the-tummy feeling and place it in a juicy scenario of your choosing. Imagine your Inner Maiden flirting her booty off! You look terrific, you feel terrific, you ARE terrific! Guess what happens next? In the middle of this flirting friskiness, your crush starts flirting back! This is your fantasy babe, so let this flirty little scene include anything that you fancy hearing. After the blush wears off, write down the frolicsome comments above on that fresh expanse of white. Include everything that was said! From "Hey, beautiful" to "You must be tired because you've been running through my mind all night." Don't miss a flirt! When you are finished, keep this reminder of your lively and lovely Maiden energies. Think about how she flirts with the night sky, growing larger and larger day-by-day in order to reach her Full Moon potential. Think about how the energy of the Maiden flirts with the Earth in Springtime, creating the space for the tender new shoots of fresh plant life to poke through the ground. Think about how our bodies flirt while in the Pre-Ovulatory Maiden Phase of the Menstrual Cycle, preparing for the precious egg of new life and new potential to travel the sacred journey into our Womb Space. Think about how the color of White flirts and invites us in, asking to be filled and accented with the vibrant hues of the color spectrum. By flirtatiously honoring our Maiden, we create the spirited possibility of rebirthing *ourselves*. This isn't about age or experience. If you have had your ovaries or uterus removed, or if you are no longer experiencing a menstrual cycle, you can still wholeheartedly participate. Allowing your heart to become aware of these energies is all it takes to create a shift in consciousness. As always, feel open to repeating this flirty fantasy again and again and again and again! Love you! Thank you for flirting with me!

Crystal Love: Kei's Crystal is the Apache Tear. These beautiful stones are a gentle variety of Obsidian (uhb-*sid*-ee-uhn). Made of volcanic glass, this Crystal initially appears dark and opaque. However, this is just a perfect reflection of the Apache Tear's healing abilities. Known for being the stone to turn to in times of grief, Apache Tears, when held to the light, become translucent. This potent magick reminds us that no matter how painful life can seem, there is always light willing to shine through, offering warmth, comfort, protection, and connection. The name of this stone also carries profound depth. It is said that the legend of the Apache Tear originates from a Native American story. In this story, the women of the tribe shed their tears upon the Earth as they grieved for their lost warriors. As they cried, their sorrow was so great that their tears immediately turned to stone. Perhaps this is why Apache Tears are recognized as providing deeper understanding for painful situations, acceptance and forgiveness around grievances, and clarity for the inexplicable hardships of life. Metaphorically, Apache Tears can shed our tears for us, cleansing the aura and grounding our Basic Chakra down into the ever-loving Heart Center of Mother Earth. Additionally, try placing an Apache Tear by your bedside to prevent feelings of bitterness and anger, and when traveling, let it protect you by creating a force field against negativity.

Suggested Reading for Empowered Healing, On All Levels, Through All Time and Space, *Theta Healing: Introducing an Extraordinary Energy-Healing Modality* by Vianna Stibal.

Additional Journaling and SPS Space

Jacqui

I'm a Feng Shui, Shaman, Healer Goddess. I am also a mom of twin seven-year-old boys, caretaker of two disabled, divorced parents, a wife, a friend, and a woman who is healing herself so that I can heal the world. I didn't realize it when I moved to Florida from Manhattan all those years ago how ready I was for change… or that I would have to lose myself to find my truth. Today I feel like I have just woken up from a very long nap. I loved living in New York, but there was an energy - a feeling - that I should always be doing more. I loved working, so left to my own devices, I became a workaholic. When my dad fell ill about fifteen years ago, my mom and I decided to move down so that I could help. I loaded up everything that mattered, hired a moving van, and headed South. Up until that point, I hadn't met anyone in my dating life that felt of substance. Believe it or not, my stepmom had a friend that she played tennis with who also had an adult son moving to Florida around the same time. They hatched a plan for a blind date. When I met my husband, it was very apparent that we were on the same page about family and marriage. That was so refreshing for me coming from New York City, where men do not typically talk about family and commitment. Meeting my husband was very different than what I was used to. When I made the decision to move, it was not only to care for my father… I also moved to reinvent myself and part of that process was finding a partner who facilitated me doing both. Through my Feng Shui work and my studies with my teacher, Dr. Jerry Epstein, I had been doing *'Bringing in a Man'* imagery work. I kept it up when I got to Florida because I thought, "I'm 39, I better get cookin'!" In my image, I kept seeing the body of a man with bare feet. That confused me because a man with bare feet was such a different direction than anything I was used to. Those bare feet in that image were my husband! Even though we were very much just friends in the beginning, it became more of a commitment when, although our backgrounds were so different, we really started to see how aligned our values and morals were. I had finally met a man who was unlike any of the other boys I had been dating. There was such synchronicity in the spiritual realm for us too, which was also new to me. We knew right away we wanted to start a family. At our ages, we decided to forgo protection, and it was kind of fun to meet this new version of myself. As a recovering Catholic girl, I thought when you *looked* at a boy you got pregnant. Trying to create a life without being married allowed a wilder and more truthful version of me to emerge. I give my husband credit for that. He helped me uncover some of the weeds and rocks that were in my Garden of Eden and together we have created something really amazing. My journey in fertility lasted about six years, and then we had twins. This was especially exciting for me having my fifth house in Gemini. As an only child caring for two disabled parents, this has given me a deep level of value for the notion of having a sibling. As I wake up from this sleep, in spite of all of the amazing things that have happened, I realize that I have lost myself in increments every time my parents have declined. It is hard to see what we don't want to see in our lives, yet I have to admit this. When I moved here, I became my father's sole caregiver. I didn't realize the scope of his situation or what caretaking for him would entail until I actually started doing it. It was like the Universe showed me the tip of the iceberg, and as I entered the world of senior caregiving, I was shown what lies beneath the surface. I didn't know anyone who had gone through anything like this. I came at it as a very privileged, very sheltered girl from Greenwich, Connecticut and I was consistently amazed about how I knew nothing in regard to caregiving for seniors. I was also consistently amazed - and consistently disappointed - to discover that this country helps with nothing. Feeling so alone, with no one to turn to, I got lost in the emotional 'saving' of my parents. My father was going through his own situation, and my mother, who had been going blind since her thirties, needed my full attention as well. My spiritual teacher would tell me that I was responsible *to* my parents, but not *for* my parents. I had a really rough time understanding that concept. I am a very loving person. I am a very caring person. I am in the healing business. I kept telling myself, "This is right up my alley!" What I am realizing all these years later is that I can't save anyone. I am here to live my path and my tribe is here to live theirs. This wisdom makes me happy and sad at the same time. It is difficult to realize that the best thing I can do to love my family is to let them go and stop trying to save them. This is the hardest part of being a healer. I continually have to remind myself to put my own oxygen mask on first - and until **I** am healed, I cannot keep giving to others that which I don't have. The lesson for me in redeveloping the Feng Shui of my new home, of putting me and my husband first, is that we are actually recreating and recalibrating the balance of healing and partnership as opposed to tipping the scales with inhuman expectations of caregiving and trying to save people who don't want to be saved. Now I realize that the only person I can save is me, and in doing so I save my tribe. It doesn't work the other way around. I am always the model. Somedays, I hate being that model. It is hard, it is heavy, and I am tired. Yet, I know that in order to get to where I want to be and live the way I want to live, my tribe is going to have to see me in a new way. Sharing your truth is only part of the process. You think, "Oh, this is great! Now, everybody is going to 'see' my truth." Then you wake up and it just doesn't happen that way. I thought I was going to make some changes for my own well-being, and everybody would happily see and support the 'new' me. Not so. I have had to train and teach my tribe how to see the new me. I also had to accept the reality that some of the people that I was working for so diligently did not, in fact, want my help. What I did start to focus on was being the change that I wanted to see in the world. That had to start with me. I had to wake up. I had to start my own peace rallies. Little by little my tribe began to join in, and we started to shift the negative Feng Shui that was making us sick: physically, emotionally, mentally and spiritually. Everything from the bottom up had to be reinvented. I had to detach from control. Whether it be my parent's health, my child's health, or my own health, I know I don't have control over these things. I have had to re-create the architecture of my life, envisioning where I would like my tribe to go, redesigning myself, and asking for help. I am still rolling up my sleeves and I have so much more work to do, but I am shifting. We are shifting. For thirteen and a half years, I kept asking the other people in my life to change. I had become convinced that if only the people in my life could see me… could see all of the work that I was doing… could see me dying on the vine… they would surely make me take better care of myself. Nope. Truth is, until I started seeing myself and what my needs were, no one else was going to, either. All of this work got concentrated when the Type 1 diabetes diagnosis came for my son on August 1st of 2017. He was just four and a half. He is my reminder to reel it in. Our energies are so in tune. So much of my life reflects my habits back to me… of doing too much and not taking care of myself. To survive, I have to keep reminding myself that I am the hologram for the whole. I am you. We are all connected. If I want to save the world, and I do, I have to save myself first. That is the real message. Don't wait any longer for anyone to save you. It's not a husband. It's not a friend. It's not therapy. It's not even a Goddess Group. Until we take care of ourselves and speak our own truths, we have nothing to give. That is my message. Be the change first. You can help others second. This philosophy of self-care will mirror everything. Heal yourself. Heal the world.

Making This Story Your Own:

Jacqui's story highlights the limitations of pouring from an empty cup.
Take a moment, breathe, and reflect.
What stands out for you when you read her words?
Is there a situation in your life that is similar to Jacqui's?
Perhaps part of her story feels connected to your own.
How can you relate her experiences to your past, present, and future?

- *My Connection to Jacqui's Story* _____

_____

_____

_____

_____

Knowing that you aren't alone, let's gently explore some other themes from Jacqui's story together:

- **Responsible *To*, Not For**
  - Are there people and situations in your life that you feel responsible *for*? Are there people and situations in your life that you feel responsible *to*? What is the difference and is this difference OK with you? What are your beliefs on personal responsibility when it comes to your family, friends, profession, and the world? When you think of these responsibilities, do they fill your cup or leave you feeling depleted? If these responsibilities are a drain, what can you do to bring them more into balance?

- **Putting Yourself First**
  - Where do *you* rank on the daily to-do list? How did you come up with this answer and is it what you'd like to be experiencing? Why, or why not? Where did you learn about self-care and valuing your needs? When you think about the world's children - our next generation - how would you like to model self-care for them? In your opinion, how important is it that children learn to value their needs? Do you value yourself and your needs with the same level of dedication and importance? If so, how do you do this? If not, why is it not equal? What would it take to make your needs more of a priority?

- **Heal Yourself, Heal the World**
  - How synonymous are the words *sacrifice* and *caretaking* in your internal dictionary? Do you hold a belief system that once everything and everyone else is taken care of *then* you can address your own needs? If so, where did you learn this? If not, how do you manage to address your needs equally? If this pattern of giving without receiving resonates, is it still working for you? Can you identify what the benefits have been from this uneven exchange? Can you identify what the benefits will be when this dynamic is shifted to become more equal?

Sacred Play Suggestions:

~SPS #1: ~

* Five Elements *

Feng Shui teaches that we can receive energy from our environment. In Feng Shui there are five Elements that, when in balance with our surroundings, can create feelings of contentment and harmony for the body, mind, and spirit. The following Elements and their characteristics are based on Jacqui's personal Feng Shui Teachings that she shared with me.

The Five Elements

- **Wood Element**: This element is strong, yet supple, and fosters personal growth through adaptation and flexibility. **Wood** offers a positive mental state and resonates with kindness, friendliness, generosity, coordination, and romantic love.
- **Fire Element:** This element is lively, spirited, cheerful, and vital to happiness and artistic expression. **Fire** offers the heat and energy necessary to create courage, zeal, joy, and general courteousness.
- **Earth Element:** This element is the supportive container of all of the other elements. **Earth** offers nourishment, transformation, fertility, receptivity, and balance.
- **Metal Element:** This element is the strong, reflective and structural reinforcement of Earth's perfection. **Metal** offers orderliness, the ability to gain wisdom, morality, justice, and rhythm.
- **Water Element:** This element is wise, intelligent, reflective, and restorative. Flowing along the path of least resistance while simultaneously embodying its intense power, **Water** offers willpower and ambition as a carrier, cleanser, and refresher of life.

Find some items in your home that can represent these five Elements. Nothing big, flashy, or specific required, just five easily accessible things to represent these wonderfully empowering and energetic, not to mention - *helpful* - Elements. Think… water in a bowl, a lit candle, a wooden spoon, soil on a small plate, a metal kitchen utensil, etc. Get creative and follow your intuition. When you have your five things, set them in front of you in the following order:

- **Wood, Fire, Earth, Metal, & Water**
  - This order represents the cycle of how these natural Earth Elements work and dance together. Another way to think of how these elements relate to each other is…
    - Wood **feeds** Fire
    - Fire **makes** Earth
    - Earth **creates** Metal
    - Metal **holds** Water
    - Water **nurtures** Wood

Get comfortable and connect into the spirit of these Elements. Visualize them coming to life before you in whatever form they take. Ask each one how they can best support you in balancing your *external* environment so that they can, in turn, also support you in balancing your *internal* environment. Write down the messages as they come forward. Employ the assistance of the Elements to create more of the life you want by asking the following questions.

    Wood, how can I balance you more so that you help me feed my personal growth?

_____

_____

_____

_____

Fire, how can I balance you more so that you help me make the
transformations and expansions I desire for my life?

_____

_____

_____

Earth, how can I balance you more so that you help me create a grounded and peaceful existence?

_____

_____

_____

Metal, how can I balance you more so that you help me hold the
mental energy of sharpness, intelligence, and acuity?

_____

_____

_____

Water, how can I balance you more so that you help me nurture the
process of letting go in order to release and renew?

_____

_____

_____

Wow! Who would have thought that connecting into these Elements could be so helpful? Remember, you can tap into this wisdom and support anywhere at any time. How lucky are we that Wood, Fire, Earth, Metal, and Water are so easily accessible and eager to help! They love you and so do I! Thanks for doing this!

~ SPS #2: ~
* Mother-Crone *

Nurturing, nourishing, and sustaining are all qualities of the *Mother*, one of the four Sacred Archetypes of Womanhood. Most of us experience some form of motherhood through our human children, fur babies, and idea children. As women, we hold within us the magickal spark to create and sustain life. However, the highest conscious expression of these magickal energies - the Divine Feminine - was never meant to be understood through the context that to *caregive* for another one must *sacrifice* the self. The creation, sustenance, and nurturing of womanhood and motherhood are meant to be gifts for both giver and receiver. That is why women, with our fluids of blood and birth - experienced as menstruation, breast milk, tears, sexual lubrication, and amniotic fluid - are so closely linked with bodies of water, the seasons, and the Moon. These larger cycling systems teach us that Feminine energy cannot be on an output all of the time. Just like Mother Moon's Dark Phase, Mother Earth's Winter, and the receding tides of Mother Ocean, our bodies, minds, and Souls also crave and depend on the down times, hibernation, and quiet solitude. Just like Jacqui's wisdom teaches us, if we are not able to replenish, we are left trying to pour from an empty cup. When that happens on a chronic basis, everyone can suffer. The Archetype of the Mother - expressed in the Lunar Cycle as the Full Moon, the seasonal cycle as Summer, and in the menstrual cycle as the time of Ovulation - balances with and is the counterpoint to the Archetype of the Crone. The Crone is expressed in the Lunar Cycle as the Dark Moon, the seasonal cycle as Winter, and in the menstrual cycle as the bleeding time, or Menstruation. We need the wisdom and energy of both of these wise Archetypes - along with their other *Sisters*, the Maiden and the Enchantress - to invoke our Divine and psychic birthrights as balanced, grounded, creative, blissful, fertile, and replenished beings. For now, let's look at the wisdom of the Crone and the Mother to see where some shifts can occur in our lives so that we can better follow these natural cycles in ways that feel more aligned with our needs. Remember, resistance is expected. We have lived for thousands of years being told that our worth is socially supported and socially defined by our embodiment of constant output, exhaustion, servitude, and sacrifice.

The Wisdom of the **Mother**	The Wisdom of the **Crone**
<ul><li>Time to care and support.</li><li>Balances the energy output with love and devotion.</li><li>Receptive, communicative, and collaborative.</li><li>Focused on needs of the group or family.</li><li>Receptive to new concepts and ideas.</li><li>Deeply connected to family, social groups, and community.</li><li>Creative energies are shared.</li></ul>	<ul><li>Time to pull in and rest.</li><li>Time to purge what is no longer serving you.</li><li>No need to please others.</li><li>Only does what is essential.</li><li>Needs of the self are most important.</li><li>Spends time alone to replenish.</li><li>Deeply connected to dreams, natural world, and psychic abilities.</li><li>Creative energies are held in.</li></ul>

Can you make a new caregiving contract that honors both your Inner Mother *and* your Inner Crone?
Try it. In the columns below, jot down all of your caregiving responsibilities. Include all of the things you do to nurture, nourish, and sustain yourself and others. Put things that require an *output* of energy in the Mother column and things requiring an *input* of energy in the Crone column.

The Wisdom of My Inner Mother	**The Wisdom of My Inner Crone**

In regard to these two powerful energies, where do things feel balanced and where could they use some extra attention? As you continue to understand what you need, connecting to the cyclical wisdom around you might be helpful. Follow the Lunar Phases and when Mother Moon is *Full* (the phase of the Mother) or *Dark* (the phase of the Crone) utilize her energy to help you with your output versus input ratios. Also pay attention to where we are on the Wheel of the Year. *Winter* (the season of the Crone) and *Summer* (the season of the Mother) can also offer much support for daily plans, schedules, and caregiving responsibilities based on your body's intuitive capacities to be influenced by the natural world. Lastly, if you are still cycling, know where you are on your menstrual cycle. If you are *Ovulating* (the time of the Mother) or *Bleeding* (the time of the Crone) your consciousness will relate to these energies in ways large and small that, when honored and respected, can be harnessed for extra energy, empowerment, and pleasure throughout all of your activities. If you are no longer experiencing a menstrual cycle, you may identify more with the monthly Lunar Cycle and feel the pull of each archetype along with Mother Moon, or the seasonal cycle, and feel the pull of each archetype as a longer multi-week experience along with Mother Earth. Lastly, connect into a body of water and let the magnetic ebb and flow of the Feminine inform and support your Crone and Mother energies. You may find that, as you listen to, work with, and invite in support from these larger Feminine entities, the concepts of sacrifice and pouring from an empty cup fade away. Small shifts and regular awareness are all it takes to make a big difference! Solidify this connection to your Inner Mother and Inner Crone by journaling for a few minutes around the following statement:

I will Honor both My Mother *and* My Crone Energies by…

_____

_____

_____

_____

_____

Thank you for taking the time to do this activity. Knowing how the energetic influences around us can support and work with the energetic influences within us is powerful! This is a cycle. It flows. It isn't static. When we flow with it, the desire to give and receive can become more organic, more natural, and more liberating. No more empty cups for us! Love you, Sister. Thank you.

~ SPS #3: ~
* Color Gift *

Colors have vibration. They can boost our energy and get us noticed at the same time. In Feng Shui, along with many other wise ways of life, everything is alive and everything is made of energy. From this perspective, you are connected to the colors you choose for your body by the way of your clothing and accessories. Think of them as over-lapping energy fields. If you are feeling sluggish one day, or maybe you need a boost in the form of a Sister-to-Sister connection, let the colors you wear help you create what you need. Below is a general list of colors and their abilities to enhance our lives. If some of the suggestions resonate, use them! If not, create your own.

Red	Try Red for Passion, Courage, Excitement, and a Connection to Mother Earth.
Orange	Try Orange for Action, Friendship, Creativity, and a Boost to Self-Esteem.
Yellow	Try Yellow for Calming and Uplifting Emotions, Happiness, and Warmth.
Green	Try Green for Peace, Relaxation, Abundance and a Connection to Nature.
Blue	Try Blue for Speaking your Truth, Security, and Soothing the Mind.
Purple	Try Purple for Increased Intuition, Nobility, and Dignity.
Pink	Try Pink for Love, Romance, Softness, and a Deep Connection to the Feminine.

For the next seven days, choose to incorporate a particular color for a particular purpose. When someone notices your color, your mission is to engage them in a conversation and tell them why you chose that particular color. This shares your wisdom of the color's vibration and creates an opportunity for meaningful conversation. Day-by-day, take note of the following:

Day 1

- Which color did I choose and why? _____

- How did I feel wearing the color? _____

- Did the color connect me to someone? _____

- What good came from wearing the color? _____

Day 2

- Which color did I choose and why? _____

- How did I feel wearing the color? _____

- Did the color connect me to someone? _____

- What good came from wearing the color? _____

Day 3

- Which color did I choose and why? _____
  _____

- How did I feel wearing the color? _____
  _____

- Did the color connect me to someone? _____
  _____

- What good came from wearing the color? _____
  _____

Day 4

- Which color did I choose and why? _____
  _____

- How did I feel wearing the color? _____
  _____

- Did the color connect me to someone? _____
  _____

- What good came from wearing the color? _____
  _____

Day 5

- Which color did I choose and why? _____
  _____

- How did I feel wearing the color? _____
  _____

- Did the color connect me to someone? _____
  _____

- What good came from wearing the color? _____
  _____

Day 6

- Which color did I choose and why? _____
  _____

- How did I feel wearing the color? _____
  _____

- Did the color connect me to someone? _____
  _____

- What good came from wearing the color? _____
  _____

Day 7

- Which color did I choose and why? _____
  _____

- How did I feel wearing the color? _____
  _____

- Did the color connect me to someone? _____
  _____

- What good came from wearing the color? _____
  _____

Great job connecting through color! Going forward, how can color continue supporting you? Afterall it *is* everywhere. We might as well use it. Thanks for taking the time to do this activity. Love you!

~ SPS #4: ~
* Bliss-Bundle-Scale *

All of our emotions have an energetic vibration. Some scales even break it down by numeric value with higher vibrations and numbers equaling an expanded existence and lower vibrations and numbers equaling a contracted existence. Take a moment and think of shame, fear, and anger. These emotions traditionally rank lower on the scale. Based on a numeric value from 0-1000, shame traditionally ranks around 20, fear ranks around 100, and anger ranks around 150. According to different schools of thought, when we consistently vibrate with these emotions we live life lower on the scale and this contracted existence can be felt within our lives and relationships as chronic suffering. However, courage - a mere 50 points from anger with a vibration value of about 200 - can boost those feelings right up. Even higher on the scale are the emotions of acceptance at 350, love at 500, and peace at 600. As you can guess, consistently vibrating with these feelings can boost the suffering up and into the realms of bliss. Sign. Me. Up! Take a moment and write down the emotions that you have experienced over the past week on the left-hand side of the diagram below. Now, taking what works for you based on the Vibration Scale already mentioned, rank your emotions from 1-1000 on the right-hand side of the diagram. Use your intuition here. Anything that hasn't felt blissful will be lower on the scale. Anything that has felt more in flow, easy, and balanced will be higher.

My Emotions	Vibration Value

When you are finished, take a look at your list. Have you been spending more time in contraction and suffering than you realized? If so, don't blame yourself. Grief and guilt will only keep you mired in the muck. Perhaps you've actually been higher on the scale than you realize… great! Be sure to give yourself credit. Willingness and reason are said to be vibing up there at around 400 and 450. Now, shift gears and think of some small, easily transportable items around your house that can remind you of these higher vibratory feelings. Find things to represent courage, neutrality, willingness, acceptance, reason, love, joy, and peace. These things can be words on a slip of paper, rocks, leaves, small toys, pieces of jewelry, refrigerator magnets… anything that calls to you. Label each item with a corresponding emotion and numeric vibration value below.

Emotion	Vibration Value	Item
Courage		
Neutrality		
Willingness		
Acceptance		
Reason		
Love		
Joy		
Peace		

Next, gather all of these things together in a small bag and voilà! You have your very own *Bundle of Bliss*. Whenever you need to raise or shift your vibe… just pull something out of the bag! When you do this, take a moment to be aware of how you are feeling and then intentionally allow the item to bring in a new feeling. Complete the process by acknowledging the shift. Even if things only shift for a brief second, it is *still* a shift in consciousness, and it counts! Keep working with your bundle and see what happens. This intentional awareness can point us toward knowing ourselves in deeper and more compassionate ways. Enlightenment - which is said to vibe all the way to 1000 - is next. Good luck! Thanks for *vibing* with me. Love you!

~ SPS #5: ~
* Be Yourself, Be the Change *

Jacqui's story offers a perspective shift from the very familiar concept of the 'wounded healer.' With much wisdom and medicine, she shares great ideas on self-empowerment, self-care, and self-dedication. Below are some of her words. Taken individually, they each make great Mantras. Together, they are a beautiful work of poetic empowerment.

I am only here to live my path.
The person I will save is me.
I am the change.
I see myself. I speak my truth.
I heal myself. I heal the world.

Let's break this down and free-write with each line. As you put pen to paper, allow anything to come up and out on the page… even if you repeat the same word over and over.

I am only here to live my path.

_____

_____

_____

The person I will save is me.

_____

_____

_____

I am the change.

_____

_____

_____

I see myself. I speak my truth.

_____

_____

_____

I heal myself. I heal the world.

_____

_____

_____

When you have explored each line, go back and reread the piece in its entirety.

I am only here to live my path.
The person I will save is me.
I am the change.
I see myself. I speak my truth.
I heal myself. I heal the world.

As a final step, journal around the following questions.

- What wisdom is still waiting for me? _____

_____

- Where can I release old ideas and beliefs around self-sacrifice? _____

_____

- How can I support myself to caregive from a place of empowerment and contentment? _____

_____

Wow, Sister… when it comes to *being* the change, you nailed it! We are always going to have the opportunity to care for others. Caregiving is a gift for both giver and receiver. It is in the *ways* that we go about *providing* that care that can prevent us from becoming exhausted, overwhelmed, and compromised. Jacqui is right, we cannot pour from an empty cup. The 'juice' is always going to come from somewhere. Your self-empowerment, self-care, and self-dedication will keep that juice cup full and flowing. When you think of it in this way, your self-love becomes an act of *selfless* love for those around you. Taking the extra forty-five minutes to get your nails ombre'd so that every time you look at your hands you are reminded of a Moroccan sunset… that isn't just for you, babe… that's for the world. ☺ Love you! Thank you!

Crystal Love: Jacqui's Crystal is the magickal, inspirational, celestial, and luminescent Labradorite (*lab-ruh-daw-rahyt*). Because of its abilities to transform into what has been labeled as a shimmering *Temple of the Stars*, this stone is said to have extra-terrestrial origins. Hold a piece in your hand, and as you experience the Labradorescence of Labradorite, allow your illusions to be dispelled, your consciousness to be raised, your imagination to be energized, and your destiny to be revealed. As a powerful protector and symbol of both the sun's vitality and the moons cyclical nature, Labradorite has long been the chosen stone of shamans, diviners, healers, and all who travel to embrace the various realms of consciousness seeking wisdom and guidance. For self-discovery, this Crystal can provoke an awakening of the inner spirit, a clarification of inner sight, an empowerment of inner wisdom, and a preservation of inner strength. As a reflector of love and light, Labradorite can also perpetuate a sense of faith when it comes to our self-reliance, supporting us to calmly and patiently transcend limitations as we cultivate our Soul's ascension process.

Suggested Reading to Step-In to Your Sovereign Divinity as a Leader and Way-Shower, *The Sophia Code: A Living Transmission from the Sophia Dragon Tribe* by Kaia Ra.

Additional Journaling and SPS Space

Mary Lu

My family immigrated to this country when I was not quite five years old. Our home in Mexico was in the mountains, a few hours' drive from the Capitol of Acapulco. Even though I was very young, I remember being aware of the courage and hard work it took my parents to bring our family here. At that time, I was the youngest of three and it was normal for my dad to be gone for two years at a time working to make money. In Mexico, it is tradition that when a woman is wed, she moves in with her husband's family and becomes the caregiver for her in-laws and any younger siblings still at home. Living with my father's family, my mom was exhausted with all of the work. My mother wanted to immigrate so that we could all have a better life. At the age of eight, most children in my village were already working. If we had stayed, I soon would have started learning how to cook and clean, training to be the kind of wife and mother accepted by my culture. After years of living this same type of subservient life, my mom was adamant that we move to California with my dad. When we got to the States, I remember feeling a mix of curiosity and fear in this new world with different languages, beliefs, and systems. Learning English didn't come easy. At that time, my parents didn't speak English. Education wasn't a priority over working to make money. My father never learned how to read or write, yet I was always amazed that he knew his directions and street names so well. He had a great memory for those sorts of things. My mom has a better handle on English now. Little by little, she started to seek out education and opportunities for herself. This caused a lot of problems between her and my dad. He had a really hard time when my mom began stepping into her power. He was so used to her being submissive. It felt good to watch my mom open her mind, but it was also scary because I could see what it was doing to my parent's relationship. I probably knew more than I should have about what was going on between my parents. I would get into the middle of their fights and try to referee. Even at twelve or thirteen years old, I could make sense of their different points of view and I would explain where my mom was coming from to my dad and vice versa. My dad would say that he didn't fit with this new independent version of my mom. Yet, as a young woman, I was inspired by watching my mom seek out any opportunity for growth and learning. At the age of eighteen, my parents finally split up. There was one huge fight that ended it all. It was traumatic for everyone. My dad was so angry that he raged out of the house threatening to drive his car off a bridge and kill himself. He told me he couldn't live like this anymore - that if he and my mom were through - he was done with living. Thankfully, I was able to calm him down and he did not drive his car off of a bridge, but this argument was a defining point where we all had to face the reality that my parent's marriage was over. Things really changed after that. My family separated. I moved with my mom and my brothers stayed with my dad. I found freedom in my mom and dad splitting up because I got rebellious. Up until this point, my parents were very strict. After the separation, I started to claim my independence. In a Latino house, when you are living at home, you are under your parent's rules no matter how old you are. After the divorce, I broke away from this, pointing the finger back at them, asking, "Who are you to tell me how to live my life?" For about four years my dad tried to reconcile with my mom, but my mom was firm. Her decision was made. She was never going back. Finally, my dad accepted that my mom wasn't going to change her mind and he told us that he was going back to Mexico to visit his mother. He came back from this visit married, to a woman younger than me, with a young child of her own. That hurt. That devastated me. At twenty-two, I had a nineteen-year-old stepmother. My dad wasn't taking care of his own kids on a consistent basis and now he had a new wife… who had a young child of her own. Soon after, when they got pregnant, my world felt like it was crashing. Things weren't perfect before, but I was always happy that my family was together. Now, I felt like I was living someone else's life. I got so angry that I stopped speaking to my father for almost two years. I was angry at him for starting over and having more children. Eventually, my dad started to make some changes. He started taking care of my younger brothers a bit more. He started to ask us if we wanted to spend time together - something that he had never done before because he was always so focused on work. It was bittersweet.

All of these changes were happening - changes that I wish had happened when my mom and dad were together - but still, I was glad that they were finally happening. I began to let my guard down. My dad and I found a peace in our relationship as I found a new way to love and accept him. I ended up living with my dad for a while during this time. Looking back, I realize that during this time I got to have the type of father-daughter relationship I had always wanted and needed. He stepped up and showed up. I knew it was temporary because my dad's new wife had already moved back to Mexico with the baby, and his plan was to move with her, but that time together was very special. I didn't support his move back to Mexico. I would question him over and over and try to remind him that his children in California still needed him, but he went anyway. The day he left was the last time I saw him. Not long after he moved, my father was murdered while working in a field. I got the call at around five o'clock in the morning from my uncle. I knew something was wrong when I saw my phone flashing. I picked up and he said, "Your dad was killed." I didn't know what to do. It felt like I was in a nightmare. I couldn't scream. I couldn't cry. No information was coming through. I just wanted to know what had happened and no one would tell me anything. I wanted to know why. Not knowing was making me crazy. Where I am from in Mexico is completely off the grid. People don't have cell phones and computers. To even make a call to the States, my family there would have to journey into the central part of the town and talk on a public phone. Because this was a murder, everyone was scared and no one wanted to say anything. I tried to stay rational, but I couldn't. I became filled with thoughts of revenge. I was so angry, and I felt like there was nothing I could do about it. As time passed, I knew that I had to find some peace. One day, my boyfriend's mom was giving away some books and one sort of jumped out at me. It was a book describing the afterlife and it talked about the concepts of energy and the potential of reincarnation. I learned through reading that book that my dad wasn't really gone. I also realized that for me to heal, I had to forgive my father's murderer. That has not been easy. Somedays I am better with it than others. What helps is my connection to myself and my beliefs in oneness. Everyone has been hurt. Everyone struggles. The man who killed my father is no different. When I can think of him with compassion and empathy, I feel much stronger. Knowing that all of life is connected helps me remember my father and know that he is with me. Believing that we are all one helps me forgive what seems unforgiveable. When I was twenty-five, I got to have six months of a relationship with my dad that I will never forget. It wasn't enough but I will forever be grateful. My relationship with my father was never perfect. There was a lot of hurt, disappointment, and guilt. If I stay rooted in that place, I am not able to see or honor all of the good that was there, too. My life changed forever the morning I got the call that my dad was gone. Of course, I would change that if I could. But I can't, so I have to transform that pain. I know that losing my dad has made me the woman I am today, and I wouldn't change her for anything.

Making This Story Your Own:

Mary Lu's story offers a perspective of peace found through forgiveness.
Take a moment, breathe, and reflect.
What stands out for you when you read her words?
Is there a situation in your life that is similar to Mary Lu's?
Perhaps part of her story feels connected to your own.
How can you relate her experiences to your past, present, and future?

- *My Connection to Mary Lu's Story* _____

_____

_____

Knowing that you aren't alone, let's gently explore some other themes from Mary Lu's story together:

- *Having the Courage to Leave*
  - Have there been situations in your life that you changed, ended, or left when you decided it was time? How did you have the courage to do this? Where did the strength come from? Have you given yourself credit for making these changes? Are there situations currently in your life that you would like to change, end, or leave? How long have you felt this way? What is keeping you from making these changes? Does maintaining the present circumstances have any benefit for you or anyone else? If so, what are the benefits? Does maintaining the present circumstances bring harm to you or anyone else? If so, what is the harm? If you desire to make a change, is there anyone or anything that can support you? How can you best support yourself?

- *Forgiving the Unforgivable*
  - What does forgiveness look and feel like for you? Have you ever forgiven anyone for anything? If so, can you recall the details? What happened? How were you able to forgive? Have you ever been forgiven? Can you recall those details? What happened and what did forgiveness feel like? In your opinion, are there certain things that are unforgivable? Why, or why not? What are the benefits of not forgiving? Who is hurt the most and who is protected the most when forgiveness remains absent? What might be the benefits of allowing forgiveness into every situation? Who would be healed the most if unconditional forgiveness were present in your life and relationships?

- *Being OK with Right Now*
  - What does contentment look like? Are you content? If so, how? Are you content with certain things and not content with others? Perhaps you are not content with anything.... If this is true for you, can you explain why? When you think back to your early years, were you given messages about what it meant to be content? Was it valued? Was it criticized? What messages were you given about your personal contentment? Are you still being given messages today? If so, from whom? How would more feelings of contentment be favorable for you and your relationships? How would they be unfavorable? If you would like more contentment, what can you either begin or end to manifest this into your life?

Sacred Play Suggestions:

<u>~ SPS #1: ~</u>
<u>* I Am Now *</u>

How often have you or someone you know said a version of the following:

"I'll be happy... *when* I lose the weight."
"I'll relax... *when* I have the time."
"I'll be fulfilled... *when* I am in a relationship."
"I'll slow down... *when* this is over."

As humans, we are goal-oriented creatures and we work well within this type of dynamic. Goals are great because they help us get stuff done. Think of how much you have already accomplished in your life and think of how much more you will accomplish in the years to come. Goals get icky when we attach a value to them that inhibits our sense of joy and peace. What if we flipped the script and instead of saying "I'll be happy when…" we start to say, "I am happy now **and** I will also be happy when - *fill in the blank* - happens." It sounds so simple, right? That's because it is. It is also just as simple to create a subconscious belief system that isn't so warm and fuzzy. Think about it. How do you talk *to* yourself and how do you talk *about* yourself? Are you consistently kind and loving? Your subconscious mind is aware, powerful, and awesome. It is listening to everything you say. It will also believe what you tell it, and it will drive your reactions and responses accordingly based on those beliefs without asking for logic or rationale from the conscious mind. So, when you catch yourself saying, "I'll feel so much better *when* I get in shape," guess what is going to happen? You *will* feel better *when* you get in shape. But what about until then? Or what if you get in shape and then get back out of shape again? Are you doomed to be unhappy until being in shape is a permanent state? The short answer is no but applying some personal empowerment will help. Your brain is like a supercomputer and your thoughts are like software that tells that supercomputer how to act. How about we write some new code for that software? Think of all the things in your life that are dangling. These are the desires, wishes, and goals that you are hoping for and working on. For example, number one on my list would be: Finish the *Soul-to-Sisterhood* book. No need to project an emotional outcome just yet. Think on it and create a list below of what you would like to happen - **for *you*.**

Desires, Wishes, and Goals
1.
2.
3.
4.
5.
6.
7.
8.
9.
10.

Now, let's work through this list with positivity, empowerment, and visualization. For each item 1-10, pick a few words from the lists below that might represent how you will feel when it is accomplished. Write the feeling words alongside your desires, wishes, and goals on the lines above.

Happy	Ready	Skillful	Perceptive	Revitalized
Relaxed	Ecstatic	Talented	Wise	Motivated
Fulfilled	Open	Complete	Transformed	Restored
Peaceful	Rewarded	Magickal	Energized	Invigorated
Joyful	Content	Loved	Strengthened	Available
Satisfied	Exuberant	Blissful	Thrilled	Present
Accomplished	Justified	Clever	Empowered	Tickled
Elated	Delighted	Organized	Tidy	Valid

Next, put each feeling that you've written on lines 1-10 into **I AM** statements and say them out loud.

- For example, if on the list above you've written words like thrilled, happy, valid, organized, delighted, or accomplished, then your **I AM** statements will be: I AM *thrilled*. I AM *happy*. I AM *valid*. I AM *organized*. I AM *delighted*. I AM *accomplished*.
  - How does it feel to verbally *claim* these things? _____

_____

Now, visualize the all of the things 1-10 on your list actually happening. In doing this, you are writing new imagination software for your supercomputer. As you visualize, see everything on your list materializing in the best way for the Highest Good.

- How does it feel to *visualize* these things happening? _____

_____

Once you have visualized the wish, desire, or goal as a reality, say "Thank you." This helps your supercomputer run the new code which allows the subconscious mind to believe that it has already happened.

- How does it feel to express *gratitude* for these things? _____

_____

Finally, let's put it all together. Choose one of your **I AM** statements and couple it with a verbal declaration of a wish, desire, or goal from your list as if it has already happened. Follow that with a visualization of your success and finish with a "**Thank you**." If I were to do this with my example from above, it would look as follows:

- I verbally claim- "I AM ecstatic! I have finished the *Soul-to-Sisterhood* book."
- I visualize this happening by imagining myself doing a happy dance as I hand over a printed copy of the book to my mom.
- I finish by expressing my gratitude with a "Thank you."

Do these steps with each item on your desires, wishes, and goals list and be sure to say them **OUT LOUD**! If it feels right, take a few more minutes to journal or reflect around the following questions.

- How did putting everything together feel? _____

_____

- What realizations came forward? _____

_____

- What was helpful about the visualizations? _____

_____

- How will the **I AM** statements offer support? _____
  _____

- How is expressing gratitude helpful? _____
  _____

Thank you. There were a lot of steps to this activity and your time is precious. I am very grateful that you dedicated this time and space to yourself. You are worth it! I love you.

~ SPS #2: ~
* Mirroring *

Eye contact is a powerful way to connect. It allows us to gauge and monitor facial expressions, body language, and the more subtle nuances of the eyes, which many agree are the windows to the Soul. Studying human behavior - either consciously or unconsciously via eye contact, facial expressions, and body language - helps us gather information and learn things from each other. It also helps us make connections. This process is known as mirroring. Mirroring, which is based on the understanding of how our Mirror Neurons work in the brain to create attachment, is vitally important to us from birth onward. How else do we, as infants, figure out how to become humans? We watch and we mirror. In fact, mirroring becomes so second nature that we do it all the time without much awareness. It's kind of like a superpower because it allows us to *know* things. Mirroring directly communicates information based on feelings that stem from the assessment, interpretation, and translation of non-verbal communication. This non-verbal exchange affords us the ability to receive very powerful messages regarding the behaviors, needs, urges, feelings, and sensations of others. Once we have this information, Mirror Neurons help us provide empathic responses. When working efficiently, this is a beautifully compassionate system for relating to ourselves and each other. When not working efficiently, the information can suffer a communication breakdown because it is now known that when under stress or duress, our mirror neurons stop functioning properly. When we are compromised, these superpowers of relatability, understanding, and considerate receptivity stop functioning at optimal capacity. No wonder our most intimate relationships suffer when we are stressed! Have you ever looked at a loved one while in the midst of an argument and thought, "Who *is* this person?" Is it any surprise that you didn't recognize them? Your mirror neurons weren't allowed to do their job because there was a hostile takeover. What about when it comes to yourself? Have you looked in the mirror and thought, "Who *is* this woman? or 'Where did I *go*?" Stress renders the accurate recognition of feelings, behaviors, sensations, and expressions extremely difficult. When we aren't closely aware of those things, how can we meet our needs? But what if we can revitalize our Mirror Neurons with self-informed self-care? Get in front of a mirror that is big enough for you to see your entire face, and with a suspension of criticism, look at yourself. Look into your eyes. What do you see? Look at your forehead, cheeks, nose, mouth, and chin. What do you notice? What do you recognize? What information do your features have for you? Try out some expressions. Mirror to yourself feeling angry, sad, happy, and lonely. Play with being silly, grumpy, tired, and wild. Be aware of what it feels like to be perfectly mirrored in every movement. As you look at yourself, begin to create a new relationship and ask…

- How do I really **feel** right now? _____

- What do I really **think** right now? _____

- What do I really **want** right now? _____
- What do I really **need** right now? _____

From this mirrored and informed place of self-care, think about how you will empathically and compassionately meet your own needs. Continue to look at yourself and recharge your Superpower of *knowing* as you visualize the Mirror Neurons in your brain being reconnected and rewired. In this moment, resolve to relate to yourself with understanding and receptivity because your feelings, thoughts, and choices are important. When you are ready, complete the following statements.

- I will honor my **feelings** by _____
  _____

- I will attentively hear my **thoughts** by _____
  _____

- I will lovingly consider my **actions** and **choices** by _____
  _____

- I will empathically meet my **needs** by _____
  _____

- I will compassionately accept my **wants** by _____
  _____

Keep a mirror close and remember, you can always revitalize your Mirror Neurons by turning-on and tuning-in to yourself. Like I said above, this is *self-informed* self-care. You see you. I see you. You love you. I love you. You get yourself a cup of coffee. You get me a cup of coffee. Just kidding. I love you. Thank you for mirroring with me.

~ SPS #3: ~
* Higher Self Support *

Who do you look up to? Who do you admire? It doesn't have to be a person you know, or even a person at all. It can be anyone or anything. This is someone whom, if they were standing in the room with you, you would be acting and responding from your Highest Self no matter what. For instance, you wouldn't want this *being* to see you losing your marbles in the grocery store because the lady in front of you is using her *all* of her coupons. Make your list and have as many on there as you need. Don't hesitate to go big. Put Ghandi and Mother Teresa on there if they resonate. God and Goddess are available. Write down a celebrity crush or two. How about a teacher? Your grandma? Your inner child? What about Mother Earth? I know I wouldn't want her to see me rushing my daughter out of the house in the morning (that version of me is *not* my best self). You can even personify an energy... what would Love and Faith look like if they were sitting in your living room? How about Growth and Transformation? Try to come up with at least 20 and make sure to include yourself.

Beings I Admire....				
1.	5.	9.	13.	17.
2.	6.	10.	14.	18.
3.	7.	11.	15.	19.
4.	8.	12.	16.	20.

Now that you have a list, pick five to ten of these beings that you want to work with over the coming days. Next, locate some small-ish items around your house that can represent them. You can choose a picture of them, a Crystal, their name written on a card, a piece of jewelry, or a piece of clothing. Anything that is evocative of them and their energy will work. If you choose an object without their name or picture, make sure you devise a way to remember who the object represents. Once you have your sacred stash, find a box or bag to store them and keep this treasure trove somewhere easily accessible. When you need to connect into your Higher Self for reactions and responses that you will admire, pull it out of the bag - *literally* - and channel in the energy of whomever or whatever you have chosen. Either utilize what you admire about them and embody that for yourself, or imagine they are standing right next to you and you consciously raise your energy and vibration to match theirs. Whatever works for you - do it. The main thing is, when life gets frustrating and you feel like you are at the end of your rope, know that you can always respond with grace, love, appreciation, and respect because all of those beings that you admire - they admire you right back. What you love and cherish about them, you also have within yourself. Channel it and own it! Love you! Thanks for doing this activity!

~ SPS #4: ~
* Surrender and Acceptance *

In her story, Mary Lu shares about a deeply personal loss. She also shares about her journey to forgiveness. Two things often talked about in regard to forgiveness are surrender and acceptance. Surrender and acceptance are awesome if you can figure out how to do them in ways that are genuine and long-lasting. Surrendering and accepting are not so awesome if they feel like a relinquishment of power and protection. Sometimes, in the pursuit of maintaining a sense of power and protection around the inexplicable and hurtful events of life, we can get hyper-focused on the details. We can become habituated to the detective work of uncovering and proving the *facts*. We may not mean to, but this search for logistics can be an unconscious way to keep us from feeling our feelings. This tethering to the particulars of a situation not only prevents us from accessing surrender and acceptance, these distractions also keep us from what neuroscience tells us is essential for healing to occur: **connection.** Trauma, which includes experiences that are unpredictable, hurtful, or scary, can make us feel isolated and convince our brains that seclusion is safer than interaction. Given the opportunity, seclusion can put us on a continual loop of reliving the facts and repeating what has happened. What if an approach to all of this - facts and details, surrender and acceptance, forgiveness and connection - could take place in steps that felt steady and safe? In no way is this activity meant to suggest that a step-by-step process is a *be-all-end-all* cure. Our lives are much more complex than that. However, if there is a situation in your life that would benefit from any of these perspectives, it might be worth giving it a try. Think of something that has happened (or that is currently happening) where you would like to employ the energies of surrender, acceptance, forgiveness, and connection. Any situation that has caused your heart to hurt is valid. Pay attention to your physical body as you decide what you'd like to work with. If something causes a catch in your breath or a kink in your tummy as you contemplate, if it feels like the time is right, use it. Now, once again, let's focus on the details.

Round One: Facts and Details

- **Who** was involved? _____
- **What** happened? _____
- **How** did it happen? _____
- **Why** did it happen? _____
- **Where** did it happen? _____
- **When** did it happen? _____

Round Two: Acceptance

- Why is it important for me to think about **who** was involved? _____
  _____

- Why is it important for me to think about **what** happened? _____
  _____

- Why is it important for me to think about **how** things happened? _____
  _____

- Why is it important for me to think about **why** this happened? _____
  _____

- Why is it important for me to think about **where** this happened? _____
  _____

- Why is it important for me to think about **when** this happened? _____
  _____

Round Three: Surrender

- Is it beneficial, or not beneficial, to remember **who** was involved? _____
  _____

- Is it beneficial, or not beneficial, to remember **what** happened? _____
  _____

- Is it beneficial, or not beneficial, to remember **how** things happened? _____
  _____

- Is it beneficial, or not beneficial, to remember **why** this happened? _____
  _____

- Is it beneficial, or not beneficial, to remember **where** this happened? _____
  _____

- Is it beneficial, or not beneficial, to remember **when** this happened? _____
  _____

Round Four: Forgiveness

- Is it in my highest good to release **who** was involved? _____
  _____

- Is it in my highest good to release **what** happened? _____
  _____

- Is it in my highest good to release **how** things happened? _____
  _____

- Is it in my highest good to release **why** this happened? _____
  _____

- Is it in my highest good to release the connection to **where** this happened? _____
  _____

- Is it in my highest good to release the connection to **when** this happened? _____
  _____

Round Five: Connection

- Who, or what, can support me in releasing the attachment to **who** was involved? _____
  _____

- Who, or what, can support me in releasing the attachment to **what** happened? _____
  _____

- Who, or what, can support me in releasing the attachment to **how** things happened? _____
  _____

- Who, or what, can support me in releasing the attachment to **why** this happened? _____
  _____

- Who, or what, can support me in releasing the attachment to **where** this happened? _____
  _____

- Who, or what, can support me in releasing the attachment to **when** this happened? _____
  _____

After you have finished, take a few quiet moments to integrate all you have done. I promise it is not my intention to bore you with question after question in the hope that you will eventually say, "Alright already! I give up! I accept and surrender! Just STOP!" This process is intricate, and it deserves time, effort, and attention. Maybe the same types of questions don't need to be repeated five times, or maybe they need to be repeated five hundred times. The point is that *you* are in charge. You are in control, empowered and protected by your own inner knowing. You decide when things feel transformed. You decide how best to heal. This activity and these questions are just guideposts. Your Higher Self, the part of you that knows without a doubt what your personal truth is, will let you know when surrender, acceptance, forgiveness, and connection are activated, actualized, and present. Thank you for doing this activity. It is exciting to think about what will be released so that new inspiration can grow. I love you.

~ SPS #5: ~
* Intentions *

For each day of the coming week ahead, set an intention for yourself. Setting intentions is a simple way to stay anchored and aligned. An intention can be anything that you would to like to embody in order to raise your energy. Fun thing about energy: when we raise ours, we also raise the energy of everyone and everything else we come into contact with. Write your daily intention on a nametag, in your calendar, text it to yourself, or claim it on Social Media. However you would like to set this intention for yourself… do it! Then do your best to live within the energy of that intention for the entire day. If this works for you, keep it up and try for a month or longer. Maybe ask colleagues and friends to join. The important part is that you choose an intention that is valid and realistic for *you*. Some examples of intentions are on the next page. When you have chosen your intention, lift it up and send it out each day by saying, "Today my intention is to live with

_____."

Joy	Openness	Authenticity	Comfort	Empathy	Forgiveness	Presence	Growth
Love	Sisterhood	Peace	Support	Productivity	Kindness	Wisdom	Goals
Bliss	Freedom	Laughter	Compassion	Intuition	Patience	Orgasms	Change
Truth	Connection	Smiles	Success	Stillness	Mercy	Strength	Security

There are only 32 ideas here, but the opportunities for living in intention are endless. Come up with more intentions in the spaces provided and have fun! As you intentionally live each day, see what happens, take notice of the shifts, and honor yourself for the daily dedication. My intention for today is love. I love **you**. I'm also grateful to you for taking this time to live your intention.

Crystal Love: Mary Lu's Crystal is the very protective and purifying Black Tourmaline (*tour*-muh-leen). This stone - revered as a shamanic talisman for ritual and guidance - can be used to clear negative thoughts, repel negative energy, clear the aura, cleanse the Chakras, and balance the right and left hemispheres of the brain. Also well-known for its abilities to create a force field around the human body for protection against environmental pollutants, Black Tourmaline can additionally offer enhanced practicality, increased vitality, stabilized emotions, sharpened intellectual acuity, and boosted creativity. Yet, the gifts of Black Tourmaline don't stop there. Try using it for a laid-back attitude with steady good spirits. Or let this stone assist you with a deeper connection to Mother Earth. Once you've felt all of these benefits, Black Tourmaline's other general contributions of promoting well-being through improved self-confidence, surplus tolerance, and extra compassion become welcome bonuses. Finally, Black Tourmaline can be empowering to those who must live or work in challenging environments, face difficult circumstances, or consistently engage with situations that feel incongruent with Soul's guidance. Play with this stone and see what happens. It just might bring about a purification so deep you'll feel like you've had a sweat lodge for your body, mind, and spirit.

Suggested Reading to Witness Life and Love Through the Lens of Feminine Spirituality, *The Feminine Face of God: The Unfolding of The Sacred in Women* by Sherry Ruth Anderson and Patricia Hopkins.

Additional Journaling and SPS Space

Pearle

I am eight years old. I love doing gymnastics and being silly. I love playing jokes and I love being a girl. Sometimes, I feel extra special because being a girl is so much fun! I'm so much fun! I know I am strong because I fly in helicopters and I do back walkovers. I am also a good friend. I think that is because I am so fun. As long as you keep having fun and as long as you are kind, people will want to play with you. That is how I know I am a good friend, because people always want to play with me. I don't remember learning how to be kind, I just started it. Now I know, being kind means that you will not be mean to other people, you will always ask them to play with you, and that you will always show them love. I do that by seeing if someone is alone on the playground and asking them to play with me. Or, noticing if someone is hurt. That way, every time you want to play with someone, someone will also want to play with you. If I see someone else being mean, I say, "Stop, I don't like that." Or, if I see someone being mean to an animal or a bug, I just tell them to "Get away!" so that everything can live happy. If you see someone trying to squash a bug, you should say, "Don't do that." The bug deserves to live. Everything needs to live the life cycle. If that bug lives, then another bug will live and then we will have a lot of bugs. When I see someone not being nice to Mother Earth, I say, "Stop it!" and, "Pick up what you dropped!" I had to talk to my friends about the Goddess. Once, we were at music class and we were watching a TV show. The show said, "God says, 'Hello.' She says, 'Hello to you.'" I told my friend standing next to me that, "God is a woman." My friend said, "No, it is just saying that on the TV show." I told her again that God is a woman, just like me. That also makes me feel strong about being a girl… knowing that I have Goddess inside of me.

Want to hear a joke?

Knock-Knock?

Who is there?

Oink, Oink.

Oink, Oink Who?

Make up your mind… are you a pig or an owl?

You really don't have to decide. It is OK to be two things at once. You can say, "Who," and you can say, "Oink, Oink, Who?" I am a girl and I am a knock-knock joke teller. I can be two things.

I say that being fun is one of my best qualities. Playing, coloring, and being with my friends are very important to me. Adults need to be better at that. They need more fun. If someone asked me for advice, I would say, don't let the sadness take over you. Just find a way and pull all of the sadness out.

Kids are going to save the Earth. We will plant more trees. We will create more oxygen.

We will teach the adults to have more fun so that when they grow up they will be more kind to others. Adults need to ask other people to come and play with them. When that happens, you are being kind.

Humans can also learn from animals. I think animals would tell humans to be more loving. I agree. I know this stuff. I am eight. I am a girl. I am fun. And, I am a good friend.

Making This Story Your Own:

Pearle's story reminds us of the importance of joy, kindness, and fun.
Take a moment, breathe, and reflect.
What stands out for you when you read her words?
Is there a situation in your life that is similar to Pearle's?
Perhaps part of her story feels connected to your own.

How can you relate her experiences to your past, present, and future?

- *My Connection to Pearle's Story* _____
  _____
  _____
  _____
  _____
  _____

Knowing that you aren't alone, let's gently explore some other themes from Pearle's story together:

- **Being Silly**
  - When was the last time you felt silly? When was the last time you acted silly? When was the last time you allowed yourself to be silly without apology, explanation, or excuse? Does being silly seem silly to you? Why, or why not? When you think about being free, wild, and playful, what feelings come up? When you think about being serious, disciplined, and subdued, what feelings come up? Is there a judgment around either set of words? If so, where did the judgment come from and is it still necessary? Can you recall what stopped your silliness when you were young? Can you remember what stopped your seriousness when you were young? What stops you from being the way you want to be now? Is this working for you? Could being silly, sillier, or acting in ways that embody more silliness, be beneficial to you and your relationships? Why or why not? Could being serious, more serious, or acting in ways that embody more seriousness be beneficial to you and your relationships? Why or why not?

- **Saying STOP**
  - How many times a day do you hold yourself back from saying "stop"? How many times a week do you hold yourself back from saying it? How many times in a month? In a year? In your lifetime? Why? Where did this suppression come from? What positive things could come from saying "stop" when you want or need to say it? What negative things could come from saying "stop" when you want or need to say it? In what way would saying "stop" shift or change your relationship to yourself? In what way would saying "stop" shift or change your relationship to others?

- **Kindness**
  - What is kindness to you? Is the kindness you give equal to the kindness you receive? If so, how have you created this dynamic? If not, why is this uneven? How has being kind benefitted you and your relationships? When you show kindness, what do you notice about yourself? When you do not show kindness, what do you feel about yourself? What inspires you to be kind to yourself and others? What stops you from being kind to yourself and others? Are there life circumstances that directly prevent you from being kind? If so, can they be shifted? If not, what are you doing to spread the energy of kindness and can you do more?

Sacred Play Suggestions:

~ SPS #1: ~
* Heart Healing *

Take a few deep breaths and visualize your heart organ. This is the organ of your continued life force. It beats and pumps rhythmically, always reminding you of its presence with just the faintest touch of the wrist or neck. Metaphysically, this organ is said to hold the pain of heartache which is often talked about and referred to as a *broken heart*. Chances are, if you heart is beating, and hopefully it is if you are reading this, you have experienced heartache and heartbreak. What do you think happens to our hearts each time we feel these big, intense feelings? Do our hearts get nicked and bruised? Do they show the wears and tears of life? What if you could create a new relationship with your heart organ that is super-easy and super-creative and what if this relationship could heal or at least *fill-in* a few of those nicks and dents? Go back to the visualization of your heart organ and ask your heart to come out of your chest for a moment. Don't worry… we are in the land of imagination and intention here, so your body won't be compromised. As your heart comes to life in front of you, really look at this magnificent organ. View it from all sides and take note of where it could use some extra tender loving care. Now, miraculously, in your left hand you have a magick wand. Take that magick wand and repair this dedicated and deserving piece of your anatomy. As you heal your heart, really *see* the nicks and dents mending. Open your ears to fully *hear* your heart rebuild where it has been bruised and broken. Zero in with your awareness and intuitively *sense* your heart restoring the pathways for love, joy, and bliss. In whatever ways these images, feelings, and messages come to mind as you visualize this healing process, trust them to be exactly what your heart needs. Once repairs are complete, let the beautifications begin! In this imaginary space of Heart Healing, you now have all of the glitter, jewels, fine fabrics, feathers, charms, and other exciting accessories that you could ever dream of! With pleasure, delight, and creativity, decorate your heart with love. Go wild! Get fancy! Have fun! Whatever your heart desires for this transformation - do it! Once the enhancements are finished, take a good look at your work. When you are ready, make a promise to your heart and write it below. End this activity with your hands on your chest, left hand closest to your skin, and say, "**Thank you. I love you**," as many times as you need. Finish by creating a promise to really see, hear, and sense what your heart needs from this moment forward.

My Heart Promise

_____

_____

_____

_____

Thank you for doing this Heart Healing exercise. Keep moving your magick wand throughout your body and ask if anything else would appreciate some healing energy. As you work, continue to really see, hear, and sense your body transforming. Don't forget the last step of beautifying and bedazzling! Love you!

~ SPS #2: ~
* Silly Selfies *

Grab your phone and take five silly selfies. Use crazy filters, graphics, apps, and other editing tools. Try to capture five different expressions. Save the pics and give each one a royally zany, silly, poetic, or empowering title that relates to a rather mundane aspect of your day. Some examples of these silly titles could be: *'Queen of Stressful Situations,' 'Goddess of Laundry,' 'Empress of Temper Tantrums,' 'Ruler of Immature Responses,'* or *'Crowned Head of Exhaustion.'* Have fun while coming up with these noble designations, and when you have taken all five photos, either print and write the titles on them or edit the photos and add the titles electronically. Next, come up with a one sentence decree for each pic based on whatever situation or issue they represent. This short proclamation for all five selfies is an amusing attempt to deal with the frustration, irritation, and general malaise these circumstances provoke. This decree isn't about censorship or maturity, it's about lettin' rip and getting as wacky and wild as you want!

For example:

- The **Imperial Decree** for the *Queen of Stressful Situations* might read:
    - When stressful situations occur, I will hide under my bed, eating chocolate chip cookies and singing "*You Are My Sunshine*" as loudly and deliberately off-key as I can, while retaining my royal right to stay there for a minimum of three hours.

- The **Imperial Decree** of the *Queen of Laundry* might command:
    - While sorting freshly laundered socks, I will purposefully toss the unmatched socks into the ceiling fan and take wagers from my children as to where in the room they will land.

Adding a layer of levity to our daily lives can help us remember that joy can be found almost anywhere. This silly selfie of you, with her silly wisdom, and silly-ness can be a reminder that you **are** fun! You **are** zany! You **are** wild! Write down your Photo Title and Imperial Decree below. Let this be proof that even when washing dirty clothes, breaking up another relentless argument, or scratching your way through yet another day of exhaustion - you got your funny going on.

- My Royally Silly Title #1 _____

    - My Totally Amusing and Wildly Entertaining Decree _____
    _____

- My Royally Silly Title #2 _____

    - My Totally Amusing and Wildly Entertaining Decree _____
    _____

- My Royally Silly Title #3 _____

    - My Totally Amusing and Wildly Entertaining Decree _____
    _____

- My Royally Silly Title #4 _____

    ○ My Totally Amusing and Wildly Entertaining Decree _____
    _____

- My Royally Silly Title #5 _____

    ○ My Totally Amusing and Wildly Entertaining Decree _____
    _____

Keep these photos handy and look at them when you need a smile. Sometimes just a short breath is all we need to pause and reset. You *are* funny and no pile of laundry is gonna take that away. Love you! Thanks for doing this!

~ SPS #3: ~
* Drawing God *

Grab a piece of paper and some art supplies and draw your interpretation of God, or Source. When you are finished, take a few moments to look at what you have created. What do you see in your work? What do you notice about line, color, image and texture? After a brief time for interpretation, read the quote on the next page.

"If we do not mean that God is male when we use masculine pronouns and imagery, then why should there be any objections to using female imagery and pronouns as well?" - **Carol P. Christ**

After reading the quote, play with adding to your drawing or creating a new drawing. Or, if you don't want to do anything, honor that as well. When you are ready, read through the next quote.

"An uneasy reaction to the word Goddess is common among women. Thousands of years of repression, hostility, and conditioning against a Divine Mother have made a deep impression on us. We've been conditioned to shrink back from the Sacred Feminine, to fear it, to think of it as sinful, to even revile it... Goddess is just a word. It simply means the divine in feminine form." -**Sue Monk Kidd**

If you are inspired, adjust your drawing to reflect any thoughts or feelings coming up or create another drawing entirely. If you do not want to change your drawing or draw something new, that is fine, too. When you are ready, read through the following quote.

"In the beginning people prayed to a Creatress of Life. At the very dawn of religion, God was a woman." – **Merlin Stone**

After reading, make any adjustments to your artwork, draw something new, or don't do anything at all. Whatever you need to do to process the feelings, thoughts, or sensations coming up, do that. When you are ready, read through the following prayer.

Our mother who art within us,
Each breath brings us to you.

Thy wisdom come, Thy will be done
as we honor your presence within us.
You give us this day all that we need.
Your bounty calls us to give and receive
all that is loving and pleasurable.
You are the courage that moves us to be true to ourselves
and we act with grace and power.
We relax into your cycles of birth, growth, death, and renewal.
Out of the womb, the darkness, the void, comes new life.
For you are the Mother of All Things.
Your body is the Sacred Earth and our bodies.
Your love nurtures us all and unites us all.
Now and forever more.
-Dale Allen

Follow your heart and do what you need to do in order to support any sensations rising to the surface of your consciousness. Layer something new onto your existing work, create a new piece, or do nothing at all. When you are ready, read through the following devotion titled, *Homecoming*.

And the Great Mother said:
Come my child and give me all that you are.
I am not afraid of your strength and darkness, of your fear and pain.
Give me your tears. They will be my rushing rivers and roaring oceans.
Give me your rage. It will erupt into my molten volcanoes and rolling thunder.
Give me your tired spirit. I will lay it to rest in my soft meadows.
Give me your hopes and dreams. I will plant a field of sunflowers and arch rainbows in the sky.
You are not too much for me.
My arms and heart welcome your true fullness.
There is room in my world for all of you, all that you are.
I will cradle you in the boughs of my ancient redwoods and the valleys of my gentle rolling hills.
My soft winds will sing you lullabies and soothe your burdened heart.
Release your deep pain.
You are not alone and you have never been alone.
-Linda Reuther

After reading, just as in the previous steps, take your time to add, create, and process. When you are ready, look at your art and reflect or journal on the following.

- Where was I inspired to make changes? _____

_____

- Why? What inspired me? _____

_____

- Where did I decide to not make any changes? _____
  _____

- Why? What inspired me to leave things as they were? _____
  _____

As you think on these questions, know that all of your answers and responses are the right answers and responses for you. They connect you deeper into yourself, your inner knowing, and your own relationship *to* and understanding *of* God and Source. Place your art where you will see it often. If you would like access to these quotes - and many more like them - they can be located in the lovely and stunning pages of the suggested reading title for this chapter, *The Girl God*, by Trista Hendren. Happy exploring! Love you! Thanks for taking the time to do this activity!

~ SPS #4: ~
* Body Wisdom *

Draw an outline of a body on a piece of paper or find one online and print it out. Make sure this body outline is a reflection of your Feminine form. Grab something to write with and answer the following either on your body outline or on the lines below. Be sure to honor your first, intuitive responses to the questions.

- Where in my body do I **feel** things? _____
  - Where do I feel joy? _____
  - Where do I feel anger? _____
  - Where do I feel rage? _____
  - Where do I feel loneliness? _____
  - Where do I feel fear? _____
  - Where do I feel peace? _____
  - Where do I feel bliss? _____
- Where in my body do I **know** things? _____
  - Where do I know when something good is about to happen? _____
  - Where do I know when something not good is about to happen? _____
- Where in my body do I **hide** things? _____
  - Where do I hide my power? _____
  - Where do I hide my voice? _____

- Where do I hide my truth? _____
- Where do I hide my thoughts? _____
- Where do I hide my feelings? _____

- Where in my body do I **show** things? _____
  - Where do I show my thoughts? _____
  - Where do I show my feelings? _____
  - Where do I show my power? _____
  - Where do I show my truth? _____
  - Where do I show my Soul? _____

With this lovely and one-of-a-kind 'map,' take a few minutes and ask the different places and spaces within you to share their wisdom. Put your hands on your body and ask, "What do I need to know right now?" After receiving from your body, reciprocate by sending gratitude, acknowledgement, and love back into all of the parts that came forward to offer messages and guidance. Thank you for opening up to your bodily wisdom in this way. I love you!

~ SPS #5: ~
* Dance Time *

Find a way to listen to music where you can easily change from song to song. This can be done with a playlist on your phone, a radio, or even a playlist found online. This is a great activity to do with kiddos if you have a few handy… if not, dancing by yourself is completely OK! Trust me, I do it all the time. Use a playlist of about twenty songs and plan on at least 20-30 seconds per song. This way your body, mind, and Soul can work together on creating moves to the music. Get started and warm up to the first few tunes to determine how long you want each song to play. Scroll through and feel the groove as you move your body to the different beats and rhythms. As you dance to these short snippets of music, notice how you move differently with different parts of your body depending on the type of song. Also pay attention to different feelings and sensations coming forward. (Feeling irritated that you are dancing counts!) Once you feel warmed up, it is time to add some creativity and silliness! There are twenty-one suggestions below for moving your body. Have fun!

Dance with just your…	Dance as if…	Dance with the feeling…
-Hands	-It is freezing cold	-Happy
-Feet	-It is pouring rain	-Embarrassed
-Hips	-It is sweltering hot	-Mad
-Tongue	-It is a super big room	-Sad
-Shoulders	-It is a super tiny room	-Lonely
-Lips	-The wind is blowing 100 mph	-Scared
-Knees	-You are an elephant	-Silly

When you are through dancing and ready to cool down, take a moment to reflect by completing the sentences below.

- At first, moving my body made me feel _____

- Switching the music, I noticed _____

- Moving different parts of my body, I felt _____

- I smiled the most when _____

- I felt most free when _____

- Once I was warmed up, moving my body was _____

Great job! Getting our bodies moving can be a big help in everything from shifting energy to processing feelings. Dancing in this way can also simultaneously stimulate the body and the imagination. This allows for different layers and levels of awareness to come forward with giggles and smiles and that is a win-win in my book! Thank you for moving, grooving, and being silly. I love seeing you smile… and I love you!

Crystal Love: Pearle's Crystal is the hypnotic Tiger's Eye. This earthy stone is said to impart courage, integrity, and the emotional maturity needed to wield the *right* use of power. With abilities to synthesize the high vibes of solar and earthly energies, the calm, soothing, and protective Tiger's Eye can promote clarity of intention, ground commitments, clear away negativity, dissolve internal conflict, and brighten our moods. Sometimes called the 'Stone of the Golden Ray,' Tiger's Eye balances with the momentum of radiance, stability, optimism, and accomplishment. If you are looking to sharpen your focus, hone your inner strength, organize your thoughts, compose your feelings, shore up your self-worth, and balance your male and female energies, get a piece in your pocket because this is the Crystal for you! Additionally, Tiger's Eye can also shift us out of the world of duality, providing new perspectives and understandings around the underlying unity behind apparent opposites. This brings us more compassion and practicality when we approach the concepts of right and wrong, good and bad, and dark and light. Just as its name implies, Tiger's Eye is ever vigilant, bringing clarity to our inner vision and a better understanding of the cause and effect of each situation. Employ this stone to encourage the wisest use of power so that various components may be brought together to form the strongest and most cohesive whole.

Suggested Reading to Playfully and Meaningfully Open Your Conscious to the Feminine Divine, *The Girl God* by Trista Hendren.

Elizabeth

I'm someone who has tried a lot of different things. Kind of like Goldilocks, I'm always looking for *just right*. I've worked in the arts. I've worked in finance. I've gone on more than 100 first dates and I've believed a few guys were *the one*. Happily, as it turns out, they were not. I didn't get married until I was 46. That has been fabulous and the greatest joy of my life. Looking back, my twenties were rough. My thirties were better. My forties were really good. Very thankfully, my fifties have been fantastic so far. It would be cool if my life story mirrored a Lifetime movie heroine's. You know… one woman's triumphant story over *fill-in-the-blank* where in the end she sells her own cancer-curing candles. Wouldn't that be amazing? But that story arc probably isn't in my cards. Committing to one path against all odds isn't my thing. My life lesson has been to change course when something isn't working. For me, pain is usually a sign to re-evaluate. Our culture tells us silly things like 'follow your passion forever.' That your first love, no matter who or what it is - Shawn Cassidy or rainbow suspenders - should be your only love. But that's dumb. What you like at 14 is not necessarily the result of a Vision Quest. Maybe you're just a kid who likes something… that should be allowed to change. In my early twenties I went through some transformative experiences. Truthfully, it was a shit storm that taught me a lot about resilience. At the time, I was pouring my energy into becoming a cellist. It was a struggle. I never believed I was good enough. Even when I won competitions, I always felt that I was an imposter. Playing for five to eight hours a day in college, I began to experience a great deal of pain. During my junior and senior year, all of my small motor movements hurt. I could hardly play. I went to doctors. I studied techniques for body awareness and pain management. Nothing helped. Emotionally, I had a lot of other stuff going on. I was in love with someone. Was he *the one*? Hugely, definitely, **NO**… but I thought he was. Unfortunately, at the time, he wasn't available. Because of the pain preventing me from practicing, I stayed at my undergraduate college for my master's rather than auditioning for a more prestigious school. I was really stressed out and sad, questioning why things weren't flowing and everything was so difficult. Instead of listening to myself, honoring my feelings and maybe changing course, I kept trudging along. Then, in the spring of my senior year I was raped at knifepoint by a man who had broken into my apartment and hid in the closet. It was a terrifying 90-minute ordeal. I remember him saying, with a weapon pointed at my back, "What have you got? What have you got?" I had two cellos at the time and he took both of them. He also stole my roommate's little stereo; ultimately that's how the police were able to identify him. They found him in possession of that little stereo with my roommate's name scratched on the back. The cellos were never recovered. Because he was a serial attacker and so many women came forward to identify him, when he was apprehended, he had no choice but to plead guilty. There was no trial. He spent seventeen years in jail. The best therapy I got - which only lasted about fifteen minutes - was when all of us women were in the same room at the police station and we started to compare notes. It was this gallows-type of humor and exactly what I needed. We were all laughing and saying, "Oh yeah, that happened to me, too." It was a reminder that I was not alone… that I wasn't the only one. It was proof that we all survived. The next few years were rough. The attack changed everything. It was like that moment in *"The Wizard of Oz"* where everything becomes technicolor but in a bad, ugly way. Suddenly, I was acutely aware of rape culture. It was - and still is - everywhere. I heard it at church from my family pastor. I saw it in movies. It felt like the world was full of giant, neon signs flashing 'USE WOMEN HERE.' I went to therapy. I read a lot of different books to help me make sense of things. Radical feminist literature took my questions and poetically flipped them so that I could better understand what I was going through. Nothing was what it had seemed. There was a lot of sadness, disappointment, and anger. During those years I continued to pursue music, but without the heart for it. Finally, I was able to admit to myself that I wasn't getting enough back and it was time to go another direction. I moved to a different state and a different school. I got an MBA and a Master of Arts in Administration. For a musician with two years of high school math, it was a culture shock and a baptism-by-fire, but the people were really friendly and I loved focusing on goals that would allow me to take care of myself. I couldn't run away from the rape - I still had to go to sleep by myself *every* night - but my coping skills got better. After I finished up the degrees, I worked in arts administration. It was not my happy ending. Over the next five years, I either got fired or quit from six different jobs. That's a LOT and I'm still kind of embarrassed… but I learned the hard way that non-profits can be a shaky world and you've got to love it enough to put up with the instability. Turns out I didn't. I switched gears again and took a job in banking. No love, no passion, no childhood dreams fulfilled. Yes!! It was calm and stable and stayed that way for fifteen years. From my thirties through my mid-forties, life was on the upswing. I was able to buy my own place, make a life, go to concerts, have friends, and date. Oh, dating…. I went on a lot of first dates. I used all kinds of dating sites. I tried speed dating. I hired a matchmaker. I was set up by friends. I dated men from work. A handful of those turned into relationships which turned into broken hearts. Then I would take a vacation from dating, only to get lonely and start up again. The worst breakup was the last one in 2008. I had developed such a rigid checklist that a guy who was great on paper could easily be terrible for me in real life. The list included: never married, lives in my city, no kids, no religion. The last guy fit my checklist to a T. Unfortunately, he was also very jealous and controlling. His mood swings were really scary. After we broke up, I was done. No more. In 2009, as the economy took a nosedive and my mom sank into stage three Alzheimer's, I decided to do something I promised myself I would never do - move home. One day, not long after moving, I saw someone I knew while grabbing a coffee. She had two of the cutest kids. I even told my dad when I got home how enjoyable her children were. She and I chatted and caught up, and I told her I had moved home to help my parents. She suggested that I date her ex-husband while I was in town. That was a first. Even though I had all these rules for dating, I figured why not? I broke them all and went out with him. We met for our first date and I felt a thunderbolt. It was the way his eyes looked into mine when he smiled. I couldn't stop the feeling. We sat and talked. He was awkward and a little nervous. I was entranced. He walked me to my car and said "goodbye" and then… nothing. He was so cute, and I was thinking, "Damn it! Ask me out again!" He had no game, and I was so used to the game that I didn't know what to think. Six weeks went by and I heard nothing from him. It sucked. Then, out of the blue he asked me out to dinner. Eighteen months later, we were married. It was all very smooth. I couldn't believe how easy it was. I kept frantically looking for red flags to underlying problems, but this time there weren't any. We just clicked. Our chemistry was - and is - fantastic. He has a huge heart and is incredibly empathic. He's a wonderful father. He's super smart. He's deep. He's very, very low key. He is completely reliable. No bullshit. He called when he said he was going to call. He would say things like, "What do you think about this?" and then he would actually listen when I would respond. My husband gets up every morning and does his yoga practice. He reads his Bible. He does his daily Catholic devotion. We are so different, and yet we are so good together. It is harmonious. Ten years later, it is still calm, easy, smooth, and very loving. I'm really thankful I took a chance on a guy who broke all my dating rules. He is the best thing that ever happened to me without a doubt. I've learned that lots of things bring me joy. I am curious about many subjects. Our culture's constant harangue to be passionate is debilitating. For me, the word *passion* is loaded. For one, it can seduce us - especially women - into working against our own self-interest. With women, I've noticed that *passion* is often code for over-functioning, long-term sacrifice, and limited rewards. On the flipside, with men it usually involves healthy compensation at work and the opportunity to enjoy it on their off hours. Also, society's relentless chorus for passion can keep us from reveling in the wonder of every day. My inner world is pretty entertaining, so I tend to avoid outside drama. I love my quiet, happy life. I still love music. It takes me to a deep place inside. Only now, other musicians take me there instead of myself and that's just fine. Much of what happened to me in my early twenties was traumatic; however, I learned lessons through those experiences that can never be taken away. I learned things about myself and the world, and I have gained perspectives that are a part of me today.

In terms of religion and spirituality, I am confidently feminist and anti-patriarchy. This is my litmus test for investing my energy. I don't need to justify myself or convince anyone of anything. For young women who are struggling, know that your life experiences can be much more complex and impactful than you may realize. Everyone's path is different. If something interests you, follow it. Don't pressure yourself to feel *passionate*. If you stop enjoying it, it is OK to let it go and pursue something else. When something big happens, be patient with yourself and know that we all heal on our own timeline. If you feel great one day, enjoy it. If you feel bad the next day, it's OK! *It is **all** OK*. Trust in that. Trust that one day, you *will* feel better. You will. Like me. You'll be 55 and interested in a whole array of things that you may not be into right now. For me that's exercise, interior decorating, reading good books, laughing at reality TV, and getting involved in good causes. Be kind to yourself, know you are enough, and honor your preferences!!! You are worth it!

Making This Story Your Own:

Elizabeth's story invites us to release that which we thought we knew.
Take a moment, breathe, and reflect.
What stands out for you when you read her words?
Is there a situation in your life that is similar to Elizabeth's?
Perhaps part of her story feels connected to your own.
How can you relate her experiences to your past, present, and future?

- *My Connection to Elizabeth's Story* _____

_____

_____

_____

_____

Knowing that you aren't alone, let's gently explore some other themes from Elizabeth's story together:

- ***Breaking Your Own Rules***
    - What are some of your *rules*? Do you have any? When you think about them, where did they come from and how useful are they? Maybe your rules are really beneficial, and they could be implemented more for increased self-worth and happiness? Maybe they *aren't* all that helpful, and they need to be revised or released? What are your rules for friendships, romantic relationships, and professional relationships? Are they in alignment with who you are? Yes or no? How can they be 'broken' in order to serve you better?

- ***No Need for Justification***
    - How often do you feel the need to justify your decisions, beliefs, thoughts, and feelings? Why? Do you feel this way because of the people in your life? Do you feel this way because of your relationship to yourself? Is justification a habituated response in order to maintain the status quo of your relationships? Is there any place in your life where you do not feel the need to justify yourself? What and who is different about these places? When you don't justify yourself what

happens? What are the positives and what are the negatives? How can you find a better balance around justification?

- ***Liberation from Passion***
  - Has passion ever left you feeling depleted, exploited, or underappreciated? Does not feeling passionately about different aspects of life make you feel inept in any way? How do you feel about just being curious and interested? Is that sufficient? Would you start a new job, relationship, or make a big life shift to merely satisfy curiosity? Or, do you feel that passion - either your idea of what constitutes passion or some else's idea of what constitutes passion - must be present in order to rationalize your choices? Thinking of passion from this context, has passion or the cultural concepts around passion worked or not worked for you in any way? Have you ever used someone else's passion or the cultural concepts around passion for your own personal gain?

Sacred Play Suggestions

~ SPS #1: ~
* First Date *

How many first dates have you been on? Regardless of personal expertise level, we've all got some pretty funny expectations, ideas, and stories around first dates. Books have been written about them, embarrassing columns in magazines are devoted to them, and a general cruise through online dating sites and apps can leave our heads spinning... never mind our hearts! So much preparation, planning, hope, and energy goes into this idea of *dating*. Time and effort spent to hopefully meet another person likable enough and compatible enough to spend more time with. What if we redirected some of that energy back toward our relationship with ourselves? Why don't we take ourselves on a few dates? This is not about the painstaking idea of going out to a restaurant and sitting alone for an entire meal in the attempts to '*get to know yourself.*' That does not sound fun, wild, or joyous at all. But, what would you really like to do if someone offered to take you out on the perfect first date? Would you want sweet and romantic, charming and funny, quiet and introspective, or adventurous and playful? Perhaps a combo of all! Let's start with a few questions for your dating profile. Fill in the following sentences.

- My most awesome hidden talent is_____

- My favorite simple pleasures are_____

- What makes me feel loved is_____

Great job! These answers may help with the second set of questions regarding where to go and what to do on this awesome date.

- The place(s) I feel most relaxed_____

- I get excited thinking about_____

- I've always wanted to go_____

Now, we move on to another important part... what. to. wear!?! This isn't about looking a certain way for someone else. This is about choosing to adorn your gorgeous self and your environment in whatever ways that make you feel relaxed, comfortable, sensual, stunning, and beautiful. When you are ready, fill in the third set of sentences.

- I feel most beautiful_____

- My body feels free when_____

- I am most in touch with my higher self when I am _____
_____

Based on all of your answers, let's make this date happen! If it isn't realistic for you to actually go on this date with yourself due to constraints around time, responsibilities, or finances... don't despair. Either IRL (in real life) or IYI (in your imagination), take yourself on this date. Get clear on the following.

- Where am I going on my date? _____

- What am I going to do once I get there? _____

- What am I going to see, hear, taste, smell, and feel on my date? _____
_____
_____

- Why is this date important for me? _____
_____

- How will I turn this first date into more dates? _____

Finally, after the date, reflect about your experience and get ready for date #2!

- On the date, I felt_____
_____

- After the date, I felt_____
_____

- I deserve this effort, energy, and attention because _____
_____

- For future dates I will_____

Hopefully taking yourself on a date will become more of a regular 'thing' because we deserve it! When we do this for ourselves, the planning, forethought, excitement, and follow through can be like foreplay for self-love and self-care. That is kind of exciting to think about! Thank you for doing this. I love you!

<u>~ SPS #2: ~</u>
<u>* 5-Pointed Star *</u>

What were the earliest hopes and dreams you had for your life? Remember that potent childhood feeling when an adult would ask, "What do you want to be when you grow up?" Can you recall what it felt like to honestly answer the question with no fear, judgement, criticism, or censorship? How *did* you answer? Can you think back and hear your sweet little voice exclaiming, "I want to be a ballet dancer... a firefighter... a pilot... a teacher... a doctor!" Why did you want that for yourself? Why did you want that for the world? Maybe there was a noble or altruistic reason why your younger self wanted to claim this destiny. Maybe there wasn't. It doesn't really matter. What *does* matter is how you can utilize this youthful wisdom and authenticity to inform, inspire, and activate the hopes and dreams you currently hold for yourself and for the world *now*. As kids, getting out of our heads and into our bodies wasn't even a thing. As adults, we strive for this kind of presence and peace daily. For this activity, let's try to tap into our bodily wisdom, intentionally moving while allowing our earliest wishes to transform into realistic ideas. Stand up and take a few deep breaths. From your core, reach out with your hands and gently spread your feet to create a 5-Pointed Star with your body. The five points are: right hand, crown of head, left hand, left foot, and right foot. This is **Position #2** and this open 5-Pointed Star represents you today. Now, hunch your back and bring your arms in to create a standing fetal position. This is **Position #1** and it will represent the younger version of you. To start, reset and stand in a neutral position. When you are ready, follow the physical prompts below and answer the following questions.

- In **Position #1,** as you are hunched over, connect to a much younger version of yourself.
  - Ask her, "*What do I want to be?*"
    - Feel the answers come from your belly.
      - Reset to a neutral standing position and record the answer.

  _____

- In **Position #2,** as your body is open to receive, consciously become aware of your **right hand**.
  - Ask, "*What do I want to be?*"
    - Feel the answer being caught in the palm of your right hand.
    - Allow the information to travel from your right hand to your Heart.
      - Reset to a neutral standing position and record the answer.

  _____

- Return to **Position #1.** Answer the following question from the perspective of your much younger self.
  - Ask, "*What do I want to change?*"
    - Feel the answers come from your belly.
      - Reset to a neutral standing position and record the answer.

  _____

- Return to **Position #2**. As your body is open to receive, consciously become aware of the <u>Crown</u> of your head.
    - Ask, "*What do I want to change?*"
        - Feel the answer coming into your Crown.
        - Allow the information to travel from your Crown to your Heart.
            - Reset to a neutral standing position and record the answer.

    _____

- Return to **Position #1** and again answer the following question from the perspective of your much younger self.
    - Ask, "*What do I love?*"
        - Feel the answers come from your belly.
            - Reset to a neutral standing position and record the answer.

    _____

- Return to **Position #2**, and as your body is open to receive, consciously become aware of your <u>left hand.</u>
    - Ask, "*What do I love?*"
        - Feel the answer being caught by the palm of your left hand.
        - Allow the information to travel from your left hand to your Heart.
            - Reset to a neutral standing position and record the answer.

    _____

- Return to **Position #1**, and again answer the following question from the perspective of your much younger self.
    - Ask, "*How will my dreams help?*"
        - Feel the answers come from your belly.
            - Reset to a neutral standing position and record the answer.

    _____

- Return to **Position #2**, and as your body is open to receive, consciously become aware of your <u>left foot.</u>
    - Ask, "*How will my dreams help?*"
        - Feel the answer being absorbed by the sole of your left foot.
        - Allow the information to travel from your left foot to your Heart.
            - Reset to a neutral standing position and record the answer.

    _____

- Return to **Position #1**, and again answer the following question from the perspective of your much younger self.
    - Ask, "*How can my dreams come true?*"
        - Feel the answers come from your belly.
            - Reset to a neutral standing position and record the answer.

    _____

- Return to **Position #2**, and as your body is open to receive, consciously become aware of your **right foot**.
  - Ask, "*How can my dreams **come true**?*"
    - Feel the answer being absorbed by the sole of your right foot.
    - Allow the information to travel from your right foot to your Heart.
      - Reset to a neutral standing position and record the answer.

After all of the information, inspiration, and guidance has come through, take a moment for integration. Reflect on the messages that have come forth from both your younger self and your current self. When it feels right, get clear on the shifts, additions, and changes that can be made within your life to better incorporate and accommodate your unique, dedicated, and valuable hopes and dreams. That was a lot! Take a few deep cleansing breaths, too. Whew! Up, on your feet, moving and grooving… channeling in the good stuff… you go, girl! Love you. Thank you!

~ SPS #3: ~
* Creative Goddess *

A very wise woman once said to me, "Creativity is our birthright." However, sometimes we get told that we aren't creative, or we infer from other people's reactions that we are not creatively talented. Nothing could be further from the truth! Due to the science of Neuroplasticity, which proves that our brains can learn new things at any age, we know that fresh neural pathways can be created at any time in our lives. So, if for some reason you were told to lip sync the words in choir because your music teacher didn't like your voice, or to avoid the arts because you couldn't color in the lines… let's leave all that behind and fire up our brains to rewire the creativity-connection.

Step 1: In the empty chart on the following page, write down ten things that you have accomplished today.
Step 2: Assign each accomplishment a color.
Step 3: Assign each a number from 1-10. Try not to think about it too much, just let the first number that comes to mind be the *right* answer. You can assign the same number to different accomplishments.
Step 4: Assign each accomplishment an easily drawable object or shape.

Here is an example.

Accomplishment	**Color**	**Number**	**Shape**
Got out of Bed	Red	10	Sad Face
Made Coffee	Brown	3	Exclamation Point
Fed Dogs	Blue	1	Happy Face
Ate Breakfast	Green	5	Circle
Got Dressed	Pink	4	Spiral
Brushed Teeth	Turquoise	3	Triangle

Now, fill in your own!

Accomplishment	Color	Number	Shape
1.			
2.			
3.			
4.			
5.			
6.			
7.			
8.			
9.			
10.			

What is this, you ask? Well… congratulations are in order! With your imaginative ingenuity, you have just created a symbol key for a brand-new original work of art. Sort of a personal *paint by numbers*. Brava! Get a piece of paper and find some markers or crayons so that you can write and draw with your chosen colors. Anywhere on your paper, begin to draw the shapes from your list in their assigned color and their assigned numerical amount. Make sure you include everything. When you are finished, take a long look at your art. See how the colors, lines, and textures dance together on the page. Infer deeper meanings as you observe how your subconscious and conscious mind worked together to create and be creative. In Neuroplasticity terms: *what fires together wires together.* Allow this artwork to represent the fiery manifestations of your newly created neural hardwiring, reinforcing that you are indeed one fine, Creative Goddess! Love you! Thank you!

~ SPS #4: ~
* Rules *

In her story, Elizabeth bravely shares about her rules for dating. She also courageously shares that when she decided to "break them all," a wonderful new opportunity presented itself. If we give it some thought, most of us have rules around different aspects of our lives and these rules often play into how we navigate relationships. But where did our rules come from, and are they still pertinent? As we explore further, let's work from the understanding that our rules came into being for really good reasons… meaning, these rules were not arbitrarily created, but were created to help us feel safe, secure, in control, and empowered. Perhaps, like Elizabeth, our rules could use some revisions and updating. Maybe, just maybe, if we do this we can open ourselves up to new possibilities and opportunities for giving and receiving love. First off, we have to identify our rules. This can be challenging because sometimes the ones in need of the most revisions are the peskiest about showing themselves. Pet peeves can be a good place to start this excavation process. Take a moment and think about your pet peeves. What drives you crazy? What makes you nuts about people and their behaviors? Everything from high decibel gum-chomping to not returning texts and phone calls is eligible. As you make this list of pet peeves, sit with them for a while and figure out what the reasons and feelings are underneath the pet peeves. We've all got personal pet peeves that we experience within the context of our relationships, and universal pet peeves that we experience within the broader social and cultural context of our lives. Some hypothetical examples of personal and universal pet peeves and the feelings underneath them are below.

Step 1: Pet Peeves

Personal Pet Peeve *example*: My friends never offer to pick up the check for me when I do it for them all the time.

- **Reason Underneath the Pet Peeve** = I feel this is uneven and unfair.
  - **How I *really* feel**....
    When this happens, I feel underappreciated, not noticed, not seen, and not heard. This makes me question my self-worth, my ability to make decisions (i.e. picking '*good*' friends), and my value.

Universal Pet Peeve *example:* I don't like it when parents let their children throw tantrums in public.

- **Reason Underneath the Pet Peeve** = When kids cry like that, it is annoying and distracting.
  - **How I *really* Feel**...
    When I see this, I am triggered by my own parenting guilt. Watching a child cry brings up moments when I wish I would have had more help and support to make better choices. It also triggers the feelings of helplessness I experienced when my daughter would do this, and those feelings are not pleasant. It is easier to judge than to really look at myself and my relationships.

What do you think? Do you get the differences between the two types of Pet Peeves? What about identifying your true feelings… the ones being hidden by the irritation and annoyance? Give it a try and fill in the boxes below. Just see what comes up.

My *Personal* Pet Peeve:	
Reason Underneath...	**How I *really* Feel...**

My *Universal* Pet Peeve:	
Reason Underneath...	**How I *really* Feel...**

Step 2: Feelings

Now take a look at all the feelings underneath the Pet Peeves and relate them to your most significant relationships.

- List your most significant relationships below. These relationships can relate to a certain **person** or a certain **aspect** of your life.

For example: The relationship to a **person** could be your relationship to your *husband, sister, best friend, boss, etc*. The relationship to a certain **aspect** of your life could be your relationship to *dating, aging, parenting, sexuality, politics, social media, etc*.

- Once you have all of your significant relationships listed, begin to connect them to the **feelings** that came up underneath your **Pet Peeves.**

For example: If one of the feelings that came up underneath a Pet Peeve is *feeling intimidated* and that feeling correlates or corresponds to your relationship with your *boss*, connect them. If another feeling that came up underneath a Pet Peeve is *fear* and that feeling correlates with your relationship to your *sexuality*, connect them.

Significant Relationships			
People		Aspects	
Name	Feeling	Relationship to…	Feeling

Step 3: Rules

- Now, in the box on the next page, write the things that you *want* to feel in these relationships.

For example: Some feelings you might want to feel in your most significant relationships could be safe, secure, beautiful, important, valued, prioritized, empowered, loved, connected, respected, cherished, prized, treasured, admired, appreciated, validated, liked, popular, calm, and peaceful.

- PS. It is absolutely **OK** to want to feel **ALL** of these things in **ALL** of your relationships.

How I Want to Feel in ALL of my Relationships…

OK, let's put all of this together and figure out how we develop rules in our efforts to feel in control. First, look at the significant relationships you have listed. Second, look at the feelings you are currently experiencing in these relationships. Third, look at the feelings you *want* to feel in these relationships. Now, answer the following questions in regard to your decisions, distractions, and choices.

Question #1: What do I use to try and control the feelings I **don't** want to feel?

_____

_____

_____

Question #2: What do I use to try and control the feelings I **do** want to feel?

_____

_____

_____

Question #3: How have these things either consciously or unconsciously become **RULES**?

_____

_____

_____

Step 4: Revisions

OK, stick with me. Let's write some of these rules down. Try to come up with at least four. Together we will see where they can be revised in order to serve you better. Create more spaces if you need.

Rule #1:_____

Rule #2: _____

Rule #3: _____

Rule #4: _____

Ask the following questions in regard to each rule.

Rule #1

- Does this rule serve me and my highest good? _____
    - If yes, how? _____
    - If no, why not? _____
- Can this rule be revised or updated in order to better serve me and my relationships? _____
_____
- What revisions and updates can be made? _____
_____
- What parts of this rule are still valid and helpful? _____
- Do I even still want or need this rule? _____

Rule #2

- Does this rule serve me and my highest good? _____
    - If yes, how? _____
    - If no, why not? _____
- Can this rule be revised or updated in order to better serve me and my relationships? _____
_____
- What revisions and updates can be made? _____
_____
- What parts of this rule are still valid and helpful? _____
- Do I even still want or need this rule? _____

Rule #3

- Does this rule serve me and my highest good? _____
    - If yes, how? _____
    - If no, why not? _____

- Can this rule be revised or updated in order to better serve me and my relationships? _____
_____

- What revisions and updates can be made? _____
_____

- What parts of this rule are still valid and helpful? _____

- Do I even still want or need this rule? _____

Rule #4

- Does this rule serve me and my highest good? _____
    - If yes, how? _____
    - If no, why not? _____

- Can this rule be revised or updated in order to better serve me and my relationships? _____
_____

- What revisions and updates can be made? _____
_____

- What parts of this rule are still valid and helpful? _____

- Do I even still want or need this rule? _____

Step 5: Release

Almost done! Last step… let's shift the rules into guidelines. Remember, if guilt and shame are present, lovingly remind yourself that those old rules were there for good reasons. You didn't know what you didn't know, right? Well, now you can't unknow what you know.

Rule #1: _____

~ **Ask**: How can I shift this **rule** into a *guideline* in order to better serve my **Highest Good**? ~

Rule #1 is now the *Gentle* Guideline: _____

Rule #2: _____

~ **Ask**: How can I shift this **rule** into a *guideline* in order to better serve my **Highest Good**? ~

Rule #2 is now the *Gentle* Guideline: _____

Rule #3: _____

~ **Ask**: How can I shift this **rule** into a *guideline* in order to better serve my **Highest Good**? ~

Rule #3 is now the *Gentle* Guideline: _____

Rule #4: _____

~ **Ask**: How can I shift this **rule** into a *guideline* in order to better serve my **Highest Good**? ~

Rule #4 is now the *Gentle* Guideline: _____

You did it! You stuck with it! Congratulations! Think of how much you just learned! Pet Peeves, feelings, relationships, rules, and guidelines are all beautiful inroads to *know thyself*. Once you know yourself, you can better understand why you do the things you do and why you feel the ways you feel. The most important part of this whole lengthy process is that you applied the energy needed to compassionately understand yourself. Now you can go forward and share this level of compassionate understanding with others. Thank you! I love you!

~ SPS #5: ~
* Peacefully – Remaining - Connected *

When we experience something traumatic, either once which is known as acute or repeatedly which is known as chronic, our bodies respond. So finely tuned to our surroundings, our bodies sense danger to our physical, emotional, mental, and spiritual well-being before we are able to cognitively process what is happening. When this takes place, a chain of events gets kick-started. It is a sophisticated biological response system, but to simplify: when danger comes our way, our brains react, communication is sent to our Nervous System, and chemicals are released as our bodies determine whether or not to stay and *fight* or to leave and *flight*. This is the 'Fight or Flight' response that we've been hearing about since Middle School biology class. A third option is also present when we cannot stand and fight, or run and flight, and that is known as *freeze*. Take a moment and think of these responses and visualize what they may look and feel like for you. As a general note, because our minds are so powerful and reflecting on these feelings and sensations can bring up a range of emotions, be sure to get reacquainted with your body and your environment by taking deep, cleansing breaths between each step of this activity.

Visualize:	Visualize:	Visualize:
• Fight	• Flight	• Freeze

When you are finished, take three deep breaths focusing on bringing pure air in for the inhale and releasing anything that isn't serving you on the exhale.

Fight, flight, and freeze are unconscious response systems. We don't have to think about them and then agree to do them; they just *do* themselves. The patterns of these response systems - similar to the feelings and sensations of the original traumatic experience - also get stored in our bodies and memories. It is this multi-dimensional storage system that creates what is known as triggers. Trigger, because it is such a good metaphor, has become a very popular word when discussing these patterned responses to our environments. Understood in this way, triggers are the stored memories, sensations, and responses, standing on the sidelines of our consciousness, waiting to run back in and help us at any time with emotional, mental, and physical reactions so that we can fight, flight, or freeze when danger is perceived. Sounds perfectly logical, doesn't it? That's because it *is* logical when danger is present. But, what about when the danger is not there? Our environments trigger us all the time… an angry boss, a crying child, a heated conversation with our partners, a firework going off, a certain cologne…. all of these things - and many more - can be triggers. The thing is, unless we become aware of the fact that what is going on *around* us provokes what is going on *inside* of us, our brains will perceive all of these triggers as actual threats. Perceiving triggers in this way - regardless of an actual threat being present - can kick start the patterned chain of events discussed above. Again, totally convenient if we need the patterned responses. Not so convenient if we are having coffee at a sidewalk café and a blast of loud music sends us into a panic. Take another moment to think of what these autonomic responses of fight, flight, and freeze look and feel like for you and then go through the following questions.

Visualize: • **Fight**	Visualize: • **Flight**	Visualize: • **Freeze**
What do I see, hear, smell, taste, and feel?	What do I see, hear, smell, taste, and feel?	What do I see, hear, smell, taste, and feel?
Which of these sensations are *real* in this moment?	Which of these sensations are *real* in this moment?	Which of these sensations are *real* in this moment?
Which of these sensations are *perceived* in this moment?	Which of these sensations are *perceived* in this moment?	Which of these sensations are *perceived* in this moment?
What are some of my **Fight** triggers?	What are some of my **Flight** triggers?	What are some of my **Freeze** triggers?

When you are finished, take three deep breaths focusing on bringing pure air in for the inhale and releasing anything that isn't serving you on the exhale.

If we aren't aware of them, these triggers can keep us in a perpetual state of fear, and our invisible response patterns can keep us in a permanent state of fighting, flighting, and freezing. This continual sequence can leave us exhausted, overwhelmed, and completely devoid of the peace, joy, and connection we seek in our interactions and relationships due to almost everything being perceived as dangerous. When this happens, our imaginations get brittle and our ability to play gets compromised. To play and to imagine, we must be relaxed and receptive. In this heightened state, relaxation and receptivity isn't realistic. Without the ingenuity and resourcefulness of imagination and play, our ability to create alternate responses to triggers - both real and perceived - can be compromised. Again, take a moment and think of these autonomic responses and then go through the following questions.

Visualize: • **Fight**	Visualize: • **Flight**	Visualize: • **Freeze**
What are my **Fight** triggers?	What are my **Flight** triggers?	What are my **Freeze** triggers?
What would someone *who cares for me see* about these triggers?	What would someone *who thinks I am smart* **hear** about these triggers?	What would someone *who wants to spend time with me* **feel** about these triggers?
What would someone *who doesn't know me* **see** about these triggers?	What would someone *who doesn't know me* **hear** about these triggers?	What would someone *who doesn't know me* **feel** about these triggers?
What can I learn from these other perspectives?	What can I learn from these other perspectives?	What can I learn from these other perspectives?

When you are finished, take three deep breaths focusing on bringing pure air in for the inhale and releasing anything that isn't serving you on the exhale.

Whether they are needed to keep us alive or not, when these trigger responses become habituated and continually engaged without the use of imaginative alternatives, this is known as hyperarousal. Hyperarousal can be beneficial in situations where there is chronic trauma. However, even in those situations, hyperarousal has a high price to pay on our health and well-being. When we are not in current chronic trauma, but in *current chronic trigger* and maintaining a state of hyperarousal, it is no surprise that our health and our relationships can suffer. Well-known trauma expert, Bessel van der Kolk, M.D., in his book, *The Body Keeps the Score: Brain, Mind, and Body in the Healing of Trauma* talks about the ability to create new and different neural pathways in order to override the habitual trigger responses, thereby hopefully reducing hypervigilance and relieving hyperarousal. This process is one that applies awareness through intentional breath, movement, and levels of engagement with self and others. Again, take a moment and think of what these autonomic responses look and feel like for you and then go through the following questions.

Visualize: • **Fight**	Visualize: • **Flight**	Visualize: • **Freeze**
Become aware of: • My **Breath** • *How am I **breathing**?*	Become aware of: • My **Movement** • *How am I **moving**?*	Become aware of: • My **Engagement** • *How am I **engaging** with my world?*
What do I **see**? • Is this real? • Is this perceived?	What do I **hear**? • Is this real? • Is this perceived?	What do I **feel**? • Is this real? • Is this perceived?
Are any **triggers** present? • What would someone I know **see** about these triggers?	Are any **triggers** present? • What would someone I know **hear** about these triggers?	Are any **triggers** present? • What would someone I know **feel** about these triggers?
Again, become aware of: • My **Breath**- Is there any difference from the way I was **breathing** before?	Again, become aware of my: • My **Movement**- Is there any difference from the way I was **moving** before?	Again, become aware of my: • My **Engagement**- Is there any difference from the way I was **engaging** before?

*When you are finished, take three deep breaths focusing on bringing pure air in
for the inhale and releasing anything that isn't serving you on the exhale.*

The declarative or explicit memory is where we store everyday memories and experiences in order to bring them up, talk, and share about them with others as we bond and try to make sense of our lives. Trauma memories get stored in the implicit memory and they aren't accessible to us at will. This means that we can't easily bring up these memories for sharing and processing. That alone would be bad enough, but in addition to preventing us from being able to share about what we have experienced, the *implicit memory* storage system can leave us feeling even more alone and isolated because of what *is* allowed to come to the surface. In place of a memory coming up to be discussed, big overwhelming feelings and sensations that cannot be expressed with mere rational conversation take the stage. When this happens often enough, we begin to believe something *unfixable* is wrong. Instead of our brains and bodies being able to connect when we need the most comfort and intimacy, this patterned response and subsequent memory recall system turn us *away* from each other instead of *toward* one another. As humans, we need to bond to feel safe and we need to feel safe in order to bond. For this to happen, our brains need the magickal bonding chemical of motherhood, also known as the magickal bonding chemical of the *Feminine*: oxytocin. When we feel safe enough to play and access our imaginations, we release oxytocin. This chemical release allows us to bond. It also allows us to tap into the ancestral wisdom of tribal interdependence and interconnection. Interdependence and interconnection are ways of being that possess the energies of bonding and coming together. They are based on human-to-human caring and caretaking. For interdependence and interconnection to be successful, a foundational belief within the group must be present. This foundational belief is one that involves trusting that individual needs will be met because there is a mutual reciprocation present for the individual to always be meeting the needs of others. This energy of reciprocation, receptivity, connection, and caretaking is - in essence - the energy of the *Feminine*. Trauma happens to us all and there is no litmus test for how we feel around what we have experienced. My trauma of a bee sting and how I interpret it may be equivalent to your trauma of a serious car accident and how you interpret that. There is no black catting in trauma, meaning you can't ever compare in order to trivialize, understand, recognize, or empathize. Yet, if we can become aware of our inner processes while we reinvigorate our imaginations and release the energy of hyperarousal - while at the same time finding a way to nurture ourselves and our relationships - trauma, triggers, and our autonomic response systems just might get a respite in favor of bonding, functionality, and harmony. Again, take a final moment and think of these automatic responses, completing this activity by going through the following questions and final journaling prompt.

Visualize: • **Fight**	Visualize: • **Flight**	Visualize: • **Freeze**
Overlap the feeling of: • **Calm**	Overlap the feeling of: • **Security**	Overlap the feeling of: • **Awareness**
Add in the feeling of: • <u>Love</u>	Add in the feeling of: • <u>Joy</u>	Add in the feeling of: • <u>Hope</u>
Layer in: • <u>**Feeling Connected**</u>	Layer in: • <u>**Feeling Grounded**</u>	Layer in: • <u>**Feeling Anchored**</u>
What *insights* do I notice?	What *differences* do I notice?	What do I notice that *happens next*?

Last step, I promise! Thanks to Elizabeth for inspiring such amazing Sacred Play Suggestions and thanks to you for sticking with me. Journal around the following statement and see what other pearls of wisdom come up. Also be sure to hug yourself. Jeez, Louise this activity took some time and you are worth it! Love you! Big time!

For myself and for all of my relationships, when it is right for me, I can choose to transform the autonomic responses of *'Fight, Flight, and Freeze'* into *'Peacefully, Remaining, Connected.'*

_____

_____

_____

When you are finished, take three deep breaths focusing on bringing pure air in for the inhale and releasing anything that isn't serving you on the exhale.

Crystal Love: Elizabeth's Crystal is the adaptive, accepting, calming, and hopeful Chrysoprase (*krise-uh-prayz*). This loving stone reminds us that we are part of the Divine Fabric of the Universe, reiterating the message that every one of us is needed, valued, and wanted. If you are feeling down and caught in a negative feedback loop (focusing on the *why* of why uncontrollable things happen), use Chrysoprase to help you find the silver lining of situations with grace, compassion, and forgiveness. This stone can also assist us in supporting independence, balancing the Masculine and Feminine energies, drawing out our creative talents, providing a needed filter for when we want to speak out in anger, and energizing our Heart Centers in order to pull love energy throughout our bodies. Additionally helpful in areas of self-judgement, Chrysoprase releases us from the perceived imperfections around how we may have handled things in the past so that we can authentically and truthfully align our choices with our spiritual philosophies. Hold a piece of this gently colored stone close to your heart for increased feelings of security, trust, and meditative peace.

Suggested Reading to Poetically Flip and Understand Questions Regarding the Denigration of the Feminine, *GynEcology, The Metaethics of Radical Feminism* by Mary Daly.

Additional Journaling and SPS Space

Jennifer

I'm a mom of three girls. Oftentimes I refer to them as "my angels." They don't really understand that, but they have given me and gifted me more strength than they will ever know. When I had my oldest daughter, she gave me the courage to end my marriage. It was a toxic situation, and at that time I couldn't do for me what I could do for her. When she was nine months old, I got strong enough to leave. Eleven years later, when I had my second daughter, she gifted me my life's purpose. Two years after that with my youngest, I was gifted the permission to fully step into my powers as a warrior momma. So much has happened over these past two decades and I am grateful for every moment. Today I can say that I love my past. I can also say that I like myself. Those may sound like simple statements, but for me they are not. It has taken me a long time to be able to say those things and really own them. I used to feel so different than everyone else. I could feel the pain of the world around me in a much bigger way than my family or my friends. People made fun of me for this and accused me of being manipulative, but I was just trying to make sense of everything. When I had my first drink at nineteen, the alcohol made me feel numb. It helped me act 'more normal' and made me feel like I could finally fit in. The drug use began when I met my first husband. Before I knew it, I had a severe substance abuse problem. Thankfully, I got off of the drugs before I got pregnant with my oldest. It was that clarity that got me out of the relationship. Fast forward three years and I was married again. I was happy. My daughter was developing and growing just fine. All seemed ok. Then I got into a car accident which left me with herniated discs and the doctor prescribed heavy narcotics. That prescription caused me to lose the next six years of my life. It wasn't really a relapse because I hadn't truly gotten clean before. I stopped using drugs, but I never stopped drinking. I never looked at why I was in abusive relationships, and I certainly didn't stop abusing myself. This time, I was off to the races. I started selling drugs. I was using quantities that should have killed me. I was lying to everyone and keeping up the façade, living a double life. My husband had no idea. I was keeping up with my responsibilities. I was a school volunteer. I couldn't be an addict if I wasn't on the streets, or so I told myself. It was early in 2009 that I decided I needed to die. I was so low and so desperate. I got our handgun, and as I was about to pull the trigger, I realized that my sweet nine-year-old daughter was sleeping just down the hall. That stopped me. I couldn't do it. Not like that. I also knew that I couldn't go on in the same way. As terrifying as it was, I had to be honest with my husband. I had tried unsuccessfully to quit on my own dozens of times and this time I needed his help. We reached out for the support of a home detox program. I made it to 76 days clean before all of the pain that I had been masking came up; but this time I didn't use. I reached out for support instead. I found a twelve-step meeting happening the next morning and that changed my life. Ten months went by and I stayed sober. I also had some big realizations. My husband had proven himself to me time and time again and yet, I was still holding things from my past over him. I didn't allow myself to trust him. One of the rules that I set at the beginning of our relationship was "no more children." Now that I was clean, I started to think about having another baby. When I went to talk with my husband about this, before the words could leave my mouth he was saying, "Yes!" over and over. We were pregnant within weeks. Sadly, this pregnancy was full of complications. I was filled with fear and guilt. I was convinced that the issues were my fault for all of the shitty things I had done when using. I thought it was my karma for being an addict and this was my payback. I don't talk about that very often. It is hard. I know different now, but at that time I was so overwhelmed and wasn't thinking clearly. Immediately after being born, my sweet little baby had severe GI issues. She needed to be held constantly to regulate. She had to sleep sitting up, her reflux was actually projectile vomiting, and it was constant. When she was almost three, she was less than 25 pounds, she was under 25 words, and she was an absolute mess. She had huge emotional responses to almost everything, didn't get along well with other children, and her digestive issues were still quite severe. We felt utterly defeated until someone suggested we go gluten-free. Within two weeks of that dietary change, we saw a difference for her digestively; within four weeks, she was speaking five-word sentences. Something unlocked for her and for me. I began to research what was going on and connecting with other families that were going through what we were going through. The only place where we didn't see much positive transformation was in her behavior… she still struggled so much. Her meltdowns sometimes lasted forty-five minutes or longer. She would hurt herself and others around her. Her bedtime routine took more than two hours. We knew something bigger was going on. Those were some of the hardest days. I am so glad that I was clean and sober, because I don't think we all would have made it otherwise. My marriage was tested. My husband and I were roommates at best. Every ounce of my energy was given to my young daughter. Yet, somehow, through it all, I had faith. I kept getting the message that this was about more than just my family's struggle. I would sit on the kitchen floor sobbing, feeling like a failure as a mother, and I would hear a voice telling me that this was all for a bigger purpose. Even being pushed to extremes and having huge emotional reactions that I had hoped not to have as a parent, I knew somehow we would get through it. I made a promise to myself that I would find a way to connect and support other parents going through similar situations. I learned about Sensory Processing Disorder on the same day that my daughter was diagnosed, and I immediately started a support group for other parents. When my daughter was six and a half, we were referred to a neurofunctional chiropractor and that has become the last piece to our puzzle. My daughter has healed completely through this treatment. No more huge emotional dysregulation. No more constant flight or fight response. My little angel has shown me a joy and a place in life that I didn't know was missing. It has all come together. My addiction and recovery along with my daughter's healing journey have empowered me to find and fulfill my purpose of connecting and healing other families going through similar situations. All three of my angels have given me so much. I mentioned before that my youngest has helped me connect to my inner Warrior Momma, and she has, but she has also been a powerful guardian for our entire family. Having had my oldest daughter as an only child for most of her life, my husband and I knew that we wanted to have a sibling close in age to our second child. We started trying and got pregnant immediately. My higher self was definitely in charge there. As our middle daughter's symptoms progressed, and as things got more challenging, I don't think we would have chosen to have another baby if we had waited. The girls are 22 months apart and our youngest child was meant to be here for so many reasons. As we continually sought answers from the medical community, doctors kept telling me that my middle daughter was only a little bit behind schedule. They dismissed my concerns regarding her milestones and told me that she would grow out of it, but my *Momma Gut* knew better and our youngest daughter became a guide for me to trust my instincts. I knew something wasn't right. As I watched our youngest grow and develop, I had living proof that something more serious was going on. My youngest grounded me in my inner knowing that I had to keep pressing forward for answers. As a guardian, her role with her sister has been to assist and support in the most incredible of ways. She has become her sister's security blanket. Going on a slide, playing on a swing, and exploring with friends were all activities that our middle daughter wanted desperately to do, but couldn't because of paralyzing fear. We used to joke that if our middle daughter wanted to try an activity but was too scared, she would send her little sister. If her sister lived to tell about it, she would participate. Because of this, their bond is incredible. As our middle daughter has healed, the relationship has strengthened and the closeness that exists between them is beautiful to witness. All of this has taken time. It has taken tears. It has taken amounts of effort and energy that I did not believe I possessed. For other parents who may be going through similar situations, know that you are never alone. So often we isolate because we feel like we have to present ourselves in a certain way, as if everything is OK… even when it isn't. Sometimes, we are so afraid to ask for help because we feel like we should be able to do it on our own, that we should be strong. We are actually taking something away from the people around us when we do that. In asking for help, we are giving a gift. In some of my darkest moments, my soul was fed as I supported and nurtured others. Reaching out takes courage. Believing that we are in this together is an act of bravery. The more we do this for ourselves, the more our children will learn to do it for themselves. When I think about all that my family and I have been through, I am so grateful. None of it would have happened if I hadn't honored myself, my sensitivity, and my sobriety. Being who I am has created the possibility for my children to fully become who they are meant to be. Because of my three angels, I love my life, I know I am not alone, I respect my children, and I totally trust my *Mommy Gut*. What they have given me I'll never be able to give back, but I don't have to. I just have to be their mom.

Making This Story Your Own:

Jennifer's story gives us a lot to think about.
Take a moment, breathe, and reflect.
What stands out for you when you read her words?
Is there a situation in your life that is similar to Jennifer's?
Perhaps part of her story feels connected to your own.
How can you relate her experiences to your past, present, and future?

- *My Connection to Jennifer's Story* _____

_____

_____

_____

_____

Knowing that you aren't alone, let's gently explore some other themes from Jennifer's story together:

- ***Honoring Yourself, Your Sensitivity, and Your Sobriety***
    - Are there thoughts, behaviors, habits, and beliefs in your life that could use some clearing up or sobering up? Do you keep yourself distracted from your inner truths, feelings, desires, and dreams in order to maintain the status quo of daily life? If so, how long has this been going on? Where did you learn this coping mechanism? What do the distractions provide for you and for those close to you? What do the distractions take away from you and from those close to you?

- ***You Are Never Alone***
    - Do you isolate in order to keep up appearances? Is it easier to project that *everything is fine* versus asking for help? If so, why? Does it feel like you always have to be strong? Does it feel like you always have to do everything on your own? Do you feel alone? Where did these feelings come from and when did they start? Have these feelings ever been proven wrong? If so, how were they proven wrong and what happened? What would need to shift in your life for you to feel safe enough to ask for help and support? What would need to shift for you to feel safe enough to be vulnerable and authentic with another person?

- ***Finding Your Life's Purpose***
    - If you could be helping, assisting, supporting, healing, or transforming anything right now, what would it be? Why? Where did this desire come from? What does this desire tell you about the

kind of person you are? Has this energy for healing and transformation come from a particular situation in your life? Are you currently pursuing this desire to help, assist, and support? If no, why not? If yes, how have you made this happen? How can you create opportunities - or continue to create additional opportunities - to fulfill your life's purpose?

Sacred Play Suggestions:

~ SPS #1: ~
* Idea Children *

In her book, *Red Moon: Understanding and Using the Creative, Sexual, and Spiritual Gifts of the Menstrual Cycle*, Miranda Gray teaches about the concept of "idea children." According to her teachings, human children enter the world through our wombs whereas idea children enter the world through our bodies, hands, feet, and voice. Thinking about our ideas in this way, idea children deserve just as much time, energy, nurturing, and sustenance as our human children. However, sometimes if our *ideas* do not translate into *products* - things that can be seen, touched, and gauged as monetarily viable - they can go unnoticed. When this occurs, the attention and care needed for both mother and child can go unnoticed, too. In a worst-case scenario, these idea children are simply abandoned or forgotten. Take a moment and reflect on your idea children. You may have already given birth to many today! Think about it. What new understandings, compassions, relationships, solutions, and energies have you birthed since waking up? You and your idea babies deserve to be honored.

- What are some of my **idea children**? _____
  _____
  - When did I last birth new **understandings**? _____
  - When did I last birth new **compassions**? _____
  - When did I last birth new **relationships**? _____
  - When did I last birth new **solutions**? _____
  - When did I last birth new **energies**? _____

Since these babies can be birthed from many different parts of our bodies, let's open ourselves to receive the guidance generating from our physical form. Start by gently placing your hands at your feet. Hold each foot and ask the questions: "What idea children have you birthed? What idea children would you like to birth?" As you hold your body, receive the wisdom offered with love and gratitude by saying, "Thank you. I love you." Continue to move up your body and let your intuition be your guide for where to receive next. Record the wise and fertile messages below. Fill in the blank spots provided with the places where you are intuitively led to go.

Left Foot	**Right Foot**
What idea children have you birthed?	What idea children have you birthed?
What idea children would you like to birth?	What idea children would you like to birth?
"Thank you. I love you."	*"Thank you. I love you."*

Left Hand	Right Hand
What idea children have you birthed? What idea children would you like to birth? *"Thank you. I love you."*	What idea children have you birthed? What idea children would you like to birth? *"Thank you. I love you."*
Your Throat and Voice	**Your Mind and Thoughts**
What idea children have you birthed? What idea children would you like to birth? *"Thank you. I love you."*	What idea children have you birthed? What idea children would you like to birth? *"Thank you. I love you."*
_____ What idea children have you birthed? What idea children would you like to birth? *"Thank you. I love you."*	_____ What idea children have you birthed? What idea children would you like to birth? *"Thank you. I love you."*
_____ What idea children have you birthed? What idea children would you like to birth? *"Thank you. I love you."*	_____ What idea children have you birthed? What idea children would you like to birth? *"Thank you. I love you."*

Whether you are a mother to human children or not, let this exercise be a reminder that *all women* are **Mother**s, giving birth to new things on a daily basis. Thank you for giving a rebirth opportunity to yourself by doing this exercise. I love you!

~ SPS #2: ~
* I Like Myself *

Jenn gifts us some potent perspectives in her story, one of them being her declaration: "Today, I can say that I love my past. I can also say that I like myself." Thinking about those statements in regard to your life, how often have you allowed yourself to simultaneously claim both? On the next page are two columns labeled **I Love My Past** and **I Like Myself**. Begin to make a list of things that come to mind for each. Start simple. For example, 'I like myself because *I am breathing*' and 'I love my past because *I lived through it*,' are perfect. When it feels right, begin to dig a little deeper. Venture back into your past as far as feels comfortable and try to get at least ten things listed in both columns.

I Love My Past	**I Like Myself**
1.	1.
2.	2.
3.	3.
4.	4.
5.	5.
6.	6.
7.	7.
8.	8.
9.	9.
10.	10.

Now, just like we used to do in Elementary School, connect Column A to Column B by drawing lines between the things in the **I Love My Past** column that relate to things in the **I Like Myself** column. Take a look at your lists and identify how the past has informed the present. How has what you have gone through made you who you are today… a person that you *like*? Reflect on your experiences - challenging or otherwise - and see if you can create new associations between then and now. It is OK if this feels a bit wonky at first. Finding ways to love and value our biggest struggles can feel weird but try to understand how you might not have one without the other. In doing this, notice how **value** can be found in *all* of your life experiences. Also, seek to release any shame or guilt that may still be present and focus more on honoring the strength it took you to survive. As a final step, complete the following sentence. Don't forget… I like you, I love you, and I am grateful for you! Thanks for doing this!

- By loving my past, I am liking myself. In doing this, I am learning _____

_____

_____

_____

~ SPS #3: ~
* Playfully Bonded *

Chronic stress and unhappiness can wreak havoc on our bodies, minds, and spirits. They can also work in tandem to make us feel alone and isolated and once here, a vicious cycle can begin. This cycle usually goes in steps. First, we feel overwhelmed. That leads to feeling guilty because we can't just 'get it together.' When we can't figure out how to get it together, we feel helpless. Once we are here experiencing the gloom of helplessness, we can begin to convince ourselves that no one understands. After that, it isn't too much of a jump to believe that no one cares. Vicious isolation cycle, yes. Permanent isolation cycle, no. Thinking about it like this, the cycle sounds pretty concrete. However, it can shift, and it doesn't take moving mountains to do so. A little dose of Oxytocin, the social hormone of bonding and relaxation, can go a long way to improve this scenario. Oxytocin is released in our brains when we feel safe and relaxed enough to bond. How do we bond, you ask? One way is to play. When human beings engage in authentic play, we do so because we feel safe and relaxed. Once there, we can begin to create attachments and then, *voila'*... let the boding begin! Think about the last time you had a really good belly laugh with someone… or the last time that you made a new friend… Oxytocin played a part in that euphoric, joyful feeling of connection. Yet in adulthood, playing gets a bad rap. Being playful isn't considered productive. We even have common nomenclature that negativizes calling someone a '*player*.' Instead of this being a compliment, when someone is labeled a 'player' it is to insinuate that they engage in sex with multiple partners for narcissistic gain. Let's forget all of that mumbo jumbo and re-remember how to play. Let's remember that we are allowed to play. Let's also remember that we can play without the use of substances to induce and excuse a 'good time had by all.' This playfulness is about finding our own ways to be playful. Let's jumpstart the process by remembering how to be playful with ourselves. Once there, we can hopefully relax enough to think of some creative ways to begin playing with others. Wherever you are, say "later gator" to isolation and "hello" to your senses!

- What do I **see**? _____
- What do I **smell**? _____
- What do I **hear**? _____
- What do I **taste**? _____
- What do I **feel** on my body? _____
    - How can I share these sensations in a playful way? _____
    _____
    - Whom can I share them with? _____

Change your environment. Get up and take a walk or switch rooms. Check in with your five senses again: What do you see, smell, hear, taste, and feel? Now, go a bit deeper with the following.

- What am I **feeling**? _____
- What am I **thinking**? _____
- What do I **want**? _____
- What do I **need**? _____
    - How can I share these insights in a playful way? _____
    _____
    - Whom can I share them with? _____

In the box below, draw how you are feeling and thinking in the upper boxes and draw what you want and need in the lower boxes. No skill required, doodle whatever comes to mind.

How I am Feeling...	How I am Thinking...
What I Want...	**What I Need...**

- How can I share the insights from these drawings in a playful way? _____
  _____

- Whom can I share them with? _____

As a last step, put on a favorite song and reflect about what came up as you were being playful. While this energy is flowing, come up with three more activities to create a safe and relaxed energy of play and playful connections.

Activities to Activate Connection

1. _____
2. _____
3. _____

You just engaged in a four-layer, multi-step process of relaxation, connection, and play. Great job for sticking with it! The isolation cycle is kind of like a train barreling down the tracks, gaining speed and momentum when left unattended. Creating playful opportunities that promote relaxation and connection remind us to take another look. When we do, we see that the big, scary train is really just a small toy, putt-putting around the track. That can be a very relaxing perspective! Thanks for going on the ride with me. You, your connections, and your special brand of playfulness are needed in this world. Love you!

~ SPS #4: ~
* Courage Conversation *

How do you define courage? The Miriam Webster Dictionary defines courage as: *mental or moral strength to venture, persevere, and withstand danger, fear, or difficulty.* Whether or not this definition resonates, take a moment and think about your connection to courage. Ask yourself the following questions and circle the most fitting answer.

I am courageous.

Always   Most of the Time   Sometimes   Almost None of the Time   Never

My courage has been helpful to me.

Always   Most of the Time   Sometimes   Almost None of the Time   Never

My courage has been helpful to others.

Always   Most of the Time   Sometimes   Almost None of the Time   Never

I can rely on my courage.

Always   Most of the Time   Sometimes   Almost None of the Time   Never

I am grateful for my courage.

Always   Most of the Time   Sometimes   Almost None of the Time   Never

Next, imagine that your courage is sitting in the chair next to you. Use your imagination to create a character. Once the image of Courage is clear, invite Courage to have a conversation. Ask Courage the following questions and feel free to come up with your own as well.

- Courage, what would you like me to know? _____

- Courage, what would you like me to begin doing? _____

- Courage, what would you like me to stop doing? _____

- Courage, how can I serve you better? _____

- Courage, how can you serve me better? _____

After having this conversation with Courage, go back and answer the initial questions a second time.

I am courageous.

Always   Most of the Time   Sometimes   Almost None of the Time   Never

My courage has been helpful to me.

Always   Most of the Time   Sometimes   Almost None of the Time   Never

My courage has been helpful to others.

Always   Most of the Time   Sometimes   Almost None of the Time   Never

I can rely on my courage.

Always   Most of the Time   Sometimes   Almost None of the Time   Never

I am grateful for my courage.

Always   Most of the Time   Sometimes   Almost None of the Time   Never

Have your answers changed? If so, why? _____

_____

_____

As a final step, play with turning the statements into a **Courage** Mantra. See how it feels to claim a new relationship with Courage. Thank you for doing this. I honor your Courage and I love you!

I AM Courageous.
My Courage is helpful to me.
My Courage is helpful to others.
My Courage is reliable.
I AM grateful for my Courage.
I AM grateful for Myself!

~ SPS #5: ~
* Good Karma *

Many wise spiritual teachers have said that the chains of karma can be broken through acts of compassion, service, and forgiveness. It has also been said that "When we praise someone, we take on their good karma; when we blame someone, we take on their negative karma." What if we turn all of this inward and think about both concepts from the context of self-love? To rephrase from that perspective, the first statement would read: 'Through *self*-compassion, *self*-service, and *self*-forgiveness, I release karma.' And the second statement would read: 'When I praise myself, I receive good karma; when I blame myself, I accept negative karma.' Journal around those two statements and see what comes up.

- Through self-compassion, self-service, and self-forgiveness, I release karma. _____
_____
_____
_____

- When I praise myself, I receive positive karma; when I blame myself, I accept negative karma.
_____
_____
_____

Thinking about karma in this way can be a total mindset shift. From this context, no longer are we helpless in regard to the things happening *to* us. Now, with dedicated self-love we are playing an active role in our destiny thereby creating things to happen *for* us. Give it a try. Journal or reflect around the following questions and see where more self-love can be present in your life.

- How can I show myself more **compassion**? _____
_____

- How can I gift myself more **acts of service**? _____
_____

- How can I show myself more **forgiveness**? _____
_____

- How can I show myself more **love**? _____
_____

Now, praise or compliment yourself in five different ways.

1. _____
2. _____
3. _____
4. _____
5. _____

What are five different ways that you can release self-blame and self-judgment?

1. _____
2. _____
3. _____
4. _____
5. _____

Go back and journal around those initial two statements and see if anything shifts.

- When I praise myself, I receive positive karma; when I blame myself, I accept negative karma.

_____
_____
_____

- Through self-compassion, self-service, and self-forgiveness, I release karma. _____

_____
_____
_____

Repeat the 'Praise and Release' parts of this activity for the next seven days. As you do, you will increase your awareness of self-compassion, self-service, and self-forgiveness daily. The important thing is just that - **awareness**! After a full week of intentionally creating this energy of dedicated self-love, see if anything feels different. As a final step, go back and reread through everything you've written for the entire activity and complete the sentence below. This took some time and you are worth it! I want you to know, I see how dedicated you are and how open you are to receiving love, compassion, forgiveness, and service. Thank you. Here is a bit more…. Love you!

As I love myself with acts of compassion, service, and forgiveness, I notice…

_____
_____
_____

Crystal Love: Jennifer's Crystal is Amethyst (**am**-uh-thist). This Crystal has been highly esteemed throughout the ages, bringing a regal sense of composure, cooperation, and fair decision making to all who employ its uses. Sought after for its stunning beauty, Amethyst is also known for its legendary powers to stimulate the mind, soothe the emotions, calm the energetic bodies, clear unkind vibrations, and stabilize the aura. Add to this Amethyst's abilities to create a complete metamorphosis, and it is no surprise that it has earned the esteemed titles of 'Stone of Spirituality,' 'Stone of Contentment,' and 'Stone of Meditation.' The name Amethyst comes from the Greek word *ametusthos* (**am**-uh-thoost-ohs), which means 'not intoxicated,' and when held on the body, can have a sobering effect on over-indulgence. This stone also encourages continued sobriety from mind-altering substances and supports us in our freedom from addictions. Very protective, very balancing, and very motivating, Amethyst stimulates the Third Eye, or Ajna Chakra, enhancing memory, accelerating the development of psychic ability, and promoting new ideas. Turn your dreams into realities with this stone's powers to dispel and transmute lower energies into useable higher frequencies. Additionally, for those of us suffering with feelings of loss and grief, Amethyst can assist you in cultivating the stability and peace needed to heal.

Suggested Reading to Turn-On Your Inner Goddess of Oxytocin and Connection, *The Tending Instinct* by Shelley E. Taylor.

Emilie

I was born a long time ago in a little town in the middle of Pennsylvania. I had a wonderful childhood. There were three of us born in three years, and our family was filled with a lot of listening, loving, and laughing. When I was ten years old, my baby brother was born. Being older and watching him grow was an education for me. He was adorable and smart and funny. I would do anything for him at any time. Nobody could believe it. I think I was old enough to witness the natural joy of childhood through him. I would choose to be with him rather than friends my own age and I still feel the same way. From him, I learned about unconditional love. My parents strongly believed in education, so when it came time for high school I went to boarding school. I missed being home. I missed my family. Yet, life opened up for me. I met many interesting people and friends. After high school, I was accepted to Wellesley College, whose motto was "Non Ministrari, Sed Ministrare." It means 'not to be ministered unto but to minister'. I have to share it because it went into my bones. I have thought about those words throughout my life. They have influenced me personally and professionally. When caring for others or doing something that I know is going to make anything better, I feel happier. After graduation from college, I married a dashing man and we had two children. His personality was domineering, which was hard to navigate in the family dynamic. Deciding to leave the marriage was not easy. Not many people divorced in those days. Yet, at the time when I was making this decision, I had a solid sense of myself. I had moved and created a new life for myself and my family seven different times. Doing this gave me the life experience to sense that the love between my husband and myself was not there. I also had the experience of watching my parents and feeling the love between them. I did not have that in my marriage. I wasn't providing that sense of love for my children. I also trusted that I would know how to handle everything when the time came, and I did. After my divorce, I took a skills and interests test. The man administering the test went over the results and told me I should be an executive. I had done so many things before while raising my children. Just like the second half of Wellesley's motto, I ministered. I was a tutor, volunteer, teacher, and I sat on the boards of different organizations. I sold real estate. I had a business placing teachers in independent schools. I had done much, and I still wanted to do much more. Around this time, I read a book about a community foundation and something clicked. I went straight to my local Community Foundation and told them that I would like to volunteer. Much of the focus was a perfect fit for me. I loved working with donors to carry out their charitable plans, helping to invest assets, and giving effective grants to organizations which are doing important work for the community. I started volunteering and got hired shortly thereafter. After five years in the Northeast, I was recruited to Maryland to serve as president. I worked with that Foundation for eight years. During that time, I met a wonderful man. We met dancing. After two hours he said, "By the way, my name is Frank." We dated for two years before we started talking about getting married, but I didn't want to get married. I had a list of pros and cons that I showed to him. He took every one of those cons and asked me point blank what I was so worried about. The cons really had nothing to do with him and everything to do with me. Frank wanted to get married. Truthfully, I didn't want him to marry anybody else, so we decided to do it. It was a wonderful idea. I had a new professional life and a kind new husband who was excited to support me in everything. He was eager to love my children and for me to love his… eager to be one big family. I responded to that. There was so much forward movement in our marriage. We loved our home. We loved our work. Our lives were good and exciting, and we had a good relationship. Six and a half years ago, when Frank was 83, things changed. It was a time when a lot of things were finishing for me. I had loose ends tied up and I was ready for something new. It turned out that 'something new' was my husband. I was at the airport when I got the call. Frank had had a stroke. He had a blocked artery on the right-hand side of his brain, and it had impacted the left-hand side of his body. It didn't affect his cognition or his speech, but due to the severity of the physical impairment, he needed round the clock care. I was devastated. It was a constant barrage of questions: *"What is a stroke?" "Will he get better?" "How long will it take?"* For me, the new normal became a process of adapting. I was heartbroken. I would burst into tears all the time, except when I was with him. I wanted to stay strong for Frank. I also thought that I should be with him every minute of every day. Balancing and managing all of it was a lot. I had never known anyone who'd had a stroke before, so it was all new to me. Slowly we got into a routine, and for five years we focused on his rehabilitation. Frank would swim every day. We would go to the movies and out to dinner together. We found a new way of being and it was enough. Last year, Frank had another stroke. This one took away what little strength he had left on his left side. Again, I was devastated. However, this time, things have been different. We are figuring it out. I don't live in fear anymore. I fear Frank's death. I do. He is as big a part of my life now as he has ever been. Maybe bigger. More than that, I think I fear the unknown between now and then. But I have learned to stay in the moment. To trust that whatever happens, it will be OK. Maybe that comes from my early experiences of really knowing who I am. Even before all of this happened with Frank, I struggled like everyone does. One particular day, I had been wrestling with an inner conflict, trying to decide if I was doing the right thing. Back and forth my mind went. Am I doing the right thing? Am I doing the wrong thing? In the middle of this, a friend came over with her Tarot Cards and we ended up with the Hangman card, the one with the man hanging upside down. My friend told me that this situation, the one I was worried about, would resolve itself in a way I could never conceive. She was right. The situation got resolved in a way that was totally upside down from anything that I could have imagined. Like the card, the stroke has been upside down. *It has turned our lives upside down.* With this way of looking at things, I ask myself daily, "Who am I to say how things are supposed to work out?" This perspective has given me peace. I do the best I can. I get the help I can. I get support from family and friends. I take the appropriate action and I have faith. That has been the biggest learning process throughout all of this: having faith that everything will be OK. It may not be OK in the way that I thought, or the way that I wanted, but I have faith that things are going to work out. I've also learned to be still and to be loving. I've learned that when things seem out of control, if I stay still and continue loving, I feel supported. We've made it through the past six and a half years by staying still and staying in love. My life with Frank has slowed way down. We don't do much. Time seems not to go as quickly. Moment by moment and day by day is how we approach things. This way of living has given me a deeper sense of the foreverness of marriage. Our marriage has weathered it all. Frank and I are a couple forever. We all promise that when we get married. I made that promise once before and did not keep it. My relationship with Frank is different. In the past, learning for me has been a very intellectual process. This learning process with Frank is different. It has been learning through feeling and through knowing. Frank is able and capable, beyond what I could have imagined. He is always considerate about what is happening around him and what is happening with me. He has never lost his sense of living. His hope. His optimism. His brain does not talk to the left side of his body. Yet, he believes that he will walk again. I hear him telling his therapists, "I want to walk, I want to show you how I can walk." He is an inspiration. He is still completely himself, only it looks different than it used to. Through all of this time and the various things that have happened, Frank has been in seven or eight different facilities. For me, every time it's an adjustment. For Frank it's another opportunity to connect. He gets to know the staff. He gets to know all of the residents, many of whom are no longer able to communicate verbally, yet he talks to them, in any way that he can, and they all like him. I love going to visit him and seeing him make these connections. I don't know many people at this stage of life, at ninety years of age, who are still so motivated and interested in everyone else. I never used to see myself as a caregiver. Even when my children were young. Today, I see myself differently. I am gratified to see myself as a caregiver. I am enjoying it. To understand myself in this context has been a gift. All of this has. It is true we've had our challenges, but I feel more love today and I am more aware of love than I ever have been in my life. As I have allowed my perspective to calm and shift, my role has shifted as well. Frank's care and managing his existence used to be my full focus. My son would look at me during those times and say, "I'm going to pray for you, Mom." I understand why he said that. When you are in the middle of it, everything is so overwhelming and you just go-go-go, doing your best every moment of the day. Nobody can

~ SPS #4: ~
* The King *

Regardless of gender, the Feminine and Masculine energies have qualities and characteristics that we feel within ourselves and every living thing. Men have Feminine traits. Women have Masculine traits. Well-known Swiss psychiatrist, Carl Jung, described these Archetypes as the Anima: the Feminine part of a man's personality, and the Animus: the Masculine part of a woman's personality. Archetypes can be thought of as universal symbols that represent recognizable patterns in human nature. A simple way to understand archetypes is to think of fairy tales. In these magical stories, there are well-known characters, situations, settings, and plotlines. After hearing these tales over and over we begin to recognize these things and either identify with or rebel against them. We can also begin to internalize the stories and unconsciously associate them with our feelings and belief systems. Think of Cinderella. Are you the 'wait-around-for-a-prince-to-save-you' kind of gal... or are you more into saving yourself? Along these same lines, the character of the King is a familiar archetype. The good king, the bad king, and the foolish king are just three easy to identify characters represented in our stories and fairy tales. How much of each do you recognize within yourself? What about your friends and family? How about authority figures and the government? When it comes to the highest conscious expression of these Masculine and Feminine energies, I like to understand them as the Divine Feminine and the Divine Masculine. More well-known, the Divine Feminine Archetypes relate to the Lunar, Seasonal, Menstrual, and Life Cycles of the Feminine and are titled Maiden, Mother, Enchantress, and Crone. The aspects of the Divine Masculine are less well-known. In their book, *King, Warrior, Magician, Lover: Discovering the Archetypes of the Mature Masculine*, Robert Moore and Douglas Gillette have created a wonderful template for understanding these energies. Instead of calling them the Divine Masculine, Moore and Gillette define the Archetypes as the Mature Masculine. Just like the anima and animus, these traits of the Divine - or *Mature* - Masculine and Feminine are present within us all. Thinking of how they identify the four archetypes of the Mature Masculine - Warrior, Lover, Magician, and King - allow your awareness to rest within the consciousness of the King. According to Moore and Gillette, some of the qualities of the King are:

- A balanced, healed, and mature '*Father*' energy.
- A consistently centered, calm, and gentle nature.
- An integral devotion to the Land and the creatures living on it.
- A selflessly created, maintained, and bountiful goodness for all.
- A wise and compassionate leadership style.
- A deep inner knowing that the individual is not personally powerful but empowered only as a conduit of the benevolent King *energy*.

Take a few minutes to think about these qualities of the King archetype. In the following columns, free-draw on the left side and journal on the right as you meditate around how these qualities are present, or how you would like them to be more present, within your life.

Draw	**Write**

Answer the following questions as a final step.

- How can the archetypal energies of the **King** best support me? _____

  _____

  _____

- How can I best support the archetypal energies of the **King**? _____

  _____

  _____

This type of awareness around the different aspects of our psyches can seem challenging and intense. It can also offer more understanding and compassion for ourselves and others. That's my goal. When I truly love myself, I am able to truly love others... and I love *you*! Thank you for doing this activity.

~SPS #5: ~
* To Minister *

Reflect for a moment on the beautiful words and sentiments of the Wellesley College motto, "Non Ministrari, Sed Ministrare" (non **min**-i-straw-ree, sed **min**-i-straw-ray). What does the translation, "not to be ministered unto, but to minister" mean for you? Connect deeper into the words and repeat them aloud: *Non Ministrari, Sed Ministrare*. Take notice of how they feel. As you continue to say them, invite your entire body to relax. Read the following to yourself or invite someone to read it for you.

> *Beginning at your toes, move your awareness slowly upward as you release the tension and create space within in your body. From your feet to your calves, up your thighs and onto your lower back, breathe deeply and bring awareness into your abdomen. Place your hands on your tummy and attune your senses to the present moment. What do you smell, see, hear, taste, and feel? In the stillness, allow your heart to open and expand with each breath. From your heart, gently focus upwards and open your crown to receive. Connecting the energy of your heart to your crown, allow your thoughts and feelings to flow down from your Soul and into your body. Receive them with breath and space. In the quiet stillness, open yourself to love. Feel love in your body. Feel love in your mind. Feel love in your spirit. As a final piece, think of Emilie's healing medicine and repeat as many times as necessary*:

I AM still. I AM loving. I AM enough. Non Ministrari, Sed Ministrare.

Thank you for taking this quiet time for yourself. Another translation of the motto is: "not to be served, but to serve." I like both interpretations. Don't forget, your self-care *is* an act of service. When you take care of you, I am your witness and I am inspired to do the same. Thank you. I love you!

Crystal Love: Emilie's Crystal is love illuminator, Rose Quartz (kwawrts). This soft, peaceful, and feminine stone offers us gifts beyond measure. Rose Quartz slows us down so that we may calmly and gently create space for deep inner healing. Pulsing like a beacon of unconditional love, Rose Quartz stimulates our most heartfelt desires for receptivity, harmony, trust, and acceptance. Filled with sensitivity and compassion, this stone will nourish all relationships while supporting us to heal emotional wounds, stimulate love energy, release trauma, and embody forgiveness. Rose Quartz also gifts us the tenderness and empathy needed to reestablish a purified and more authentic state of self-love. Wear this crystal on your body to remove negativity, to bring clarity of emotion, and to attune your aura to the highest conscious expression of Divine loving energy. Place Rose Quartz around your home to increase feelings of beauty, peace, and connection. This stone will attract love, it will help you feel calm amidst chaos, and it will activate your heart to open wide. Working with this stone is not only transformative, it is inspirational. Gazing into Rose Quartz's spectacular vistas of splendid, glowing, rosy pink reminds us that we can all strive to **be the Rose Quartz** in every moment of every day.

Suggested Reading to Attune your Awareness to more Love Energy, *The Path to Love: Spiritual Strategies for Healing* by Deepak Chopra

Connie

I've been told I carry joy and love into every situation that I am in. If this is so, I think I owe that ability to my father. He was a single dad. He taught my brother and me that the glass is always half full. He was a whistle-while-you-work kind of guy. Even though we had our financial struggles, my brother and I were never aware of them. My dad was an artist and I remember his art studio in the basement smelling of linseed oil and paint. He would spend hours in the evening painting and drawing. I hung out there and had access to whatever I wanted. Growing up, he never judged or criticized me and always supported my decisions. Looking back, I imagine he must have been a bit nervous about many of them, but he knew the best way to build my self-esteem was to give me the opportunity to find the solutions to my own mistakes. He did the best he could, yet still my heart struggled with certain aspects of my childhood. Growing up, I loved church. I went to Catholic school until 7th grade, so I was in church every day. The stained-glass windows, the smells of frankincense and myrrh, the music… I loved the whole atmosphere. It was the teachings of 'God created man in his own image' that confused me. The image I was given of God was that of an old disciplinarian in the sky. It just didn't work for me. By the time I reached adulthood, I'd lost my sense of connection to any spiritual path. Nothing made the kind of sense that I needed to understand what God was and to feel connected to God. I knew I had to take responsibility for my own spiritual life. As I did this, I also began to take responsibility for my heart. I kind of just figured out that we are here for love. The 'image of God' that we were created to be like had nothing to do with a man in the sky. It had nothing to do with a physical image at all. What that image truly began to reflect to me were the qualities of love, compassion, forgiveness, and generosity. For me, God is Love and Love is God. *That* energy of love **is** the most important thing. When you really cultivate a loving heart, there is so much peace. A loving heart contains a natural sense of non-judgment, kindness, and responding from a peaceful and loving place. Cultivating this love in the heart is something I started exploring when I began my journey on the Sufi Path. That is where I learned practices about how to carry this love into everyday life. There are teachings from the Sufi Path intended for daily use. They start with an awareness of connecting the love in your heart to the love of the Universe - the love of the *Divine*. This is the way of carrying all of the qualities of being human into a space of non-judgment, kindness, compassion, divine discernment, and creativity. The Sufi Path gave me a better understanding of the idea that we are created in the image of God because God is within us. Therefore, if God is this huge, big, supportive, loving, and compassionate energy of non-judgment and forgiveness, then we can be the same for our fellow human beings and ourselves. As people, we too have been created to carry all of these qualities. It is important to clear the heart of anger, resentment, pain, and suffering… the things that we carry from our pasts, or from any moment of any day. When we clear these things, we are left with the light within the heart. That is who we truly are. That is what we are meant to share with others. That is how we can honestly connect with other living beings, and once we start sharing this love, we receive it back. Then, there is no reason not to love and support other people. To do all of this, I learned prayers that are meant to be practiced multiple times a day. If I get really busy and crazy with life and I don't pray, I can get pretty selfish and trite. Then it slips in… a few gossipy words here and there… I catch myself, but it doesn't feel good when it happens. I make sacred prayer beads that I wear to remind me that God is present 24/7. They sort of snap me back into alignment. This isn't something that I talk about often because I feel that the best way I can love is to be an example of love. I have to be the love. When I got married at the age of 47, I had a really good opportunity to use all that I had been practicing and praying about for years. It was easy in my small artist's studio to live a very loving and peaceful existence, but when a blended family and all of the relationship dynamics got added into my life, they provided a really good opportunity for me to test these qualities and philosophies that I had been studying and living. I had to step back. I had to release my need to be in the middle of it all. When I married my husband, I became the woman of our home, but there was a huge history of a family with parents and three children that existed before me. I had to let go of my need to be the woman in charge of all of that. I had to step back and love them all without judgment. I was very careful about giving my opinion and my perspective about choices and decisions that were being made. I let the parents of my stepchildren be *the parents* and I purposefully became a supportive character in the background. I didn't become a doormat. I would speak up if I saw something going on that wasn't healthy, and sometimes even that wasn't welcome. When I made the decision to step into that family, I had to let go of my ego. It wasn't just about what I needed anymore. I had already built a full life for myself: I had my art, my business, and my friends. Yet, when I was faced with these relationships, they were a test. They were a real eye-opener. I relied heavily on what I had learned from my Sufi teachers and I thought, if this path is really what I am here to do… always… all the time… then here is the perfect opportunity. Do I want to be forgiving? Well, then be forgiving. Do I want to be compassionate? Well, then be compassionate. I would think to myself, "If this is really who you say you are, be it with these people." It hasn't been easy. It hasn't been perfect. It hasn't always gone according to plan. Yet, all I can do is love without judgment. Over time, I realized that through all of this I still have my self-respect. At the time, I didn't know what I was doing. I didn't know what all of it would lead to, but I stayed true to who I knew myself to be. All of us can do this. No matter the situation. We can always be who we want to be in our authentic Souls. We are the ones who cultivate that. We are Souls in this life. We are Souls in this body. Do you want to grow your Soul, or do you want to compress it? Answer the question and then be prepared to make the choices from day to day that support that. We can all bring love and peace. It really is up to us how we want to live our days. It is about integrity. My father taught my brother and me to live with integrity. We don't find that outside of ourselves. We have to find that within. I have found that. I finally am listening to my Soul - directly *to* my Soul - and I not only have found that love and peace, I have found that I am truly my own blessing.

Making This Story Your Own:

Connie's story gives us many opportunities for contemplation.
Take a moment, breathe, and reflect.
What stands out for you when you read her words?
Is there a situation in your life that is similar to Connie's?
Perhaps part of her story feels connected to your own.
How can you relate her experiences to your past, present, and future?

- *My Connection to Connie's Story* _____

_____

_____

_____

Knowing that you aren't alone, let's gently explore some other themes from Connie's story together:

- ***Taking Responsibility***
    - Who is responsible for your joy? Who is responsible for your heart? Who is responsible for your Soul? Are you completely confident in your answers to these questions? If someone or something other than you is being given responsibility for the joy, love, and connection to spirit

within your life and relationships - who or what are they, when did this happen, and why did this happen? Taking the initial three questions a little deeper, what is your *core* sense of joy? What is your *core* sense of love? What is your *core* sense of spirit? How do you identify these things? Again, are they truly yours to maintain and manifest? If so, *how* are they truly yours? If not, is there a way you can begin to lovingly reclaim them and take responsibility for them?

- **Relationships**
  - In your life, do you have relationships in need of resolution, transformation, or healing? If so, how do you go about doing this? How much responsibility do you take on for managing your relationships? Is it more than half? Is it less than half? Are there certain relationships where you feel like you must be in charge? Are there other relationships where you feel like someone else is in charge? Why? When did this start? Is this your choice? Is this how you want it to be? If you would like the dynamics of your relationships to shift, what are a few small things you can try?

- **Love is the Most Important Thing**
  - Where is love present in your life? Can you create more? Where has love gone missing? Can you find it? Where is love nonexistent? Can you recreate it? Are you an example of love? If so, how? If not, why? Is love a driving force for you? Is it a driving force in all aspects of life, or just in some? How does love influence your creativity, compassion, and connection? How does love influence your hurt, anger, and fear? Do you love yourself? How? Do you love others? How? Have you received unconditional love? Can you give unconditional love? How can you carry more love into every aspect of your life?

Sacred Play Suggestions:

~ SPS #1: ~
* Prayer Power *

Prayer is powerful. It is also easy. So easy, we can overlook prayer's importance in our daily lives. In many religious and spiritual traditions, prayers are said multiple times per day. For the Sufi Tradition (a form of Islamic mysticism that practices purity of heart, detachment from material things, and a loving surrender to God) prayers are said five times per day. Can you imagine what your day would be like if you stopped what you were doing and said a prayer five different times? With all of our commitments, it can feel like we don't have the time or the space to pray. However, with just a few minutes and with very little effort, prayer - or a prayer-like meditative state - can do wonders to relax and rejuvenate us. Most of us spend more time and energy than we realize with our minds running scripts that aren't useful. Let's flip that and create a new habit. Instead of worrying about this, that, and the other, let's re-allocate a few precious moments per day to prayer. The only thing to keep in mind for this activity is: Your prayer is YOURS. Many of us have been turned off to prayer by the rules and limitations forced on us regarding the '*right*' way to pray. That is not the kind of prayer we are talking about here. *There is no right way to pray.* There is only **your** way. This is a prayer to anyone about anything and it can be said in any way for any amount of time. Just follow your heart and set the intention for the *Greatest and Highest Good to come forward for All*. The daily suggestions below to create a personal prayer practice are just that: *suggestions*. Use them if it feels right or create your own if that feels better. This prayer practice is completely up to you.

- **Day 1:** Write your prayer. _____
  _____

- **Day 2:** Write your prayer *twice* today. _____
  _____
  _____

- **Day 3**: Write your prayer. _____
  _____

  - Say your prayer aloud *three* times today.

- **Day 4:** Write your prayer. _____
  _____

  - Find an item to hold in each hand as you pray. Pray your prayer aloud *four* times today.
    - Keep the items close by. They are infused with the energy of your prayer and are now sacred. Yippee!

- **Day 5:** Write your prayer. _____
  _____

  - Set your sacred items from yesterday on a shelf or counter to create an Altar.
  - Take a picture of the Altar so that you have it on your phone.
  - Pray either at your Altar or at the picture of your Altar *five* times today.

- **Day 6:** Write your prayer. _____
  _____

  - Pray five times today at your Altar or at the picture of your Altar.
  - Find one additional time today when your mind is running or racing on something unproductive. Shift that unproductive mental energy into your *sixth* prayer.

- **Day 7:** Write your prayer. _____
  _____

  - Pray five times today at your Altar or at the picture of your Altar.
  - Find two additional times today when your mind is running or racing on something unproductive. Shift that mental energy into your *sixth* and *seventh* prayers.

Wow! Congratulations! Seven days is a great start to creating a new habit. Your prayer energy is powerful. I can feel it. I also need it. The whole world does. When you take a moment and make that moment sacred, everything benefits. Thank you. My prayer is that you feel my love and gratitude. When you are ready, take a moment to journal and reflect on these final questions.

- How does it feel to incorporate a prayer practice into your schedule? _____
  _____

- What differences did you notice? _____
  _____

- How can you maintain this daily devotional? _____
  _____

- Why is prayer important for you? _____
  _____

~ SPS #2: ~
* Love Heals *

Did you know that just looking at a picture of something you consider to be loving can raise your Immune System Responses? In his book, *The Path to Love: Spiritual Strategies for Healing*, Deepak Chopra gives a wonderful example of this by citing a study that involved Mother Teresa. In this study, participants watched films of Mother Teresa doing her work in India. The footage they observed showed her hugging and embracing children living in horrible conditions and oftentimes the children shown were suffering from debilitating diseases. After watching the films, the participants were tested and it was discovered that even if they did not personally agree with what Mother Teresa was doing, they experienced a rise in certain chemical indicators that were indicative of enhanced immune responses. Isn't that amazing? It is like our Souls recognize love and hit us with a dose of the feel-good-feels when we see it. Maybe this explains why all of those baby animal videos get millions of views? Witnessing something sweet and loving is like getting a super charge to the heart. Tears spring to our eyes, our breath catches in our throats, our minds stop racing… we slow down and focus on *love*. That is really powerful! Think about it… what happened the last time you saw a picture that reminded you of love, made you feel loved, or inspired you to give love? It may have been just an instant, but the energy around your heart probably changed. It grew is what it did! That growth process not only feels delicious, but it roots us in our pure essence: love. The reclamation of love energy - which we all recognize no matter how hardened we think our hearts to be - provokes feelings of comfort, compassion, and mercy. Those things help human beings not only feel better, but as Deepak Chopra proves, actually *be* better. They heal. *Love* heals. And since this healing process is a journey, not a destination, let's do it together. Take a moment and locate five images that connect you to the feeling of love. These images can be from magazines, online, personal pictures, drawings… whatever feels right to you. Arrange the images in order from 1-5 and create a personal prayer of love for each one. No need to think too much about this prayer. Let it flow from how the images inspire your consciousness. For example, if one of your images is of a beautiful flower, your prayer could be to notice natural beauty as Universal love. Or, if you have chosen a picture of a cherished family member, your prayer could be to unconditionally give and receive love. Write down your prayers for each of the five images.

- Image One Prayer: _____
  _____

- Image Two Prayer: _____
  _____

- Image Three Prayer: _____
  _____

- Image Four Prayer: _____
  _____

- Image Five Prayer: _____
  _____

Next, if you have printed images or images from a magazine, rip or cut out them out. Get a glue stick, some tape, or a stapler and make a collage of your five images - creating your own personal piece of 'Love Prayer Art.' Hang this beautiful representation of your love where you can see it often. Notice how it makes you feel and let it be a reminder of how powerful, pure, and healing *your* love is. It ***is***! I can feel it from here and I'm sending you loads of love right back. Thank you for taking the time to get your *love-prayer-art* on!

~ SPS #3: ~
* Creating Compassion *

Below, fill in the left-hand column with the names of people in your life who receive most of your time and energy. Start with the obvious - kids, partners, siblings, friends, colleagues, etc. Then move on to include people you may not speak to or relate to any longer, but still devote mental and emotional energy to. Next, ask yourself the following two questions in regard to these relationships. Some answers may be easier to pinpoint than others… but sit with the questions for a moment and see what comes up.

Relationship	Am I judging this person?	What am I most afraid of?

Read through your answers and see if the columns correlate in any way.

- Do the fears fuel the judgments? _____
  _____
  _____

- Do the judgments fuel the fears? _____
  _____
  _____

For the same relationships identified above, repeat the process and answer the next two questions.

Relationship	Where can I release control?	Where can I show compassion?

Read through your answers and again see if the columns correlate.

- Can compassion release control? _____
  _____
  _____

- Can releasing control create compassion? _____
  _____
  _____

For the final step, repeat the exercise with your name in the left-hand column.

Name	Am I judging myself?	What am I most afraid of?
	Where can I release control?	Where can I show compassion?

To finish, read aloud the names you have listed followed by the statement: "**Thank you for being one of my greatest teachers**." When you come to yourself, don't forget to add in some extra love. Put some in there from me, too. Thanks for doing this activity! Love you!

~ SPS #4: ~

* I AM Love *

Sit quietly for a moment and let your awareness travel to the middle of your chest. Breathe into this part of your body and visualize a beautiful green light shining like an emerald. In your imagination, witness this emerald at your chest beaming a vivid green ray of light. This light is received in the back of your body and is given from the front. As you breathe in and as you breathe out, allow the light on both sides to grow and dance on your skin. This area is your Heart Energy Center, or Heart Chakra. The color of this Chakra is green, and this sacred wheel of energy is all about unconditionally giving and receiving love, our ability to be loving and express our lovingness, our will and the emotional maturity needed to not force it upon others, and group consciousness as it relates to the collective needs and love of the group. What a mouthful, huh? With this awareness, connect back into your Heart Chakra. What do you notice?

- My Heart Chakra feels _____
  _____

- My Heart Chakra needs _____
  _____

- The back, where I receive love is _____
  _____

- The front, where I give love is _____
  _____

- My Heart Chakra wants me to know _____
  _____

As your connection to this Energy Center deepens, visualize the green ray of light infusing every cell of your body. Ask your Heart Chakra to send loving energy to the different levels of your consciousness: Physical, Emotional, Mental, Personality, and Soul.

- When my Heart Chakra connects to my **Physical** Consciousness, I notice _____
  _____

- When my Heart Chakra connects to my **Emotional** Consciousness, I notice _____
  _____

- When my Heart Chakra connects to my **Mental** Consciousness, I notice _____

  _____

- When my Heart Chakra connects to my **Personality** Consciousness, I notice _____

  _____

- When my Heart Chakra connects to my **Soul** Consciousness, I notice _____

  _____

In this place of heart-centered connection, repeat to yourself a version of Connie's wise and loving understanding of: "God is Love - Love is God."

I AM Love - Love IS ME

Sit for a few precious moments and allow yourself to be held in this love energy. You are love. We all are. Thank you for taking the time to do this Heart Centered Activity. I love you.

~ SPS #5: ~

* Core Sense of Joy *

Free write around Connie's very wise question: "What is my core sense of joy?" Put the pen on the paper, and without direction or censorship, allow your hand to write for you.

What is my _core sense_ of joy?

When it comes to your core sense of joy, have you given any power or responsibility to anyone other than yourself? It is OK if you have. Sometimes it is almost impossible not to… but it doesn't have to stay that way. Try free writing again and play with the statement: **I AM my own core sense of joy!** See what inner magick is revealed when you take full responsibility.

I AM my own core sense of joy!

What kind of things came up? Any surprises? Now, as a final step, think of three realistic things you can do *right now* to embody your core sense of joy.

- 1. _____
- 2. _____
- 3. _____

You are glowing! Thank you for doing this activity. The more you dance with your joy, the more I dance with mine. I love you!

Crystal Love: Connie's Crystal is the soft, celestial, and ethereal Selenite (*sel*-uh-nahyt). Possessing a very fine and very high vibration, Selenite can bring clarity of mind, expanded awareness of self, and powerful connections to the Angelic Realms. This stone purifies the physical, etheric, and energetic bodies by removing blockages. Polish a piece up and get it in front of you because Selenite can also act as a mirror to reflect our Divine Inner Light. A great anchor for the spiritual aspects of our awareness, Selenite offers us protection against outside influences when they are not in keeping with our Greatest and Highest Good. This ancient and powerful stone is known to open our Crown Chakra and our Higher Celestial Chakras so that we may be a symbol of cosmic justice. Knowing peace and embodying bliss is not far-fetched when you work with this Crystal. Selenite carries with it the imprint of all that has happened in the physical world and can be used to gain access into larger libraries of stored Akashic information. Use it for prayer and meditation to see the deeper meanings of things and to increase your sense of Metaphysical support or just keep a big slab close by. It can't hurt.

Suggested Reading to Release Judgment and Reclaim Joy, *Making Love to God: The Path to Divine Sex* by Ananda through Tina Louise Spalding.

Additional Journaling and SPS Space

Allison

I am a momma of two boys. I am married, second time around, for almost ten years. And, I am a twin. I am older by a minute and my mom says that I made sure to let everyone know that as we were growing up. I was the first to walk. The first to talk. The first one with hair. I was the instigator and my twin brother was my assistant. My parents told us they got a boy and a girl in one shot, so they were done. We got into a lot of trouble together as kids. We even had our own language. We are fraternal twins and we were typical until we were almost seventeen. My brother struggled quite a bit academically and socially. He was diagnosed with Learning Disabilities and ADD. Even back then he was prescribed Ritalin, although he never took it. He gave it to our dog who promptly spit it out… I hope. Yet, my brother was very, very gifted. From the age of fourteen, he was a drummer in professional bands. When he would let me tag along with him and we would drive to his gigs with the other musicians, I would watch him drum on the sunroof of the car and I was blown away at his talent. He was also a pilot. He loved aviation and flying. At the age of 16, which is the youngest age possible, he got his pilot's license. When we were little, he would always make our living room into a cockpit and I would be his co-pilot. He had the goofiest sense of humor. Nobody could make me laugh like he could. At the end of our sixteenth year, my brother had a brain aneurism. He had been sick and was on intravenous antibiotics for months. I can remember my parents fighting about giving him those medications; they were so stressed. We had to have a sterile room in our house, and he kept clogging up the port in his arm because he was always drumming. On the night it happened, it was about 1:30 in the morning. I heard this sound that woke me up. It was a sound like a wild animal would make. I ran into my brother's room. My cat, Tigger, was already there. She put her paw on his hand and as soon as she pulled it away, he started having violent seizures. It was terrifying. The ambulance came and I remember being so angry with them because it seemed like it was taking them forever get him down the stairs. We followed the ambulance to the hospital. Again, it seemed like everything was in slow motion. I was so upset and so scared. Once he was stabilized, a doctor came to talk with us. My brother was suffering from a brain aneurism and he needed immediate surgery to stop the bleeding and relieve the pressure. When we were able to see him for the first time, they had shaved his head and all of these tubes were coming in and going out. His eyes were just gaping open and machines were breathing for him. After the surgery, he was in a coma for around six weeks. From watching movies, you think that when someone comes out of a coma they just bounce back. I expected him to wake up, look at me, and say what he always said, "Hey, ya big boof!" It was much slower than that. One day he would move his thumb, the next his eyes. It was a very long and very difficult process for all of us. Years later there was a lawsuit and I had to testify. The lawyers wanted the jury to hear my story for the 'sympathetic approach.' I had to go up on the stand and talk about what our lives *could* have been like, had this not happened. It took almost a year before my brother was able to come home. So much happened during this time. My parents split up. I went from loving school to just wanting to be at the hospital every day. Some mornings, I would wake up and trick myself that I had imagined it all. Then, I would walk past our front door. From the windows, I could still see the tracks left in the grass from the stretcher. All of it would come crashing back in. This nightmare was real. I tried to maintain some sense of normalcy by staying as close to my brother as I could. His hospital room looked like a dorm room. I hung my own art pieces - which were mostly dark images with charcoal as the medium - everywhere. I played loud music. Groups of our friends would meet at the hospital before school dances. Even though I was in a really dark place, I coped where I could and somehow kept it together. Going back to school sucked. I felt all of these expectations to just be normal. No one knew what to say. People assumed I didn't want to talk about it because I was upset. They were right, I was upset… I was *always* upset. I was doing my best to make sure that both my brother and I had the most typical teenage experience possible, but there was nothing typical about what we were going through. Somehow, I graduated and went as far away as I could for college. That first year, I was so sad and angry about everything. I wanted to begin the healing process and I knew that I needed to try something different. I found a spiritual healer. I had never done anything like that before. I told her what happened to my brother and that I couldn't get over him basically dying. As she worked with me, I felt a presence. It was a feminine entity. She told me that she was with me to teach me and protect me. It was so powerful. It felt like a new beginning. The presence gave me peace and I left the healing session with a deep connection to the concept that everything does happen for a reason. I was so excited to share this with our parents. During the heartbreak of everything that happened, both of them had given up on God. I wanted to share with them what I had learned during the healing because I hoped that maybe it would help. They weren't really able to understand, so I tucked the experience away for myself. Now that I am in my forties, I have spent another birthday with my brother in the hospital. Last year for our 41st, he was in the ICU again. After the aneurism when we were teenagers, my brother was severely physically injured and suffered cognitive impairment as well. Yet, there was still so much he could do. He could write. He could walk. He and my mom would go on cruises together. This time, he had gotten into the liquor cabinet and went for twenty plus minutes without oxygen to his brain due to alcohol poisoning. Once again, we thought we were going to lose him and once again he came through… only now he is much worse off. He is blind. He cannot walk. He doesn't really know if I am there. An analogy that is sometimes used for those who have suffered a traumatic brain injury is the empty coffin. This resonates with me. It has been this way since I was seventeen, but it is definitely even more so now. My brother is gone and the body that is left is nothing like the person who left it. I can never have another conversation with him like we used to. He will never again confide in me like he did when he lost his virginity or when he would tell me about experimenting with drugs. He will never again ask to sleep at the end of my bed just so that we can be close. That part of his brain is gone. The person that I had is gone. I have his body, but I will never have my brother back. People don't understand this. They see him and think, "Oh, he looks good, he must be better." He isn't, he won't ever be. Even with the healing presence that came forward all of those years ago, a presence who I still feel around me to this day, this situation is awful. At the same time, if my brother were here… *really* here with me today, I would say, "Thank you." He has taught me so much. Through all of this, I have come to know myself extremely well. I can recognize the good and the bad, and I am so proud of who I am. I definitely know empathy. I can put myself in someone else's shoes. I can also value that most moments are teachable moments. I wouldn't choose to do it over again, but I am a better person for having gone through this life experience. My brother lived his shortened life to the fullest. I don't manage to do it all the time, but I try to live like that too. Today, I ask the uncomfortable questions to avoid assumptions and judgments. I see my children following my lead on this. They aren't afraid to find out why someone is different. When they ask questions, I don't shut them down or get embarrassed. Our differences make us who we are. If we hide them, or are ashamed of them, they become something much different. I am not OK with that. I do this because I want to authentically connect. I want to genuinely listen. Sometimes people get irritated with me, but life is too short not to follow my heart. My personal mantra today is: 'Be the kind of person I would have liked to have had around me when I was a little girl.' In this way, my brother is influencing my professional life. I am a full-time therapist for teenagers and I love my work. I don't know if I am trying to go back and change my past, or even trying to save myself by working with this age group, but if I help one student it has been worth it. When we were going through all of this the first time around, my parents handled themselves the best they could. My dad was so sad. That was hard. My mom didn't show any emotion. That was even harder. They couldn't handle the tragedy of it all and they separated. However, as my brother metamorphosed into what he is now, it has given my parents' permission to live their lives as they were supposed to. My father had suppressed his known status of a gay man since he was a tween. With the lesson received after my brother's fate, he decided to come out and now lives his truth. This has also influenced me to be open and honest with my children. Because of what I have been through, I am dedicated to parents being honest - in age-appropriate ways - with their children. Trust me, kids know much more than you give them credit for. Even when it seems so confusing and so hard, kids deserve communication and support to make sense of everything. I didn't have that. As a teenager, I had to talk with the doctors myself to find out what was going on. That hurt then and it still hurts now. I still struggle with the pain of all of this. I even struggle with being around my brother. His constant need for care is overwhelming. But I know I have to be patient and understanding with myself like I am with my clients. In this way, I take care of me. When I am not conscious of that kind of self-care, I put on a mask and compartmentalize my feelings. I get wrapped up in the future. I become that younger version of myself trying to create a typical high school experience in the ICU... staying busy and focused on anything but my feelings, my relationships, and me. I still have a long way to go, but I am at peace knowing my brother would be at peace with how things have turned out. I think he would also be at peace with how I have turned out.

Making This Story Your Own:

Allison's story shares how hardship and heartbreak can bring forth connection and healing.
Take a moment, breathe, and reflect.
What stands out for you when you read her words?
Is there a situation in your life that is similar to Allison's?
Perhaps part of her story feels connected to your own.
How can you relate her experiences to your past, present, and future?

- *My Connection to Allison's Story* _____

_____

_____

_____

_____

Knowing that you aren't alone, let's gently explore some other themes from Allison's story together:

- **The Toughest Gratitude**
    - What have been some of the most challenging situations in your life? Do you have gratitude for what has happened? Is it OK with you to have gratitude about some parts of the situation and not about other parts of the situation? Why or why not? What would it take to have gratitude about everything and everyone involved? When you reflect back on what you have been through, can you identify any silver linings? What are they? When it comes to these difficult experiences, what feelings other than gratitude are present? Are these feelings helpful? Would it be beneficial if they shifted in any way? If so, when you begin the process of transforming the feelings, what will be the first thing that you notice has changed?

- **Loving What is Lost**
    - In your life, what have you lost and what has been your process for dealing with that loss? What happens when it feels like something has been taken from you? What about when a situation or a relationship is over before you're ready to let go? Are your *inner* thoughts and feelings compatible with your *shared* thoughts and feelings? Is there a way to allow more love, understanding, and forgiveness to be present? How would shifting your relationship to what is lost shift your relationship to yourself and others?

- ***Teachable Moments***
  - Do you notice the teachable moments in your day? Do you often find yourself in situations that offer new perspectives, fresh insights, or unique understandings? Do you feel in charge of these moments, like they are happening *for* you... or does it feel a bit different, like these moments are happening *to* you? Which is a better fit and why? Would it be beneficial if your awareness of the teachable moments was different? Would you like more empowerment around them? Would you like to recognize them in new ways? Would you like to be more receptive? If so, how can you do these things in ways that bring about the best and highest good for all?

Sacred Play Suggestions:

~ SPS #1: ~
* Answering Your Own Prayer *

I was once lucky enough to get to participate in a ceremony honoring the Goddess Artemis. There were about 14 women in our circle, including my young daughter and myself. In this circle, we danced, sang, shared, and talked. It was a truly beautiful experience. At the end, the woman facilitating the ceremony had us take a piece of woolen yarn. Her direction for us was to ask another participant in the circle to tie this yarn around our wrist. As we did this final piece of the ceremony, the Sister tying the yarn was guided to whisper loving and empowering intentions as she wrapped and knotted the wool. That piece of yarn stayed on my wrist for months. It was such a wonderful reminder of Sisterhood and female empowerment that I didn't want to take it off. In fact, it is still wrapped around a Crystal in my office. Let's do our own version of this ceremony. Go scavenging around your house and find some yarn, thread, ribbon, or thin strips of fabric. When you have located your materials, choose three distinct pieces. Make sure these three pieces are long enough to be wrapped around your wrist and ankle. These little beauties are going to become subtle reminders of your love, value, and empowerment. Choose the first piece of yarn or fabric that you would like to work with. This piece is going to represent your **prayer**. Maybe you know what this prayer is immediately. Perhaps you would like to give it some thought. Either way, take a few minutes and journal around this first question.

What is my Prayer?

_____

_____

_____

Ok, now take your prayer and speak it into the first piece of yarn. In your mind, visualize this very important prayer as a warm ***Golden Light***. Witness this Golden Light wrapping around every fiber and see its luminosity weave around, through, and within as you create this new piece of **Divine Jewelry**.

- When you have spoken your prayer, finish by tying this piece of yarn around your **left wrist**.
  - We tie around our left wrist because this is the Feminine side of the physical body. We tie here so that our prayers are received with **compassion** and **mercy**, two loving qualities of the Divine Feminine.

(Note: Be sure your piece of yarn is long enough. Tying things around our own wrists can be challenging. The longer the yarn, the easier it is. You can do it!)

Now, grab your second piece of yarn. This piece is going to be the reminder of **why** your prayers are **important.** Our prayers are always important and needed. However, the chronic pull of daily life can sometimes convince us that prayers are just wishful thinking and not worthy of our time and energy in light of everything else we have to do. This is NOT TRUE! Take a few minutes and journal around this second question.

Why is my Prayer important?

_____

_____

_____

When you are ready, speak your very valid and significant reasons into this second piece of yarn. Visualize your intentional motivations for making our world a better place as a bright ***Silver Light.*** Witness this Silver Light wrapping around every fiber and see its iridescent radiance weave around, though, and within as you create this new piece of **Divine Jewelry**.

- Finish by tying this piece of yarn around your **right wrist**.
  - Our right side is the Masculine side of the physical body. We tie here so that our reasons are protected and supported with **confidence** and **strength**, two dedicated qualities of the Divine Masculine.

Onto the third and most important piece! This piece is going to represent how you will become the answer to your own prayer. I know! Crazy, right? We are so used to praying to an outside source that relying on ourselves and our own Divinity can seem otherworldly. Yet, it isn't. Many religious and spiritual practices contain teachings that Source, or however you would like to refer to this energy or entity, is **within**. That Divine Spark of creation, life, empowerment, love, and so much more is ***within us.*** So, why can't we become the answer to our own prayers? Take a few minutes and journal around this third, and final, question.

How will I become the answer to my own Prayer?

_____

_____

_____

When you are ready, speak your very clear intentions for becoming the answer to your own prayer into this third piece of yarn. Visualize these deep and profound inspirations for authenticity and love as a direct and masterful ***Platinum Light.*** Witness this Platinum Light wrapping around every fiber and see its gleaming glow weave around, though, and within as you create this new piece of **Divine Jewelry**.

- Finish by tying this piece of yarn around your **left ankle**.
  - As you already know, the left side of the body represents the Feminine. It is also said to represent the Heart. Leading with our left foot is a decisive commitment to step forward with consciousness around our **thoughts** and **emotions**. The left foot is also said to represent the Goddess Isis and her powers of **regeneration** and **new beginnings**.

You are beautiful! Proudly wear these three pieces of Divine Jewelry as a loving reminder of your prayer, your value, and your Divinity. What to do when they fall off or if you must to take them off? Your choice! It is up to you to create your next best step as you continue to cultivate your empowered relationship to your prayer. Thank you for taking the time to do this activity and to create these beautiful pieces of living prayer. You are glowing! Love you!

~ SPS #2: ~
* Angel Wings *

What would you say if I asked to see your Angel Wings? Some version of "Who? Me? An angel… I'm *no* angel!" might come out of your mouth and your reaction is understandable. A lot of us have been conditioned to question our goodness. Culturally, it is not supported for us to believe that we are pure of heart. And, hey - nobody is perfect, but that is not what this is about. Doesn't it make at least a little sense to put some attention towards reminding ourselves that we *do* care, we *are* loving, and we *desire* peace? Perhaps if we approach this Angel Wing idea with the notion that we do indeed possess Angelic qualities, it can become more manageable. Ready to give it a try? Find a quiet spot, and as you inhale and exhale, let your eyes soften - breath by breath - until they are gently closed. Bring your awareness to rest between your shoulder blades. As you do this, play with rolling your shoulders a few times, flexing them forward and backward and up and down to loosen up your muscles and bones. Next, visualize your Heart Chakra, the energetic center which rests at the center of your chest. This Energy Center allows us to give and receive love freely and unconditionally. Witness your Heart Chakra glowing a bright green as it pulsates in rhythm to the beat of your heart. With each pulse, you feel a sensation at the back of your chest. It is an open and expansive feeling that is simultaneously heavy and light. With each heartbeat, the sensation grounds and lifts, offering you a knowing that is both new and ancient. This is your Angel Wings opening and unfurling. Take a moment and record what is happening.

- What are my **thoughts**? _____
- What are my **feelings**? _____
- What other **physical sensations** are taking place? _____
  _____

As your Wings continue to unfurl and grow to their full and glorious potential, notice their characteristics. Observe color patterns, shape, size, and any other defining attributes. When you have taken in all of the Divine features of your fully expanded Angel Wings, spend a few moments either thinking about or journaling around the following.

- The **colors** of my Wings are_____
  - These colors represent_____

- The **size and shape** of my Wings are_____
  - This size and shape represent_____
- My Wings will **help me**_____
- My Wings will **help others**_____
- My Wings have this **guidance**_____
- Today, I will **use** my Wings_____

Congratulations, Angel! Your Wings are stunning. They are securely rooted and constantly present… always there to remind you of your loving, caring, and authentic *goodness*. As a final step, draw your Wings below.

My Angel Wings

Wow! Your wings are beautiful! Just like you! They are open and they are activated. Don't forget to use them when you need them. I'm right there with you, Sister. Wing tip to wing tip. Love you! Thank you!

~ SPS #3: ~
* Fairy Tale *

Have you ever made up your own fairy tale? A lot of us have probably fantasized about turning our lives into more of a fairy tale-*esque* type of scenario… but what about intentionally creating a personal fairy tale? A fantasy complete with anything and everything imaginable to be utilized for our own joy, empowerment, and freedom? It's easier than you might think. Creating a fairy tale is a well-known improvisation game. If you have kids, chances are they've probably played this in school. Kids are a great inspiration for this activity because they have no filter, no restraint, and they don't make excuses or backpedal when their ideas aren't *realistic*. You were once a little girl too, you know. What sorts of things did you dream about? Think back to that version of yourself, somewhere between the ages of six and ten, and connect into her. Remember what you looked like at this age, what kind of clothes you wore, where you lived, and what you were interested in. If for any reason you don't have a clear recollection from this time of your life, create her now. Be your younger self. Step into her consciousness. Feel her feelings. Think her thoughts. Smell her smells. Taste her tastes. When you are ready, from the perspective of your younger self, create a personal fairy tale using the prompts below.

- Once upon a time… _____.
- And, everyday… _____.

- Until one day... _____.

- And because of that... _____.

- And because of that... _____.

- And because of that... _____.

- And because of that... _____.

- And because of that... _____.

- And because of that... _____.

- And because of that... _____.

- Until finally... _____.

- And then, after that... _____.

You can turn any part of your life into a fairy tale. This activity is about joyfully and playfully utilizing our imaginations to create new ideas, solutions, and opportunities. Don't worry, you won't actually lose your grip and get lost in an alternate reality. However, releasing the restrictions on our creativity in order to step more fully into a masterful collaboration of our lives is a great way to feel reenergized and re-empowered. Asking the wisdom from our younger self to be involved is just a bonus! Concretize the activity by answering the questions below.

- Why is my fairy tale important? _____
  _____

- What did I learn from my fairy tale? _____
  _____

- How can I implement my fairy tale into my life? _____
  _____

- What is my next fairy tale going to be about? _____
  _____

What a creative creatrix you are! When fashioned and produced by us, living our own fairy tale is a testament to our empowered, capable, generative, and Divinely Feminine sovereignty. We get to play all of the characters, make all of the script revisions, and collect all of the box office proceeds. We are leading by example, way-showing with self-love, and forging a path with outstanding confidence, competence, and capability. No longer is "You act like you are living in a fairy tale!" a negative. Nope. That statement is now a compliment of the highest order. Own it. Love you! Thank you!

~ SPS #4: ~
* Inside – Outside *

Visualize your beautiful face and really see what you look like. Study your eyes, skin, nose, and lips. Consider the unique way your features fit together to make the perfect work of art that is you. Next, take a few moments and think about the face you present to the world. These are the expressions you feel most comfortable showing. We will call this version of you the '**Outside**.'

- What is my 'Outside' expression when I run into someone I know? _____
  _____

- What is my 'Outside' expression when I am stopped at a light in traffic? _____
  _____

- What is my 'Outside' expression while at work? _____
  _____

- What 'Outside' expression do I mostly show friends and family? _____
  _____

In the box below, with some pens or markers, and other crafty items that call to you, draw this 'Outside' version of your face. If you aren't a great artist, no worries! The most important thing is to honestly represent the 'Outside' face that you present to the world.

My Outside Face

Next, begin to envision how your face looks when you are showing your true feelings. This is the side of you that - when you can and are aware - you consciously hide or camouflage. These expressions are the ones you attempt to conceal with the 'Outside.' This is the vulnerable and authentic face that honestly shows how you are feeling. This is the '**Inside**.'

- What is my 'Inside' expression when I am alone? _____
  _____

- What is my 'Inside' expression when I turn away from the people and things that cause me to feel upset and hurt? _____
_____

- What is my 'Inside' expression when I drop the camouflage? _____
_____

- What is my 'Inside' expression while I sleep? _____
_____

Draw this version of your 'Inside' face. Remember, no worries about being a great artist. Just draw to honestly express this version of you.

My Inside Face

Now you have two distinct and authentic versions of you: the 'Outside' and the 'Inside.' As you look at them, think about the following questions.

- What wisdom do both have for me? _____
_____

- How are both sides valid? _____
_____

- How are both sides valuable? _____
_____

- Is there a way I can bring more balance to these sides of myself? _____
_____

- Is there a way I can bring more respect to these sides of myself? _____
_____

When you are finished, take a long look at your works of 'Inside-Outside' art and let them be reminders of your inner and outer truth and wisdom. As a final step, draw a third picture that is a respectful and balanced expression of both your 'Inside' and your 'Outside.' Give this blended version a befitting title that honors all sides of you and your feelings. Love you! Thank you for doing this!

~ SPS #5: ~
* Visible Connections *

One of my favorite principles of Drama Therapy is: 'What unites us will always be stronger than what divides us.' This statement has given me much peace over the years and if you want proof of its truth, you need look no further than a High School theatre department or a local Community Theatre. The magick of theatre can virtually extinguish perceived differences. Through the rituals of singing, dancing, and performing, friendships and connections that might never have happened elsewhere tend to flourish. When working with a cast and crew to accomplish the shared goal of getting a show up on its feet, the lines of diversity remain respected but become invisible in deference to the more important objective of producing a good show. We can all become producers with an objective like this. Instead of highlighting what makes us different, we can focus more on what makes us similar. When we do this, the objective shifts from invisible division to indivisible unity, an essential requirement for any successful production. Start simple and begin to notice the common threads. Think about it, what if you made a deliberate attempt to find and share something you have in common with someone? What might happen if your powers of observation noticed a similarity and you didn't just keep it to yourself, but you brought attention to it? The second parts of the previous two sentences - *bringing attention to* and *sharing* - are the most important and both will help to make this activity more meaningful. Not only are we going to spot things, we are going to **bring attention** to them and **share** them in the hopes of making newer and deeper connections.

Step One: Footwear

Whenever you come across anyone who has on shoes like yours (*flip-flops, tennis shoes, flats, boots, etc.*), give notice and bring attention to your similar footwear.

- If they respond and if it feels OK, find out a second thing you have in common.

    o How did this feel? _____

    _____

- What did you learn about yourself? _____
  _____

• If they don't respond, that is great, too! See what feelings come up for you around no response.

- How did it feel to get no response? _____
  _____

- What did you learn about yourself? _____
  _____

Step Two: <u>Clothing</u>

Whenever you come across someone that has on clothing similar to yours (*color, logo, style, etc.*), give notice and bring attention to your similar fashion choices.

• If they respond and if it feels OK, try asking them a question.

- What are your thoughts about connecting in this way? _____
  _____

- What did you notice about your perceptions and observations? _____
  _____

- Did any memories surface? _____
  _____

Step Three: <u>Accessories and Activities</u>

Whenever you come across someone that is wearing an accessory similar to yours (*necklace, purse, backpack, watch, earrings, phone, etc.*), or engaging in an activity similar to yours (*exercising, working on the computer, walking the dog, checking the mail, etc.*), give notice and bring attention to the similar accessory and/or the shared experience.

• If they respond and it feels OK, share something about yourself.

- What did you notice about yourself when you were sharing? _____
  _____

- What did you notice about the other person when they shared? _____
  _____

Step Four: <u>Reflection</u>

After experiencing these unique and somewhat silly opportunities for sharing and connection, take a moment to reflect or journal around the Drama Therapy Principle we started with. Thanks for taking the time to do this activity. Connection matters! I bet *we* have loads of things in common. ☺ Love you!

What Unites Us Will Always Be Stronger Than What Divides Us.

_____

_____

_____

_____

<u>Crystal Love:</u> Allison's Crystal is the highly protective, rejuvenating, and harmonizing Angel Aura Quartz (kwawrts). This type of iridescent, shimmery Quartz is created when platinum, silver, gold, or other trace minerals are bonded to the surface in a high-pressure environment. This Crystal, and its multi-hued, gossamer-like angelic presence holds intense energy for connection to both the magickal and the Divine Realms of consciousness. This stone can be used to activate the Throat Chakra, gifting us the ability to clearly and authentically communicate from our Higher Selves. Try holding this stone at your heart for increased feelings of joy and optimism. Allow the Angel Aura Quartz to work on releasing negativity while providing a welcome sense of freedom from the self-imposed limitations to creative, spiritual, and energetic potential. This stone, like the wings of an angel, is a powerful transmitter of Angelic energy which reminds us that we are indeed beings capable of calm, peaceful purity in body, mind, and spirit. As a Quartz, this crystal is a great enhancer and amplifier to use with other crystals for increased mental focus and redirecting energy. Finally, if all of that hasn't convinced you to get some Angel Aura Quartz in your life, this stone can also alleviate the doldrums by dusting off the dull and listless parts of existence and offering us a renewed enthusiasm for life, love, humanity, and the world.

<u>Suggested Reading</u> for Peace, Perspective, and Personal Empowerment, *The Four Agreements: A Practical Guide to Personal Freedom* by don Miguel Ruiz.

Michelle

My parents split up when I was four years old. When I was in kindergarten the following year, I remember going to my mom and saying, "OK, I'm ready. I'm a big girl now. You can tell me. I know that I'm adopted." My mom was shocked! Of course, she told me that I was indeed her daughter, but I just felt so different from her. I definitely felt like I had come from my dad, but when it came to my mom, I felt like I didn't belong. Like I had been plopped in a family and left there. After my parents divorced, visitation with my dad was good for about five years. My sister and I lived with my mom and stepdad in Oregon and we would see my dad and my stepmom in Vegas for holidays and summer breaks. When I was with my dad, everything was an adventure. I was so much like him. My personality. My looks. I really was daddy's little girl. I can remember loving to spend time with him. We would work together for hours in the garage. We were always building something or fixing something. I was fascinated by hanging out with him. My sister would ask me to come inside and play Barbies with her and I would say, "No, let's hang out with dad in the garage! It is way more fun!" One summer, my dad refused to put us back on a plane to Oregon. He wanted to see us more and he didn't feel like my mom was taking good enough care of my sister and me. There was a court case and I had to go and talk to the judge. The judge said to me, "You make the decision for you and your sister. Do you want to be with your dad, or do you want to be with your mom?" That was so much pressure. I wanted to be with my dad, but I knew that if said that my mom would know and it would break her heart. So I sat there crying and I didn't say anything at all. The courts decided that we were to live with our mother. I was devastated. I kept convincing myself that I should have said something… anything. After the trial, we went back to Oregon and I started sixth grade. Even though my dad still had custodial rights, I never saw him again. I talked to him on the phone quite a bit over the next two years, but my mom was terrified of ever putting us on a plane to visit him again. At the end of January during my seventh-grade year, my stepmom called my school. I knew something bad had happened, because she had never called me at school before. It was like she was in shock and didn't realize what she had done until she actually heard my voice. When I got home from school that day, my mom told me that my dad had died of a heart attack. I was so angry. Angry with my mother for not letting me see my dad for two years, and now he was gone! Now he was taken away from me! I was in so much grief. I felt so abandoned. I coped by creating a story in my head that this was all a rouse created by my dad to get me back to him. It wasn't that I was trying to change my reality or create a new reality, the story in my head was actually the beginning of my own understanding of how powerful our minds are. Believing that story didn't make things OK, but it did make them bearable. It also gave me the wisdom to identify my relationship to my thoughts. From that moment on, I have lived with the belief and the intention that my dad is an angel watching over me. That probably kept me out of quite a bit of trouble when I was younger. It has also given me comfort because it keeps my dad very present in my life. Losing him, and how I coped, really changed everything. As I got older, I lived from a very free-spirited perspective. I knew how short life could be, and that made me want to live my best life. To live as present as possible. I appreciated the importance of telling people how much I loved them because I had first-hand experience of not knowing how long they would be here. As I did more research and reading into these philosophies, I surrendered more into the acceptance of who I was: an extremely intuitive person who could sense and know things. As I continued to open up to this side of myself, accepting my power to create my own reality and to connect into different realms, my dad - who had already been coming to me in my dreams - started coming to me in my daily life. As a single mother of a son today, I embody all of this through my parenting. When my son was first born, I was terrified that I was going to lose him. I knew these fears were from what I had been through with my dad. I couldn't sleep, and I wouldn't step away from constantly watching over my son. Finally, I couldn't keep it up and I thought to myself, "What can I create that will make this all feel OK?" I got the answer to turn to my dad. So, I did and I trusted that he would take care of both of us. I connected to him and said, "I'll go to sleep, you watch over the baby… wake me up if you need me." I still do this today. If I get anxious, I ask my dad to protect my son. This gives me so much peace. Allowing my dad in to care for us helps me feel like everything really is going to be OK. Living in this way, as presently as possible, from my perspective as a mother, means that I am big on my son experiencing things. I know that our shared experiences can give him things that toys cannot. I am also dedicated to having him experience being appreciated, supported, validated, and loved. This means that I am there to share in his feelings with him. To nurture him through with the certainty that his feelings are OK, that talking about them is OK, and that he is allowed to feel however he feels. I do this so that he will have the confidence to handle things in ways that empower him when I am not there. As an eight-year-old, he is already very articulate. I get feedback from his teachers that he openly shares about how he is feeling in class. I smile when I hear this because he is just doing what he has been taught to do. He is such a conscious child. Some of it, his sweetness and his kindness, are just who he is. Some of it is because he is mirroring back to me the sweetness and kindness that I have modeled for him. Because he shares my intuitive gifts, my son is also is a great reminder of the power of the human mind. There are times when he will say something in response to me and I will be stunned because I know I didn't say anything out loud. That makes me very mindful of my thoughts. If he can read what is going on in my head, I don't want there to be a discrepancy between what I'm saying and what I'm thinking. Through him, I am teaching and learning authenticity at the same time. Mothering him in this way, we are both finding our balance without sacrificing our truth. Step by step, with each stage of his development, I see the deepening of his attunement to himself. I witness his growing masculinity as he identifies what he needs and what he doesn't. I gently guide him to the best of my abilities, surrendering and letting go at certain points because, truthfully, I have no idea what it is like to figure out the thoughts and feelings involved in being male in our world today. I don't know what it is like to grow up as a boy. I don't know what it is like to become a man. I can only follow his lead and support us both as we ask, "What do we do next?" That simple question has helped me in so many ways. The relationship with my son's father has been challenging and may continue to be that way. To deal with that, I have to honor all of the facets of myself, which means honoring all of my gifts. I have this interesting dichotomy to my personality where I am extremely traditional and extremely wild at heart at the same time. One side of me wants explanations and will become obsessive about acquiring information, and the other side is very whimsical, spiritual, and free. These two very different people are inside of me and I've learned how to mesh them together. When I was engaged in a conflictual divorce and custody situation, I became obsessive. I learned everything I needed to know about ending a marriage. I studied up on my parental rights. I worked with a therapist. I researched how to understand the Law. I also dove into the other side of me, creating the mental headspace and mental empowerment required to produce the outcome I needed for myself and my son. I meditated every day. I focused on cultivating the powers that I knew were available to support me. I called my Angels, Spirit Guides, and those who have come before me, those who walk with me now, and those who will come after me as I prepared and allowed the power of my thoughts to lay the foundation for what I wanted to create. I had faith. It was easier said than done, but we all have a lot more power than we give ourselves credit for. For me now, this place of power is a place of neutrality and I got to this place by doing a lot of work. It wasn't magic. Some moments were easier and some moments were harder than others, but what I've come to through this perspective of neutrality is that there is no place of right and wrong. I'm allowed to have it all together sometimes and sometimes not to have anything together. I push through when I have to, and I veg out when I have to. I am open to it all and no longer resist who I know myself to be. When I think about this in relation to my dad and my journey as a woman and a mother, it all works together. I share this with my son. I let him know that no matter what, he and I will always be connected just like my dad and I are always connected. Even when he can no longer see and touch me we are always together, in this lifetime and in all lifetimes. He is not alone, and he never will be. Neither am I. Neither is anybody. Not everyone knows this, or believes it, or lives like this. They don't have to. I just want everyone to know that they *can* if they *choose* to.

Making This Story Your Own:

Michelle's story accentuates the power of living authentically.
Take a moment, breathe, and reflect.
What stands out for you when you read her words?
Is there a situation in your life that is similar to Michelle's?
Perhaps part of her story feels connected to your own.
How can you relate her experiences to your past, present, and future?

- *My Connection to Michelle's Story* _____
  _____
  _____

Knowing that you aren't alone, let's gently explore some other themes from Michelle's story together:

- **Our Minds Are Powerful**
  - How aware are you of your thoughts? What percentage of your thoughts is focused on the positive things that you would like to bring into your life? Is this percentage enough for you? Why, or why not? What percentage of your thoughts is focused on the negative situations of your life? Is this percentage acceptable to you? Why, or why not? If you were to allocate more time and energy towards thinking positively, is there anything that you suspect might change regarding your life and relationships? If you were to allocate less time and energy to negative thinking, is there anything that you suspect might change? Where do your ideas about a positive or negative mindset come from? Are they yours? If they are solely yours, how were they created and are they working for your highest good? If they are not yours, how were they created and are *they* working for your highest good?

- **Honoring Gifts**
  - What are your gifts? What positive attributes do others notice about you? What aspects of yourself do you freely show and share with the world? How did you come to realize that these characteristics were favorable and who helped you identify these traits? What aspects of yourself and your gifts do you not freely show and share with the world? Why do you not share these? Who assisted you in creating the belief that these attributes should remain hidden? Is hiding them in alignment with who you are today or who you would like to become? What *benefit* comes from allowing these aspects of yourself to remain unseen and unnoticed? What *benefit* might come from allowing these aspects of you to be fully seen and heard?

- **Living the Best Life**
  - Can today be your best day? Can this moment capture your best life? Would you have regrets if your life was over? Why? What would you still *need* to do? What would you still *want* to do? What is keeping you from doing these things? Do you live with the idea that there will *always* be enough time, that there is *never* enough time, or that sometimes there *is* and sometimes there *isn't* enough time? If so, where did you learn to live this way and how is this embodied in your daily living? Is this way of living functional for you and your relationships? Is this way of living optimal for the relationship you have with yourself? Would you like more balance in your daily routine? What would it take to design the best life possible and what is one small thing you can do right now to work toward this?

Sacred Play Suggestions

~ SPS #1: ~
* The Whole You *

One of my favorite lyrics is in a musical by Stephen Schwartz called, *Pippin*. The lyric is from a song called "Love Song" and goes, "They say the whole is greater than the sum of the parts it's made of." Thinking about this lyric, can you apply the principle of honoring the 'whole' versus the 'sum of the parts' when it comes to how you view yourself? When you take this theory into consideration, does it give you a different perspective on certain situations and events in your life, or maybe even a different perspective on personal judgements and criticisms? You are a dynamic being with infinite aspects to your personality, psyche, and consciousness. How often do you honor and value all of these sides of yourself? Are there sides to you that you like better than others? Are those *more likeable* sides always helpful? Do you make efforts to keep your perceived *unlikeable* sides hidden? For this activity, let's play with the possibility that all of our parts and pieces - functional, dysfunctional, likeable, unlikeable, and otherwise - have been created for good reasons. Like mentioned above, there are infinite sides to all of us. For now, let's focus on two valid and needed parts of our personalities that most of us can identify with: *The Protective Side* and *The Peaceful Side*. Just like the matching worksheets from our younger years, let's have some fun with this process. Below there are two lists. One side represents some qualities that might be expressed as our *Protective Side*, the other represents some qualities that might be expressed as our *Peaceful Side*. Draw a line between the two columns and match the qualities based on your perception of how they correlate. For example, your *Serious* self may feel a connection to your *Enthusiastic* self. If this is true for you, draw a line and connect the two words. Keep going. Your *Sarcastic* self may be related to your *Friendly* self. Your *Methodical* self might really need your *Quiet* self to feel balanced. Connect as many as feels comfortable and add additional qualities in the blank spaces provided.

The Protective Side	**The Peaceful Side**
Assertive	Loving
Determined	Supportive
Focused	Compassionate
Uncompromising	Warm
Sharp	Friendly
Critical	Secure
Sarcastic	Quiet
Analytical	Constructive
Serious	Accepting
Judicious	Playful
Independent	Connected
Investigative	Free Flowing
Methodical	Amenable
Destructive	Willing
Precise	Enthusiastic
Orderly	Cooperative
Disciplined	Open
Controlled	Caring
Correct	Empathetic
Measured	Accommodating
-	-
-	-
-	-

Take a look at the connections from both columns. Are there any surprises? Now, pick a handful of these connections to explore further. We are going to use our imaginations and create a dialogue between you and these two sides of your personality. For instance, if your *Orderly* self is connected to your *Secure* self, allow both sides to come to life in front of you so that the three of you can have a little chat. If this was your chosen scenario, you would now be sitting with the *Orderly* self of your personality and the *Secure* self of your personality. When you are ready, pick two correlating aspects of yourself from above to have a conversation with. Use the following questions and free-write from their perspectives to dive deeper into the valuation, validation, and acceptance of the *whole* you.

- **Ask: Aspect #1** _____ **& Aspect #2**_____

    - Why do you two correlate? _____
    _____
    _____

    - How do you two support each other? _____
    _____
    _____

    - What would both of you like me to know? _____
    _____
    _____

    - What would each of you like the other to know? _____
    _____
    _____

    - Are either of you out of balance? _____
    _____

    - If so, what do you need to feel in balance? _____
    _____
    _____

Finish by thanking each side for their participation and reiterate the following affirmations to both.

I see you. I hear you. I hold you. I am you. I love you.
You are valued. You are needed. You are not alone.

Keep working through as many scenarios as you want asking the questions above to the various facets of your personality. See what new information and insight comes up. The *whole* you is definitely greater than the sum of the parts it's made of. You, *all of you*, are also a unique and glorious representation of your own perfection. I see you. I hear you. I hold you. I value you. I need you. I love you. I am grateful for you. You are never alone!

~ SPS #2: ~

* Magickal Senses *

What would you like to manifest into your life? Think of at least one thing and then take a few minutes to answer the following questions as if it has already happened.

- What is different for me now that this has happened? _____
    - How do I **look** different? _____
    - How do I **think** different? _____
    - How do I **feel** different? _____
- Who else notices, and what is their reaction? _____
- What is the larger benefit for the world now that I have manifested this into my life? _____
  _____

Now, designate five places in the room to represent your five senses. You can grab different items and objects to help with remembering. The key here is that the five locations are spread out so that you have to move your body to access them. For example, the blanket on the couch could represent your sense of touch. The picture on the wall could represent your sense of sight. The flowers in the vase could represent your sense of smell. The stereo could represent your sense of hearing. The green book on the shelf could represent your sense of taste. You get what I'm saying. Be creative and have fun!

- Go to the **Sight** spot of your room. Once again visualize what you want to manifest.
- In your visualization, **see** what is happening.
    - See what you see right *before* it manifests.
    - See what you see *as* it is manifesting.
    - See what you see right *after* it has manifested.
        - As you visualize, notice *colors, shapes, images, objects, people, locations, etc.*
        - Take a few deep breaths and allow this **scene** to solidify in your consciousness.

- Go to the **Hearing** spot of your room. Once again visualize what you want to manifest.
- In your visualization, tune in and **hear** what is happening.
    - Hear what you hear right *before* it manifests.
    - Hear what you hear *as* it is manifesting.
    - Hear what you hear right *after* it has manifested.
        - Notice *sounds, rhythms, melodies, instruments, volume, clarity, etc.*
        - Take a few deep breaths and allow this **soundtrack** to solidify in your consciousness.

- Go to the **Taste** spot of your room. Once again visualize what you want to manifest.
- In your visualization, become aware of what you **taste** as you witness what is happening.
  - Taste what you taste right *before* it manifests.
  - Taste what you taste *as* it is manifesting.
  - Taste what you taste right *after* it has manifested.
    - Pay attention to *sweet, savory, sour, bitter, astringent, or pungent tastes.*
    - Take a few deep breaths and allow these **tastes** to solidify in your consciousness.

- Go to the **Smell** spot of your room. Once again visualize what you want to manifest.
- In your visualization, become aware of what you **smell** as you witness what is happening.
  - Smell what you smell right *before* it manifests.
  - Smell what you smell *as* it is manifesting.
  - Smell what you smell right *after* it has manifested.
    - Pay attention to the different smells... what they remind you of and how they make you feel, and their category: *fragrant, fruity, citrus, woody, chemical, sweet, minty, etc.*
    - Take a few deep breaths and allow these **smells** to solidify in your consciousness.

- Go to the **Touch** spot of your room. Once again visualize what you want to manifest.
- In your visualization, become aware of what you **feel** on your body and *in* your body as you witness what is happening.
  - Feel what you feel right *before* it manifests.
  - Feel what you feel *as* it is manifesting.
  - Feel what you feel right *after* it has manifested.
    - For feelings *of* the body, pay attention to *stiffness, flexibility, pain, constriction, temperature, ease, etc.* For feelings *in* the body, pay attention to *emotions, nausea, heart rate, pulse, breathing, blockages, etc.*
    - Take a few deep breaths and allow all of these **feelings** to solidify in your consciousness.

Once you've experienced this through all of your senses, give yourself a few deep cleansing breaths for integration. Now, go back and answer the original journaling prompts again as if what you want has already happened.

- What is different for me now that this has happened? _____
  _____

  - How do I **look** different? _____

  - How do I **think** different? _____

  - How do I **feel** different? _____

- Who else notices, and what is their reaction? _____

- What is the larger benefit for the world now that I have manifested this into my life? _____
  _____

Read through your writing from the first and second set of journaling questions. Complete this activity by solidifying the wisdom that has come through from start to finish.

- What do I notice between my first and my second responses to the journaling questions? _____
_____

- What are the differences? _____

- What are the similarities? _____

- What guidance has come through? _____
_____

- What support is already presenting itself? _____
_____

- How can this exercise assist me in manifesting other things into my life? _____
_____

Well, hello beautiful! How do you feel after all of this wildly powerful work? Thank you for sticking with this. No matter how many of the steps you did, or how you did them, you just devoted time and space to yourself and that is reason to celebrate. I'm doing a happy dance right now. Love you!

~ SPS #3: ~

* Yes, And… *

Saying no can be a fantastically empowering thing. Repeatedly saying no to *ourselves*… that's a different story. Always deferring to the *'no'* can be disempowering and keep us stuck in a negative loop. Even a *'yes, but…'* can be deceptively unconstructive. In improvisation, we have an activity called, **Yes, AND…** This simple game is not only fun, it is also useful. **Yes, AND…** utilizes the powers of creativity while sparking our imaginations to produce unlimited possibilities. This is a game that builds us up and is productive on stage and in life. For example, a round of **Yes, AND…** might look like this:

<u>Step #1</u>- **Create your opening statement relating to what you want and say it out loud.**

- "I will apply for my dream job."

<u>Steps #2 through 10</u>- **Produce the unlimited possibilities.**

- "**Yes, AND**, I will have an amazing interview."
- "**Yes, AND**, during the interview, I will be asked about my idea to save the company thousands of dollars."
- "**Yes, AND**, the whole team will love it!"
- "**Yes, AND**, they will give me a job right there on the spot."

- "**Yes, AND,** they will offer me a raise before I even start."
- "**Yes, AND,** they will throw a company-wide party for my first day."
- "**Yes, AND,** I will be accepted, valued, seen, and appreciated for my talents and gifts."
- "**Yes, AND,** my workspace will be perfectly comfortable and creative."
- "**Yes, AND,** everyone will be flexible with my schedule."
- "**Yes, AND,** this job will provide for all of my personal and professional needs."

Give it a try. Remember, dream BIG and let your imagination do the talking. Try out the following idea generator sentences. Play with finishing the sentences with big and bold wishes, dreams and desires. Continue to generate a positive loop by creating at least five to ten unique **Yes, AND**... statements after each idea generator for each round.

<div align="center">**Idea Generator Sentences**</div>	
<ul><li>I will fulfill my wish of...</li><li>I will manifest my desires of...</li><li>I will make my dreams come true by...</li><li>I will succeed at...</li><li>I will satisfy my craving for...</li></ul>	<ul><li>Today I will...</li><li>Tomorrow I will...</li><li>My hopes will become reality when I...</li><li>I will meet my needs by...</li><li>I will become all I aspire by...</li></ul>

Step #1-

- Idea Generator Sentence: "_____"

Step #2 through 10-

- "**Yes, AND**.... _____"
- "**Yes, AND**.... _____"
- "**Yes, AND**.... _____"
- "**Yes, AND**.... _____"
- "**Yes, AND**.... _____"
- "**Yes, AND**.... _____"
- "**Yes, AND**.... _____"
- "**Yes, AND**.... _____"
- "**Yes, AND**.... _____"
- "**Yes, AND**.... _____"

Step #1, Take #2-

- Idea Generator Sentence: "_____"

Step #2 through 10-

- "Yes, AND.... _____"
- "Yes, AND.... _____"
- "Yes, AND.... _____"
- "Yes, AND.... _____"
- "Yes, AND.... _____"
- "Yes, AND.... _____"
- "Yes, AND.... _____"
- "Yes, AND.... _____"
- "Yes, AND.... _____"
- "Yes, AND.... _____"

If you enjoyed **Yes, AND...** try it with friends! This is a great activity for families, couples, and groups because everyone gets to have fun creating solution strategies. **Yes, AND...** also makes us feel more connected, empowered, playful, and loved. Win-Win! Love you! Thank you for **Yes, AND...**ing with me!

~ SPS #4: ~
* Neutrality *

Michelle shares some potent wisdom about the powers of the mind and how to harness those powers through meditation. When there is less loud energy dedicated to the outside world, more quiet space can become available for the inner world. This connection to our inner worlds can also connect us to our inner knowing. Deepening the connection to ourselves in this way can lead to new ideas, solutions, inspirations, and more. However, meditation can seem like a distant land to a weary traveler if time, space, and peace are compromised... although that is usually when we need meditation the most! For this activity we will also implement Michelle's other tidbit of wisdom: neutrality. As defined by its secondary definition, neutrality - for our immediate purposes - is "the absence of decided views, expressed opinions, and strong feelings." Why is neutrality useful? Neutrality helps us release judgement. It gifts us a space to liberate the ego's desire to assign hierarchy, duality, and separation. Neutrality reminds us that *everything* is of value and *all* is connected. In a neutral space we can remember that these qualities, feelings, judgments, and values are *of* the world we live in but are not indicative of our *true* nature. So, if you love this experience, great! If you hate this experience, great! I'm totally neutral about it... seriously, though... however permanent or temporary this release of judgment might be, let's see if we can quietly get to a place of meditative neutrality. As my Esoteric Healing teacher used to say, "Worst case, you'll feel nothing, best case, you'll feel better."

Find a quiet, comfortable spot.
Play some soft music if you'd like.

For a series of seven breaths, align your inhale and exhale to your etheric body, *or* Chakra Systems.
*Inhale and bring your awareness to the base of your **spine**.*
*Exhale and connect the color **red** to your* Basic Chakra.
*Inhale and bring your awareness to your **lower abdomen**.*
*Exhale and connect the color **orange** to your* Sacral Chakra.
*Inhale and bring your awareness to your **navel**.*
*Exhale and connect the color **yellow** to your* Solar Plexus Chakra.
*Inhale and bring your awareness to your **chest**.*
*Exhale and connect the color **green** to your* Heart Chakra.
*Inhale and bring your awareness to your **throat**.*
*Exhale and connect the color **blue** to your* Throat Chakra.
*Inhale and bring your awareness to your **forehead**.*
*Exhale and connect the color **purple** to your* Ajna Chakra.
*Inhale and bring your awareness to the **crown of your head**.*
*Exhale and connect the color **lavender** to your* Crown Chakra.
Connect your body, mind, and spirit to the energies of Source *and* Center.
Visualize your consciousness resting in a vast spacious area.
Envision the following words, concepts, and ideas.
*Read through them aloud and allow yourself to see, feel, and embody the perceived divisions.
*Read through the words again and for the second time through, imagine the words, concepts, and ideas coming together in perfect harmony.
Lastly, read through the words for a third time. With all aspects of your awareness, co-create a new active and livable version of **neutrality where the words hold no value other than the value of their existence.*

Good - Bad	Honest - Dishonest	Male – Female
Long - Short	Life - Death	Heaven – Hell
Old - Young	Idealism – Realism	Together – Apart
Right - Wrong	Complete – Incomplete	Love – Hate
Black – White	Perfect – Imperfect	All – None
Up – Down	Decided – Undecided	Big - Small
High – Low	Committed – Uncommitted	Out – In
Expanded – Contracted	Soft – Hard	Kind – Unkind
Concentrated - Diffuse	Quick - Slow	Same - Opposite

When you are finished with the meditation, take a few moments to reacquaint yourself with your physical space and your physical body. Tightly wrap your arms around your shoulders. With gratitude, acknowledge the powers of your mind and with respect, salute your graceful travels to the inner world of your inner knowing. Complete this exercise by journaling around the following.

- My inner world offers me _____

_____

_____

- My inner knowing offers me _____
  _____
  _____

- My neutrality offers me _____
  _____
  _____

The energy of neutrality is what it is…. I mean, I'm OK either way. There really is no ending or beginning when you think about it. It's neither here nor there. Pretty equal in my book. Everything happens for a reason, right? Hopefully you are smiling at least a little bit right now. Love you. Thank you for doing this activity. ☺

~ SPS #5: ~
* Spirit Messages *

Messages from the Spirit World are everywhere. Unfortunately, most of us don't regularly notice them. Think about it, have you ever thanked a Guardian Angel? Or, like Michelle, have you ever communicated with someone who has left the Earth Plane? Maybe animals come to you with messages. Maybe numbers are more your thing. Perhaps you work with Ascended Masters. Maybe you do all of this and more. Maybe you don't. A teacher of mine who was a Medium used to say that our ancestors liked to ride around in the car with us. Hey, whatever works, right? For right now, let's utilize the powers of our creativity to communicate with that which cannot be seen, but can be sensed, felt, and *known*. Collaging is a great way to get our creative juices flowing. Looking through magazines - not to be sold anything, but to find colors, textures, words, and images that strike our fancy - is like going to an arts and crafts store and picking out what we want for *free*. That is my kind of retail therapy! Try it. Grab a magazine that you have lying around the house - one that you don't mind ripping out pages from - and give it a try. As you leaf through and begin to rip or cut out the things that catch your attention, hold in your mind who you would like to communicate with and receive messages from. This can be anyone or anything that isn't readily available for you to sit and physically chat with in the present moment. When you have a nice pile, cut your pieces to size, get a glue stick or tape, and prepare to assemble. Assembly is your oyster. You can stick the images to a piece of paper, poster board, or cardboard, decoupage them with some liquid adhesive, staple them together, or even get an old wire hanger and make a mobile. What you make is not as important as what you have chosen and how you put those images together for interpretation. From your pile, randomly pick out ten pieces. Spread them out and place them in order, assigning each a numeric value from 1-10. Make yourself a cheat sheet so you can remember which pieces correlate with which number. In any order, collage your pieces together to create this original work of art. Have fun playing with how the images flow together, how they touch, color patterns, word play, etc. When you have all ten pieces on your chosen background, let this work of art begin to speak to you. Have the cheat sheet for your images and their corresponding numbers nearby. Numbers have spiritual connotations and colors have psychological implications. If it feels like a fit, use the lists below, along with your own internal wisdom for receiving guidance through your chosen images and words, as you interpret your artwork. Keep holding the person, place, or thing that you originally intended to communicate with in your mind as you welcome the messages.

Numbers	Colors
1 - New Beginnings, Motivation	Red - Passion, Courage
2 - Divine Purpose, Love	Orange - Creativity, Excitement
3 - Inspiration, Manifestation	Yellow - Spontaneity, Happiness
4 - Practicality, Solid Foundations	Green - Renewal, Stability
5 - Freedom, Lessons, Choices	Blue - Loyalty, Integrity
6 - Unconditional Love, Empathy	Purple - Spirituality, Imagination
7 - Spiritual Awakening, Enlightenment	White - Purity, New Life
8 - Inner Wisdom, Abundance	Black - Empowerment, Formality
9 - Universal Love and Service	Pink - Love, Tranquility
0 - Infinity, Wholeness	Brown - Reliability, Warmth

Knowing what you know and using your collage as a channel, talk to yourself from your chosen entity's perspective. With translations coming in from the images, numbers, and colors, ask any questions you may have. Ask for deeper clarification around certain issues or situations. Ask for specific support and guidance for your life. When the channeling feels complete, add in anything else that still feels like it needs to be said and conclude this activity however you would like. Some ideas for resolution without disconnection are: hang your collage where you can see it, gift your collage to someone who will appreciate its meanings and messages, bury your collage as an offering, burn your collage in a firepit (or other safe burning receptacle), or place it lovingly in a box or drawer to be brought out and appreciated later. Write down any messages and guidance that came through below so you don't forget! Thank you for doing this! Love you!

My Messages from the Spirit World

_____

_____

_____

_____

Crystal Love: Michelle's Crystal is Hawk's Eye, also known as Blue Tiger's Eye. Hawk's Eye is a stone to use when you want to increase your psychic abilities, clairvoyance, and aptitudes for Astral Travel. Because of these high vibratory talents, Hawk's Eye can stimulate and invigorate the physical body while balancing the Masculine and Feminine energies. This Crystal can promote clear thinking and deep insight while clearing the Throat Chakra so that intuitive truth may be clearly communicated, and the support doesn't stop there. Hawk's Eye is also a powerful emotional healer and can disperse negative thought patterns, melt away undesirable behaviors, resurface buried emotions, reveal new perspectives on old issues, release cynicism, and offer support for the authentic reflection needed to identify blockages in the emotional body. Additionally, Hawk's Eye wants us to prosper in all areas of life… so play with wearing this stone to attract monetary abundance, riches of the heart, and affluence of the spirit. Furthermore, try burying this stone in your garden or gifting it to a tree as Hawk's Eye is also known to be a wonderful healer of Mother Earth.

Suggested Reading to Rev Up, Enhance, and Miraculously Inspire the Powers of Your Mind, *The Universe Has Your Back: Transform Fear to Faith* by Gabrielle Bernstein

Nisla

My story of motherhood has shaped and transformed me. The lessons I've come to understand through this journey are universal. Although the unique incidents of my life are mine, I know that the collective experience is not. As women, we live through so many of the same things and share so many of the same feelings. While our personal stories are important, it is more important to know that we have a sisterhood to support us. We are definitely not in this alone. So often we feel this way, but that is not the case. For me, raising children is powerful, transformative magick, especially when we are dedicated to doing it in a different way than has been done before. Breaking negative patterns and cycles is challenging. My partner and I met when we were in our early twenties and married soon thereafter. Because we were both children of divorce, we decided to wait until we were in our thirties to have children. We really wanted to be sure of who we were and that our relationship was solid before we brought a child into the world. My daughter's birth was an emergency situation and both of us nearly died. After 36 hours of intense labor, an emergency cesarean was performed because the umbilical cord was wrapped around her neck. It was all so scary, but I know we survived for a reason. Being her mother has been one of my greatest teachings. I struggled to raise her in the early years. As a child, I was subjected to a lot of trauma in the forms of sexual and physical abuse, divorce, and growing up in a household with addiction. I did not want my daughter to be exposed to any of those things and I made a conscious choice to protect her; however, I went too far. I was afraid to take her anywhere, so I sheltered her. I didn't do anything with her. It was a process of deliberately attempting to keep her safe, but at the same time I didn't let her grow. I had a really hard time trusting anyone or anything. I was so terrified to let her go out and play in the neighborhood because I was convinced that someone would get to her. With the arrival of my son when my daughter was twelve, everything changed. After the birth trauma of my daughter, I was fine with having only one child. I was too afraid to even consider having another baby. Then, my daughter started telling my husband and me, "I want a little brother or sister." We thought about it and were actually coming around to the idea when - little did we know - our daughter snuck a fertility Goddess that she had sculpted into our bedroom. She was eleven at the time. Looking back, I realize that this child is a master-manifestor. When she wants something, she gets it. Soon I started having hot flashes and feeling very hormonal. I was approaching forty and I thought I was going through the beginning stages of menopause. It wasn't until almost the end of the first trimester that it finally dawned on me that I could be pregnant. I was working with a chiropractor, and one day I dragged myself into his office convinced that something was really wrong with me. He did a thorough exam, and at the end, he said, "Nisla, you're pregnant!" Even then, I still didn't believe it. Five pregnancy tests later, I showed them to my husband. He replied in shock, "How did that happen?" Finding out we were pregnant was a big surprise to everyone but my daughter. The whole pregnancy with my son was easy. I felt great. I loved my doctor. I worked up until the day I had him. The birth was beautiful. The planned cesarean was gentle, and he was on my chest and at my breast within minutes of his arrival. I even left the hospital early. Everything seemed perfect. Unfortunately, within the first few months of my son's life, the walls that I had built - literally and figuratively - came tumbling down. At his four-month doctor's visit, my son suffered a vaccine related injury. His brain swelled, causing him to develop a severe sleep disturbance along with multiple allergies and other issues. This threw me into a tailspin. I had to quit my job to stay home with him. We decided to move to another state to be closer to family. We lost our home to a foreclosure. It was all beyond stressful. I felt so guilty about everything. I felt responsible for my son's injury. After we made the move, my husband took a pay-the-bills job that was really hard on him. I felt responsible for that, too… like I had failed my daughter, my family, and myself. I became suicidal. I was so low that I started to believe everything I had done was a huge mistake and the world would be better off without me. One particular day, after listening to my son's screams night after night, I wanted to load him up in a car and drive us off a bridge. By some grace, at that moment, I ran into another mother who told me about a family organization in town which helped support parents and children going through all sorts of transitions and issues. I drove myself and my infant son to the place she had mentioned. I sat in that family room for what seemed like hours and wept openly on the couch. Eventually, I was connected to a few other support networks through this agency. Then my journey of healing through this phase of my life began. It was so powerful finding out that other women were going through similar things and feeling the same kinds of things that I was feeling. I found a sisterhood with these women. I found a way to fill my cup. They all helped me uncover the path back to myself. Slowly, I started a reclamation process of the woman I knew myself to be. I also found a desire to help other women by sharing my story. No matter what our individual traumas are, I know that we need each other. How we feel and how we internalize our pain can be transformed and healed when we share it. There were times when I would listen to other women's stories in the different groups that I participated in and think to myself, "I would have died if I had gone through what she's been through." There is no doubt that I have had a unique trauma history. I've been through a lot, but hearing other women courageously share their life stories reminded me that no matter how different we seem, we are all in this together. Their strength is my strength. Everybody is going through something. Even if you think you are making every mistake in the world, share your truth and trust that the right ears will hear it. Luckily, at seven years old my son is fine and we have healed his injury. I wouldn't have been able to access the resources and support needed to heal him if I had not shared my story. By transforming the pain that I was feeling, I found the strength to help my family. For women out there who are struggling with feelings of guilt or fear, look to your resources. That morning, when I sat crying on the couch, I allowed my community to come in and hold me. I was so low and filled with guilt that it felt like the most powerful thing in my life. Yet now, I've come to realize that guilt is just misplaced energy. We all waste our energy feeling guilty about things that may or may not have been in our control. No matter how much you feel that you are to blame, you aren't. No matter how much it feels like the pain is unbearable, it isn't. No matter how much you feel like nobody would miss you, I guarantee people will miss you. Nothing is ever the end of the world. There is always somebody else going through a similar experience. Find them and share your story. When you do, you open up to a world of endless possibilities.

Making This Story Your Own:

Nisla's story highlights the importance of community.
Take a moment, breathe, and reflect.
What stands out for you when you read her words?
Is there a situation in your life that is similar to Nisla's?
Perhaps part of her story feels connected to your own.
How can you relate her experiences to your past, present, and future?

- *My Connection to Nisla's Story* _____

_____

_____

_____

Knowing that you aren't alone, let's gently explore some other themes from Nisla's story together:

- ***We Are in This Together***
    - From 0-100%, how responsible do you feel for the successes in your life? How responsible do you feel for the failures? Who else in your life might also be responsible for these things? Do you share with others about your accomplishments and mistakes? Do other people share with you about these things? How does it make you feel when this happens? When you share, do you censor yourself? Do you think others do this with you? Would you like this process to shift in any way and if so, how? Would sharing with others in more open and authentic ways be beneficial for you? When others share with you, can you receive and reciprocate in ways that promote more connection and community?

- ***Breaking Negative Cycles***
    - As an adult, can you look back and identify the functional and dysfunctional patterns demonstrated by the adults in your life when you were younger? As you reflect on this, are any of these patterns being consciously or unconsciously repeated in your current relationships? Is this OK with you? When you think about it in this way, has there been any benefit in repeating these patterns? Has there been any harm in repeating these patterns? In regard to these cycles, what are you ready to let go of completely? What are some learned behaviors that you would like to change or stop? What are some learned behaviors that you would like to implement or continue?

- ***Look to Your Resources***
    - Could you use some extra support? Where in your life would additional assistance be helpful? Have you researched available community resources? If so, have you utilized these resources? If not, what keeps you from taking advantage of these services? What cultural messages have you received about asking for help? Are these messages consciously or unconsciously inhibiting you from receiving the support that you want and need?

Sacred Play Suggestions:

~ SPS #1: ~
* Extraordinary Life *

Have you ever thought about guilt and all of the things you feel guilty about? What about shame? What are you ashamed of? Not a fun way to begin a Scared Play Suggestion, I know, but think about it… guilt and shame are powerful! If you are human, you've had them. Kind of like lice - they are a rite of passage. Guilt and shame can drive us to do things that are absolutely beautiful and straight up bat shit crazy… and everything in between. There are a lot of times when we are aware of the guilt and the shame that we carry. There are also a lot of times when we are completely unaware and both scenarios can offer gifts and challenges. However, guilt and shame of any kind impedes our ability to feel pleasure. They also mess up the whole 'livin' in bliss' goal. Let's peel this onion layer-by-layer and see what we can shed when it comes to guilt and shame. They may not be ready to fully leave us and that is OK. This activity is about being open and aware. Think of guilt and shame and ask them to be present to this potential transformation. In your imagination, allow the energy of these two entities to come to life before you. They may spring forward as one character, they may be two, or even many. Whatever is created from your imagination is yours and it is valuable. You are going to be the writer, actor, director, and producer of this scene. That means you hold all of the power and empowerment needed for this experience to create your Greatest and Highest Good for this moment and for this time. Just like all talented writers and actors, you are going to 'step-in' to these characters and generate material from their perspectives. With both Guilt and Shame standing on the internal stage of your consciousness, let's begin.

- *Step-in* to the character of **Guilt** and journal from Guilt's consciousness for the following.
  - Guilt's *Character* Backstory involves the fear and pain for having done something wrong, the fear of being found out for mistakes and wrong-doings, and the fear and pain around intending to do something wrong.

I am here because of…

_____
_____
_____

I am physically and emotionally felt as…

_____
_____
_____

My beautiful gifts are manifested as…

_____
_____
_____

My bat-shit crazy challenges are manifested as…

_____
_____
_____

Next, work with the character of **Shame.**

- *Step-in* to the character of **Shame** and journal from Shame's consciousness for the following.
  - Shame's *Character* Backstory involves the feelings and pervasive beliefs of being bad, unworthy, unlovable, and broken.

I am here because of…

_____

_____

_____

I am physically and emotionally felt as…

_____

_____

_____

My beautiful gifts are manifested as…

_____

_____

_____

My bat-shit crazy challenges are manifested as…

_____

_____

_____

OK, what have you discovered about Guilt and Shame? Hopefully some helpful things came to the surface, but no worries if not. These two characters are phenomenal at their craft and getting them to open up may not be easy. Let's switch gears just a bit and explore what Georg Feuerstein refers to in his book, *Sacred Sexuality: The Erotic Spirit in the World's Great Religions*, as the "Ordinary Life." According to him, when we live with Guilt and Shame, we live the ordinary life. This existence is one in which we trade in constant joy and pleasure for short bursts of socially acceptable fun. To deal with the steady companionship of Guilt and Shame, we distract ourselves with satisfactory experiences that temporarily meet our needs for happiness. These distractions come in all forms and can really fool us into believing that they are as good as it gets. Concerts, vacations, work success, exercising, parties, and other surface level experiences that come and go offer us the illusion of joy but really keep us living below our potential for regular and reliable bliss. For some, this can be even more problematic as they seek comfort in food, sex, alcohol, shopping, drugs, gambling, etc. Kind of crazy to think about it like this, isn't it? Ready to peel back another layer of the onion? This time, as director and producer of the scene, you will interview Guilt and Shame and ask them a few questions. In your imagination, ask the following and record the answers you receive below.

<u>**You**</u>: Guilt, what do you do to keep me distracted?

Guilt: _____

_____

You: Shame, what do you do to keep me distracted?

Shame: _____

_____

You: How do both of you keep me living the 'Ordinary Life?'

Guilt and Shame: _____

_____

You: What would it take to let you go?

Guilt and Shame: _____

_____

OK, good news! Guess what? A new producer with unlimited funding has stepped up to work with you on this project and her name is Bliss. She just has one stipulation. She wants Guilt and Shame to be recast with two new actors. These new talents are both genius protégés of Bliss and their names are Joy and Pleasure. Another bit of good news… Guilt and Shame have both told their agents that if you decide to cast Joy and Pleasure in their roles, they want to be released from their contracts. Pleasure and Joy are here right now to audition for you. Ready? In your imagination, visualize the two most stunning creatures walking toward you. They look familiar. They radiate so much light that it is hard to make out their features, but once they get close enough… you realize that these two Goddesses are *you*! Joy auditions first with her monologue. As she speaks, your consciousness merges with hers and you are able to know what she is going to say before she says it. Fill in the blanks below with your inner knowing of Joy.

Joy: I am here because _____. You deserve me in your life unconditionally because you are _____.

When you need me, you just need to _____. You will know I am present when _____. Because we are one, your body will _____. Because I am here, your heart will feel _____

_____. Because I am close, your mind will know _____

_____. Because we are in harmony, your soul will allow _____

_____.

Now that was an excellent audition! Ready for Pleasure? Again, with Pleasure's monologue your consciousness merges with hers and you know what she is going to say before she says it. Fill in the blanks below with your inner knowing of Pleasure.

Pleasure: I am here because _____. You deserve me in your life unconditionally because you are _____. When you need me you just need to _____. You will know I am present when _____. Because we are one, your body will _____. Because I am here, your heart will feel _____. Because I am close, your mind will know _____. Because we are in harmony, your soul will allow _____.

Ready to sign contracts? I suggest as a change from the "Ordinary Life," we name our production "The Extraordinary Life." The last step is to work out the particulars with your new business partner, Bliss. This is going to be a fantastic work of art. You have worked very hard and you deserve all of the accolades that follow. I want you to know, I love you. Channel in these new arrangements from your inner knowing of Bliss and sign on the dotted line! Thank you for doing this!

~ **For the Production of *"The Extraordinary Life,"* the bonding pacts are as follows.** ~

- To avoid distraction, Bliss and I will _____

- To honor our obligations to Joy and Pleasure, Bliss and I will _____

- To maintain personal and professional distance when Guilt and Shame want their jobs back, Bliss and I will _____

- To stay diligently devoted to our contractual arrangements, Bliss and I will _____

- To stay dedicated to Bliss, I vow _____

- To stay dedicated to me, Bliss vows _____

Signed & Dated by Me: _____

Signed & Dated by Bliss: _____

~ SPS #2: ~
* Reaching Out *

Reaching out for help can be really hard. Sometimes it is easier to ask people we know and other times to ask people we don't. Sometimes, we can even convince ourselves that it is easier to handle things on our own rather than depend on another person for support. How sad, right? If someone you love was feeling this way, wouldn't you want to go to them, hug them tight, and remind them - "Hey, I am right here! Let me help!" Nisla offers so much wisdom in her story when she shares about letting her community support her. Take a moment and think about that. What would it look and feel like to let your community support you? Fill in the following three-sentence story and see what comes up.

I want to connect to _____ **because I need** _____
_____.

I haven't reached out because I am afraid _____
_____.

Yet, when I do reach out, I have faith _____
_____.

Now, reread through the three sentences above and imagine that you are hearing these words come from a beloved friend or family member. With an awareness of your feelings, finish the following sentences.

- When I imagine this need for support being expressed from someone I love and care about…

    o **I feel** _____

    o **I think** _____

    o **I hope** _____

OK, here is a loaded question, and I bet you know where I am headed with this…

**How much more reactive and responsive are you to this need for
support when you envision it coming from someone else?**

_____

Why?

_____

_____

If there is any tug to admonish yourself right now, take a deep breath and pause. Wrap your arms around your shoulders and know that you are doing the best you can, always, all the time, in any given situation. Cultivating trust in our communities and the available resources may take some time, and that is OK! Nisla offers us another wonderful bit of wisdom when she shares that "Hearing other women courageously share their life stories reminded me that no matter how different we seem, we are all in this together. Their strength *is* my strength." Wow. Think about that. Your strength *is* my strength and my strength *is* yours… we are in this *together*. When I witness you allow the support and help you need into your life, you give me permission to do the same. Let's change the original three-sentence story a bit and see if anything shifts. Fill in the blanks one more time.

When I reach out, I have faith _____

_____. **I am no longer afraid** _____

_____.

Because of _____ **I will connect**

to _____.

Great job! Take a deep breath and connect into your Higher Self. Let your awareness travel up, around, and through your consciousness and enter into the loving, supportive, capable, and all-knowing energy of your Soul. From this magickal, intuitive aspect of you that holds both the intention and motivation for your best and highest good, read through what you just wrote. Now, from your Higher Self's perspective, answer the following questions.

- When witnessing this need for support being expressed from myself, someone I deeply love and care about…

    o **I know** _____

    o **I will** _____

    o **I AM** _____

Last step! Read through the following three-sentence Mantra and create your own new three-sentence story in response.

I love and care about myself.
I respond to my needs.
I allow my community to support me.

_____

_____

Congratulations! This is powerful work and you did it. Your strength *is* my strength. Thank you… love you!

~ SPS #3: ~
* I Know This is True *

Have you ever come out on the other side of a particularly taxing time and realized that your fears and anxieties made you believe a whole bunch of stuff that wasn't true? Jeez… I sure have. I have created epic multi-series, made-for-TV movie events and, after the dust settled, realized that almost none of the created crap was true. However, as *untrue* as I came to know all of that stuff to be, in the moment, the story was extremely powerful! Not to mention exhausting, draining, and demoralizing. Even going forward, as I became aware of this pattern, I oftentimes felt helpless to stop it. Have you ever heard of the concept that for healing to occur it has to happen in the present moment? My Esoteric Healing teacher used to tell us that in class all the time. The truth of her words never really hit me until I became aware of how the pain of the past and the pressure of the future play such a big role in creating the 'stories' of our lives. I know it may sound overly simple, but when that inner screen writer gets a tad too energized, you can regroup and reground with the "I Know This is True" game. Give it a try. Use one of your hands, and for each finger name five 'true' things that you can actually **see**. For example, the five things I see at this moment are: I see my blue shirt. I see the outer rims of my glasses. I see my chair. I see the computer screen. I see my white purse on the floor. Name five things that you **see** below.

5 Things That I See

1. _____
2. _____
3. _____
4. _____
5. _____

Next, move on to five things that you can **hear**. Be sure to keep using your fingers so that the mind-body connection is still present. For this round, try breathing in between each one.

5 Things That I Hear

1. _____(Breathe)
2. _____(Breathe)
3. _____(Breathe)
4. _____(Breathe)
5. _____(Breathe)

Playing "I Know This is True" can slow us down a bit and get our minds focused on what truly is happening right now versus what happened in the past or what might happen in the future. Taking five deep breaths helps, too. Let's go on to the senses of smell and taste. These might take a bit longer to identify and that is OK. We are going to add in some hand mudras to help us with concentration. A mudra (*moo*-druh) is a symbolic hand gesture that is used to channel the body's energy in specific ways. Often seen in meditation, there are over 100 known hand mudras, and they are very helpful in pulling mental focus inwards to cultivate concentration, empowerment, and focus. The first mudra we will use for identifying five things that we smell will be the **Gyan** (*guy*-an) Mudra. This mudra is said to assist us as we seek to gain knowledge and you've probably seen it before. Try it by holding the tips of your thumbs and your index fingers together while the other three fingers are out straight. It sort of looks like an 'OK' sign. When holding this Mudra with your palms up, this is for lightness. With your palms down, that is for grounding. Now, with both of your hands in the **Gyan** Mudra, identify five things that you smell. Don't forget to keep up with the deep breaths in between each one.

5 Things That I Smell

1. _____ (Breathe)
2. _____ (Breathe)
3. _____ (Breathe)
4. _____ (Breathe)
5. _____ (Breathe)

For taste, we will try the **Surya** (sir-eee-*yuh*) Mudra which is known to be a mudra for metabolism and digestion. For this mudra, bend your ring finger towards your palm and touch in between both knuckles with the pad of your thumb. Play around with this one to find the position that feels most comfortable. When you are ready, stretch your other three fingers out straight. Hold this mudra with both hands as you identify five things that you can taste. Again, don't forget to breathe!

5 Things That I Taste

1. _____ (Breathe)
2. _____ (Breathe)
3. _____ (Breathe)
4. _____ (Breathe)
5. _____ (Breathe)

How are you doing? Have you been thinking about the past or the future? If not, great! If you have, no worries… we are in this together and we are going to keep going. For the rest of this exercise, we are going to be holding our hands in the **Anjali** (un-*jah*-lee) Mudra. This is also known as the prayer mudra. To do it, simply bring your palms together with your fingers aligned in front of your Heart Center in the center of your chest. This mudra connects us to the energies of love, gratitude, and respect. When we intentionally hold our hands in the **Anjali** Mudra, we are honoring ourselves and all living things. OK, with the help of this mudra, we are going to add in the last topping of the "I Know This is True" sundae and explore what we are thinking and feeling. Only this time, as we identify our fabulous five, we are going to filter it through a layer of consciousness to determine if what we are experiencing is coming from our Soul (the present) or our Ego (the past and future.) I know… this sounds complex. And it is! Our Souls and Egos are huge entities within our psyches. But we are going to keep this as simple as we can. Try working with the following filters and see if they resonate.

- If any thought or feeling comes with a side order of shame, fear, guilt, self-loathing, or negativity, it is coming from the **Ego**.
- If any thought or feeling comes with a side order of positivity, self-love, compassion, forgiveness, peace, or bliss, it is coming from the **Soul**.

Ready? With your hands in the **Anjali** Mudra, identify five things you are feeling right now.

5 Things I am Feeling

1. I am feeling_____ (Breathe)

    - Ask: "Does this feeling come with any shame, fear, guilt, self-loathing, or negativity?"
        - If so, release it from your **Ego** by saying, *"Thank you, I am choosing a different path."*
    - Imagine this feeling being washed over by positivity, self-love, compassion, peace, and bliss.
        - Accept the wisdom of your **Soul** by saying, *"Thank you for showing me the way."*

2. I am feeling_____ (Breathe)

    - Ask: "Does this feeling come with any shame, fear, guilt, self-loathing, or negativity?"
        - If so, release it from your **Ego** by saying, *"Thank you, I am choosing a different path."*
    - Imagine this feeling being washed over by positivity, self-love, compassion, peace, and bliss.
        - Accept the wisdom of your **Soul** by saying, *"Thank you for showing me the way."*

3. I am feeling_____ (Breathe)

    - Ask: "Does this feeling come with any shame, fear, guilt, self-loathing, or negativity?"
        - If so, release it from your **Ego** by saying, *"Thank you, I am choosing a different path."*
    - Imagine this feeling being washed over by positivity, self-love, compassion, peace, and bliss.
        - Accept the wisdom of your **Soul** by saying, *"Thank you for showing me the way."*

4. I am feeling_____ (Breathe)

    - Ask: "Does this feeling come with any shame, fear, guilt, self-loathing, or negativity?"
        - If so, release it from your **Ego** by saying, *"Thank you, I am choosing a different path."*
    - Imagine this feeling being washed over by positivity, self-love, compassion, peace, and bliss.
        - Accept the wisdom of your **Soul** by saying, *"Thank you for showing me the way."*

5. I am feeling_____ (Breathe)

    - Ask: "Does this feeling come with any shame, fear, guilt, self-loathing, or negativity?"
        - If so, release it from your **Ego** by saying, *"Thank you, I am choosing a different path."*

- Imagine this feeling being washed over by positivity, self-love, compassion, peace, and bliss.
  - Accept the wisdom of your **Soul** by saying, *"Thank you for showing me the way."*

You are amazing! Now, go on to your **thoughts.**

5 Things I am Thinking

1. I am thinking_____ **(Breathe)**

   - Ask: "Does this thought come with any shame, fear, guilt, self-loathing, or negativity?"
     - If so, release it from your **Ego** by saying, *"Thank you, I am choosing a different path."*
   - Imagine this thought being washed over by positivity, self-love, compassion, peace, and bliss.
     - Accept the wisdom of your **Soul** by saying, *"Thank you for showing me the way."*

2. I am thinking_____ **(Breathe)**

   - Ask: "Does this thought come with any shame, fear, guilt, self-loathing, or negativity?"
     - If so, release it from your **Ego** by saying, *"Thank you, I am choosing a different path."*
   - Imagine this thought being washed over by positivity, self-love, compassion, peace, and bliss.
     - Accept the wisdom of your **Soul** by saying, *"Thank you for showing me the way."*

3. I am thinking_____ **(Breathe)**

   - Ask: "Does this thought come with any shame, fear, guilt, self-loathing, or negativity?"
     - If so, release it from your **Ego** by saying, *"Thank you, I am choosing a different path."*
   - Imagine this thought being washed over by positivity, self-love, compassion, peace, and bliss.
     - Accept the wisdom of your **Soul** by saying, *"Thank you for showing me the way."*

4. I am thinking_____ **(Breathe)**

   - Ask: "Does this thought come with any shame, fear, guilt, self-loathing, or negativity?"
     - If so, release it from your **Ego** by saying, *"Thank you, I am choosing a different path."*
   - Imagine this thought being washed over by positivity, self-love, compassion, peace, and bliss.
     - Accept the wisdom of your **Soul** by saying, *"Thank you for showing me the way."*

5. I am thinking_____ **(Breathe)**

   - Ask: "Does this thought come with any shame, fear, guilt, self-loathing, or negativity?"
     - If so, release it from your **Ego** by saying, *"Thank you, I am choosing a different path."*
   - Imagine this thought being washed over by positivity, self-love, compassion, peace, and bliss.
     - Accept the wisdom of your **Soul** by saying, *"Thank you for showing me the way."*

Wow. Just, wow! How do you feel? Hopefully present and clear without a 'story'! OK. Last, last thing. How can you keep the energy of this *presence* going with the mudras, the filters, the awareness to your senses, and the dedication to the present moment? Breathe and ***know… know*** and breathe. You got this! I love you! Thank you for doing this activity!

~ SPS #4: ~
* Sacred Circles *

Sometimes, actually seeing something on paper can help us to integrate it into our lives. Let's try an exercise together in the box below. As you work, feel free to grab another piece of paper if you run out of space.

- **Step One**: Draw a small circle in the center of the box and label it 'Me.'

- **Step Two**: Draw a second circle around yours. In the space between the two, write in the names of the people in your life who are helpful or supportive in some way. Don't forget, pets and plants are people, too.
- **Step Three**: Draw a third circle around the first two. In this space, list the organizations in your community that have been helpful or that you are interested in getting more information from which could be beneficial in the future.
- **Step Four**: Draw a fourth circle around the others and pause to do a little online research. Locate some support such as social media groups, list serves, newsletters, chats, etc. that feel interesting to you. This doesn't mean that you have to access these options or even use them. Sometimes just knowing what is available is comforting.
- **Step Five**: The fifth and final circle goes around the all of the others. Let this space be about what you would like to create in your life. List any goal, desire, or wish that you dream about creating for yourself.

Take a look at your five circles and the spaces between. Can you make any connections through the layers? For example, maybe a certain person in level two can help you connect to an organization listed in level three that can connect you to an additional online resource from level four which might lead you to creating something new in your life listed on level five. Grab your pen and start connecting the dots! No worries if a potential connection feels unrealistic; keep connecting and see what happens. You never know what ideas and insights might come to life as you open your mind and heart to the possibilities. Once you have connected all the dots, look over the circles again and take in what you have already created. Also focus on that fifth layer and continue to call in what you want to bring forth. For **Step Six**: read through the following Mantra and journal any additional thoughts and feelings. I am so grateful to you for doing this. Love you!

I AM Connected.
I AM Resourceful.
I AM a Creatrix of Meaningful Support.

~ SPS #5: ~
* Self-Care Practice *

A self-care practice is so nice to think about, isn't it? Just yesterday, I was daydreaming in the shower that when this book is finished, I will dedicate at least an hour a week to a massage. Before the daydream was over, I had created a schedule in my head that every Friday, I would set aside time for a mani-pedi, a massage, maybe a facial, and some sort of energy healing treatment. I think I came back to reality as I was shaving my legs. Yeah, right! A full day of spa treatments once a week. Hello self-care *practice*! That would be a practice makes perfect kind of scenario. Truth is - the last time I had a massage was last year for my 44th birthday. It has been over a year since I last got my nails done and a facial…. shoot, what's a facial? My point is that sometimes self-care feels impossible to fit in with all of our daily responsibilities. But that doesn't mean we don't need it or that we can't make it happen. We do and we can! Sometimes, we just need to use a little creativity to figure out how we can incorporate simple self-care ideas that don't take a lot of time, energy, or cash. My Friday daydream is an all-day affair. And guess what… if I *really, really* wanted it, I could and would make it happen. But obviously it isn't 100 percent in alignment with me or I would be doing that. What *is* in alignment is a recalibration around my self-care '*practice*.' And that recalibration needs to be realistic, easy, and inexpensive. Lucky for all of us, we are Creative Genius Goddesses, so figuring this out together shouldn't be too hard. Work your way through the following questions.

- What gets in my way when it comes to my current self-care practice? _____

_____

_____

Self-Care Now	Self-Care A-NEW!
What I do **now** for my: • Physical Body • Emotional Body • Mental Body • Spiritual Body	What I would **like** to do for my: • Physical Body • Emotional Body • Mental Body • Spiritual Body

- What negative coping strategies do I use instead of a dedicated self-care practice? _____

_____

_____

- What can I do to shift this? _____

_____

- How can I find a realistic balance between what I am doing now and what I know I want for my future?

_____

_____

Hopefully some ideas for a balanced and realistic self-care practice are percolating. As a final step, let's address the potential challenges before we get to the good stuff of actually making a self-care agreement. No matter how hard self-care seems, you deserve it. When you take care of you, you love yourself. Since we are connected, that means that you are loving me, too. Thank you and I love you right back!

- What do I suspect will still get in the way of my new self-care practice? _____

_____

- How will I gently and lovingly address these things? _____

_____

- Even when it feels impossible, how will I stay devoted to myself and to this practice? _____

_____

My New, Realistic, Balanced, and Well-Deserved *Self-Care Practice* Agreement
What I **will** do for my:
• Physical Body
• Emotional Body
• Mental Body
• Spiritual Body

Crystal Love: Nisla's Crystal is Unakite (*oohn*-a-kahyt) which is also referred to as the 'Stone of Vision.' Placed over the Ajna, Unakite's calm and gentle energy can promote the meditative and psychic visualizations needed to rebirth new versions of ourselves. This crystal grounds us in the present and facilitates a balancing of our emotional resonance with our desired spiritual resonance. Known for releasing blockages, Unakite also helps bring forth insight and awareness regarding past experiences and aids us in eliminating exhaustive thought patterns and negative feedback loops. Use this beautiful, earthy stone to determine where you could use some compromise and fairness in your life and relationships since it is wonderful at reframing problems and issues. Whether in the realistic or metaphorical sense, utilize Unakite's abilities to facilitate a deeper understanding of birth, life, death, and renewal as you release and purify the cycles and patterns no longer in alignment with your values. Play with keeping a piece of this stone close, either in your pocket or worn as jewelry, for translating your body's wise communication into a language that can be both seen and heard by others.

Suggested Reading to Connect into your Metaphysical Community of Support, *The Spiral Dance: A Rebirth of the Ancient Religion of the Great Goddess* by Starhawk.

Kim

I've always identified with my inner child. She is sweet. She is also wise. I haven't honored her as much as I would have liked, but I'm getting there. I believe we come forth with all of the knowing that we could ever need in this life. Back when I was younger, I was aware of this and I trusted that wisdom; however, I was simultaneously taught from outside influences to look outside of myself for connection to the Divine. I can remember at seven and eight years old being given messages from my wise inner self. Sometimes they were clear, like when my bedroom caught fire. Before I even smelled the smoke, I was told to get out of the house. Sometimes they weren't so clear. But I can identify that the early religious teachings I received splintered me away from my inner knowing and my intuition. None of my early religious education felt right to me, but I was so young that I didn't know how to communicate or clearly understand why. At nine, my father died, leaving my mother a widow and single parent of four. Because I was the oldest, I immediately stepped into the caregiver role. My body even followed along, jumping ahead of itself, and I started my menstrual cycle that same year. I was so young for that to happen. A time that should have been celebrated, my becoming a woman, went by unnoticed, forever associated with the death of my father. I felt like my childhood was over. Like I had lost my connection to that sweet, wise girl. I know now that my inner child didn't go away, but she did get very quiet and she stayed silent for a very long time. Only about ten years ago did I begin to reconnect to her when I started attending women's retreats. At the first retreat, the leader incorporated hand drumming. Those drumming sessions opened something for me. I started collecting drums. I found churches that used drums in their services. It struck something deep within me… a feeling of knowing that this was how I was going to connect with other people. It was the way back to my sweet, wise inner child. Ironically, the only people in my life, at that time, who were open to me and my drumming were children. We would have big family dinners and events, and afterwards, I would gather all the children around me, and we would drum and tell stories. None of the adults wanted to participate and that was fine. When given permission to really speak, I found that the wisdom that came forth from these little beings was profound. Their inner child was present and empowered. They said beautiful things to me and to each other. They could visualize the bigger picture, and honored events that had taken place during the day. They spoke openly and honestly about how they felt. They were my little teachers. Through drumming, I created space to allow this wisdom to pour out of them. That felt really good. It completed something in me. My family all thought I was a weirdo. I was made fun of. I was mocked, but I kept with it. One day, a friend witnessed me holding these circles with children and said to me, "Kim, this is your calling." I didn't quite know where to begin, but I researched therapeutic drumming and found a training happening across the country. I wanted to go and was met with a lot of resistance. I think, before I even recognized it myself, my family felt me shifting. Somehow, they could sense things were going to change. Going to that training was the first time in my life I stood up for myself. I basically told my husband and my two adult daughters that I was doing it whether or not they approved. I went, and they were right: everything changed. A man walked in on the first day and instantly I knew in my heart that I had known him for lifetimes. It all unfolded rather irrationally because the feelings I felt for him were so strong. Almost immediately, I made the decision to leave my marriage. I can look back now and see that everything that transpired was less about my husband, or this new person in my life, and more about me. I was opening up to a part of myself that had laid hidden for a very long time. It took so much courage for me to follow my heart. The whole situation was very hard, and for that, I am terribly sorry to all who were involved. I had been married 29 years, my children were adults, and everyone felt the pain from my decision. Looking back, I can identify that the illusion of the happy family - an illusion that I created - was understandably very painful for my family to release. Everyone felt the illusion crumbling apart with the choices I was making; yet somehow I kept forging ahead, listening to my soul, and knew that I had to make these changes. There was no way I could keep living the way I was living. Through this process, I have grown into the woman that I am supposed to be. For my whole life, I have always been scared. From the first day of the drumming workshop when this man, my beloved, walked into my life, that feeling changed. Following my path and living my truth has allowed me to find the safety I have always been seeking. Not because of him, but because of me. That security is within me now because I trust myself. I feel beautiful now, too. Before, I had such a skewed perspective. I didn't allow myself to feel beautiful. Through all of this, I have found my inner and outer beauty. I believe it when my beloved tells me that I am beautiful. I never taught this to my children. I fawned over them and told them they were fantastic, but they never saw me living that for myself. They never saw me embodying my beauty, and I realize what a mistake that was. I mothered these two amazing, beautiful, and successful daughters and yet they never experienced me loving myself. Ending my marriage, creating new relationships, and making huge life changes shifted all of that. I see myself differently. I relate to myself differently. By following my heart, I've started thriving instead of merely surviving. Now, four years into this new chapter of my life, I am being called back home to engage in an emergency custody battle for my adolescent niece, stepping back into the role of mother, and a cycle that I have been in for almost five decades. Only, this time, I'm different. Because of my journey, I can now mother in a new way. My niece is aware of things that would have scared me before. Maybe I would have shut her down. Now, I am conscious enough to meet her where she is. To honor her gifts. To parent her in a completely new way. By finding a way to speak my authentic truth, I am able to allow my niece to fully live hers. None of this would be possible if I hadn't found my way back to my inner child. If I hadn't followed my heart and gone to that drumming workshop. If I hadn't listened to my soul's calling and ended my marriage. That inner voice is such a strong part of my life now. I rest when she tells me to rest. I slow down when she tells me to slow down. By finding her again, I have truly found myself. My path may not be yours. That is fine. But all of us have an opportunity to reconnect to our truth. To reconnect to that inner wisdom that we were born with. For me, I couldn't be a creature of the routine if I was to grow and expand. Living from a place of integrity and authenticity isn't always easy, but it is always meaningful. Has my inner child been with me the whole time? Yes. Have I been with her? No. But I've come back to that loving, wise, and connected younger version of myself with the realization that the adult version of me is pretty powerful, creative, and amazing, too.

Making This Story Your Own:

Kim's story shares the importance of following your own path.
Take a moment, breathe, and reflect.
What stands out for you when you read her words?
Is there a situation in your life that is similar to Kim's?
Perhaps part of her story feels connected to your own.
How can you relate her experiences to your past, present, and future?

- *My Connection to Kim's Story* _____

_____

_____

_____

_____

Knowing that you aren't alone, let's gently explore some other themes from Kim's story together:

- **Connecting to Your Inner Child**
    - What image comes up when you think of your inner child? When you listen for her voice, what do you hear? Do you regularly talk to her? Does she regularly talk to you? When you reflect back on your childhood, what feelings come up? When you reflect back on this younger version of yourself, what feelings come up? Do you trust your inner child? Do you feel loved by her? Do you love her? Can you explain why, or why not? Would creating a relationship with your inner child - or recreating the relationship you already have with her - be beneficial for you in anyway?

- **Letting Go of Limiting Belief Systems**
    - What do you believe in? When you think about the world that we live in, what are your beliefs in regard to life and love? What are your beliefs about spirituality? What about right and wrong? What about moral versus immoral? How did you come by all of these beliefs? Are they all yours, or have they been given to you by someone or something else? Can you think back to when these beliefs began? Are they still in alignment with who you are today? Why, or why not? Do your beliefs completely support you, your relationships, and the life you want to create? If so, how do they provide this support? If not, how can they be shifted?

- **Owning Your Beauty**
    - How beautiful are you? Is it easy to answer that question? Why, or why not? When someone notices your inner and outer beauty, are you good at accepting the compliment? If yes, how did you become good at accepting compliments like this? If no, why is it difficult and when did this start? What *is* beautiful to you and how has this notion of beauty been created? How beautiful is your mind? How beautiful is your heart? How beautiful is your Soul? When you think of your beauty from this perspective, do you value your inner beauty differently than your outer beauty? Where did this value system come from? Is it in alignment with your best and highest good?

Sacred Play Suggestions:

~ SPS #1: ~
* Authentic Feelings *

Sometimes, following our hearts can be as simple as following our feelings. When it comes to honoring feelings, Kim offers us a blueprint for this wisdom. Out of a desire for emotional authenticity, she shares that she has made many needed life changes. Perhaps a life change isn't in order for all of us, but maybe a shift around recognizing, valuing, and honoring our feelings is. Let's give it a try. Circle the first five words below that jump out at you.

- Sad - Joyful - Embarrassed - Mischievous - Lonely - Happy	- Playful - Exhausted - Exhilarated - Connected - Loving - Enraged	- Lethargic - Disenfranchised - Blissful - Angry - Starving - Turned On

Why did those five feelings catch your attention just now?

_____

_____

Now, write down five more feeling words in the box below. If you'd like, feel free to use the examples from above.

┌───┐
│   │
│   │
│   │
│   │
└───┘

Now, *draw* five more feeling words in the following box. Get creative and have fun! Create images or designs to represent the feelings. Write them using bubble letters and curly cues. Try out different colors and play with markers, crayons, and colored pencils. Cover the space however you feel called and when you are finished, sit with what you have created. Read through the words again and allow each one a chance to resonate.

┌───┐
│   │
│   │
│   │
│   │
└───┘

Think back to a time when you have felt any of the feelings that have come forward during this activity. Take a deep breath and allow those past memories to connect to more recent times when you have felt the same or similar. Take a moment to journal and reflect around the following questions.

- What are the differences and similarities between my past and my present *experiences?* _____

_____

- What are the differences and similarities between my past and my present *feelings?* _____

_____

- How am I different now? _____

_____

_____

- What have I changed? _____
  _____

- Where have I grown? _____
  _____

- Where could I grow some more? _____
  _____

In honor of your past and present, fill in the following sentences. As you do, hold an awareness of following your feelings and ultimately, following your heart.

- The next time I feel_____ I will _____
  _____

- The next time I feel_____ I will _____
  _____

- The next time I feel_____ I will _____
  _____

- The next time I feel_____ I will _____
  _____

- The next time I feel_____ I will _____
  _____

When you are finished, read your sentences aloud. Claim your feelings and their authenticity with empowerment, dedication, and the wisdom that they are *yours* and they are here for very valid reasons. You are amazing! Thank you for doing this. Honoring our feelings is important. Taking this time for yourself reminds me that I can, too! Love you!

~ SPS #2: ~
* Inner Child *

Getting to know our Inner Child has recently become a popular topic for good reason. Connecting to this younger version of ourselves can be freeing and empowering. Add to that the childlike wisdom, honesty, and spontaneity that can come forward, and this youthful aspect of our consciousness can offer our adult sensibilities a welcome respite. Accessing this innocent inner dreamer is actually easier than you might think. Many different techniques exist to help you with this connection, but simply opening a heartfelt invitation within your mind is effective. Take a moment and let your memory drift back to your childhood. Allow the different moments in time to fade in and out. From your earliest memories to your young adult years, picture these versions of yourself. Observe this part of you - your Inner Child - as she smiles without hesitation, remains playful despite stress or worry, and doesn't second guess her instincts. Now, allow an aspect of you to come forward that is approximately between six and eight years old. As she stands before you, take the time to really see her. Write the answers to the following questions so that you remember the details.

- How old is she? _____
- What is she wearing? _____
- How is her hair? _____
- What has just happened to her? _____
- What expression does she have on her face? _____
- What is she thinking? _____
- What is she feeling? _____

~ Gaze into her eyes. ~
~ From your adult-self, thank her for being here and tell her you love her. ~
~ Wrap her in your arms and let her know that she is safe because you are here and in control. ~
~ Prepare to honestly listen. ~

As you ask her the following questions, allow your pen to move freely without censorship or attempts to control the process. Permit your Inner Child to communicate with you in any way she chooses.

- How can we have more joy? _____
  _____
- How can we have more connection? _____
  _____
- How can we feel more secure? _____
  _____
- How can we remember our innocence? _____
  _____
- How can we take better care of each other? _____
  _____

- What else can I do for you? _____
  _____

When you bring your intuitive writing to a close, take a moment and read over what you have written. Once again, connect to your Inner Child and send her love and gratitude. With her input, come up with a special activity that you can do for yourself today in honor of your Inner Child's continued love, devotion, and trust. Write your activity below as an official agreement.

- Today, my Inner Child and I will_____

For the last step, continue this process and journal your intended plan to respect, love, and value this sacred relationship. Your Inner Child loves you. Always know that. I do, too, and I am so grateful for you!

From this moment forward, I will honor my Inner Child by...

_____
_____
_____

~ SPS #3: ~
* One Year Left *

In the book, *A Year to Live: How to Live This Year as If It Were Your Last*, author Stephen Levine asks the question, "What would you do if you only had one year left to live?" This is a tough question. It is also a good question. *Really* think about it. If you only had one year left to live, what would you be doing differently? Go through the questions on the next page and write down the first answer that comes to you. Be honest and be authentic. One thing to keep in mind as you answer these questions: **This is about YOU**. These answers are not about preparing your family. They are not about making sure that everyone and everything will be taken care of after you pop the mortal coil. This is only about YOU... YOUR wants... YOUR desires... YOUR needs... and, what you would be doing differently for yourself if you only had a limited amount of time left on Earth.

If I only had one year left to live....

- What would I start doing? _____

- What would I stop doing? _____

- What would I think about? _____

- What wouldn't I think about? _____

- Who would I spend time with? _____

- Who wouldn't I spend time with? _____
- What would I spend my time on? _____
- What would I not spend my time on? _____
- What unfinished business would I take care of? _____
- Which relationships would I repair? _____
- Which relationships would I end? _____
- How would I fulfill my existence for the next 365 days to feel fully alive and present?
  _____
  _____

Give your list another read and with a focus on your wants, desires, and needs, get clear on the following.

- Today I will **release** _____
- Tomorrow I will **release** _____
- Next week I will **release** _____
- Next month I will **release** _____
- Today I will **begin** _____
- Tomorrow I will **begin** _____
- Next week I will **begin** _____
- Next month I will **begin** _____

Keep this close and read it often as a reminder of what you **do** want, what you **do** desire, and what you **do** need. Now breathe, it was only an exercise! I can't wait to see what new things you are going to birth into your life with all of these new endings and beginnings. You are an inspiration, Sister. Love you!

~ SPS #4: ~
* Soft Belly *

In the same book mentioned above, Stephen Levine suggests a soft belly meditation for release and letting go. If you think about it, the more we constrict our bodies, minds, and hearts, the less comfortable we feel. When we aren't able to feel comfortable, we aren't able to relax. When this happens, being mentally, emotionally, or spiritually present - popularly referred to as *'being in the moment* - becomes virtually impossible. Yet, if we aren't in the present moment, where are we? Many books and many teachers have studied this topic. It seems to be the general consensus that when we are prevented from 'being in the moment,' we are experiencing a mixed bag of unconsciously and consciously reliving the past while simultaneously fretting about the future. No fun! Yet, if we intentionally expand and soften our physical bodies - especially around our hearts and bellies - we can create space for a much-needed pause. We can relax, get comfy, and slow the mind to focus back into the present moment. Let's give it a try. Put on some soothing, instrumental music if you would like, and prepare yourself for the soft belly meditation below which is based on Levine's work. Softly read it to yourself or ask someone to read it to you.

Take a few deep breaths with your hands on your abdomen.
As you expand and contract with your in-breath and out-breath,
let your hands begin to gently massage and relax the skin and muscles of your belly.
Become aware of the beginning, middle, and ending of each breath.
...Breathe in... Hold...and Breathe out....
As you become more and more aware of the sensations of your own touch,
begin to let your body soften in response.
Breathe and soften your skin to receive.
Breathe and soften your muscles to receive.
Breathe and soften your organs to receive.
...Breathe in... Hold...and Breathe out....
With each inhale and each exhale, continue softening your tissues and your flesh to receive.
Let go of what you have been holding onto for a lifetime.
...Breathe in... Hold...Breathe out....and Let go....
Let the hardness dissolve and float away.
...Breathe in... Hold...Breathe out....and Dissolve...
Release the fear, the pain, and the hurt.
...Breathe in... Hold...Breathe out....and Release...
Allow your soft and merciful belly to be filled with grace, kindness, and compassion.
Allow your soft and tender belly to receive.
In this place of softness, be present.
In this place of softness, be still.
In this place of softness, be you.
...Breathe in... Hold...and Breathe out....

Spend as much time as you need in this soft-belly-state of awareness. If thoughts, feelings, or sensations arise, allow them to come and go at will. As you become present to the present, know that your softness and receptivity will create a butterfly effect of softness and receptivity for those around you. Thank you for doing this. I am so grateful that you did. I love you. Continue with the needed time for integration, and when you are ready, take a few moments to reflect or journal about your experience.

In My Soft-Belly State I...

_____

_____

_____

~ SPS #5: ~
* You Are Beautiful *

Recently, the science of Infant Mental Health (IMH) has focused on the developing brain. Turns out, there is a huge amount of neurological magick happening in utero and our first 1,000 days of life. During our first few years, our environments and our experiences work together with our brains to literally carve out neural pathways. This carving out, or elimination based on need, is a process known as pruning which is also a gardening term that refers to the cutting back of plants in order to make them grow in certain ways. When you are born, you have the capacity to learn any language. Your brain works with your environment to identify which language(s) you need based on what is being spoken around you. Once this is determined, the other neural pathways for learning other languages are removed or pruned. This process is the foundation for all of our academic, social, and emotional learning. Most specialists agree that our brains have done a major amount of neurological pruning by the age of three. Does this mean that we can't learn new things as we get older? Not at all. To use the example of learning language once again, the countless programs for adults to learn foreign languages are proof that we can learn anything at any age. Yet, identifying that we want to learn a new language is a pretty common cultural construct. There are TV commercials and other forms of advertising bombarding our psyches with the idea all the time. But where are the commercials advertising how to learn self-love as an adult? What about advertising how to develop a strong sense of self-worth? How about a marketing campaign to assist us in recognizing and celebrating our unique inner and outer beauty? Yes, some of these things do exist. But we could use much, much more when it comes to creating new neural pathways for functional and optimal ways of being in relationship to ourselves and others. Kim generously shares with us that for many years she did not fully recognize or embody her inner and outer beauty. Today, she courageously identifies that this no can no longer work for her Greatest and Highest Good. Take a moment and think back to your earliest memories of your inner and outer beauty. Consider the following in relation to the pruning that may have taken place when you were younger:

What were you taught in relation to your own beauty? _____

_____

_____

- Did validation come from an outside source? _____
- Was validation taught to come from within? _____
- Was validation absent? _____

Things to Ponder

If you were never taught or shown how to have a loving and supportive relationship
with your beauty, your brain may not know how to recognize, accept, and assimilate
an appreciation for how beautiful you are. It's OK… you can shift this!

How did these early experiences influence your current ideals and standards of beauty? _____

_____

_____

- Are these standards and ideals yours? _____
- Are they from someone or something else? _____
- Are they a mixture? _____

Things to Ponder

Our subconscious beliefs and standards - which relate to our current behaviors and choices - can be hidden in plain sight. You may not even realize that you feel this way because the feelings are deeply habituated. Awareness is key in this release and recalibration process.

How can you begin to recognize your inner and outer beauty in ways that feel authentic and consistent?

_____

_____

_____

- How can your inner critic be loved into peaceful satisfaction? _____
  _____

- How are the perceived flaws really your greatest gifts? _____
  _____

- How can you become your own inner and outer beauty muse? _____
  _____

Things to Ponder

This is about practice and repetition. Think of digging an irrigation ditch in your brain so that the flow of thoughts goes on a different journey... a journey that you are consciously choosing for yourself. From now on, every time you intentionally think about recognizing and honoring your unique beauty, another shovel-full of Earth is removed to create a new neural pathway for self-love. As a final step, to relearn, re-develop, and recreate a loving relationship to yourself, finish the following statement.

**From this moment forward,
I will recognize, appreciate, and accept my inner and outer beauty by...**

_____

_____

_____

You are truly beautiful. Stunning! Inside and out. Shine that light, my love. The unique and Divine artistry that makes you so special is a gift for the world. Thank you for being you. I love you.

Crystal Love: Kim's Crystal is the beautiful pink heart mender, Rhodochrosite (roh-duh-***kroh***-sahyt). This healing stone promotes love throughout all time and space. As a true stone of the heart, Rhodochrosite brings forward emotional wounds to be healed so that the connection to our Divine Purpose may be revealed and activated. This connection gifts us the opportunity to let go of that which has been weighing us down while increasing the feelings of replenishment and revitalization. As this invigorating process occurs, Rhodochrosite keeps up with the unconditional love by gifting a spirit of liberated forgiveness as it supports us to release co-dependent relational patterns. Hold a piece in your hand and play with setting intentions for balanced and grounded human-to-human connection. Try wearing a piece of Rhodochrosite to create at your highest and wildest levels of potential. Don't worry, this newfound creative freedom won't come as a surprise to the system because Rhodochrosite is actually known to alleviate feelings of shock and panic. As a profound nurturer, Rhodochrosite reconnects us to our inner child, allowing us to genuinely comfort her while listening to her needs. Finally, this is just an all-around great stone to have in the house because it brings on the energies of purpose, cooperation, altruism, and generosity.

Suggested Reading to Connect to you Inner Rhythmic Goddess: *When the Drummers Were Women: A Spiritual History of Rhythm* by Lane Redmond.

Additional Journaling and SPS Space

Nancy

I was born in Mexico City and came to the U.S. when I was five years old. In Mexico, we were Catholic, but when we came to the States, my parents found a very strict Christian church. Our family was the only Latino family at this church and I remember struggling because we experienced quite a lot of racism. We didn't know the language or the culture and we were judged. It was a very rigid upbringing trying to fit into all of the boxes. In this particular church, the message for women was one of subservience to men, suppression, and shame. In this church, sex was only for procreation. At a very young age, my mother caught me masturbating. She was so upset, and I got a ration of shit from her and my father. My mom was an incredibly loving woman, but because of all the religious teachings that she and my dad believed, they told me that I was bad and that it was a major sin pleasuring myself. In spite of that, I kept masturbating because it felt so delicious and pleasuring my body felt right - even though the guilt and shame would creep in and I would cry and pray for God's forgiveness afterward. Looking back, it was this defining time that began the suppression of my sacred sexuality… which breaks my heart because I am such a sexual being! For me, as the adult woman I am today, my sexuality is more than just sex; it is the source of my creative power and spirituality. For so many years, I hid this side of myself. I was ashamed of what I wanted. I was ashamed of my body. At nineteen, I blindly entered into what became an unhappy marriage. We were both young, and he was raised in the same strict church environment. Neither of us had any experience with our bodies or any way to understand sensual desire or passion. I went into that marriage a virgin, with all of these desires and expectations of romance and love. When that didn't happen, I was crushed. The sex was extremely painful and there was no loving connection. My mom had explained some things about sex, but she passed away when I was sixteen. I knew logistically what was going to happen, but I had no one to help me understand the loving, intimate side of sex with my husband. I shut myself down and created the belief system that sex was something I didn't want in my life because it felt awful. The marriage ended and my lack of connection to myself led to many other bad relationships. Even when I did have a pleasurable experience, I was scared. I didn't know who I was. I didn't know how to voice what I wanted in sex, or in life. As a Latina, I was also taught that a woman's purpose is to serve men. I was never to put myself above men. My wants and needs didn't matter. I was here to cook and clean and sex was just one more thing I provided. When I entered into my second marriage, it was the same scenario of 'serve and put myself last.' I had no idea how to express what I wanted, and I lost myself even more. This went on for years. Deep down, I knew something was missing. I knew there was more *to* me and more *for* me, I just couldn't pinpoint what it was. One day, I was listening to a webinar on the treadmill. It was all about women in business and female empowerment. After listening, I was filled with these questions of, "Who am I?" "What do I want to do with my life?" "What do I want to be?" I broke down. I was in tears trying to answer these questions and I had no idea where to start. Right before my mom died, she said to me, "You are a healer and you are meant to help many people." I had no idea what it meant at the time, but as I was weeping on that treadmill her words came back to me. I opened myself and at that moment it felt like the Universe poured into me. Soon after that, things started shifting and coming into alignment. I went to an event for my business and I met this incredible person. He looked at me and said, "There is fire within you. You are a beautiful, sexy Latina. Own it." Hearing those words, that I was not only beautiful - but sexy too - was a pivotal moment for me because for the first time, I agreed! It finally clicked for me that I was indeed a beautiful, fiery, passionate being with so much to give. With that statement, I found the permission I needed to claim my right as a sensual, creative, and sexual woman. The mirror was held up for me to see the truth of my being - *my whole being* - and I stepped in. I started exploring my body. I bought sex toys. I had so much fun finding out what gave me pleasure. This process of discovery was something that I did solely for myself. As I became more dedicated to honoring my sensuality, it also became clear that my marriage was over. I needed to be true to who I was and what I wanted. I couldn't serve anymore. I could not stay in a relationship where I wasn't touched in the way I wanted and needed to be touched. I could not stay in a relationship where I wasn't loved in the way I wanted and needed to be loved. I separated from my husband, and after some time of focusing on myself and doing my own healing, I met someone. I had asked the Universe to bring someone into my life who aligned with me. Someone in tune with who I was and what I wanted. I asked for someone passionate, someone who saw the best in me, and someone I could have blissful, soulful sex with. I had no idea it would happen so quickly. One night, I was out with a friend, and this beautiful man came up to me. Before saying a word, he kissed me. I mean who does that? Any other time, I would have slapped someone, but this felt different. This felt familiar. This felt passionate. We ended up kissing for hours. I had never been kissed like that before. The connection I felt with him and what I was experiencing was deep and profound. That evening, I made a conscious choice. Somehow, in a short span of time this man helped me create a space for myself to just let it all go. And I did. I released all of the shame, limiting beliefs, and guilt that I had been holding onto for decades. We went home together and made love for hours. I didn't know sex like that existed. The passion between us was physical, but it also felt like so much more. Somehow, completely naked and vulnerable, I felt seen and accepted for the first time. Being with him in that way, it felt right. It felt like home. Since having this experience, and many more like it, I feel more creative, more fiery, bolder, and fiercer. Yes, fear is still present, but I am much freer to be the woman I am meant to be. I have finally found my voice. I have finally stepped into my value. Just like my mother said to me all those years ago, I **am** a healer. I know that I am meant to help others heal with this knowledge of sexual freedom, creative power, and sacred sexuality. This level of sexual awakening is truly sacred. Now, I ask for what I want and feel strong in my non-negotiables. I will no longer serve without asking for my pleasure in return. This whole experience has shifted every aspect of my life. Physically, I am fitter and stronger than I've ever been. My food choices nourish my body for its highest good. My body, mind, and soul are open and receptive. I walk differently. I move differently. I inspire differently. I am more at ease with who I am. Every aspect of me, from my thighs to my intuition, from my stretch marks to my soul, is alive and amplified. My business flows free and in abundance. My creativity is richer. I teach my daughter self-love and body confidence with authenticity because not only do I believe it is important, I practice it daily and lead by example. As women, I want all of us to let go of our inhibitions and insecurities. I want us to allow our bodies to be loved as they are. Our breasts are perfect. Our tummies are perfect. Let's get out of our heads. Let's stop questioning and looking for what is *wrong*. Let's let it all go and allow ourselves the permission to really receive what it is that we *want*. We can start by asking for our needs to be met, sexually and otherwise. When we do this, it will spill over into every aspect of our lives. Living this way is truly orgasmic. I know, because I live like this and the payoffs are endless. Not only do I pleasure myself and gift myself multiple orgasms a day… orgasms with my partner are longer, deeper, richer and the sort of time-stopping experiences that I thought only happened in the movies. In allowing myself this freedom, I have discovered many new and surprising things about me both in and out of the bedroom. I am so grateful that I have been awakened through the spiritual connection of allowing my pleasure and my orgasms to come forward. So much of my life has opened up in ways that I never imagined possible. I have found strength in the raw vulnerability of just being me, and this magic is available to us all. Ladies, we've got 8,000 nerve endings in our vaginas… 8,000 nerve endings all designed to give us pleasure. This is nothing to be ashamed of. This is something to be celebrated! Divine sex is Divine Love. Why else would we be created in this way? Own the skin you are in. Ask for what you want. Tap into your sexuality. Say yes. Say no. Say whatever you want. Living this way - as a sensual, sexual, and soulful woman - involves my whole being. I love it. I absolutely love it and I want all women to know that they can live and love like this, too.

Making This Story Your Own:

Nancy's story reminds us of the importance of the body, mind, spirit connection.
Take a moment, breathe, and reflect.
What stands out for you when you read her words?
Is there a situation in your life that is similar to Nancy's?
Perhaps part of her story feels connected to your own.
How can you relate her experiences to your past, present, and future?

- *My Connection to Nancy's Story* _____
_____
_____
_____
_____
_____

Knowing that you aren't alone, let's gently explore some other themes from Nancy's story together:

- **There is Fire Within You**
    - Are you fiery? When you hear the words fierce, bold, sexy, brilliant, and wild... do they remind you of yourself? Do you want them to? Where do you feel these words in your body? When was the last time you spoke with passion, acted with passion, and loved with passion? Are there untamed, unruly, uninhibited, and uncontainable places within your consciousness asking to be set free? Can you oblige? What makes you furious? What turns you on? What brings you to your knees in despair? What fills your spirit with ecstasy? How satisfied are you with your connection to these deep and powerful feelings? What can you spark to life right now to begin burning brightly from within?

- **Asking for What You Desire**
    - What gives you pleasure and how do you like to receive it? How do you like your body to be touched? How do you indulge your heart? What stimulates your mind? Do you give voice to your desires? Do you ask for what you want? Why, or why not? Do you feel comfortable exploring what turns you on? Are you open to doing this with yourself or with a partner? What about exploring your relationship to your Orgasm? Is your sensual contentment and sexual satisfaction something that you would like to give more attention to? If so, what are a few small ways you can begin appointing more energy to this side of yourself?

- **Sacred Sexuality**
    - Is your sexuality connected to your spirituality? Is sex sacred for you? Can it be? Is your Orgasm a Divine Experience? Why, or why not? When you honor the sensual and sexual sides of yourself, what happens? What feelings come up before, during, and after these aspects of you are allowed to come forward? Is your relationship to your sensuality, sexuality, and spirituality fulfilling? Is there any need for healing, soothing, or rebalancing? If so, how can you begin the process of enhancing the connection you have to these sides of yourself?

Sacred Play Suggestions:

~ SPS #1: ~
* Pleasure *

Our bodies are really magickal when you think about how the various systems work together to create feelings and sensations. Take a second and gently rub your right hand over your left palm. How does that feel? Now, slowly bring your fingertips up over your wrist and onto your forearm. Stroke up and down with the lightest of touch, and then let your index finger trace the crease of your elbow back and forth a few times. Hmmmmmm… how do you feel now? Keep going! Touch your body the way you want to be touched and take notice of what happens. Move from your arm to your shoulder, letting your fingers dance across your chest and up towards your cheeks. Play with the softest of touches over your ears, eyes, and forehead. When you are ready, move down and tickle your ribs one by one. Explore your beautiful body. Get to know yourself in a different way. Give and receive pleasure however you want to give and receive pleasure. As you continue to open yourself up to this experience, take note of what is going on within you. What are you thinking? What do you feel *on* your body? How do you feel *in* your body? Take a few deep breaths and keep going. Rediscover every inch of your exquisite self. Let this connection to your sensuality and your pleasure awaken you to other aspects of your consciousness. Pause for a moment and think…

What does my *body* want and need right now?

_____

_____

What does my *heart* want and need right now?

_____

_____

What does my *mind* want and need right now?

_____

_____

What does my *Soul* want and need right now?

_____

_____

Now, look around where you are sitting and find three different items with three different textures. You have complete mastery over this entire experience so choose whatever strikes your fancy. A blanket, a scarf, a piece of ice, a soft brush, some lotion… all are great examples of what may be convenient and accessible for a pleasurable encounter. Our bodies are wonderful transmitters of Divine information. Our skin, with all of its sensitivities, can show and tell us much in the form of bodily wisdom, instinct, and intuition. Our unique desires and our subsequent reactions and responses to feeling pleasure are just another example of how remarkable we are. Begin to lightly touch your skin again. As you do, explore how the various textures of these three items feel. Play with pressure and movement as you glide these things over your miraculous body. With a dedication only to what feels good, investigate how the different items evoke different sensations. Allow the pleasure you are feeling to permeate the layers of your awareness and, with genuine sincerity, complete the following sentences.

- When I experience pleasure, **physically** I am _____
  _____

- When I experience pleasure, **emotionally** I am_____
  _____

- When I experience pleasure, **mentally** I am_____
  _____

- When I experience pleasure, **spiritually** I am_____
  _____

Continue on and begin to massage your loyal feet. As you touch the skin of your feet and toes, become aware of how reliable and dependable these two parts of your body are. Ask your feet what would give them the most pleasure. When you receive the answer, oblige and pour pleasure into your feet. As you do this, repeat the Mantra below and record any messages that come forward.

As I give pleasure to my Body,
I receive my Body's wisdom for my Divine Purpose.

_____

_____

Next move on to your mid-section. As you touch the skin of your belly and your chest, become aware of how empowered and loving these parts of your body are. Ask your belly and your chest what would give them the most pleasure. When you receive the answer, oblige and pour pleasure into them. As you do this, repeat the Mantra below and record any messages that come forward.

As I give pleasure to my Heart,
I receive my Heart's wisdom for my Divine Purpose.

_____

_____

Keep moving up and let one hand rest at your throat and the other at your mid-brow. As you touch the skin of your throat and forehead, become aware of how wise and energized these parts of your body are. Ask your throat and your mid-brow what would give them the most pleasure. When you receive the answer, oblige and pour pleasure into them. As you do this, repeat the Mantra below and record any messages that come forward.

**As I give pleasure to my Mind,
I receive my Mind's wisdom for my Divine Purpose.**

_____

_____

Finally, let all ten fingertips tickle your scalp and from your temples to your crown and on down to the base of your skull, massage your head. As you rub, become aware of how awakened and connected this part of your body is. Ask your head what would give it the most pleasure. When you receive the answer, oblige and pour pleasure into it. As you do this, repeat the Mantra below and record any messages that come forward.

**As I give pleasure to my Soul,
I receive my Soul's wisdom for my Divine Purpose.**

_____

_____

Wow, Sister. Thank you. Thank you for devoting time and energy to your pleasure. Your Divine Purpose is amazing, and it is so very needed in our world today. You are an inspiration! I love you!

~ SPS #2: ~
* Clitoris Conversation *

If thinking about sensual and sexual pleasure feels a bit weird to you, don't worry. We have been taught to turn away from our body's natural wisdom and capacity for pleasure for thousands of years. However, think about this: our Clitoris is filled with over 8,000 nerve endings. This part of our anatomy is dedicated to pleasure - ***our*** pleasure - and it has nothing at all to do with procreation. Let's get to know her! Yep, you read it right. I just said, "Let's get to know our Clitoris," and I am not joking. I am totally serious. Come on, we can do this! It will be fun! I promise! I get it… it may seem a bit odd talking to your Clitoris… but trust me - you do want *her* to talk to *you* - or better yet, you want her to **SING** to you when the time comes for her to be a willing participant in your Orgasms, right? So, how about getting to know this anatomically small - yet ecstatically huge - powerhouse in a new way? Do what you need to do to get comfortable. Create privacy. Play relaxing music. Light a candle. Diffuse essential oils. Breathe and smile… smile and breathe…. OK, first things first, how are you feeling about all of this? Take a minute to journal around anything and everything that is coming up.

What feelings are present as I am preparing to meet my Clitoris?

_____

_____

Way to go! All right, are you ready to be pleasurably playful? Good! Relax your eyes and release any tension you may be holding in your body. With each in-breath and out-breath, step deeper into the realm of your imagination. When you are ready, visualize the physical embodiment of your Clitoris standing before you. Pay close attention to her details and characteristics and record them below so that you don't forget.

- How old is she? _____
- How tall is she? _____
- What body type does she have? _____
- What color is her skin? _____
- What color is her hair? _____
- What color are her eyes? _____
- What kind of clothing is she wearing? _____
- Does she remind you of anyone? _____
- From where and what time period does she come from? _____

_____

Make eye contact with her and introduce yourself. What is her name?

Thank her for being here with you and ask her what wisdom she has for you. Record her words below.

My Clitoris' Wisdom

_____

_____

Now, with this connection to your Clitoris, can you create a Sacred Contract for your pleasure? Give it a try. Sink back into the internal world of your visualization and imagine an improvised banter taking place between you two Goddesses.

Sacred Pleasure Contract	
My Wants, Needs, and Desires…	**Clitoris' Wants, Needs, and Desires…**
1.	1.
2.	2.
3.	3.
4.	4.
5.	5.

Dang! How crazy is that? Did you ever even think that when you picked up this book you would be making a '*Sacred Pleasure Contract*' with your Clitoris? I mean… who does that? **We do** - that's who! Because our pleasure is paramount, and nobody is going to make it a priority but us! OK, last step for this activity, but feel free to hang out with your Clitoris as long as you want. Close your eyes and connect back into her. As you do, she smiles warmly and hands you something. It is a gift. You hug her with gratitude and tell her goodbye for now. In preparation to leave, you make a date to see her again soon. When you are ready, bring your awareness back into your body and your physical environment. Reacquaint yourself to the present moment and record the gift she gave you as well as the date for your next encounter. Thank you for taking the time to do this! Love you!

My Gift

_____

_____

Our Next Date: _____

~ SPS #3: ~
* Enchantress *

The Enchantress is probably one of the most misunderstood, misinterpreted, and yet most needed of the Feminine archetypes. Even the word, *Enchantress*, conjures up some pretty specific images. What comes up for you when you hear it? Take a moment to draw or free write in the box below and see what comes forward.

Enchantress

Typically, in our fairy tales and stories, the Enchantress is depicted as a witchy woman who is up to no good. Alternating between horrid hag and beautiful temptress, she usually wants to kill the fair Maiden or at least keep her away from Prince Charming at all costs, denying us our happy ending. She is powerful, uncontrollable, cunning, and aggressive. As the beautiful seductress, her beauty makes her mysterious and wicked. As the hag, her repulsiveness makes her easy to hate and fear. What we are not told in our stories is that the hostile potency of the Enchantress is our own unbridled, uncaged, and extraordinary Feminine intuition and POWER. *Of course* she wants to protect us from marrying Prince Charming! An immature, spoiled dude living in a patriarchal world of female servitude who obviously has no idea how to create any true intimacy but is applauded because he can wield a sword and kill things… ugghhh…. Sister, for *reals*? Do you really want to hook your wagon up to *that*? Our Inner Enchantress takes one look, says, "Oh, *hell* no!" and then creates the destruction needed to prevent it from coming true. The Enchantress relates us to our sexuality, our pleasure for pleasure's sake, and our natural ebbs and flows of hormones, psychic awareness, and emotional intelligence. She is not always pretty, but she is always authentic. Like the other three archetypes of the Sacred Feminine - Maiden, Mother, and Crone - she relates to Mother Moon, Mother Earth, our menstrual cycle, and our physical life stage. As the Waning Moon, she reminds us that all things must slow and diminish in order to be replenished and renewed. As the Season of Fall, the Enchantress reminds us to prepare for the never-ending eventuality of Winter's death. As the Luteal, or PMS, phase of our menstrual cycle, she forces us towards isolation and quietue in order for us to rest as our uterine lining sheds. As the physical age and stage of perimenopause and menopause, she reminds us of our wisdom and power and will not be denied by society's current cultural obsession with and deification of youth. We need our Inner Enchantress because she loves us unconditionally as a fierce, protective, mature, well-rounded, and badass momma bear. She gets vilified because in our world today there still is much confusion and fear around a woman standing in her truth, her power, her cyclical wisdom, her sexuality, her sensuality, her wisdom, her beauty, her emotional authenticity, her needs, her wants, her pleasure, her wisdom, and her strength. Now, take another moment, and draw or free write about what comes up for you regarding the energy of your Inner Enchantress. No matter how old you are, you feel her. She is there and she comes to you on silvery threads of moon beams and crisp night air. She roils and boils through your veins as rage, anger, and the purifying weight of a gut-wrenching scream. She energizes you equally through both your orgasms and your sobs. You see her when you catch the beautiful angle of a cheek in the mirror and pause to think, "Who *is* that beautiful woman?" … Only to realize that the Goddess in the looking glass is YOU.

I AM ~Enchantress~ I AM

When respected, understood, and honored, our Enchantress Energy can be expressed, recognized and channeled as wildly inspired creativity, mysterious and thrilling sensuality, bold and vivid empowerment, and dynamic intuition that is equally prophetic and shamanic. With this wisdom in our minds, let's drop it down into our bodies and channel our Inner Enchantress. With her dramatic flair, she can help us destroy what is no longer serving us when it comes to belief systems about our power, pleasure, needs, and truth. If you've got a favorite sexy song to play or some rhythmic drumming to move to, go ahead and put it on. When you are ready, stand with your feet a little wider than shoulder width apart and begin to move your hips in a figure eight. Move slowly and breathe deeply. Feel the sensuous heat being created in your body as you move your hips, buttocks, and *yoni* in round, circular patterns. Play with allowing your arms and hands to flow and dance to the natural rhythms you are creating. Touch your body, and with gentle compression, press this energy into your skin, muscles, and bones. Keep your movement steady as you connect into the deep, purging, and powerful energies of your Enchantress. Based on your inspired intuition, when it feels right, play with claiming the following statements aloud. Chant and move, as you allow this stimulating energy to sink into your consciousness.

Enchantress Chants

I am a dynamic, powerful, bold, and beautiful woman.
My sexuality, sensuality, and lush creativity are a gift for all creation.
I declare and welcome my passions, desires, and pleasures with no explanations and no apologies.
I honor my needs. I speak my truth. I command my authenticity.
I pronounce authority over my body, my cycles, my rhythms, and my natural womanly abundance.
My dynamic, Divine, and Feminine empowerment is mine and it is worthy!

Well, hello you fine, Divine Mommy! Woo-Hoo! That was awesome. Keep moving and keep claiming your Enchantress Chants. Create your own below. If I were there, I'd be drumming, chanting, singing, and dancing right along with you! I love you. You are beautiful! Thank you!

My Enchantress Chants

_____

_____

_____

_____

~ SPS #4: ~
* Temple of You *

At sacred and historical sites across the globe, there have been temples and structures built in honor of the Great Goddess. These sites reflect the beauty, fertility, fecundity, and verdant richness of the female body in both form and design. Some sacred sites were built in areas where the natural beauty of the Earth reflected breasts, a full pregnant belly, and had a cave or opening to represent the vagina and birth canal. Thinking of your own form from this divine perspective, your body *is* a temple. What would the *'Temple of You'* honor? Your goodness? Your ability to birth new life? Your compassion? The *Temple of You* would probably honor many of the wonderful things that make you special. If you can, get a compass and lie down to do this activity. These ancient sites were built with specific aspects of the structures relating to specific directions for astrological and geological purposes. This was done to harness the energy of the Earth and the Sky. Well, Goddess, you are deserving of the same devotion and attention. Lie down with your feet to the South, with your right arm pointing West, your left arm pointing East, and your head facing North. Get comfortable and read through the following guided visualization.

*As you relax, begin to blend your energy with the energy of Mother Earth. Feel the reciprocal exchange of life-force being fused with the timeless creation wisdom of love and nurturance. Let your awareness travel **South** to the direction of the **Emotions**. As you connect into the emotional layer of your consciousness, bring energy up into your feet and legs.*
This is the entryway into the Temple of You.
Imagine a great song being sung at the Temple Gates in celebration of your emotional wisdom. Breathe and know the words to this exultant Mantra below.

My Mantra of Emotion

---

*Let your awareness now travel to the **East**, the direction of **Spirituality**. As you connect into the Spiritual layer of your consciousness, bring energy around and into your left arm and shoulder. This is the great hall of your Soul. You hear another melody being sung in honor of your essence. Breathe and know the words to this exultant Mantra below.*

My Mantra of Spirit

---

*Your awareness now grounds itself in the **West**, the direction of **Physicality**. As you connect into the physical layer of your consciousness, bring energy around and into your right arm and shoulder. This is the great hall of your instincts and senses. Again, another chorus drifts over you exclaiming your keen bodily wisdom. Breathe and know the words to this exultant Mantra on the next page.*

My Mantra of Body

---

*Now, you are drawn to the **North**, the direction of **Intellect**. As you connect into this mental layer of your consciousness, bring energy up to your head and crown. This is the great library of your temple. In this place you hear many different languages and tongues in Divine descant praising your knowledge. Breathe and know the words to this exultant Mantra below.*

My Mantra of Mind

---

*Finally, you are drawn into the **innermost chamber** of your great temple, the place of **Source and Center**. This powerful vortex is your Sacred Pubic Triangle and all life emanates from here. As you connect into this layer of your divinity, bring energy into your womb center. In this sacred space, innumerable voices from innumerable worlds gratefully chant in honor of the glory that is you. Breathe and know the words to this exultant Mantra below.*

My Mantra of Divinity

Allow this to integrate as you walk back through the Temple. Your emotional, mental, and spiritual energy has shifted to assimilate this deserved respect and warranted reverence. You exit the inner-chamber and walk toward the library. Continuing onward through the great halls, you finally arrive back at the entryway. Once you have crossed the temple gates, turn around and feel the open, unconditional welcome that is eternally yours. Walk back into your physical space and your physical body. Wrap your arms tightly around your shoulders and take three deep breaths. When you are ready for reentry, stand up slowly and begin to move, reacquainting yourself with present moment.

Whoa, that went a lot deeper than I expected! Was it as good for you as it was for me? ☺ You are a temple, Sister. So am I! We all are! Thanks for taking the time. I appreciate you and I love you.

~ SPS #5: ~
* Inner Lover *

The idea of the 'Lover' brings up many images. For each one of us, based on our individual experiences and understandings, those images can connect us to different memories, longings, stories, characters, and characteristics. I remember my friend telling me once that she was struck silent in the middle of a big social gathering when her Scottish beau, in his lilting brogue, introduced her to everyone as his *Lover*. Obviously, I was struck too, because that conversation was probably fifteen years ago, and I still remember it like it was yesterday. His *lover*, huh? What exactly did that *mean*? When I was a kid, when someone was your lover, it meant you were having an affair with them. You had a husband or wife, sure, but, if you had a *lover*, that person was from the other side of the tracks. That was who you were *having sex* with and that person was *bad news*. Not really a great way for a kid to understand love, especially the love between intimate partners. Thankfully, I have a new understanding of the Lover that is more aligned with my spiritual principles and personal philosophies. This new context, informed by the work of Robert Moore and Douglas Gillette, is rooted in their concept which identifies four archetypes of the Mature Masculine as King, Warrior, Magician, and Lover. According to them, the Lover is the living expression of love. Regardless of gender, this version of the Lover represents love and the energy of love in many forms. Platonic love, erotic love, romantic love, soulful love, sexual love, brotherly love, sisterly love - and more - combine together to create the Lover's libido for all of creation. This Lover aspect of the Masculine feels vivid and alive, passionate and primal, sensitive and empathic, and he does it all without shame or apology. He knows that his hunger for true connection, nourishment, and creation comes with extreme highs and lows and he freely embraces all of the processes of life from joy to sorrow and back again. This way of being is one of connection to the world through feeling, not intellect. He reminds us that life is sometimes messy and unconventional… like a grand representation of the finest work of art. If we open to our Lover, this Masculine side of our psyches will support us as we cherish our sensuality and pleasure. Thinking about the Lover in this new way, I want to be on his side of the tracks! Let's try it! Let's see the world through the eyes of the Lover. Place your hands on your body where your Inner Lover lives. Let your body and hands work together with your intuition and instinct and try not think about it too much. Close your eyes and let the picture of your Inner Lover come to life in your imagination. This is the deeply mystical part of your Masculine Side that is expressive and dramatic. He is driven to satisfy hungers and urges while remaining dedicated to the creation of love and life. A rebel *with* a cause, he is a devotee of pleasure, and a consummate seeker and master of sensual, sexual, and spiritual intimacy. He is amazing and he is *you*. Continue to create this visualization, and when he is clearly and fully standing in front of you, enter his body. Step into him and see the world through *his* eyes. Hear through *his* ears. Feel through *his* heart. Taste through *his* tongue. Smell through *his* nose. Record anything of note below.

My Inner Lover is…

_____

_____

_____

- Through his **eyes**, I see _____

- Through his **ears**, I hear_____

- Through his **nose**, I smell _____

- Through his **tongue**, I taste _____

- Through his **heart**, I feel _____

From this Divinely Masculine point of view, continue to channel in guidance. Talk with your Inner Lover like you would a lover. Below are some ideas for a dialogue as well as space to create your own.

<u>**You:**</u> How can I become more enthusiastic and connected in my life and work?

<u>**Lover Answers:**</u> _____

_____

<u>**You:**</u> How can I intensify and cherish my relationships?

<u>**Lover Answers:**</u> _____

_____

You: How can I bring deep purpose and love to my endeavors?

<u>**Lover Answers:**</u> _____

_____

<u>**You:**</u> How can I energize the things I do with pleasure and sensuality?

<u>**Lover Answers:**</u> _____

_____

You: _____

Lover Answers: _____

_____

You: _____

Lover Answers: _____

_____

When the conversation feels complete, thank your Inner Lover for being here and for sharing his wisdom. Again, place your hands on your body where he dwells and press to fully integrate his awareness into your own. Make an agreement to communicate with him often and finish with a deep, cleansing breath. Know that you can *turn him on* in order to look, hear, smell, taste, feel, and love through his senses whenever and however you choose. From my Inner Lover to yours, I am grateful for you and I love you.

Crystal Love: Nancy's Crystal is the powerful, dynamic, and fiery Dragon's Eye, also known as Red Tiger's Eye. This stone balances our Basic Chakra and helps us make our desires clearly known so that we may bolster the vitality, passion, stamina, and motivation needed to enhance our self-esteem, self-worth, and self-confidence. A great releaser of fear and anxiety, Dragon's Eye can support us in creating space for resolution around issues of sexuality, sensuality, and pleasure within all of our relationships. This Crystal also sends energy into the lower organs of the body which can help with sluggishness, procrastination, and anything else that keeps us from witnessing and incorporating the sensual and invigorating beauties of life. Needless to say, this stone is full of intensity! Get a piece near your body to heat up the areas of your life that you wish to transform. Once this warming up and transformational process gets rolling, Dragon's Eye offers the additional gifts of increased personal integrity, a balanced sex drive, and a re-focus of energy to protect our wealth, happiness and peace.

Suggested Reading to Re-Claim your Orgasmic Life *Pussy: A Reclamation* by Regena Thomashauer.

Additional Journaling and SPS Space

Kristin

One of the things that has helped me the most is realizing that I am not alone. I went through a period of time when I was in a verbally abusive relationship and was ostracized from my family and I didn't have anybody to talk to or, go back to. I was living this existence where I felt like I was just a food gathering person and a mom. This relationship lasted four years, and this is the father of my children, so this is someone I still have to deal with. That has been one of my biggest struggles with self-worth and empowerment, something I have to overcome every day, because I have to interact with him on a consistent basis. It is hard having to deal with someone always talking down to me… always trying to incite an argument. Becoming a mother was the first step of really setting myself apart from this situation. It gave me the strength to know that I wanted to be my own person. That I wanted to find my own power. I wanted to become a great example for my children. It was definitely a gradual thing because I didn't think very highly of myself at the time. I didn't like who I was. I didn't like where I was. I wanted to change, but it was still so hard. I left the relationship a couple of times. After I got pregnant the first time, I tried to leave. After my daughter turned four months, I tried to leave again. I always got roped back in and that was my cycle of abuse. I would get to the point of, 'I'm done, I can't do this anymore.' Then, it would get better, and things would calm down, only to ramp back up again into more dysfunction. The whole cycle takes a while. I was ready to leave again when I got pregnant with my second child. Believe me, I wasn't trying to have two. I got pregnant with an IUD and while nursing. Ending up with two little babies in this situation, I felt so isolated and alone. Then, suddenly, my dad died. His heart just stopped. He took a nap one day at his store and never woke up. That was pretty devastating. He had been my go-to person and then he was just gone. He had a heart problem that he never took seriously. His death was a shock to everyone. I am so grateful that there wasn't a lot of suffering and that it wasn't long and drawn out. He just, very surprisingly, died. I can still imagine his voice saying, "Damnit… Damnit!" over his body, completely pissed that it happened. Losing him at this time was hard but it also confirmed some of my spiritual philosophies about death. I know now that it is not an ending. I still feel his support around me even though he isn't *here*. I can feel him talking to me, giving me messages through different things like music and symbols. That has been the most reassuring thing in dealing with his death - realizing it is not final. That has given me so much comfort over the past few years because my journey has been about realizing what I have been through and finding my strength. Around the same time that all of this happened, I found the Divine Mommy Group, and it really helped. Hearing that there are other women who have their own stories of challenges and struggles helped me to see that I wasn't completely alone. I started to realize that my walls could come down a little bit and that I didn't have to handle everything by myself. A year later, I left the relationship. I moved in with my mom and, for four years now, this has been the new normal. My kids and I share a room. That has been close. Closer than I'd like sometimes, but it is all my youngest has known. In the first year that I left their father, the aftermath of leaving was severe. I got 23,000 text messages. The 'running away' from the situation just wouldn't work. I had to stand and face it and deal with it. That has been so hard because I still have the post-traumatic stress-like feelings of never knowing what is coming my way or what will happen next. I've had to learn how to address the situations with my ex, but not take the hook of the argument that is dangled right there for every single interaction. It has taken a while, but now I know that I have the strength not to react. To be in control of my own actions. My kids are such a great inspiration here, because I always try to deflect my energy towards them and what is best for them. I don't want them seeing me freaking out and arguing with their dad all the time. Which I do, sometimes; I'm not perfect. I have bad days. I get stressed. My resources get low and I grab the hook. I fight back. Now I'm getting so much better at just hanging up the phone and walking away. Once I saw a video about how to deal with a bully. They said to just agree, so I did that…. "Yeah, I agree, I am being terrible, right now… according to you…" I don't take it on, but I validate him. After that, where can he go with his argument? It isn't easy, but sometimes it's the little things that just help me keep going. Tools like that have really helped. Finding a group of women who support me as I work on other things has helped as well. My aggression and anger and what I am repressing… to really work through some of those things has been like a weight coming off. That is why this whole process has felt like such a journey. I have been in survival mode for so long. Now, I am beginning to discover my own voice, my own creativity. Before it was a struggle, hour by hour, to get by. I used to tell myself, "Just get through this day… just make it through this moment…" Now, I feel grounded and only have little glimpses of that. Talking about my experiences has really given me a sense of strength. It has helped me discover that I have been through a lot and I have survived. I also read a lot. When I catch myself thinking this or that person has been through so much, and that they are so strong, I also realize that my story is similar. That I, too, am strong and have come through so much. I've accomplished self-healing. I'm working on forgiveness. These aspects of my journey have also been a huge step towards owning my empowerment. I take comfort in the fact that I am no longer getting wrapped up in the small-mindedness of this situation. It is hard, but to release through forgiveness has been huge. It feels good to be able to let go of the adrenaline-fueled feelings of vindictiveness. It is like a weight has been lifted. I also know that this strength is a result of me tapping into something greater than myself. To not engage in the fight. To not hold it in, but to let it all out. The more it flows for me, the more I know I am connected to a higher power. This allows me to step more authentically into my feelings. This sense of a higher power also helps me to connect into other women and to know that I am not alone. To believe that their strength is my strength. To trust that someone else will have my back. To know that I've got my own back, and that powers greater than me have my back. I have this strength because I am connected. Now I can focus on letting things just be, even if they aren't perfect. I am what I am. I nurture that with awareness. I bring something to the table in whatever situation I am in. Noticing my own power has been a process, but I've got something worthy to share. I want all women to know this, too. No matter what, know that you are beautiful inside and out. You are powerful beyond recognition. You are not alone.

Making This Story Your Own:

Kristin's story brings a balanced perspective to empowerment and vulnerability.
Take a moment, breathe, and reflect.
What stands out for you when you read her words?
Is there a situation in your life that is similar to Kristin's?
Perhaps part of her story feels connected to your own.
How can you relate her experiences to your past, present, and future?

- *My Connection to Kristin's Story* _____

_____

_____

_____

_____

Knowing that you aren't alone, let's gently explore some other themes from Kristin's story together:

- ***Letting Things Be***
  - Can you walk away from a situation without telling your side of the story? What about walking away from a *conflict* without telling your side of the story? If you answered yes to either question, how do you manage to do this? If you answered no, can you explain why it is so hard to walk away? When expressing yourself, or when arguing a point, is it important to be validated by an outside source? Is it important to feel like you've won? If so, when did this start? What would be different if all that you needed was your own validation? What would be different if winning and losing weren't important?

- ***Surviving Survival Mode***
  - Does living in survival mode sound familiar? In general, how much do you feel like you are just *surviving*? How does this *work* or *not work* for you and your relationships? If you were to slow down and relax enough so that your system could come out of survival mode, what would happen? What would you be doing differently? What about your life would change? Who in your life would benefit the most and who would benefit the least? Who else besides you would notice? If coming out of survival mode would be beneficial, what is one small step you can take to create some well-deserved relief?

- ***You Are Powerful***
  - Do you see yourself as powerful? Why, or why not? What is your definition of powerful and does it include a realistic perspective of you, your talents, and your abilities? If so, where did this definition of powerful come from? If not, where did a definition of powerful that *does not* include you, your talents, and abilities come from? Are there ways in which you would like to be more powerful in your life? What is keeping you from this? Would embodying your power change existing dynamics that are either functional or dysfunctional within your personal and professional relationships? Would these potential changes be welcome or unwelcome? Why?

Sacred Play Suggestions:

~ SPS #1: ~
* Thrival Mode *

Survival mode is awesome if we need to run away from an irate tiger. Survival mode sucks if it's a way of life. Our biology has great processes in place to survive danger. Our biology gets highjacked when those processes are habitually applied to everyday *stuff*. When this happens, our health can be compromised and life can feel like a hamster wheel of hard labor. If you feel like you are living in survival mode and you would like some relief around the constant needs of daily responsibilities, a therapeutic concept known as reframing might help. Reframing is looking at a situation differently to discover more beneficial perspectives. See if you can reframe some of your daily responsibilities. What are some things that you do not look forward to doing? Can you identify any benefits as to *why* you do them? Sometimes just this little shift in the way we think can create big differences in the way we feel. Try applying this to more *stuff*. In the following columns, play with listing things in each category. *Must Do* is the column for the non-negotiables. *Have To* is the column for what you have to do but isn't urgent. *Want To* is the column for things you actually want to do. *Won't Do* is for stuff you won't be doing anymore because it isn't your responsibility. (Be patient - the *Won't Do* column may stay sparse for a while.)

Must Do	Have To	Want To	Won't Do (anymore...)
•	•	•	•
•	•	•	•
•	•	•	•
•	•	•	•
•	•	•	•
•	•	•	•
•	•	•	•
•	•	•	•
•	•	•	•
•	•	•	•
•	•	•	•
•	•	•	•

After filling in the columns, go back and take a really honest look at all of that *stuff*. Does anything in the *Must Do* and *Have To* columns need to be moved over to *Want To* or *Won't Do?* These are the things that you may not remember choosing, and they may not feel like a choice anymore, but ultimately these things originated as *stuff* because **you** decided to do them. If so, go ahead and move them over. Another way to survive Survival Mode is to release the idea that all of this *stuff* has to be done immediately. Next, go through the columns again and label each item with a realistic timeframe. Today, tomorrow, next week, next month, next year, and never are all valid options. As you do this, ask where the current timelines have come from. If they are self-imposed, release the immediacy and replace it with a realistic goal that is more in tune with your needs. Now, on to the reframe. For each column and for each item listed in each column, find a positive or beneficial reason for why you do these things. These reasons can be about you, the people you are doing the things for, or the world at large. One Universal reframe that encompasses it all - the good, the bad, and the ugly - is that ALL of this *stuff* is part of a growth process. It's all part of the learning curve for becoming better versions of ourselves. Discovering why we do things and then making empowered choices to either stop or continue doing them is a lesson in self-mastery. Yeah, there are always going to be things that we aren't thrilled about, but when we alleviate the resentment and self-punishment, we propel ourselves out of survival mode and into *thrival* mode... a mode of standing firm in our choices, our authenticity, and our freedom. And yes, I totally made that word up. Love you! Thanks for doing this activity.

~ SPS #2: ~
* Labels *

What is hanging around that you would like to release? Labels, relationships, negative self-talk... things in your life that are no longer serving you. Take a minute and identify what is ready to be let loose so that something new can come forward. Following are three areas to bring pen to paper and discover what is holding you down. Labels to let go of might be stressed, bitchy, tired, brittle, irritable, or frustrated. Relationships to release might be to a person, substance, or activity. Beliefs to banish might be 'I don't deserve abundance,' or 'I don't deserve happiness.'

What Can Be Released?		
Labels	**Relationships**	**Beliefs**

Great job! Now shift gears and find an empty jar with an airtight lid. Make sure the jar is clean and fill it about three quarters to the top with tap water. Next, get some scrap paper and cut it into strips about an inch or two wide. On these strips, write down all that you would like to release. Use your writing from above and add another layer… after putting down what is going *out*, claim what is coming *in*. Below are a few examples.

- I **release** negative self-talk so that I can *regenerate* self-love.
- I **let go** of my relationship to unhealthy food so that I can *rebirth* a strong and healthy body.
- I **shed** the label of stressed and *transform* it to accomplished.
- I **banish** the belief that other people's well-being is my responsibility and *birth* the inner knowing that I can only heal myself.
- I **liberate** what others think and *restore* trust in my own truth.

Below are a few words to play with for the *first* half of the sentence.

• Discharge	• Liberate	• Eradicate	• Exonerate
• Clear	• Absolve	• Liquidate	• Dismiss
• Eject	• Banish	• Shed	• Release
• Evict	• Eliminate	• Discard	• Exile

Below are a few words to play with for the *second* half of the sentence.

• Rebirth	• Regenerate	• Restore	• Release
• Revitalize	• Reinforce	• Revive	• Restart
• Rekindle	• Redevelop	• Revamp	• Renew
• Rejuvenate	• Reignite	• Reinvigorate	• Recover

Once the strips of paper are filled with everything needing to be released, transformed, and rebirthed, fold them and drop them into the jar of water. Make sure they are completely saturated and then screw the lid back on, giving the jar a shake to ensure the lid is tight. Now shake the jar again… shake it hard! Shake it with your whole body. Let your energy, momentum, and force begin to decimate the paper into smaller and smaller pieces while transforming those strips into something new. As you shake it, verbalize what you are releasing and reclaiming. Set your intentions out loud. Sing the *why* of wanting this rebirth. Speak your plan to awaken, refresh, and restore the Goddess within. You will know when you are finished because the paper will begin to break down. Congratulations! This is hard work on many levels, and you did it! You stuck with it because you are worth it. In the coming days, keep this jar close for more shaking and notice what happens in your life as the paper continues to transform. Love you! Thank you!

<u>~ SPS #3: ~</u>
<u>* Kundalini Rising *</u>

Kundalini (**koon**-duh-**lee**-nee) is a Sanskrit term that has recently become very popular. This energy resides within us and awareness of our Kundalini energy can be beneficial. You might not have known the name, but chances are you have already felt the sensations of your Kundalini opening and activating. This is the profound feeling we experience when we are aligned and attuned with our Higher Selves. For a visual, Kundalini is often described as a snake coiled at the base of the spine. Moving and activating this energy is said to bring us closer to enlightenment, because as the Kundalini snake uncoils and travels upwards so, too, does our consciousness. Sounds pretty amazing, right? It is! And - because it is so *awe-mazing* - it can also result in big feelings ranging from bliss to overwhelm and everything in between. For this activity, as we open our Energetic Centers and visualize the Kundalini energy, be sure to take it slow and go easy on yourself. P.S.… If the whole snake visual creeps you out, here is a reframe: snakes have been associated with the Divine Feminine and the highest forms of femininity for a very, very long time. Think about it… they coil in a spiral, which is one of the oldest shapes associated with the Feminine. Their intuition is off the charts. They can sense even the slightest change or vibration in their environments. They shed their skin - which is metaphorically linked to the shedding of the uterine lining during the Menstrual Cycle. And they make their homes within the dark the womb of Mother Earth. When you look at them in this way, snakes are a wonderful totem for Feminine wisdom, empowerment, and magick. Woot-woot! Go Snakes! Aaaaaand, focus… ☺

Take a few deep breaths and allow your consciousness to rest at your lower back. Sense an opening here that connects the base of your spine to the crown of your head. At the bottom of this opening rests your Kundalini Snake. Allow this gorgeous creature to come to life. See her and feel her.
In your imagination, decorate this grand space that your Kundalini energy will use to rise.
As you visualize this beauty within, also give your attention to your seven Energy Centers, raising in rainbow hue from red, to orange, to yellow, to green, to blue, to purple, and finally to lavender, or white.
Read aloud the following as an active meditation.

- *As this rainbow dances and swirls together, I witness my Kundalini energy rise and coil to my* Basic Chakra*. The color is red. This energetic support system, located at the base of my spine, is my gateway to* **abundance, security,** *and* **grounding***. In this space of Sacred Connection, I ask my* **Basic Chakra** *to come into balance in the best and highest way. Now, I gently activate this Chakra by allowing it to spin clockwise, blossoming open like a beautiful Lotus Flower.*

- *I witness my Kundalini energy rising and coiling, taking with it the activated red energy of my Basic onto my* Sacral Chakra*. The color is orange. This creative system, located in my lower abdomen, is my gateway to creating* **new life, relationships,** *and* **sexuality***. In this space of Sacred Connection, I ask my* **Sacral Chakra** *to come into balance in the best and highest way. Now, I gently activate this Chakra by allowing it to spin clockwise, blossoming open like a beautiful Lotus Flower.*

- *I witness my Kundalini energy rising and coiling upwards, taking with it the activated red and orange energies of my Basic and Sacral as it continues onward to my* Solar Plexus Chakra*. The color is yellow. This emotional system, located at my navel, is my* **power center for processing feelings** *and* *moving through life in an empowered, empathic way. In this space of Sacred Connection, I ask my **Solar Plexus Chakra** to come into balance in the best and highest way. Now, I gently activate this Chakra by allowing it to spin clockwise, blossoming open like a beautiful Lotus Flower.*

- *I witness my Kundalini energy rising and coiling upwards, taking with it the activated red, orange, and yellow energies of my Basic, Sacral, and Solar Plexus as it continues onward to my Heart Chakra. The color is green. This loving system, located at my chest, is my **unconditional love center for giving and receiving love in equal measure**. In this space of Sacred Connection, I ask my **Heart Chakra** to come into balance in the best and highest way. Now, I gently activate this Chakra by allowing it to spin clockwise, blossoming open like a beautiful Lotus Flower.*

- *I witness my Kundalini energy rising and coiling upwards, taking with it the activated red, orange, yellow, and green energies of my Basic, Sacral, Solar Plexus, and Heart as it continues onward to my Throat Chakra. The color is blue. This communication system, located at my throat, is my **driving center for thought creation, belief systems,** and **authentic communication**. In this space of Sacred Connection, I ask my **Throat Chakra** to come into balance in the best and highest way. Now, I gently activate this Chakra by allowing it to spin clockwise, blossoming open like a beautiful Lotus Flower.*

- *I witness my Kundalini energy rising and coiling upwards, taking with it the activated red, orange, yellow, green, and blue energies of my Basic, Sacral, Solar Plexus, Heart, and Throat as it continues onward to my Ajna Chakra. The color is purple. This intuitive system, located at my forehead, is my **intuition center for receiving guidance, wisdom,** and **messages from my Higher Self,** and **any other High Vibratory Energies**. In this space of Sacred Connection, I ask my **Ajna** to come into balance in the best and highest way. Now, I gently activate this Chakra by allowing it to spin clockwise, blossoming open like a beautiful Lotus Flower.*

- *I witness my Kundalini energy rising and coiling upwards, taking with it the activated red, orange, yellow, blue, green, and purple energies of my Basic, Sacral, Solar Plexus, Heart, Throat, and Ajna as it continues onward to my Crown Chakra. The color is lavender, or white. This spiritual system, located at the crown of my head, is my **bliss center for awareness, enlightenment, peace,** and **an opening to the oneness of all that is**. In this space of Sacred Connection, I ask my **Crown Chakra** to come into balance in the best and highest way. Now, I gently activate this Chakra by allowing it to spin clockwise, blossoming open like a beautiful Lotus Flower.*

Finally, with intention and attention, visualize your Kundalini energy connecting to and rising through each Chakra. Gently place your hands over your Basic Chakra and then move to the Sacral, the Solar Plexus, the Heart, the Throat, the Ajna, and up onto the Crown.
Breathe into this connection and breathe into this energetic channel.
Once again look at your Kundalini Snake. See her. Feel her. Thank her. Love her.
Take a few moments to enjoy this activation as your Kundalini continues to open and energize.
Journal any messages, guidance, or wisdom that comes through.

Messages from My Kundalini Energy

_____

_____

_____

Go snakes! Sorry… had to sneak that in one more time. Go *you*! How do you feel? Check in with your snakey-sense. What is going on with your intuition? How is your vibration? Are you ready to shed your skin and go be held within the dark womb of Mother Earth? Me too! Meet you in 5? Cool. See you there. Love you. Thank you!

~ SPS #4: ~
* New Love Mantra *

What would be your Mantra to open your heart to *new* love? New love can come to us in various forms, and most of us can agree that we still have spaces and places available for love within our consciousness. A lot of us are pouring out love on a daily basis, so this isn't a Mantra about creating more love within us to *give*… rather this is about creating more love for us to *receive*. Perhaps this Mantra can be about opening to receive love that is already there but not quite yet noticed. A good example of this can be the unconditional amounts of love coming our way from animals and plants. Perhaps this can be about opening our hearts to receive the full amount of love coming from other people. Even the Universe, Source, or whatever you call your Higher Power, has infinite amounts of love just for you. Are you as open as you can be to receive it? Maybe a Mantra is already brewing. If so, great! Maybe some idea generators would be helpful. Try finishing the following sentences and see what comes to light.

- I deserve new love _____

- I want new love _____

- I need new love _____

- I have space for new love _____

- I welcome new love _____

- I am open to new love _____

- I receive new love _____

Once you have finished writing, read through your words and begin to simmer them down into a sentence or two below.

Simmered Down Mantra Starter

_____

_____

Now, with this condensed version, concentrate your thoughts even more into a short, clear statement.

New Love Mantra

If your *New Love Mantra* surprises you, that is OK! Writing our thoughts and feelings taps into different layers and levels of our consciousness. Sometimes feelings are hibernating down there, and we don't even know it. Empowerment and transformation come from bringing these deep feelings up to be seen, honored, loved, and validated. Congratulations on your **New Love Mantra.** You can chant with your Mantra. You can write it on another piece of paper and hang it where you will see it often. You can even write it down, put it in your pocket, and forget about it. Trust that your **New Love Mantra** will begin working for you in whatever way you need. In fact, it is working right now! Get ready to receive my love…. I love you! Thank you for doing this!

~ SPS #5: ~
* Prayer Basket *

In all of my groups, I always have a prayer basket. A prayer basket can be a great addition around the home or workplace because it can offer small, short reminders that anything and everything can be lifted up in prayer. Use any basket, bowl, box, or bag that you have and decorate it if you want to. Next, find some scrap paper and cut or tear it into strips a few inches wide. These will be your prayer sheets. Make a good-sized stack so that you have enough. Now, begin writing your prayers. Pray to anyone or anything about anyone or anything. There is no '*right*' way to do this; there is only *your* way. Once each prayer is written, fold it and put it in your basket with the energy of sending it to wherever you choose in whatever way you choose. If this prayer basket is just for you, create Sacred Boundaries based on your needs. If this prayer basket will be shared with others, create a Sacred Boundary of confidentiality around the prayers, meaning that once they are folded safely in the basket they are never reopened and read. Once the prayer basket feels full, decide on your own or as a group what to do with the prayers. You can transform the prayers and send them up by burning them. (If you do this, please do it carefully with the proper equipment, space, and expertise to ensure safety for all.) You can bury the prayers someplace and allow Mother Earth to transform them using her magick of Holy Compost. Or, you can create something completely new by recycling them into fresh sheets of homemade paper. To do this, search '*simple steps to recycle your own paper*' online and you will find some great ideas and tutorials. When you are ready, start the beautiful process all over again and know that your prayers have a place, they are received, they are heard, and they are transformed - all by **you**! Thanks for doing this. I feel your prayers and so does every other living thing. Love you!

Crystal Love: Kristin's Crystal is the gorgeous, transformative, adventurous, and bold Malachite (*mal*-uh-kahyt). This stone is an extremely powerful metaphysical stone because it can amplify both the positive and the negative aspects of any given situation. This metaphysical gift from Malachite is done as a fast track resolution tactic so that we can get back to harmony, peace, and unconditional love. However, just as it needs to be handled with caution due to its toxicity in raw form, know that when using Malachite things can get intense. This stone will rebirth us, but it does so with its own unique brand of love, which can sometimes be tough. If you are calling in transformation, Malachite is the stone to alleviate shyness, release inhibitions, intensify moods, magnify emotions, draw out deep belief systems, break unwanted patterns, encourage risk taking, inspire change, stimulate dreams, escalate powers of observation, and multiply messages coming through from the subconscious. Due to this attunement and reawakening of personal truth, Malachite can additionally ground our Spiritual energies to assist us in identifying blockages on the path to ascension. Thank goodness Malachite is also known for absorbing negativity, clearing and activating the Chakra Systems, and releasing the mind of negative feedback loops… because with all that it can do for us, we will need it!

Suggested Reading to Boldly Declare and Valiantly Assert that Wise, Powerful Inner Goddess, *Shakti Woman: Feeling Our Fire, Healing Our World, The New Female Shamanism* by Vicki Noble.

Jaana

When I was young, I remember watching a television special about a family who had adopted a bunch of children. This family was a blend of ethnicities and cultures. Even at that young age, the beauty of what this family had done touched me deeply. It gave me the idea that family could be created in many different ways. That moment impacted me, and from then on I talked about adopting. For as long as I can remember, I've never been attached to the concept that my child has to come from my body. The notion of getting pregnant - or of being pregnant - never really mattered to me when I thought about how I would become a parent. I knew that there was a child out there for me, and that however that child came to me, they would be my child no matter what. When I met my husband, he was in agreement. Although he did want to try and have at least one biological child. I understood that. Lucky for us, his company paid for three IVF treatments. We went through two IVF procedures, and after the second one, I developed lumps in my breast from the hormone treatments that had to be removed surgically. At that point, I was done with drugs. After watching me go through those two very difficult treatments, my husband was in agreement and we started getting serious about adoption. We researched adoption agencies and the countries open for international adoption. Finally, we stumbled upon a local agency. They told us that Nepal would be opening up soon. When I heard Nepal, I knew that was where we were headed. I just had this feeling. I had always held a fascination with the country and felt such a connection to Nepal. Thank goodness my husband and I were so optimistic and so positive. In the beginning, we thought we would just go through the process and adopt a child. Our naivete turned out to be a good thing. There were incredible amounts of tedious paperwork and long months of waiting for information. Through the process, I heard so many heart-breaking stories. All told, our adoption started with a dossier of paperwork in August of 2008. Nepal officially opened for adoption in the beginning of 2009. We were matched with a child two days after my birthday in September of 2009. We got permission to travel two days before my husband's birthday in April of 2010, and we brought our daughter home the next month in May. In terms of international adoption, ours was relatively quick and provided us both with birthday presents. During the process, we joined a few different online groups. These groups were great for information about the adoption situation in Nepal because there were members from all over the world. From those groups, we formed an even smaller group with people who had gotten matched with children around the same time. We knew another local family was adopting from Nepal. In fact, they were number one to get their paperwork in and we were number two from our local agency. When we got our match that September, I can't even describe how it felt. We received an email with one picture and a few bits of information. When my husband and I saw the picture we were jumping up and down. It was like, "Oh my gosh! That is our kid!" I imagine it is like seeing your baby's face for the first time, only our baby was fourteen months old. We kept looking and staring at her. We had no idea what her life had been like. We showed that picture to everyone, but not everyone was totally supportive. My family had a hard time with it. My grandfather struggled with the mixing of races. My parents were worried about the problems that could arise from an international adoption. I understood. My husband and I had our own concerns. We had no idea what was going to happen... no idea what our child could come home like. We didn't know what to expect either. Of course, my family instantly fell in love when they met her. The seven months between getting her picture and leaving to go to Nepal were the longest seven months of my life. We knew she was there waiting, and we were here waiting for a signature. In April of 2010, we got word that the head of the Ministry for Women and Children had signed our papers and that we needed to be in Nepal as quickly as possible. Due to my husband's work schedule, he only got a certain amount of days off. Together, we decided that he would wait and take that time off when my daughter and I returned. My mother traveled with me. Emotionally, this part of the process was hard. All of this time had passed. I was getting on a plane. I was going to meet my child. I just wanted to see her and hug her and take her home. It didn't quite happen that way. After several days of traveling, my mother and I flew into Katmandu. We had some time to acclimate before going to the village where my daughter was staying. This was actually a really good thing. I got to get a sense of the culture and of the Nepalese people. We also got to meet some of the other families from our online group who were there at the same time adopting. It was so nice to get to know everyone face-to-face after months of interacting online. The day we were taken to the home to meet her for the first time, I had so much anxiety. She was 21 months old now and I was so curious about who this little person would be. I couldn't wait to hear her voice, to know what she sounded like. As she was being carried in by the Didi - which is the name they give for the women who care for the children in these homes and literally translates to "older sister" - I was trying to take everything in. What the land looked like. How clean the home was. I saw her and wanted to grab her and hold her, but I knew that I couldn't. She had no idea who I was. I probably looked strange and smelled weird. I was speaking a foreign language. It was this combination of trying to hold it all together and be respectful while playing with her and approaching her on her terms. Then the visit ended, and it was time to go. I wasn't upset about leaving because I respected that this had to be done in steps. We came back the next day, and as soon as my daughter saw my mother and I, she started screaming, "Ni, ni, ni, ni, ni!" Which means "no" in Nepali. For all of the following visits, my daughter screamed and cried the entire time. The workers in the home had no idea what to do because they had never seen a child react like that. Soon, it became clear that my child was very bonded with the woman taking care of her. I found out that her Didi had been taking care of her since she was one week old. I started to ask myself if I was doing the right thing taking her from the woman who, for the most part, had been her mother. Was I doing the right thing taking her from her culture? Ultimately, I knew I was doing a good thing, and it was the right thing. Thank goodness for my background in early childhood education. Although the crying was awful, I knew that it was a positive sign. It meant that my daughter could create a secure attachment to a caregiver. I knew that if she could attach and bond with her Didi, she could attach and bond with me. The other interesting thing was that several of the workers in the home kept remarking that my daughter looked like me. One of the women asked me if I believed in fate. I replied, "I do." The woman responded, "She looks like you. She is meant to be your child." I was like, "Well, she *is* my child!" In the midst of the visits, there were also so many other things to do. So many appointments. So many papers to get signed. Doctor's visits to schedule. Passport photos to take. Our visas were running out, so my mom and I had to get new ones issued. On the day of the actual adoption, my daughter was hysterical. Her Didi was hysterical. I was feeling hysterical but was trying not to cry. I kept thinking, "I am a mom now. I can't believe it. I have a child." It all started to sink in. That first night, we were back at the hotel and could not get her to calm down. I held her. I sang to her. I rocked her. She eventually quit crying, but anytime I stopped moving she would start back up again. For hours, I rocked, walked, and sang to her. I have no idea how long it was, but I finally got her to sleep in her crib. When I got into bed, the tears came flooding out of me. All of it. I had held so much in. I kept thinking about the Didi crying. I had a child, who was now sleeping peacefully, but who would not stop crying when she was awake. In the middle of this, the thought hit me that for the rest of my life everything would change. Everything that had happened before was no longer. This was the pivotal moment. Now that she was here, what do I do next? That question was answered by the Nepalese government shutting down and going on strike. It was terrifying. We had no information. We could only leave our hotel at certain times. The American Embassy was closed. We had no idea how long the strike would be. We didn't know quite what to do. Through a connection of one of my mom's friends, we finally got somebody to talk to somebody. Then all of a sudden we got some movement. A person from the embassy came to our hotel. As he was talking to us, he explained that they would get the Americans out of Nepal if the situation got worse. I asked about my daughter. He told us that she would have to stay because she was not an American citizen. I looked at him like he was crazy. If he thought I was leaving my daughter in a war-torn country, he was nuts. It was all so surreal. I had spent my first Mother's Day in Nepal. My mom had her birthday in Nepal. Luckily, the strike came and went within a week. Finally, we were able to head home. Through all of this I have learned that I am definitely a resilient woman. All of the experiences that I had to go through to get my daughter, I stuck with it all. I never faltered in my thinking that I was going to have a child. And, once I got her, I knew instantly that I was going to fiercely protect her. She was mine. I was her mother. No question. This journey has been so interesting. Getting her was only the beginning. Once we had her, I had to figure out how to become the parent that I wanted to be. That took a lot of work, too! I had to get really clear about what I wanted for my daughter. Then I had to get clear on how to become the kind of parent to make that happen. Today, she is in Middle School and our reality is different. She is very proud to be from Nepal, but with school and social stuff, her interest level in her ethnicity comes and goes. I am very aware that I have a girl child of a different race. We talk a lot about this. We talk about how people of different races have been treated in the past. We talk about how some things have gotten better and how other things have not. I try to approach all of this with awareness and honesty because I want to prepare her to have the best future possible. She is a girl from a different race. Her story is unique. Her best friend to this day is the little girl that the other local family adopted from Nepal. So when they are together, race is not a big deal. I recognize that it is hard for my daughter to grasp the fact that there are parents who gave birth to her whom she will probably never meet. Having this as part of her story is another challenge. From my perspective as her parent, knowing that story is difficult. But, I wouldn't be her mom if they hadn't made that decision and I choose to believe that they made their choice out of love... not because they didn't love her, but because they loved her so much. I know people struggle with adoption. It can be a hard decision to make. But your child is your child. Children come to us. It doesn't matter how. That is how I see it. That is why I share my story so openly. I want others to know how enriching adoption can be. How powerful it can be to become a parent in this way. If I could talk to my ten-year-old self, I would tell her thank you. I am so grateful she was open to that story on the TV all those years ago and that she allowed it to have such an influence on her life. That program showed me a different way to create a family. Today, with my life and in my work, I show others that we are all capable of giving unconditional love to a child.

Making This Story Your Own:

Jaana's story reminds us that family and love are both heartfelt choices.
Take a moment, breathe, and reflect.
What stands out for you when you read her words?
Is there a situation in your life that is similar to Jaana's?
Perhaps part of her story feels connected to your own.
How can you relate her experiences to your past, present, and future?

- *My Connection to Jaana's Story* _____

_____

_____

_____

Knowing that you aren't alone, let's gently explore some other themes from Jaana's story together:

- *Resilience*
    - Is the word resilient a word you would use to describe yourself? Why, or why not? When you think of your life, what have you survived, what have you accomplished, and where have you thrived? In spite of the challenges, where and when have you kept going? What qualities within you gave you

the strength to do these things? Have you given yourself enough credit for all that you have been through? If you were witnessing or hearing about these life events as if they belonged to someone else, would you feel that *they* were resilient? Would you give them more credit than you are giving yourself? Why, or why not? What are some small ways that you can begin honoring yourself more for all that you have accomplished and survived and the ways in which you have thrived?

- **The Parent You Want to Be**
  - What kind of parent are you? Are you the kind of parent that you thought you would be? If yes, how? If not, why? Are you the kind of parent that you **want** to be? If so, how do you do this? If you aren't the kind of parent you would like to be, do you know why? Where do your ideas and ideals about parenting come from? Were you - and are you currently - parented in the way that you want to be? Do these past and present experiences affect the way that you parent your children? Is the effect positive, negative, or a mixture of both? Are there ways in which you can *parent yourself* that would be beneficial to you and your family? If yes, what would parenting yourself look like for you and what are some small, manageable things that can be done to begin this process?

- **Making Choices Out of Love**
  - What are some of the hardest choices you have made in your life? When you think about these choices and what led you to make them, what feelings come up? Do you, or did you, hold any judgment against yourself or others in regard to these situations? If so, how has this judgement been beneficial and how has it been destructive? Thinking about these decisions now, regardless of the outcome, can you identify where love and hope were present? Looking at other people's choices, even if they seem inexplicable and easy to judge, would discovering the love and hope offer beneficial opportunities for perspective?

Sacred Play Suggestions:

~ SPS #1: ~
* Honorable Harvest *

In the beautiful book, *Braiding Sweetgrass, Indigenous Wisdom, Scientific Knowledge, and the Teachings of Plants*, author Robin Wall Kimmerer discusses many rich perspectives, including the ethical practice of the "Honorable Harvest." This elegant protocol is a respectful, reciprocal, and easily applied tradition that helps us become aware of our choices, especially when it comes to our choices about expecting Mother Earth to sustain our needs. According to Kimmerer, the four main tenets of the "Honorable Harvest" are:

> *"Take only what is given.*
> *Use it well.*
> *Be grateful for the gift.*
> *Reciprocate the gift."*

Not necessarily a rule, but more a way of life, the "Honorable Harvest" requests that we consciously ask, "What do I need? Why do I need it? Who do I thank? Where can I return the favor?" One of the easiest ways to make sense of this concept is to think about our relationship to food. For most of us, our food-gathering typically involves going to the grocery store, pushing around a big metal cart, and filling it to the brim with what we think we might need. We then give money to the cashier and lug everything home to be unloaded and maybe used… maybe not. However, think about how far this removes us from the processes of preparing the land, planting the seeds, growing the food, harvesting the fruits and vegetables, and then sharing what we've grown with our communities. There are pros and cons, sure, but what are we missing by cutting ourselves out of this relationship to the Earth and nature? What else could be gained if we applied the "Honorable Harvest" ideology to all aspects of our lives? How can we follow those four lines as we go about getting our personal and professional needs met? In her book, Robin Wall Kimmerer also offers some other suggestions for implementing the ways of the "Honorable Harvest." They are:

- Ask for permission and always abide by the answer.
- Never take the first. Never take the last.
- Harvest in a way that minimizes harm.
- Take only what you need and leave some for others.
- Use everything that you take.
- Take only that which is given to you.
- Share what you have received.
- Be grateful.
- Reciprocate the gift.
- Sustain the one who sustains you.

Think about how you get your needs met physically, emotionally, mentally, and spiritually. How can you apply the "Honorable Harvest" to all facets of your life? Let's go through it together and see what comes up.

What are my *Physical* needs?

_____

_____

What are my *Emotional* needs?

_____

_____

What are my *Mental* needs?

_____

_____

What are my *Spiritual* needs?

_____

_____

In meeting these needs, how can I embody the "Honorable Harvest," by:

~ Taking only what is given. ~
~ Using it well. ~
~ Being grateful for the gift. ~
~ Reciprocating the gift. ~

_____
_____
_____
_____
_____

Take this wisdom even deeper by reflecting or journaling on the following questions related to Robin Wall Kimmerer's additional guidelines of the "Honorable Harvest." As you answer, keep in mind your Physical, Emotional, Mental, and Spiritual needs.

- What do I really need? _____

- How can I ask for permission and always abide by the answer? _____
  _____

- How can I be conscious of never taking the first or the last? _____
  _____

- How can I harvest in a way that minimizes harm? _____
  _____

- How can I take only what I need so that I leave plenty for others? _____
  _____

- How can I take only that which is given to me? _____
  _____

- How can I use everything I take? _____
  _____

- Who do I thank once I have received what I need? _____
  _____

- How can I express my gratitude? _____
  _____

- How can I pay it forward? _____
  _____

- How can I share what I have received? _____
  _____

- How can I reciprocate the gift? _____
  _____

- How can I sustain the one who has sustained me? _____
  _____

Once you have completed your "Honorable Harvest" process for the Physical, Emotional, Mental, and Spiritual layers of your consciousness, take a moment for integration. Clearly identify where you can release, shift, adopt, and assimilate this new way of being. As you sit, aware of your breath, grab this new energy with your hands and press it gently into your body, solidifying your transformation. With love and gratitude for yourself, open your consciousness to receive the love and gratitude coming your way from Mother Earth, every living thing, and me! I am very grateful for you and I love you. Together, our love will change the world, one "Honorable Harvest" at a time.

~ SPS #2: ~
* Cherish Yourself *

The Dalai Lama has a beautiful quote:

"As you breathe in, cherish yourself.
As you breathe out, cherish all Beings."

Along with your in-breath and your out-breath, read through the quote a few times, following along with the instructions to *cherish yourself* on the **inhale** and *cherish all Beings* on the **exhale**. Take notice of any sensations you feel within your body as you do this. Next, let's have some fun and create our own quote. Fill in the blanks for the following two sentences.

As I breathe in, I_____ myself.

As I breathe out, I _____ all Beings.

Following your own instructions for both the inhale and exhale, read through your quote a few times and take notice of any physical, emotional, or mental sensations. Now, create five more personal quotes by filling in the statements below with other things that you would like to manifest for yourself and for all Beings. According to most habit-change research, to achieve the lasting results when integrating something new into our lives, it needs to be obvious, attractive, easy, and satisfying. Since these quotes aren't just lip-service, let's apply the wisdom below as we create.

- **Step One**: Make the quotes *Obvious*.
  - Trust in yourself. These quotes are *obvious* to you because you know what you need, and you know what you would like to see in the world.

- **Step Two:** Make the quotes *Attractive*.
  - Trust in yourself. Your quotes are *attractive* because they reflect your pure heart. That is not only attractive, that is STUNNING!

- **Step Three:** Make the quotes *Easy*.
  - Trust in yourself. Your intentions for what you would like to create for yourself and for the world will be *easy* because they are yours.

- **Step Four:** Make the quotes *Satisfying*.
  - Trust in yourself. This is YOU! These are your needs, desires, hopes, and dreams for making this world a better place. No one but you came up with these miraculous ideas and they are perfect! They connect you to yourself as well as the larger, more *satisfying* concept of oneness, which reminds us that we are never alone.

As I breathe in, I_____ myself.

As I breathe out, I _____ all Beings.

As I breathe in, I_____ myself.

As I breathe out, I _____ all Beings.

As I breathe in, I_____ myself.

As I breathe out, I _____ all Beings.

As I breathe in, I_____ myself.

As I breathe out, I _____ all Beings.

As I breathe in, I_____ myself.

As I breathe out, I _____ all Beings.

Amazing! You have such a generous heart! This world is lucky to have you. *I'm* lucky to have you. Thank you for taking the time to put this beautiful energy into the Universe. Love you!

~ SPS #3: ~
* Mandantra *

A Yantra is a geometric pattern used as an instrument or tool to support our consciousness through meditation, contemplation, and spiritual liberation. In Sanskrit, the word yantra comes from the root words 'yam,' which means *instrument* or *support* and 'tra,' which means *release from bondage*. A Mandala, which is very similar to a Yantra, is also a geometric pattern, loosely translated in classical Sanskrit to mean *circle*. Mandalas also support us in our spiritual liberation and remind us of wholeness and our relationship to the infinite world that extends beyond our minds and bodies. A Yantra can be conveyed as a *principle* (think of it as a prayer) and a Mandala can be conveyed as an *expression* (your intention for answering your prayer). With so much creative potency available in both, let's combine the two and make a **Mandantra**!

- Locate an area in your yard, on the floor of your living space, or on your counter… you can even use a piece of aluminum foil or paper. Whatever your chosen medium, this is now the Sacred Space to create your unique work of spiritually infused art.
    - With energy and creativity, we are going to charge this **Mandantra** with your *prayers* and your *intentions* for answering those prayers.

- Next collect the **Mandantra** decorations. Choose anything you would like based on your available space and accessibility of items. You can use flowers, rocks, crystals, sticks, stuffed animals, sacred objects, ornaments, books, stickers, oracle cards, images and shapes that you draw and cut out, etc. Let your imagination run free and gather quite a lot to ensure that you have enough.

You have your space. You have your items. Now let's do some Divine Designing!

- **Step One:** Create a large outer square with some of your objects.
    - This is the border of your **Mandantra**.

- **Step Two:** With more of your chosen objects, try filling the outer square with a few nested circles.
    - Nested circles are circles that get consistently smaller as you work towards the very center of your design.

Keep moving inward and as you design, play with adding different shapes like stars and triangles to the inner-most area.

- **Step Three:** Charge your **Mandantra** with your *prayers* and your *intentions* for answering your prayers.
    - To infuse or charge an object or group of objects within your **Mandantra** design, use a physical and energetic connection.
        - As you hold or touch the object - or hold your hands above the object - visualize your prayers and intentions being absorbed into the form and structure of the object.
            - Your prayers are *yours*. They are personal and they are valid. Have as many or as few as you want. You can choose certain objects to represent prayers and others to represent intentions, or you can have objects that simultaneously represent both. This is *your* **Mandantra**!

- Some example *intentions* to send into your objects as answers to your prayers are: love, peace, communication, energy, perspective, healing, transformation, grace, or flow.

As you create your **Mandantra**, get as detailed and specific as you want. Either while designing or afterwards during reflection and contemplation, take note of other significant design elements and choices as they relate to color, direction, location, and shape. Some common correlations are below.

Color, Chakra, and Psychological Contribution	**Direction**
Lavender - Crown Chakra - Bliss	East - Spirituality
Purple - Ajna Chakra - Intuition	North - Intellect
Blue - Throat Chakra - Communication	South - Emotions
Green - Heart Chakra - Love	West - Physical Body
Yellow - Solar Plexus Chakra - Emotions	Above - Source
Orange - Sacral Chakra - Relationships	Below - Center
Red - Basic Chakra - Security	Within - Higher Self
Location	**Shape**
Right Upper Corner - Partnership	Circle - Cycles
Left Upper Corner - Abundance	Square - Protection
Right Center - Completion	Triangle - Sacred Womb
Left Center - New Beginnings	Star - Celestial Connection
Right Lower Corner - Support	Spirals - Divine Feminine
Left Lower Corner - Inner Wisdom	Zig-Zag - Goddess
Center - Peace	Crescent - Lunar Wisdom

Once your **Mandantra** is complete, step back and allow this personal expression of prayer and intention to work its magick. Take a picture, journal, free write, or just sit quietly and be inspired by your creativity and Divinity. Open your awareness to receive all that comes forward in the form of answered prayers, insight, liberation, peace, and self-love. This **Mandantra** is yours. Enjoy it! Thank you. I love you.

~ SPS #4: ~
* Family Circle *

Who is your family? When you think of this group, who is there with you in this sacred circle? Relatives, friends, fur babies, and ancestors might come to mind. If it feels right, allow your Spirit Guides and Angels to join. Goddesses and Gods, too. Maybe you would like to include the Soul of someone, or something that has not yet manifested into your life yet. For example, this could be a new lover, a new friend, a new baby, or any *new* relationship. Keep adding to your *family circle* and in your mind, create a round table for all of them to join you. If your Family Circle is big, write down everyone's names to help you remember who all is here. In your imagination, visualize all of these wonderful beings sitting at the table of your Family Circle. These beings are here because you have chosen them and because they have chosen you. For people whom you know or have known, allow their Highest Selves to be present at this Family Circle Round Table. This means that when they communicate with you, or when you communicate with them, there is no judgement or criticism… only loving words spoken for the Greatest and Highest Good. Does this mean that unfinished business, uncleared patterns, or family cycles in need of a tune-up aren't allowed at this table? Absolutely not. It just means that everyone present is here to bring about the Greatest and Highest Good - and that includes *your* Greatest and Highest Good - so all communication must be filtered through the three Golden Gates by asking: 1.) Is it necessary? 2.) Is it honest? and 3.) Is it kind? Now, let the conversation begin! Below are some ideas of things to give and receive during this conversation. You might want to create a running order of taking turns or going around the table in order to give everyone a chance to speak.

- Ask a question and allow everyone in your Family Circle to respond.
- Express how you are feeling and allow everyone in your Family Circle to do the same.
- Offer an observation about what is going right in the world and allow everyone in your Family Circle to follow suit.
- Give gratitude to everyone in your Family Circle and allow them to return the gratitude to you.
- Say what you love about everyone in your Family Circle and allow them to say what they love about you.
- Ask for your needs to be met by everyone in your Family Circle and allow them to reply, specifically stating how they will meet them.

When the conversation feels complete, take a moment to thank everyone for their participation. When you are ready, bring your awareness back to the present time and space. Take a few deep breaths to ground your energy and allow a few moments for integration. A lot of information came to you just now and you may want to journal or take notes below. Remember, you can come back to your Family Circle at any time and your Family Circle can grow and shift with you and your needs.

Family Circle Wisdom and Insight

_____

_____

_____

Thank you for taking the time to do this activity. These relationships are present for our continued growth. The rate, amount, and way in which we grow is up to us. Love you. Thank you for doing this!

~ SPS #5: ~
* Verse and Chorus *

Have you ever made up a song? A whole song? With verses and a chorus? Believe it or not, it isn't as difficult as you might think. With a little guidance on structure and some of your creative genius, a simple tune can be born in no time. Think of some songs that you like. What are the first words that come to mind? Most Likely, those words are the hook, which is part of the chorus, and is the phrase that the song is built around... almost like the song's *Mantra*. What would your song's *Mantra* be? Let it be a simple phrase that is rooted in your feelings. Think about what you want and need, and then build a short phrase around that. You can start your hook with "I want....," "I feel....," "I need...." or "I think..." Let it be a simple phrase and - if you can - let it end with a word that is easy to rhyme.

- **My Hook Line:** _____

Once you have your hook, now you can structure the chorus. The chorus is the repeated section that goes in between the verses and carries the big meanings of what your song is about. Typically, a chorus is four lyric lines that are similar in length or syllables. Below are three options for chorus structures. Use them, or you make up your own.

Chorus #1- Hook Line: I want to live my *Dream*	Example
1. Hook Line	I want to live my **DREAM**
2. Second Line (*option to rhyme with last word of Fourth Line*)	Feet firmly on the *Earth*
3. Third Line (*last word can rhyme with last word of Hook Line*)	Where things are as they **SEEM**
4. Fourth Line (*option to rhyme with last word of Second Line*)	Clear life and clear *rebirth*

Chorus #2- Hook Line: I want to live my *Dream*	Example
1. Hook Line	I want to live my **DREAM**
2. Hook Line	I want to live my **DREAM**
3. Different Lyric Line (*option to rhyme or not*)	Where things are as they **SEEM**
4. Hook Line	I want to live my **DREAM**

Chorus #3- Hook Line: I want to live my *Dream*	Example
1. First Line (*line 2 from Option #1, rhymes with Line 3*)	Feet firmly on the *Earth*
2. Second Line (*line 3 from Option. #1, rhymes with Hook Line*)	Where things are as they **SEEM**
3. Third Line (*line 4 from Option #1, rhymes with Line 1*)	Clear life and clear *rebirth*
4. Hook Line	I want to live my **DREAM**

Your Original Chorus:
HookLine:_____

Line 1:

Line 2:

Line 3:

Line 4:

Now on to the verses. This is the *story* of your song. Here is where you can rhyme or not rhyme and follow structure or not follow structure. Verses are a bit more loosey-goosey. They are the reason why you are writing this tune in the first place and they are filled with feelings. Most songs have several verses that go between the choruses. Let's go for at least three. An easy way to create the verses is to think of the reasons **why** your Hook Line is important and then give three examples of **how** those reasons are presenting in your life. The reasons and the three examples become the four lines of your verse. For the three verses, to create a story arc, play with breaking them down into three categories.

- **Verse 1- Category 1**: You don't have what you want…
  - Based on the *original* Hook Line - *I **want** to live my dream.*

- **Verse 2 - Category 2:** How you are going to get what you want...
  - Now, turn your Hook Line into a *question* - **How can I live my dream?**

- **Verse 3 - Category 3:** What life will be like when that happens...
  - Here, your Hook Line becomes a *wish* for the future - **I am my own dream.**

Verse 1 - Category 1: You don't have what you want. You want to live your dream, but you're not. Figure out why is this important to you and how it is affecting your life. For Verse #1, we focus on:

*~ I **want** to live my dream, but I am **not** living my dream. ~*

Why is this important-	3 Reasons **how** I am unhappy:
• Because living this way makes me **unhappy**.	• I'm **lonely**. • I'm **unfulfilled**. • Yet, I'm still **hopeful**.

Verse #1 Example

-What does **unhappy** look like for me?	**Line 1:** *I walk all day, in a haze, I wonder where I'm going.*
-What does it feel like when I am **lonely**?	**Line 2:** *Alone and tired, itchy in my skin, just no way of knowing.*
-What does it feel like when I am **unfulfilled**?	**Line 3:** *Something else is just right there... just beyond my reach.*
- What does **hopeful** look like for me?	**Line 4:** *I'm climbing up... clawing through... my light will be unleashed.*

Now, you try.

Verse 1 - Category 1: What is it that you want, but that you don't have?

~ _____ ~

Why this is important:	3 Reasons how this is presenting in my life:
•	• • •

Your Original First Verse

Line 1:
Line 2:
Line 3:
Line 4:

Verse 2 – Category 2: Turn your what you want – your Hook Line - into a question:

*~ I **want** to live my dream.... **How** can I live my dream? ~*

<u>**Why**</u> this is important-	3 Things ***will happen*** when I am whole:
• When this happens, I will be **whole**.	• I will be **authentic**. • I will be **empowered**. • I will be **connected**.

Verse #2 Example

-What will being **whole** look like for me? -What will it feel like when I am **authentic**? -What will it feel like when I am **empowered**? - What will being **connected** look like for me?	**Line 1:** *There's another way for us all to live, another way to be* **Line 2:** *Connected with our hearts and souls, empowered, bold, and free* **Line 3:** *Together we will walk and laugh, together hand in hand* **Line 4:** *Trusting in each other, in truth, in love, and in the land*

Your turn.

Verse 2 – Category 2: Turn your Hook Line into a question and then figure out how you are going to get what you want.

~_____~

<u>**Why**</u> this is important-	3 Things ***will happen*** when you figure this out:
•	• • •

<u>**Your Original Second Verse**</u>
Line 1:
Line 2:
Line 3:
Line 4:

Verse 3 – Category 3: What is your wish and what is life like now that it has come true?

*~ I **want** to live my dream.... **I AM** my own dream. ~*

Why this is important-	**3 Things that I _will be_:**
• I am *whole*.	• I am **happy**. • I am **myself**. • I am **connected**.

Verse #3 Example

-I am **whole** and this is how I know. - I am **authentic** and this is how I know. - I am **empowered** and this is how I know. - I am **connected** and this is how I show it.	**Line 1:** *This happiness is mine and yours to cherish and to hold.* **Line 2:** *Knowing deep within our Souls, we've always been whole.* **Line 3:** *Hold my hand, we're flying now, to Heaven and beyond.* **Line 4:** *Look around, sing out our song, invite others to come along.*

OK, Third Verse.

Verse 3 – Category 3: This is your wish come true.

~_____~

Why this is important-	**3 Things that _I AM_ now:**
•	• •

Your Original Third Verse
Line 1:
Line 2:
Line 3:
Line 4:

Now it is time to put it all together! You've got your Hook Line, your Chorus, and the variations on your chorus - if you've chosen to do that - and three original verses! Congratulations, you amazing lyricist, you! Take a look below. This is a suggestion for structure, but follow your gut as you put your song together. Lastly, don't forget to title this phenomenal creation!!

Title: *"Live My Dream"*

Structure Suggestion	*"Live My Dream"*
Chorus #1	I want to live my **DREAM** Feet firmly on the Earth Where things are as they **SEEM** Clear life and clear rebirth
Verse #1	I walk all day, in a haze, wondering where I'm going. Alone and tired, itchy in my skin, just no way of knowing. Something else, is just right there, just beyond my reach. I'm climbing up, clawing through, my light will be unleashed.
Chorus #2 *(with, or without variation)*	I want to live my **DREAM** I want to live my **DREAM** Where things are as they **SEEM** How can I live my **DREAM** *(note lyric variation)*
Verse #2	There's another way for us all to live, another way to be. Connected with our hearts and souls, empowered, bold, and free. Together we will walk and laugh, together hand in hand. Trusting in each other, in truth, in love, and in the land.
Chorus #3 *(with, or without variation)*	Feet firmly on the Earth Where things are as they **SEEM** Clear life and clear rebirth I want to live my **DREAM**
Verse #3	This happiness is mine and yours to cherish and to hold. Knowing deep within our Souls, we've always been whole. Hold my hand, we're flying now, to Heaven and beyond. Look around, sing out our song, invite others to come along.
Final Chorus- *Finish with as many choruses as you want, in any variation that you want.*	I want to live my **DREAM** Feet firmly on the Earth Where things are as they **SEEM** Clear life and clear rebirth ~~~~~~~~~~~~~~~~~~~~~~~~~ Feet firmly on the Earth Things are as they **SEEM** *(note lyric variation)* Clear life and clear rebirth I will live my **DREAM** *(note lyric variation)* ~~~~~~~~~~~~~~~~~~~~~~~~~ I am my own **DREAM** *(note lyric variation)* I am my own **DREAM** Things are as they **SEEM** I am my own **DREAM**

Title: "_____"

Chorus #1
Verse #1
Chorus #2
Verse #2
Chorus #3
Verse #3
Final Chorus

One of the most helpful hints I can give for this whole process is to use an online rhyming dictionary where you can search for rhymes, near rhymes, and synonyms. As for the music, if you are a musician and can compose your own tune, that is amazing! If not, no worries You probably already feel a musical connection to what you have written. Sing through your tune a few times to get familiar with whatever melody is percolating. You can do this while recording yourself on your phone. This helps with remembering the notes and rhythms. You can also work with a local musician to help you create the music. There are some online resources, too. www.freemusicarchivec.org is a great place to start. Good luck, have fun, and in the immortal words of Gypsy Rose Lee, "Sing out, Louise!" Love you! Thank you for sharing your creativity!

Crystal Love: Jaana's Crystal is Jade, the highly prized stone of wisdom, purity, serenity, and tranquility. Coming in many different colors, Jade can help us channel our inner teachers, aiding us in reducing the perceived difficulty of situations and concepts while stimulating new ideas and awareness. If you are feeling irritable, try holding a piece of Jade. If your self-confidence could use a boost, try using Jade to gently release limitations while opening your heart to Divine potential, opportunity, and purpose. If empathy and attunement to the needs of others would be useful, try carrying a piece of Jade in your pocket to access the deep reserves of the nourishing and stabilizing energy of your Heart Chakra. Revered in many ancient cultures, Jade reminds us that although Spiritual Integration is optimal for living an awakened life, we are still human beings experiencing our own Spirituality, and sometimes that might not look or feel picture-perfect. When this happens, try using Jade in meditation to bring about clarification, understanding, and perspective. This stone can also be very helpful with manifesting and remembering specific dreams. Try placing a piece on your bedside table to release, cleanse, and soothe through the dreamscape. Lastly, known to many as a Good Luck charm, Jade can vibe in financial abundance and prosperity as well as the superior riches of friendship, emotional intimacy, and fellowship.

Suggested Reading to Compassionately Nurture the Minds of Children, as well as Your Own Inner Child, *The Whole-Brain Child: 12 Evolutional Strategies To Nurture Your Child's Developing Mind* by Daniel J. Siegel, M.D., and Tina Payne Bryson, Ph.D.

Additional Journaling and SPS Space

Katia

I took my power back the moment I started being true to myself. After years and years of being disconnected, my soul started screaming. I think the disconnect started much earlier. I'm not exactly sure when, but before I realized it, I was looking for validation from other people. I began forming opinions about myself based on what others thought of me. This thought process became really clear to me towards the end of my relationship with my children's father. I knew I needed to be out of this toxic relationship, but how? In my culture, success for a woman is almost always defined by her relationship to a man. If I left, I would be a single mom. That was scary. The other fear for me was financial. For most people from my country, they come here with the financial motive to make money. That is fine. That is why they come. Honestly, I lived my life like this, too, for many years. However, after realizing that this was not in alignment with my values, I began to recognize that life success is measured by much more than what kind of car you drive, what kind of house you live in, and what kind of job you have. I understand. I have to make money and I like to have nice things, but there are other things I feel are more important. My children's father had the mentality that since we came here to work, I should be working and producing and making money all the time. For him, being busy and productive was valued over everything else. Yet, I couldn't be busy working and making money because we have a son with special needs. With him, I really had to *be* with him. I had to stay home with him. He needed me. Money couldn't come first and family second because his needs weren't about money. No amount of money could fix them. That was the breaking point. I put my foot down and said "no" to going back to work and putting our child wherever – anywhere - just so that I could make money. In doing that, my son has taught me so much about what is important. I really have to think outside of the box with him. For both of my children, taking my power back has been very important. To model this for them, I have to have a better relationship with myself. Self-care has become my guide back to me. In my culture, women are supposed to give and give and give. It is like moms are not supposed to have a 'girl's night' or 'girl's trip.' It is seen as being irresponsible, but moms with special needs kids need self-care the most! So, I started doing self-care and I got a lot of push back. It felt as if people thought I should be even *more* dedicated and *more* devoted because my son has special needs. But, how can I give more if I don't have it? I really struggled with this in the beginning. People don't realize how hurtful they can be when they give an opinion and then say, "Oh, I was just trying to help." I try to take all of this as information. As a lesson. Not a lesson in the sense of 'I deserve this…' but a lesson in the sense of constantly learning and continuing to follow the path that is right for me and my kids. It can be hard. I have rough moments. I'm in a better situation than I was, but it isn't perfect. To think beyond Katia 'The Mother' is still difficult. I'm still discovering who I am, and I like the way I'm heading. I'm open to the possibility of being in a relationship again. This time, I know I won't repeat the same situation because I have grown. I'm working on me. Like I said, everything is information. Good or bad, if it triggers me, I know it is something that I need to work on. Having a group of women as 'sisters' to support me as I go through this has been really helpful. Knowing that there are other women out there on a similar path, on a similar journey of discovering themselves… that is really comforting. Now, what I used to see as weakness I see as strength. My feminine qualities. My compassion. My empathy. My stillness. I've always needed those things so much, but I didn't value them before. I do now. Giving back to myself has changed everything. Having a better relationship with myself and making time for me has made all the difference in the world. Even my kids know it is crucial. How can I give to them what I don't give to myself? There is a saying in my country that goes, "Puedes rehacer tu vida," which literally translates to "You can rebuild your life." But, what it *really* means is that you will find someone else, because ultimately your success as a woman is defined by your relationship with a man. When the relationship with my children's father was ending, people used to say that to me all the time. It didn't make me feel good at all. I've got a new phrase for me: "Puedes reinventarte en todo momento de tu vida." It means, "You can reinvent yourself at any point in your life." That is what I know, that is what I live, and *that* is beautiful!

Making This Story Your Own:

Katia's story helps us define what is truly important in our lives.
Take a moment, breathe, and reflect.
What stands out for you when you read her words?
Is there a situation in your life that is similar to Katia's?
Perhaps part of her story feels connected to your own.
How can you relate her experiences to your past, present, and future?

- *My Connection to Katia's Story* _____

_____

_____

_____

Knowing that you aren't alone, let's gently explore some other themes from Katia's story together:

- ***Success***
  - How do you define success? What does it look and feel like in your life and relationships? How much does money play into your understanding of personal and professional success? Are there things in your life that you value more than money? Is your happiness or contentment based on something that you can purchase like a car, a vacation, or a house? What makes you feel secure and do these feelings of security rely on financial success? Is there any part of you that would like to view success - financial or otherwise - differently? If so, how would you like to begin defining success for yourself and others?

- ***Social and Cultural Boundaries***
  - What cultural and social boundaries do you feel influenced by? Are there certain belief systems within these social and cultural boundaries that are in alignment with how you want to live your life? If so, what are they and how are they in alignment? Are there certain belief systems within these social and cultural boundaries that are *not* in alignment with how you want to live your life? If so, what are they and how are they not in alignment? What can you shift in your life to address these social and cultural boundaries so that they feel more authentic and aligned?

- ***Self-Care***
  - What is self-care? What does it mean *to* you and *for* you? Are your ideas about self-care consistent with your efforts to actually incorporate self-care into your life? If yes, how do you manage this? If no, how can you manage this in a better way? Does the thought of spending time and energy on yourself feel unwarranted for any reason? Is there anyone in your life, past or present, that has made you feel this way? Are these feelings and beliefs about self-care working for you? Would you like them to shift in any way? If so, what are a few small things you can do today to begin implementing self-care?

Sacred Play Suggestions:

~ SPS #1: ~
* Who Am I *

Who are you? Kind of a weird question, right? Who... *are*... you? Let's try to answer it together. In the box below, make of list of everything that defines who you are in this world. Include titles, accomplishments, certifications, and roles. Nothing is too small and everything counts. That straight-A report card in the second grade is just as important as running a marathon, so dig deep. There are twenty spaces. If you need more - and I am sure that you will - grab another piece of scrap paper and continue on.

Who Am I...	
What Makes Me, *Me*...	**What This Says About Me...**
1.	1.
2.	2.
3.	3.
4.	4.
5.	5.
6.	6.
7.	7.
8.	8.
9.	9.
10.	10.
11.	11.
12.	12.
13.	13.
14.	14.
15.	15.
16.	16.
17.	17.
18.	18.
19.	19.
20.	20.

For each amazing thing you have listed, write in the next column an answer for 'What this says about me...' When coming up with this answer, self-censoring and self-deprecation are not invited to the party. Imagine how your Fairy Godmother would respond and go from there. For example, if you listed on number fifteen that you went skydiving, your answer to 'What this says about me...' might be something like "This says that I am brave, exciting, adventurous, and bold!" When you are finished writing all of the amazing things that make you - *you,* grab something to cover the 'What Makes Me, *Me*' column. Now, with just the right-hand column visible, think of the opening question, 'Who are you?' Try answering by reading each line in this column aloud. Begin with, "I am..." and work your way through this glorious list of the things that make you special and unique. Read it a couple of times. Sing it. Dance it, too, if that feels good. Honey, you are all of this and more! Own it, claim it, and never forget it! Love you! Thank you for doing this for *you.*

~ SPS #2: ~
* Masculine – Feminine *

Masculine and Feminine energy are present within every living thing, regardless of gender, and each one of us is an exceptional example of varying degrees of these qualities. However, oftentimes we are forced, culturally and socially, to undervalue one side of ourselves and overvalue the other. This out-of-balance expression can lead us to do and feel all sorts of things that aren't in alignment with our authentic selves. In their beautiful book, *Into the Heart of the Feminine: An Archetypal Journey to Renew Strength, Love, and Creativity,* Massimilla Harris, Ph.D. and Bud Harris, Ph.D., give great examples on how this imbalance can wreak havoc in all of our relationships and experiences. Throughout the book, they also give examples of generally felt and understood qualities that relate to the Feminine and Masculine. Following is a list that I have created based on the qualities they outline. I love looking at this list because it helps me identify where I am overvaluing and undervaluing specific aspects of myself in deference to what I have been taught is *good, acceptable,* and *valuable*. Take a few deep breaths, give it a read-through, and see what feelings, thoughts, and sensations come up.

Qualities of the Feminine	Qualities of the Masculine
Nurturing	Protective
Compassionate	Identity Oriented
Relatedness	Goals
Presence	Success
Open-Heart	Personal Achievement
Warmth	Growth
Patience	Production and Productivity
Trusting	Work
Gentle	Strength
Loving	Meeting Expectations
Emotionally Secure	Forward Movement
Attentive	Change
Healing	Progress
Merciful	Rationality
Kindness	Efficiency
Acceptance	Self-Reliant
Alternative Consciousness	Analytic Thought
Nourishing	Accomplishments
Transformational	Autonomous
Able to Hold and Contain	Power
Awareness	Winning
Innate Wisdom	Personal Empowerment
Intuition and Instincts	Logic
Interdependent	Independent
Stillness	Multi-Tasking

As you read through the qualities, what happened? Did certain ones provoke particular feelings? Maybe memories came up? Did any qualities make you uncomfortable? All feelings, thoughts, and sensations are OK! Think about it, our DNA has had several thousand years to acculturate an overvaluation of the

Masculine. It makes sense that we would evolve to value logic, independence, and productivity very highly. Those things have been held as the pinnacle of what our modern world defines as success. Yet, how much more successful are we as humans - as beings who need love and connection to survive - when we are able to maintain states of compassion, mercy, and kindness? Do you see where we've been led astray? Our Feminine qualities keep us thriving and healthy… body, mind, *and* spirt! We can't fully realize the things on the right side of the list if we don't have the foundation of the Feminine. We don't put a price tag on hugs, but that doesn't mean we don't need them. Perhaps an internal journey of rediscovering balance and value would be beneficial. Remember, these qualities have no relation to gender. They are available, expressed, and experienced within all living things. The way they are expressed is unique to each individual and that in itself is a gift. When you are ready, journal or reflect on the following questions. Be gentle with yourself and take your time. Awareness may come in stages. Answer the questions in ways that feel most comfortable for you as you honor both the Feminine and Masculine sides of your consciousness.

- Which qualities do you most identify with? _____
  _____
  _____

- Which qualities are most awarded and valued by society? _____
  _____

- Which qualities are most awarded and valued by your peers and colleagues? _____
  _____

- Which qualities are most awarded and valued by your family? _____
  _____

- Which qualities are most awarded and valued by you? _____
  _____

- Where are you out of balance when it comes to the **valuation** of the Masculine and the Feminine?
  _____
  _____

- How has this affected you? _____

- Where are you in balance when it comes to the **valuation** of the Masculine and the Feminine?
  _____
  _____

- How has *this* affected you? _____

- Where are you out of balance when it comes to the **expression** of the Masculine and the Feminine?
  _____
  _____

- How has this affected you? _____

- Where are you in balance when it comes to the **expression** of the Masculine and the Feminine?
  _____
  _____

- How has *this* affected you? _____

- Do you recognize a need for more qualities of the Feminine to be present in your life? _____
  _____

- How can you honor this? _____
  _____

- Do you recognize a need for more qualities of the Masculine to be present in your life? _____
  _____

- How can you honor this? _____
  _____

Wow! How do you feel? I feel great just typing this! Embodying this balance with awareness is key. When people around you start to notice a shift, keep on *keeping on*. I've heard it said that a miracle is created when one heart begins to live in love. Living in this type of balanced self-love and self-acceptance might just be contagious… and you won't even have to say a word! Woot-woot! Love you! Thank you!

~ SPS #3: ~
* Names and Nicknames *

What is your name? How do people address you? Play with saying your name a few times in your head and then saying it out loud. How does it feel? Say your *full* name. What kinds of thoughts and feelings does *that* bring up? What about a nickname? Do you have one or a few? Write down these different versions of how people connect to you on the next page and really look at them. Look at the letters. Look at the words. Your name is something that you have heard and said yourself countless times, but how often have you really thought about it?

My Names and Nicknames

Your name is special, and it is yours. Have fun answering the following questions.

- What is the story of your name? _____

  _____

- Are you named after someone? _____

  _____

- Does your name mean something in another language? _____

  _____

- Is there a specific reason why you were given your name? _____

  _____

- Do you like your name? _____

- What about your nickname(s)? Do you like them? _____

  _____

- Have you ever changed your name and if so, why? _____

  _____

- If you could give yourself a new name, what would it be? _____

  _____

Now, close your eyes and think back to a tiny infant version of yourself... the you who received your name when it was first given. In your mind, see that small, vulnerable, open, and loving being. Wrap her in your arms. Feel the weight and the potential of this moment. Look down at her precious face from your current place of wisdom, empowerment, love, and protection, and gift her your name. Whisper it into her sweet ear and tell her all that you wish for her life. Prepare her, with compassion and love, to become YOU. Kiss her on her forehead and hold her tight, heartbeat to heartbeat. Stay in this moment for as long as you need. For some of us, our names can bring up very difficult emotions. If some support around these feelings is needed, reach out and talk to someone. If that isn't a fit, perhaps some more journaling or reflecting might help. Always know that your needs are valuable and worth meeting. Thank you for taking the time to do this activity. Love you!

~ SPS #4: ~
* Boundaries *

Social and cultural boundaries can be thought of as a created set of standards, rules, and agreements that we navigate throughout our lives. These standards, rules, and agreements can be spoken or unspoken, conscious or unconscious, clear or unclear, known or unknown. Suffice it to say that they are helpful at times, unpredictable at times, debilitating at times, confusing at times, and oh so very powerful **ALL** of the time when it comes to how we evaluate, compartmentalize, and create the criteria for what is considered '*good*' and '*right*' by the world at large. Sometimes we aren't even aware of how we fit into this complex dynamic until we break it down and get clear on how we have been influenced by these standards, rules, and agreements. We may not realize how much we hold others accountable based on these standards, rules, and agreements, until we break it down, too. Try going through the following in regard to the social and cultural boundaries that you have been navigating and see what comes up to be revealed and released.

From Your Family of Origin**,** what is considered good, bad, acceptable, unacceptable, to be rewarded, or to be punished?

Good, Acceptable, and Rewarded	**Bad, Unacceptable, and Punished**

Are these Standards, Rules, and Agreements:
Clear or Unclear, Known or Unknown, Spoken or Unspoken, Conscious or Unconscious?

_____

_____

_____

What can be **released**? _____

What can be **claimed**? _____

What can be **reinforced?** _____

What can be **transformed**? _____

From Your Culture or Ethnicity, what is considered good, bad, acceptable, unacceptable, to be rewarded, or to be punished?

Good, Acceptable, and Rewarded	Bad, Unacceptable, and Punished

Are these Standards, Rules, and Agreements:
Clear or Unclear, Known or Unknown, Spoken or Unspoken, Conscious or Unconscious?

_____

_____

_____

What can be **released**? _____

What can be **claimed**? _____

What can be **reinforced?** _____

What can be **transformed**? _____

From Your Geographic Location, what is considered good, bad, acceptable, unacceptable, to be rewarded, or to be punished?

Good, Acceptable, and Rewarded	Bad, Unacceptable, and Punished

Are these Standards, Rules, and Agreements:
Clear or Unclear, Known or Unknown, Spoken or Unspoken, Conscious or Unconscious?

_____

_____

_____

What can be **released**? _____

What can be **claimed**? _____

What can be **reinforced?** _____

What can be **transformed**? _____

From Your Religious or Spiritual Background, what is considered good, bad, acceptable, unacceptable, to be rewarded, or to be punished?

Good, Acceptable, and Rewarded	Bad, Unacceptable, and Punished

Are these Standards, Rules, and Agreements:
Clear or Unclear, Known or Unknown, Spoken or Unspoken, Conscious or Unconscious?

_____

_____

_____

What can be **released**? _____

What can be **claimed**? _____

What can be **reinforced?** _____

What can be **transformed**? _____

From Your Political Background, what is considered good, bad, acceptable, unacceptable, to be rewarded, or to be punished?

Good, Acceptable, and Rewarded	Bad, Unacceptable, and Punished

Are these Standards, Rules, and Agreements:
Clear or Unclear, Known or Unknown, Spoken or Unspoken, Conscious or Unconscious?

_____

_____

_____

What can be **released**? _____

What can be **claimed**? _____

What can be **reinforced**? _____

What can be **transformed**? _____

From Your Professional Background, what is considered good, bad, acceptable, unacceptable, to be rewarded, or to be punished?

Good, Acceptable, and Rewarded	Bad, Unacceptable, and Punished

**Are these Standards, Rules, and Agreements:
Clear or Unclear, Known or Unknown, Spoken or Unspoken, Conscious or Unconscious?**

_____

_____

_____

What can be **released**? _____

What can be **claimed**? _____

What can be **reinforced?** _____

What can be **transformed**? _____

From Your Personal Beliefs and Philosophies, what is considered good, bad, acceptable, unacceptable, to be rewarded, or to be punished?

Good, Acceptable, and Rewarded	Bad, Unacceptable, and Punished

**Are these Standards, Rules, and Agreements:
Clear or Unclear, Known or Unknown, Spoken or Unspoken, Conscious or Unconscious?**

_____

_____

_____

What can be **released**? _____

What can be **claimed**? _____

What can be **reinforced?** _____

What can be **transformed**? _____

Wow… you are amazing! What a lot of stuff to wade through… and you did it! Now, with all of this newfound awareness, what will you shift? Within the context of what social and cultural boundaries would have us believe is '*good*' or '*right*,' how will you *keep on keeping on* as the wonderful woman you are with no apologies and no explanations? I think doing this activity makes us *Wonder Women*! Who has their leotard and gold cuffs ready? I do, I do! I just need my headband and lasso. I'll see you in the costume aisle, Sister. Love you! Thank you for taking the time to do this!

~ SPS #5: ~
* Radiance *

When was the last time you felt radiant? Do you remember? What stars were aligning to bring out your radiance? Radiance is such an important word in regard to our Feminine energy because it is a potent reminder of female spirituality, bliss, ecstasy, and empowerment. When we feel radiant, we literally *radiate* beauty, love, strength, and wisdom. We are magnetic. Others notice. We notice. We are lit from the inside out and the magick of the impossible becoming possible doesn't really seem all that far-fetched. In her book, *Pussy: A Reclamation,* Regena Thomashauer talks about how an "altar without candles is just a shelf." She goes on to liken this to our Feminine divinity and identifies that without our radiance, we don't glow with life force energy. We forget our pleasure. We forget our power. We forget our wild connection to the world around us. We forget to remember that these things - pleasure, empowerment, and connection - are ours to claim and to have at will as much as we damned well please! I veto the idea of me being a dusty old shelf any longer! I want to re-light my candles and open my portal to inner bliss and ecstasy. I want to become my own altar. Who is with me? Let's start by finding the best spot to create this sacred personal space. Is there somewhere in your home or yard that feels especially good and comfy? Not necessarily because it is a comfortable place to sit or lie down, but in this place the *energy* is comfortable. The energy here fits you and whether you feel upbeat and ready to be productive, or tired and in need of a recharge, this is your place. If you do have a place like this - wonderful! If not, let's make one. Find a nook, cranny, chair, corner, or other spot that you can dedicate to this process. Here in this space, come up with the intentions of how this particular place will support your radiance. Energy follows thought, so claim anything. Don't censor. Let your intuition guide you. If for instance you are in a closet hiding away from the rest of the fam and you feel more *silly* than *sublime*, don't fake-it, *faith-it* until it feels more real. Trust in yourself. You are a Goddess, remember?

- This place will support my **bliss** by _____

- This place will support my **ecstasy** by _____

- This place will support my **spirituality** by _____

- This place will support my **empowerment** by _____

In this place, I *step into* my RADIANCE by…

_____

_____

_____

Now, light the candles on your altar. In your imagination, visualize where the physical portals on your beautiful body are located for the sacred flames of radiance to be lit. Activate and warm your hands by rubbing them together. Either by holding your hands a few inches above your skin, or by gently placing your hands on your skin, intentionally light your fire! Visualize your physical body coming to life as each light begins to flicker and flame.

- The **bliss** portal on my body is _____

- The **ecstasy** portal on my body is _____

- The **spiritual** portal on my body is _____

- The **empowerment** portal on my body is _____

In this place, I *activate* the RADIANCE of my body by...

_____

_____

Most altars have sacred items that channel, contain, and imbue energy. Your gorgeous heart and your brilliant mind are two wonderful places to unearth these precious objects. Think of your feelings as priceless treasures and your thoughts as exquisite adornments. Breathe several times - connecting your heart to your mind - and in your imagination, decorate your altar with delightful embellishments.

- My thoughts and feelings bring me to my **bliss** by _____

  _____

- My thoughts and feelings bring me to my **ecstasy** by _____

  _____

- My thoughts and feelings bring me to my **spirituality** by _____

  _____

- My thoughts and feelings bring me to my **empowerment** by _____

  _____

In this place, I *feel* and *know* the RADIANCE of my *heart* and *mind* by...

_____

_____

_____

How are you feeling? Hopefully awesome! OK, last step. We have created a radiance consciousness for the embodiment of bliss, ecstasy, empowerment, and spiritual connection around our physical space, our physical bodies, our thoughts, and our feelings. Let's finalize this process by stimulating our Souls. Wowza! Just typing that feels sensuous! Take a few more deep breaths and connect into your Soul. This is your Higher Self. This is the aspect of you that is always radiant because your Higher Self knows no other way of being. Your Higher Self unconditionally radiates beauty, love, strength, and wisdom because it is consistently in a state of bliss, ecstasy, empowerment, and connection. Your Higher Self is purely connected to Source because it *IS* Source. And, you know what that means… if your Higher Self *IS* Source then **SO ARE YOU!**

- In my Soul, **I AM** my own **Bliss** by _____

_____

- In my Soul, **I AM** my own **Ecstasy** by _____

_____

- In my Soul, **I AM** my own **Spirituality** by _____

_____

- In my Soul, **I AM** my own **Empowerment** by _____

_____

If it feels right, finish by reading aloud and reflecting or journaling around the following.

In this place, I AM RADIANCE.
In this place, I AM Bliss.
In this place, I AM Ecstasy.
In this place, I AM Spirituality.
In this place, I AM Empowerment.
In this place, I AM my Soul.
In this place, I AM my Higher Self.
In this place, I RADIATE beauty, love, strength, and wisdom always and in ALL ways.

_____

_____

_____

Woo-hoo! Way to go baby-cakes! This may take a few run-throughs and you will probably get interrupted one or fifty times, but don't forget this: **YOU** are the sacred candles, objects, energies, and intentions of your Altar. **YOU** are your own Radiance. All you have to do is be yourself because you are *enough*. Now, go and play with your radiance. Have fun and have pleasure! You deserve it! Love you! Thank you!

Crystal Love: Katia's Crystal is Cinnabar (***sin**-uh-bahr*) and this stone is all about expansion and abundance. Because of its perceived powers to acquire and maintain a state of wealth, Cinnabar was known in ancient times to be a 'Merchant's Stone.' Today, we use this Crystal to reinforce the belief that true wealth is a state of being, for Cinnabar can escalate fluency of communication, clarity of mind, elegance of demeanor, and create ease for the work-life balance. Also supporting us in the realm of expansion, Cinnabar can increase assertiveness in those wishing to give, as well as increasing receptivity for those wishing to receive. Additionally, this stone assists us in organizing community work - infusing our team with dignity and power - so that we may create the lasting and needed changes of peace, mutual respect, joy, and interdependence. At the spiritual level, Cinnabar can connect us into the Soul-based wisdom that everything is as it should be, and everything is in perfect, Divine order. Use this stone, or get a piece in your pocket, to expedite the focus, flow, and facilitation of service to the Divine!

Suggested Reading to Understand, Assimilate and Revalue the Feminine, *Into the Heart of the Feminine: An Archetypal Journey to Renew Strength, Love, and Creativity* by Massimilla Harris, Ph.D. and Bud Harris, Ph.D.

Additional Journaling and SPS Space

Matilda

I'm eleven years old. I've moved a lot and moving has taught me that it is hard to leave my friends, but I will always remember them and I trust that I will make new friends. I know that sometimes it can be hard to be friends with someone. If a friend feels like they aren't getting enough of your attention and they are doing something you don't like, you shouldn't get mad at them. Everyone can make bad decisions and it isn't worth getting all worked up about it. Take some time off from them to think differently and what they are doing won't make you as mad or upset. Then you can try again and be a better kind of friend. People can change and they do. My friends today are different and that is good. I have two friends that are a lot like me. They are both quiet. The other two friends want a bunch of attention. Both types of personalities are fun. We don't all have to be the same to get along. I look for truth in people that are going to be my friends. I don't want to be around people who are trying to be cool. I want to be around friends that aren't afraid to be themselves, who like to play, and who like to have fun. We all should be doing more of that! It is so much fun to sit down and play because when we do that together, we find out what we have in common. Exploring and baking are fun. When I am exploring, if I like what I try, I want to do more of it. If I don't like it, I move on. With baking, it passes the time and then you get a fun reward when you are done. It feels really neat to create something. I like being creative. I also like being surprised, like when I got a phone. I was really surprised because I got it two years early. I got it because I am so responsible. I don't make bad choices. I do the right thing even when no one is looking. Even when my parents aren't around. I learned to do this by watching kids at school. Sometimes they do things that they aren't supposed to do. Sometimes they get caught and sometimes they don't. I don't think I could do that. I couldn't do something bad and be OK with it. Even if I didn't get caught. Even if no one found out, I would not be happy with myself. I think I feel this way because of my heart, my brain, and my soul. It is a mixture. My heart is full of love, my brain makes me think, and my soul is my personality. They all help me think about new ideas. Like our world being vegan. I think about that a lot. My wish is for everybody in the world to know the truth about animals. Animals have the same emotions, feelings, and qualities as humans. They shouldn't be treated any differently. Why do we eat them? I'm not sure what adults know, but I want them to know the truth about animals and slaughterhouses. They always show happy cows on milk containers and that is not the case. I know the truth about how animals are treated when they are killed for meat and I want to tell other people. So does my family. It is important for us to tell the truth about why we are vegan. It makes us stronger. I'm already helping people change their minds about how they eat. In my class at school, I brought vegan treats for my birthday and everyone loved them. My friend just came for a sleepover and told me she wants to go vegan for a week. I never feel afraid about telling the truth for animals. I don't care if I am left out or if people say they don't like me because of it; this is important to me. This is my mission. I also think the world should be equal. That means everybody, all people, men and women. All of these words have 'man,' in them; wo-man, hu-man. Or, the word, his-story. If I could make changes, I would say our-story. This is important for me. I don't like it when I see people feeling left out or feeling not important. Especially girls. I am so glad that I am a girl. I can do so many things. I can have a baby. Being a girl is very special. I get to become a mom. I haven't thought about how many babies I want to have, but I get excited thinking that my body can make a new life. Girls have a lot of power. So many girls have changed the world. I don't know if I will be one of those girls, but maybe. I do know that I am kind. I am also helpful. I like doing these things because I can see that they make other people happy. When my little brother is upset and not wanting to do something, I help him out and his feelings change. He feels better. When people say, thank you, it makes me feel better, too. I want to remind adults that there is always going to be a positive and negative side to everything. It is like being the oldest kid in our house. I get to do everything first, but my brother and sister won't have to wait as long to do the same things. That is OK. I wouldn't want to be any other age. I want to be the oldest no matter what. Everything can have a good and a bad side. That doesn't mean we have to give up or walk away. We can all say "please" and "thank you." We can all make good choices. We can all be responsible. I do this. I know this about myself: I don't give up. I know there are still a lot of things out there for me to learn, but that goes for everybody. My hope for the future is Veganism and Equality. What is yours?

Making This Story Your Own:

Matilda's story is an inspiration for doing the right thing.
Take a moment, breathe, and reflect.
What stands out for you when you read her words?
Is there a situation in your life that is similar to Matilda's?
Perhaps part of her story feels connected to your own.
How can you relate her experiences to your past, present, and future?

- *My Connection to Matilda's Story* _____

  _____

  _____

  _____

  _____

Knowing that you aren't alone, let's gently explore some other themes from Matilda's story together:

- ***Everyone Makes Mistakes***
    - What are your thoughts on making mistakes? Do you have a rating system where some mistakes are more significant than others? How was this rating system created and where did it come from? How do you handle it when your friends make mistakes? How do you handle it when your partner makes mistakes? How do you handle it when your children make mistakes? How do you handle it when *you* make mistakes? Are your responses different for different people, or are they similar? If they are different, why? If they are similar, why? When someone else makes a mistake, how do you want them to go about correcting it? When you make a mistake, what is your process for repair? Where did you learn this process, and is it still working for you? If you don't have a repair process, how can you begin to create one that is in alignment with who you are today?

- ***Living Your Truth***
    - What is really important for you when it comes to values, ethics, and morals? How do they apply to your daily life, your community involvement, and your interaction with the world at large? How do you express yourself in regard to these important values, ethics, and morals? Do you share your thoughts and feelings with like-minded people? Do you share your thoughts and feelings with people who might disagree? When it comes to speaking, living, and embodying these important principles, do you have a role model or mentor for living this way? If so, who is it? If not, can you give yourself credit for being your own role model and mentor? How can you

be a role model or mentor for others when it comes to them speaking, living, and embodying their own values, morals, and ethics?

- **Don't Give Up**
    - What important goal, dream, or life path have you given up or put on hold? Why have you made this decision? What were the influencing factors? Do these factors still apply today? Can you make revisions to these goals and dreams so that they are more realistic, manageable, and applicable to you and your life now? When you reflect on your early years, what were the messages you received about following your dreams and reaching your goals? Do these messages still influence you? If so, how, and is the impact beneficial or not beneficial?

Sacred Play Suggestions:

~ SPS #1: ~
* Body Talk *

Would you believe that your body can sometimes tell your truth better than your mind can? This can be remarkably true for hidden belief systems. Our mature, rational minds may think we feel a certain way only to discover upon deeper investigation that a very different subconscious program is running. Let's give it a try and see what comes up. First, make sure you are hydrated. This way all of your cells can be answering together in a way that is fluid (sorry, bad joke) and uncompromised. There is an actual form of alternative medicine that is based upon our body's ability to give feedback called Applied Kinesiology. For this activity's feedback, let's play with taking a step forward for an answer of *"yes,"* and taking a step backward for an answer of *"no."* Let your neutral spot be depicted by standing at a certain place on the floor which can be easily returned to for a reset in between questions. For example, this neutral place could be a particular tile, a design on a rug, or some tape marking an 'x' on the floor. Once you've got your neutral spot, read the statements below out loud and without letting your mind lead, let your body do the talking.

I deserve love.	I create my own love.	I give and receive love.	I am love.
I deserve happiness.	I create my own happiness.	I give and receive happiness.	I am happiness.
I deserve health.	I create my own health.	I give and receive health.	I am health.
I deserve abundance.	I create my own abundance.	I give and receive abundance.	I am abundance.
I deserve peace.	I create my own peace.	I give and receive peace.	I am peace.

What happened? If your body gave even the slightest tug in a direction different than what your mind *thought* you should answer, honor your body. If your answers were surprising, or have left you feeling the least bit worried, don't fret. This is good! You are uncovering old belief systems. These old belief systems can subconsciously cause us to create dynamics in our lives that manifest situations to make them *feel* true. However, that doesn't mean that they *are* true. Now that you know these programs are running, you've got the power to change them. You can't unknow what you know - and now that you know - you can consciously create a different reality for yourself… a reality that is more congruent with how you *want* to live rather than how you were *taught* to live. To finish, create your own clear statements below that reflect your new consciousness and your new beliefs. Stay positive and omit any negative language such as can't, don't, won't, or isn't. Repeat these statements often to solidify your choice of living in empowered truth from this moment forward.

I deserve	I create	I give and receive	I am
I deserve	I create	I give and receive	I am
I deserve	I create	I give and receive	I am
I deserve	I create	I give and receive	I am
I deserve	I create	I give and receive	I am

If you would like to learn more about releasing belief systems, check out Vianna Stibal's Theta Healing Modality. Her work is filled with love and light. So are you and so am I! I love you! Thank you!

~ SPS #2: ~
* Stereotypes *

We live in a world that is seeking to bust through stereotypes. Yet, just like anything we see quite a bit of - think "Real Men Wear Pink" - our brains can start to file it away under *everyday stuff*. When that happens, we can forget and forego the reasons behind why the statement or movement is powerful for us in the first place. Sometimes, we don't even realize that we are holding onto stereotypes. These can be stereotypes handed down from our families. They can be related to the geography of where we grew up. They can also be from someone or something in our lives that was or is influential. However, what stereotypes cannot do is stick around if we know they are there and know that we want to them to change. Below are some words. Read through them and label them with the first association that comes to mind for either **girl**, **boy**, **man**, or **woman**.

Glitter	Manicure	Martial Arts	Pink	Jewelry
Construction	Running	Making Money	Pilot	Shopping
Building	Hammer	Nurse	Dirt	Talking
Blue	Overalls	Flowers	Fist Fight	Sky Diving
Cooking	Owner	Secretary	Valedictorian	Smelly
High Tops	Purse	Doll	Billfold	Doctor
CEO	Dancing	Diets	Hair Bows	Video Games
Tough	History	Beer	Singing	Farm
Spiritual	Drugs	Blood	Athletic	Religious

Take a look at your word associations. Are any surprising? Whether they are or not, let it just be *information*. This activity is not about pointing the finger to highlight where we are wrong or to give pats on the back for where we are right. It is about bringing awareness to that which is hidden. If we are not aware that we have certain feelings, regardless of if they actually fit with who we think ourselves to be, we can unknowingly act and react from a place that maintains hurtful labels and categorizations. Yet, bringing this stuff up to take a deeper look is a great way to self-reflect, grow, and transform. Go back through the list of words and see how you can make them apply to all human beings regardless of gender, age, nationality, ethnicity, education level, or socio-economic status. Thank you for doing this. Every little bit of excavation helps. Love you!

~ SPS #3: ~
* You Are Amazing *

Matilda shares with us her exemplification of the C. S. Lewis quote, "Integrity is doing the right thing, even when no one is watching." How have you embodied this philosophy in your life? Chances are, you've embodied it more than you realize. You have probably acted with integrity, with no witness present, more than you can appreciate or comprehend. This is easy to do. We live, and have been living for a long time, in a culture that values shared misery over shared success. This energy is especially prevalent in our smaller familial and social groups. When you really think about it, it's easy to see how much more we accept communal commiseration than a sharing of our talents, successes, joys, and general amazingness. In fact, we learn very early not to toot our own horns for fear of the backlash. No one wants to be called a braggart, full of themselves, or a showoff. However, keeping our lights dimmed can have other more dangerous effects. When we don't bring attention to our goodness, we can forget to remember how truly *good* we are. Just like the flower that wilts and dies with no water, the very parts of us dedicated to doing what is right can dry up and die as well. That image may be a bit dramatic, but our good, healthy parts - those that are not only compassionate and empathetic, but ones that are also energized to be integral *no matter* the outcome - need to be recognized. They deserve to be appreciated and shared. When we do this, a beautiful pattern comes to life where we inspire others and they inspire us in return. It can be such a win-win! Make a list of the good things that you have done today since you've been awake. Water that plant, Sister, and keep going. Make a list of the good things that you have done in the past week… the past month… the past year… your whole life! After all, why did you get that Good Samaritan Award in second grade? It counts. It does! Don't diminish any of it. Don't downplay the goodness that is *you*. The more you notice how beautiful your heart is, the more beautiful and kind things you will do. To keep with the plant metaphor, doing this is like fertilizer for good deeds. Now, here is the deal. You have to tell someone. Start small. The next time you are with your friends, ask them what is going right in their lives and tell them what is going right in yours. Tell your partner about a choice you made that helped someone. Share with colleagues about a great parenting moment you had with your children. Don't dilute. This isn't about bragging; this is about authentically sharing what a blessing you are to the world. Stop rolling your eyes. You *are*! You *are* a blessing. The more you own it for yourself, the more others can own it for themselves, too.

My Good-Hearted and Inspirational Amazingness	
Good Stuff I Did Today…	**Good Stuff I Did Yesterday…**

Good Stuff I Did Last Week	Good Stuff I Did Last Month
Good Stuff I Did Last Year	**All the other Good Stuff I've Done in My Life**

Thank you for doing this! Multiply this good momentum by continuing to share what is going right. Take notice of how others begin to follow. Way to go, you Way-Shower, you! What a beautiful thing to be: someone who shines their light so bright that you inspire others to do that same. I say "Huz-Zah" to that and I say "Huz-Zah" to *you*! Love you!

~ SPS #4: ~
* Breath of Fire *

There is an Ayurvedic breathing technique called Kapalabhati (kah-pah-luh-**bah**-tee), or 'Breath of Fire,' that feels a little like the breathing techniques taught for labor and delivery. Both ways of breathing are intended to invigorate the body, increase life force, focus the mind, generate strength, and provide release. To breathe the 'Breath of Fire,' inhale and exhale through your nose quickly, filling your belly on the inhale and releasing the breath by bringing your navel towards your spine on the exhale, and repeat twelve times. Follow this with several long slow Ujjayi (*oo*-**jai**-yee) breaths. These breaths are also through your nose, with deep inhalations and long exhalations. When exhaling for these Ujjayi breaths, slightly constrict the back of your throat to produce a "HAAAAHHHH" sound. This sound is sort of like the sound you would make if you were using your breath to fog up a window or mirror. As women, yes, we breathe. No question about that. As women, we also hold the magick of birth within our bodies, minds, hearts, and spirits. We birth human children from our wombs. Yet, we birth many other 'children' on a regular basis in the form of ideas, relationships, perspectives, initiatives, movements, education, and enlightenment. Let's honor this Divinely Feminine birth magick with some Mantras and breathing and see what we can *deliver*. Grab a glass of water to rehydrate in case you start to feel dizzy or lightheaded. Put your hands on your lower abdomen and visualize a connection from your heart to your womb. When you are ready, begin the practice of chanting the Mantras below, in order *and* in the amount listed, followed by the Kapalabhati breaths and Ujjayi breaths. Take note: the number of Mantras equals **108** and the number of combined breaths also equals **108**. This is to honor the Mantra Practice of different spiritual traditions in which a mantra is chanted

108 times around the mala. The number 108 is sacred because the 1 represents you, the 0 represents your relationship to Source, or God, and the 8 represents the infinite nature of that relationship. OK, ready? Let's chant, breathe, and birth! Use your fingers to count.

- **I am prepared. I am ready.**
  - Chant the Mantra **15** times.
  - Follow with **12** rapid Kapalabhati breaths and **3** slow Ujjayi Breaths.

- **I am perfect for this.**
  - Chant the Mantra **15** times.
  - Follow with **12** rapid Kapalabhati breaths and **3** slow Ujjayi Breaths.

- **I trust my body, mind, and soul to give birth to this new life.**
  - Chant the Mantra **15** times.
  - Follow with **12** rapid Kapalabhati breaths and **3** slow Ujjayi Breaths.

- **I will follow my natural instincts.**
  - Chant the Mantra **15** times.
  - Follow with **12** rapid Kapalabhati breaths and **3** slow Ujjayi Breaths.

- **I birth in the way that I desire.**
  - Chant the Mantra **15** times.
  - Follow with **12** rapid Kapalabhati breaths and **3** slow Ujjayi Breaths.

- **I birth new life with pleasure.**
  - Chant the Mantra **15** times.
  - Follow with **12** rapid Kapalabhati breaths and **3** slow Ujjayi Breaths

- **I relax, breathe, and open.**
  - Chant the Mantra **_18_** times
  - Follow with **12** rapid Kapalabhati breaths and **_6_** slow Ujjayi Breaths

Whew! Take a moment and center yourself. If you feel dizzy, gently let your breath return to normal and take a sip or two from your glass of water. Once your systems have become reacquainted to the present moment, allow yourself time to rest and relax. Birth magick is demanding and beautiful work and you did it! You are amazing! Thank you! Love you! When you are ready, reflect or journal about what beautiful new life you will be bringing into the world.

The Beautiful New Life I Will Birth

_____

_____

_____

_____

~ SPS #5: ~
OurStory Logo

'Healer, heal thyself,' is an often shared and well-known philosophy. So is, 'Be the change you want to see.' Matilda inspires us all to step into this place of self-reflection and self-empowerment with her hope for a more equitable world. Just like she says, this is not just about '*his*-story,' it's about making '*Our*-Story.' To have a little fun with this, let's get evocative with imagery. Image is so powerful to the human psyche. Think of advertising, art, and iconography. We adorn our bodies daily with imagery in our clothes, jewelry, and tattoos. Our dwellings are filled not just with photos, but with meaningful items, art, and images. Logos are a huge part of this conversation. We have so familiarized ourselves with certain colors, fonts, and designs that we can see a logo and know exactly what it represents in terms of the product, but also in terms of how the product relates to our lives and lifestyles. Right now, let's craft our own Logo for the world we would like to create… a world based on Equality, Peace, and Partnership…. A world that tells *Our*-Story. We will work with three steps for release, embodiment, and transformation. Grab something to draw on and some things to draw with. Get as fancy as you want.

- **Step #1. The Mind**
  - This is the first part of the Logo design.
    - For this part of the image, we are stepping out of the existing socio-cultural patterns of societal formation to create something new.
      - Our Modern Age is referred to as a Patriarchy.
        - Patriarchy is simply defined as a system of society or government in which the father or eldest male is head of the family and descent is traced through the male line.
      - Before the last five thousand years of Patriarchy, her-storians have identified that humans lived within the values of a Matriarchy.
        - Matriarchy is simply defined as a family, society, community, or state governed by women in which descent is traced through the female line.

- Draw: Thinking of and identifying the differences between the two ways of organizing society, can you create an initial image that blends the best of both and represents your understanding of what a Humanarchy (a world where familial and societal organization is governed not by gender, but by the values of mutual kindness, love, respect, and community) could be?
  - Allow your imagination to work through your hand, and without censorship or editing, draw this first part of your Logo.

- **Step #2. The Heart**
  - This is the second part of the Logo design.
    - For this part of the image, we will explore releasing *independence* (success for the self) to create a newfound sense of interdependence *(success for the tribe).*
      - If we think of our Society or Culture as a parental figure, the type of parenting currently represented is Authoritarian, in which a dominant style of leadership is characterized by high demands and low responsiveness. This type of *parenting* lacks comfort, support, or love to balance the pressure to perform and leaves us feeling insecurely attached. When this happens, we can become fixated on individual success, protection, and productivity while simultaneously feeling lonely, isolated, and disconnected. The following sums it up perfectly:

- - - "The boy who is not embraced by the village will burn it down just to feel its warmth." - **African Proverb**
  - Yet, if we can embody a Partnership, or Authoritative Societal Style of 'Parenting' in which high demands and high responsiveness are equivalent, we can create more secure attachments. This type of *parenting* instills an intrinsic trust that the world is good and will meet our needs. Within this type of organization, our dedication to the self is expressed and met through our dedication to the tribe.
  - The following quote sums this perspective up:
    - "Love makes us remember our true identity." - **Riane Eisler**

- Draw: Thinking of and identifying a world where we are connected in *Partnership* by our responsiveness to one another, can you create and blend a second image with your first drawing that honors equality, connection, and security?
  - Allow your imagination to work through your hand, and without censorship or editing, draw this second part of your Logo.

- **Step #3. The Spirit**
  - This is the third part of the Logo design.
    - For this final part of the image, we will balance qualities of the Masculine and Feminine within to birth a fresh and empowered Social Paradigm.
      - Some qualities of the *Masculine*, when balanced and expressed, can look like:
        - Strong and Protective
        - Linear and Rational
        - Independent, Successful, and Productive
        - Efficient with Forward Movement and Momentum
        - Dedicated and Able to Receive Support from the Feminine
      - Some qualities of the *Feminine*, when balanced and expressed, can look like:
        - Compassionate and Connected
        - Able to Relate and Empathize
        - Powerful, Intuitive, and Instinctual
        - Creative and Abundant
        - Nourishing and Fertile
        - Dedicated to and Merciful Healer of the Masculine

- Draw: Thinking of and identifying how you can fully embrace, embody, and express all of these Masculine and Feminine qualities to become a way-shower of empowered equality and interconnectedness, can you create a final image, correlating it to the first two, which honors all life?
  - Allow your imagination to work through your hand, and without censorship or editing, draw this third and final part of your Logo.

Once you are finished with your Logo, give yourself a hug. That was hard work! Hang it up so that you can be consistently reminded of what a powerful Creatrix you are. Wow! That image is amazing. Show it off if you feel comfortable. Your Logo, just like a good picture, will not only inspire a thousand words, but a thousand feelings, thoughts, and ideas. Way to go! Love you! Thank you for taking the time to create such a motivational image for Equality, Peace, and Partnership.

Crystal Love: Matilda's Crystal is Andalusite (an-da-*loo*-sahyt), sometimes referred to as Chiastolite (kahy-*as*-ta-lahyt). Legend holds that as monks carried these stones and touched them with daily dedication, the oils from their skin brought about a polishing effect, revealing the equilateral cross formation within. Let this symbol of equality from Andalusite reawaken your Spiritual Wisdom to the balance, value, perspective, and memory of all things. This Crystal is also a wonderful reminder that rationale can be applied in all situations, offering us the ability to moderate our emotional responses while holding an unbiased feeling about the results. Because of these abilities for well-rounded physical, emotional, spiritual, and psychic assessments, Andalusite can additionally help with recovering our balance, aligning our Chakras, understanding messages from the Spiritual Realm, and offering support to authentically view our character. Sit with Andalusite to process a point of view that believes no one event, experience, or thing is more important than the other. Hold Andalusite to appreciate the value of oneness. Finally, this stone may help you maintain a sense of calm with its wisdom that self-sacrifice is sometimes OK, but never required.

Suggested Reading to Renew and Revive Your Love for Animals, Mother Earth, and Yourself, *Dear Children of the Earth: A Letter from Home* by Schim Schimmel.

Additional Journaling and SPS Space

Misty

On June 7, 2019, I was in a car accident as I was heading home from work around 7:00 pm. I was making a left turn and the other driver, who was intoxicated, was going extremely fast. I still don't understand how I didn't see his car coming. When our cars collided, the combination of the airbags deploying and metal smashing was the loudest sound I'd ever heard. My first thought was: "Oh my gosh, what just happened?" My ears were ringing. I blacked out within seconds. The crunched hood prevented me from seeing the extensive damage before paramedics took me from the scene. When I arrived at the tow yard to get my belongings the next day, I stopped in my tracks. I immediately began crying when I saw the mangled mess that remained of my car and thought, "How the hell did I survive that with nothing more than a dislocated rib and minor burns and cuts on my hands?!" I didn't realize it, but up until that point I had become like a robot going through my days. I had been divorced ten months and had gotten so accustomed to the feelings of hatred and resentment that I didn't even notice them anymore. When my marriage got really rocky the year prior, marriage counseling helped, but not much. My husband and I agreed that we needed to work on ourselves individually in order to become good partners for each other. At that time, we had been together twelve years, married six, and had a three-year-old daughter. It quickly became apparent that I desperately needed to work through a lot of repressed emotions, and I was grateful to have an incredible clinician walk with me on that journey. I began to understand how all of the pain and anger I was carrying around from my past was impacting the way I interacted with the world. Without explanation, my husband chose not to hold up his end of our agreement. As I learned to value myself and my self-confidence grew, so did the divide between us. I believe that he knew I wasn't going to remain in a marriage with someone who didn't treat me with respect and kindness much longer. As I was slowly gaining the confidence to pursue a divorce, he beat me to the punch. In the months prior, he chose to have an affair while we were in the process of refinancing our house. The ink was barely dry on the loan documents when he came home drunk and announced that we were getting a divorce. Quite honestly, I was in shock, but not completely surprised. At this point, I am grateful to him because I don't believe I would have had the courage to leave for months, maybe years. I am a determined person and quitting is not in my nature. Despite knowing deep down that the emotional abuse he spewed was hurting me and was also harmful to our daughter's growth and development, I was torn. I had been fighting for her to have what we didn't: a stable, safe, financially secure, two-parent home. I felt like the rug had been pulled out from under my feet. Not only was my marriage ending, but I had to leave my fourteen-year-old dog and the home we had built as a family. I not only felt betrayed, I felt used and thrown away. It was a living nightmare. There was a lot of rage. I. Wanted. Revenge. Realizing that I was never going to recoup the energy I had put into the relationship was insanely painful. I had kept all of my promises, and he hadn't. I felt so stupid. Naïve. Tricked. I developed painful ulcers in my mouth. I cried often. I thought about suicide, not only to end my pain but to free my daughter *from me*. I tried to focus on work but would cry it out on the floor in my office, hoping no one knocked on the door. I took out some of the anger I had towards him on my daughter during that time, which is still tough to admit. One thing I want to touch on is - for the first year of her life - I struggled with Post-Partum Depression. I was a complete and utter mess. I felt supremely guilty. I just couldn't understand why I didn't instantly love her. Why I didn't want to spend every minute with her. Why I often wished I were dead, or that she had never been born. Saying this out loud is so hard. If I don't understand something, I dig in, do the research, and figure it out. I found a book that focused on early childhood trauma and learned about how our experiences during those years have a major impact on our relationships and parenting. This book provided so much clarity for me. When I was three months old, my mom had just regained custody of four of my five brothers who had been in foster care while she rebuilt her life after fleeing domestic violence. She worked two jobs and was often stressed. She struggled with mental illness stemming from 30 years of physical, sexual, and emotional abuse. My mom kicked my dad out when I was nine months old because he refused to take care of me. As a young child, I was sexually abused by my older brother, which I discovered after my therapist encouraged me to request my records from the Department of Children and Families. Reading this book as I was receiving therapy to process all of that trauma helped me understand why I developed Post-Partum Depression, which enabled me to forgive myself. Then, I was able to develop a healthy relationship with my amazing daughter, and our bond is stronger than I ever thought it could be. All of this - the concentration of all of these experiences - came crashing in on me during the days following the accident. It was like a lightning bolt hit me. I realized how fortunate I was. It was a stark reminder of just how short life is. I knew - right then and there - that I had to let go of the anger, hate, and resentment. I recognized that these lingering feelings were weighing me down, causing me to lash out at those I loved, and preventing me from being kind, patient, and loving toward myself. I started journaling again. I reached out to old friends. I picked up some powerful books that have helped me heal. Most importantly, I have learned to slow down, enjoy the little things, and live in the moment. In the evenings, I used to let my daughter play by herself while I did chores; now, I relax and enjoy spending time with her. I am so much closer to being the person and mother I have always wanted to be. Rather than continue to hate my dad, brother, and ex-husband, I have learned to dislike the choices they made which caused me so much pain. This has enabled me to release the anger that was rooted in that pain, and to cope in healthier ways when similar situations arise in the context of other relationships. I can tell you that Mark Twain had it right when he said: "Anger is an acid that can do more harm to the vessel in which it is stored than to anything on which it is poured." The dark feelings that I have released have opened up space for so much peace and joy. I notice all of the beauty around me and am grateful for that. Reluctantly, I've started dating again. Before the accident, my heart was completely closed. Being vulnerable and letting go of the fear that I will be taken advantage of again is difficult. Yet, I recognize that we are both hurt and healed in the context of relationships, so I press on. I listen to my heart more than my head. When I was going through all of this, I felt weak. Looking back, I recognize the strength and courage I had. I know that I have inherited these qualities from my mom, who is the most resilient person I have ever known. As a Social Worker, the perspective and wisdom I gain from clients further strengthens and empowers me. When my daughter is older and reads this, I want her to know that having her in my life has made me more resilient, patient with myself and others, and has enabled me to accept my limitations rather than perceive them as weaknesses that I must overcome. In large part because of her, I am proud of the woman that I am today. I have learned to love myself and can now lead by example so that she learns how to love herself as well. My hope is that she will know her worth and that - combined with her self-love - will prevent her from settling with a partner who is undeserving of her. The mental walls we build in an attempt to protect ourselves from pain trap the light and darkness that we all carry inside of us. One day, I hope that I will learn to fully trust myself, because only then will I be able to trust others and thus have the courage to tear my walls down and once again let my light shine so that others will be inspired to do the same.

Making This Story Your Own:

Misty's story reminds us that sometimes endings are really beginnings.
Take a moment, breathe, and reflect.
What stands out for you when you read her words?
Is there a situation in your life that is similar to Misty's?
Perhaps part of her story feels connected to your own.
How can you relate her experiences to your past, present, and future?

- *My Connection to Misty's Story* _____

  _____

  _____

  _____

Knowing that you aren't alone, let's gently explore some other themes from Misty's story together:

- **Releasing the Pain**
    - When you think about your life, are there any unresolved issues where you are holding on to pain or where it feels like pain is holding on to you? If so, how do you identify the pain and how does it show up? When you think about these situations, does the pain offer you anything? Has it been useful in any way? Or is the pain prohibiting you from anything and does it get in the way of your life and relationships? Perhaps the pain has been both... offering some positives and some negatives? When you think about it even deeper, are the *perceived* positives really negatives in disguise? Or are the *perceived* negatives really positives in disguise? If so, what are a few small things you can begin doing for relief and release?

- **Be Kind, Patient, and Loving Toward Yourself**
    - How often are you kind to others? How often are you patient with others? How often are you loving to others? How often are you kind, patient, and loving to *yourself*? Is this amount equal to, higher, or lower than the kindness, patience, and love you show others? If it is equal, how do you do this? If it is lower or higher, why? Where did this notion of being kind, patient, and loving come from? What are the benefits of relating to yourself and others in these ways? What are the drawbacks?

- **We are Hurt and Healed in Relationship**
    - When was your last genuine belly laugh? What was happening? Who else was there? Can you remember a time when you felt unconditional love? How did you recognize the feeling? Have you ever suffered abandonment and isolation? What was going on? Who wasn't there for you? When was the last time your heart knew disappointment? Can you recall what happened? Knowing that these things were felt within the context of the relationships you have with yourself and others, how does the notion *'we are hurt and healed in relationship'* feel for you? How do you make sense of it? How *does* it work or *not* work within your life and could it be working for you in better or different ways?

Sacred Play Suggestions:

~ SPS #1: ~

* Compassion Fatigue *

Many of us deal with something known as Compassion Fatigue. You may or may not be familiar with this term. If you have heard it, chances are you've heard it with another term - Burnout. Compassion Fatigue is the physical, emotional, mental, and spiritual deterioration that takes place when *'the helpers'* (aka: *you*) are unable to properly and sufficiently restore, refuel, and regenerate. Whether you are in a *service to others* dynamic or not, we can all experience varying levels of Compassion Fatigue just by turning on the news or scrolling through our social media feeds. Have you ever had a conversation with someone in which they shared about stressful life circumstances and as a result, felt completely drained and exhausted? That exhaustion can be an indicator of Compassion Fatigue. How about feeling numb after seeing or hearing about a terrible event? That numbness can be an indicator of Burnout and both of these conditions share a series of symptoms that accompany feeling overly taxed and under-relaxed. Put a different way, if you are in a personal or professional cycle of compassionate output without consistent and effective self-care, you could experience Compassion Fatigue and Burnout. If any of this resonates, take a moment and journal around the following statements.

- I notice a change in my ability to be empathic. _____

  _____

- I am more cynical than usual. _____

  _____

- I am often angry and irritable. _____

  _____

- I don't enjoy things as much anymore. _____

  _____

Take a breath and sit with your words. Your truth is important, and this is a judgement-free zone. My Granny Illa used to say, "We are just talking here." Right now, that is all we are doing… just talking and discovering. Take another few deep breaths and continue to journal around the next set of statements.

- I feel physically and emotionally exhausted. _____

  _____

- I feel like I don't cope as well as I used to. _____

  _____

- I feel powerless to do anything about how overwhelming life is. _____

  _____

- I feel differently about the world. Things aren't as good as I thought. _____

  _____

Great job! Honestly exploring these things is not easy. We live in a glossy world of '*shoulds*' and oftentimes those expectations (created by ourselves and others) leave little room for us to authentically step into the aspects of our lives that don't look or feel *pretty*. Well, I say, "Don't *should* on yourself!" I can't give Granny Illa credit for that phrase, but she probably would agree if she were here. Let's put these signs of Compassion Fatigue together with the symptoms of Burnout and turn them into a prayer. Most experts in this field agree that the way to heal from this type of exhaustion is dedicated self-care. However, this self-care practice must be created around sensible interventions that are *easily doable* and *realistically sustainable*. This can't be the self-care of New Year's resolutions. This is about a committed self-care practice that integrates a practical approach to balance our *work-life-output-input* roles, transitions, and stressors. Who better to make this prayerful plan than *you*? Fill in the sentences below with your inner wisdom and see where your prayer takes you.

- Dear_____ (Send this prayer to whomever or whatever you want.)

- Choose a sentence (or sentences) from the first journaling prompts or write your own.

    - I notice a change in my ability to be empathic.

    - I am more cynical than usual.

    - I am often angry and irritable.

    - I don't enjoy things as much anymore.

    - _____

- Connect the first sentence with a sentence (or sentences) from the second journaling prompts or write your own.

    - And, I feel physically and emotionally exhausted.

    - And, I feel like I don't cope as well as I used to.

    - And, I feel powerless to do anything about how overwhelming life is.

    - And, I feel differently about the world. Things aren't as good as I thought.

    - And, _____

- This is because_____

- And, I know I need_____

- In order to_____

- The three ways I can incorporate this into my daily responsibilities and routines are:

    - _____

    - _____

    - _____

- I deserve this_____

- I will solidify this commitment to self-love and self-care because _____

- Thank you_____

When you are finished with your prayer, read it out loud a few times. This will offer your subconscious mind the opportunity to clearly hear how much you value yourself and your well-being. As a final step, shift the perspective of the first two sections and with your empowered prayer, lovingly reclaim your energy and compassion.

- When I notice a change in my ability to be empathic, I will _____

- When I feel cynical, I will shift that by _____

- If I feel angry and irritable, I will _____

- If stop enjoying things, I will _____

- When I feel physically and emotionally exhausted, I will _____

- If I start to feel like I don't cope as well as I used to, I will _____

- When I start to feel powerless about how overwhelming life is, I will _____

- If I begin to feel differently about the world, I will _____

Thank you for doing this activity. Your compassion is needed, it is valuable, and it is worthy of rest and replenishment. Fill your cup, darling. You fill so many others. This is your time. Love you!

~ SPS #2: ~
* Failure on Purpose *

How do you feel about failure? Funny question, right? But what if through failure, an opening into a new perspective was actually found? This happens all the time. Transforming something that goes awry into something that goes better than originally planned is a sweet gift of life and one that often happens completely independent from us and our contributions. Yet, most of us don't actually start out trying to consciously fail. If failure was an option from the get-go, what might be different? Ready to see what happens if we *try* to fail? "Woo-Hoo… Count me in for failure!" Said no one ever… until now. Find a work of art. Look up images online or actually crack open that coffee table book you bought a couple of decades ago. Find some ideas that strike you as beautiful and artistic. Pick one masterpiece to recreate in the space below. Only, don't try to succeed. Don't try to emulate what you see. Don't *try* at all. Make crazy choices. Draw outside of the lines. Choose random colors. Design this endeavor to fail and commit to that failure wholeheartedly. Sketch, cut, paint, and craft this work of art with the intention to create a colossal '*oops*.' Don't forget to title your piece and as you work, answer the questions below during the beginning, middle, and end of the activity.

Beginning:

- Which three words express how I am feeling right now? _____

_____

- What do I want to learn? _____

_____

- Do I trust in my creativity? _____

_____

- Do I trust in myself? _____

_____

Middle:

- Which three words express how I am feeling *now*? _____
  _____

- What am I learning? _____
  _____

- Do I trust in my creativity? _____
  _____

- Do I trust in myself? _____
  _____

End

- Which three words express how I am feeling *now*? _____
  _____

- What have I learned? _____
  _____

- Do I trust in my creativity? _____
  _____

- Do I trust in myself? _____
  _____

- How is my *failure* really a triumph? _____
  _____

After you have finished your artwork and answered the questions, identify three or four places in your life where you've been feeling a little let down. Now think, how can this type of *malfunction* energy turn these places and spaces into *masterpieces*? Sit quietly for a moment and reflect on your courage to even *attempt* failure. I mean, come on! Give yourself some massive kudos here. When you are ready, draw these transformations on the next page and see what happens. Love you! Thanks for doing this activity!

From Malfunction to Masterpiece	**From Malfunction to Masterpiece**
From Malfunction to Masterpiece	**From Malfunction to Masterpiece**

~ SPS #3: ~
* Soulmates *

Dr. Dan Siegel, well-known author, psychiatrist, and director of the Mindful Awareness Research Center, says that "Relationships are the number one factor that determines our well-being." Taking this into consideration, think of a few significant relationships in your life. These are the relationships that are not necessarily the most fulfilling, but are the ones you put most of your time and energy into. They may very well be your 'soul-mates,' but not in the way that most of us have been led by Hollywood to believe that soul-mates manifest. These relationships are not about finishing each other's sentences and running through fields of daisies together. These soul mate relationships are significant in the way that author and Medical Intuitive, Carolyn Myss, explains as "the person that causes your soul to grow the *most*." Yet, for a lot of us, these significant relationships that cause us to grow the most come with their fair share of *growing pains*. Where does that leave us and our well-being if our experiences in these relationships aren't filled with bliss? Try not to give up quite so easily because the quick answer is: this leaves us in a place of possibility. With some diligent creativity and industrious focus, maybe we can *shift our perspective **ON** our perspective*. Think of the significant relationships of your life. Again, these are not the easy relationships, but the noteworthy ones. Beginning with the first one that comes to mind and cycling on through as many as you feel comfortable, go through the following:

- **Visualize this person sitting across from you.**

    o   Name one positive thing about this person. _____

    o   Name two positive things that you have learned from this person. _____

    _____

- Name three positive things that you have learned about yourself from this person. _____
  _____
  _____

- Name four positive things your relationship with this person has inspired you to do. _____
  _____
  _____

- Name five positive things that your relationship with this person will inspire you to do in the future.
  _____
  _____

Does the energy around the relationship feel shifted or transformed? If not, try repeating the steps. There are spaces below to explore at least two more of these significant relationships. Don't feel like you have to stop at two if you don't want to… keep going on another sheet of paper!

- **Visualize this person sitting across from you.**

  - Name one positive thing about this person. _____

  - Name two positive things that you have learned from this person. _____
    _____

  - Name three positive things that you have learned about yourself from this person. _____
    _____
    _____

  - Name four positive things your relationship with this person has inspired you to do. _____
    _____
    _____

  - Name five positive things that your relationship with this person will inspire you to do in the future.
    _____
    _____

- **Visualize this person sitting across from you.**
    - Name one positive thing about this person. _____
    - Name two positive things that you have learned from this person. _____

    _____

    - Name three positive things that you have learned about yourself from this person. _____

    _____

    _____

    - Name four positive things your relationship with this person has inspired you to do. _____

    _____

    _____

    - Name five positive things that your relationship with this person will inspire you to do in the future.

    _____

    _____

Finally, allow the relationship you have with **yourself** to be the last '*significant*' relationship you explore. Go through the following.

- **Visualize a version of *yourself* sitting across from you.**
    - Name one positive thing about you. _____
    - Name two positive things that you have learned from yourself. _____

    _____

    - Name three positive things that you know others have learned from you. _____

    _____

    _____

    - Name four positive things your relationship to yourself has inspired you to do. _____

    _____

    _____

- Name five positive things that your relationship to yourself will inspire you to do in the future.

_____

_____

_____

To deepen the transformations and shifts, repeat the questions above as many times as you want and need. You may never feel like running through daisies with these people and that is OK! Just seek to shift the energy around the relationship. However, you will probably want to run through some daisies with yourself. Go for it! **You** are where the real magick is. Thank you! Love you!

~ SPS #4: ~
* Ghost Pepper *

All of our feelings have wisdom. Unfortunately, not all of our feelings are regarded as valuable. Remember the nursery rhyme:

> What are little boys made of?
> What are little boys made of?
> Snips and snails
> And puppy-dogs' tails
> That's what little boys are made of.
> What are little girls made of?
> What are little girls made of?
> Sugar and spice
> And all things nice
> That's what little girls are made of.

How many of us have had this ditty parroted back in some fashion as we've attempted to cry, rant, rave, express, and make sense of our feelings? These feelings - big feelings that Misty so courageously and honestly talks about - are universal. We *all* feel them. They are a gift of the human experience and they are anything but sugar, spice, and all things *nice*. Well, maybe they are spicy, but they are a lot more Ghost Pepper than Cinnamon. These feelings are hurricanes and bungee jumps, raging torrents and stampeding elephants. They are uncontrollable, thundering, explosive, boiling, and raw. They are powerful. They are cleansing. They are purifying. They destroy the old so that *we* can create the new. They are needed forces within our bodies, hearts, and minds. Rage, anger, resentment, hatred, loneliness, and isolation… we recognize them, feel them, and crave their unique and authentic expression. Yet the devaluation of these feelings has prevented us from being able to safely express, securely process, and responsibly handle the situations which provoked the feelings in the first place. If these big feelings aren't validated, we don't learn what to do with them the next time. Their destructive capacity - no longer purifying and cathartic - becomes insidious and dangerous. A little overdramatic, you say? Think about it: when the potential for destruction gets turned inward, denied in a way that is damaging beyond the purification process, it can become host to many different things in our lives, none of which feel good, productive, or healing in the long term. In his book, *The Untethered Soul: The Journey Beyond Yourself,* Michael A. Singer talks about how the barrier places of our emotions and the darkness that we experience can feel like an abyss… which is a place most of us don't want to go. But he goes on to explain that if we sit with the darkness and give ourselves permission to actually be *in* it, we realize that the darkness is only a wall blocking the light. And guess what? That wall that can be removed! At the risk of sounding like a Simon and Garfunkel song, are you ready to break down some walls and say, "Hello darkness, my old friend?" Let's try it. Let's dialogue with our big feelings - our big, needed, and valuable feelings - and see what wisdom comes up. Below are some examples of feelings that might fall into the 'darkness' category. If they work for you, awesome. If you want to come up with some of your own, use the empty spaces.

Rageful	Angry	Indignant	Seething	Wrathful	Resentful
Hateful	Bitter	Offensive	Loathing	Disgusted	Horrified
Nauseous	Revolted	Repulsed	Snubbed	Repelled	Sickened
Forceful	Ireful	Isolated	Irritated	Furious	Outraged
Livid	Fuming	Annoyed	Frustrated	Irate	Ferocious
Brutal	Savage	Wild	Aggressive	Vicious	Intense
Unstoppable	Unrestrained	Harsh	Untamed	Severe	Defiant

When you are ready, find a quiet spot. Take a few deep breaths. Ground your feet to the floor by letting roots grow from your soles down into the layers and levels of Mother Earth. Next, connect the crown of your head into your Higher Power. This way, you are anchored and aligned as we work. Now, visualize one of the feelings from above coming to life. Witness the feeling becoming manifest from a part of your body and watch as the feeling sits down across from you. Take notice of the feeling's appearance and observe body type, size, shape, facial features, hair, clothing, demeanor, voice, mannerisms, and other descriptive characteristics. When you are ready, talk to the feeling and see what insights present themselves as the feeling's responses. Below is a script. Use it if it resonates or create your own if it doesn't. The most important aspect of this activity is that these feelings are validated, seen, heard, and respected in order for them to step into their Divine Purpose of empowered transformation and emotional alchemy. In other words, as we fully honor these feelings, they in turn are able to utilize the full spectrum of their powers to destroy and create for the Greatest and Highest Good. In your imagination, speak your lines and wait for the Feeling, your scene partner, to answer.

You: Hello_____ (*Insert feeling*) _____. I am glad you are here.

Feeling:_____.

You: I see you.

Feeling:_____.

You: I hear you.

Feeling: _____.

You: Have there been times in my life when you have felt honored and validated?

Feeling:_____.

You: Have there been times in my life when you have **not** felt honored and validated?

Feeling:_____.

You: When I feel you, what wisdom do you have for me?

Feeling:_____.

You: When I feel you, what do you feel from me?

Feeling:_____.

You: When I feel you, what do you *want* to feel from me?

Feeling:_____.

You: How can I express you in ways that feel honest, authentic, complete, and safe?

Feeling: _____.

You: How can I open up to more freely accept your love and wisdom?

Feeling:_____.

You: How can I break down the walls of darkness to experience the infinite light?

Feeling: _____.

You: Thank you. Is there anything else you would like me to know?

Feeling:_____.

Repeat this scene as often as you need, inviting all of your feelings to come forward and share their wisdom. When the conversations feel complete, take a moment and allow the information to integrate. Regroup and reground with more deep breaths, more intentional connection to the Earth, and more dedicated anchoring to your Higher Power. Read back through the script and reflect on anything that came up and out through this exercise. End with a big tight squeeze of gratitude around your shoulders for having the courage to break down the barriers so that you can feel the light. Thank you. I love you.

~ SPS #5: ~
* Moon-Bath *

Have you ever heard of Moon-Bathing? Don't worry, no sunscreen is needed for this free and soothing medicine of the Soul. Simply put, Moon Bathing is just what it sounds like: allowing the silvery essence of Mother Moon to bathe over your body and your consciousness. Nothing is needed other than your gorgeous, glorious self and our gorgeous, glorious Mother Moon. For us, let's incorporate some Lunar Wisdom into this Moon Bathing experience and invoke the Archetype of the Lunar Phase as it correlates to the Seasonal

Cycle, the Menstrual Cycle, and the corresponding Archetype of Womanhood. First things first, you've got to determine what Lunar Phase Mother Moon is in for you right now: Dark, Waxing, Full, or Waning. A quick internet search can answer this, and once you've determined where Mother Moon is in your sky, you can begin. It doesn't have to be completely dark, but it is best to start when the sunlight is dimming and Mother Moon is visible. Set yourself up either outside or by a window where you can purposefully gaze at her and alternately feel her energy being absorbed. If she is in her Dark Moon phase, find a place either indoors or outdoors where you can *feel* her. As you bathe, let your intuition be your guide and gift yourself this much deserved experience for as long as you need. Enjoy!

Moon Phase: Dark
~Associated Color~
- Black

My Intention for this Dark Moon Bath

_____

Correlating Season: Winter
~Seasonal Wisdom~
- Hibernation
- Pulling in
- Old Must Die for the New to Grow

My Winter Wisdom

_____

Correlating Menstrual Phase: Bleeding
~Menstrual Wisdom~
- Slow Mental Energy and High Emotional Energy
- Comfort is a Necessity
- Deep Psychic Abilities

My Menstrual Wisdom

_____

Archetype: Crone
~Archetypal Wisdom~
- No Need to Please Others
- Outspoken
- Aware of Wisdom and Power

My Crone Wisdom

_____

Associated Goddess: Hecate
~Goddess Wisdom~
- Hecate is the Goddess of past, present, and future. She stands at a crossroads for decisions, life and death, and darkness and light. She is patroness of Witches and a deep holder of wisdom, knowledge, and power. She is psychically connected to all realms.

My Goddess Wisdom

_____

My Dark Moon Bath Wisdom as I hold the Knowledge of *Purging*, *Intuition*, and *Truth*...

_____
_____
_____

~ ~ ~

Moon Phase: Waxing
~Associated Color~
- White

My Intention for this Waxing Moon Bath

_____

Correlating Season: Spring
~Seasonal Wisdom~
- Fresh and Flirty
- Joyful Sexual Energy
- Time to Plant New Seeds for New Life

My Spring Wisdom

_____

Correlating Menstrual Phase: Follicular (Pre-Ovulatory)
~Menstrual Wisdom~
- Very Playful
- Time to Give Insights and Ideas Expression
- Renewed Strength and Confidence

My Menstrual Wisdom

_____

Archetype: Maiden
~Archetypal Wisdom~
- Complete unto Herself
- Dynamic and Enthusiastic
- Bold Seeker of Knowledge

My Maiden Wisdom
_____

Associated Goddess: Persephone
~Goddess Wisdom~
- **Persephone** is the empowered Goddess of personal choice. Embodies gentleness and fierceness in equal measure. Brings newfound respect to youth, simplicity, and sovereignty. Knows herself, what she wants, and honors her extroverted exuberance.

My Goddess Wisdom
_____

My Waxing Moon Bath Wisdom as I hold the Knowledge of *Freedom*, *Confidence*, and *Focus*...
_____
_____
_____

~ ~ ~

Moon Phase: Full
~Associated Color~
- Red

My Intention for this Full Moon Bath
_____

Correlating Season: Summer
~Seasonal Wisdom~
- Full of Life and Fertility
- Time of Outward Expression
- Contentment

My Summer Wisdom
_____

Correlating Menstrual Phase: Ovulation
~Menstrual Wisdom~
- Nurturing and Sustaining
- Powerful Connection to Mother Earth
- Very Creative

My Menstrual Wisdom

_____

Archetype: Mother
~Archetypal Wisdom~
- Spiritually Whole and Empowered
- Soul-Based Sexuality
- Confident in Supporting the Family and Community

My Mother Wisdom

_____

Associated Goddess: Ishtar
~Goddess Wisdom~
- Ishtar is the powerful Mother Goddess who brings fertility, love, and sexuality out to play. Her potentials of creation and destruction are significant. She combines the sensuality needed to create life with the nurturance needed to sustain life.

My Goddess Wisdom

_____

My Full Moon Bath Wisdom as I hold the Knowledge of *Receptivity*, *Self-Worth*, and *Harmony*...

_____
_____
_____

~ ~ ~

Moon Phase: Waning
~Associated Color~
- Purple

My Intention for this Waning Moon Bath

_____

Correlating Season: Fall

~Seasonal Wisdom~
- Slowing Down
- Withdrawing
- Preparing to Become Empty

My Fall Wisdom

_____

Correlating Menstrual Phase: Luteal (Pre-Menstrual)

~Menstrual Wisdom~
- Energy is Directed Inward
- Deeply Connected to the Sprit World
- Must Feel the Full Spectrum of Feelings

My Menstrual Wisdom

_____

Archetype: Enchantress

~Archetypal Wisdom~
- Mysterious and Dramatic
- Sexually Intense and Primal
- Pulled in to Experience the Deep, Dark Inner Realms

My Enchantress Wisdom

_____

Associated Goddess: Demeter

~Goddess Wisdom~
- Demeter is the strong and determined embodiment of the feminine psyche. She is the Goddess of cyclical wisdom: wild, emotional, and free while maintaining a generous and generative spirit. She reminds us to honor all of our attributes.

My Goddess Wisdom

_____

**My Waning Moon Bath Wisdom as I hold the Knowledge
of *Authenticity*, *Prophecy*, and *Awareness*...**

_____
_____
_____

Four delicious Moon-Baths for a delicious quadruple Goddess! Woot-woot! Take it all in, love. You deserve this kind of attentive reverence every moment of every day. Thank you for doing this activity and accessing your deep inner wells of wisdom, clarity, expression, creativity, and authenticity. I love you!

Crystal Love: Misty's Crystal is the loving but butt-kicking Red Jasper. This wonderfully grounding stone has the momentum to keep us working towards growth, spiritual maturity, emotional maturity, and self-love, while offering us the safety and security needed to stay firmly put when those old wounding patterns come up and scream "RUN!" Thank goodness this strong and beautiful Crystal is also from the nurturing family of Jaspers which can provide a soft and merciful energy from root to crown as it helps to instill a sense of calm and intentional focus. This energetic balance comes in handy as Red Jasper assists us in bringing up issues for resolution, pulling forth guidance and messages from dreams, and stepping firmly into the understanding that our all of our choices are our responsibility. All of this culminates as support for Red Jasper's influential energies, which ask us to bring justice to unjust situations and dissolution to the general tensions and conflicts of life. This sometimes not-so-gentle, but *oh-so-needed* approach offers us all a re-birthing and a re-forming of the soul.

Suggested Reading to Authentically and Whole-Heartedly Engage the World You Live In, *The Gifts of Imperfection: Let Go of Who You Think You are Supposed to Be and Embrace Who You Are* by Brene' Brown.

Additional Journaling and SPS Space

Elizabeth D.

I had a really great mentor who, when someone would say or do something off-putting, she would say to me, "Consider the source." When she said this, she wasn't trying to imply that this person was bad, she was saying to consider the source by considering the *whole person*. She was asking me to think, "How did this person grow up?" and "What could have led this person to do that?" She was helping me to understand someone before labeling and judging them. My mentor was trying to teach me how to build a bridge instead of tearing one down. When I was in the military, that really gave me something to think about. Now, as a parent and foster parent, her words have become extremely relevant. I know that what I say really matters. I know that if I want something enduring, it has to be based on trust. It has to be based on a relationship. When dealing with a child or one of the guys in my unit - if I wanted to have an influence on their behavior that was meaningful rather than punitive and anxiety provoking - I had to tap into my own reserves of empathy and ask, "How can I build trust? How can I build a bridge?" It is this level of empathy that I want to help everyone access. Right now, I'm studying for my master's degree in criminology and my hope is to go on for my Ph.D. When I am finished, I plan to use my knowledge and life experiences to do the kind of research that will inform policy and hopefully change the way we treat trauma in children and adults. There are so many ways we can improve how we relate to people in our various 'systems'. If we can put ourselves in someone else's shoes, we can begin a true healing process that considers the whole person and includes their life history. Responding from a place of rehabilitation will help to reduce recidivism and reoffending. When I was in Baghdad, I had a young soldier in my unit. He did something one day, I can't even remember what it was, and I said to him, "Hey, I am really proud of you!" He stopped, turned, looked at me and said, "No one has ever said that to me before." He was telling the truth. No one had ever told him they were proud of him. That moment in time really got my attention. Having that experience in the beginning of my career made me take my job much more seriously. I realized that I wasn't just a manager or a technical expert... I was a *leader*. I was responsible to these people in a more holistic way than making sure they did their job and got to work on time. I was responsible for making sure they were OK. As a Platoon Leader and Commander, if I felt something wasn't right I would stop and ask "Hey, are you OK?" Every time I stopped and asked that, I found someone who needed to be listened to. Sometimes, people would even break down and cry they needed to talk so badly. I really liked hearing everyone's stories. Everyone has such an interesting story of where they have come from and how they have made the decisions to get where they are. I had a fold out chair by my desk that I called my 'therapy chair.' Soldiers would come in and sit down and talk to me about their lives. They would talk while I worked. Even when I couldn't respond, they would talk at length about everything. There was always somebody in that chair. When I joined the army in 2006, I never expected to have the incredible experiences that I had. I guess joining was kind of an impulsive decision, although that really isn't the right word for it. I just thought about it one day and drove to the recruiting station, walked in the door, and said I wanted to join. I even told the recruiter, "I don't need the big spiel, just show me where to sign." He looked at me like I was crazy. About two weeks later, I was in basic training. From there, I went to Officer Candidate School and got branched into the Ordnance Corps. Because the Ordnance Corps primarily deals with weapons systems and munitions, it wasn't my first choice. But then I found out that within the Ordnance Corps I could apply for Explosive Ordnance Disposal School. I got selected for EOD school and finished the year-long program when I was about 25 years old. My first assignment was as Platoon Leader for the 787th EOD Company, and we deployed to Baghdad in 2009. My second deployment was to Basra, Iraq as the Partnership Chief for the Iraqi Bomb Squad in the Nine Southern Provinces. It was an interesting position because my work was driven by the Department of State Mission to 'Strengthen the Rule of Law in Iraq.' The mission wasn't punitive. It was focused on education for proper evidence collection guidelines and prevention of contamination. I was working with Police Department and Bomb Squad Chiefs. It was a very alpha-male type of field - and yet as a woman - I didn't have any issues working with the Iraqi people. I wondered in the beginning what these men were going to think of me, but all of the people I worked with made me feel welcome. In Basra, I also got linked up with a local Women's Rights Activist Group under the Department of State. On Sundays, they held a meeting at the airport. Usually it was me and three or four other American or British women in uniform and six or eight Iraqi women in their traditional dress. These Iraqi women were either involved in local politics or they wanted to be. I still think about them every day, and my time with them is what made my second tour so impactful. These women were incredible. They were all so well-educated, so passionate, and so determined to broaden their horizons. They came to our group under the premise of wanting to learn to speak better English, but they all spoke English beautifully. Together, we talked about everything. They would bring in the things they were writing and ask us to help with the spelling and grammar. They loved Oprah, and one day after seeing something on Oprah about yoga, they asked if we knew how to do yoga and if we would teach them some poses. After that, we would do yoga together for the last fifteen to twenty minutes of each group. One of my favorite moments ever was when we were all standing close in a circle in Warrior One Pose. Our arms were all pointed towards the center with our hands touching in the middle. It was one of those moments I wish I had a picture of, or that I was an artist, so I could paint it. We stood in that circle, hands touching, making eye contact, and it was powerful! In that moment, we were just human beings connecting to one another. There were no differences, no barriers… just a group of women supporting each other as friends. It could have been anywhere at any time. I was in Basra for 11 months. I actually came back to the states with the intention of leaving the Army. I had never intended to stay in that long and - after what I experienced - I was done. I was used to dealing with a sort of low-grade sexism all the time. But sometimes, because of leadership, it not only felt overt, it felt intentional. For me at that time, getting a Company Commander position was the best job I could have. It was actually said to me that women shouldn't be in EOD, women shouldn't be in the army, and that no matter how good of a job I did, I would never get recommended for Company Command. I was enjoying my job and I wanted to do it well no matter what, but I knew what I heard was true. I also realized that although there are a lot of policies in place against sexism in the Army, in a small organization like EOD, people will band together and it is really hard to tell your story without retribution. So, I left Basra mid-tour and dropped my resignation packet as soon as I got back. Because they still needed troops and there was a loophole in some education benefits that I had used, my resignation was declined. I was told that I would have to stay on for another six months. Because of the mental state that I was in, another six months felt like an eternity. Thank goodness there ended up being a change, and we got a new Commander. Come to find out the Executive Commander told the new Commander that even though I had been treated unfairly, I had performed very well while in Basra. The new Commander offered me a Company Command position. Since the position was a 12-month contract, I decided to stay and was placed in Command of the 710th EOD Company for a total of 27 months with 9 months of active duty in Afghanistan. Two weeks into my new position, we got deployment orders. When we left, I deployed with 45 soldiers which consisted of 9 EOD teams and a staff. When I took command, this unit had called themselves the 'last all-male unit of EOD.' Here I was not only breaking up the band, but in charge of them all. It was hard in the beginning because there were people in the Company who were legitimately bad at their jobs. They were unsafe. I knew I had to get it together because we were deploying to the Horn of Panjwai, the birthplace of the Taliban. Our job was going to be emergency response to roadside bombs, and we were going to be on foot. I knew there were going to be life or death situations. To keep my Company safe, some people had to lose their jobs. If they couldn't do the work, it was not helpful to keep them in positions where they wouldn't succeed. This was met with much consternation from the other leaders in my unit. The Commander before me had been friends with many of the men. They went out drinking together and had a different type of relationship than what I was trying to create. When I took Command, I took small groups of team leaders and asked them if they felt safe with certain people. When there was unanimous agreement, I would fire that person. I am not sure what the soldiers thought I was going to do with the information they were telling me. So often the guys would say, "You can't fire him. How is he going to support his wife?" I would reply, "He won't be able to support his wife when he is dead." We had some rocky times in the beginning. I am pretty laid back. I don't yell. But, once I've made a decision, the decision is made. I don't hem and haw over things and I don't want to hear a bunch of griping. That seemed to take the men in my unit by surprise. Before we deployed, I got a female Team Leader. She and I became really good friends and we are still friends to this day. She was very well read on the topic of Women in Leadership. She would share different articles with me, and we would study them together. When things would get difficult, she would remind me about what we were studying. For instance, the perception is that when men are abrupt in their decision making, they are being good, strong leaders; however, when women do the same we are often perceived as being a bitch. It was neat to have her voice of support during those times because she helped me tune out the nonsense and the noise. Eventually, my whole unit ended up having a great rapport. A lot of the younger soldiers called me 'mom,' which was adorable. But there were a lot of lessons from that time about team building and finding a state of mental clarity to make decisions. This part of Afghanistan was the most hostile area that I had ever been to. Nobody was happy to see us anywhere we went. All of these people were looking to me to make decisions. If I seemed indecisive or like I was freaking out, morale would have gone way down. I had to carve out space every day to meditate so that I could access an inner calm to lead us through whatever scenario came our way. I am so grateful for all of those experiences and I am happy to say that we all came back home safely. Shortly after we returned to the states, I resigned again. This time, I was allowed to go. I was so glad that my first resignation was denied. I didn't leave angry. I left ready. That was such a good lesson for me about not being driven by anger in my decision-making processes. If I had left the Army when I was angry, I might have stayed angry. When I left, it was on my own terms and there was no resentment. Leaving that way, I got to have a fresh start. My partner at the time agreed that we should move back home to Florida. Once we got settled, we started the process to become Foster Parents. When the guys in my unit found out I was going to be a foster mom, they joked that I would be a natural since I had already been a mom to 45 wayward boys. They were right. Being their Commander has given me much perspective as a parent. So far, I've adopted three of the children I've fostered and I am in the process of adopting the fourth. I feel so lucky. All of these kids have unique stories and backgrounds and so do their parents. These families in the system need support and kindness. For a lot of them, the trauma spans multiple generations. When a child or a parent is labeled through the foster care or juvenile system, it becomes part of their self-image and is very difficult to shed. At that point, it is a pretty easy jump for things to seem completely hopeless. You figure everyone around you has already given up on you so you wonder how there can possibly be anything to gain? I have had foster kids come to me that at the age of three and four years old having been taught to shoplift. I would have to shake them down leaving the grocery store. If you reduce that child down to a label or a set of perceptions without any interventions, and that kid gets to 18 only to be punished as an adult for repeating the same survival strategies that they've been employing their whole lives, the catastrophic failure happened way before that moment. And it is not their fault. For kids and adults in our systems, we have to heal the roots of trauma. Instead of trying to control behavior, we have to heal what the behavior stems from. When we do that, we will be way more effective. That is what I am interested in. We all respond to trauma differently. When you experience trauma at a young age, it gets encapsulated in your psyche. It becomes the only way you know how to cope. Then, when you experience trauma as an adult, you may respond in ways that seem very irrational to those around you. The way our system works, you get punished for using the tools in your toolkit. We are all worthy of healing this. We are all worthy of releasing the negative labels. It is possible to recreate a sense of self-esteem and self-love. As a community, when we really sit down and try to understand someone else's experience, we will all start to think more about our actions and choices. We may not ever agree about what the problem is, but if we can listen with empathy, we can respectfully relate to each other, and things won't feel so hopeless. We can overcome the cycles of self-abuse and abuse to others. There are always other options. That is my message. We don't have to be defined by our decisions, by our mistakes, by our choices, or even a moment in time. No matter what. We can all keep moving forward. It might be hard, but redemption is possible. It is up to every one of us to rebuild the bridges of kindness and empathy. Just like my mentor used to say, "Consider the source… the *whole* source." Start there, and we can work together, one brick at a time.

Making This Story Your Own:

Elizabeth D's story invites us to consider our strengths and abilities as empowered leaders and way-showers. Take a moment, breathe, and reflect.
What stands out for you when you read her words?
Is there a situation in your life that is similar to Elizabeth D's?
Perhaps part of her story feels connected to your own.
How can you relate her experiences to your past, present, and future?

- *My Connection to Elizabeth D.'s Story* _____
_____
_____

Knowing that you aren't alone, let's gently explore some other themes from Elizabeth D.'s story together:

- **What I Say Matters**
    - How often do you consider what you are saying? Not only the words, but the meanings behind them? Are you prone to letting things fly out in the heat of the moment without an awareness of how they might affect someone else? Maybe you are aware of this but in certain circumstances feel that no-filter is acceptable? Have you ever stopped to think about how what you say affects *you*? The last time you let loose in a fit of passion or anger, how did you feel afterwards? Did you apologize to those involved? Did you apologize to yourself? Maybe you speak to yourself like this all of the time? How could more awareness around the words you say - and the way you say them - be beneficial for you and your relationships?

- **Don't Leave Angry**
    - Have you ever left a situation angry? Maybe a job, relationship, or conversation? What happened? Was it easy to let it go and walk away, or was it more difficult to find closure? Did you feel empowered? Did the feelings of empowerment last? If not, how can this dynamic be shifted in the future? How can more awareness around ending a situation peacefully, or at least ending your side of things peacefully, become a reality?

- **Women in Leadership**
    - What are your beliefs about women in leadership? Where did those beliefs come from? Are they cultivated purely by you? Have they been influenced by someone or something else? What would it feel like for you to be led by a woman? What would it feel like for you to see others led by a woman? What would it feel like for you to lead? What thoughts and feelings come up around envisioning yourself as a leader? Are these thoughts and feelings motivated by the paradigms of the world we live in today? Or are they motivated by the world you want to create for tomorrow?

Sacred Play Suggestions:

~ SPS #1: ~
* Interdependent *

Elizabeth D. shares some potent wisdom on leadership. Unfortunately, the external pressures to her leadership efficacy are a very old and familiar story for a lot of us. For about the last five thousand years, the Feminine has been denigrated and the fallout can still be felt today within most of our personal and professional interactions. As outlined by archeomythologist, Marija Gumbutas, and many other Feminist herstorians, when human culture switched from Matriarchal Gift Economies to Patriarchal War Economies, a very brutal destruction to the empowerment of the Feminine was methodically employed. Thanks to you, me, the Soul-to-Sisterhood Tribe, and other fabulous individuals all over the world, we are changing this by dedicating ourselves to uncovering, embodying, and sharing the power of the Feminine. As we collectively heal from this wounding to the female energies inherent within every living thing, it is interesting to take a look at leadership dynamics. First off, you *are* a leader. We all are. In our own unique ways, each of us is a way-shower, influencer, and leader for our friends, families, and professional endeavors. We may not be assigned titles and responsibilities typically understood as such, but that does not deny our leadership roles. Although it may seem a little unrelated at the moment, journal around the following question and see what comes forward.

How often have I opted to be *liked* over being *effective*?

Give yourself some grace around this. Being liked is a pretty universal desire. Yet, taken into context with what we have been discussing, think about these next questions.

- How does striving to be *liked* compromise my *effectiveness*? _____
  _____

- Is being *liked* equivalent to staying *small*? _____
  _____

- Is staying *small* equivalent to staying *safe*? _____
  _____

Again, approach this with compassion for yourself. Knowing what we know about epigenetics - the science that has proven our environment shapes our genes - our DNA is still working from the very real memories and very dangerous reality that our power can bring us great harm. From the witch trials to modern day

Middle School, we have been taught to systematically deny our intellect, instinct, intelligence, and intuition to be accepted. In nature, and that includes human nature, being accepted as part of the pack usually offers protection - protection at a price sometimes - but protection, nonetheless. No wonder we will do almost anything to be liked and accepted. Recently this dynamic has been related to two different styles of leadership: Codependent Leadership and Interdependent Leadership. I first learned about these two Leadership Styles while studying with the creator of the Sophia Code Feminine Christ Consciousness International Ministry, Kaia Ra. Codependent Leadership involves compromising ourselves for the perceived needs of others. Interdependent Leadership does not. Interdependent Leadership focuses on secure empowerment with mutual respect, emotional integrity, healthy boundaries, and spiritual maturity. Look over some of the qualities of Codependent and Interdependent Leadership below. Feel free to add your own ideas.

Codependent Leadership		Interdependent Leadership	
Defensive	Filled with Expectations	Vulnerable	Flexible
Judgmental	Immature	Compassionate	Mature
Inauthentic	Lacking	Authentic	Abundant
Fear-Based	Unclear	Courageous	Conscious
Repellant	Resentful	Connected	Fulfilled
Stagnant	Diffuse Boundaries	Energizing	Clear Boundaries
Lonely	Insecure Attachment	Magnetic	Securely Attached
Disempowered	Never Beginning	Empowered	Never Ending
Hard	Blocked	Clear	Open
Exchange Economy	Wounded	Gift Economy	Healed
Insecure	Dysfunctional	Secure	Functional
Exhausted	Self- Sabotage	Open-Hearted	Self-Mastery
Rigid	Limiting	Soft	Loving
-	-	-	-
-	-	-	-
-	-	-	-

Pretty crazy to think about leadership like this, huh? The qualities needed for Interdependent Leadership - mutual respect, emotional integrity, healthy boundaries, and spiritual maturity - can't really coexist with the qualities under the Codependent column. Answer the following questions.

- How has **Codependent Leadership** been present in my life? _____

_____

- How has **Interdependent Leadership** been present in my life? _____

_____

Finally, let's lighten this conversation and play fill-in-the-blank. Hopefully some different interaction will deepen the excavation process and continue to enrich all of our leadership opportunities and styles. In the first blank, pick a quality from the **Codependent Leadership** column. In the second blank, pick a quality from the **Interdependent Leadership** column. You may need to revise the words a little bit so that they make sense within the sentences. For example, 'vulnerable' may need to become – *vulnerability*, or 'loving' may need to become - *love*. Trust your gut and know that there is no right way, only **your** way. ☺

When I led from a place that was _____ I dimmed my Leadership light.

Now I will lead from a place of _____ and my Leadership light will shine bright!

When I led from a place that was _____ I made my Leadership small.

Now I will lead from a place of _____ and my Leadership will be as BIG as it needs to be!

When I led from a place of _____ I compromised my Leadership.

Now, I will lead from a place of _____ and my Leadership will no longer be compromised by anyone or anything- *especially* me!

When I led from a place of _____ I was trying to please everyone.

Now, I will lead from a place of _____ and know that I don't have to please anyone, and that is OK!

When I led from a place of _____ I wanted to feel in control.

Now, I will lead from a place of _____ and know that the only thing I can control is *myself*!

When I led from a place of _____ I was playing it safe to be liked.

Now, I will lead from a place of _____ and trust that **I AM** unconditionally *loved* and *supported*!

When I led from a place of _____ I was playing it dumb to be accepted.

Now, I will lead from a place of _____ and trust that *I* can provide what *I* need for myself.

When I led from a place of _____ I didn't listen to my instincts.

Now, I will lead from a place of _____ and step *fully* into my Divine Feminine Power.

When I led from a place of _____ I didn't follow my intuition.

Now, I will lead from a place of _____ and I will *trust* my Intrapsychic Superpowers!

When I led from a place of _____ I was just trying to make everyone happy.

Now, I will lead from a place of _____ and I will *create* my own joy!

With great self-empowerment comes great self-love. Read through the above statements aloud. Hear your voice claiming and proclaiming your Interdependent Leadership Role. Remember, this is not the leadership of self-sacrifice. To step into this role, you don't have to *do* anything. You only have to *be*. As a living embodiment of your awareness, your empowerment will lead the way. Thank you for doing this activity. Thank you for being you. I love you!

~ SPS #2: ~
* Security Circle *

There is a great parenting intervention model co-originated by Glen Cooper, Kent Hoffman, and Bert Powell called the Circle of Security. This model, which is based on several psychotherapeutic attachment models, provides a visual map of attachment that helps parents and caregivers reflect on a child's attachment needs in order to create a secure attachment bond. Becoming trained in the model and working from the *Circle of Security* framework was a highlight of my clinical career. There are many, many powerful and transformative components to this model, but one of my favorites for understanding a child's behavior is: "Being difficult is just too difficult." To take it further, this theory turns crying, acting out, tantrums, and other behavioral difficulties - typically recognized as *bad* behavior - away from that interpretation (which cultivates disconnect) and into a gentler interpretation (which inspires connection). Within the context of *Circle of Security,* these behaviors represent a child's attempt to communicate a need that is not being met. Basic human needs are simple no matter the age. We have physiological needs like food, warmth, rest, shelter, and safety. We have psychological needs of wanting to feel connected and loved. We also have fulfillment needs of feeling worthy, accomplished, and capable of achieving our potential. Putting it all together, *Circle of Security* asks us to consider the source - the *whole source* of the person - and that includes how their history *has* and *is* shaping their behavior. Use your life experiences for an example and think back… when were you expressing an unmet need and it was perceived negatively either by you or someone else? This isn't about supporting destructive or dysfunctional behavior; this is about understanding the *how* of how the behaviors came forward in the first place. Since we are all works in progress, hopefully this perspective can offer some self-compassion, self-forgiveness, and as Elizabeth says in her story, "build a bridge" back to you. Let your mind rest for a few breaths. As you begin to feel relaxed, think of a situation that you wish you could change because of the way you conducted yourself.

- What was the situation? _____

- What were your behaviors? _____

Now, let's go a little deeper into the *'how'* of the situation.

- What was going on with you before this situation occurred? _____
  _____

    - How were you feeling *in general*? _____

        - How were you feeling about **yourself**? _____

    - What were your thoughts *in general*? _____

        - What were your thoughts about **yourself**? _____

- What need(s) were you trying to get met? _____

    - How were you doing this? _____

    - What could you have done differently? _____

Finally, let's begin to *'build the bridge.'*

- What are your thoughts and feelings about things now? _____
  _____

    - What are your thoughts and feelings about yourself now? _____
      _____

- Can the situation be repaired? _____

    - If so, how? _____

    - If not, how can you be OK with this? _____

- How can you meet your own needs going forward? _____
  _____

- How can you have more compassion, understanding, and forgiveness for yourself? ___
  _____
  _____

Keep going with this and reflect on additional situations from your life and relationships. Self-compassion and self-forgiveness are integral ingredients in the recipe for a bliss-filled existence. Once you have explored this for your own unmet needs, try applying this level of understanding to the needs of friends and loved ones. Keep going from there and interpret other behavior through this lens. A deeper understanding of the needs bombarding us every day can create an energetic force field against negativity and that includes our own negative reactions and responses as well. Looking at things this way can be like an infinity loop of love. Nice image, right? Love you! Thanks for doing this!

~ SPS #3: ~
* Are You OK *

"Are you OK?" is such a powerful question. Take a moment and ask it of yourself. Place your hands on your heart and genuinely inquire, "Am I OK?" What comes up? As things come to mind, write them down below.

_____

_____

_____

These three words can carry a lot of weight. At times we ask out of genuine concern. Other times, we don't truly want the answer. Sometimes expressing anger is our motive and out of irritation we ask, "Are you OK?" … hoping that our tone of voice will be enough to jolt someone into getting it together. Try asking this question with various subtexts (the feelings and motivations) underneath the words. You can pretend you are talking with someone specific or you can just with play with asking the question.

- Ask: "*Are you OK?*" with the subtext of **fear.**

    o What do you notice? _____

    o How familiar is the feeling of **fear** when asking this question? _____
    _____

- Ask: "*Are you OK?*" with the subtext of **encouragement.**

    o What do you notice? _____

    o How familiar is the feeling of **encouragement** when asking this question? _____
    _____

- Ask: "*Are you OK?*" with the subtext of **concern.**

    o What do you notice? _____

    o How familiar is the feeling of **concern** when asking this question? _____
    _____

- Ask: *"Are you OK?"* with the subtext of **frustration.**
    - What do you notice? _____
    - How familiar is the feeling of **frustration** when asking this question? _____
    _____

- Ask: *"Are you OK?"* with the subtext of **hope.**
    - What do you notice? _____
    - How familiar is the feeling of **hope** when asking this question? _____
    _____

Great job! Playing with subtext is a fun way to create a deeper awareness around habituated and repetitive response patterns. Sometimes those response patterns work wonderfully and sometimes they don't. Think again about these three simple words: **Are… You… OK…?**

- Would you like to ask them more? _____
- Would you like to ask them less? _____
- Would you like to ask them differently? _____
- Do they ever deflect or distract from your true feelings? _____
- What do they teach you about yourself? _____

Once more, place your hands over your heart again and ask, "Am I OK?" What comes up now? As things come to mind, write them down.

_____
_____
_____
_____
_____

Pause here for a moment and let this work sink in. Take a few deep, cleansing breaths and shake this wisdom into your body. That's right. I said, shake it. Shimmy, too, if you want! Move your physical body in ways that will accommodate and assimilate this wisdom. Thanks for doing this activity. Oh… don't stop shakin' it… you look awesome! I just want to add a "thank you" and an "I love you" into the mix!

~ SPS #4: ~
* Sympath – Empath *

Energy and emotions can be contagious. Think about the last time you were around someone who was really angry. You may or may not have actually *caught* the anger, but regardless, your system probably reacted in some way. When we are around another person who is experiencing anger, we sense danger and begin the process of protecting ourselves. Unless we are aware of what is happening, the tipping point of joining in that anger can happen rapidly. As human beings, we share our feelings verbally and energetically. Sadness, embarrassment, grief, and joy are just a few of the emotions that we can collectively recognize, mirror, and embody. Yet, as helpful as this seems for our fellow humans, what about us? Catching joy and happiness - awesome - sign me up! Catching sadness and anger - boo - not so much. My Esoteric Healing teacher used to say, "Are you a sympath or an empath?" Maybe this question can't be answered by the traditional dictionary definitions of the words, but what I think she meant was, can you support someone as they feel what they are feeling without catching the feelings and compromising your own energy? Being empathic has commonly been referred to as being able to walk in someone else's shoes. But, if we are walking in someone else's shoes with them, how can we maintain the levels of objectivity and neutrality needed to be supportive? According to this perspective, walking in someone else's shoes and allowing their experiences to become our own is not empathic, but more *sympathic*. Being a sympath can give us the unconscious belief system that in order to understand someone else, we must feel their feelings with them. Engaging with someone in this way can be energetically draining and dangerous for our well-being. Below are some qualities of both types of support: empath and sympath. Please do not mistake these qualities as blanket descriptions for either empathy or sympathy. Thinking about the ways in which we offer support in this context is different than an emotional state of being or a character trait.

An Empath…	**A Sympath…**
Is not connected to an outcome	Attempts to control the outcome
Understands feelings	Feels the feelings with someone else
Can separate self	Cannot separate self from feelings or situation
Is clear on boundaries around time and energy	Has unclear boundaries around time and energy
Is energizing	Can feel exhausted
Is not trying to fix anything	Tries to fix things
Support is purely about the other person	Correlates to something within the self
Does not compromise other relationships	Can compromise other relationships
Sees a choice, not a responsibility	Feels a responsibility, not a choice
Is objective	Is subjective
Remains neutral	Is biased
Is compassionate	Is passionate
'Not about you' mentality	'About you' mentality
Is responsive	Is reactive

Genuinely supporting someone without it becoming a detriment to the self can be a fine line to walk, but we can do it. Just knowing the difference between the two types of support can be helpful. Clarification on personal boundaries doesn't hurt and a sincere look at why we are doing what we are doing is also valuable. Take a few moments and journal around the following statements.

I am an Empath when…	I am a Sympath when…

After journaling, sit with this new level of awareness and give yourself credit for all that you have given to others in the form of support, comfort, and compassion. As a final step, complete the following two sentences.

- When I offer support, my intentions for **myself** are _____

  _____

- When I offer support, my intentions for **others** are _____

  _____

Thank you. This Empath vs. Sympath work can bring quite a bit to the surface. As you process, gently and patiently love yourself. This new way of offering support might feel foreign at first. That is OK. This is a new *way of being.* Give yourself time. Love you.

~ SPS #5: ~
* Both, And *

The concept of 'both and' resonated with me when I was in graduate school to become a marriage and family therapist. Often times when we are discussing our feelings - especially when the situation is emotionally elevated - to make sense of things and to simplify, we attempt to compartmentalize. It helps us feel safer when we can explain our thoughts and feelings as either one way or another. In the heat of an argument we say to each other, "How do you feel?" "What do you want?" "Where is your head?" These questions imply an *either-or* dynamic. You either feel good or bad. You either want this or that. Your thoughts are either here or there. Obviously, there are many combinations of answers, but when given the opportunity to get clear and process about how we feel, it usually isn't completely one or the other, but a mixture of both. The *and* of the *both and* concept is the new and third possibility that arises from honoring both states simultaneously. Another way that we do this in life is with people. We categorize each other to efficiently organize complexities. When I was working professionally as an actor, this happened all the time. Agents, Casting Directors, and Managers would ask, "What *type* are you?" They wanted me to help define what types of characters I would most likely be cast to play. I always had trouble answering this because it felt so limiting! They didn't agree. They wanted the guesswork taken out of it. It was way easier if I told my agent to submit me for auditions that were for a 'girl-next-door-young-mom-teacher-waitress-sexy-funny-girlfriend-kind-of-type who could sing.' No one in the business was trying to be offensive; they were just asking me to typecast myself. They were streamlining what we do to ourselves and others on a daily basis. They were having me typecast myself by labeling myself. Think about it, how have you been typecast? What labels have you been given? What labels have you given others in attempts to *take out the guesswork?* What about the labels you've given yourself? We do this to make it easier for people and also as a defense mechanism. Our hearts feel a lot safer around labels and limitations if we've beaten someone to the punch. Labels can limit us into a false sense of security with the simplification of an *either-or* perspective, but always – ALWAYS - we are way more *both and.* Below are some options of *either-or* labels. Circle the ones that resonate and add in whatever else comes to mind in the available space on the next page.

Sensitive-Insensitive	Authentic-Superficial	Strong-Weak	Easy-Difficult
Likable-Offensive	Considerate-Careless	Victim-Survivor	Attractive-Repulsive
Wild-Virtuous	Creative-Unimaginative	Assertive-Timid	Sweet-Foul
Confident-Insecure	Aggressive-Passive	Protective-Neglectful	Affectionate-Cold
Brave-Scared	Supportive-Opposing	Selfless-Selfish	Present-Unfocused
Whole-Broken	Abundant-Inadequate	Casual-Formal	Vivacious-Boring
Connected-Isolated	Controlling-Nonchalant	Cheery-Depressed	Carefree-Serious
Able-Incompetent	Wise-Reckless	Crazy-Sensible	Warm-Unfriendly
Sensual-Severe	Harsh-Lenient	Provider-Taker	Spiteful-Charitable
Energetic-Lethargic	Respected-Disregarded	Inspired-Discouraged	Loving-Detached

The world we live in would have us believe that if we are one, we are not the other. That is not true. At various times in my life, I have been every one of these characteristics… and countless more. I have been insensitive, offensive, selfish, and foul. Does that mean I am those things? No. Not at all. In any given situation, I may be offensive, but I may also be likeable. I can be *both of those and* sensitive and insensitive, too! We all feel, behave, and make choices that reflect every quality and characteristic out there. When my daughter is being difficult, does that mean she is a difficult person? No. But, I only have to say a few times, "Ugh…. You are *such* a difficult child!" for it to invisibly implant in her consciousness. Pretty soon that label of '*difficult*' is part of her self-image. In an *either-or* context, if she is difficult, what is she not? She isn't *easy.* She isn't *easy* going. She isn't *easy* to get along with. What is valued more in society? Being difficult or being easy? It is a silly question. You get my point. Ready to *both and*? Pick ten *either-or* combos from above. Play with the sentences below and fill in the blanks with the *either-or* characteristics that feel right for you. The third blank in each sentence is open for you to claim your empowered state of being through simultaneously embodying your *both and.* Some ideas for the third blank could be:

• I am perfectly me.	• That is totally cool.
• That is OK!	• I love myself for both!
• Both are valid.	• The world needs both sides of me.
• I claim both.	• This makes me- **me!**
• I am allowed.	• How lucky am I?!?
• They both serve my highest good.	• They both fuel my creativity.
• That is just how life goes.	• I am a Goddess!
• I am fine with that.	• I honor all aspects of me.

Here are a few examples of how you can fill in all three blanks.

Sometimes I am **energetic** and sometimes I am **lethargic,** and ***that is just how life goes.***
Sometimes I am **whole** and sometimes I am **broken,** and ***I am fine with that.***

Sometimes I am _____ and sometimes I am _____, and _____.

Sometimes I am _____ and sometimes I am _____, and _____.

Sometimes I am _____ and sometimes I am _____, and _____.

Sometimes I am _____ and sometimes I am _____, and _____.

Sometimes I am _____ and sometimes I am _____, and _____.

Sometimes I am _____ and sometimes I am _____, and _____.

Sometimes I am _____ and sometimes I am _____, and _____.

Sometimes I am _____ and sometimes I am _____, and _____.

Sometimes I am _____ and sometimes I am _____, and _____.

Sometimes I am _____ and sometimes I am _____, and _____.

How does it feel to claim your *both and?* Keep going! Keep claiming your unique, dynamic, complex, and beautiful gifts. There is only one you in this whole world, and we need *you*. We need you with all of your exceptional and distinctive qualities that only you can offer. Love you! Thank you!

Crystal Love: Elizabeth D.'s Crystal is the calming, purifying, boundary breaking, and limitation busting Snowflake Obsidian (uhb-*sid*-ee-uhn). This glossy black stone with its snowflake-like patterns is actually molten lava that was forced to cool so quickly, it didn't have time to crystallize. A very protective stone, Snowflake Obsidian works with us to implode toxic thought patterns and dysfunctional wounding cycles so that we may discover the value of mistakes, the benefits of isolation, and the courage to follow intuitive guidance in order to do what is *right* versus what is easy. Known as a 'Stone of Purity,' personal and spiritual authenticity are a must when working with Snowflake Obsidian. Generally recognized to be enormously powerful and lighting quick, collaborating with Obsidians can take some getting used to. Be sure to prepare yourself for their quick and clear insights into the truth of things. Just like the colossal force of an erupting volcano, these stones can bring everything - good, bad, and ugly - to the surface for clarity, transformation, and release. This process, which can feel very volatile, is actually needed to clear the path for love, beauty, and serenity. Hold a piece of Snowflake Obsidian and play with the feelings of receptivity that may come forward. Wear a piece as a pendant against your heart and ask for guidance from the deep inner realms of your Soul. The more we work with this formidable stone, the more we recalibrate and purify body, mind, and spirit.

Suggested Reading to Reclaim and Repossess the Empowered Feminine Energy and Leadership Present Throughout the Timespan of Humanity's Development, *The Chalice and The Blade: Our History, Our Future* by Riane Eisler.

Kialey and Kristin

We are best friends. Together, we've been through nine years of recovery, motherhood, marriage, and more. Although at times we might have questioned it, we have always had each other's unconditional love and support. We are family. Sometimes it is hard to believe, but this type of friendship is possible. It takes work, and it has taken us both choosing to not give up, but it is worth it. Even when things get difficult… *especially* when things get difficult, we have learned to open up and talk about the hard stuff.

Kristin: We met in an addiction treatment facility. We were in the same dorm room. I was 19. Kialey was 22. It is typical to make friendships in rehab, but it isn't typical for friendships to last. Usually people will go their separate ways. Either one person stays clean and the other one doesn't, or they both go back out together.

Kialey: Our friendship was special because we were both dedicated to our recovery. We were dedicated to this new way of figuring life out. I'm sure when Kristin first saw me, she was probably thinking, "Oh my gosh, what is wrong with that girl?" I had just gotten out of jail. I was homeless. I had been living on the streets. Life was hard and I didn't think I was going to make it. This was my second time in treatment, but it was the first time I had chosen help. I was grateful to have another chance.

Kristin: Kialey was just sitting there with this headband on and when she introduced herself, she seemed so happy and grateful. I felt like those things had been stripped away from me. I was not in a good place at all… so angry, not feeling good, trying to make sense of things… I couldn't understand what was so great about being in treatment.

Kialey: Looking back, when we commenced from the program, our friendship changed from 'friends in treatment' to actual friends.

Kristin: Graduating and having this friendship was so good for us. Together, we got to be kids again. We got a chance to do things over… clean.

Kialey: When we got out of the program, we got to go back and relive our teenage years. We would go to our morning meeting, and then come back to my house, make lunch, and watch movies. We would take naps. We would go out to sushi. It was so much fun!

Kristin: It was during this time that Kialey met her husband… and I had to check him out. When I did, I really liked him! He reminded me of me. I even moved in with them for a bit. But when I saw how serious Kialey was about this relationship, things started to change. When Kialey got pregnant, I felt like her life was moving on and mine wasn't. I started feeling like I was losing my friend.

Kialey: When Kristin moved out of our apartment and into another apartment in the same complex, things got really painful and uncomfortable between us. We didn't talk about what was going on because we didn't have the relationship skills. We had never been taught how to maturely speak like adults about the awkward things that happen in friendships… the things that need to be said so you don't walk around carrying them. She felt like she had lost me. I felt like I had been shunned. It was so hard. I would drive in and see her on her porch and think, "She doesn't even want to talk to me anymore."

Kristin: Believe me, I was happy for her about the baby. I wanted that for her. I just didn't know how to talk to her about what was going on with our friendship. I didn't know what to say. The separation felt terrible. I felt so alone. I just thought, "Well, I've lost her, too." One night, thinking it was a really great idea, I made an effort and asked her to go bowling.

Kialey: My daughter was crawling at the time. It was almost 9:00 pm at night. We were in such different places. When she called and asked me, I was happy, but I was also thinking, "Yeah, that is just what you do with a crawling baby at this time of night!"

Kristin: We both wanted it so badly, but we just couldn't figure out the painful parts. In a lot of ways, we were still showing up for each other, but we weren't addressing what was really going on or how we were really feeling. It took us a couple of years to get back on track. I finally approached Kialey and told her that I wanted to clear the air. I was so scared of losing her, it took me a long time to even say that. I figured I could bring things up, and our friendship would be over, or I could bring things up, and we would get past them. When I initiated that conversation, we started to find our way back to each other.

Kialey: Kristin came to me and said, "Let's talk about the resentments we've both been carrying." I guess it never occurred to me to have a conversation. In my family, there are loads of things that we should talk about but don't ever discuss. I was afraid of ruining what little we had left, what little we were holding on to, if we did bring everything up.

Kristin: I had planned it all out. I told Kialey, "I'll say something and then I'll let you say something." I am a talker and I wanted to be sure that she got time to say what she needed to say.

Kialey: I think, being in recovery, we are both solution-based people. So, once the subject was open, we were both ready.

Kristin: It took a little while to trust that we could be totally honest with each other. It was still weird for a time. But we were eventually able to let it all go.

Kialey: That is why I am so proud of this relationship! A lot of people, when it gets hard like that, they decide they can't work on it, and they walk away. To this day, if there is something that is bothering us, we get it out of the way as quickly as possible. Even if it is awkward. Even if it is hard. We say it. We bring it up. Most times, we are completely oblivious that we've done something upsetting, but that doesn't matter. We address it because we are dedicated to being best friends. Little things happen in all relationships. Especially when we start running things through the jaded filter of our past experiences. I know this is true for me. I have a rough time processing things, especially when it involves someone I love. I will think, "What is wrong with me? Have I done something?" Or I will think that someone is trying to hurt me when they're not.

Kristin: Now, we talk each other off the ledge. I'll say, "Come on, they didn't mean that." Or Kialey will say to me, "Really? That's not real." We help each other stay grounded.

Kialey: I love that about us. It's fine if we say things to each other that don't sound like we have it all together. We know we are crazy!

Kristin: We get so much love and laughter from this friendship. We have been through and accomplished so much together. Kialey has consistently been there for me, no matter what. Trusting that she would and always will be there for me is a really big deal.

Kialey: Over the past seven years, we have shared pregnancies and marriages. I would get pregnant and have a baby, and then Kristin would get pregnant and have a baby. We have maintained this friendship through husbands and kids, our lives, and our responsibilities.

Kristin: After my first child was born, I went through a dark, dark time with Post-Partum Distress. I didn't know how to express what was happening to me. Nobody I knew had ever gone through what I was going through, or if they had I didn't know about it. I was afraid to tell a doctor. I was afraid if I talked about what was going on inside of me I would be locked up and my baby would be taken away. I was so ashamed, and I didn't want people to see me, even Kialey. It was like when I was getting clean. I would meet people and think, "If you only knew what I've done, you wouldn't want to be around me." I felt the same way after I had my son. I was so filled with guilt. I would meet other moms and think, "If you only knew how I felt about myself, if you only knew what kind of mother I *really* was, you wouldn't want to be around me." I felt like I couldn't trust anybody.

Kialey: After my second child was born, I went through Post-Partum Distress, too. I ended up being hospitalized when he was six months old. I knew something wasn't right. My feelings weren't "I'm going to give up, I can't take care of this baby." I felt rage… *intense* rage. Nobody was talking to me about that as a symptom of the baby blues. Doctors would ask if I cried a lot or if I had problems getting out of bed. I was fine getting out of bed. I had no problem with that. I would tell my husband how frustrated I was with our three-year-old. I'd say, "I shouldn't have been like that with her today." He would say, "You just need more sleep. You need a schedule." I tried everything and nothing helped. Kristin showed up for me during this time. It was the most beautiful thing because I needed her so much. We would talk and talk. I would say, "I know something is wrong with me," and she would say, "I know what you are going through." Having her right there, knowing she understood me, knowing she could talk to me about what I was going through, and knowing that she wasn't leaving… that was a powerful thing.

Kristin: It wasn't until I got pregnant with my daughter three years later that I told my doctor. I told them that I had lied before when I said that everything was OK. I told them, "I need help now before this happens again." I knew I wouldn't survive the depression and the feelings of despair. Having babies is supposed to be this beautiful thing. What I went though was not beautiful at all.

Kialey: And, this is just another way we support each other. Kristin is my person. I tell her all of my secrets. No matter if it is good, bad, or indifferent. I tell her everything.

Kristin: We took a picture the other day with all of our kids. You can only see our faces above the little ones, but I love that picture because it reminds me of how far we've come. We have been through so much together. When I first got clean, I didn't believe in myself. I didn't trust other women. I didn't know if I would make it.

Kialey: Today, as I am pregnant with my fourth, I can't believe how much we have been through. Over the past nine years, I have not stayed clean. My husband doesn't think I have really had a relapse, but I do. Today, being honest and having integrity is the most important thing about my recovery. After I had my first baby, I took the pain medication more than I should have. I also haven't been completely honest about my levels of pain going through the procedures to address my gallbladder issues. During all of this, I have picked up white key tags two different times. They signify my surrender and starting over, and Kristin has been with me through it all. Even today, when I need to take medication, I still fear the chance of relapse. My brain is so sneaky when it tries to tell me that my health problems are a free pass to use. When this happens, I call

Kristin and she talks me through it. If there were a relapse, we would figure that out together and decide what to do about it together; no judgement. I know I have to have this type of vigilance for the rest of my life.

Kristin: Opening up and sharing more about what is really going on has given us a new level of maturity. I called Kialey one day and said, "I don't know how to clean my house. I can't do it." She came right over. She helped me clean. She helped me organize. It was great for me because I had to admit there are a lot of things I don't know how to do. Sure, it was embarrassing, but Kialey stepped right in and helped me with ideas for organization and cleaning. She is the only person I can trust with this side of myself. I know she can see this part of me and not think that I am a disgusting person who can't keep her house clean. It may sound weird, but this is really hard for me. It is something I really struggle with.

Kialey: The struggle Kristin helps me with is parenting. I don't want to be an angry parent. I want to be the peaceful, positive parent. I pray and I wonder, "Why does it come so easy to some people?" I call Kristin and honestly tell her about how I am as a parent. I tell her the truth, instead of what I think she wants to hear so that she will think I'm a 'good' mom. I am completely real with her; I'll say "I don't like what I did today."

Kristin: When we do this, we are finding solutions together. I tell her what I have tried, and what has worked. I encourage her. She encourages me. We have to be totally honest with each other for it to work.

Kialey: About a year ago, we had another beautiful turning point. We started supporting each other in our spirituality.

Kristin: I had no spiritual foundation growing up. My parents would take me to church on Christmas. I wasn't against it, it just felt phony. I just didn't believe there was anything to believe in. I went back and forth for a long time. In recovery, I would pray that prayer for someone or something to please help me because I knew I couldn't do it on my own, but that was it. It has taken a while, but I've realized that I don't have to be like everyone else.

Kialey: I've always had a strong Christian belief. In our program, you have the freedom to explore for yourself and come to a relationship with God or a Higher Power on your own terms. So, for the last year and a half, I have been fighting with myself to figure out if God is a boy or a girl. This is my attempt to come out of my box and create a relationship with God that works for me, and I've really begun to question what I have been told. I've recently started to think if I don't feel good about something someone has told me, I don't have to believe it.

Kristin: It has actually been fun. We have been sharing books and ideas back and forth. Through this journey of self-discovery, we have realized that we don't need a structure or a building to validate our spirituality.

Kialey: This spiritual journey has also helped with our other relationships. It has helped with everything. It has been powerful and beautiful. For us, it has made our bond even stronger. Doors have started opening, we have had new adventures, and we found the Divine Mommy Group together.

Kristin: I'm no longer afraid to explore this side of myself. Yes, I have been through a lot. But I am equal. I am not less than. The confidence that was stripped away during the Post-Partum Distress has all started coming back as Kialey and I have discovered our spiritual selves together.

Kialey: This has been the most beautiful journey.

Kristin: I want others to know that this type of friendship is possible. I didn't believe that for a long time. I was living in fear. But it is.

Kialey: Yes, this kind of friendship needs work, but it is *so* worth it. Female friendships are worth it.

Kristin: And they are important. We need each other!

Kialey: All those years ago, I could never have imagined the life I have today. Where I've come from. What I've made it through. Being in that dorm room with Kristin, I wasn't sure I would live, let alone become the kind of woman and mother I am, having just celebrated four honest years of recovery.

Kristin: I remember laughing. Laughing for real for the very first time without being on anything. Thinking of that feeling today, it is crazy how far we have come. It is crazy to think how far we will go!

Kialey: I may tag Kristin to have another baby. After this one, it *is* her turn….

Kristin: I don't know if *that* will happen… maybe I'll follow her lead and go back to school.

> We are best friends. We are family. We know there will be more struggles and more challenges. Life can be hard, but people will help you through the pain if you let them. We've learned how to be best friends by *being* best friends to each other. Recovery, motherhood, marriage, spirituality…. It is worth it to be vulnerable about these things. It is worth it to open up. We have each other's unconditional love and we never have to walk alone.
> That level of support is amazing! So are we!

Making This Story Your Own:

Kialey's and Kristin's story invites us to remember the importance of female friendships.
Take a moment, breathe, and reflect.
What stands out for you when you read their words?
Is there a situation in your life that is similar to Kialey's and Kristin's?
Perhaps part of their story feels connected to your own.
How can you relate their experiences to your past, present, and future?

- *My Connection to Kialey's and Kristin's Story* _____

_____

_____

Knowing that you aren't alone, let's gently explore some other themes from Kialey's and Kristin's story together:

- ***Giving and Receiving Love***
    - When you think of love, do you value *giving* love as much as *receiving* love? If yes, how do you value them equally? If not, why? In reality, do you actively create opportunities for receiving love that are equal in measure to the love that you give to others? Why, or why not? Do your words,

in regard to the value you place on *receiving* love, match your actions when it comes to *accepting* love into your life? If so, how did you learn to do this? If not, where could you use some support?

- **Second Chances**
    - Where in your life would you like a second chance? What is keeping you from creating this opportunity? Would it help to be more vulnerable? What would vulnerability around this situation look and feel like? Might it help to be more vulnerable with yourself about choices and feelings? Is there a way in which you could be more vulnerable with others about your choices and feelings? What would it take for you to feel safe enough to *honestly* and *authentically* express your opinions, impressions, beliefs, concerns, suspicions, and ideas in regard to these situations? How would authentically expressing these things be productive for you, the situation, and your relationships?

- **Discovering Your Spiritual Self**
    - What are your Spiritual beliefs? Who is your Spiritual Self? Where did this Spiritual part of you come from and how has your Spirituality come into being? When you think back to your earliest memories and teachings around Spirituality, what comes to mind? Tracking your Spiritual Journey from those early times until now, what does that journey look like? Has this journey been completely yours? Who else has been involved? Are there places and spaces where old belief systems can be released? Are there places and spaces still available for new beliefs? How would you like your Spirituality and your Spiritual Self to evolve? Taking into account your Spirituality today, can you give yourself credit for creating this aspect of your consciousness? Why, or why not? If you would like to be able to give yourself credit, or to give yourself more credit, what are a few small things you can do?

Sacred Play Suggestions:

~ SPS #1: ~
* Higher Self to Higher Self *

What relationships in your life could use a tune up? Is there anyone from your past or present that you would like to clear the air with? Maybe there have been some hurts or disappointments with a friend, and now things just feel wonky? If these questions resonate, don't beat yourself up. Sure, you may have some responsibility to take, but try not to be mean to yourself. When you already feel badly because something is hurting an important relationship in your life, adding more blame and shame to the mix won't help. Blame and shame keep things on lock down and don't provide the forward momentum to create shifts and resolution. Because they are our biggest teachers, our relationships will traverse into the quirky land of conflict - all. the. time. - for the *rest* of our lives. We are meant to grow from our relationships and sometimes the growing pains are painful. However, we need not suffer. Getting things back on track and saying what needs to be said can seem impossible. When we are in the midst of feeling all of the feelings, our defense mechanisms convince us to let things go unsaid in the hopes that peace will re-establish itself. That might happen, but how long will it last and how genuine will it feel? Like Kialey and Kristin, most of us aren't taught how to communicate in a calm, respectful, and emotionally mature manner when it comes to hurt feelings. That is OK! This stuff is really hard! But when you take the time to get clear about what you *would* like to say and set the intentions for the Greatest and Highest Good to come forward *while* you say it... it becomes easier. It also helps that - for this activity - we are going to imagine the other person is sitting with us, eager to listen and ready to participate. I got this idea from a friend of mine. I was speaking to her about some long lasting and sucky energy I felt between myself and another friend. She said, "You know, you can always have a conversation with her Higher Self." When she said that, a light bulb went off. I had already spent loads of mental head space having hypothetical conversations with this friend in my mind. But these exhaustive conversations went nowhere, and nothing got resolved. Talking Soul-to-Soul felt different. It felt empowering. By creating a space to communicate Higher Self to Higher Self, I relaxed into the possibilities of reconnection and resolution, even though I didn't have a blueprint for exactly how this was going to happen. The following is based upon the traditional Aligning, Attuning, and Allowing (AAA) practice of an Esoteric Energy Healing Session. This energetic connection, based on the work of Alice Bailey, facilitates connecting to someone in mind, body, and spirit. In doing this, we 'Align' with the higher vibratory energies of Spirit, 'Attune' our consciousness to receive, and 'Allow' the guidance to pour forth. Let's try it!

- Take a few deep breaths to relax while sitting comfortably or lying down.
    - Tune in to your body and become aware of any tension or stiffness.
        - If they are present, ask for them to be released.
- When you are ready, think of a relationship that you would like to shift for the better.
    - Close your eyes and visualize this person sitting across from you.
        - Connect with them Heart to Heart
            - Do this by visualizing a **green** ray of light going from the center of your chest to the center of their chest.
        - Connect with them Mind to Mind.
            - Do this by visualizing a **purple** ray of light going from your forehead to their forehead.
        - Connect with them Soul to Soul.
            - Do this by visualizing a **white** ray of light going from just above the crown of your head to just above the crown of their head.
        - Either in your head or out loud, set the intention for '*the Greatest and Highest **Good** to come forward and the Greatest and Highest **Choice** to come forward.*'
- Speak honestly and clearly to the person sitting across from you in your imagination.
    - Say everything that you need and want to say. Don't censor.
        - Trust yourself. Remember, you have aligned and attuned with your Higher Self so that the exact right words and feelings can come forward.
            - Take note of what you say and how you say it. This way of communicating may be useful should this conversation happen in real life.
- In your imagination, allow the other person to respond with their thoughts, feelings, and answers to your questions.
    - Take note of what they say and how they say it. This may give you empathic insight to understand how they are feeling.
- When the conversation feels complete, finish with the Ancient Hawaiian Practice of Forgiveness, Ho'oponopono, and repeat the following Mantra three times:

I'm sorry, please forgive me, thank you, I love you.
I'm sorry, please forgive me, thank you, I love you.
I'm sorry, please forgive me, thank you, I love you.

Bring your awareness back to your physical body and reconnect to your breath. Again, gauge any physical sensations, taking note if any additional relief from the tension and stiffness has occurred. As a final step, journal or reflect on the guidance that has come through for repair to the relationship and resolution to the conflict.

Higher Self to Higher Self Wisdom and Guidance

_____

_____

_____

_____

One heart focused on healing can bring about many magickal outcomes. Just by doing this activity, you shift your energy toward the situation. Because *you* are different, the situation is now different as well. It may still need some time and space, but you can keep holding these Higher Self to Higher Self conversations. Keep raising your vibration and you never know what might happen. Thank you for your dedication to peace and resolution. I love you!

~ SPS #2: ~
* Gratitude Tree *

Is there anywhere in your space that could use some sprucing up? Gratitude is a great design essential for any environment. No doubt, holding an awareness of gratitude within our consciousness is beneficial. Expressing gratitude with our voices is also very helpful. Bringing gratitude front and center to be visually recognized and interacted with multiple times a day… that can bring about a whole new level of *thanksgiving*. The materials for this activity are going to be found in your trash and recycling. Go ahead and locate any reusable cardboard boxes and paper bags that you may have. If you don't have recyclables at the moment, find things that are already lying around the house. Scrap paper, magazines, newspapers, old books, and cards will also work great! Now, choose the special spot in your home. Choose a wall, the fridge, a door, a cabinet… anywhere that you and your family will pass by as you go about your day. This will be the spot for your original work of gratitude art. Start by creating the trunk of a tree. Follow your creative intuition here. Out of the materials you have gathered, cut, collage, paste, glue, and color this strong and sturdy trunk. Your tree trunk can be any shape, size, color, or texture. Once the trunk is complete, tape or attach it to your chosen spot. Be sure to leave plenty of room above to create the crown of your tree which includes all of the leaves and branches. With the left-over materials, cut out the leaves for your Gratitude Tree. Again, these can be any shape or size; just be sure they are big enough for you and your family members to write on. Once you have a large stack of leaves, put them in a container next to the trunk. Set a marker and some tape next to the leaves and offer everyone the opportunity to write what they are grateful for as they pass by. Once the leaf is complete, tape it up. Soon, the crown will be filled with jewels of gratitude. Every so often, stop and read all of the thankful thoughts. As you tape the leaves up, witness how your tree grows and notice the daily energy of gratitude building within your household. Enjoy! Love you!

~ SPS #3: ~
* Duh *

Identifying how we feel about things can be really difficult. When emotions run high and we are asked to reflect, finding the clarity about situations isn't always easy. A similar phenomenon can take place when something hasn't gone according to plan. When big feelings are present and we are asked to project what we would have *preferred* to happen, the answer is usually something like – "Uhm…I don't know…. Obviously not this... duh…" and *"Duh"* is actually a pretty perfect answer here. Grappling with the hurt feelings and confusion of life doesn't always lead to eloquently verbose perspectives… and maybe it's not meant to. Maybe the '*duh*' moments are meant to slow us down? Maybe the *not knowing* how to make sense of something is the gift? Maybe the confusion is there to stop the momentum and offer us some space? We live in a world of instant gratification. We are so used to not waiting or wanting for things. Our creature comforts can be satiated with very little effort and time. Want something for your latest project? Bam - it is delivered to your door in under 24 hours. Feeling a smidge hungry? Click on the latest food delivery app and – boom! A delicious meal arrives. It makes sense that we would consciously and unconsciously expect that the same processes with fast results, minimum effort, and instant fulfillment to apply to our relationships and feelings. But think about it: how much of this glorious human experience would we miss if everything could be known, processed, and fixed instantly? Would we forget the important things? Love takes time. Trust is built. Conflict isn't resolved by a touch screen. We get clear on our feelings by taking the time and putting forth the effort. There is no prewritten timeline for that. How and when this happens is unique for each person and each situation. Think about it, can you be OK with not having the answers? Can you handle a crunchy situation staying crunchy for a while? Can you manage feeling your feelings? In our world of faster, bigger, newer, and better, allowing this space can seem counterproductive and counterintuitive. But it is not. Let's give it a try. Think of a situation where repair is needed. This can be any situation or relationship that doesn't fall into the bliss category. Take a moment and identify the things you know:

- Who and what is/was involved? _____
  _____

- What has happened or is happening? _____
  _____

Take a look at what you have written. For a few moments just be aware of these *known* circumstances. Visualize the players and events moving and interacting in slow motion. Without working towards a goal or outcome, let your thoughts come and go. Try doing this for at least two minutes. Next, slightly change directions, and as you maintain a conscious connection to the situation, reflect and journal around the following:

- What might be the gift of *not knowing*? _____
  _____

- What might be the gift of *confusion*? _____
  _____

- What might be the gift of *slowing down?* _____
  _____

- What might be the gift of *no resolution?* _____
  _____

Continuing with the conscious connection to the situation, let your thoughts flow for a few more minutes. Still, with no objective to find answers or solutions, reflect and journal around this final set of statements. The purpose here is to develop new ideas and explore possibilities.

- I will know I am ready to get **clear** when_____
  _____

- I will know I am ready to **identify** my feelings when_____
  _____

- I will know it is safe to **feel** my feelings when_____
  _____

- I will know what the next **best step** is when_____
  _____

- I will know there has been **resolution** when_____
  _____

How did this activity feel? It wasn't fast or direct, but was it productive and did it honor your intuition? Take your time to answer ☺. Love you. Thank you.

~ SPS #4: ~
* Really Talk, Really Listen *

One of the best bits of advice I ever got as an actor was to '*really talk and really listen.*' It sounds so easy. Sure! I really talk and really listen all the time! But think about it… as an actor, on a set, with costumes, speaking memorized lines that someone else has written, in character, talking to someone else who is also in character, with bright lights, in front of several hundred strangers… *really talking* and *really listening* is close to impossible. Not only is it unnatural, there is also so much else for our brains to focus on. Yet, really talking and really listening is exactly what an actor has to do to be fully in character and in the moment… two essential things that create a good and believable performance. Take this concept and translate it to the *scenes* of our lives. Kialey and Kristin offer us much wisdom around this when, in their story, they share about the breakdown of their close friendship. In an attempt at repairing the relationship, they planned a time to talk and Kristin created a running order of: "I'll say something and then you'll say something." The plan was to *really talk* and *really listen*! Even though this scene provided much outside stimulus to pull focus - hurt feelings, misunderstandings, fear, anxiety, etc. - they were able to successfully create a space for vulnerability, honesty, and clarity. Wow! Cool, right? So, here is the question put into the context of our own relationships: How can we create the same vulnerability, honesty, and clarity in order to really talk and really listen, especially when the scene is emotionally charged? Taking another cue from acting class, maybe writing our backstories might help. A backstory is the details that make you, ***you***. In acting, we create a backstory, partly pulled from information the playwright gives, and partly pulled from our own imaginations as we develop our characters. For this activity, you know yourself better than anyone, so you are actor and playwright in one. Let's start with some generals.

- How old am I? _____ Where am I from? _____

- Where did I go to school? _____ What is my favorite food? _____

- What is my body type? _____

- What are my most important relationships? _____
  _____

- What are my relationships like? (personal and professional) _____
  _____

- What do I do for work? _____

- What are my hobbies? _____

- What kind of music do I like? _____

- Who are my friends? _____

- What am I good at? _____

- What am I not good at? _____

- What are my hopes and dreams? _____

- What is the most important thing that has ever happened to me? _____
  _____

- What do I want more than anything? _____

- What do I think of myself? _____
  _____

Feel free to add more to your backstory. Once it feels full, let's talk objective. In every scene, the characters have what is called an *objective*, which is the overall goal of the scene. The *objective* for our scene - which is the reparative conversation - is **to *really talk* and *really listen*.** Motivation is what the actors use to reach the objective. Our *motivations* are to be **vulnerable, honest, and clear.** To productively play the *motivations* in our scene, it is equally important to discover what helps and what hinders us in doing so. Work with the following questions and take note of what comes to light in regard to the **objectives** *(the goal)* and **motivations** *(how we **reach** the goal).* As you answer these questions, do so from the perspective that the *'Scene'* is the emotionally charged argument or conversation, and your *Scene Partner* is whoever you are talking to: spouse, friend, colleague, child, parent, sibling, etc.

When I am in a *Scene* with my *Scene Partner,* to play the motivation of '*vulnerability*'…

- What helps me to be vulnerable? _____

- What hinders my vulnerability? _____

- How can I be more vulnerable? _____

- When will I know that I have successfully and effectively reached the **objective** of really talking and really listening though my vulnerability?

_____

When I am in a *Scene* with my *Scene Partner,* to play the motivation of '*honesty*'…

- What helps me to be honest? _____

- What hinders my honesty? _____

- How can I be more honest? _____

- When will I know that I have successfully and effectively reached the **objective** of really talking and really listening through my honesty?

_____

When I am in a *Scene* with my *Scene partner,* to play the motivation of '*clarity*'…

- What helps me to be clear? _____

- What hinders my clarity? _____

- How can I be clearer? _____

- When will I know that I have successfully and effectively reached the **objective** of really talking and really listening through my ability to be clear?

_____

Wow! Great job *fleshing* all of this out. To flesh it out is a theatrical term which translates to: putting the flesh on the body of the piece by creating and designing all of the production elements. As you have *fleshed out* your acting homework, complete your scene prep by reflecting or journaling on the following questions.

What have I learned about myself?

_____

_____

_____

How does my backstory influence my ability to play my motivations and meet my objectives?

_____

_____

_____

How can I apply *really talking* and *really listening* to all of my relationships?

_____

_____

_____

How can I apply *really talking* and *really listening* to the relationship I have with myself?

_____

_____

_____

If you feel stuck around a certain part of this activity, give yourself some time. The healing process will be supported by your creativity; however, it will not be forced. If you find yourself feeling blocked, move your body to get the energy flowing again. Take a walk around the room, do some jumping jacks, or touch your toes. Also get reacquainted with your breath. A few deep breaths will support you in finishing this work of understanding the motivations and objectives played out within the scenes of our lives and relationships. Now, don't even think I'm going to let you forget about the cast party. Following the opening night of a show, there is always an after party. This is the time to celebrate everyone's hard work with salutations, toasts, hugs, and shared appreciation. You, my dear, have done it all, and you deserve a party! Now, how are you going to celebrate? I'll serenade you with an original song… all you have to do is ask. Love you! Thank you!

~ SPS #5: ~
* Chi *

Many Eastern philosophies include perspectives on how to move the energy or Chi throughout our bodies. The idea is that once the chi is optimally flowing, we feel better in mind, body, and spirit. Moving the Chi in this way can be simple and easy. It just requires choreographing your breath to a visualization that intentionally moves the energy around your body in a specific pattern. Let's give it a try. In whatever way that feels right to you, visualize energy gathering at the base of your spine. As you inhale, bring that energy up the back of your body and into your head. Once at your head, send that energy into your brain. Then exhale, bringing the energy down the front of your body. As the final step, connect the energy back into the source of energy resting at the base of your spine. Try this breathing pattern at least three times. Once you are finished, record what you notice.

- **Physically,** I feel _____
    - I notice a shift in _____
- **Emotionally,** I feel _____
    - I notice a shift in _____
- **Mentally,** I feel _____
    - I notice a shift in _____
- **Spiritually,** I feel _____
    - I notice a shift in _____

For the next round, let's include another layer and let's vibe in **love**. However you are aware of love energy, during this next breath cycle, invite and allow love into your consciousness. Once again, inhale and bring the energy from the base of your spine up the back of your body. When you get to your mid-back, between your shoulder blades, open your awareness to receive love energy. Continue with your inhale and feel the love as it infuses every cell of your body. Continuing on with the breath, as you reach the crown of your head, send energy into your brain. Now begin your exhale and bring the energy down the front of your body. Once you get to the center of your chest, visualize the love energy streaming forth from your heart and out into the world. Finally, connect the energy circuit back into the source energy resting at the base of your spine. Repeat this breathing pattern at least three times. Once you are finished, record what you notice.

- **Physically,** I feel _____
    - I notice a shift in _____
- **Emotionally,** I feel _____
    - I notice a shift in _____

- **Mentally,** I feel _____
    - I notice a shift in _____
- **Spiritually,** I feel _____
    - I notice a shift in _____

For the final round, let's ask our Higher Selves to participate. Inhale and bring the energy from the base of the spine up the back of your body. Open your awareness to receive love as you travel up between the shoulder blades. Once your reach the crown of your head, visualize opening your crown to connect to your Soul. As you receive guidance for the Greatest and Highest Good, send this energy into your brain. Begin your exhale and bring the energy and guidance down the front of your body. At the center of your chest, once again visualize the love energy streaming forth from your heart and out into the world. Finally, connect the energy circuit back into the source energy resting at the base of your spine. Repeat this breathing pattern at least three times. Once you are finished, record what you notice.

- **Physically,** I feel _____
    - I notice a shift in _____
- **Emotionally,** I feel _____
    - I notice a shift in _____
- **Mentally,** I feel _____
    - I notice a shift in _____
- **Spiritually,** I feel _____
    - I notice a shift in _____

Go back and read through your thoughts from the three breath cycles. The first cycle opened the levels of your body and mind. The second cycle stimulated the awareness of love within your heart. The third cycle connected you to your spiritual consciousness. Putting it all together, journal and reflect on the questions below.

- How did the cycles build upon each other? _____
- What was similar? _____
- What was different? _____
- How would incorporating this into my daily routine be beneficial for me? _____

_____

- How can I share this practice? _____

_____

Your Chi is flowing, and it is gorgeous! *You* are gorgeous! Thank you for doing this activity. Bringing forth the energy of the body, mind, and spirit connection infuses you with love so that you can go forth and infuse the world. Rock on, Sis! Love you.

Crystal Love: Kialey and Kristin's Crystal is the soft, milky, reflective, fertile, and Divinely Feminine Peach Moonstone. This beautifully calm, balancing, and introspective stone connects our deep intrapsychic instincts to the cycles of the female body, the cycles of Mother Moon, the cycles of Mother Earth, and the ever wise and ever-loving creational cycles of birth, life, death, and renewal. Use this Crystal for grace to handle the constant ups and downs and ebbs and flows of life. If some attunement to your destiny is what you seek, try holding a stone in your hand while speaking your wildest wishes and most heartfelt hopes into its brilliant chatoyancy. If your relationships are feeling muddy and co-dependent, try asking Peach Moonstone (or any of the Moonstones) for empathic discernment and compassionate insight. Perhaps an exploration of your Shadow Self is being called for? If so, ask this Crystal for support and protection as you travel the murky depths of your unconscious and bring back to the surface of your awareness the much-needed transformational wisdom for personal rebirth, regeneration, and rejuvenation. Also known as a talisman of good fortune, this stone is empowering for women and for the Feminine energies embodied throughout all of creation. When we allow this powerful recalibration and realignment with the Feminine to be felt throughout our daily interactions, choices, and relationships… the good fortune of fertility, connection, receptivity, and reciprocation can be felt by all.

Suggested Reading to Embody Your Fertility, Grace, and Transformation Through the Female Anatomy and Female Consciousness, *Red Moon: Understanding and Using the Creative, Sexual, and Spiritual Gifts of the Menstrual Cycle* by Miranda Gray.

Additional Journaling and SPS Space

Mindy

I am a forty-year-old woman now, which seems odd because with everything I've been through, I didn't know if I was going to make it to forty. I had a rocky childhood. My parents divorced when I was two years old. My mom, sister, and I had a challenging relationship. My mom's mom moved in to help with raising us and living expenses. I leaned on my grandma a lot when I was younger. I still do, even though she isn't here anymore. My grandma died when I was eighteen from breast cancer and I was at a loss without her. She was my go-to person for everything. That same year, I had a cyst removed from my right ovary. I was told that it may be the kind of cyst that could grow teeth and hair. I was also told there could be a chance I would wake up minus an ovary. It was devastating to think I might not be able to have children one day. Thank goodness it didn't turn out that way. I had dodged that bullet, and by the ripe age of twenty-one I was married to my high school sweetheart and became a mommy. I never imagined that being a mommy could bring so much heartache and joy. The delivery was intense, and my newborn daughter suffered a birth trauma. She was diagnosed with Erb's palsy, a damage to the brachial plexus nerves which connects the spinal cord to the extremities. The nerves in her neck were injured so severely during the delivery because she had been hung up on my pelvic bone. The entire birth was traumatic. My husband referred to it as brutal. He said the doctor even put her foot up on the bed and began to pull at our daughter's head. She never tried to do an episiotomy. She never tried to turn the baby away from my pelvic bone with her hands. It took hours and hours. I was in and out of consciousness. They would tell me to push and I would try, but I didn't know that I was really making it worse, stretching her little neck even further. When they brought her to me for the first time, she was so terribly bruised and swollen and I thought, "What the hell happened to my baby?" Her little arm was completely limp. The nurses would look at me and pose the question, "Maybe her arm is broken?" I was getting so many scary mixed messages. Finally, a woman came in and told me what my baby was being diagnosed with. She then went down a list and proceeded to tell me all the things my daughter would never be able to do. All of that threw me into a deep depression. I blamed myself for a long, long time. I would cry and cry and cry, asking God, "Why? Why did that happen to my baby?" It bothered me that my husband didn't cry and show as much emotion as I did. Then the depression morphed into something worse. I got mean. Really, really mean. I was hurtful to myself. I started drinking and doing other things I shouldn't have been doing. I couldn't deal with everything and it was the downfall of my marriage. I didn't know how to cope, and my husband didn't either. Now that I am older and a little wiser, I know he was dealing with it in his own way. He was trying to be strong and brave for me because he could sense how broken I was. As time went on, we tried to get pregnant again. I suffered three miscarriages. In the first one there was no longer a heartbeat. In the second and third, both were blighted ovums, a condition that occurs when a gestational sack develops without an embryo. It all got to be too much. Pretty soon, we stopped talking. We stopped trying. And we both just gave up. I felt so utterly alone, and I got involved with someone else. I'm not proud that I had an affair, but it does happen. It did happen. And, I got pregnant again. This time, the pregnancy and delivery were perfect. I had a planned c-section. The sad part was, this baby's father chose to walk away from us and live a different lifestyle. I became a single mom of two girls. I dated off and on for ten years. Then I met someone different than all the rest. He didn't fit my type, but he was so sweet and thoughtful. There was a sense of comfort and safety about him. He took me to the beach one evening to watch the sunset. We sat down in the sand and he asked me to marry him with a ring he had made out of a vine from our backyard. I said no and gave him a list of reasons why he didn't want to marry me. He stopped me and told me to quit trying to talk him out of wanting to be my husband. He said that I was the best thing that had ever happened to him. So we eloped, and I became pregnant with our first child. The only issue with this pregnancy was that I developed gestational diabetes. My son's birth and c-section were successful. The nurses referred to him as 'Quiet Wyatt,' because he didn't cry until they started to clean him up. Fifteen months later, I was expecting another baby. Early into the pregnancy, it was discovered that my placenta was growing into my uterus. I was told I had a serious condition that occurs when all or part of the placenta attaches abnormally to the muscular layer of the uterine wall. There are three levels to this condition, and I had the most severe, Percreta. With this diagnosis, I had no idea what I was in for. For the bulk of the pregnancy, I was on pelvic rest. There was no heavy lifting and no sex. I had to be very careful because there was a high risk of hemorrhaging. My doctor was very concerned because my condition could be life threatening. There were multiple appointments and procedures to monitor what was going on because the placenta can attach itself to your other internal organs. I was so nervous. Emotionally this time was very difficult. I was never sure what to do. I didn't know if I should live like I was dying. I wondered if I should create videos for the kids so that they knew how much I loved them and never wanted to leave them. This took a toll on my marriage. My husband and I were both so stressed and scared. He was being told he could lose his wife and have to raise a newborn alone. When the time came to have the baby, it felt like I was a ticking time bomb. I didn't know what to do or how to feel. My doctor and the hospital prepared for the worst. Once I checked into the hospital, I was so nervous because I didn't know if I would be walking back out. I would be awake for the entire procedure so the physicians would be able to monitor me better. At first, my husband was not going to be able to be in the operating room, but one of the attending doctors went to bat to have that changed. There were so many nurses and specialist in the room… it was intimidating and terrifying. I hadn't gotten much sleep in the days leading up to the surgery, and as I was lying on the table I began to drift off into a sort of wakeful sleep. They were getting ready to cut me open when they finally brought my husband into the room. It was in that moment that I came out of a dream and said, "We are having a girl! I saw her and her name is Lillee." That vision still plays in my head sometimes. It was so clear. I was laughing and smiling while holding her in my arms and calling her Lillee. We hadn't been told the sex of the baby so we could have at least one surprise to look forward to amidst all the worry and stress. They held the baby up, and sure enough, it was a girl. My husband said, "It IS a girl!" I was crying and asking if she was OK. I only got to see her for a quick second as they were whisking her off to the NICU because my surgery was to last another 8-9 hours. It was grueling. I could hear everything the doctors and nurses were saying. I could hear them saying I needed more blood. Finally, it came to an end. I knew I was going to survive because of the dream, but there were moments when I wasn't sure. Those first days in the hospital were awful. A few days after the surgery, my husband went home to be with our son. That night, alone in my room, I bled out. I was soaked in blood at the site of the bulb that was in my abdomen to collect the fluid. The on-call doctor was called by the attending nurse, and I was at the mercy of the professionals once again. I was rushed off to have an MRI because the doctor was concerned that I had internal bleeding. Then they brought me back in my room and performed an x-ray. I was in so much pain from all the movement. A specialist was called in to put a port in my neck so that I could receive blood transfusions and fluids. My arms were so bruised from the infiltration of the IV during surgery and the nurse's inability to put an IV in my arm. Finally, I was moved to post-op. My hospital stay lasted nine days. Lillee stayed in the NICU for thirteen days. I didn't even get to see her until she was four days old. I was so weak and in terrible pain. To make matters worse, I was sent home with a catheter which I ended up calling my ball and chain. I had to live with that for the next four months. The spasms were miserable. I wish I could say my marriage grew stronger after the trauma, but everything was too overwhelming. Our marriage suffered greatly. I was diagnosed with PTSD, Anxiety, and Depression. My husband's unwillingness to understand and be patient with me made me feel very sad and alone. Yet the vision I had kept me going, along with the need to be a strong mother to my children. That dream let me know that there is a Divine Source, a Universal Source, that connects us all. It is this perseverance that I've tried to pass on to anyone who is suffering. With a little faith and perseverance, we can get through anything. As long as we can see a light at the end of the tunnel, we can keep going. It is hard. It is really hard. The recovery from all of that trauma has been harrowing. A lot of times I felt like I was in a deep dark hole. But I got through it. I made it through to the survivor's side and I am forever changed from it all. There is a light all around us, a Higher Power that is always here for us, giving us signs. We just have to slow down enough to see them and believe them.

Making This Story Your Own:

Mindy's story takes us on a journey of determination.
Take a moment, breathe, and reflect.
What stands out for you when you read her words?
Is there a situation in your life that is similar to Mindy's?
Perhaps part of her story feels connected to your own.
How can you relate her experiences to your past, present, and future?

- *My Connection to Mindy's Story* _____

_____

_____

_____

Knowing that you aren't alone, let's gently explore some other themes from Mindy's story together:

- ***Perseverance***
    - When have you been called on to persevere? How did you do it and where did the strength come from? Is perseverance a personality trait of yours? When you've persevered through challenging times, what have you noticed about yourself? What have others noticed about you? How do you feel about your determination and dedication? Is it easy or difficult to accept these qualities about yourself when other people see them in you? When that happens, what is it like to know that you and your actions are inspiring? Have you given yourself enough credit for all that you have lived through? Is there a way that you can become your own best witness... noticing and giving yourself credit where credit is due? How can you begin to truly honor your perseverance?

- ***Releasing Other's Advice, Opinions, and Expertise***
    - Whose opinions influence you? What advice or expertise impacts your decisions? The media? Is it a colleague, co-worker, or family member? Maybe a friend? When did this begin and is it still working for you? What would it look like if you didn't listen to anyone else and relied solely on your own counsel? What might happen? Can you imagine doing this for a day? A week? A month? Do you trust yourself enough to try it? Why, or why not? Do you offer your opinions, advice, and expertise? Is this solicited or unsolicited? What would it look like for you to refrain from doing this... trusting the people in your life to rely on their own counsel, too? Would trying this out be useful in any way? Would it not? Would you or anyone else benefit from this sort of trust and empowerment?

- ***Trusting in a Higher Power***
    - What gives you a sense of peace and purpose when it comes to the inexplicable situations in your life and the lives of others? Who or what do you turn to when you need strength to get through

the tough times? Where does this presence or energy exist? How do you connect to it? Are you comfortable enough with this connection to allow others the space to cultivate and create their own connection... even if it is no connection? Thinking of this as a mutually respectful and judgement-free dynamic, how can you maintain your connection in your own unique way while allowing others to do the same?

Sacred Play Suggestions:

~ SPS #1: ~
* Four Corners *

In the room where you are sitting, let the four corners of the room represent four different things in your life that influence you. This can be friends, family members, social media groups, television shows, news anchors, celebrities, teachers, gurus, spirit guides, energies, etc. Be as broad or specific as you want and assign each to a corner. For example, the corner closest to you could represent your spouse, another corner your mother, another the news, and the fourth corner could represent a teacher. When you have your four corners decided, write them down below.

- _____ #_____
- _____ #_____
- _____ #_____
- _____ #_____

Next, write these four names or entities on different pieces of paper and tape the papers up in their respective corners. Now, stand in the middle of the room and rank them in order of influence from one to four, with one being the most influential and four being the least. You can jot these numbers down on the lines provided above. OK, now you are going to work your way around the room. As you stand in each corner, fill-in and journal around the following questions.

#1.

Why does_____ have such influence?

_____

_____

When did this start?

_____

_____

_____

Do I still want or need this?

_____

_____

#2.

Why does_____**have such influence?**

_____

_____

When did this start?

_____

_____

Do I still want or need this?

_____

_____

#3.

Why does_____**have such influence?**

_____

_____

When did this start?

_____

_____

Do I still want or need this?

_____

_____

#4.

Why does _____ **have such influence?**

_____

_____

When did this start?

_____

_____

Do I still want or need this?

_____

_____

Alright, what came to the surface after taking some time to determine why these things are so influential and if you even need them anymore?

What bubbled up, Buttercup?

_____

_____

_____

Get ready to switch roles. Yep, you are going to step into the consciousness of this fab four. Take a second and ground yourself. Breathe deeply and feel your feet firmly on the floor with your heart and head open to receive. Start with #1, and journal answers to the following questions from each perspective.

#1. *Step into the consciousness of this person or entity and answer from their perspective. Put your name in the first blank and then fill in the rest as if they are talking through you.*

I have such influence in _____**'s life because**_____

_____.

I started to have influence in _____**'s life when** _____

_____.

Although I still want to support _____**, I trust that she no longer needs**

460

my influence as much because _____

_____.

#2. *Step into the consciousness of this person or entity and answer from their perspective. Put your name in the first blank and then fill in the rest as if they are talking through you.*

I have such influence in _____**'s life because**_____

_____.

I started to have influence in _____**'s life when** _____

_____.

Although I still want to support _____**, I trust that she no longer needs**

my influence as much because _____

_____.

#3. *Step into the consciousness of this person or entity and answer from their perspective. Put your name in the first blank and then fill in the rest as if they are talking through you.*

I have such influence in _____**'s life because**_____

_____.

I started to have influence in _____**'s life when** _____

_____.

Although I still want to support _____**, I trust that she no longer needs**

my influence as much because _____

_____.

#4. *Step into the consciousness of this person or entity and answer from their perspective. Put your name in the first blank and then fill in the rest as if they are talking through you.*

I have such influence in _____**'s life because**_____

_____.

I started to have influence in _____**'s life when** _____

_____.

Although I still want to support _____, **I trust that she no longer needs**

my influence as much because _____

_____.

How was that? Sometimes stepping into another's consciousness can give us increased understanding, empathy, and compassion. You know yourself. You know what you need. You know if the influencing factors of your life are in alignment with your Greatest and Highest Good. You do YOU, babe. You are perfection. Thank you! Love you! Oh, don't forget, you still have papers taped in the corners.

~ SPS #2: ~
* Sacral Chakra *

In many different healing traditions and modalities, the anatomical structures of the body are known to have psychological contributions. Esoteric Healing, a modality of Energy Work based on the writings of Alice Bailey that I talk about a lot in this book, teaches that our reproductive organs correlate to the energy center in the body known as the Sacral Chakra. The Sacral Chakra lies on the midline, or center of the body, and is located in the mid-belly between the base of the spine and the navel. The color associated with the Sacral Chakra is orange. This Chakra receives energy from the back and gives energy from the front. Pause, and as you take a few deep breaths, visualize a radiant orange beam of light streaming from this place on your body. With each in-breath and out-breath, let the light become brighter at your lower back and abdomen. Now, let the orange beam shift in texture and quality to reflect how you give and receive from this energy center. What do you notice?

- In back, where I **receive** energy, my Sacral Chakra is _____
  _____

- In front, where I **give** energy, my Sacral Chakra is _____
  _____

Notice how I haven't said what this Energy Center is all about yet? That was on purpose. Even if you are a Chakra Expert, sometimes it can be helpful to just *feel* the energy versus adding in the complexity of our brains 'knowing what we know' about it. OK, what is the Sacral Chakra all about? Well, to be really thorough, it would take pages and pages… and please, continue this further and do your own research for a deeper dive. But in very simple terms, our Sacral Chakra is all about birthing relationships, creativity, sexuality, self-worth, a connection to Mother Earth, and our ability to manifest what we want for our lives. See why I didn't say anything before? That is a shed load to think about! With just those basics, once again connect into the energy of your Sacral Chakra and feel the quality of the energy from front to back. If it helps, close your eyes and visualize the orange light beaming from your lower back and belly. What do you notice?

- Holding an awareness of my **relationships,** my Sacral Chakra _____
  _____

- Holding an awareness of my **creativity,** my Sacral Chakra _____
  _____

- Holding an awareness of my **sexuality,** my Sacral Chakra _____
  _____

- Holding an awareness of my **self-worth,** my Sacral Chakra _____
  _____

- Holding an awareness of my **connection to Mother Earth,** my Sacral Chakra _____
  _____

- Holding an awareness of my **ability to manifest** what I want in my life, my Sacral Chakra _____
  _____

Our ovaries, fallopian tubes, womb, birth canal, and vagina are all energetically influenced by the Sacral Chakra. That is how the superpowers of creativity, sexuality, manifestation, and connection are all *birthed into being* from our consciousness. If the Sacral Chakra is open, balanced, and vibing at its highest conscious expression, we are golden, birthing away all day every day. However, living this experience called *life* puts nicks, dents, filters, dirt, and muck all over that sacred orange light beam. This sludge prevents it and us from shining to the fullest. So, what do we do about it? We take our energetic sovereignty into our own hands and we balance that shit with love. Juuuust checking if you are still with me...☺ Seriously though, you are a Goddess. Try it and see what happens. FYI, if you have had any of these parts of your reproductive system removed, that is OK. The energy of your anatomy is still there, wildly powerful and potently present! Let's start with our wombs. This is the magickal spot for all new life to grow with safety, security, and protection. Our wombs are the sacred incubators which hold the promise and reality of new life being birthed into existence. Again, take a few deep breaths. Close your eyes if it helps and hover your hands about six inches above your womb. When you feel a connection, or even if you don't, intentionally send love into your womb. What do you notice?

- By giving love to my **womb,** I receive _____
  _____

Branch out to the right and left, and as your hands continue to hover… gently move them back and forth, connecting into your fallopian tubes. These regal roads are like miniscule superhighways, hosting the initial travels of new life into the physical world. Like your favorite paths in nature, these two passageways are to be honored, loved, and cherished. As you continue to connect, intentionally send love into your fallopian tubes, paying close attention to the differences and similarities felt on both the left and right side. What do you notice?

- By giving love to my **fallopian tubes,** I receive _____

_____

_____

Now, feel your ovaries. These precious glands contain the seeds for new life and these seeds include the divine blueprints for both human and idea children alike. Take a few deep breaths and allow your hands to provide an open conduit of connection from your awareness to your right and left ovaries. Sense if there are any differences or messages coming to you from either side and intentionally send love into each one. What do you notice?

- By giving love to my **ovaries,** I receive _____

_____

_____

Let your hands come together and move in a downward motion as if following the path of your birth canal. As your hands hover, envision this sacred space of your body as the final preparation place for new life before entering into the physical world. See the layers of love, wisdom, nourishment, protection, and guidance in this great canal. When your connection to this part of your body feels strong, intentionally send love into your birth canal. As you do this, imagine being held and rocked within the warmth of this soft darkness and prepare to rebirth yourself. What do you notice?

- By giving love to my **birth canal,** I receive _____

_____

_____

Lastly, let your hands hover over and send energy into your vagina. This beautiful entryway is the welcoming point for new life to enter your body and the exit point for new life to enter the world. This miraculous gateway is designed to offer bliss as an invitation to creation. Visualize a new, aligned connection to this part of your body. A relationship that is completely yours. A bond that is empowered and emboldened. When this new connection feels strong and full, intentionally send love into your labia, clitoris, and vaginal opening. What do you notice?

- By giving love to my **vagina,** I receive _____

_____

_____

Let's put this all together and see if anything has shifted with our Sacral Chakras. Connect back into that vivid orange beam of light coming in through your lower back and going out through your lower abdomen. Take another deep breath, and in your mind, begin to energetically knit these pieces together. Start at your back, where the Sacral energy is received. Connect that Sacral energy into your right ovary, down into the right fallopian tube, over into the left fallopian tube, and on to the left ovary. Continue on and bring all of those energies together, letting them rest and replenish in your womb. Once refreshed, take another deep breath and bring the energy down into the birth canal and on to your vagina, finally tethering it to the front of your Sacral Chakra. Hold this space for just a moment as you visualize your anatomy and your Chakra coming into their highest conscious expression of love, whatever that may be for you at this moment. What do you notice?

- In back, where I **receive** energy, my Sacral Chakra is _____
  _____

- In front, where I **give** energy, my Sacral Chakra is _____
  _____

I love you. Have I told you that lately? Well, I do. I am also super grateful that you took this time for yourself. Last step, what are you going to birth? Read the following statement aloud and see if anything else rises to the surface.

**With the energy and wisdom of my Sacral Chakra,
Ovaries, Fallopian Tubes, Womb, Birth Canal, and Vagina,
I give Birth and Rebirth to my Superpowers of
Creativity, Sexuality, Connection, and Manifestation.**

_____

_____

~ SPS #3: ~
* Self-Love *

When you gift self-care and self-love to yourself, it is a radical act of unconditional love for the world. I know it may sound contradictory to what you've been told, but it is true. We are all connected. All of life. When your heart beats with joy, so does mine. When you ache with loneliness and despair, I do, too. The collected feelings and sensations we get from others may not even register most of the time. But when you intentionally open your awareness and connect to another living being, you can definitely share in the energy of their emotional, mental, and spiritual resonance. When was the last time you got a *feeling* from someone and thought, "I am going to keep my distance." What about when you followed your intuition and got in touch with a friend only to have them say, "Thank you, I needed to hear that!" It goes the other way as well, and people pick up on these subtle nuances from us. When was the last time someone called or texted out of the blue with just the right message at just the right time? In fact, we are all so good at this, we forget to remember how sensitive we are to one another. Peace and joy are good for us. Connection and love are transitive. When we feel these feelings, it is easier for us to share them in intentional and empowering ways. When we feel better, we do better. Everything benefits. When your cup is full of self-love, it doth runneth over… and it doesn't take loads of money or time to get there. Take a look at the following list. Choose at least one thing to do in the next hour, and two things to do in the next 24 hours. Spend a few minutes thinking about each suggestion. Some of them might not feel like an act of self-love at first. As you connect in deeper to yourself and to the potential, see if any shifts or insights come forward.

Suggestion #1. Call an old friend.

- Who would you call? _____
- Why would it be good to talk to them? _____
  _____

Suggestion #2. Spend 20 minutes with someone and give them your undivided attention.

- Who would you spend time with? _____
- Why would this be a good idea? _____
  _____

Suggestion #3. Silently observe something beautiful for 5 minutes.

- What would you observe? _____
- How would this be beneficial? _____
  _____

Suggestion #4. Send loving energy into Mother Earth.

- How would you do this? _____
- Why would this be good for you? _____
  _____

Suggestion #5. Write yourself a love note.

- What loving words do you want and need to hear? _____
  _____
- How would this help? _____
  _____

Suggestion #6. Invite a new friend to lunch.

- Who would you invite? _____
- Why is this a good idea? _____
  _____

Suggestion #7. Surprise a friend by gifting them something of yours.

- What do you have to give? _____

- How would this help with feeling loved and connected? _____
  _____

Suggestion #8. Sing and dance for 10 minutes.

- Where can you do this? _____

- How would this bring relaxation? _____
  _____

Suggestion #9. Look at old photos.

- What photos would you like to look at? _____

- How would this bring joy and peace? _____
  _____

Suggestion #10. Take a walk.

- Where would you walk? _____

- Why is this a good idea? _____
  _____

Choose one suggestion that you are going to try right now, and two that you will do in the next 24 hours. Pay close attention to how these three acts of love and self-love affect you and the world around you.

Self-Love Suggestion #1: _____

My self-care and self-love are radical acts of unconditional love for the world.

I know this to be true because _____
_____

Self-Love Suggestion #2: _____

My self-care and self-love are radical acts of unconditional love for the world.

I know this to be true because _____
_____

Self-Love Suggestion #3: _____

My self-care and self-love are radical acts of unconditional love for the world.

I know this to be true because _____

_____

Keep going! Use these suggestions and come up with your own to work with over the following week. Small, dedicated acts of love and self-love can be powerful beyond measure. Repeating them solidifies the belief system that peace, joy, relaxation, love, and connection are natural ways of being… not just something reserved for special occasions. We deserve this every moment of every day… as does every other living thing! Thank you for loving yourself. When you do that, I feel it. And I love you right back!

~ SPS #4: ~
* Fire *

Fire is powerful. No doubt about that. It is destructive, purifying, illuminating, and regenerative. It turns raw food into cooked food. It keeps us warm when it's cold outside. No matter how mystical and magickal fire is to us, we humans are inexplicably drawn to it. Safety, connection, transformation, and inspiration are just a few of the things we can feel while sitting around a fire. As we watch it burn, fire connects us to the wild, fierce, and dangerous sides of ourselves. Listening to its soft crackle, fire connects us to the peaceful, relaxed, and quiet inner worlds of solitude. Even the smells and tastes of fire are evocative. Having a big bonfire out in nature is wonderful, but the simple act of lighting a candle at home can be pretty wonderful, too. There are many ways through ritual and ceremony to light and use candles in order to bring forth specific energy. Let's try one that utilizes intention and visualization. Get a candle and something to light it with. A good friend of mine always uses matches. For her, the fire at the end of the matchstick represents the origination of fire as a bolt of lightning striking and setting fire to a tree. If you have matches, great! If you don't, use what you've got. Most important, stay smart and safe. Burn only candles that are appropriate and make sure the area where you place your candle is clear of anything flammable. When you are ready, strike your match. As you light the candle, verbally call out three intentions: one for yourself, one for your loved ones, and one for the world. Record them below.

My Three Intentions

For Myself_____

For My Loved Ones_____

For the World_____

Sit for a minute or two, allowing the soft light to illuminate the space of the room and the space of your heart. As you gaze at the flame, bring awareness to your breathing and - with an imaginary paintbrush - connect your heart to your mind and Soul. Now with this imaginary paintbrush, paint out in all directions. Up, down, left, right, forward, and backward… connect your awareness to everything. Let your spirit soar as it travels all the way around the globe, sharing your loving energy throughout all space and time. Connect up and down to Source and Center. Connect left and right to the Feminine and Masculine energies. Connect front and back to past and future. Let the energy spiral in and out of you in waves, curving upon itself as it comes and goes through your consciousness. When you feel a connection to every living thing that has ever - or will ever - witness the beauty of fire, set your three intentions one more time.

My Three Intentions

For Myself_____

For My Loved Ones_____

For the World_____

As you create your intentions, say them aloud and visualize them already happening. When you are finished, say "Thank you." You can either blow your candle out as a final step or leave it burning. Just know that whatever you do, you have shifted energy, opened awareness, and lifted spirits by intentionally declaring love for yourself, others, and the world. Thank you. Love you!

~ SPS #5 ~
* Dreamscape *

Mindy's dream while waiting on the operating table to deliver her daughter via emergency Cesarean was potent and powerful, so much so that she attributes the clear vision of holding and smiling at her infant daughter as being the beginning of her very long and grueling healing process. Mindy gifts us a wonderful example of how prophetic and shamanic our dreams can be. Those who have come before us knew of this power and they took it very seriously. Throughout the ages, our abilities for psychic visioning through the dreamscape have been respected and regarded as not only compelling information, but formidable counsel! All the way back to the Upper Paleolithic period, our early ancestors and ancestresses were aware of the messages, prophecy, and guidance that came through dreams. Up until a few thousand years ago, many of these early civilizations depicted the importance of dreams by carving and creating figures of women sleeping. In her amazing book, *Shakti Woman: Feeling Our Fire, Healing Our World: The New Female Shamanism,* author Vicki Noble talks about many pertinent things, but her chapter on dreamwork - specifically women's dreamwork - is not to be missed. The following exercise is based on Vicki's suggestions for interpreting dreams. You can work with a recurring dream or the dream you had last night. If it is difficult to remember your dreams, try keeping a notebook close to your bedside so that you can record specifics about your dreams as soon as you wake up. Once you start creating space within your consciousness to remember your dreams, it should become easier to retain some or most of the information. Alternately, if you prefer to use a recent vision or recurring daydream, that is fine, too. When you are ready, get comfortable and allow your breathing to become slow and deep. Give yourself permission to have an experience and know that whatever presents itself is just *information*. When you have your chosen dream or vision, prepare to step into that world. Let your mind relax as it sets the stage and recreates an entry point for you to enter into the dreamscape. Record anything you would like as it comes up or after you have finished the activity.

Enter the dream with your senses ready to receive.

- Check in with what you see, hear, smell, taste, and feel. _____

_____

- How much **realistic information** is in the dream and can be taken at face value? _____
  _____
  _____

- How much **unrealistic information** is in the dream and must be interpreted? _____
  _____
  _____

Associate the symbolism of the dream.

- Allow your imagination and associative mind to get active and feel into the **people** of your dream.

    - Who is there? _____
      _____

    - What does each person make you think, feel, and want? _____
      _____
      _____
      _____

    - What does each person represent? _____
      _____
      _____

- Feel into the **places** of your dream.

    - Where are you? _____
      _____

    - What does the location make you think, feel, and want? _____
      _____
      _____
      _____

- What does each place represent? _____
  _____
  _____

- Feel into the **objects** of your dream.
  - What things do you notice? _____
    _____
  - What do these things make you think, feel, and want? _____
    _____
    _____
    _____
  - What does each thing represent? _____
    _____
    _____

- Feel into the **situations** of your dream.
  - What is happening? _____
    _____
  - What do these situations make you think, feel, and want? _____
    _____
    _____
    _____
  - What does each situation represent? _____
    _____
    _____

Embody the dream characters and objects.

- In your imagination, allow the people, places, things, and situations of your dream to become characters. Dialogue with them. As you make statements and ask questions, respectfully listen to their replies and answers. Record any pertinent information below.

  _____
  _____
  _____
  _____

- Now, step in and blend the consciousness of the people, places, things, and situations of your dream(s) with your own. Let them speak through you. Allow them to make statements and ask questions while you offer respectful replies and answers. Record any pertinent information below.

  _____
  _____
  _____
  _____

Intentionally change or revisit the dream for more information.

- Calmly re-enter the dream narrative and make lucid choices that create different dream scenarios. From this empowered place, imprint your desires onto the dream for new outcomes.

  o What dream dynamics changed? _____
  _____

  o What was the new outcome? _____
  _____

Wow! Our dreams are not only powerful, they also have much wisdom and guidance to share. Because of their power, some of us have been taught to fear our dreams... internalizing every aspect of the narrative as an indicator of a bad omen or something wrong with us. When we can release that old story, we can step into a new way of relating to and being in relationship with our dreams. Hey, we are with them every night so we might as well enjoy it! Dream big, Sister. I will, too. Love you! Thank you for dreaming with me!

Crystal Love: Mindy's Crystal is Howlite (***howl**-ahyt*). Howlite is oftentimes overlooked because of its subtle coloring, yet it is a wonderfully calming, inspiring, and encouraging stone. Howlite slows us down to clearly communicate, prepares us to receive, and links us to the wisdom of our past lives by strengthening our multi-dimensional memories. A huge benefit for conflict resolution, Howlite helps us to dissolve our internal anger and rage while deflecting the anger and rage directed towards us from outside sources. Also use Howlite to help identify your positive personal traits and innate decency as you formulate the goals and ambitions needed to fulfill your Divine Purpose. A promoter of the Divine Feminine, Holwite will increase your natural connection to your women's wisdom, intuition, and instinct. As a promoter of the Divine Masculine, Howlite can create a protective and strong container around people, places, and things. Put all of this together, and you've got a stone that helps with stress, encourages emotional release, alleviates insomnia, and teaches patience. Get some Howlite in your pocket... heck, get some in both pockets and see what kind of magick this powerful and understated healer has in store for you.

<u>Suggested Reading</u> to Awaken Your Timeless, Fertile, Connected, and Empowered Self, *Uncoiling the Snake: Ancient Patterns in Contemporary Women's Lives* by Vicki Noble.

Monika

I grew up about ten kilometers outside of Stockholm. As a child, my father worked during the day and my mother worked as a night nurse for the elderly. My siblings and I never saw her as a working mom. With her schedule, she would arrive home at 7:00 in the morning and she didn't leave the house until later in the evening. She did this for fourteen nights a month, and in Sweden that is considered working full-time. My mother took care of everything for us. If she was exhausted, we never saw it. I don't know how she managed. When we came home from school, she was always there to listen to everything we had to tell her. I loved school. It was very easy for me. We have a system in Sweden where children go to school for nine years from age seven to sixteen. Continuing with your education in what we would call Senior High School is usually reserved for students who are on an exclusive academic track. I was definitely on that track, but I did not continue on it right away. When I was fifteen, I turned into a real teenager. It was 1964 and I wanted to wear makeup. I wanted freedom. I wanted to party. Sometimes, I didn't even go to school. At sixteen, I decided to quit and not go on for the final three years. This was considered acceptable because most children only did the nine years of schooling. It was at this age that I got a job and moved out of my parent's house. It felt so good to be able to support myself. I loved it! I loved living on my own. My family was very religious, and we were part of a very strict church. The rules were no makeup, no earrings, nothing that could change the way God had created me. I wanted to break free from that. When I moved out, I dyed my long blonde hair dark black. It was so dark! Even my ears got dyed black. My father was so upset with me that he tried to wash the dye out himself, but couldn't. It was my revolution. When I turned eighteen, I realized that I wanted to go on to Senior High School. I continued working full-time and went to school part-time in the evenings. It took six years to complete the three-year curriculum. When I went back to school, it was *for me*. I wanted to go further and create more opportunities for myself. I had my own life and I knew that I could have more freedom to decide my future by being successful in school. When I was finished, I decided to keep studying, and I went to Stockholm University. The more I studied, the better my jobs got. I was on my own for about nine years when I met my husband at a dance restaurant. Most people who went there didn't eat, they just danced and drank beer; yet here sat this handsome man eating a salad! That caught my attention. I was with a girlfriend and when I pointed him out to her she said, "I know him, we are in school together!" She introduced me, and from that night we have been together. I knew when I saw him that this man was going to be my husband. We talked from the beginning about getting married. He was very keen on that because I think he knew as well. Today, we've been married almost 45 years. The same thing happened when it came to children. We didn't even discuss it. We just knew that we wanted to have a family. Balancing my work with motherhood wasn't easy, but we did it. My husband and I agreed to share responsibilities 50-50 when it came to parenting. We wanted to be very equal. At that time, it was not so typical for men and women to share parenting responsibilities. My husband and I were very unique. When our daughter was in school, I would drop her off in the morning and he would pick her up. This was good for his company and his fellow employees to see a father taking care of his child. It sent a good message that taking care of your children is very important. I know I missed a lot. When our daughter was very young, she did go to a nanny during the day. She took her first steps with this other family and there were times when I was jealous. But I wanted to work. It was very important that my husband and I both worked. We wanted to have more children, but when our daughter was just a few years old we realized that was not going to happen. In those days, there wasn't the medical support or fertility help that we have today. I just accepted that I could not have another baby. When we realized this, I thought maybe I would like to begin studying again. I applied to the Stockholm School of Economics. At the time, I didn't really understand how prestigious this school was or how difficult it was to get accepted. When I got in, I wasn't surprised. I knew I had the scores and the points. During our studies, my fellow students would ask me to join them at the pub after class and I would say, "no." It wasn't in my best interest to do that. Not only was I ten years older than most of them with a young child at home, I wanted more for myself and I knew I was capable of more. When I graduated, I went back to the same company that I had been working for, but in a new position. I returned as the Head of Accounting for the Swedish Dairies Association. After that, my next promotion was to Chief Financial Officer and I worked for this company for 37 years. Throughout my career, I did have the support of friends and family, although there were many questions about why I wanted to keep advancing. I can remember my mother asking me why I wanted to study so much when I was already a secretary. To her, being a secretary was a very good job, and it was for me as well, but I had such a passion for learning and knowledge. During coffee and lunchtime breaks at my company, I would hear other employees discussing literature, current events, and different philosophies… things I had never heard of. I wanted to be a part of that. I wanted to know those things, too. I didn't want to be the one questioning what everything was. I loved these new and interesting conversations. I read all of the books I could find written by Noble Prize winners. It was sometimes difficult reading, but I wanted to know so much more. For younger women today who are entering business or who are businesswomen - don't ever lose your passion for learning, don't lose your courage, and don't take any shit. In Swedish it is said differently, but it essentially means the same thing: take no shit. In my studies and work, I have seen sexism. I haven't experienced it directly, but I have heard other students and colleagues talk about how hurtful it is. My fellow female students would say, "If I am equally qualified, there should be no problem!" I agree. We can't let that or any other pressure wear us down. We must believe in ourselves, our education, and our experience. The more we do this, the more we can claim our strengths. We should all let people know how good we are at what we do without feeling too shy or ashamed. This is not bragging; it is about owning our hard work and success. We cannot be afraid of our own accomplishments. My husband and I have worked very hard to give this sense of independence and confidence to our daughter. We were dedicated to bringing her up in this way so that she would have the courage to follow her heart. In this way, my professional life has really influenced my mothering. To give our daughter the opportunities and life experiences of studying internationally and traveling, we had to work hard. It has been worth it. When my daughter focuses her mind on something, she goes for it and won't stop until she has accomplished her goal. She is like me in that way. She is so brave, and I am so proud of her. She lives in a different country now, which is hard because I would like to have her closer. Yet, I like to think that our traveling as a family helped her have the courage to do this. Early in my career, I used to feel that if women didn't work outside of the home they were missing something. I feel differently now. I understand what an important job it is to take care of our children. Although I would ask all women to think about this, regardless of where they work: please plan for your financial future. My feelings about this come from being a mother and my background in economics. We still live in a time when - if someone isn't earning a paycheck - little gets put back for their retirement. That makes us so very vulnerable. As women, we must find ways to ensure that we have financial freedom and security for our present and our future. That way we are not dependent on anyone or anything. We can still have our hopes and dreams and be realistic, too. We can find ways to take better care of ourselves. When we do that, we are actually taking better care of everyone.

Making This Story Your Own:

Monika's story brings up topics for us to look at more deeply.
Take a moment, breathe, and reflect.
What stands out for you when you read her words?
Is there a situation in your life that is similar to Monika's?

Perhaps part of her story feels connected to your own.
How can you relate her experiences to your past, present, and future?

- My Connection to Monika's Story _____

_____

_____

_____

_____

Knowing that you aren't alone, let's gently explore some other themes from Monika's story together:

- **Doing Things for YOU**
  - When was the last time you made a commitment to yourself? Did you follow through? Why, or why not? What happened next? How did you feel and what did you do? Is there a new idea or opportunity tugging at your consciousness and asking to be given attention? If so, what is it and how have you made it real? Have you told someone? Have you done research? Have you checked the calendar? How are you making a plan to fulfill this personal commitment? Does focusing on doing something for yourself feel empowering? Why, or why not? What are a few things you can do right now to begin devoting time and energy back towards yourself?

- **Trust in Yourself, Your Education, and Your Experience**
  - Do you openly claim your strengths? When asked, are you honest about your levels of expertise, experience, and education? If not, can you determine why you are reticent to openly talk about your talents and abilities? When did this begin and does this happen all the time, or only in certain situations? Does downplaying your gifts offer any advantages in your professional and personal relationships? What about disadvantages? What would need to happen for you to feel comfortable enough to always share openly about yourself and what you bring to the table?

- **Plan for Your Future**
  - What comes up for you when you think about the future? Do you feel that you can prepare yourself? What about when it comes to money and finances? How empowered do you feel regarding your financial security? Is this OK with you? Would you like it to change? If so, what are a few steps you can take to attain financial freedom and financial confidence? What needs to happen and what will it look like when you feel prepared?

Sacred Play Suggestion:

~ SPS #1: ~
* Goals *

What have you always wanted to learn? A new language? A new skill? Maybe a new academic pursuit? How about traveling to a distant land? Anything goes! These are your dreams and they are valuable. Your heart's desires are important for you and for everyone because when you follow your heart, you give me permission to follow mine. Figuring out a way to make your wishes come true helps everyone else figure out how to do the same thing. What makes your breath quicken might or might not make my heart skip a beat and that isn't the point. What *is* the point is witnessing you as you work to meet your goals. The energy of self-love is all over that kind of dedication - and when you internally and externally focus on that powerful commitment, you heal the world. The people, places, and things in your life cannot help but be affected by you and what you have accomplished. So often we can convince ourselves that self-growth or attention on our wants and needs is selfish. That couldn't be further from the truth! Every time you focus on what you want and need, you fill your own cup. You raise your energy. You shift, change, and transform. When you do that, you forge a path for everyone else to do the same and people *will* pay attention. When you offer motivation and encouragement in this way you are not simply giving lip-service to an idea… you are grounding your authenticity in *action*. That action sends out a shockwave. Take a moment to think of at least five things that fall into the category of *life goals* and list them below.

What I Want for Myself
1.
2.
3.
4.
5.

How does it feel to write these things down? As you look at your list, let's keep working to identify the potential shockwaves. Remember, this dedication to the self is an act of generosity not only for you, but for everyone else in your life. Keep focusing on that if you start to feel mired down in the details.

Goal #1:

Start Date: _____

- Who will be the first to notice that I have started working on this for myself? _____

_____

- How will I inspire others by doing this for myself? _____

_____

- What will I transform in my relationships by doing this for myself? _____

_____

- What will I shift in the world by doing this for myself? _____
  _____
  _____

Goal #2:

Start Date: _____

- Who will be the first to notice that I have started working on this for myself? _____
  _____

- How will I inspire others by doing this for myself? _____
  _____
  _____

- What will I transform in my relationships by doing this for myself? _____
  _____
  _____

- What will I shift in the world by doing this for myself? _____
  _____
  _____

Goal #3:

Start Date: _____

- Who will be the first to notice that I have started working on this for myself? _____
  _____

- How will I inspire others by doing this for myself? _____
  _____
  _____

- What will I transform in my relationships by doing this for myself? _____
  _____
  _____

- What will I shift in the world by doing this for myself? _____
_____
_____

Goal #4:

Start Date: _____

- Who will be the first to notice that I have started working on this for myself? _____
_____

- How will I inspire others by doing this for myself? _____
_____

- What will I transform in my relationships by doing this for myself? _____
_____

- What will I shift in the world by doing this for myself? _____
_____

Goal #5:

Start Date: _____

- Who will be the first to notice that I have started working on this for myself? _____
_____

- How will I inspire others by doing this for myself? _____
_____
_____

- What will I transform in my relationships by doing this for myself? _____
_____
_____

- What will I shift in the world by doing this for myself? _____
_____
_____

How amazing are you? Dang, lady! Did you realize how powerful you are? I hope so, because we need you to be doing *you* - in all of your gloriousness - so that the rest of us can follow suit. OK, now let's keep grounding these five Goals so that we can get them off of this page and onto the *stage* of life.

Goal #1: _____

- What are the first 3 steps I will take to begin making this happen?

    o _____

    o _____

    o _____

- What will I notice about myself when I start working on this? _____

_____

_____

~ What is my **Goal** Mantra to remind me how important this is? ~

_____

- What will be different when I have accomplished this for myself? _____

_____

_____

Goal #2: _____

- What are the first 3 steps I will take to begin making this happen?

    o _____

    o _____

    o _____

- What will I notice about myself when I start working on this? _____

_____

_____

~ What is my **Goal Mantra** to remind me how important this is? ~

_____

- What will be different when I have accomplished this for myself? _____
  _____
  _____

Goal #3: _____

- What are the first 3 steps I will take to begin making this happen?
  - _____
  - _____
  - _____

- What will I notice about myself when I start working on this? _____
  _____
  _____

~ What is my **Goal Mantra** to remind me how important this is? ~

_____

- What will be different when I have accomplished this for myself? _____
  _____
  _____

Goal #4: _____

- What are the first 3 steps I will take to begin making this happen?
  - _____
  - _____
  - _____

- What will I notice about myself when I start working on this? _____
  _____
  _____

~ What is my **Goal Mantra** to remind me how important this is? ~

_____

- What will be different when I have accomplished this for myself? _____

_____

_____

Goal #5: _____

- What are the first 3 steps I will take to begin making this happen?

    o _____

    o _____

    o _____

- What will I notice about myself when I start working on this? _____

_____

_____

~ What is my **Goal Mantra** to remind me how important this is? ~

_____

- What will be different when I have accomplished this for myself? _____

_____

_____

Great job! Keep working with this. When *you* love yourself enough to follow through on something that sets your soul on fire… *I* watch and learn. Everyone does. If any sense of guilt or unease creeps in as you are putting *you* first, remember - when you do this for yourself, you are doing it for all of us. Thank you. I love you!

~ SPS #2: ~
* Love Yourself *

What would you say to your younger self if she were sitting next to you? From your worldly wisdom and life experience, how would you build her up so that she is prepared to become you? Take a moment and visualize yourself through the ages and stages of life. As you do this, from tiny infant to the *you* of just a few moments ago, hold yourself in light. When you are ready, create loving and compassionate messages for these different versions of you below. When you get to an age that is beyond your current years, create a loving and compassionate message to your future self.

To My Infant Self

To My Young Child Self

To My Girl Self

To My Adolescent Self

To My Teenage Self

To My Young Adult Self

To My Twenty-Five-Year-Old Self

To My Thirty-Year-Old Self

To My Forty-Year-Old Self

_____

_____

To My Fifty-Year-Old Self

_____

_____

To My Sixty-Year-Old Self

_____

_____

To My Seventy-Year-Old Self

_____

_____

To My Eighty-Year-Old Self

_____

_____

To My Ninety-Year-Old Self

_____

_____

To My One-Hundred-Year-Old Self

_____

_____

When you have all of these messages written, read them aloud as if they are one long love letter. If you can, do this while making eye contact with yourself in a mirror. When you are finished reading, place your hands on your heart and intentionally send love back to the younger versions of you. Next, send love forward to your future self. Keep these words close by as a reminder of self-love, self-dedication, and self-mastery. Finish with a big hug around your shoulders and send love into the _you_ of this present moment. Know that you are loved. I love you! I am very grateful for you, too!

~ SPS #3: ~
* Compliments *

The word *compliment* is defined as "a polite expression of praise or admiration." Forget the 'polite expression' part and think, how often do you do this? How often do you give yourself compliments where you identify and validate - with praise and admiration - something that you like about yourself? Chances are, most of us need to work out this compliment muscle. We need to get it a bit stronger so that one, it is easy to locate and two, it is strong enough to be used on a consistent basis. We come by this lack of a compliment muscle honestly. Socially and culturally, it is much more acceptable for us to connect over our faults and miseries than it is to connect over what makes us amazing and special. The sad thing is, you might never know what makes someone else so incredible because everyone is too darned scared to publicly claim their gifts. Try giving yourself a compliment right now. Express some praise and admiration for yourself out loud and see what happens. How did that feel? Now think about the last time you heard someone else giving themselves a compliment. How did that feel? While doing this exercise, bring awareness to your reactions when you hear these compliments for yourself and others. Always listen to your inner monologue and gauge whether it is accepting or judgmental. If the judgement is there, don't be critical. Those feelings might be a message that it is time to release some old ways of being that are no longer serving you. The main goal is to be gentle with yourself during this whole process. OK, ready to work out your compliment muscle?

- **Step One**: Verbally compliment yourself three times right now.

    - You can be on your own for this one. Practice with your plants and pets. They love it!

        - **Compliment #1** _____
        _____

        - **Compliment #2** _____
        _____

        - **Compliment #3** _____
        _____

- **Step Two**: Publicly compliment yourself at least three times today.

    - Give yourself a giggle and try this out with people you don't know personally. Share with the pharmacist how crafty and creative you are. Tell the coffee barista that you are so proud of yourself for finishing a project. While on the phone with a customer service representative, share a hidden talent. Slip in these opportunities for personal praise and admiration and see what happens.

        - **Public Compliment #1** _____
        _____

- **Public Compliment #2** _____

  _____

- **Public Compliment #3** _____

  _____

○ How did I feel complimenting myself in this way? _____

_____

- **Step Three**: Give someone you know a compliment within the next hour.

  ○ Pay close attention to how they receive the compliment. If they return the favor, pay close attention to how you receive the compliment.

  - **Shared Compliment** _____

    _____

  ○ How did I feel giving a compliment? _____

  _____

- **Step Four:** Over the next 24 hours, when talking to a loved one or someone you have a close relationship with, compliment them and then compliment yourself.

  ○ Good luck! You can do it! Those early belief systems of dimming our light can be powerful! Remember, we are creating a new muscle here. Give yourself loads of credit!

  - **My Compliment for Them** _____

    _____

  - **My Compliment for Me** _____

    _____

  ○ What did I learn about myself giving and receiving in this way? _____

  _____

  ○ What did I learn about others giving and receiving in this way? _____

  _____

Now, put it all together and repeat! With awareness of your feelings, give and receive compliments as much as you can and see what happens. Remember, you are fantastic! The more you own it and share it, the more others will feel comfortable owning and sharing their delicious awesomeness, too. Raise up the collective vibe, Sister. We need you! Thank you! Love you!

~ SPS #4: ~
* Earth Star Chakra *

Take your shoes off and get your bare feet on the ground or floor. Did you know we have energy centers on the bottoms of our feet? Amazing, right? These centers are places on our physical body where we can give and receive energy. Much more can also happen via these energetic channels, but for right now, let's create an awareness to intentionally open these energy centers - also known as Chakras - on our soles. (I know there is a joke here… 'sole-to-soul' and all that jazz… but I have to stay focused!) This sweet spot that connects to our toesies rests about 12 inches down in the ground and is known as our Earth Star Chakra. Is that the coolest name or what? Take a few deep breaths and allow your mind to picture what your Earth Star Chakra *looks* and *feels* like. To cultivate and strengthen this connection to these energy centers, record the details below. Draw, write, and doodle whatever comes into your heart, mind, and soul.

My Earth Star Chakra	
~Looks Like~	~Feels Like~

Now, in your imagination, see your Earth Star Chakra open to receive the energy of Mother Earth. As Mother Earth's nurturing energy spirals up your legs and into your body, take notice of what happens for you physically, emotionally, mentally and spiritually and record it below.

- As I receive nurturance from Mother Earth through my Earth Star Chakra…

    o **Physically** I notice _____

    o **Emotionally** I notice _____

    o **Mentally** I notice _____

    o **Spiritually** I notice _____

Next, we are going to allow this loving energy from Mother Earth to **activate** all of our Chakras. These Major Energy Centers are located from the base of the spine to the crown of the head and they rest on the midline of the body. In order from one to seven, they are: the Basic Chakra (also called the Root Chakra), the Sacral

Chakra, the Solar Plexus Chakra, the Heart Chakra, the Throat Chakra, the Ajna Chakra, and the Crown Chakra. Read through the following activations and answer the questions. The answers may come to you as images, sounds, feelings, smells, tastes, or an inner sense of just *knowing*.

The Basic Chakra

With awareness resting at the base of your spine, think of the color **red** and connect into your first Energy Center. See the energy of Mother Earth coming up through your **Earth Star Chakra** to activate your **Basic Chakra**.

As these energies connect, what Sacred Images come to mind?	
My Activation Image *Looks* Like	**My Activation Image *Feels* Like**

Maintaining this connection to Mother Earth, open your consciousness to *receive* from her on your next **inhale** and reciprocate by *giving energy back* to her on your next **exhale**.

With your wisdom of **Grounding, Presence,** and **Instinct**, ask from the awareness of your **Basic Chakra**: "What do I need to know at this moment at this time?"

_____

_____

The Sacral Chakra

With awareness resting at your lower abdomen, think of the color **orange** and connect into your second Energy Center. See the energy of Mother Earth coming up through your **Earth Star Chakra** to activate your **Sacral Chakra**.

As these energies connect, what Sacred Images come to mind?	
My Activation Image *Looks* Like	**My Activation Image *Feels* Like**

Maintaining this connection to Mother Earth, open your consciousness to *receive* from her on your next **inhale** and reciprocate by *giving energy back* to her on your next **exhale**.

With your wisdom of **Creativity, Fertility**, and **Connection**, ask from the awareness of your **Sacral Chakra**: "What do I need to know at this moment at this time?"

_____

_____

The Solar Plexus Chakra

With awareness resting at your navel, think of the color **yellow** and connect into your third Energy Center. See the energy of Mother Earth coming up through your **Earth Star Chakra** to activate your **Solar Plexus Chakra.**

As these energies connect, what Sacred Images come to mind?	
My Activation Image *Looks* Like	**My Activation Image *Feels* Like**

Maintaining this connection to Mother Earth, open your consciousness to *receive* from her on your next **inhale** and reciprocate by *giving energy back* to her on your next **exhale**.

With your wisdom of **Resonance, Emotional Integrity**, and **Empowerment**, ask from the awareness of your **Solar Plexus Chakra**: "What do I need to know at this moment at this time?"

_____

_____

The Heart Chakra

With awareness resting at the center of your chest, think of the color **green** and connect into your Heart Center. See the energy of Mother Earth coming up through your **Earth Star Chakra** to activate your **Heart Chakra.**

As these energies connect, what Sacred Images come to mind?	
My Activation Image *Looks* Like	**My Activation Image *Feels* Like**

Maintaining this connection to Mother Earth, open your consciousness to *receive* from her on your next **inhale** and reciprocate by *giving energy back* to her on your next **exhale**.

With your wisdom of **Giving and Receiving Love, Unconditional Love,** and **Divine Love,** ask from the awareness of your **Heart Chakra**: "What do I need to know at this moment at this time?"

The Throat Chakra

With awareness resting at the middle of your neck, think of the color **blue** and connect into your Throat Center. See the energy of Mother Earth coming up through your **Earth Star Chakra** to activate your **Throat Chakra**.

As these energies connect, what Sacred Images come to mind?	
My Activation Image *Looks* Like	**My Activation Image *Feels* Like**

Maintaining this connection to Mother Earth, open your consciousness to *receive* from her on your next **inhale** and reciprocate by *giving energy back* to her on your next **exhale**.

With your wisdom of **Truth, Communication,** and **Sovereignty,** ask from the awareness of your **Throat Chakra***:* "What do I need to know at this moment at this time?"

The Ajna Chakra

With awareness resting at your forehead, think of the color **purple** and connect into your Third Eye Energy Center. See the energy of Mother Earth coming up through your **Earth Star Chakra** to activate your **Ajna Chakra.**

As these energies connect, what Sacred Images come to mind?	
My Activation Image *Looks* Like	**My Activation Image *Feels* Like**

Maintaining this connection to Mother Earth, open your consciousness to *receive* from her on your next **inhale** and reciprocate by *giving energy back* to her on your next **exhale**.

With your wisdom of **Intuition**, **your Higher Self**, and **Divine Guidance**, ask from the awareness of your **Ajna Chakra**: "What do I need to know at this moment at this time?"

___

___

The Crown Chakra

With awareness resting at the crown of your head, think of the color **white** and connect into your Crown Center. See the energy of Mother Earth coming up through your **Earth Star Chakra** to activate your **Crown Chakra**.

As these energies connect, what Sacred Images come to mind?	
My Activation Image *Looks* Like	**My Activation Image *Feels* Like**

Maintaining this connection to Mother Earth, open your consciousness to *receive* from her on your next **inhale** and reciprocate by *giving energy back* to her on your next **exhale.**

With your wisdom of **Bliss**, **your Divine Purpose**, and **Oneness**, ask from the awareness of your **Crown Chakra**: "What do I need to know at this moment at this time?"

___

___

You are rocking this Earth Star Activation! How do you feel? Let's put it all together. Go back and read through all of your words and look at your eight drawings. As a final step, speak the words of wisdom from each Chakra and complete this process by declaring your next best step for embodying this activation. Don't forget, I love you! Thank you for doing this!

With my wisdom of ***Grounding*, *Presence*, and *Instinct*,** I AM

___

With my wisdom of ***Creativity*, *Fertility*, and *Connection***, I AM

___

With my wisdom of *Resonance, Emotional Integrity, and Empowerment*, I AM

_____

With my wisdom of *Giving and Receiving Love, Unconditional Love, and Divine Love*, I AM

_____

With my wisdom of *Truth, Communication, and Sovereignty*, I AM

_____

With my wisdom of *Intuition, my Higher Self, and Divine Guidance*, I AM

_____

With my wisdom of *Bliss, my Divine Purpose, and Oneness*, I AM

_____

~ SPS #5: ~
Money Mantras

Let's talk money. Monika so wisely reminds us that our financial freedom, security, and responsibility are under our control. Yet money - like politics, religion, and education - is such a mercurial and secretive subject. It drives us. It can fill us with bliss and comfort. It can reduce us to a terrified heap on the floor. It can make us feel generous. It can make us feel bitter. We have such interesting vernacular around it, too. From "I'm gonna make it rain in here!" to "He would squeeze a buffalo nickel to make it shit." Money drives how we talk, feel, engage, and relate. So how do you feel about money? Not in the sense of "Well, I like it when I have it and don't like it when I don't," but how does your relationship to money - even the hidden aspects of your belief systems around money - drive you? Hopefully, this activity will provide a small glimpse of awareness into a very, very large topic. If something really resonates, maybe it is a clue to explore further. For now, let's see what comes up. Take a moment and journal for a few minutes on the following two phrases. Remember, don't censor. Someone else's voice may be in there driving your ideas and beliefs about money and you may not even know it! This is the time to excavate and exorcise for your highest good.

Money is the root of all evil.

_____

_____

Money makes the world go around.

_____

_____

What came up? Were there any surprises? Based on what you wrote, can you create a new Money Mantra that is more in alignment with you and your beliefs?

My Money Mantra

_____

OK, let's keep digging. How we grew up and our parent's beliefs and behaviors around money can have a big effect on us. Sometimes we don't even realize that we are running those old programs. Take your time to journal and reflect on the following.

- What are your earliest memories regarding money and finances? _____
_____
_____
_____

- What **positive** things did your parents and caregivers pass on to you regarding money and finances?
_____
_____
_____

- What **negative** things did your parents and caregivers pass on to you regarding money and finances?
_____
_____
_____

Did anything insightful come to the surface from these questions? When you think about these early experiences around money, how have they shaped your belief systems today and are these belief systems still working for you? Can these old stories be turned into new narratives? Give it a try. See what comes up. Don't edit. Let it flow and see what happens as you begin to create this new relationship with money.

Today, I Claim as My Money Narrative…

_____
_____
_____

OK, now we are going to switch gears as we tunnel and dig a bit more. Journal around the statements below.

Money equals power.

_____

_____

Money equals greed.

_____

_____

Money equals transformation.

_____

_____

Money equals survival.

_____

_____

Money equals freedom.

_____

_____

Do some of the statements resonate more than the others? As your feelings and ideas came up, did any offer helpful awareness? Can you create a new statement for yourself that is even more in alignment with your financial values?

<u>My Financial Values</u>

_____

_____

Lastly, does it feel like a fit to shift your money awareness to an awareness of abundance? How do those two words - money and abundance - work for you? Can they be interchangeable and mutually reciprocal? Does one flow more easily into the other? What benefit would it be to blend your financial consciousness with your abundance consciousness? Journal for a few minutes on the following Abundance Affirmations. Again, no editing or censoring. Be gentle with yourself.

Infinite abundance is mine.

_____

_____

I attract wealth and prosperity in all my relations.

_____

_____

All of my needs are always met by my understanding of abundance.

_____

_____

I AM Infinitely abundant.

_____

_____

Last time I ask this for this activity, promise! What came up? Do these Affirmations resonate with you? Why, or why not? Can you create an Abundance Affirmation that is in alignment with your relationship to money, wealth, and prosperity?

<u>My Abundance Affirmation</u>

_____

_____

Now, go back and locate your four new money statements from this activity and write them below.

- My **Money Mantra** _____
- My **Money Narrative** _____
- My **Financial Values** _____
- My **Abundance Affirmation** _____

Can these four lines become your new Money Mission Statement? Are there still revisions needed? If so, think a bit more and see what else comes up. When you feel that you have four empowered and authentic statements, write them below. Way to go! Thank you for taking this time for _you_! Love you!

My Money Mission Statement

_____

_____

_____

_____

Crystal Love: Monika's Crystal is Pyrite (*pie*-rahyt). Pyrite is commonly known as fool's gold, but that silly label couldn't be further from the truth! Not a fool at all, this stone is a fantastic protector against negativity, a great guardian against pollutants, a powerful stimulator of the intellect, and a mighty cheerleader when it comes to reminding us that we are truly the creatrixes of our own wealth. Helping us to see the higher truths of words, situations, and actions, Pyrite leads by example with its unwavering refusal to be seen as less-than. Allow its golden warmth to connect you to the constant presence of the Sun, and just like the reliable solar energies, use Pyrite for the patience and security needed to let things unfold naturally. Known to some as a 'Stone of Ambition and Commitment,' allow Pyrite to infuse you with glowing confidence so that you can follow through and complete your goals. With a close connection to creative potential, this stone also continues to break down barriers while teaching us to identify the beauty within all disciplines of thought and expression. Get a piece of Pyrite in your pocket if you need some extra courage to live boldly and to stand up for what you believe in.

Suggested Reading to Develop your Inner Corporate Goddess, *Sacred Commerce: Business as a Path of Awakening* by Matthew and Terces Engelhart

Kristine

Having children has been my most empowering experience of womanhood. They have definitely taken me on a journey of becoming who I am. Through them, I have gone from only trusting in the Western Medical Model to now trusting that I know best when it comes to my health. With my first pregnancy, I was so scared the whole time because everything I encountered was fear-based. It was as if had to go to a doctor because I was 'sick'. Instead of being viewed as natural, being pregnant felt like a condition. Even trying to get pregnant was hard. Without the proper knowledge of what my body could do, I was convinced that I had to be helped by medical intervention. I felt like I couldn't do it on my own. That was my state of mind. In the end, for all three pregnancies, we got pregnant on our own. It was when we were trying to get pregnant with our second child, doing all the fertility treatments, that I finally said "no." Up until that point, it felt like I was on this conveyor belt of: see the doctor, take this medicine, see the doctor again. When I changed my mindset, everything else changed, too. I did acupuncture. I got a book about natural fertility. And it happened. I got pregnant on my own. I guess I needed to do those things to start trusting myself, to start trusting in my body, and to start trusting in nature. I no longer needed medicine as a crutch. By my third pregnancy, I just enjoyed the feeling of being healthy. I had faith that my body knew what it was supposed to do. I was confident that I was growing this baby and taking care of her in the most perfect way possible. I had a natural birth at home, and it was amazing. I could eat and walk around. I wasn't strapped to machines. There was no waiting for the doctor. There was no pressure. I had all the time in the world for my body to do what it needed to do. That experience opened my eyes so much. If I could birth a baby on my own, what else could I do? How else could I begin to heal my body? I wondered if perhaps I was wrong about my need for Western Medicine, maybe I was also wrong about how we were treating my son's asthma. I started to look at the foods we were eating. I learned that plants have enough protein, nutrients, and fiber to completely replace animal products. This opened me up to a new world. For the first time, I began realizing that we really are capable of healing ourselves. We don't have to rely on medicine anymore as our only treatment for dis-ease. Now in my family, if someone gets a cold, we make a high vitamin C smoothie or a healthy juice. Miraculously, my son's asthma is gone, my back pain is gone, and my allergies are gone. I feel like I solved a puzzle. I became vegan first and my family followed. I let my compassion and love guide me and now I feel this sense of joy because my values and my choices are in alignment. I had always felt that treating an animal like a commodity wasn't right. Now, my part in that process didn't have to be 'the norm' because consuming animal products is 'just what you do.' No longer did I have to turn off the part of me that could sense the pain, the fear, and the tears. I didn't have to keep pretending that animals didn't have feelings. I had always known this in my heart, and now I could actually act on it by making different choices for my lifestyle. I began authentically living my truth and healing my family at the same time. In that way, for me, veganism and motherhood go hand in hand. They are both about compassion and doing the right thing. I am teaching my children how they can heal themselves, and by making compassionate and informed choices, they can heal the world. I am teaching them that their actions and their words are important. My marriage is better and stronger now, too. My husband and I work together as a team. Veganism is our shared joy and passion for making the world a better place. We have let food lead us as a family, and we have met some amazing people. This is not a diet for me. This is forever. This is my way of giving back. This is my way of making a difference. At least three times a day, I choose to heal myself with my food intake. That is so empowering. Now that I have found my voice, I share this empowerment with others. It is so easy to give up and say, "One person can't make a difference." I am only one person, but I'm not alone. This web of empathy and awareness for animals is growing and it is creating big change. I've found that for myself and for others, when you let compassion lead, it isn't hard to make the right choice.

Making This Story Your Own:

Kristine's story emphasizes how compassionate choices can become a compassionate lifestyle.
Take a moment, breathe, and reflect.
What stands out for you when you read her words?
Is there a situation in your life that is similar to Kristine's?
Perhaps part of her story feels connected to your own.
How can you relate her experiences to your past, present, and future?

- *My Connection to Kristine's Story* _____

_____

_____

_____

_____

Knowing that you aren't alone, let's gently explore some other themes from Kristine's story together:

- **Becoming Who You Are**
    - What have been some of the most important moments of your life and how have they made you who you are today? Can you recall specific details? Thinking back to these experiences, what can you identify about yourself? How were you receptive and was your receptivity part of the significance? How were you intolerant and was your intolerance part of the significance? Reflecting on all that you have been through and experienced, what would you like next for personal development? Who would you like to become in five, ten, or twenty years? What things can you begin doing today to embrace this vision for your long-term expansion and growth?

- **Trusting in Your Body**
    - What is your relationship like with your body? Do you trust your body and think of your body as a partner? Do you not trust your body and think of your body as an adversary? Maybe it is a mixture of both? Is your body something you *have* to take care of, or do you *want* to take care of it? Does it take care of you? Where did these belief systems come from? Are they completely yours or were they given to you by an outside source? Are these beliefs and feelings about your body still serving you? If so, in what way? Is there any way you can strengthen and nurture this relationship in order to make life more enjoyable, pleasurable, and gratifying? If so, what are some things you can do?

- **Letting Love be Your Guide**
    - What is *love* to you? What is your relationship to giving and receiving love? How do you express love and how do you recognize love? Does the concept of '*letting love be your guide*' feel realistic? If so, how? Does it feel unrealistic? If so, why? Where did your ideas about love come from? What are your principles around love? Do you show your love differently to different people? Does your love depend on the situation? Do you love yourself? If so, how? Would you like your

connection to love to shift in any way? Would you like love to be present within your life and relationships in different ways? If so, how would you like it to be different and what can you do to make this happen?

Sacred Play Suggestions:

~ SPS #1: ~
* Mission Statement *

Businesses, non-profits, and organizations have Mission Statements. The definition of a Mission Statement is "a formal summary of the aims and values of a company, organization, or individual." The word individual is in the definition, yet how often do we create Mission Statements for ourselves? It can be challenging to think about. Crafting a thoughtful, easy to understand summary of our personal aims and values can seem overwhelming. Yet, when you have the time to quietly reflect… what *are* your values? What *is* the aim of your life? What are your plans for manifesting the hopes you hold for yourself, loved ones, and the world? Now quick, put that into three sentences or less… and, curtain! Just kidding. Let's do it together and let's do it in steps.

- **Step 1.** Take a moment and focus on your breathing. Take three long, deep inhales and exhales. When you are ready, imagine roots growing down from your feet into the Earth. As your roots grow, open your consciousness to receive energy from Mother Earth. This energy presents as a gentle red river of light flowing up through your feet, around your legs, and taking root at the base of your spine. When this connection feels strong, contemplate and journal for a few minutes around the following question.

    o **What am I?** _____
    _____
    _____

- **Step 2.** Focus the attention back to your breath. Take three long, deep inhales and exhales. When you are ready, imagine the softest, most comforting orange cloth lightly draping itself around your lower abdomen. Experience the smooth warmth of this fabric against your skin. Visualize the orange colors dancing around your belly and mid back. The energy flows equally in both directions. When this connection feels strong, contemplate and journal for a few minutes around the following question.

    o **What do I want?** _____
    _____
    _____

- **Step 3.** Focus the attention back to your breath. Take three long, deep inhales and exhales. When you are ready, imagine a golden yellow beam of sun hitting your navel. Feel the dependable and balanced power of this solar ray as it heats up and activates your body. Visualize tiny sparks of empowerment against your skin as the sun's dedication reaches your physical body. When this connection feels strong, contemplate and journal for a few minutes around the following question.

- **What do I feel?** _____
  _____
  _____

- **Step 4**. Focus the attention back to your breath. Take three long, deep inhales and exhales. When you are ready, imagine a bright green emerald beaming from your chest. The stone is so pure and so big that it shines out equally from the front and from the back. Like a magnifying glass, this emerald brings love into your body and supports you in giving unconditional love from your heart without sacrifice or exhaustion. When this connection feels strong, contemplate and journal for a few minutes around the following question.

  - **What do I love?** _____
    _____
    _____

- **Step 5**. Focus the attention back to your breath. Take three long, deep inhales and exhales. When you are ready, imagine an expansive blue sky coming to rest within your throat. This is the clearest, bluest sky you have ever seen. Within this space you feel peaceful, validated, and safe. Any constriction or restriction that you have felt fades away as your mind becomes bright, free, and open. When this connection feels strong, contemplate and journal for a few minutes around the following question.

  - **What do I believe?** _____
    _____
    _____

- **Step 6**. Focus the attention back to your breath. Take three long, deep inhales and exhales. When you are ready, your Higher Self comes forward and places an opulent, flawless amethyst at your mid-brow. When this happens, your entire awareness awakens and is flooded with crystal-clear wisdom and guidance. Questions no longer need answers in this space and a calm serenity cushions your spirit. When this connection feels strong, contemplate and journal for a few minutes around the following question.

  - **What do I know?** _____
    _____
    _____

- **Step 7.** Focus the attention back to your breath. Take three long, deep inhales and exhales. When you are ready, you sense your Source Energy soaring above the crown of your head. The most beautiful diamond floats delicately in the balance as it connects you to your inner Divinity. The gem reflects a dazzling spectrum of gentle violet light rays which drift down over your body. As you open to receive, pure bliss fills your consciousness. When this connection feels strong, contemplate and journal for a few minutes around the following question.

  o **What do I dream?** _____

  _____

  _____

After the seven steps, gift yourself some time for integration. Continue with an awareness of your inbreath and outbreath and as you reacclimate, gently return your attention to your physical space. When you are ready, read over what you have written in response to the questions above. Notice the themes and similarities as you pull out important words and phrases. Concentrate the essence of your writing and begin to create your Personal Mission Statement without censorship or judgement. When you are ready, write your Personal Mission Statement below. Your values, aims, plans, hopes, and dreams are amazing! This world is very lucky to have you. *I'm* very lucky to have you! Thank you for taking the time to do this! I love you!

My Personal Mission Statement

_____

_____

_____

_____

~ SPS #2: ~
* Who Are You *

Who are you? Having a Personal Mission Statement can help with that answer. But really, who are you? And who are all of these people around you? Getting to the core of who someone is takes time and dedication. For practicalities' sake, most social interactions don't allow for this type of genuine perspective to be created. What oftentimes happens is a quick presumption of who we *think* people are based on limited observations. Both sides of this dynamic have probably happened to all of us at some time or another… we either presume or get presumed. Maybe we are so used to making these assumptions that we even do it to *ourselves*. What happens when someone says, "So, tell me about *you*." Do you freeze up? Do you have a stock answer? Do you avoid the question? If you met yourself at a party, what would you think? Would you fall head over heels in love? For the very general questions below, allow anything to come up and out. See what percolates to the surface as you put pen to paper and free write on the lines. Let's answer this "Who are you?" question together.

Who are you in *body*?

- What you look like... where you are from... where you live... what your occupation is, etc. _____
_____
_____
_____

Who are you in *mind*?

- What are your thoughts and beliefs? _____
_____
_____
_____

Who are you in *heart*?

- What do you care about? _____
_____
_____
_____

Who are you in *spirit*?

- What are your philosophies and values? _____
_____
_____
_____

Great job. What do you think about your answers to the questions? Did anything surprising come up? Now let's move on to the next set and discover who are you *not*.

- **What are you *not* like?** _____
_____
_____
_____

- **What do you *not* believe in?** _____
_____
_____
_____

- What do you *not* care about? _____

  _____

  _____

- What do you *not* hold as philosophies and values? _____

  _____

  _____

Taking it a bit further than the two categories of 'I am' and 'I am not,' what part of you are you hiding? *Ewwww*...right? Who wants to go there? But our shame and guilt drive us and are a part of us just as much as the other stuff. Make a list of all the attributes and characteristics you'd rather not have on a resume. Be gentle and don't force anything. Take your time as you give these parts permission to become visible.

- What do you keep *hidden* about your body? _____

  _____

  _____

- What do you keep *hidden* about your thoughts and your past? _____

  _____

  _____

- What do you keep *hidden* about your feelings and your relationships? _____

  _____

  _____

- What do you keep *hidden* about your imperfections and mistakes? _____

  _____

  _____

Hug yourself right now. This is hard work and you deserve a hug. A *big* one. Taking all of these things that you have listed into the context that they are part of the past - and the *past* can literally mean one second ago - what do you want to inform who you are choosing to become *right now*? Try taking each of the things that came up during the previous questions - who you are, who you are not, and what you keep hidden - and look at them from the perspectives of the following questions.

What *did* I *know*?

- What were my resources? _____
  _____

- What were my strengths? _____
  _____

- What were my limitations? _____
  _____

What *do* I *know*?

- What are my resources? _____
  _____

- What are my strengths? _____
  _____

- What are my limitations? _____
  _____

What *do* I *release*?

- What are my resources? _____
  _____

- What are my strengths? _____
  _____

- What are my limitations? _____
  _____

What *do* I *choose*?

- What are my resources? _____
  _____

- What are my strengths? _____
  _____

- What are my limitations? _____
  _____

From this empowered place, when you take into consideration all that you are, all that you are not, all that you release, and all that you choose… Who are you? Besides being someone that I love and that am super grateful for… and other than being *totally freaking **amazing!*** Who are you?

I AM…

_____
_____
_____
_____
_____
_____

~ SPS #3: ~
* The Magician *

In the book, *King, Warrior, Magician, Lover: Rediscovering the Archetypes of the Mature Masculine* by Robert Moore and Douglas Gillette, four main archetypes are given for both the Immature and Mature Masculine. In other *Soul-to-Sisterhood* Sacred Play Suggestions, we explore the Mature Masculine archetypes of "The King" and "The Lover" and in the S2S Oracle Card Deck, we also include the archetype of "The Warrior." Because of Kristine's dedication to share her passion and wisdom on compassionate living, this activity will focus on the Mature, or adult Masculine archetype of "The Magician" and its immature, or boyhood aspect, "The Precocious Child." Keep in mind that these are Masculine *Energies* and the use of the adjectives mature and immature are only meant to be descriptive of age, not personality. In their work, these eight main archetypes also lead to sixteen other Shadow poles. That's alotta archetypes! If this way of understanding the Masculine is interesting to you, please take a look at their book and discover your own way of relating to the 24 possibilities of expression. For us right now, keep in mind that the younger, immature aspect – when nurtured and given the opportunity to optimally develop – grows into the older, mature aspect. Additionally, while doing this activity remember that we all possess traits of both Masculine and Feminine energies regardless of gender. Below are my understandings of what Moore and Gillette define in their work as "The Precocious Child" and "The Magician." Take a look at the different characteristics and see what feels like a fit for you.

The Precocious Child	**The Magician**
• Is eager to learn and eager to share. • Adventures into the world of ideas. • Wants to know the 'why' & 'how' of everything. • Is a great student. • The child prodigy. • Is an explorer of the unknown, strange, and mysterious. • Tends to be introverted and introspective. • Is reflective and often able to see hidden connections. • Also is extroverted and eager to share insights and talents with others. • Is seen as a helper.	• Is wise and capable. • Dedicated to healing and deep thought. • A Seer or Prophet. • Is consistently questing for enlightenment. • A channeler and container of great power and energy • Always sees self as an initiate and feels their task is to ritually initiate others. • Holds the specialty of knowing something others do not and seeks to share the knowledge. • Is the archetype of awareness and insight; thoughtfulness and reflection. • Always seeking to use their knowledge for the benefit of all.

As you read through the characteristics of "The Precocious Child," envision a younger version of yourself. What about these qualities resonates? Take a moment to journal around the following questions.

- What do I need to know at this time from my Inner **Precocious Child?** _____

_____

_____

- How can this connection to my **Precocious Child** support me? _____

_____

_____

- How can this connection to my **Precocious Child** support my relationships? _____

_____

_____

- How can I *lovingly* and *respectfully* share this wisdom? _____

_____

_____

Next, read through the qualities of "The Magician" and take a moment to identify, honor, and claim these within yourself.

- What do I need to know at this time from my Inner **Magician?** _____
  _____
  _____

- How can this connection to my inner **Magician** support me? _____
  _____
  _____

- How can this connection to my inner **Magician** support my relationships? _____
  _____
  _____

- How can I *lovingly* and *respectfully* share this wisdom? _____
  _____
  _____

Found within both of these archetypes is the theme of sharing wisdom and knowledge for the greater good. What can both your Inner Precocious Child and your Inner Magician inspire you to teach and share to create a better world for us all? Sit with both Masculine versions of yourself and ask them for guidance. As you align with these sides of your consciousness, finish the following statement.

**With my wise and enlightened awareness,
I will share my talents and insights for the greater good of all living things by…**

_____

_____

_____

Thank you for taking the time to optimally nurture and allow for the ideal expression of these two powerful Masculine energies. If this activity felt like a fit, keep exploring! Moore's and Gillette's book is a treasure chest of opportunities for deeper exploration into the various aspects of the Masculine. According to them, "when transformed and enriched by life's experiences, the archetype of "The Hero" matures into "The Warrior," "The Oedipal Child" matures into "The Lover," and "The Divine Child" matures into "The King."" Have fun discovering! Love you! Thank you!

~ SPS #4: ~
* Water *

Water has long been associated with the Feminine. Our ancient Paleolithic and Neolithic Ancestors and Ancestresses knew that water sustained and nourished all of life. They correlated these understandings of the powerful, life-giving waters of the Oceans, Lakes, Rivers, and Streams to that of the powerful, life-giving waters of the human female. For them, the magick of menstrual blood, breast milk, amniotic fluid, sexual lubrication, and tears were equally as valuable as the Oceans that produced fish, the streams that yielded plant life, the rains that made the forests, and the lakes that watered the animals. They honored and valued the living world as a Great Mother and understood how all of life could be nourished and fed within this symbiotic and Feminine exchange. If you look at ancient art from these time periods, explained and shown brilliantly by Marija Gimbutas in her work, *The Language of the Goddess*, much of the artistic expression was in honor of this correlation tying the bodies of water on our Mother Earth to that of a Great Mother Goddess Creatrix, which in turn was understood to be embodied by the incarnate Feminine, or the female of all species. Thinking of your body in this revered way, grab a bowl and fill it with drinkable water. Hold the bowl in your hands and gaze into it. Make a mental, emotional, and spiritual connection from your body to the life-giving and life-sustaining waters of Mother Earth. Energetically connect the moisture of your tears, the warmth of your breast milk, the wisdom of your menstrual blood, the bliss of your sexual lubrication, and the miracle of your amniotic fluid to the water in your bowl. If you have never held a baby at your breast, remain here. If you have never felt the delight of sacred sexuality, remain here. If you have never felt the rush of life emerge from your body, remain here. If you have never tasted the salt of your tears, remain here. If you have never prized the cyclical love of your blood magick, remain here. This exercise is to reawaken, revitalize, reconnect, and re-empower the Feminine within. This is not about perceiving where we are different. This is not about creating a boundary around what we have or have not experienced. This is about stepping into the Feminine energies of Mother Earth and the Embodied Female. No matter our gender, no matter our politics, no matter our age… we can all find a way to venerate and respect the very life-giving qualities of the Feminine that sustain all of creation. As you hold your bowl of water - the sacred liquid that connects you to every living thing - speak a prayer into this sacred vessel. Pray for whatever your heart desires and take as long as you need. There are no rules and no *right ways* to pray… only *your* way. When your prayer is complete, drink your prayer-filled water. Sip by sip, as you invite this beauty into your consciousness, allow each cell of your body to be hydrated, nourished, comforted, valued, and loved. When you have drunk all of the water in your bowl, sit quietly for a moment and sense the energy of the water traveling outwards from your navel, connecting your physical body to all bodies of water upon Mother Earth. Allow this energy to return to you purified, cleansed, and replenished as it flows into your belly and down over your Womb. As a final step, warm this area of your body by placing your hands over your Sacred Pubic Triangle. As you send love and light into this holy place of life and creation, know that you are valued and cherished by me and by many. Thank you. I love you. Finish by recording and reflecting on your Sacred Prayer below.

My Sacred Prayer

_____

_____

_____

What I Give

_____

_____

_____

What I Receive

_____

_____

_____

~ SPS #5: ~
* Sacred Sex *

Unless we go looking for it, Sacred Sexuality isn't something we hear a lot about. Depending on our religious and cultural upbringing, it can seem like a contradiction in terms. Sex is everywhere. It bombards us. Yet, thinking of sex as '*Sacred*' can be a major leap of faith. For this activity, go slow. There is an amazing song with words and music by Karen Drucker and chorus by Robyn Posin called, "Gentle with Myself." Some of the lyrics read:

I will be gentle with myself
And I will hold myself like a newborn baby child
I will be tender with my heart
And I will hold my heart like a newborn baby child
And I will only go as fast
As the slowest part of me feels safe to go
I will be easy on myself
And I love myself like a newborn baby child

If we can approach this topic with that energy, we just might be able to dance and sing with the concepts of Sacred Sexuality in ways that feel safe, secure, and empowering. The truth is, a lot of us have been really hurt and deeply wounded when it comes to our sexuality. The statistics are staggering when it comes to sexual abuse and sexual violence, not to mention the denigration of the Feminine that has been perpetuated over the last 5,000 plus years. Is it any wonder that we are where we are today in terms of balanced and healthy - not to mention orgasmic and blissful - sexuality and sexual expression? This activity and the entire *Soul-to-Sisterhood* book is about healing this. It is my hope and desire that together we can heal the Feminine and the Masculine aspects *within* in order to create a Sacred Union of Souls that meets functionally, respectfully, healthfully, and lovingly *between*. Let's start with an understanding of what Sacred Sexuality is.

Sacred Sexuality can be explained as a bliss-filled love experience that transcends our typical notions of partner intimacy by jettisoning us into a fully expressed and fully actualized balancing of the celebrated Feminine and Masculine energies in order to access, expand, and ascend into deep spiritual connections with all of life, throughout every layer of existence, and every level of consciousness.

What is it like to think about *sex* in this *Sacred* way?

_____
_____
_____

As you continue to allow the concept of Sacred Sexuality to dance in your consciousness, write down the first five to ten words that express how you are feeling.

Sit with these words for a moment and discover their significance. Ask yourself:

- **Where** did they come from? _____
_____

- **Why** are they here? _____
_____

- How are they **beneficial**? _____
_____

- How are they **destructive**? _____
_____

If we get biological about female sexuality... female orgasm and female anatomy can be an interesting addition to the conversation. The clitoris is said to have approximately 8,000 nerve endings in a small localized spot that is dedicated to pleasure, not reproduction. The penis has less than half of the amount of nerve endings spread over a much larger surface area. There is little reproductive value in the female orgasm, meaning that a woman does not have to climax to become pregnant. The situation is the opposite for men. To release the sperm for fertilization, ejaculation through orgasm traditionally needs to occur. Women can also have multiple orgasms, with no time limit as to how long the orgasms last, and typically need little rest in between. Again, this is not the standard experience for most men. So, what is the deal with female orgasm? Many wise people throughout history have revered the female orgasm as a Shamanic Experience. When you think about female orgasm from this spiritual perspective, it becomes much richer. From this context, orgasm can connect us into a level of consciousness that harnesses the multi-dimensional mind-body-spirit-connection as both our choice and our gift. Our orgasmic pleasure becomes nothing less than a magickal encounter for manifestation, bliss, healing, and much, much more! Take a moment and write down five to ten words that come forward as you think about female orgasm in this way.

Now, sit with these words for a moment and discover their significance. Ask yourself:

- **Where** did they come from? _____
  _____

- **Why** are they here? _____
  _____

- How are they **beneficial**? _____
  _____

- How are they **destructive**? _____
  _____

You now have two distinct sets of words and many more from the journaling questions. Combine your own with the words provided below and create a Mantra to embody your Sacred Sexuality.

Open	Love	Respect	Awareness	Pleasure	Release
Bliss	Comfort	Powerful	Conscious	Wild	Woman
Intimacy	Orgasm	Spirit	Body	Connection	Expansion
Stars	Moon	Earth	Life	Freedom	Sovereignty
Deep	Transformation	Peace	Empowered	Sacred	Sexuality
Gentle	Sensual	Transformative	Feminine	Masculine	Sex
Union	Beauty	Womb	Energy	Healing	Manifest
Expression	Ecstasy	Breath	Confident	Dynamic	Bold
Fertile	Productive	Fresh	Joy	Light	Embrace
Enchantment	Authentic	Communion	Consciousness	Communication	Positive
Balanced	Revolution	Partnership	Tenderness	Devotion	Passion

My Sacred Sexuality Mantra

_____

_____

_____

When your Sacred Sexuality Mantra is complete, honor your work by repeating it several times to recognize, respect, adore, and cherish your sensuality and sexuality, your sexual security, and sexual sovereignty. Finish by once again reading or saying aloud the beautiful lyrics to "Gentle with Myself."

I will be gentle with myself
And I will hold myself like a newborn baby child
I will be tender with my heart
And I will hold my heart like a newborn baby child
And I will only go as fast
As the slowest part of me feels safe to go
I will be easy on myself
And I love myself like a newborn baby child

For more of Karen Drucker's work, be sure to visit her website www.karendrucker.com. You will feel inspired and loved by her lyrics and melodies. Until then, feel inspired and loved by me. Thank you and I love you!

Crystal Love: Kristine's Crystal is Garnet. Because of its awesome healing and keen regenerative powers, this stone is dually known as the 'Stone of Commitment' and 'The Stone of Health.' Utilize the speed and power of Garnet, said to contain lightning within, for enhancing the inner fires of passion, transmuting negative energy, regenerating intellectual functions, and producing a stable sense of calm for situations involving great change. This stone simultaneously anchors and connects and additionally assists us in balancing our need for freedom with our need for responsibility, activating survival instincts in order to turn crises into challenges, all while offering courage, hope, warmth, and understanding. Hold a piece of Garnet and feel the Kundalini energy flow as it amplifies your deep connection to Mother Earth. Wear a piece of Garnet and feel supported as you change old behaviors, move past obsolete ideas, liberate inhibitions, and find the clarity needed to step away from culturally supported taboos. Correlating to the Basic Chakra, Garnet can balance fears - rational and otherwise - to enable our bodies a chance at relaxation. When this happens, our nervous systems can take a break and we can open our Crown Chakras to bliss. This bliss, which is a great inspiration to relax into physical intimacy with ourselves or a partner, can also bolster confidence, bringing forth the energies of our wise, empowered Inner Medicine Women.

Suggested Reading to Activate and Amplify your Inner High Priestess of Healing, Empowerment, and Transformation, *Medicine Woman* by Lucy H. Pearce.

Additional Journaling and SPS Space

Jacki

We've all got the potential to awaken to the beauty available to us in this life. We all have an intuitive self, a knowing, of how to live in this beauty. Some of us know this from the time we are very small. Society tries to force us to unlearn this inner knowing. The world tells us not to listen to our intuition, but to internalize to whatever is being projected *out there*. We suffer when we don't listen to ourselves. Look at us… we live in a world of sickness, mental illness, and rampant anxiety. This comes from people not listening to or taking care of themselves. Not treating themselves as if they are valuable. When we awaken, we realize that there is an opening to a bright clear world ahead where we can listen to the inner voice and take it seriously. There will always be negativity. There will always be bad things in this world and bad things that happen to us, but the key is not to embrace it. Don't live in fear. This can be very hard, but we can't let our desire to control things perpetuate the negativity. It is much easier to recluse, ignore the world, and numb with TV and electronics. I say turn off the devices. Get outside. Get connected to nature. Hug a tree. Find a body of water. Find some like-minded people. It may take time and effort to get to this point - especially when we don't have a strong sense of who we are - but connecting to our intuition frees us and helps us to release our attachment to what other people think of us. I used to be very close with my older sister, who recently passed away. We were never able to reconnect before she died and although this was her choice, I am at peace with it. When she was living, she suffered from addiction and other problems. The relationship became toxic. Because I listened to my inner voice, I knew that I had to set a clear boundary with her and cease contact. This created a very profound and hostile reaction. Other people in our family would make a point to tell me what she had said that was mean or cruel. My response finally became, "I don't care." Believe me, I cared about my sister, I just stopped caring about the negative things she was saying. Her words and her feelings about me didn't change my life. Thank goodness I came to realize that my reaction to her feelings and words *could have*. What she was saying had everything to do with her and nothing to do with me. When someone says something unkind, we can take it to heart and get upset, or we can stop and think, "Where is this really coming from? Is it really directed at me, or is it more of a reflection of how this person is feeling about themselves?" Once I figured that out, I was truly free. I still get pulled back in. I'm human. I think this is a very hard thing for us to learn, especially as women. We are taught to value ourselves based upon the opinions of others. Yet, other people's feelings about us and their actions toward us actually have nothing to do with us. How we feel about ourselves is what is important. Finding people that support us in being free to be who we are is critical. You see, I spent a lifetime trying to be this perfect person who did everything for everybody and took care of everyone… all to my detriment. Trying to live life this way was exhausting, anxiety-inducing, and depressing. No matter how hard I tried, I couldn't make everybody happy. Then, I had my children. When they became adults, I realized that I had nothing left. I had put everything into them. This has been difficult, but I have learned that mothers should not put their lives on hold for their children. I did this. I don't regret it per se, but it has been a major lesson. I have three children. Right now, two of them have chosen not to have contact with me. I'm not really sure why they have made this decision, but I know they are working through something. They know my love is unwavering and I will be here for them when they are ready to come back. Before, I would have taken this so seriously and let it affect me deeply. Truthfully, it has to an extent. However, by finding a way to not take this so personally, I have also found a way to accept their decisions without blame and anger. This is about them. It isn't about me. Not seeing my young grandson has been the most painful piece. I think about him all the time. As much as I am able to apply the philosophy of not taking things personally, where my grandson is concerned, I'm not quite there. I was a big part of the first two years of his life. Today, just walking into his room at my house makes me cry. I miss him terribly, but I also know that because I have given him so much love, he is protected. Knowing that helps me begin to let it go. I know my fear makes me want to try to control this situation. It makes me believe that I'll never see him again. Yet, I also know that if I stay focused on my fears, they will most likely come true. The less time I spend worrying and the more time I spend releasing - *knowing* that I don't have to understand why everything is happening this way - the more I can focus on what it is that I do want. I want to be in my grandson's life. It isn't happening now and that is allowing me to be free to pursue other things. I needed a break from taking care of others to step into this new stage of my life. Now, I can teach and guide without sacrificing myself. I take it all one step at a time. One day, I will feel really great about everything… solid in what I know. The next, I will feel terrible. I've learned to allow myself to have the highs and lows, to let myself have bad days. I just don't wallow in it. To maintain physical and mental health, I take my time to feel how I feel. I sit on the couch and eat chocolate. So what? One bad day - or even one bad week - doesn't define me. All of this, my past, present, and future, does not create my identity. We all have baggage. I used to dwell on trying to figure out why my childhood was so hard, asking "Why did this happen?" When I listen to my intuition, the answer is always that I went through what I went through to become the woman I am now. Learning this lesson has helped me let go of resentment. My parents did their best. Doing your best, in any given situation, depends on so many variables. How can I judge them? Blaming them or anyone only hurts me. I know there are many of us out there who have been or currently are in bad relationships, but it is all a lesson. Don't beat yourself up. Just take responsibility and make a change. There are so many resources out there for all of us. I firmly believe we are all as strong as we want to be, but we live in a world that tries to convince us otherwise. The cultural messages are always trying to tell us that we are inferior or weak. All of that is so untrue. We *can* do it all. Think of all that we do as women! We *DO* do it all, we just need to remember that! It is hard to be human: emotionally, mentally, physically, you name it. The key is not living in the hardship. Find what is good today…. in *this* moment. My goal is to share with women that we can be happy no matter what. I know this because I come from a family where almost no one is happy. My family of origin was and remains negative, angry, mistrustful, and full of blame. I have lived long enough to know that this is no way to live. I want to live a full life of joy. A quote that I love is "I will grow older, but I refuse to grow up." That is me. Life will never be perfect. That doesn't mean I am going to stop playing, dancing, and sitting with my toes in the ocean. This is a world that we all can live in and we all can have our own way of how to get there with no apologies. Let's focus on that. Let's share that. I am who I am. I don't pretend to be anybody else. For those out there who can accept me being me, we're all good.

Making This Story Your Own:

Jacki's story offers us the gift of release.
Take a moment, breathe, and reflect.
What stands out for you when you read her words?
Is there a situation in your life that is similar to Jacki's?
Perhaps part of her story feels connected to your own.
How can you relate her experiences to your past, present, and future?

- *My Connection to Jacki's Story* _____

_____

_____

_____

Knowing that you aren't alone, let's gently explore some other themes from Jacki's story together:

- *Living in Beauty*
    - What are your thoughts on being human? Is life filled with gifts? With sorrow? Perhaps you feel it's a combination of both? Where did these beliefs come from? Did you learn them on your own or were they taught to you from someone else? Are they in alignment with who you are or who you would like to become? How often do you notice the beauty around you? Inside of you? Would you like to notice it more? How can you begin to do this and what will be different when more beauty is present within your life and consciousness?

- *Releasing* Toxicity
    - What situations, relationships, and aspects of your life are not fulfilling and what lets you know this? Is it your feelings? Thoughts? Reactions? Maybe even your habits? Can you identify any benefit that these unfulfilling things bring to your life? Do they benefit anyone else? Is there a way to release them and let them go? If releasing them is not an option, can these relationships be shifted, and if so, how? When change does occur, who will be the first to notice and how will you know that you have successfully shifted things to be more fulfilling and functional?

- *Focus on What You Want*
    - What do you *really* want? When you think about that question, what comes to mind? Can you break it down and identify what you want personally and professionally? What about your wants for your physical body? Your heart? Your mind? Your spirit? Expanding even bigger, what are your wants for the Earth? For humanity? For the future? When you give name to this and claim it for yourself, what happens? Does your focus stay motivated on creating what you want to see, feel, and experience? Do you begin to question yourself, allowing doubt, fear, and worry to creep in? How can you refocus your energy and breathe new life into your dreams and desires? How can you focus on what you *really* want and make it happen?

Sacred Play Suggestions:

~ SPS #1: ~
* Heart to Heart *

Not taking things personally is much easier said than done. Sometimes it might feel as if we have it mastered and then, boom! A new lesson arrives and it's even harder than the previous one. As these lessons get more challenging, we realize that we have more work to do. For me, when I am at this juncture, I also know that I've got some choices to make. I can choose to be hard on myself and add more insult to the already painful injury, or I can compassionately witness my processes with patience and understanding and, like Jacki did, work to release the blame and anger. I know this is hard. When really hurtful things happen, we search for the *why*. We look for ways to assign responsibility. We try to make sense of what happened and sometimes in our efforts, we can be unkind to ourselves and others. While I was writing this book, a very close friendship of mine significantly changed. This is someone whom I love. We have shared many personal and professional highs and lows. We have supported one another in all sorts of endeavors and for several years, this relationship has epitomized Sisterhood for me. Then something happened. Actually, *a lot* of somethings happened and now our relationship is in a stage where there is no contact. Am I hurting? Hell yes. Has this situation made me explore a lot of deep, dark things about myself? Yep. Have I felt rage and despair and everything in between?

Affirmative. Am I grateful that this happened? Not quite… but I will get there. What has helped me is that since our last conversation about a year ago, I have made it a daily practice to send her love and to faithfully pray for both of us. OK, I have to be honest and let you know that this process has been helped by a totally random occurrence. One time she and I were talking, and she told me about a website that sells organic cotton underwear. Well, I ordered some, and I am now on their mailing list. Daily, as I sit and write at my computer, a 7:00 am advertisement email comes through and that is my prayer reminder. I know, ran-dom! But it has worked! Sometimes, the Angels offer us silly little gifts like that, and we can either choose to use them or not. I am so glad that I did. This daily devotion of love and prayer has not necessarily given me answers or been a magick wand to cure my hurting heart, but it has offered me daily opportunities for compassion and empathy. It has also given me faith. No doubt, this is a tough lesson. One that for me, as I write a book titled "*Soul-to-Sisterhood*," has made me question *everything*! Yet, as I accept the lesson of learning how not to take this personally, my understanding becomes clearer as to why I manifested this situation into my life. I have some lessons to learn about how I hold and deal with anger, blame, and resentment. As the creator and facilitator of women's groups, and as the creator of this book, a Sisterhood wound cuts right to the core of who I know myself to be. This particular type of wound could have rocked the very foundation of my Divine Purpose: *Service to Others*. Have I felt like a fraud over the last six months because I am looking for somewhere to place my anger, blame, and resentment? Yes. Have I had fantasies about conversations in which I prove my righteousness? Yes. Have I tried to pretend that I can forget what our friendship means to me? Yes. But in addition to those things, I have also held my faith that although our connection looks and feels different, it isn't gone. Even in death life recreates itself. Our Sisterhood isn't lost, it is just transforming. I have had to release control and accept that I don't know what is going to happen while still trusting that it is all going to be OK. Ready to try it with me? Think of a relationship in your life where there is suffering, unfinished business, and conflict. Once you have this relationship in mind, take a moment and envision both of you being held in love and light. Imagine a beautiful golden force field surrounding you, and when it feels right, see a beam of that golden light connecting you to one another at your mid-chest or Heart Chakra. Take some deep breaths to solidify this image and when you are ready, invite faith to join you and begin to set the intentions for your prayer.

Which relationship are you connected to?

_____

_____

What is your intention for this connection?

_____

_____

Send a bright beam of **light** from your heart to theirs.
Send a bright beam of **love** from your heart to theirs.

What is your prayer?

_____

_____

What is the lesson?

_____

_____

What will be your daily reminder to pray this prayer?

_____

_____

When will you know things have shifted?

_____

_____

When will you know the lesson has been learned?

_____

_____

This isn't easy. Finding a space of non-aggression when we have been hurt and want to react defensively is what my therapist refers to as "graduate level relationship stuff." Congratulations! You made this level of growth a priority and the Universe thanks you. So many of the mystical, metaphysical, and spiritual lineages of teaching maintain that the aggression, violence, and ugliness we witness happening *around* us is only a mirror of the aggression, violence, and ugliness we feel *within* us. As we work together to shift this internally, our external world gets a breather… a time to relax and be the beautiful, blissful place it was always meant to be. Thank you for taking the time! I love you!

~ SPS #2: ~
* Perfectly You *

What would the perfectly supportive relationship look like for you? Romantic or platonic, how would this relationship fill your cup? Always present and available, able to be both comforting and authentic while prioritizing and validating your needs, this relationship is fulfilling and reminds you daily of your worth and value. What are ten things that make this relationship ideal?

1. _____

2. _____

3. _____

4. _____

5. _____

6. _____

7. _____

8. _____

9. _____

10. _____

Let's get our minds and hearts working together and playfully bring this relationship to life. In your imagination, allow answers for the following questions to spring into your consciousness. Don't labor and attempt to force an answer. Let it land from your intuition and go with it. If nothing comes forward, skip it and move on.

- What is this being's name? _____

- How did you meet? _____

- What is their favorite color? _____

- What do you two enjoy doing together? _____

- What big plans do you two have? _____

Take a moment and reread the ten ideal qualities identified above. As you read them one by one, think of a time in your life when you have embodied this for someone else. Now, in your imagination, see this perfect partner standing in front of you. Make eye contact with them. When you feel connected, visualize them stepping into you. When this happens, the simultaneous actions of *blending* and *becoming* alternately *show* you and *remind* you that you are this perfectly supportive person for yourself and that you always have been. Now, clear the dust from your vision and take a moment to fully claim the ideal perfection that is *you*. From this moment forward, you know that you are your own perfect partner and you trust that you are your own perfect relationship. Does this mean that you won't or can't experience this level of support and connection with another person? Absolutely not! The world is our mirror and now that we know our own capacities for presence, availability, comfort, authenticity, validation, and prioritization, we can manifest them in someone else. In fact, call me! Better yet, what are you doing later? Let's get together and kick up our heels. I love you, lady, and I'm so glad you are here! Thank you for seeing your value and worth. You hold the mirror up for me to see mine.

~ SPS #3: ~
* Why *

In her story, Jacki shares personal wisdom on finding her answer to one of the most frequently asked questions of life: "Why did this happen?" Think about how many times we ask this question and how much time we spend trying to make sense of *why* things happen the way they do. Seldom is there a clear-cut answer. Sometimes it is really difficult to figure out why things transpire the way they do. Sometimes the answer is there, but it isn't what we want to hear. Sometimes it can feel vague and disconnected to the situation. Either way, it's all a part of our journey. Jacki's answer, "I went through what I went through to become the woman I am today," takes a lot of trust and understanding to accept. This type of answer can feel good when we are on the other side of the situation, but in the midst of the storm, it can feel like a pretty crappy cop-out. What if we can open up our perspectives a little and create our own answers to the question? Answers that feel more concrete, clear, and useful. Let's try it. Think of a situation in your life that you would like to change and definitely warrants the "Why did this happen?" question. Get clear on the circumstances of the situation and answer the following questions from *your* perspective. Be as honest as you can and don't censor your viewpoint.

- Who was involved? _____
- What happened? _____
  _____
- When did this happen? _____
- Where did it happen? _____
- Why did it happen? _____
  _____
- Who or what got the **most** benefit from this happening? _____
- Who or what got the **least** benefit? _____
- What were the **worst** moments of the situation? _____
  _____
- What were the **best** moments? _____
  _____
- Would anything **remedy** this situation? _____
  _____

How was that? OK, for the first question above, you listed who was involved. Now, answer the same set of questions from their viewpoint. Step into their consciousness and answer from their perspective. You might be thinking, "How in the heck am I supposed to do that?" Actually, pretty easily. With what you know about this other person, imagine that you are them. Feel their wants, needs, and desires. Remember, this is not your *perception* of them. Your perception is biased, and your answers will reflect your assumptions and characterizations... *especially* if you are upset. To the best of your abilities, stay neutral and genuine and allow your intuition to be your guide as you answer from their perspective.

- Who was involved? _____

- What happened? _____
  _____

- When did this happen? _____

- Where did it happen? _____

- Why did it happen? _____
  _____

- Who or what got the **most** benefit from this happening? _____

- Who or what got the **least** benefit? _____

- What were the **worst** moments of the situation? _____
- _____

- What were the **best** moments of the situation? _____
  _____

- Would anything **remedy** this situation? _____
  _____

How did that go? Did any insights or understanding come forward? OK, last step. Think of a totally uninvolved person... a person whom you admire. This person's observations and assessments are typically helpful for you and you respect their opinions. Imagine that this person has witnessed the entire situation. Every exchange, every word, every feeling - they are aware of it all. This person accurately understands everyone's involvement and, without judgement, their only desire is to impartially recount what they have seen. Third time is a charm, right? Answer the same questions from this person's perspective and see what else comes up. Step into this alternate consciousness just like you did for step two.

- Who was involved? _____

- What happened? _____
  _____

- When did this happen? _____

- Where did it happen? _____

- Why did it happen? _____
  _____

- Who or what got the **most** benefit from this happening? _____

- Who or what got the **least** benefit? _____

- What were the **worst** moments of the situation? _____
  _____

- What were the **best** moments of the situation? _____
  _____

- Would anything **remedy** this situation? _____
  _____

Read all three perspectives. You've probably heard the saying that there are two sides to every story and the truth lies somewhere in the middle. Use this philosophy to determine what rests in the middle of this situation. What can be considered for useful and concrete clarity as to *why this happened*? Layer all three perspectives together and create the answer for yourself.

Why did this happen?

_____

_____

_____

_____

Congratulations! Maybe you did all of the steps, maybe you only did a few. The main thing is, you did this for yourself and the more you continue to stand firm in your own inner knowing, the more you can continue to release the yucky feelings associated with conflict. You look beautiful, by the way! Freer, lighter, and ready to soar. Have fun! Thank you! Love you!

~ SPS #4: ~
* Ego and Soul *

Have you ever had one of those moments where big feelings just took over and you thought to yourself, "What the heck was *that*?" Or maybe a day of reactions and interactions left you feeling crummy, out of sorts, and not like yourself at all. Maybe the opposite has happened, and you've experienced a feeling of freedom and love when looking at a beautiful landscape. Or perhaps a sense of unlikely calm washed over you in the midst of a very intense exchange. I like to think of these little surprise moments as gifts. Even if they don't feel particularly awesome, they remind me that I am part of something much bigger and greater than just my day-to-day endeavors. They make me feel connected to the entire human experience, sort of like what well-known Swiss psychiatrist and psychoanalyst, Carl Jung taught with his concept of the collective unconscious. According to Jung (and to many who practice and explore his work) a simple understanding of this phenomena is that the collective unconscious is common to all human beings and is responsible for many deep-seated human belief systems and instincts. It is a collection of unconscious knowledge and imagery that every person is born with and includes certain relational and archetypal understandings… kind of like how we all have an image pop into our head when we think of 'Mother and Child' or 'Father and Child.' It also includes even greater representations of human behaviors and experiences such as birth, death, sex, and religion. Add in our collective symbolism for dreams, money, personalities, and power, and you've got a system of imprinting that isn't necessarily our choice, but can be explored and understood for further growth, ascension, and transformation. I like to think of those surprise moments mentioned above as my way of connecting into the collective. I guess it is more like the collective connecting into me because although it *is* welcome, it *is not* sought-after and it isn't always a *positive* experience. Funny enough, I was reading a wonderful book called *Eros Ascending: The Life Transforming Power of Sacred Sexuality*, by John Maxwell Taylor when I came upon his nuanced description of the collective unconscious. According to his writings, there are actually two facets to the collective unconscious: the collective Ego and the collective Soul. Mind blown! I had never thought of it like that before, but it makes so much sense! As women, due to our energetic receptivity to the influencing factors of the seasonal cycle, the lunar cycle, our menstrual cycle, and the Feminine archetypal cycle, we are intra-psychically linked to the world around us. We are affected by so many dynamic properties of the natural world. The huge amounts of continuous information coming to us through our intuition and instincts could fill a shelf of Encyclopedia Britannica's every *day*! In short, you can say that we are energetically sensitive. We sense things which cannot be quantifiably 'seen' and 'known,' and we sense them in different gradients, amounts, and levels depending on where any of those aforementioned cycles happen to be. This sensitivity includes the collective energy of the human experience as well! After reading Taylor's book, I started thinking, "I want to be more aware of this energetic influence and if it *is* coming in from the collective Ego, I want to shift it to the collective Soul." As we work on this, remember this energy of the collective isn't a choice that we are making. But it if we want to vibe higher - and I do - it **is** my choice to intentionally recalibrate where this energetic influence is coming from and realign my consciousness with the *Soul*, not the Ego. So, a few guidelines to think about. The collective energy of the entire human experience - which includes all of humanity throughout all time and distance - is available to us. Through our Feminine Superpowers of intuition and instinct we can use visualization and awareness to intentionally understand, connect to, and utilize the vibration and wisdom of the collective Soul. Lastly, based on our connection to our emotions and our abilities to discern our experiences, we can distinguish which layer of consciousness we are connecting to and receiving from and make an empowered choice at that moment to either stay or shift. Let's create our own map for working with these two levels of the collective unconscious.

- When connected to the **collective Ego**, feelings may range from restless to fragile, confused, irritable, disturbed, constricted, inadequate, and miserable.
  - The collective ego feels <u>*small.*</u>

What other feelings come up for you when you think of the collective *Ego*?

_____

_____

- When connected to the **collective Soul**, feelings may range from content to empowered, clear, peaceful, stable, free, capable, and joyful.
  - The collective soul feels <u>*big.*</u>

What other feelings come up for you when you think of the collective *Soul*?

_____

_____

- How will you know when you are connected to the ***collective Ego?*** _____

_____

- How will you know when you are connected to the ***collective Soul?*** _____

_____

**When you choose, how will you make an empowered shift from the
collective *Ego* to the collective *Soul*?**

_____

_____

Great job! OK, if this collective energy speaks to us through belief systems, images, relationships, knowledge, intuition, and instincts, let's make our map more specific so that it is easier for us to follow, especially when we are experiencing the powerful feelings of the Ego.

- What *belief systems* are present for me when I am plugged into the ***collective Ego?*** _____

_____

~ **What *belief systems* are present for me when I am plugged into the <u>*collective Soul*</u>?** ~

_____

- What *images* are present for me when I am plugged into the ***collective Ego?*** _____

_____

~ **What *images* are present for me when I am plugged into the <u>collective Soul</u>?** ~
_____

- What do I notice about my *relationships* when I am plugged into the **collective Ego**? _____
_____

~ **What do I notice about my *relationships* when I am plugged into the <u>collective Soul</u>?** ~
_____

- What *wisdom* and *knowledge* are present when I am plugged into the **collective Ego**? _____
_____

~ **What *wisdom* and *knowledge* are present when I am plugged into the <u>collective Soul</u>?** ~
_____

- What do my *intuition* and *instincts* tell me when I am plugged into the **collective Ego**? _____
_____

~ **What do my *intuition* and *instincts* tell me when I am plugged into the <u>collective Soul</u>?** ~
_____

Keep working with this awareness and see what shifts occur. I've been playing with requesting a connection to the collective Soul when life circumstances get stressful. This supports me in showing up as my best self. With a little help from my '*friends*,' it is easier for me to respond from a place of empowerment and peace during the challenging times. Have fun and get creative. How you work with these energies to vibe in more good, juicy feelings and experiences is totally up to you! Count me in as part of your Collective Soul Sisterhood Network of Support. I've got your back and I know you've got mine! Thanks for doing this activity. Love you!

~ SPS #5: ~
* Positive Good *

What is good, or what wouldn't you change about today? Being able to breathe counts! Breathing is a gift! In her story, Jacki shares that focusing on what she *does* want versus what she *doesn't* allows her to be more fully aware of the **good** in life. Most of us have heard this information because it is pretty commonplace. Yet, implementing it is an entirely different ballgame. The last time something was going wrong, were you aware and/or were you able to stop the thoughts accompanying the negative situation? If so, awesome! If not, awesome, we are going to work on this together! Without conscious intervention, when something is not going well, focusing on the negative is biological. Noticing danger has kept us alive as a species. When a situation isn't turning out optimally, our systems react and the feelings accompanying this experience are usually based in fear. Once the fear starts, the thoughts follow, and we can become afraid of a gagillion different things. We experience the fear of being wrong, the fear of being punished, the fear of being physically hurt, the fear of being emotionally hurt, the fear of losing someone, the fear of the unknown, the fear of fear, etc.… all understandable… and all reactions that can create and reinforce the negative narratives in our heads which may or may not be true. Enter hungry wild animal with big gnashing teeth ready to gnaw our arms off. Yikes! What happens next? We run, attack, or drop and play dead. All three are amazing response systems evolutionarily engineered to keep us alive when there is an actual threat of being eaten alive. All three are not so good for keeping us calm and connected to ourselves and others when trying to make sense of emotionally charged situations which can have similar feelings and thoughts. No question, our biology is beautiful and sophisticated, and our big brains love us so much they will do anything to try to keep our arms from being gnawed off. However, within that desire for safety at all costs, when we react to our fears in the moment, the subsequent fallout can be even worse than what caused us to feel afraid in the first place. Like gremlins fed after midnight, the consequences of the fallout can multiply… fast! They dig irrigation ditches in our brains and, without even being aware of it, our thoughts begin to flow down those deep pathways and create habituated response patterns to the world around us. Similar to the process we witness in nature, every time a thought follows this path, it gets deeper and deeper. Before we know it, we have a Grand Canyon of negativity in our minds. No fun, right? OK, let's fire the wild animal from the cast and change the script. In our new story, both arms are safe, and we are the directors of the show. We decide how this new narrative is going to look and feel because we have the final say-so over all design elements. First order of business is the intervention of highlighting a positive. Let's go back to that original question:

What is good, or what wouldn't you change, about today?
(Remember, breathing counts!)

_____

_____

Maybe we forget this is an option because 'positive thinking' gets a bad rap. I've heard it all…. "It's too simple." "It isn't how the world works." "It makes us sounds silly." "Stop being such a Pollyanna." Sure, sometimes positive thinking isn't supported by the world around us but think positive! It can change! See how I snuck that in there ☺ It *is* simple, and maybe the world around us isn't following suit, and sure someone might have something snarky to say, but come on, Sister! When have we ever let *that* stop us? Highlighting the positives (however small they seem) can help our brains begin to recalibrate so that we start noticing what is going *right* versus always noticing what is going wrong. Focusing on the positives can amp up our brain biology. It can modernize our response systems. It not only helps us stay rooted in the present moment, but it also helps us stay focused on creating the life we want. Try it again with a few more questions.

What has been good, or what wouldn't you change, about *yesterday*?

_____

_____

What has been good, or what wouldn't you change, about *last week*?

_____

_____

What has been good, or what wouldn't you change, about the *last month*?

_____
_____
_____
_____

What has been good, or what wouldn't you change, about the *last year*?

_____
_____
_____
_____

What do you notice right now about the way your body feels? How about your mind and your heart? What about your Soul? Is there the slightest hint of release or relaxation? If so, your brain is beginning to shift into the safe zone. Brava! You are feeling secure enough to notice the good! This dynamic is like an irrigation ditch, too, only it feels more like an infinity loop: the calmer you feel, the more you notice the positives; the more you notice the positives, the calmer you feel. Keep going.

What has been good, or what wouldn't you change, about the last *hour*?

_____
_____

What has been good, or what wouldn't you change, about the last *minute*?

_____
_____

What has been good, or what wouldn't you change, about the last *second*?

_____
_____

Still feeling comfy and relaxed? I hope so! For our last step, stop for a moment and visualize a golden light around your head. This light is warm, comforting, nurturing, and *positive.* In your imagination, see that golden light going down into your scalp on through to your brain organ. Now allow that light to permeate every cell and the space between the cells. See it flowing around and through all of the various parts of your neurology and allow it to just be present. When you are ready, let your inner-director channel in job security and create space for a sequel.

What will be great, fantastic, and amazing in the *next hour*?

_____

_____

What will be great, fantastic, and amazing *today*?

_____

_____

What will be great, fantastic, and amazing *tomorrow*?

_____

_____

What will be great, fantastic, and amazing *next week*?

_____

_____

What will be great, fantastic, and amazing *next month*?

_____

_____

What will be great, fantastic, and amazing in the *next year*?

_____

_____

Look at us! We are like sparkly unicorns with rainbows coming out of our butts! We are positivity times infinity google! Keep going! All of this positive energy is contagious. The naysayers who told us to "get real" need us right now. Go and spread some of your sparkle, darling. Real quick, though, before you go, put your hands on your heart and send yourself gratitude. Know that I am grateful for you, too. This world needs you and the special brand of magick only you can bring. Thank you. I love you!

Crystal Love: Jacki's Crystal is Aquamarine (ah-kwuh-muh-***reen***) and this gentle, calming, and compassionate stone is one to use in almost any situation. Known as a 'Stone of Courage,' Aquamarine encourages us to feel dynamic with its abilities to bring harmony into conflictual situations and to promote tolerance without judgment. In ancient lore, Aquamarine was believed to be the treasure of mermaids, and was used by sailors as a talisman of good luck, fearlessness, and protection. Connected to the Throat Chakra, we know today that Aquamarine can also clear blocked communication, promote self-expression, bring order to feelings of overwhelm, sharpen intellectual responses, and nurture desires for higher level intra-personal learning. A stone of eternal youth and happiness, Aquamarine can additionally safeguard all who travel by, over, or near water. Perhaps most important, this stone encourages service to humanity so that all life may develop an attunement for universal healing. Try playing with a piece to summon clairvoyance, emotional and intellectual stability, and closure. Get a piece on your body, either in your pocket or as a necklace, to feel the deep, mystical and purifying empowerment of this stone. When you do, don't look down, your legs might just turn into a tail and fins! Lucky you… Mermaid Goddess!

Suggested Reading to Call Forth a Life that Lives in Beauty, *Braiding Sweetgrass: Indigenous Wisdom, Scientific Knowledge, and the Teaching of Plants* by Robin Wall Kimmerer.

Additional Journaling and SPS Space

__Stella__

My life has been a story of learning to receive the love all around me. It's really a love story. My blessings have always outweighed my hardships. All of the big and little miracles that have happened to me, there is no currency of deserving these things. I haven't had to earn the love; I've just had to learn to receive it. I guess because we live in an earthly world where the perspective is based on earning, trading, and working in order to deserve the things we have, being able to fully receive love has been my biggest lesson. It is also the area I'm still working on. These gifts I speak of - my family, my kids, my sister, my dearest friends - they have been given to me from a Creator who loves me unconditionally. Yet, receiving these gifts hasn't always been easy. Opening my heart to receive love has been a process. For a long time, I was in a mode of not receiving love. That became my truth. I thought I was unworthy, and if I hadn't sacrificed or worked my tail off to make something happen, then it wasn't real. I filtered everything through that lens of 'undeservedness,' and I had to be shattered open to see my real truth. Today, even though I'm still a work in progress, I am choosing to focus on the blessings. For twenty-three years, I have had a best friend who has been with me through everything. You could say that it was an extraordinary set of coincidences that brought us together, but I don't really believe in that. I believe that everything in this Universe is perfectly planned. My best friend has been there with me through it all: my marriage, the births of my children, my divorce, new beginnings, starting chapters, ending chapters... Joy is her name, and it couldn't be more fitting. People observing Joy and I together always remarked on our special connection. Some would even say, "That horse knows what you are thinking!" Amazingly, she does and she loves me anyway. I have always had a safe place to go to rest my head in her flaxen mane. With her, in the place that smells like sweet sunshine mixed with Earth and happiness, I can talk right from my heart. It is in these moments - when we are connected and my heart is really open - that I receive the same two messages from my horse. She tells me that I can give and receive love freely and that I am connected to all things. She repeats these messages to me over and over and I repeat them to myself. She is my heart-horse. My spirit animal. My guide to a better version of me. Thinking back, I can't remember a time when I didn't love horses. My earliest memories of horses are all sensory. I remember their smell, the softness of their coats, and the warmth of their breath on my skin. With horses, even in those early, early years, I felt whole. I still feel that way. No matter what else is going on, when I am around my horses, my heart is happy. I have been so blessed to have these beautiful animals, my horse family, in my life. Their spirits have chosen me, and they have been the perfect spiritual teachers... always coming forth to guide me for as long as I can remember. They've helped me understand my human interactions in ways that I wouldn't have been able to if I had not had the equine connection first. I know how lucky I am to have this. Although I've had some painful parts to my life, if I reflect back on all of the moments, good and bad, I realize that I am just an average person who has been extraordinarily blessed. The events that have led me to this place, as a single mom of three kids, have been devastating. They have also been extremely beautiful. The rejection, betrayal, and abandonment I experienced during the dissolution of my marriage took away the hopes and dreams I had, not only for myself, but for the future of my family. Ending my marriage forced me to find a more authentic dream that was more in alignment with my destiny. Now I realize that it was always supposed to be this way. Remaining in an emotionally abusive and loveless marriage put a spiritual lock on me that kept my heart in a permanent jail cell. When I was that unhappy, I couldn't truly experience life. I was also over a thousand miles away from my family. Being so removed didn't facilitate space for me to do the needed and painful work around my own childhood experiences. In my marriage, I was blocked emotionally and geographically from healing. When everything changed, I moved home. I started over. I stepped into the light. Being at home, I got to know my parents in a deeper and richer way. I received the gift of having their love showered over me time and time again, in every way imaginable. Standing witness to them loving my children has also been very healing. My parents have shown up and loved my kids unconditionally. They have made sure my kids have their every need met. Experiencing this outpouring of love, I have begun to appreciate the fact that there are two parts to loving relationships. There is the person doing the loving and the person receiving the loving. For a large part of my life, I have not been fully receiving the love being offered to me. I mean it when I say that I stepped into the light. The gift in moving home is seeing that the love has always been there. The connection to my family has always been there. I genuinely feel it. I'm not perfect. Like I said, I am a work in progress. Today I am more open and more capable of giving and receiving love than ever before… not only to and from my parents, but to and from everyone. Before I was born, I was blessed with having my sister be my sister. Again, having a gift like this can only lead me to the knowing that I am so loved by the Creator. I don't know how people get through their lives without a sister. I really don't. One of my earliest memories is of being very young and wanting to hold her hand. Even then, I knew that if I could hold her hand I would be braver, better, stronger, and faster. I still feel that way. We live 1,300 miles apart, but I know that our love and spiritual connection created all those years ago still makes me feel braver, better, stronger, and faster. Opening my heart to receive love in this way - to see all the places where I have been blessed - I wish I could go back and talk to my younger self. I'd have so much to tell her about life! I remember being a young woman and mourning for my friends when they got pregnant. I was so glad that it wasn't me. I didn't know what miracles children were. Since then, I've been blessed to be the Mom of three amazing beings. My children teach me and love me daily, and they are the best things that have ever happened to me. Being their mom inspires me every day to live better, to love better, to receive better, and to be more authentic. When I was pregnant with my youngest, I was told that she was incompatible for life outside the womb. At 14 weeks in utero, she was diagnosed with a genetic disorder called Trisomy 18. My doctors told me that if she survived the pregnancy and was born, her life expectancy would be minutes. I prepared for the worst. I picked out a place in the cemetery. I set up the 'end of life care' for after her birth. Miraculously, my baby was born healthy and she did not have this disorder. I can't explain this miracle. I remember the doctors coming to tell me about the hole in my baby's heart and laughing with tears of joy because my baby was OK. Her problem was fixable. I'm sure that reaction seemed inappropriate to them, but to me, a hole in her heart was wonderful news! During the emotional roller coaster of her birth, I let my own health slip. I wasn't paying attention to my body. I was so overjoyed to have a healthy baby that the rest was inconsequential! After her birth, my c-section kept opening and eviscerating. The doctors tried to glue me back together. They tried to cauterize me back together. Nothing worked. Finally, my skin healed, but my abdominal muscles did not. They never reclosed like they should have. Since then, I have been living with a huge hernia. To be more graphic, I live with my guts on the outside. Living like this is disfiguring. The pain is at best overwhelming, and at worst unbearable. I have been living this way for almost five years and it is a visceral experience. And yet… here is another way that I'm choosing to believe I am infinitely blessed… I am coming to see my hernia as another gift. What looks like a disability at first glance is really a superpower. I know that cracks are always where the light shines through. Sometimes I imagine that I am like one of those fancy Japanese vases. They are the broken vessels put back together with gold, creating a unique mending process with precious metals which becomes an artform unto itself. For now, after one failed repair surgery, I'm choosing to believe that the cracks in my body are like the cracks in those vessels. Only my cracks are where the love shines in and out. My unique mending process has helped cleared the blockages to my giving and receiving of love. Once, I had given up the idea of ever having a fulfilling and intimate partnership. I shut down my hopes and convinced myself that it wasn't important and that I didn't need this type of connection. Thankfully my plan - or what I thought was my plan - wasn't nearly as good as what the Universe and the Creator had in store for me. Someone has come into my life, and he means a great deal. As this new love and new energy has presented itself through the tenderness, mercy, and care that this man has shown me and my family, it has opened me up to yet another way of giving and receiving love. My heart-horse continues to be right. Even when I think I can't open my heart again, or open it any wider, she is always there to remind me that I can. I think I've done some great things and some not so great things in my life, and if you plotted them on a graph, it would average out to a straight line. In spite of that, I have lived a life of abundant blessings. Blessings that have come from a Creator who loves me more than I will ever comprehend. I don't know how I got so lucky, but I am filled with gratitude. I am so grateful for these gifts. I am so grateful for the consistent presence showing me, no matter how much I've tried to resist, how to step into the grand plan of freely giving and freely receiving love. In honor of that, I choose all of my blessings and all of my JOY.

Making This Story Your Own:

Stella's story reminds us that sometimes the most magick can be found where we least expect it.
Take a moment, breathe, and reflect.
What stands out for you when you read her words?
Is there a situation in your life that is similar to Stella's?
Perhaps part of her story feels connected to your own.
How can you relate her experiences to your past, present, and future?

- *My Connection to Stella's Story* _____

_____

_____

_____

_____

Knowing that you aren't alone, let's gently explore some other themes from Stella's story together:

- **Choosing the Gifts**
    - When you think about the gifts of life, what comes to mind? What about the gifts of *your* life? As you reflect on these gifts, what do you notice? How does your body feel? Does your breathing change? Where do your thoughts go? How does your heart respond? Do these gifts have any guidance and support for you? When things feel like they are going *right,* how easy is it to access this guidance and support? When things feel like they are going *wrong,* how easy is it to access? When the present moment feels like anything **but** a gift, how can you refocus and reconnect to the support and guidance coming through from your gifts?

- **The Universe has a Plan**
    - When you make your to-do list for the day, do you expect to be in total control or do you take into consideration that other factors might have an impact? What about when you make your plans for the week? The month? The year? How about the plans for your life? When you think about this, does it seem like an outside force has had more of a plan for you than you have had for yourself? Have there been times when this other plan has felt *too* different or *too* difficult?

What do you make of this? How has everything worked out? Does the belief system that the Universe, God, or another Spiritual Entity has a plan for you feel comforting? If so, why does it feel comforting? Does it feel anything other than comforting? If so, what does it feel like for you?

- **Stepping into the Light**
  - What does 'stepping into the light' mean for you? When you think of shifting consciousness from the darkness to the light, what comes up? Is there resistance? Is there relief? How about fear or hope? What other feelings do you feel and why are they present? Has the dark been beneficial? If so, how? If not, why? Will the light be beneficial? If so, how? If not, why? If stepping into the light feels in alignment for you, who else can witness and support this process? What is one small step you can make to begin this transformation?

Sacred Play Suggestions:

~ SPS #1: ~
* Epona Goddess *

When you were little, do you remember asking for a horse or a pony? I do. I loved horses. I still do! I also remember my little sister asking over and over for a Palomino pony. Every chance she got, she reminded us of her dream to have a little yellow horsey. There is something that connects our little girl spirits to horses and it's not as inexplicable as we've been led to believe. In her book, *The Tao of Equus*, Linda Kohanov talks about this connection. She states:

> "These sensitive, non-predatory beings respond to the world in ways that are traditionally associated with feminine values…. Horses and women also seem to have instinctually powerful bonds that can develop into relationships with potent healing qualities. For horses, as prey and pack animals, are extremely feminine. The equine existence emphasizes emotion over thought, intuition over logic, relationship over territory, process over goal, and collaboration over force. A horse can and will also embody a human's exact emotional truth. Horses literally have a legitimate phenomenon, or sixth sense, that when kicked into gear, can nourish humans psychically, mentally, creatively, and spiritually while inspiring increased sensory and extrasensory awareness."

What a perspective! Connecting the Feminine to the equine can be a great way to think about why we love horses. It can also provide a deeper understanding of our emotional authenticity, our non-verbal communication, our hidden feelings, and our intuitive, instinctual wisdom. Let your imagination work with your memory and think back to a time when you felt connected to a horse or horses. Maybe it was a movie or a photograph. Perhaps you used to ride, or your neighbors had horses. Maybe you still do ride. Whatever comes to mind, build on those images and take a few deep breaths to reconnect into this part of yourself, your horse-self. As you relax into your thoughts, feel your body begin to transform. Your feet and hands become hard and hoof-like. Your body becomes big, round, and strong. Your skin, a freshly brushed coat of fine hair, glistens in the sun. Your neck elongates as you gracefully shake your wild mane back and forth, tickling your withers in the process. Your ears are up and alert. Your eyes can see with a wide panorama of periphery. You take a deep, cleansing breath and you can feel your rib cage expand in a new way, filling up your big lungs all the way to your belly. As you wiggle your hips side to side, you feel your long silken tail brush your hocks and fetlocks. Your body has changed. Your perceptions have changed. Your awareness has changed. It is you, only different. You stand proudly, strongly, and firmly on four powerful and swift legs. Looking down, you notice your beautiful coloring: Bay, Black, Sorrel, Chestnut, Paint, Palomino, Buckskin, or Appaloosa. Every cell of you is open to receive the messages from the human and what author David Abram calls the "more than human" worlds. You now embody your sensory and extrasensory horse-self. Take a walk around. Feel your weight. Feel your strength. Run a bit. Playfully rear up. When you land, kick your back legs out and feel what it feels like to extend and move your body in this way. Cutting through space, you run, jump, stretch, and expand back into this naturally known and remembered wildness. Hear your hooves as they pound into the ground of Mother Earth. Smell the fragrance of sweetgrass being released as you gallop through meadows. Drink in the colors of the wildflowers rushing past as you run faster and faster for no reason other than the pure joy of it. Stay with that feeling of exuberance and, when you are ready, slow down to a trot as you enter into the woods. The smells, sounds, and sights are comfortable and familiar. You walk a bit further and see your safe resting place. Walking towards the soft leaves on the forest floor, you sense that the time is right to receive your horse-self's wisdom. As your body continues to calm and your heart continues to slow, you stand perfectly still, absorbing the world around you from your equine consciousness. In this place, ask your inner Epona Goddess to share her guidance. Inquire how and where your life and relationships could benefit from valuing emotions over thoughts and intuition over logic. Ask her to show you where your relationships and connections can be prioritized over territory and things. Open your heart to her direction regarding the significance of your processes over the importance of your goals. Request her guidance to shift the energies of force toward the energies of collaboration. Finally, ask to be shown your hidden truths, your emotional authenticity, and the wisdom of your body's non-verbal communication. As each message and each answer comes forward, breathe out a long sigh, expelling the tension and stress on the out breath as you signal to your human self that all is safe and all is secure. Keep breathing deeply, and as you incorporate and integrate your horse-sense, let another aspect of your consciousness begin to return you to your human form. Your hands and feet now both possess their respective appendages. Your skin is soft and back to its original coloring. Your neck shrinks back to its normal length and gently holds your head with its two human sized ears and two human shaped eyes. With two legs instead of four, you feel the weight of your human form resting within your clothes, noticing the touch of the fabric on your body. Right before you open your eyes, you realize that one thing either in or on your body doesn't change back into its human form. This is your secret spot to access your Equine Energy anytime that you choose. When you are ready, prepare for re-entry into whatever you have next on your agenda for the day. Enjoy!

- What wisdom did your horse-self have for you? _____

  _____

  _____

- Where is your secret spot of Equine Energy located? _____

  _____

- How will you use this magickal spot of intuition and connection? _____

  _____

Sleek, stunning, strong, elegant, graceful, and exquisite are just a few words that come to mind as I envision you embodying your horse-self. If it feels right, allow your Equine Energy to support you as you go about your days. Horses are magnificent and being 'of service' to humans has been their conscious choice. In her book, Linda Kohanov also talks about this sacred inter-species contract. When we can step away from the historical misinterpretations of this contract and see it not as one of servitude, but as one of liberal and sovereign generosity, perhaps we will begin relating to the Epona spirit differently. The Equine majesty is in your veins, too. Treat yourself accordingly. I'll start now. Thank you, Sister Goddess. I honor your dedication, loyalty, courage, and beauty of spirit. I love you.

~ SPS #2: ~
* Kintsugi *

Take a page out of a magazine, book, or use a plain piece of scrap paper. Rip the page into ten or fifteen smaller pieces and shuffle the pieces to mix them up. Next, find another medium on which to glue the smaller pieces. This can be another piece of paper, a balloon, a cardboard box, a folder cover, a piece of aluminum foil… anything goes. Let your creativity guide you. When you have chosen your medium, grab some glue, tape, or a stapler. This is the beginning of our version of recreating the centuries old Japanese artform of Kintsugi, or Kintsukuroi, which beautifully translates to "golden joinery." Unlike traditional repair attempts that seek to mend broken vessels in ways that hide the breakage, the Kintsugi technique celebrates the cracks of each piece of by using precious metals for restoration. Instead of disguising the flaws, this technique highlights the perfect imperfections with stunning seams of gold, platinum, and silver to honor the unique history, story, experience, and beauty held within each piece of pottery. The philosophy is that with Kintsugi, everything is eligible and deserving of a second chance - a second life - and through this, we realize the beauty held within the flaws and the mistakes. Just like Stella, we all have cracks and crevices that we may feel are anything but beautiful. Yet, when held through the perspective of Kintsugi, these experiences are the very cracks where the beauty of life can shine through the brightest. Take a look at your torn-up pieces of paper and let them represent the pieces of you that are perfectly imperfect in their unique history, story, and beauty. Decorate them, label them, or leave them blank. When you are ready - in any random order - begin to put your smaller pieces back together. Adhere them to the surface with your selected sticking agent to create a new piece of unique and reflective art. To highlight the *'Golden Joinery'* of your Kintsugi practice, you can fill the cracks between the pieces with marker, glitter glue, gel pens, colored pencils, etc. Wherever it feels right and however you feel called, begin to draw and trace the lines between each of your smaller pieces, emphasizing the cracks and breaks with color, splendor, and loving attention. When your piece feels complete, take a good look at what has been created. As you see how the pieces fit together in this new way, notice the precious details between them. Honor the beauty, mistakes, and connections. Honor the second chances. Honor yourself and all that you have been through. This stunning work of art is your unique mending process, and nobody could have done it but you. Finish with a big hug around your own shoulders. Thank you. I love you.

~ SPS #3: ~
* Blessings Bag *

Grab an old purse or bag that you have hanging in your closet and get some scrap paper, a pen, and a pair of scissors. We are going to create a *'Blessings Bag'* to use for 30 days. Cut the sheets of paper so that you have 30 individual strips to write your intended blessings on. On each piece of paper, choose one of the five sentences below to fill in and claim what you want to receive over the next month. Fill in the five sentences six different times with unique blessings for each day, giving you a total of 30. When you are finished, fold the 30 blessings and put them into your bag. For the next 30 days, pull out one blessing per day and read it aloud as many times as you choose.

- Today, I will **receive**_____
- Today, I will **feel**_____
- Today, I will **know**_____
- Today, I will **see**_____
- Today, I will **hear**_____

Each day take a quick minute to write down your blessings.

Today I received,	Today I felt,	Today I knew,
Today I saw,	Today I heard,	Today I received,
Today I felt,	Today I knew,	Today I saw,
Today I heard,	Today I received,	Today I felt,
Today I knew,	Today I saw,	Today I heard,
Today I received,	Today I felt,	Today I knew,
Today I saw,	Today I heard,	Today I received,
Today I felt,	Today I knew,	Today I saw,
Today I heard,	Today I received,	Today I felt,

Today I knew,	Today I saw,	Today I heard,

Thirty days is a long time to implement any extra step into your routine. Congratulations on your dedication! What do you notice now that you have created and claimed all of these blessings? Finish this activity by completing the following sentence.

As I Create and Claim my Blessings, I…

_____

_____

_____

Don't forget to include yourself as one of your blessings. I count you as one of mine! Doing these activities and honoring yourself in this way is a blessing to everyone. Thank you! I love you.

~ SPS #4: ~
* Equal Energy *

In different modalities of energy work, our Energy Systems or Chakras can balance with one another. In the Esoteric Healing Work that I have studied, the Crown balances with the Basic (or *Root*), the Sacral balances with the Throat, and the Heart balances with the Solar Plexus. This can be a really helpful perspective to hold as we work with our Chakras because it reminds us to value the seven Centers equally. Sometimes, because the Heart deals with love, the Ajna deals with intuition, and the Crown deals with bliss, they can be the main focus. However, all of our Chakras are important, and they all work together in beautifully symbiotic ways. Let's have some fun with our Chakras and see what guidance these fantastically functional relationships can offer. When you are ready, take a few deep breaths and quiet your mind. Become aware of your physical body, emotions, thoughts, Ego, and Soul. Let your awareness create an open conduit of exchange between these levels of your consciousness for guidance, love, and energy to be both given and received.

- Begin with the connection of your **Crown Chakra** to your **Basic Chakra**.
  - Allow your consciousness to simultaneously rest at the crown of your head for your **Crown Chakra** and the base of your spine (or perineum) for your **Basic Chakra**. The correlating colors are lavender for the Crown and red for the Basic. Visualize the colors and allow them to dance together in your imagination. See them blending and swirling as if you were pouring them onto an empty canvas.
    - *The **Crown Chakra** connects us to our bliss and our divinity. This energetic center opens and supports our facilitation and transformation from human beings into spiritual beings.*
    - *The **Basic Chakra** connects us to our will and grounds us in the present moment. It can be activated and over-activated by stress, fear, and anxiety. This energetic center responds with flight, fight, or freeze.*

- With this information:
  - Ask your **Crown** and your **Basic Chakras** to come into Balance.
  - Ask to be shown how they work together in perfect harmony.
  - Ask to be shown how they can be held in the highest conscious expression of love.
  - Ask for new ways to connect, express, feel, and intuit them in order to bring about the Greatest and the Highest Good.

- Next, bring your awareness to the connection between your **Sacral Chakra** and your **Throat Chakra**.
  - Allow your consciousness to simultaneously rest at your lower abdomen, between your navel and the base of your spine, for your **Sacral Chakra** and your mid-throat for your **Throat Chakra**. The correlating colors are orange for the Sacral and blue for the Throat. Visualize the colors and allow them to dance together in your imagination. Pour them - witnessing as they blend and swirl onto your already beautiful canvas - adding them to the lavender and red.
    - *The **Sacral Chakra** connects us to our creativity, sexuality, and our ability to manifest new life into the world. This energetic center deals with all of our relationships, especially the one we have with ourselves.*
    - *The **Throat Chakra** is the seat of our mental body and holds all of our belief systems. This energetic center is about honest, authentic, and clear communication.*
      - With this information:
        - Ask your **Sacral** and your **Throat Chakras** to come into Balance.
        - Ask to be shown how they work together in perfect harmony.
        - Ask to be shown how they can be held in the highest conscious expression of love.
        - Ask for new ways to connect, express, feel, and intuit them in order to bring about the Greatest and the Highest Good.

- Next, bring your awareness to the connection between your **Heart Chakra** and your **Solar Plexus Chakra**.
  - Allow your consciousness to simultaneously rest at your mid-chest or between your breasts for your **Heart Chakra** and your navel for your **Solar Plexus Chakra**. The correlating colors are green for the Heart and yellow for the Solar Plexus. Visualize the colors and allow them to dance together in your imagination. Pour them - witnessing as they blend and swirl onto your already beautiful canvas - adding them to the lavender, red, orange, and blue.
    - *The **Heart Chakra** reflects our abilities to unconditionally give and receive love. This energetic center deals with how we express love both to ourselves and to others. It also deals with the energies of group consciousness.*
    - *The **Solar Plexus Chakra** is the seat of our emotional body and is known as a power center. This energetic center is all about emotions, emotional expression, and emotional authenticity.*
      - With this information:
        - Ask your **Heart** and your **Solar Plexus Chakras** to come into Balance.
        - Ask to be shown how they work together in perfect harmony.
        - Ask to be shown how they can be held in the highest conscious expression of love.
        - Ask for new ways to connect, express, feel, and intuit them in order to bring about the Greatest and the Highest Good.

- Finally, bring your awareness to your Third Eye, or **Ajna Chakra**.
  - Allow your consciousness to rest at your mid-brow or forehead and connect into the energy of your **Ajna Chakra**. The correlating color is purple. Visualize the color and allow it to dance in your imagination. Pour the vibrant purple onto your beautiful canvas, witnessing as it blends and swirls with the lavender, red, orange, blue, green, and yellow.
    - *The **Ajna Chakra** is where our intuitive guidance comes in. This Energy Center does not have just one partner, it partners and balances with all of the other Centers on the body. The balance and clarity of the **Ajna** is a direct reflection of the balance and clarity of the **Basic, Sacral, Solar Plexus, Heart, and Throat Chakras**.*
      - With this information:
        - Ask your **Ajna** to come into balance with your **Basic, Sacral, Solar Plexus, Heart, and Throat**.
        - Ask to be shown how this system works together in perfect harmony.
        - Ask to be shown how all of your **Chakras** can be held in the highest conscious expression of love.
        - Ask for new ways to connect, express, feel, and intuit your Energy Centers in order to bring about the Greatest and the Highest Good.

- As a last step before completion, gently reconnect all of your Chakras. Visualize the tendrils of energy flowing between, around, through, and underneath them. In your imagination, allow your understanding of these Energy Centers to once again be infused with equality, expression, connection, and love.

Thank you. This work is like tossing a pebble into a pond… it can ripple out and make a big difference in the way things look and feel. It is also a gift. As your energetic vibration shifts to be more aligned with love, others will sense it and want to make a shift, too. It may be small and it may be unconscious, but it is a start! I love you!

~ SPS #5: ~
* Seven Directions *

The directions of the compass - North, South, East, and West - have long been known to hold spiritual significance. Based on their connection to the Natural World, these directions have powerful wisdom to share regarding our physical, emotional, mental, relational, and spiritual health. Long practiced in many different Native and Indigenous cultures, the ceremonial creation of ritual to acclimate and assimilate guidance from the directions has offered support, comfort, and connection for individuals and groups alike. When you are ready - from within your home environment - locate seven different items to represent the four directions of the compass and the three additional directions of Above, Below, and Within. These items can be small, meaningful things that are easily transportable and OK to set on the ground. Let your intuition be your guide as you locate these things to represent: North, South, East, West, Above, Below, and Within. Now that you have your sacred items, find a place either outside or by a window so that you may gaze upon the natural beauty of Mother Earth. If either of these options are unavailable, that is OK! Do this ceremony wherever you can. Sit comfortably and place your items in their respective directions of N, S, E, & W (helpful hint: use the compass application on your phone to find your directions). Place the item for Above directly in front of you, the item for Below directly behind you, and the item for Within in your lap. As you continue to get comfortable, let your breathing become slower and deeper. Soften your eyes and let your gaze fall upon the beauty around you. As you become aware of the connection between your heart and the heart of every living thing, begin.

- Set three prayerful intentions and speak them out loud. Some examples are: peace, love, connection, bliss, joy, and authenticity.
  - Begin in the Direction of the **East.** The East is the direction of the rising sun, birth, and new beginnings. The East offers us the teachings of **courageous trust, radiant purity,** and **peaceful leadership.**
    - The Color associated with the East is **Yellow.**
    - The Element associated with the East is **Air.**
      - *Visualize yourself soaring high on the currents of warm air and landing on a mountaintop. As you look out, ask to see with the eyes of your Heart. As the eyes of your heart open, create your prayer to the* **East.**
        - Speak your prayer while holding the item that represents the East, which will infuse it with Divine Energy.
          - When your prayer is complete, set the item down.

  - Move to the Direction of the **South.** The South is the direction of the mid-day sun, healing, and comfort. The South offers us the teachings of **sensitive generosity,** sovereign loyalty, and **creative expression.**
    - The Color Associated with the South is **Red.**
    - The Element associated with the South is **Fire.**
      - *Visualize yourself lying on a bed of soft, new grass. As you sink into this innocence, ask for ease and support as walk your path with creativity and strength. With this newfound strength and innocence, create your prayer to the* **South.**
        - Speak your prayer while holding the item that represents the South, which will infuse it with **Divine Energy.**
          - When your prayer is complete, set the item down.

  - Move to the direction of the **West.** The West is the direction of darkness, cleansing, and personal awareness. The West offers us the teachings **of meditative visioning, luminous dreaming,** and **steadfast authenticity.**
    - The Color Associated with the West is **Black.**
    - The Element associated with the West is **Water.**
      - *Visualize yourself floating on cool water under a Full Moon. As you hold your hand at your heart, ask for the intuitive clarity to know your* Divine Purpose. *With this clear vision of purpose and path, create your prayer to the* **West.**
        - Speak your prayer while holding the item that represents the West, which will infuse it with **Divine Energy.**
          - When your prayer is complete, set the item down.

  - Move to the Direction of the **North.** The North is the direction of abundance, completion, and wholeness. The North offers us the teachings of **intellectual wisdom, timeless gratitude,** and **ancient connections.**

- - - The Color Associated with the North is **White**.
    - The Element Associated with the North is **Earth**.
      - *Visualize yourself standing on a steep rocky outcrop. With your left foot claiming connection to the old, and your right foot claiming connection to the new, ask for replenishment so that you may continue your path of service. With a full heart, create your prayer to the **North**.*
        - Speak your prayer while holding the item that represents the North, which will infuse it with **Divine Energy**.
          - When your prayer is complete, set the item down.

  - Move to the direction of **Above**. Above is the direction of our vast sky, where linear Father Sun and cyclical Mother Moon reside. Life Force and Life Rhythm are both protected and regulated here. Above offers us the teachings of **ardent dependability, expansive commitment,** and **resolute grace**.
    - *Visualize yourself sitting with Father Sun and Mother Moon. They both face you with unconditional love, admiration, and respect. In this safe and secure space of absolute acceptance, you breathe deeply, knowing your own perfection. From the connection of this empowered trinity, create your prayer to **Above**.*
      - Speak your prayer while holding the item that represents Above, which will infuse it with **Divine Energy**.
        - When your prayer is complete, set the item down.

  - Move to the direction of **Below**. Below is the direction of our Mother Earth with all of her sustenance, compassion, and mercy. In this warm and inviting womb of rebirth, your whole being relaxes into the preciousness of the moment. Below offers us the teachings of **radical nourishment, uncompromised sanctuary,** and **exquisite beauty**.
    - *Visualize yourself being held and cradled by Mother Earth. Your body and your consciousness melt into the magickal, milky waters of her vastness, releasing anything that is no longer serving you. As you float in her dark womb, create your prayer to **Below**.*
      - Speak your prayer while holding the item that represents Below, which will infuse it with **Divine Energy**.
        - When your prayer is complete, set the item down.

  - As the final step, become connected to the direction of **Within.** Within is the direction of Spirit. This is where all dimensions and all universes converge, existing as a macrocosm within the microcosm of your individual consciousness. Within offers us the teachings of **ecstatic balance, resplendent bliss,** and **jubilant oneness**.
    - *Visualize yourself expanding beyond all time and space, throughout all lifetimes, and past any known or unknown restrictions. Feel your ascension journey as it unfolds before you, once again reiterating the message that you are a Divine Being of Love and Light. From this zero-point of oneness, create your prayer to **Within**.*
      - Speak your prayer while holding the item that represents Within, which will infuse it with **Divine Energy**.
        - When your prayer is complete, set the item down.

As you complete your sacred circle, once again become aware of the energy tethering you to every other living thing throughout all time and space. Let your awareness rest again on your inbreath and outbreath, taking slow, deep breaths as you reacclimate yourself to your environment. Gently open your eyes and slowly bring your soft gaze back to a focused clarity. Collect your seven sacred items and verbally re-declare your three intentions from the beginning of this activity. Place your seven items on an altar or in some other special place in your home to remind you of this sacred ceremony. Thank you for doing this beautiful ritual. Throughout all time and space, I send you gratitude and love.

Crystal Love: Stella's Crystal, Bloodstone, is also known as the 'Stone of Courage.' This purifying and cleansing stone has long been used for its revitalizing gifts of heightened intuition, reduced irritability, increased creativity, advanced detoxification, and empowered healing. Both grounding and protective, Bloodstone offers us an interesting perspective of mature flexibility to handle life's ups and downs. Mix this with Bloodstone's abilities to deflect negativity, and you've got dual fortification to stay rooted in the heart-centered energy of love - which promotes the momentum of peace and harmony - while reducing the burdens of aggression, impatience, and resistance. A very mystical stone, this Crystal can connect us to our dreams, dispel confusion, enhance spiritual wisdom, and root us to the present moment as we cultivate our potentials for magick. Also regarded as a gem of noble sacrifice, Bloodstone is truly the stone of the Spiritual Activist, offering solace and support to all who are called to give of themselves in service to others. When in the midst of emotional, mental, and spiritual turmoil due to the processes of awakening, ascension, and expansion, use Bloodstone to access the higher levels of masterful sight needed to understand the value of surrender. In Ancient times, Bloodstone was regarded as an audible oracle, giving off sound as a means of guidance. As you work with this Crystal and patiently wait for Bloodstone to speak its wisdom, intentionally ask for a calm, balanced alignment so that you may continue the work of bringing about the Greatest and Highest Good for All.

Suggested Reading to Experience, Feel, and be Transformed by the Epona Equine Magick, *The Tao of Equus: A Woman's Journey of Healing and Transformation through the Way of the Horse* by Linda Kohanov.

Jamie

My life has always been one of change and big decisions going hand in hand to produce destiny. Listening to my intuition isn't what I would have called it twenty years ago, but that is exactly what I've been doing. I think a lot about that younger version of me. I laugh sometimes because she seems so unrecognizable to the woman I am today. I bet she would laugh at me, too, because I am so different from her. Although I know that when I connect into younger versions of myself and other versions of myself, they are grateful to have my wisdom and love. I know they need it. I need it from them, too. Being able to send love out into the multi-dimensional field – what I call wisdom teachings - came to me about two years ago. It started the week after Summer Solstice. I should have known something big was going to hit the fan when a baby owl took a nose-dive in our yard. Thankfully, after a few minutes of stunned confusion, he was fine. That was a Saturday, and by the following Thursday, I started to experience feelings of deep devastation. It was dark and extreme, and I had no idea where it was coming from. Even today, I have a hard time reading my writings from back then. I was a shell of myself. I wanted to leave the Earth. I kept having overwhelming thoughts and feelings of being *done*, wanting to go home – wherever that was – and knowing that my family would be fine without me. Not that they wouldn't miss me… but that if I somehow spontaneously combusted, which is what I was hoping would happen, it was their sacred contract, too, right? I know that sounds glib in light of something so serious, but I'm being completely honest. That is the space I was in and it persisted - off and on - for months. One day, I was in the kitchen putting dishes away, and out of nowhere I received some information that helped pull me out of it. The way this information was shared was so peaceful and simple. Was it my Higher Self? Was it Angels? Maybe Ascended Masters? I say "yes" to all three, and more. What I do know for sure is that this benevolent Source wanted me to know that sometimes overwhelming feelings come in through the energy fields around us. For me that day, I was being shown how these feelings can come in from concurrent versions of ourselves. I was also shown that we can agree to receive these feelings with sovereignty, or we can decide to decline them with sovereignty. We can also intentionally connect into the multi-verse and send our love out. We can even request for love to be sent back to us when we need a little boost. I didn't question what I was being told. In fact, since I've opened myself up to receiving guidance, I haven't questioned any of it. There is a sense of calm, easy grace present when I hear or channel things in from the Divine. In those moments, there is pure, empowered peace. And the guidance has always been beneficial. Sometimes it's that sense of timeless grace, and the gratitude that I even notice it at all, that keeps me going. It's also pretty cool to know that I am an empowered being who can reach out to simultaneously give and receive healing. I can hear that twenty-year old version of me laughing right now and saying, "If you tell people this, you are going to get laughed off the face of the Earth!" My present self opens my arms to her and says, "Come here, darling. We don't live our life based on what others think anymore, remember?" It was a trip to Egypt that led me onto this path all those years ago. Prior to it, a five-year relationship had ended. I had moved myself and my two dogs across the country to take an unstable job in a field that I knew very little about. I had no family close by and only a handful of friends. I was thirty, single, floating untethered, and ready to check out. Living in paradise helped. Little did I know that my life was about to take a major turn. About ten years before, when I graduated college, I was sure that I was going to be on Broadway. So sure, that after graduation, I moved to New York City. I was so tenacious and wild. Not wild in the sense of making bad choices. I was wild in that I knew what I wanted, and I was going to figure out how to make it happen. Thankfully, my wild hasn't left me. It has transformed a bit, but I've still got it. The first apartment I found to sublet in New York turned out to be a disaster. After about 10 days, the girl I was renting from locked me out and refused to let me back in to get my things without a police escort. Welcome to NYC. That night, I sat on a park bench in Queens, and put ideas together on how to stay in the Big Apple so that I could make my dreams come true. By morning, I had figured it out. I remembered that I had friends. I had a network that I had created doing Summer Stock. Those 'real, live actors from New York City' that I called and told my family about when I got cast in my first professional theatre job, they gathered together and helped me, and I had a new place within 48 hours. I didn't know it then, but that sense of family, that sense of being connected, it allowed me to release the trauma of what had happened. Sure, the apartment fiasco was short lived, but it was nonetheless terrifying. All of the money I had saved, all of the pavement I had pounded to find a place - and believe me nobody wanted to sublet to a first timer - all of the hopes I had, not to mention all my belongings held hostage in this woman's apartment… it all could have disappeared if I had let myself believe what the voice of fear was trying to tell me. The night that woman locked me out, I begged her to change her mind. She said some awful things to me that could have found real estate within my consciousness. Somehow, I was able to insulate myself against her words and not let them become part of me. My hope protected me. My hopes were so strong that I wasn't about to accept what I was being told. I had big things to do and I wasn't going to be derailed by her or anybody. Turns out she was running a scam, so the sweet NYPD officers who helped me get my things told me. They suggested small claims court to get my money back, but I couldn't wait around for that. I had a gig! An out-of-town gig, but that didn't matter. That gig led to another and another and that led to a life of me living and loving in New York City for several years. When I got what I thought was my 'you've made it' job, everything changed, and not for the better. After months of working on a show as the lead, I was replaced, and made to understudy the part. I was devastated. I tried to act cool, but I wasn't. I know this kind of thing happens all the time, but it was the first time it had happened to me, and it broke my heart. So much so that my heart got brittle. I didn't know then what I know now, and the wound made me mean. I kept at acting for another year and a half or so, but when I had the opportunity to move and start over, I jumped. Not because I didn't absolutely love performing, but because I knew my heart was too tender to continue on in an industry that created such competitiveness, jealousy, and self-loathing within me. Today, I know that I allowed all of that to happen. Of course, if you had told me that then, I would have fought you on it. But, by going through all of that, I ultimately learned how to choose love for myself over a career path that was no longer a fit. My hopes and dreams were shifting, and I had to allow the metamorphosis. I couldn't grow into the new me while holding on to the old self. I had to let go and trust that I would fly. It took me a while, but I got a jolt when I saw that brochure for the trip to Egypt. From the moment I read the words "Spiritual Pilgrimage," I knew I was going. There was no doubt. I lived on credit cards and paid the installments to secure my spot in cash. I knew very little about the trip, only that I had to get a ticket to JFK Airport in order to catch my flight to Cairo. When I landed, I was overcome with the feeling that everything was about to change. I had never even heard of a Chakra, and there I was in a small group of master level energy healers getting ready to hit the sacred sites of Mother Egypt. It was amazing! I meditated for the first time. I activated aspects of my being that brought forth past life memories. Most important, on the Isle of Philae in the Temple of Isis, I met the Goddess. I didn't realize it at the time. I still very much believed that God was a man who lived outside of me. But when Isis talked to me, although I wasn't conscious of hearing her call as an awakening to the Divine Feminine within, that is exactly what happened. She flat out told me, "You are not going to work as a professional actor anymore. You are going to work helping others." This time I heard what I was told, and it did garner some mental real estate. A lot of it. I got home from the trip. I started teaching adult acting classes. That led to utilizing the connective and healing tools of theatre and drama with younger populations. Next, I went back to graduate school to become a Drama Therapist and Marriage and Family Therapist and I haven't looked back. I believe it when I tell people that Isis is my homegirl because she has been with me every step of the way. I have been working, being *of service*, since coming back from Egypt. Has it been an easy path? Nope. But I've found that the more I follow my path, the more I love myself, and the more I love myself, the more I discover my

Divine Purpose. Doing that takes huge amounts of trust in my intuition. Like the grace I mentioned before, it's the same with my intuition. When that peaceful, loving inner voice communicates with me, I perk up and pay attention. Is following my intuition always easy? No. Sometimes my intuition guides me to places I have no desire to go… or at least I think I don't. Yet, when I really get honest with myself, my intuition is always right. Accepting this consistent invitation has been what one of my teachers calls "a dragon ride." I can't think of a better way to explain it. Sometimes growth - which can come from doing nothing – feels anything but comfortable and safe. Regardless, I've managed to hang on, and after all of these go arounds on the dragon, I know my Divine Purpose is a path of healing and service. I also know that for me to stay rooted on this path, I have to stay rooted in self-love. That has taken practice and dedication. Not the serving and healing part. I'm a natural at that. It's the self-love practice that I have to remind myself of every day. I joke that this is my 'Earth-School-Amnesia.' Maybe that resonates, maybe that doesn't, but I know my human being is only capable of so much. I forget what I've learned. Sometimes I forget on a daily basis. If I don't approach this Divine Purpose from the foundation of self-compassion, self-understanding, self-forgiveness, and self-acceptance, then the whole structure crumbles. I get depleted. I lead from my wounded-self. I become attached to outcomes. I take things personally. I let my internal punisher talk louder than my intuitive Higher Self. When I am in those places, I am not in my purpose. Does this mean I am joyful 24/7? No. But, living this way, I am living within the vibration of joy a whole lot more than if I wasn't. All of it. The me's of yesterday… my experiences, hopes, dreams, weaknesses, and disappointments... they have all come together to weave the tapestry of my current self. That tapestry is a beautiful work of art and that is what I want to share. We are all beautiful tapestries. We are all unique, Divine, perfectly imperfect works of art. We've been through what we've been through to make us *us,* and the world needs us just as we are. With all of our mistakes and mishaps. With all of our wisdom and growth. Leading from that level of self-love and self-acceptance inspires others to do the same. When enough of us are vibing that vibe, *everything* shifts and reflects that vibration back. That is the magick we all possess. The more I love myself, the more I love you. The more you love yourself, the more you love me. When I find my way to that sovereign pocket of security, I am filled with gratitude. I am here and there is no place else I'd rather be.

Making This Story Your Own:

Jamie's story shines a light on the Divinity of our human experiences.
Take a moment, breathe, and reflect.
What stands out for you when you read her words?
Is there a situation in your life that is similar to Jamie's?
Perhaps part of her story feels connected to your own.
How can you relate her experiences to your past, present, and future?

- *My Connection to Jamie's Story* _____

_____

_____

_____

_____

Knowing that you aren't alone, let's gently explore some other themes from Jamie's story together:

- **Grace**
    - Are you aware of grace? Why, or why not? What are your thoughts when you hear that word? How do you associate it with yourself? Are you graceful? Are you full of grace? Are you both? Are you neither? When it comes to embodying grace within your life and relationships, does it come naturally? Does it feel necessary to push or force grace? What if you only have to continue being who you already are to have it? How might you begin to recognize the grace around and within you? Is there an easy way to access and claim this grace? How will you trust it? How will you know that grace is always present?

- **Your Past is Past**
    - How much does your past influence your present? When you engage with your life and relationships, is every moment a new opportunity? If not, can it be? Where would you like a fresh start? In what relationships and situations would you like a do-over? Who might like a do-over with *you*? Can releasing the past offer freedom? Does thinking about the past as a past life sound beneficial? How might it work if the past offered only support and assistance with no restrictions or imprisonment? If you could start over with everyone and everything, what would be different? If you could start over with yourself, what would be different? If these differences would be helpful, where and how can you begin this fresh start?

- **Tapestry of You**
    - How often do you laugh, not *at*, but *with* yourself? How often do you provide comfort for yourself through the messy parts of life? How often are you your own best friend, even when you're down? What if **all** of your experiences – good, bad, and otherwise - made up the softest, most reassuring blanket? Would you wrap that blanket around your shoulders for warmth and relief? Would you be able to take a moment and enjoy just being you? Do you enjoy your complete self? If yes, how and if no, why not? If you do enjoy the total tapestry of you, how does this affect the rest of your life? If you do not, how does this affect you and can this change? How would liking, loving, and enjoying yourself – **all** of yourself - more be beneficial for you and for others? What can you begin doing today that will provide more opportunities for laughter, love, and enjoyment with the tapestry of you?

Sacred Play Suggestions:

~ SPS #1: ~
* Your Sign *

What does your sign say? Not your astrological sign, or the sign out in front of your business, but your sign… the *energy* that you project onto all of your relationships. Not until two years into this project, four years into facilitating the Divine Mommy Groups, and five years into being a marriage and family therapist did I realize that my sign says, "I'm not enough." I discovered this while listening to a class online where the facilitator was talking about following guidance for generosity, love, and connection. As I was furiously taking notes, my immediate reaction was, "Ahh jeez…. I'm not generous…. I'm not loving…. I'm not connected…. I have *got* to find a way to do *more* of those things… and *fast*!" Even as I was saying these things to myself, my internal voice sounded weepy, helpless, and totally deflated. As the class kept going, I began making lists in my head of all the ways I could begin incorporating more generosity, love, and connection into my life and my relationships. Those lists quickly turned into fantasies… only these weren't pleasant fantasies. They were punishment fantasies. In a glimpse, I had highlighted all of my perceived mistakes, limitations, and faults and turned them inward. I put my lack up in lights and it was easy-peasy-lemon-squeezy because I have been doing it for over four decades. The scariest part was, I wasn't even aware I was doing it because leading with my sign is second nature. To say I am an expert at this is this a huge understatement. It wasn't until the facilitator said "Maybe it's time to write that book… start that group… or take that course…" did I jolt out of the punishment fantasy and realize, "Holy shit! I HAVE been doing these things. I HAVE been listening to guidance. I HAVE dedicated myself to others. I AM generous. I AM loving. I AM connected!" That realization left me numb and I had to sit with it for a while to think about some things. When I vulnerably admitted to myself that one of my core limiting beliefs is *I am not enough, nor will I ever be*, a lot of things started to make sense. Personal and professional relationships that had left me questioning were now easier to understand. I began to recognize why I was somewhat turned off by connections that were mutually respectful, beneficial, and fulfilling. Those types of relationships didn't fit with my sign. They didn't support my core belief. Therefore, my punishment fantasy wouldn't allow them much real estate because they didn't reinforce my lack. These relationships mirrored my abundance, talents, and gifts and my Ego was having none of that. I was drawn to the relationships that felt punishing and familiar. So, what's *your* sign? Let's explore together. Think about some themes of your personal and professional relationships. Remember, these aren't your Mantras. These are core beliefs - the limiting ones - that keep you from living a bliss-filled life. These relationships can be new or old, functional or dysfunctional. They can be with friends, colleagues, family members, lovers, etc. They can also be active, meaning they are still happening. Or, they can be inactive, and not happening any longer.

- **Our Relationships:**
    - What do you notice about the beginning of your relationships? _____

    _____

    _____

    - What do you notice about the middle of your relationships? _____

    _____

    _____

    - What do you notice when there is conflict in your relationships? _____

    _____

    _____

    - What do you notice when your relationships end or transform? _____

    _____

    _____

- Looking at all of the answers, what do you think your sign is? _____
_____

Ok, let's keep excavating. For this next group of questions, write whatever comes to mind first without editing or censoring.

- **Our Inner Voices:**
    - When someone gives you a compliment, what does the voice inside your head say?
    _____

    - When you accomplish something or experience success, what does the voice inside your head say?
    _____
    _____

    - When you feel love or contentment, what does the voice inside your head say?
    _____
    _____

    - When someone is kind to you, what does the voice inside your head say?
    _____

    - When you want to be kind to yourself, what does the voice inside your head say?
    _____
    _____

    - Whose voice is inside your head? _____
    _____

- Looking at these answers, what is your sign? _____
_____

- Is this different than what you originally thought? If so, why? _____
_____

Now, onto fantasyland. We won't stay here long, I promise.

- **Our Fantasies:**
    - What are some of your internal punishment fantasies? _____

    _____

    _____

    _____

    - Where did they come from? _____

    _____

    - How do they influence your sign? _____

    _____

- Looking at these answers, what is your sign? _____

    _____

- Is this different than the other two? If so, why? _____

    _____

Ready to put it all together? Look back over everything you have written, simmer it down, and answer…

What is your sign?

_____

Now it's your turn for a holy shit moment.

- Why isn't this sign *valid*? _____
    - Please give examples. _____

    _____

- Why isn't this sign *true*? _____
    - Please give examples. _____

    _____

- Why isn't this sign *accurate*? _____
    - Please give examples. _____
    _____

- Why isn't this sign *right*? _____
    - Please give examples. _____
    _____

- Why isn't this sign *genuine*? _____
    - Please give examples. _____
    _____

- Why isn't this sign *real*? _____
    - Please give examples. _____
    _____

Just a few more steps until the creation of your new sign. These parts of you, the way you navigate relationships, the inner voice, and the punishment fantasy… believe it or not, they weren't manifested to make you miserable. They were created with really good intentions and for really good reasons. They just got a little off course. Let's find a way to release them with gratitude.

- ***Misdirected* Relationship Wisdom:**
    - How has your relationship wisdom been helpful until now? _____
    _____
    - How has your relationship wisdom been protective until now? _____
    _____
    - How can you release this relationship wisdom with gratitude? _____
    _____
    - What is your new relationship wisdom? _____
    _____

- *Misguided* **Inner Voice Support:**
    - How has your inner voice been helpful until now? _____
    _____

    - How has your inner voice been protective until now? _____
    _____

    - How can you release this inner voice with gratitude? _____
    _____

    - What does your new inner voice sound like? _____
    _____

- *Misapplied* **Fantasy Creation:**
    - How has your punishment fantasy been beneficial until now? _____
    _____

    - How has your punishment fantasy been protective until now? _____
    _____

    - How can you release this punishment fantasy with gratitude? _____
    _____

    - What is your new fantasy? _____
    _____
    _____

Are you ready? From this moment forward, what are you going to lead with? What is the empowering and positive message that you will choose to energetically influence every interaction? Isn't this exciting?!? You've done the work. Give yourself the credit. My new sign is simple. It is "I AM ENOUGH!" What is yours?

My New Sign
_____

Woo-hoo! That is an awesome sign! Go and give it a test-drive. See what happens. As you get used to this new sign, so will those around you. You might not be able to see this new sign with your eyes, but you will feel it in your heart. Thanks for doing this. I love you!

~ SPS #2: ~
* No Pushing *

Where are you on the path of growth, evolution, and spirituality, and what are you doing that is letting you know you are on this path? Maybe you read books and take classes. Maybe you have a regular practice or daily devotional. Take a breath and think of all of the things that have led you to being *you* at this very moment. Wow, you are awesome! You are! Accept the compliment! Now take a breath and think about this: where on the path have you - or are you - *pushing* for growth? Only you can answer this question because no one else truly knows your experiences other than you. Try answering the question again: where are you pushing? It is understandable why we do this. We live in a world that values productivity. The routine of 'producing to be of value' is so habituated that most of us don't even notice it anymore. It is a belief system that goes down to our genetic coding and it is supported everywhere. Even our individual evolution and ascension processes have been highjacked. But, do we really need to be doing all of this stuff? If we have established an awareness of the path, do we need to do anything else? It is hard. My mind instantly thinks of a retort. I can list all of the reasons why we have to do something to achieve growth. But maybe that is where I am off base. Can this kind of growth ever be *achieved*? Or is this something we *receive*? I giggle as I think about this because it makes me remember my sweet Grandma. My Grammy was an amazing woman in so many ways that it would take me pages and pages to write about all of her gifts and talents. She didn't yell, raise her voice, or speak crossly. I have no idea how she did it. I only heard her cuss one time and that was at my Grandpa when he was fussing at her about her backing out of the driveway. Although I knew she was really irritated, she even did this in a sweet and even-tempered way. She said, "Well, what the shit does Grandpa want?" The reason I mention her is that when it comes to this question of growth, I can hear her soft, sweet voice telling me, "Stop. No pushing. Sit down. Be quiet. Don't do anything." I probably hear those words now because I heard them a million times when I was a kid. She did have to break up a lot of fights between the cousins. Anyhoo, try it. Channel your inner Grammy. With your kindest, sweetest inner voice, repeat those words and just be aware of *being you* for a moment.

Stop. No pushing. Sit down. Be quiet. Don't do anything.

The irony is not lost on me that this book has 179 other suggestions of *stuff* to *do*. However, the intention for this book is to create such a strong relationship to our intuition that we ONLY do what is for our best and highest good. Whenever you feel the *push* creeping back in, reset with Grammy. Breathe and repeat.

Stop. No pushing. Sit down. Be quiet. Don't do anything.
Stop. No pushing. Sit down. Be quiet. Don't do anything.
Stop. No pushing. Sit down. Be quiet. Don't do anything.

And just receive. Oh, I love you. Be sure to receive that, too! And thank you!

~ SPS #3: ~
* Moldy Molds *

What molds do you feel like you have to fit into? These molds are sometimes dictated by the rules, restrictions, and constraints of the world we live in and are oftentimes different for the different roles we play. But do we really have to live by these molds, or have we just forgotten that we can chuck them in the trash? Sometimes these molds give us a sense of comfort because they are familiar. Sometimes these molds are painful, and we know that they aren't right for us. Sometimes they are unconscious, and we don't even realize how hard we try to fit into them. I would venture to say that no matter how these molds are manifesting within our lives, they keep us from our joy because they aren't completely *ours*. We didn't create them, but for some reason, we live by them. Why do we do this if they aren't 100% right for us? Let's identify some of these molds together. While digging deep for this information, don't forget to take into consideration the hidden societal messages bombarding us as socially acceptable paradigms. One of these socially accepted paradigms that has been so painful for me to realize and release in regard to my role as a woman, mother, and partner is: *Sacrifice is Noble*. What a bunch of BS! Sacrifice isn't noble. Sacrifice sucks! I am ready to let that moldy-old-stinky-sock-of-a-belief-system go! How about you? Let's explore together and see what comes up.

Moldy Molds

- What has been my **Motherhood** mold? _____
  _____

  - What is familiar and comfortable about this mold? _____
    _____

  - What is painful and uncomfortable about this mold? _____
    _____

  - What is clear about this mold? _____
    _____

  - What is unclear or hidden about this mold? _____
    _____

  - What are some sayings, quotes, and commonly held belief systems that support these molds of **Motherhood**?
    _____
    _____

  - How can I transform these old *molds* into ***beautiful new frames***? _____
    _____

  - How will these new frames be more in alignment for me? _____
    _____

- What has been my **Partnerhood** mold? _____
  _____

  o What is familiar and comfortable about this mold? _____
  _____

  o What is painful and uncomfortable about this mold? _____
  _____

  o What is clear about this mold? _____
  _____

  o What is unclear or hidden about this mold? _____
  _____

  o What are some sayings, quotes, and commonly held belief systems that support these molds of **Partnering**?
  _____
  _____
  _____

  o How can I transform these old *molds* into **beautiful new frames**? _____
  _____

  o How will these new frames be more in alignment for me? _____
  _____

- What has been my **Womanhood** mold? _____
  _____

  o What is familiar and comfortable about this mold? _____
  _____

  o What is painful and uncomfortable about this mold? _____
  _____

- What is clear about this mold? _____
  _____

- What is unclear or hidden about this mold? _____
  _____

- What are some sayings, quotes, and commonly held belief systems that support these molds of **being a woman**?
  _____
  _____
  _____

- How can I transform these old *molds* into **beautiful new frames**? ____
  _____

- How will these new frames be more in alignment for me? _____
  _____

You can answer questions like these for many more of the roles and molds that you play and fit into on a daily basis. Sometimes bringing awareness is enough to know that these things aren't working for us anymore. Sometimes we need more powerful reminders. Be sure to give yourself credit: socially accepted belief systems are powerful. Keep your thoughts and insights close as you create, recreate, and *re-frame* this new way of being. Love you! Thank you for doing this!

~ SPS #4: ~
* Crystal Force Field *

Sadly, while working on this project we lost our fifteen-year-old pit bull pup, Lydia. She was the greatest dog. A fabulous big sister to our daughter and a wonderful teacher of unconditional love, understanding, and forgiveness, she had a smile that could light up a room… or clear it, as her smile looked somewhat like a pre-pounce grimace with her lips pulled back and her teeth glaring. She was a big dog, and more than once as she sauntered to the door 'smiling,' we had to explain to guests, "We promise she isn't growling. She is just *really* excited to meet you!" The week before she died, we had a scare in which she acted as if she couldn't move her back legs. Thankfully we already had vet appointments for both of our dogs that day. When we left the office after a steroid shot, we were optimistic, and for the next week, Lyds slowly recovered. She even watched movies with us on the couch the night before she died. When I woke up the next morning and saw her, I knew without a doubt that she had decided it was her time. She looked at me from the couch and clearly told me she was ready to go. Because it was so early in the morning, Lyds and I were together for a few hours on our own. It was during this time that she gifted me some very useful wisdom. Forehead to forehead we sat, and as I continued to pour love into her, she shared with me how to energetically prepare for her transformation from the Earth Plane. As she communicated with me, she had no fear, only peace and love. She guided me on Mantras to sing, where to place my hands on her body, and how to begin preparing a portal for her Soul to travel onward. She also gave me some really useful Crystal wisdom. From this book, you can tell, I love Crystals. I use them, study them, work with them, talk to them, channel information from them, and much more. How do I get them? I buy them. Like every other Crystal lover who doesn't live with a Crystal mine in their backyard, I spend my moolah on rocks. Beautiful, magickal, healing, and inspiring rocks, yes, but that isn't the point. The point is, I love Crystals and I always want *more*. Big ones, small ones, cheap ones, expensive ones... it doesn't matter, I want to bring them all home with me. Early that morning as I sat preparing my canine baby to leave this physical world, she looked at me and said, "Mom, you don't need to have all of these Crystals." What? My head was in a lot of different places, obviously, and I thought maybe I had made that up. I looked at Lydia again, and clear as a bell, she gifted me the message that my energy around Crystals is one of possession. That, she advised, is the Ego. She went on to share that the Crystalline Realm is here for us all to use at will. We only have to ask, and they will come to be with us. We don't have to buy them or own them. Of course, there is no judgment on their part. They happily love and support us in whatever way we choose. From their unconditionally loving perspective, our perfection matches their own and however we want to commune with them is fine. Lydia's wisdom for me wasn't about that. It was about releasing my own mental script that was telling me that to work with a Crystal, I needed to own it and have it in front of me. She was also letting me know that my desire to possess 'things' was not of my Soul but of my Ego. Collecting the 'stuff' of life and holding onto it was keeping me tethered to the belief system that more, more, more equals happy, happy, happy. Desiring, wanting, seeking, and lusting after *stuff*, no matter what kind of *stuff* it is - Crystals, designer purses, cars, jewelry, books, plants, antiques, *whatever* - is the fear of the Ego trying to convince us that we are not enough... that we need all of this to be *safe*. Lydia then went on to show me how to work with Crystals in a way that - for me - was going to be more in alignment with my Soul. Now, before I get into the *how*, I want to clarify *why* I am sharing this bit of wisdom from Lydia. I am not trying to tell you what to do. Shoot... buy all the Crystals you want! Build a Crystal palace and invite me over. I only share this to offer a glimpse of my lesson around releasing Ego attachments. My attachment to *stuff* is my way of staying small and I don't want to do that anymore. As an initial step for this activity, take a moment, journal around your attachments to stuff, and see what comes up.

My Attachment to *Stuff*...
What does it look like and where can it be released?

_____

_____

_____

_____

Now, let's dive into the Crystal wisdom Lydia shared. It isn't complicated. You don't need certifications or degrees. All you have to do is ask the Crystal to be present and it will be. Lydia gifted me the visual of creating a layered force field of crystal love around myself. She also gifted me the knowledge of creating different *recipes* for the layers. For instance, yesterday on a long car ride I was experiencing fear around this book... irrational fears about the book being successful, unsuccessful, and everything in between. Alone on the road with my mind racing, I employed Lydia's force field recipe idea and asked for Moldavite (**mohl-d***uh*-**vahyt**),

Malachite, and Labradorite to crystallize - in that order - as a force field around my body. In my imagination, I visualized those beautiful Crystals swirling and forming a three-tiered crust around my energetic field. Once complete, the Crystals remained in place but became invisible. As I did this, my mind slowed, the irrational thoughts dissipated, and I began to feel better. I don't know if Lydia's Crystal wisdom will work for you, but there are 36 Crystals at your disposal right now on the pages of this book. Want to give it a try? For my force field, three stones came to mind. **Crystal Love** on Malachite and Labradorite can be found in Kristin's and Jacqui's chapters. Moldavite is not in the book, but I think it came to mind because it is a meteoric stone of incredible transformation energy and psychic protection… two things I really needed as I was spiraling in my fear fantasies. Obviously, there are many more Crystals than the stunners featured in our book. If you know Crystals, let them come to mind as you do this. If you aren't familiar with a lot of Crystals, you can use a Crystal Oracle Card Deck as a reference, you can search online, or you can let this book lead. It is up to you. Let's create our first force field.

- Close your eyes and take a few deep, cleansing breaths. When you are ready, ask your Crystal Force Field to come forward and gift you what you need at this moment at this time. If you are working with this book as your reference, let your intuition guide you to a Chapter. That Chapter's Crystal is yours for right now.

    o What is my Force Field Crystal? _____

        ▪ What wisdom, medicine, and guidance does this Crystal have for me right now?

        _____

        _____

        _____

- Visualize this Crystal forming an outer layer around your physical body. When the Crystal field is complete, allow it to seep into your body and your consciousness. Finish by expressing your gratitude to the Crystal. As you go about your day, pay attention to what happens, what you notice, and if the Crystal's force field wisdom, medicine, and guidance has been helpful.

Now, let's create some recipes! These force field recipes are your personalized works of support, art, transformation, and love. Let's start with a recipe for the Divine Feminine. Let your Higher Self and the Crystalline Realm work together on this one and allow the Crystals to present themselves to you. Don't think about it; just let it flow. If you are using this book as your reference point, connect into each Archetype of the Feminine as directed below, let the book fall open, and trust that that Chapter's Crystal is yours for right now. If you get the same Crystal for more than one layer, lucky you!

Divine Feminine Crystal Force Field

- Connect into the energy of the **Crone**. This is the Feminine Archetype of *profound wisdom, quiet solitude,* psychic purging, and *unapologetic authenticity.*

    o Breathe deeply and allow a Crystal to come forward and represent your Inner **Crone** energy.

- What is my **Crone** Force Field Crystal? _____

- What wisdom, medicine, and guidance does this Crystal have for me right now?

  _____
  _____

- Connect into the energy of the **Maiden**. This is the Feminine Archetype of *upbeat and playful energy, courageous activism, planting seeds of new life,* and *renewed confidence.*

  - Breathe deeply and allow a Crystal to come forward and represent your Inner **Maiden** energy.

    - What is my **Maiden** Force Field Crystal? _____

    - What wisdom, medicine, and guidance does this Crystal have for me right now?

      _____
      _____

- Connect into the energy of the **Mother**. This is the Feminine Archetype of *radiant fertility, ripe expression and creativity, content nurturance,* and *the birthing of new life.*

  - Breathe deeply and allow a Crystal to come forward and represent your Inner **Mother** energy.

    - What is my **Mother** Force Field Crystal? _____

    - What wisdom, medicine, and guidance does this Crystal have for me right now?

      _____
      _____

- Connect into the energy of the **Enchantress**. This is the Feminine Archetype of *dynamic emotion, intimate mystery, empowered sexuality,* and *wild self-acceptance.*

  - Breathe deeply and allow a Crystal to come forward and represent your Inner **Enchantress** energy.

    - What is my **Enchantress** Force Field Crystal? _____

    - What wisdom, medicine, and guidance does this Crystal have for me right now?

      _____
      _____

- Finally, visualize the four layers of your Crystal force field swirling together to create a solid crust. When it feels complete, allow the Crystal love to seep deeply into the layers of your consciousness. Although this force field is invisible, it is present with you for as long as you need. Solidify your force field by sending gratitude to each of the four Crystals. When you no longer need this force field, you can consciously release it, or trust that the Crystals will release themselves. Utilize this unique and personal support system as needed.

OK, now think about what other force field recipes you want to create. The other day, I created a force field to embody my Inner Isis. The recipe was **Carnelian** (found in DeWanda's Chapter), Lapis, Red Coral, and **Amethyst** (found in Jennifer's Chapter). It felt glorious! Some other ideas for Crystal force field recipes are: Forgiveness, Grace, the Divine Masculine (the Archetypes are *King, Warrior, Lover, Magician*), Sisterhood, Love, and Bliss. Let your Higher Self have a ball with the possibilities. With your brilliance, dedication, and follow through… they really are endless! Thank you for doing this activity. I can't wait to hear about your recipes. I love you and Lydia does, too!

~ SPS #5: ~
* Ascetic Hedonism *

Over the years as I've studied different things, I've come across the notion of ascetism. Living life as an ascetic used to be, and still is, a highly regarded path to ascension in many different spiritual modalities. The idea is that, as an ascetic, one practices severe self-discipline and abstinence when it comes to indulgence and pleasure. This denial is typically reserved for the sensual goodies of life and seeks to extinguish all physical and psychological desires in order to obtain a spiritual ideal. To live this way, worldly comforts are denied and although considered austere, ascetism is traditionally viewed as a spartan existence fed by a spartan diet. Hmmmmm… I'm just gonna pause for a minute and collect myself before going on. Like our mommas always say, "If you don't have anything nice to say, don't say anything at all." Breathe with me… in and out... in and out…. OK, I'm collected. How about you? A denial of the pleasures of life? Nope. Not gonna happen here with this Goddess. See, the way of the Goddess *is* one of sensual pleasure and joyful indulgence. We amplify our very Divinely Feminine empowerment by living, loving, and orgasming with our world, over and over and over. We create our bliss through our own bliss of creation. Sign me up for *that* kind of ascension. I will not starve myself from my own Garden of Eden to seek a paradise elsewhere. I wonder what it would look like to flip this whole ascetic script a bit. Hedonism, traditionally reviled among the upper crust of spiritual seekers, *is* the pursuit of pleasure and self-indulgence. What if we actually sought to be hedonistic and indulged in wild amounts of empowerment, self-love, authenticity, pleasure, orgasm, Divinity, and sovereignty? And, what if we followed that with an ascetic diet to address self-criticism, denial of our power, disconnection, distraction from our divinity, the numbing of our feelings and intuition, apologies for our blood and birth magick, and the wounding of our wild, untidy, and instinctual natures? That kind of abstinence I would sign up for! Let's explore these two options a bit further and see what comes up. Journal around ascetism and hedonism and how they might look and feel like for you.

My Ascetic Approach…

_____

_____

_____

My Hedonistic Brilliance...

_____
_____
_____
_____
_____
_____

Next, a little lighting round. Write down the first things that come to mind as you fill in the statements below.

- As an **ascetic** against all that doesn't serve me, I will **abstain** from the following in the following ways:

    ○ I will abstain from **self-criticism** by _____
    _____

    ○ I will abstain from the **denial of my power** by _____
    _____

    ○ I will abstain from **disconnection** by _____
    _____

    ○ I will abstain from **distractions from my Divinity** by _____
    _____

    ○ I will abstain from **numbing my feelings and intuition** by _____
    _____

    ○ I will abstain from **apologizing for my blood and birth magick** by _____
    _____

    ○ I will abstain from **wounding my wild, untidy, and instinctual nature** by _____
    _____

I kind of like being an ascetic now. Go Divinely Feminine powers of transformation! Woo-hoo! OK, onto hedonism.

- As a **hedonist** for all that does serve my highest good, I will **indulge** in the following in the following ways:
    - I will indulge my **empowerment** by _____
    _____
    - I will indulge my **self-love** by _____
    _____
    - I will indulge my **authenticity** by _____
    _____
    - I will indulge my **pleasure** by _____
    _____
    - I will indulge my **orgasms** by _____
    _____
    - I will indulge my **Divinity** by _____
    _____
    - I will indulge my **sovereignty** by _____
    _____

No surprise, I love being a hedonist when it comes the pursuit of our pleasure. I love this not because it is self-serving, but because it is an *act of service*. The more pleasure we are in, Sister, the more we share it. Our pleasure becomes our vibe and it is one of self-love, self-compassion, self-understanding, self-forgiveness, and self-mastery. The more we embody this way of being, the more we inspire others to do the same. Wrap your arms around your shoulders and squeeze tight. Close your eyes and feel my gratitude and love for you mixing with your own. Thank you. Thank you for being you. As Sister Goddess Jacqui says, "Thank you for being me." I love you.

Crystal Love: Jamie's Crystal is Astrophyllite (a-stro-*file*-ahyt), a stone dedicated to our development and progress. Manifesting a true rebirthing process from the inside out, Astrophyllite works to protect its keeper by infusing the system with light in order to offer judgement-free support as we fully clarify and claim our spiritual identity, Divine destiny, and conscious sovereignty. This stone can also help us find hidden reserves of love and strength so that we may clearly see opportunities, reframe limitations, welcome changes, and make quick moves upon the path of life's journey. The energy of this Crystal is very sincere and, when used with romantic or platonic partnerships, is known to promote honesty, fidelity, and intimacy. This sincerity can also apply to the intra-personal partnership with ourselves as Astrophyllite purges that which is not in alignment for our highest good, refines and enhances our psychic sensitivities, and opens us to the guidance of our own inner wisdom. Working in tandem, all of Astrophyllite's gifts can offer a calming and reassured perspective as we assess our full spiritual potential within this human experience and jump into the quantum talents of Astral Travel. Go forth and prosper! Just be sure to take a piece of Astrophyllite with you!

Suggested Reading to Experience your Inner Wild, *Women Who Run With the Wolves: Myths and Stories of the Wild Woman Archetype* by Clarissa Pinkola Estes, Ph.D.

Glossary

Thanks for taking a look back here. Throughout the chapters, there are highlighted words which you will find definitions to in this Glossary. These definitions contextually relate to where you found them. They may not be congruent with a dictionary definition, your personal definition, or someone else's definition, and that is OK. Different words, concepts, schools of thought, and principles garner many different understandings - and thank goodness for that! My Grammy always used to say, "I am grateful we are all so different… this world would be pretty boring otherwise!" I agree. These definitions are here to help explain where I am coming from in the 'Making This Story Your Own,' 'Sacred Play Suggestions,' and 'Crystal Love' sections of this book. If they work for you and help you to better understand something, that is wonderful! If they don't work for you, that is also wonderful - go and find definitions that do. My only intention in creating this Glossary is to provide extra support, clarity, and maybe even a few giggles. I love you! Thank you for being here!

~ A ~

Abhyanga is an Ayurvedic oil massage. Recommended daily to maintain overall health and well-being, this nourishing practice is said to calm, replenish, revitalize, and restore the entire system. Traditionally done with cold-pressed, organic sesame oil, this regular practice focuses on allowing our skin - the largest organ of our bodies - the support needed to efficiently remove toxins and absorb nourishment. To find out more information or to seek additional support in the ancient healing tradition of Ayurveda, get in touch with Soul-to-Sisterhood Goddess Maria at: www.atomica-arts.com.

Aboriginal relates to the Aborigines, the Indigenous people of Australia. For our understanding, this term also encapsulates a principle form of wisdom from the land and the beings on that land who existed there before colonialization and before what we understand as recorded *his*tory. This is a genetic and cellularly held memory of life and our existence before '*time*' began.

Abundance The mindset, belief, or way of living that embodies the notion that everything you could, would, or should ever need or want for your Greatest and Highest Good is either on its way to you or you already possess it.

Acculturate is a process by which we adopt, adjust, or assimilate to something. This can be a new relationship, a new way of living, a new culturally or socially enforced belief system, or even a new way of thinking. By acculturating ourselves to something, we are stepping into a new *culture* - a new paradigm - and living from that contextual framework with our actions, reactions, and responses.

Actualize(d) literally means to make *actual* or to *realize*. For our work together, for parts of us to be fully actualized, they must be completely and totally honored, seen, valued, heard, and allowed to be made manifest. This relates to our Feminine Side, our Masculine Side, our full range of feelings, our Wounded Self, our Higher Self, our Inner Child, our Inner Archetypes of the Masculine and Feminine, our blood magick, our birth magick, and much, much more. When we allow all of the beauty that makes us **us** to come forward - no matter what we may have been told to think about it or what judgments, fears, and/or vulnerabilities we may have around it - we functionally actualize the entirety of our being. Nothing remains hidden. By courageously bringing things to the forefront of our existence, we can live more authentically, more intimately, and more joyfully.

Acute Trauma is a single traumatic incident that can come in the form of many varied experiences. Witnessing violence, having an accident, or suffering anything that threatens our physical, emotional, mental, and/or spiritual safety can equate to trauma. Everyone's individual experience of trauma - the initial acute incident and the subsequent aftereffects to one's life, daily living, and relationships - is unique and personal.

Affirmations are words, phrases, literary passages, and thoughts used regularly to affirm encouragement, connection, comfort, and support.

Ajna (*ah*-jnah), or Ajna Chakra, is often referred to as the external point of the Third Eye. Located in the center of the forehead, this part of the Ajna Center is not anatomical, but etheric and energetic. You may not see it with your eyes, but you can intuitively sense it and energetically connect to it. The correlating colors are commonly known as purple or indigo and twenty-three lines of concentric energy cross here aptly earning the Ajna Energy Center the title of a 'Major Energy Center.' The Ajna channels in all of our intuitive guidance and coordinates the activities of the body to create harmony within the whole. The Ajna contains a reflection of the lower five Chakras (Basic, Sacral, Solar Plexus, Heart, and Throat) and when all of them act in unison, the Ajna can function fully as the highest and most powerful creative center. When open and activated, the Ajna can balance the ego's willingness to cooperate and integrate with our Higher Self.

Akashic is a Sanskrit word for 'ether' and often refers to the energetic field or *library* - as in the *Akashic Records* - of all recorded events including the thoughts, emotions, words, intentions, and actions of every living thing for the past, present, and future throughout all time and space. This is a non-physical plane of existence and can be conceptualized as an infinite database for all events happening throughout all co-existing Universes. In this endless etheric encyclopedia of vibrational support and wisdom for all Souls, rules of time don't apply, the records are open and available to anyone choosing to learn how to enter and read them, and there is no judgement for anyone or anything… only information and knowledge.

Alchemize is a process of transforming the nature or properties of something into something else by a seemingly magickal process.

Alice Bailey was born in Manchester, England, in 1880 and wrote more than twenty-four books, nineteen of which were channeled via telepathy from the Tibetan Master, Djwal Kuhl. This relationship with the theosophical master began in 1919 and lasted until her death in 1949. Her writing, known as Esoteric Philosophy, is considered to be the birth of modern-day Esoteric Healing and teachings. During her life, she started an esoteric school called The Arcane School, and also created the Lucis Trust and the Lucis Publishing Company.

Aligned is to be in alignment with something. This ease is based on the mutual cooperation, agreement, support, and authenticity of the relationship.

AAA (Aligning, Attuning, & Allowing) is the first step of any Esoteric Healing Practical or treatment and can be used in any situation to create a higher vibratory dynamic or relationship. When aligning, attuning, and allowing, you are superseding the Ego to connect directly via the Soul. This is done by energetically connecting Ajna to Ajna, Heart to Heart, and Soul Light to Soul Light, thereby aligning the energetic frequencies of the physical plane to attune to the higher vibrations of the Spiritual Plane and intentionally allowing the pure spiritual energy to flow into one's Physical, Emotional, Mental, and Spiritual layers of consciousness.

Alta is a Minor Energy Center located at the back of the head. This Minor Chakra is considered to regulate the Nervous System. Fourteen lines of concentric energy cross at the Alta and the color typically associated with it is yellow. Not able to be seen anatomically, connecting to the Alta and sensing it energetically is a protocol of Esoteric Healing.

Altar is a special space designated to embody worshipful and purposeful energy in order to connect into the Divine. Used in many different religions, spiritual practices, and modalities, Altars offer a portal for deeper connection. Oftentimes created as an intentional offering to honor Gods, Goddesses, Ascended Masters, Realms of Consciousness, Angels, Spirit Worlds, or anything else the creator of the Altar chooses to connect with, they can be decorated, crafted, activated, and designed in many different ways.

Angelic Energy is the energy felt from Angels and the Angelic Realms. Typically understood to be comforting, supportive, and transformational, this energy can also be uplifting, inspiring, and motivational.

Angelic Realms are the realms of consciousness that host all Angelic Energy. Easily accessible to humans, the Angelic Realm is devoted to all living things.

Anima/Animus are terms coined by Swiss psychiatrist, psychoanalyst, and creator of analytical psychology, Carl Jung, to better understand the Feminine and Masculine. Thought to be inner forces and sometimes described as behavioral archetypes, the Anima is the expression of femininity within the male and the Animus is the expression of masculinity within the female. Like their counterparts of Feminine and Masculine Energy, when fully actualized the Anima and Animus can be balanced and integrated, offering many different beneficial qualities. Additionally, when repressed, hidden, or misunderstood, these two inner-energies can become imbalanced, displaced, and expressed as dysfunction, dis-ease, and challenges in relatability.

Animal Spirits are the spirits of an entire animal species which come forward to commune with the Human Realm offering guidance, wisdom, protection, loyalty, and love. Animal Spirits can come to us in life, dreams, and other forms of imagery.

Applied Kinesiology is based in biomechanics (the study of body movement) and is a diagnostic methodology used to treat different dis-eases manifesting in the physical body by muscle strength testing. This muscle testing is not done to gauge actual strength, but is performed to better understand muscle function and nervous system interaction based on the holistic belief that our various musculature is connected to different anatomical and physiological components of our bodies. It is also known to be a good indicator of overall health.

Archeomythology is the interdisciplinary study and dedication to cultural research with particular importance allocated to the beliefs, rituals, social structure, systems of communication, and symbolism of past and present societies. Formulated by archaeologist and Archeomythologist, Marija Gumbutas, this field of study focuses on understanding the varied expressions of human culture by utilizing the methodologies of many different scientific traditions and disciplines. More information can be found on the website of The Institute for Archeomythology at: www.archeomythology.org.

Archetype can be related to the original, prototypical pattern or model of a commonly held belief, understanding, characterization, idea, thought system, or image. Many stories, myths, narratives, historical models, and cultural constructs carry forth Archetypes and Archetypal images that we consciously and unconsciously assimilate. For example, the story of Cinderella, the myth of Medusa, the narrative that exhaustion equals worth, the historical implications of Joan of Arc, and the commonly held cultural belief system that supports the experience of Motherhood to be an experience of sacrifice. These all create very specific feelings, reactions, and responses based upon the Archetypal understandings and can manifest either collectively, individually, or as a combination of both.

Archetypal Mothering Energies when actualized, honored, and valued, these energies are expressed and experienced as the highly conscious and highly vibratory Feminine energies of Mothering and of Mothers. Compassionate, nurturing, sustaining, merciful, warm, comforting, and caring are just a few of these expressions of this 'Archetypal' - or patterned - image and understanding of 'The Mother.' The Mother is one of four Feminine Archetypes. The other three are: Crone, Maiden, and Enchantress. While all four are equally valuable, powerful, and needed, the Mother is the most well-known, understood, embodied, expressed, and sought-after. However, due to such social and cultural pressures around the perfection of the Motherhood role and the constructed conditioning and rules of that role, Mothering energies can get displaced and dysfunctional. This is what Massimilla Harris Ph.D. and Bud Harris Ph.D. explain in their book, *Into the Heart of the Feminine: An Archetypal Journey to Renew Strength, Love, and Creativity,* as the "Death Mother." Although much more complex than this, the "Death Mother" can be thought of as the opposite of what is typically sought after when seeking the Archetypal Mothering Energies.

Artemis is a wild and empowered Greek Goddess, also known in Roman Mythology as Diana. Free, strong, capable, and brilliant, this child of Zeus and well-known lover of animals was a beloved guardian of nature, spiritual protector of the woods and trees, and deep-thinking woman of focus, intention, and manifestation. Twin Sister of the Sun God Apollo, and daughter of Leto - a Great Mother Goddess who was born of the Titans - Artemis offers support for intense concentration and the ability to trust that all of our needs are being met

Ascended Masters are beings who have dedicated their existence to assisting Humanity in becoming the answer to humanity's own prayer. Often times having an incarnated Earth-School experience, these Masters have ascended through the lessons of life to become the ultimate integration of Soul, Higher Self, Oversoul, and God-Goddess Consciousness. They are dedicated to all of life and are always present, eager to assist and support all beings in becoming the best and highest expressions of ourselves so that we may bring about the best and highest good for others.

Ascension Journey is the process of life as a mystery school where every life lesson is a teachable opportunity toward growth, expansion, and the bliss existence that can come from the marriage of Ego's integration into pure Soul. As a journey, this ascension can take many lifetimes and is the birthright of all living beings.

Ascension Process (of the Soul) is the innerworkings of the Ascension Journey. As our Souls transform and fully integrate our human consciousness with our divinity consciousness, this process gifts us opportunities for continued integration and transcendence. All of these opportunities can be understood and experienced as life lessons, growing pains, 'a-ha' moments, insights, epiphanies, connections, and the continuous exploration of the euphoric wisdom that Source energy is not an entity residing somewhere outside of our being, but truly an energy that lovingly and absolutely resides within.

Asceticism is a lifestyle practice that is devoted to the abstinence of pleasure and sensuality. Typically pursued for spiritual, religious, or philosophical reasons, this type of self-discipline through avoidance of any indulgence is a manner of life intended to jettison one closer to a higher moral state, or closer to God. Oftentimes a person practicing these principles - known as an Ascetic - will engage in rigorous self-denial and self-mortification as a form of personal austerity and virtue.

Astral Travel or Astral *Projection* is the traveling of one's consciousness - also referred to as the Soul or Astral Body - out of the physical body to different times, spaces, locations, universes, galaxies, and dimensions. This type of travel is commonly referred to as an Out-of-Body Experience and is thought to be both voluntary and involuntary.

Attachment is the psychological theory made famous by the work of John Bowlby in the 1950's (and in later decades many other clinicians, researchers, and scientists, specifically Mary Ainsworth), of the deep and enduring emotional bonds that living things create to one another across time and space. Initially understood through the context of infant development, Attachment Theory worked to highlight the importance of attachment behaviors, such as crying and searching for an attachment figure in order for the infant to secure the comfort, care, and protection needed for physical survival and optimal emotional functioning. Understanding infant attachment and its developmental benefits as well as the potential damage that may occur when it is absent or improperly ascribed has created a whole field of study for adult relatability, functionality, and relational success.

Attuned is to be *in-tune* with something. When attuned, we are receptive, responsive, and aware. This can feel like a reciprocal match of vibe, flow, and sensitivity.

Aura is the field of energy surrounding every living thing. Regarded as an essential part of any being, our auras can be seen in colors, textures, and patterns. Certain cameras can even detect and capture an image of this awesome, multi-layered vibrational field.

Authentic Self is the deepest core of you that honors your full truth. Your Authentic Self feels your every feeling, explores your every instinct, and values your every intuition. When living in this way, your actions and deeds align with your words and beliefs. Your Highest Self is in the lead when embodying your Authentic Self, and although still a human being having a spiritual experience, Soul's Guidance is unconditionally honored in all facets of life.

Authenticate is to prove or *show* the truth or authenticity of something. This can be subjective. What is authentically true for you may not be authentically true for someone else. Following the guidance from your Higher Self will offer you a perspective on how to authenticate your thoughts, beliefs, words, actions, and deeds.

Authoritarian is a leadership style that favors strict obedience, a lack of critical thinking, and total submission. This can be experienced in governments, businesses, organizations, religions, and parenting and is often enforced at the expense of personal freedom. In parenting, this is considered a 'style,' and is often characterized as a boot-camp type of dynamic where there is little responsiveness, warmth, or nurturing from parent to child. Instead, what presents itself in the parental hierarchy is an attempt to control with little encouragement of reciprocal communication and scant explanation for rules, punishments, and expectations. Affection and love are often withheld, and large, angry explosive reactions are standard.

Authoritative is a leadership style that favors collaboration and is characterized by reasonable demands and high responsiveness. High expectations are present, however so are the resources and support needed to meet them. In regard to parenting, this style is warm, nurturing, and sensitive, yet firm when boundaries and consequences are called for. Reasoning and positive reinforcement are employed to inspire cooperation, positive communication, and a recognition of the child's sense of autonomy. Authoritative parents lead by example and embody self-discipline, maturity, and respect for others as motivation for their children to do the same.

Autonomic Response Systems are the control systems of the body that act largely unconsciously to regulate bodily functions. This is known to be part of the peripheral nervous system and is responsible for involuntary or Autonomic Response functions such as heartbeat, blood flow, breathing, digestion, and the responses of fight, flight, or freeze. This system is divided into three parts: the sympathetic division of the nervous system, the parasympathetic division of the nervous system, and the enteric nervous system. The sympathetic division speeds us up for a fight or flight reaction. The parasympathetic division slows us down for a freeze reaction. The enteric system relates to the gastrointestinal tract. The sympathetic and parasympathetic systems operate by receiving information from the environment and then going right into action. When functioning optimally, they also tend to regulate one another by working in tandem to heighten responses for mobilizing the body and then dampening responses to calm the body.

Awareness is everything that you are aware of on every level of your Physical, Emotional, Mental, Ego, Soul, and Spiritual consciousness. It can also relate to a way of being as in *acting from* a state of awareness depending on the perception, understanding, and embodiment of either a low level of awareness (a contracted existence) or a high level of awareness (an expanded existence). Through our awareness we are cognizant of the events, dynamics, sensations, and feelings of everything going on around and within us. Through our awareness we directly *know* both the *known* - the tangible *given* circumstances - and the *unknown*, the intuited, sensed, felt, realized, and recognized circumstances.

Ayurveda is an ancient healing science which originated in India more than 5,000 years ago. In Sanskrit, the word Ayurveda translates to "The Science of Life" and is often referred to as the 'Mother of All Healing.' This healing practice places great emphasis on prevention and fosters the maintenance of health through the balance of one's diet, daily activities, thinking, movement, herbs, and attention to the individual constitution. To find out more information or to seek additional support in the ancient healing tradition of Ayurveda, get in touch with Soul-to-Sisterhood Goddess, Maria at: www.atomica-arts.com.

~ B ~

Backstory is the acting homework that focuses on creating the unique, specific, and detailed history of a character. By doing a backstory, an actor takes what the playwright has given as character traits and then adds to them to fully bring the character to life. In doing this, the actor utilizes creativity and ingenuity to lift the character off of the page and onto the stage for a performance that is well-rounded, grounded, authentic, and real.

Basic Chakra, Basic Center is the Major Energy Center located anatomically at the base of the spine or perineum. Associated with the color red, the Basic Energy Center is also referred to as our First Chakra. Not visible to the eye, this Energy Center can be sensed, felt, and *known*. The Basic Chakra connects us to our will to be in the present moment. It can be over-activated by stress, fear, and anxiety and is the Center responsible for our responses of fight, flight, or freeze. Balancing with the Crown Chakra, the importance of the Basic Chakra is paramount, reminding us to ground and connect to the Center in order to be open and aware of our Bliss. In this text, I use the name Basic Chakra instead of the more familiar name, Root Chakra. This is because I was taught by my Esoteric Healing Teachers to call this Energy Center the Basic Chakra. However, the name Root is a wonderful visual for this Center. Like the strong, stalwart, and steadfast roots of a tree... the deeper one anchors, the higher she can grow.

Belief Systems are the created lenses by which we view, conceptualize, categorize, and attempt to understand our lives. Crafted out of our experiences, belief systems can be thought of as the set of interconnected and influential factors that govern our behavior. Based on our principles and ideologies, these systems of belief - born out of our interactions - can be helpful in making sense of difficult topics and situations and can either be rigid or diffuse and have typically helped humans to speed up cultural evolution. These systems can be very limiting or freeing, depending on perspective, and go down to the core root of who we think ourselves to be. Able to be dually held in the space of the conscious and/or unconscious awareness, individual belief systems can be known or unknown. When incongruent, outdated, or dysfunctional, they can bring about relational strife, life stress, psychopathology, and general dissatisfaction.

Biological is the association of the various interactions, cycles, processes, and functions relating to the development and evolution of the anatomical and physiological aspects of the living organism.

Birth Magick relates to the mystical, miraculous, incredible, and creative energies of the Feminine to grow, birth, and sustain new life. Nothing less than shamanic, the magickal process of *birthing* takes us to the very brink of life and death and back again so that we can continue to regenerate, revitalize, and restore ourselves and our tribes. Birth magick is to be respected, honored, and revered as the wondrous process that it is.

Black Catting is a way of always trying to be better or more important than someone or something else. For example, if someone were to say in conversation, "My knees are really hurting me," and the other person replied, "Your knees? *MY* knees have been killing me for years!" that person has just 'black catted' by not acknowledging the other person, expressing their needs over the other person's needs, and degrading the original statement by displaying a lack of empathy, sympathy, or care.

Black Out Poetry is the artform of blacking out certain words on a page of text to create an original work of poetry.

Bleeding Time is the phase of Menstruation within the four phases of the Menstrual Cycle. The other phases are the Follicular or Pre-Ovulatory Phase, the Phase of Ovulation, and the Luteal Phase, more commonly referred to as P.M.S. or pre-menstrual syndrome. In many cultures, a woman's bleeding time was a time to celebrate with rest and replenishment. Considered the most psychically powerful phase, women were given a comfortable and nourishing place for relaxation and meditation when bleeding. During this time, her visions, divinations, and guidance were eagerly understood and recognized as oracular prophecy for the sustainability of her people.

Blood Magick is the magick of our Menstrual Cycle. Correlating our physical, emotional, spiritual, and psychic sensitivities to that of the seen and unseen worlds, our monthly blood cycle is literally a magickal opportunity to harness the powerful, dynamic, ever-changing, and transformative energy of the inner and outer realms. Flowing with the continuously shifting dynamics of our creativity, sexuality, sensuality, physical stamina, and emotional resonance - when respected, actualized, and embodied - our Blood Magick offers empowering, loving, appreciative, and everlasting ways of relating to our body, mind, and spirit.

Bodily Wisdom is the wisdom of our body. Each aspect of our anatomy has physical, emotional, and energetic wisdom that - when asked - can come forth as guidance. This guidance is offered as a way to be fully in alignment with our Greatest and Highest Good.

Both, and is a clinical concept of understanding that honors the different states of being we may feel, embody, or express at any given time. *Both, and* allows us to feel two things at once while also allowing space for a third, new way of being that is the unique result of the blending of the first two original states. For example, I may feel *both* happy and sad about my daughter growing up *and* feeling both of those things also leaves me a bit perplexed. Ergo, I feel both happy and sad and also perplexed.

Burnout is a state typically felt when we experience prolonged exposure to stress. Physical, emotional, and mental exhaustion, overwhelm, cynicism, and a lack of perceived professional abilities are just some of the byproducts of burnout. When we feel this way, our overall health can suffer and we may experience feelings of alienation and an increased inability to meet personal and professional demands.

~ C ~

Carl Jung is the founder of analytic psychology. He is also is one of the most well-known pioneers of modern-day psychoanalysis. Born in Switzerland in 1875, through his tireless research and dedicated work with patients, Jung created ideas and methods which offer a rich understanding of conscious and unconscious human behavior, social dynamics, the energies of the human Soul, and the somewhat inexplicable and oftentimes dysfunctional patterns of life. Since his passing in 1961, the broad body of work he left behind has continued to influence clinicians, clients, professionals, seekers, creatives, and all other beings attempting to authenticate and deepen their relationships as well as enrich the very experience of being human.

Cathartic/Catharsis is something that provides physical, emotional, mental, and/or spiritual relief through the witnessing, embodying, or experiencing of something that provokes expression, purging, and/or purification.

Celestial can relate to a Heavenly or visibly skyward perspective referring to stars and other celestial bodies. It can also relate to a sense of Divinity felt when connecting to higher realms of consciousness such as Heaven, the Angelic Realms, Source Energy, Ascended Masters, and Celestial Beings. Celestial consciousness, which many believe all of life possesses, comes to us from what is called a Starseed lineage and is part of our Celestial DNA. Many spiritual teachings expound that this Divine energy is contained within the smallest known particles of life, similar to the concept of the entire Universe being reflected and holographically reimagined within the nucleus of a living cell. Alongside this belief is that if all of life is a mirror of Divinity, then Divinity is within, and there is no need to seek an outward experience of the Divine.

Celestial Connection is the connection we feel to Celestial energies, beings, nations, bodies, masters, lineages, ancestry, genetics, and ways of being.

Cellularly Held is the concept that our cells hold memories of every lived, ancestral, and collective experience. This can inform and affect our daily lives, dreams, beliefs, fears, desires, phobias, repulsions, connections, and choices. It is believed that many women still hold cellularly held traumas from the burnings and torturous times of the Witch Trials. In support of these beliefs, one could conceptualize that the many acts of intra- and inter-personal violence we experience are cellularly held traumas being played out on the stage of modern-day life. It is also held that when we as women come together to collectively heal, we heal all of those who came before us and all of those who will come after us. This is known as 'healing the bloodline.' When this can occur within the Sacred Heart of Sisterhood and the energies of the Divine Feminine, the cellularly held memories can be rewritten with a script that inspires fearless empowerment, bold authenticity, wild sensuality, unbridled psychic abilities, and a powerful, unapologetic ownership of our femininity, Feminine *her*story, and Divinely Feminine potential.

Center is the deep anchoring to the Center of our Great Mother Earth. Just like the tallest of trees, we too can grow our roots deeply and firmly within the flesh of our Great Mother as we ascend and traverse the highest of spiritual heights. Oftentimes this centering practice can also include a connection into the Central Crystal or Womb of Mother Earth.

Center is another name for Chakra. This interchangeable title can relate to a Major Energy Center or a Minor Energy Center.

Chakra(s)- is the word used to describe the energetic centers of the body. Chakra translates to *wheel* or *circle* in the ancient language of Sanskrit and in various teachings are referred to as the flowers, discs, portals, and/or openings through which we give and receive energy. The Major Chakras lie at various points on the center of the body where 23 lines of concentric energy cross. Each of these Major Chakras relates to a Physiological System, an Endocrine System, and has a correlating Psychological Contribution. The 7 well-known Major Chakras - Basic, Sacral, Solar Plexus, Heart, Throat, Ajna, and Crown - as well as the 5 lesser well-known Major Chakras - Earth Star, Central Crystal (also known as the Central Diamond Core), Celestial, Solar, and Galactic - are represented by a color. For the 7 Chakras on the body, the energy flows from back to front, except for the Ajna, where the energy flows into the forehead and out the top of the head behind the Crown. Chakras cannot be seen, but they can be energetically felt, sensed, and *known*. According to the Esoteric Teachings, in addition to the 12 Major Chakras, there are also 70 Minor Chakras where 14 lines of concentric energy cross. Of these 70 Minors, 21 are considered Major Minors and 49 are considered Lesser Minors. When in balance and allowed to flow unencumbered, it is understood that the energy of our Chakras supports us in creating optimal levels of health in mind, body, and spirit that is free from dis-ease.

Channeling can occur when we open our consciousness to connect into and receive information from the different Realms. All of life is capable of channeling in different wisdom and guidance from the various layers of consciousness; however, some Channels are talented in specific ways or tend to work with a chosen energy, entity, Realm, or Level.

Chatoyancy is the optical reflection that appears as a band of light which can be seen within a Crystal, oftentimes giving a sense that the light is moving just beneath the surface of the stone. Appearing to be shiny, wavy, milky, or iridescent, this beautiful and joyful happenstance is an additional gift from the Crystalline Realm to offer us whimsy and splendor.

Chi is the Eastern word for the vital life force energy of the Universe that resides within every living thing.

Chorus is the part of a song that is the most memorable. It is repeated throughout the tune and usually holds the reason for the song. In typical song structures, the chorus is sung in between all of the verses and will usually end the song in various combinations of lyrics and melodic structure. Sometimes it is reflected in the title of the song. If you know at least some of the words to a song, chances are you know the chorus.

Chronic Trauma is the long-term, continuous exposure to trauma or multiple incidents of related or unrelated trauma that can come from many varied situations, experiences, and dynamics. Ongoing suffering or any circumstances that regularly threaten physical, emotional, mental, and/or spiritual safety can equate to chronic trauma. Everyone's individual experience of trauma - which can include an initial acute incident or a series of repeated and sustained incidents, and the subsequent aftereffects as they pertain to one's life, daily living, and relationships - is unique and personal.

Circle of Security is a fabulous intervention of support, introspection, and insight for caregivers, parents, children, and families. Focusing on the creation of secure relationships between caregivers, parents, and children, its co-originators - Kent Hoffman, Glenn Cooper, and Bert Howell - have created a visual map of attachment that is understandable, practical, realistic, and easy to implement. Circle of Security offers programs for parents, organizations, and caregivers as well as specialized professional training programs which can cater to both clinical and non-clinical needs. Visit: www.circleofsecurityinternational.com for more information.

Clairvoyance is the ability to perceive things through sight, sound, touch, and intuition that are typically beyond what is considered a typical sensory experience.

Codependency is a way of being in relationship where there is a dependency created in the exchange between the parties to keep the 'status quo,' no matter how dysfunctional and how uneven the status quo might be. While it is often reduced down to needy or clingy behavior, there really is a lot more to it. In this type of Codependent dynamic, both sides of the relationship enable unideal behavioral patterns, allowing them to persist and perpetuate. From this perspective, both entities are simultaneously dependent while continuing to enable their own and the other's dysfunctional behaviors. Over time, this pattern can turn into ingrained cycles that feel frozen and habituated and Codependency can look and feel different for everyone. Initially, the term was used to describe the partner of an addict. In this example, the non-using partner enables the partner's addictive behavior by creating circumstances which maintain the status quo of the addiction. However, Codependency has expanded to include many other relational dynamics. It can also be one-sided in which a person is looking to get all of their emotional needs met by another person or thing and all perception of self-esteem and self-worth are based upon pleasing the other entity at all costs. Additionally, Codependency can manifest as intense reactivity to the emotional states of others, whereby the Codependent person is continuously defensive and exhausted. It can appear as caretaking to a point of self-harm, and it can also look like very diffuse boundaries with a Codependent person seldom creating personal guidelines which honor their time, space, efforts, and physical, emotional, and/or spiritual well-being. At the core of Codependency is the need to feel safe and secure and that is oftentimes demonstrated as striving for control over situations and relationships through any means necessary. No matter how harmful to the self, this oftentimes appears as an excessive belief that one must gain the approval of others to maintain a sense of identity.

Codependent Leadership is a style of leadership that is based on people-pleasing, being liked, and compromising leadership efficacy for the perceived needs of others. While many codependent leaders are very successful, full potential is seldom reached due to the consistent energy expenditure needed for unnecessary caretaking, over-compensating, managing organizational dysfunction, and the lack of professional boundaries. This type of leadership is hard to detect because some tenets of effective leadership - often depicted as things like *teamwork* and *successful customer service* - can disguise themselves as functional when in actuality they are not. Teamwork and successful customer service are parts of Interdependent Leadership as well; however, the differences can be identified within the subtlety of implementation. When there is a sacrifice of empowerment, authenticity, responsibility, or respect in an effort to promote, force, or create teamwork or happy customers within any level of an organization, the leadership style is most likely codependent in nature. This can create systemic problems in communication, fulfilling responsibilities, growth potential, and issues stemming from attempting to control behavior to avoid feelings of fear, failure, and powerlessness.

Cognitive refers to the mental processes employed in an attempt to become aware of, accomplish, shift, or make sense of something. When we are cognitive, we are conscious, and we relate accordingly. When we use our Cognition, we are using what we know. When we are Cognitively approaching something, we are relating in ways that are based on what we know. We are also able to cognitively relate in ways that we know might change what we know or, depending on how convincing the new cognition, what we *knew*.

Collective Ego is the notion that the human collective (or all of humanity) has a larger entity of collected Ego energy. This energy is a simultaneous representation of the whole and the sum of its parts, which means that this collective energy will embody and express mixtures and dynamics of the human Ego as individualized and homogenized aspects throughout all of time, space, and existence. This energy affects us individually and collectively as living beings. Because this is the energy of the Ego - the part of the human psyche or personality that is focused on fear, staying small, materialism, isolation, wounding patterns, and perpetuating dysfunctionality - this energy can be felt as limiting, negative, scornful, cynical, hurtful, and/or judgmental.

Collective Soul is the same notion as the Collective Ego above, only this energy is of the Soul. The Collective Soul is also a collection of energies representing the individual and collective aspects of the human Soul throughout all time, space, and existence. However, this energy, because it is of the Soul, is focused on inner-wisdom, intuition, expansion, Inner Divinity, sovereignty, and the Greatest and Highest Good for all of life. It can be felt and experienced as God, Goddess, or Source, guidance, wisdom, a channeling of information, or just a sense of inner knowing. The energy is positive, loving, compassionate, forgiving, understanding, uplifting, and masterful.

Collective Unconscious is the Jungian psychological theory that there are common unconscious understandings, beliefs, experiences, knowledge, imagery, memories, narratives, and impulses that are ancestrally inherited from the collective human experience. This can be true for all of humanity as well as for other species. It is also said that many human beings are not aware of the collective unconscious or its potential for influence within their lives and relationships.

Compassion Fatigue is a state of being in which we are so emotionally and physically exhausted, overwhelmed, and stressed, that we perceive a lack in our abilities to be compassionate. This is a set of symptoms that typically occurs when our caregiving output is not matched by our self-care input. This strain can be felt for many different reasons and can manifest in our lives in many different ways. Compassion Fatigue oftentimes co-exists with burnout; however, it has its own unique set of experiences which can include depersonalization, isolation, existential despair, decreased cognitive ability, and increased emotionality.

Compassion Fatigue can take years to surface. Its seriousness can go undetected and it can be misunderstood as just a low-level yet persistent inability to show care and concern compatible with previous displays of personal and/or professional compassion. This understanding can lead to even more isolation as we tend to internalize this with blame and shame. However, Compassion Fatigue is a very real and very serious complication of the 'service to others' industries and vocations. To lovingly shift these symptoms, realistic and consistent efforts toward self-care must be diligently applied.

Conscious Sovereignty is the steadfast awareness and embodiment of living from personal authority as it relates to all aspects of physical, emotional, mental, and spiritual health and well-being. All personal and professional relationships are navigated through this lens. In living this way, one unconditionally trusts their own counsel above all others.

Consciousness is the awareness of our internal and external existence. It is everything that we experience, perceive, project, adopt, relate to, and connect with. There are also different levels of interrelated consciousness which are recognized throughout many different spiritual and esoteric philosophies.

Construct is a foundation of thought or belief that can be constructed from social and cultural influences as well as personal experiences. This type of ideology can be held individually as well as in small or large groups.

Contracted Existence is a way of living that is based in fear, isolation, and separation. It is sometimes referred to as living from the Ego versus the Soul.

Core Limiting Beliefs are beliefs that keep us small, scared, and separated. Although created to maintain the illusion of safety and security, they can be painful, instigating extremely dysfunctional dynamics within our relationships to others and ourselves. These types of Limiting Beliefs can come from our families of origin, our social experiences, or even larger cultural influences. They can be personalized, such as the belief system: 'I am not enough.' They can be generalized, for example the common belief system: 'To be a loving parent you must sacrifice yourself.' And they can be broad, as evidenced by the historically recognizable belief system: 'Anyone who looks different than me is not to be trusted.' These limiting core belief systems are destructive and divisive.

Cosmic Justice is a Divine template of justice. This type of justice supersedes our traditional human constructs of law and order. Cosmic Justice is the high vibration consciousness of the unconditional 'right' that is always dedicated to the best and highest good coming forward for all living beings throughout all universes.

Counterintuitive is something that goes against our intuition. It just doesn't feel right. Our Feminine intuition is one of our Superpowers and when something isn't cool – or counter to our intuition - we sense it.

Creatrix is the Feminine expression of Creator. For many wounded by organized religions that perpetuate the patriarchal image of the 'Creator of All Life' as a strong, punishing, and/or judgmental male figurehead, Creatrix offers a female embodiment in its place. This notion of the Feminine as the Creatrix of all life is based upon the recognizable characteristics of the Divine Feminine. Sustenance, compassion, and nurturing are present. The body of the female, where all of life is conceived and unless you are a Seahorse, Pipefish, or Sea Dragon - *birthed* – is revered and honored for its true life-giving capacities. This term can also apply to our abilities for creation, creativity, and creating as well as our cyclical wisdom for death, destruction, renewal, and regeneration.

Crone is one of the four Archetypes of the Divine Feminine. The other three are: Maiden, Mother, and Enchantress. These expressions of the Feminine work together with the other influential cycles of the Moon, the Seasons, and our Menstrual Cycles. Each Archetype has wisdom, empowerment, and support to share and impart through the experience of womanhood as well as the larger unified human experience. The Crone correlates with the Season of Winter, the Phase of the Dark Moon, and our Bleeding Time. Oftentimes viewed as an age or stage of life, the Crone energy also offers a deeper understanding of our physical, emotional, mental, and psychic needs no matter how old we are. The Crone reminds us to pull in and replenish. She takes away the fear of death and replaces it with the cyclical wisdom of going Dark, or barren as in Winter, in order to birth new life. Her power takes us deep into the recesses of our Shadow-Self and invites us to dream the dreams of purging, authenticity, comfort, and awareness. When dancing with Crone, there is no apologizing for our needs, there is no shrinking of our power, and there are no explanations required for our comfort. We are unafraid to demonstrate our knowledge, outspoken in our liberation, and astute in our clear judgement of destruction for the Greatest and Highest Good.

Crown is the Major Chakra located at the crown of the head and the colors most often associated with it are lavender and white. This Center is also referred to as the Seventh Chakra. Although it cannot be physically seen or touched, it can be energetically felt, sensed, and *known*. The Crown opens us up to higher states of consciousness, connects us to our bliss, and fully aligns us with the Divine wisdom of oneness and interconnectedness. It is here in the open, activated, and balanced Crown that our human awareness fully integrates with our Soul's guidance and we become Spiritual Beings. According to Esoteric Healing, the Crown anatomically relates to the Pineal Gland, where the thread of consciousness is said to be anchored. The Esoteric teachings also hold that our Crown Chakras balance with our Basic Chakras. When we intentionally connect to our Crown energy, we securely ground and anchor to this human experience, thereby clarifying our Divine Purpose.

Crystal Oracle Card Deck are cards similar to other decks of spiritual, self-help, and tarot cards that share the wisdom of Crystals. These types of cards can be found in metaphysical shops, online stores, and other fun places. Like this book and like the Soul-to-Sisterhood Oracle Card Deck, you can infuse your deck of cards with your energy. In doing this, your cards are aligned and attuned with you, your Soul, and your Greatest and Highest Good.

Crystalline Realm is the realm of Crystal consciousness. It is from here that Crystals choose to engage with the Human Realm to share their wisdom, guidance, support, and medicine.

Cultural Boundaries are defined as ethnographic boundaries and have typically been understood as the lines that separate us based on our ethnicity, religion, and/or language. However, these boundaries tend to go much deeper. Without considerable effort to become conscious of them, cultural boundaries can affect our choices, belief systems, thought processes, behavioral patterns, and general ways of relating without our knowledge. Knowing yourself, your biases, and your general relatability to all things based upon your cultural upbringing and identity can offer a sense of liberation in that you are consciously choosing your cultural boundaries instead of them unconsciously choosing you.

Cultural Construct is a foundation of thoughts and beliefs influenced by common cultural characteristics. Cultural constructs are usually reserved for how we make sense of culturally defined entities and other social categories. Think of gender and race or of other larger human experiences like birth and death. We have culturally held constructs about socially acceptable ways to navigate these topics which are simultaneously processed and experienced internally and externally. Due to this, they can be complex: sometimes invisible, other times glaring, and all the time worthy of personal consideration and exploration.

Cultural Context is how we make sense of things, literally putting them into context and figuring them out with our cultural wisdom, know-how, identity, and experience. It is in this place of contextualizing that we construct our basis for relating and reacting to our environments with our thoughts, emotions, and behaviors.

Cultural Messages are the messages we get about how to be in our worlds based on cultural values, beliefs, rules, and standards. These messages can be both external and internal. For instance, cultural messages about beauty, purity, and morality can affect how we feel about ourselves and others. Cultural messages around events like dating, work ethics, or how to celebrate holidays can affect our daily choices. Larger cultural messages regarding the '-*isms*' (such as classism, sexism, racism, etc.), can affect how we navigate all of our interactions.

Currency of Adult Relationships is the relational give and take exchange of adulthood. This currency is based on emotional maturity and is outlined by clearly and consistently asking for your needs to be met in order to extinguish the potential damage brought about by silent expectations and resulting resentments. When asking, the request is able to be met with a yes or no. It is then up to the requester to decide if this response is OK. If the response to the request is not OK, it is also up to the person asking for their needs to be met to communicate openly about their feelings. At this point the participants can then decide to create future boundaries that feel more in alignment. This could mean that the relationship shifts or ends to accommodate the new boundaries.

Currency of Parent-Child Relationships is the relational exchange between a parent and child where the clear communication of needs from child to parent is not required in order for the child's needs to be met. In this dynamic, the expectation for a parent to meet their child's needs without any communication is OK. This example is ideal and seldom is it realistic for parents to automatically know and meet all of their child's needs. However, perfection is not needed for functionality. If a parent and child have a secure attachment, the parent can meet the child's needs *enough* (some parenting theories posit that if this happens only 30% of the time, it is sufficient) to foster safety, security, and connection within the parent-child dynamic. It is believed that this secure relational currency created in childhood actually perpetuates the emotional intimacy, maturity, and positive sense-of-self needed to efficiently utilize and implement clear and open communication within Adult Relationships.

Cyclical Wisdom is the practical application of the varied, complex, and influential knowledge of the never-ending cycles of life as they apply to all of our relations. This includes but is not limited to: our Menstrual Cycle, the Lunar Cycle, the Seasonal Cycle, the Cycles of the Archetypes of Womanhood, Astrological Cycles, and Celestial Cycles. The *wisdom* surfaces when we can understand and identify how each cycle is manifesting within us and use the benefits of each to bring about the Greatest and Highest Good for all.

~ D ~

Dark Moon is the first phase of the Lunar Cycle and is sometimes referred to as the New Moon. Going completely dark in the sky, this phase correlates to the Archetype of the Crone, the season of Winter, and the Bleeding Time of the Menstrual Cycle. This time of darkness reminds us to pull in and release that which is no longer serving us. During the Dark Moon we may also feel the need to isolate. This desire for solitude is an offer of respite and regeneration amidst the busy and hectic schedules that so many of us keep. Dreams can be very powerful and psychic abilities may be enhanced during this time.

Decree is an official order usually given by someone with legal authority or power to enforce the rule of law.

Deity is a Divine Being of Divine Status. Goddess, God, Source, Universe, Universal Energy Source, You, etc., can all be thought of as deities.

Deification is to make something God or Goddess-like, or to give something Divine Status through the actions by which it is treated, referred, and related to.

Demeter is celebrated as the Greek Harvest Goddess, Goddess of Agriculture, or Corn Goddess. Representing the duality of creation and destruction through her embodiment of the cycles of birth, life, death, and renewal, Demeter reminds us to proudly own our vast and varied emotional states and personal attributes. A fierce badass warrioress momma, she took on the Pantheon when they refused to help her rescue her daughter Persephone who was stolen by Hades, God of the Underworld. Heartbroken, she turned her back on the fertility of the crops and refused to let anything grow until her daughter was returned. Fighting for what she held most dear, she was wild, unruly, unmanageable, untamed, and generally deemed *bad* by the establishment. Undeterred, she continued her quest for what she knew in her heart she needed and did not stop until she had struck a deal with Hades to have her daughter returned, unharmed, for part of the year. Like the archetype of the Enchantress, she is misunderstood and mislabeled for sharp authenticity and deep desires. However, within the very act of withdrawal she renders Mother Earth barren - not forever - but as an act of regeneration in order for the crops to grow lush and full on a rested and replenished body.

Descant is an independent melody line usually sung by one or a few voices above the traditional melody line of a song. This additional piece of music - which is layered over the original tune and sung during the final verses - can sound like an Angelic voice singing from the heavens and tickling your ears with its Divinity.

Dialogue is a conversation between two or more people. Typically witnessed on the stage, screen, or page, this theatrical term has also grown to include our everyday conversations.

Dimming Our Light is the act of reducing ourselves in order to promote the comfort of others. This can include reducing our empowerment, intelligence, talent, beauty, charisma, sensuality, wisdom, power, consciousness, etc. The messages we receive about dimming our lights to fit in can be powerful, painful, and extremely effective.

Dis-ease is a term that I learned from my Esoteric Healing teacher which encompasses anything that is less than optimal physical, emotional, mental, and spiritual health. This can include everything from a broken limb to a cold to a life-threatening condition.

Divine Birthright is the Divine Purpose that we were born for. It is complete and sovereign success, bliss, creativity, divinity, and empowerment. It is also the unwavering belief that we are pure hearted and that our word is good - always in **all** ways - no matter what. No argument, no waffling.

Divine Blueprint is the Divine Architecture of our genetics, the fabric and foundation of all of life and life's interactions, as well as our destinies.

Divine Child is one of the four main archetypes of the Immature Masculine - or "boyhood psychology" - presented in the book, *King, Warrior, Magician, and Lover: Discovering the Archetypes of the Mature Masculine* by Robert Moore and Douglas Gillette. My understanding of their work is what follows. The Divine Child is the youthful expression of its mature counterpart, the King. This young aspect is fresh, innocent, and a miraculous source of life that represents an emerging identity which can be an indicator of the potential his mature self carries. The Divine Child is very mysterious, very powerful, and yet totally in need of comfort and care to survive. His enthusiasm and capacities for greatness must be protected and encouraged to ensure optimal development. If not acknowledged in a balanced way, the Divine Child can be expressed as a Shadow Pole which represents either an over - or an under - identification with the archetype.

Divine Declaration is a formal announcement that is either channeled from a Divine Source, from the Divine Source Directly (which can be You because You are Divine), or is Divine in intent.

Divine Destiny is the preordained life experience that we choose through Sacred Contracts and Sacred Unions to fulfill our Divine Purpose. This transcends the karmic notion of cause and effect and pushes us into the realm of everything not only happening for a reason, but everything happening for everything else in order to manifest the Divine Purpose for all living beings throughout all time and space. Our Divine Destiny is created, experienced, and fulfilled within the field of oneness and is our unique expression of Source experiencing itself… an expression that we have collaboratively co-conceived with Source. Since Source is within sharing our experiences with us, we are Source and part of our Divine Destiny is to remember that.

Divine Energy is all of energy that we experience. Yes, Divine Energy is from the Divine and usually we expect that to feel amazing… and most times, it does. However, if all of our experiences have been manifested to guide, teach, transform, and love us into becoming the highest conscious expressions of ourselves… then aren't they *all* Divine, no matter how we experience them?

Divine Experience is life. All of it. The experiences that we would typically understand as *Divine* help us to understand the absolute nature of our infinite existence and that includes everything: the cool stuff, the not-so-cool stuff, and everything else in between. If we didn't have the Divine Experiences of seeing life in a raindrop, of feeling Angels around us, or of talking to Ascended Masters for needed guidance, we probably wouldn't be able to change that poopy diaper with gratitude, handle our crabby spouse with grace, or honor our children's tantrums with understanding. Everything affects everything and thankfully, it's *all* Divine, no matter how it may feel in the moment.

Divine Fabric is the invisible thread of life weaved throughout all of existence which connects us together through all time and space. It's like the great blankie of consciousness that we can hold and snuggle with whenever we need to be reminded that we are not alone, we are all one, and we are in this together.

Divine Feminine is the amazing, awe-inspiring, fertile, life-giving, and life-sustaining energy of Mother God, Feminine Christ Consciousness, Feminine Energy, Mother Earth, the Female, and YOU. In fact, I can hardly express it with mere words. I need to dance. Dance with me and shake this inner wisdom into being! Let's move our bodies and reclaim this empowered, powerful, and transformative magick. Let's shake this into our hearts, minds, and souls together. Better? Me too. The Divine Feminine is what we have been taught to turn away from because when we own it, especially when we own it through the unbreakable bonds of Spiritually Mature Sisterhood, we are an unstoppable, unshakable, unrelenting, and unescapable force for good and just interdependence, egalitarianism, love, and LIFE! When we stand strong in our femininity, sexuality, blood and birth magick, psychic abilities, energy, compassion, mercy, and capacities for simultaneously creating and destroying for the Greatest and Highest Good, we are The Mother, birthing in a new paradigm of existence. We are The Maiden, planting the seeds of peace. We are The Enchantress, proudly claiming all aspects of ourselves. We are The Crone, stepping into the shadows so that we may be reborn again and again and again. This energy asks us to turn toward one another. To understand and value our world, our children, our life, and our essence. The Divine Feminine is within every living thing and she is our creative connection to life, love, and bliss. Oh, and orgasms. Lots of orgasms. Just sayin'….

Divine Feminine Archetypes are the four Divine expressions of womanhood: Crone, Maiden, Mother, and Enchantress. We feel these energies in various capacities based on our age, the Lunar Cycle, the Seasonal Cycle, and our Menstrual Cycles. Although the influence and impact of these energies can be felt in different ways, we all feel them no matter our age, life stage, or awareness. Each Archetype brings its own unique wisdom and our ability to engage with the four energies in a balanced and supportive manner depends upon how we internally and externally honor, express, and value them.

Divine Healing Light is the sense of light or warmth that we can get when we feel a healing presence. This presence can be whatever you want or need it to be: your Higher Self, Oversoul, Source, Angels, Ascended Masters, God, Goddess, the Universe, etc. Your healing and how you heal is up to you. This light is available to every living thing and exists within every living thing. As we step more fully into our capacities as Healers, Oracles, and Medicine Women, we can learn to utilize and work with this light. However, our healing and our abilities to heal are an external reflection of our internal processes, belief systems, and self-love. We can heal without loving ourselves. It is possible. However, our true Divine gifts for healing will not totally be achieved if we hold onto dysfunctional patterns that challenge our self-worth, self-acceptance, self-compassion, self-forgiveness, and self-mastery. Sure, we may feel like we can hold onto these things and help others, but that is just another trope of the wounded healer paradigm. It has to go for us to grow. Love yourself, love the world. And, just like S2S Sister Goddess Jacqui says, "Heal yourself. Heal the world."

Divine Inner Light is the pure, authentic, and loving *core* you. This is the innocent, empowered, accepting, forgiving, wise, and connected part of you that knows your Divine Nature and never doubts it. This is the infant you. This is the infinite you. The is the you that was born so perfectly, as such a perfect expression of perfection, the Angels sang of your arrival so that all of life could celebrate. And guess what, she is still in there! When you feel that you are in the flow and sense your own inner beauty glowing around you, your Divine Inner Light is shining. When you feel terrible, like you want a giant, red 'end' button to just make everything disappear because life feels like a pile of poop, your Divine Inner Light is shining. The trick is seeing it in all of the places and spaces within you no matter what. I see it. Girl, you're gorgeous. Go get your glow on. It doesn't matter that you haven't changed out of your yoga pants in three days. Glow, baby, GLOW!

Divine Masculine is the strong, protective, regenerative, life-promoting, and life-stimulating energy of Father God, Masculine Christ Consciousness, Masculine Energy, Father Sky, the Male, and YOU. This amazing Masculine energy holds the Feminine with such tenderness and heroic courage that new life can be born, nurtured, and sustained. Humanity has been taught to turn away from authentic Masculine Divinity in favor of a more violent and brutal representation. Yet, the Divine Masculine is not interested in creating warfare to steal and take. The Divine Masculine is devoted to the surrender of deep healing so that his line can live on truly healthy, happy, and free. The Divine Masculine also understands that domination and ruthless destruction are mere fallacies created by the illusions of power. For the good of the many, this energy leads by creating a balanced relationship with feelings, passions, and ego to ensure that peace, prosperity, and production is brought about by empowered choice versus punishing force. This energy works in tandem with the Feminine - accepting softness, comfort, and support - while responding in-kind by cherishing, worshipping, and providing for her so that the infinite and intertwined partnership of creation can continuously form and reproduce. This proactive, confident, and present energy is within every living thing, regardless of gender.

Divine Masculine Archetypes are the four Divine expressions of mature manhood: King, Warrior, Lover, and Magician. These four names are taken from the Mature Masculine archetypes outlined by Robert Moore and Douglas Gillette in their book, *King, Warrior, Magician, Lover: Rediscovering the Archetypes of the Mature Masculine*. Although others have used these particular names (and many more such as Sage, Priest, God, Father, Jester, Ruler, Explorer, etc.) as descriptors of the Divine Masculine, I chose to focus on Moore's and Gillette's names because we explore their work throughout several of the Sacred Play Suggestions. We feel these archetypal energies within us and within all of our relationships. Based on their balanced and empowered actualization, these Archetypes can come forward and offer much understanding, compassion, and relief for our conceptualization of the Masculine. Each Archetype brings its own unique perspective to power, productivity, and potency and our abilities to engage with them depend on how we internally and externally honor, express, and value them.

Divine Purpose is our ultimate purpose for being incarnate on Earth. Some believe that this purpose has been decided upon and specifically fashioned for us before birth. Others believe it is a mixture of Divine Will and Free Will forming this purpose in tandem through our daily interactions. It could also be a combination of both. Intuitively living from Soul's guidance can help our human minds understand and feel that we are either in or headed toward our Divine Purpose. Yet, you just being *you* is pretty Divine. Maybe we don't have to push it? Kind of like our Divine Birthright, if we can deeply accept and believe our purity of heart in both word and deed, we can embody a self-love that is not only inspirational but contagious. Perhaps it is only our conditioning to accept that a Divine Purpose must be lived through what our world would have us understand as being 'great' or 'successful.' What if a Divine Purpose can be lived from the couch, doing nothing but loving and accepting our whole selves? No book tours, no influential prize-winning works, no notoriety or fame… only self-love and a connection to the Divinity within. Pretty cool to think about.

Divine Realm(s) of Consciousness are all realms of consciousness because all of consciousness is Divine. Although some amazing teachers and way-showers typically refer to these levels as above our physical world (the Third Dimension) and describe them as the Fourth, Fifth, Sixth, Seventh (and on up) Dimensions or Levels. Suffice it to say, you will know when you are connected into a Divine Level of Consciousness because it won't feel judge-y, complain-y, or ego-y at all. This Consciousness is of Soul, Source, the Universe, and other high vibratory levels of energy. It exists within you and outside of you simultaneously. Accessing these levels utilizes a different type of awareness than mere physical awareness because this consciousness is energetic.

Divine Timing is when it all works out. Some would argue that everything - no matter if it feels good or bad - is in Divine Timing. Whether our human minds realize it or not, it is *always* working out in *all ways* according to the Divine Plan. Kind of like a 'no mistakes, no coincidences, no matter what' sort of perspective.

Diviners are the Souls that can channel in Divine Guidance. This guidance can come from any Divine Source and it is done so as a form of support, healing, transformation, and opportunity for individuals and tribes alike. The process of Divination can look and feel different for various practitioners, groups, rituals, ceremonies, etc. As women, due to our dynamic relationships with the Cycles of Womanhood, the Lunar

Cycles, the Seasonal Cycles, our Blood and Birth Magick, and our natural psychic abilities, we are Diviners by nature. How many times have you told your kids that you have eyes in the back of your head? Or, how often do you sense, intuit, or just *know* things? Some of us just go with it and others want to formalize this talent. You do your *Diviner* Self, Sister. ☺

Drama Therapy is an active and experiential form of Expressive Arts Therapy that uses dramatic techniques and principles to meet therapeutic goals, create therapeutic results, and bring about desired change. This form of therapy is great for all populations and is thought to be very effective in creating profound and beneficial insights for clients that are applicable, useful, and transformational. The Drama Therapy work is multi-dimensional and inter-disciplinary in nature. It is also a very studied, researched, and complex form of therapy with over 30 different models in practice. Drama Therapy works beautifully with other types of therapeutic interventions and is not performance-based, although the Ritual of Performance can be a component if deemed clinically advantageous to the client or group.

Dream Narrative is the *story* that we experience, live, witness, participate in, and embody while dreaming.

Dreamscape is the landscape of our Dreamworld. This is the setting that hosts all interactions, aspects, and involvement happening within our dreams. Quite like another realm of consciousness, the Dreamscape is vast and full of infinite possibilities.

Duality is the concept of *either-or* which creates a dual nature, contrast, or opposition between two things.

Dysfunctional Cycles are the behavioral patterns playing out in our relationships that are less than optimal. These cycles can be handed down from our families of origin, we can create them ourselves, or they can be witnessed in others and then adopted as our own. They may be conscious or unconscious. These cycles keep us rooted in what we don't want, what isn't in our alignment, and are the opposite of Soul's Guidance. However, they are tricky because they can become so familiar and habituated that we don't even realize we are doing them. Or we can get so used to them that even in their discomfort they seem safer than the unknown. Awareness of these cycles can be the key to shifting them, if we want to. Empowerment can come from knowing they are there and making the choice to do things differently.

Earth Plane is the physical world that we live in and is considered to be the Realm of humans. To most human sensibilities, this world is tangible, quantifiable, and realistic to our brains in the sense that we can actually observe and touch what we see and feel. Oftentimes, the Earth Plane is called the Third Dimension and is different than that of the Spiritual Plane.

Earth Star Chakra is the magickal Energy Center located underneath our feet. Sometimes understood to rest just about 12 inches below our feet within the flesh of Mother Earth, this Chakra is also known as 'Gaia's Anchor' and correlates with the colors of pink and turquoise. This Energy Center deeply tethers our seven other Chakras to the greater grounding and stabilizing energies of both the Earth and the Universe. As with all of our other Energy Centers, these places on our bodies are not anatomically visible but they can be energetically and intuitively felt, sensed, and *known*. To get this Energy Center nice and juiced up, take your shoes off and put your bare feet on the ground. Connect into Mother Earth and make an offering to consider her as you go about your days, making your decisions, and generally being more aware of your relationship to the natural world. Our Earth Star Chakra can also gift us a solid sense of well-being, connection, and oneness. When we activate this Center, we activate our awareness of humanity's collective consciousness, the Crystalline Realm, and the vast field of 'All That Is' to bring healing energy and powerful purification into our daily lives.

Earthly Energies are the energies' characteristic of our Earthly existence. This can include the energies of our Sun, Moon, and Earth. It can also include both our positive and negative human energies. Sometimes these energies can feel rooted in the Ego, sometimes they can feel connected to the Soul. It is up to each one of us to decide how we interact with these energies, learn from them, and transform them - or not - for the Greatest and Highest Good.

Ego is the part of our personality or psyche that involves the processes and reactions from the perspective of I, me, or mine. Socially, the word Ego has become a pejorative label used to ascribe selfish, self-centered, and/or self-serving traits and is the literal English translation of the Latin word 'I.' When we look at something from our Ego, we are typically perceiving, understanding, and acting from a mixture of our physical vantage point, personal interests, and evaluations, which tend to fit with our beliefs, biases, and experiences. In many Spiritual teachings, the Ego is considered in need of quieting in order to fully walk within Soul's or Source's Guidance. For me, I love my Ego. I understand that my sense of 'I' is a sense of separation born out of my Human Consciousness as well as the wounds I've experienced through this lifetime. However, if I try to exorcise my Ego or consistently hold it in a negative space, I feel that I am pushing it from the realm of *shadow* into the realm of *secret* and that is a space where my Ego sits and putrefies, not purifies. I want to know my Ego, hold it, and love it into being. I want to stroke it until it purrs… because to do that means I have embarked on a healing quest where no part of me will be left unseen, unloved, or unheard. When I view my world from the lens of 'I,' I am in fear, staying small, trying to protect myself with only the insight of my anxiety reiterating the toxic message that I am alone. When I accept my Ego and see it for who it truly is, I can compassionately witness it without surrendering to it.

Ego Attachments are the 'I - Me - Mine' attachments to the things that our Egos would convince us we need to in order to stay safe, powerful, in control, secure, and strong. These can be material items, belief systems, relationship dynamics, life choices… really they can be anything and everything that keeps us disconnected from ourselves, our empowerment, each other, and every other living thing.

Embodied Action is intentional and purposeful movement of the body to internalize, externalize, process, and transform frozen, stuck, or unconscious behavioral and thought patterns pertaining to our emotional states, awareness, and growth in order to create beneficial shifts, meet therapeutic goals, and strengthen the body, mind, spirit connection to ultimately move towards more optimal life functioning.

Emotional Alchemy is the process of consciously transforming emotional states that feel lower in vibration to emotional states that feel higher in vibration. This is done by honoring, feeling, and respecting the wisdom from all states of being and then - with awareness and empowerment - allowing them to shift into something new which promotes pure relational functionality, ascension, and bliss. When emotional alchemy takes place, it is said to be a state of pure love and light.

Emotional Authenticity is being totally and completely authentic with how you are feeling at all times no matter what. To be emotionally authentic, you must know and recognize your feelings, honor them, and be able to honestly express them in ways that don't projectile vomit your dysfunction all over everyone and everything else. You are your own best authority for this one. To be living from a place of Emotional Authenticity, you have to monitor yourself with razor sharp precision to maintain an indisputable sense of personal integrity and honesty.

Emotional Intelligence is the ability to understand, recognize, express, and honor our own feelings and the feelings of others. To be emotionally intelligent, you don't need to agree with the feelings, but sensitivity, compassion, and empathy are definitely helpful in holding space for the feelings and creating a dynamic where the relationship can either continue with or work towards ideal health and functionality.

Emotional Maturity is the way in which we handle our own and other's feelings with respect, acceptance, and accountability. This type of emotional interaction deescalates situations and is very useful for relationships of all kinds.

Emotional Resonance is when you feel an emotional state and react accordingly to be of service. This resonance can be toward yourself or others and can be identical, where you actually feel what the other person is feeling, or reactive where you empathize with what the other person is feeling. The whole 'react accordingly' and 'be of service' points mentioned in the first sentence is kind of where the Spiritual Maturity rubber hits the road because these two things are so subjective. Sometimes just energetically holding someone in love and light is more than enough Emotional Resonance. Other times, more action is needed. The 'accordingly' is up to you and your Higher Self. As always, bringing about the Greatest and Highest good is the pinnacle of any resonance, emotional or otherwise.

Emotional Sobriety is the sobering up process of becoming really clear about how you *really* feel. So many things keep us distracted, hazy, fuzzy, and unclear about our emotions. Emotional Sobriety is where that confusion stops. It can come from stopping the use of a particular substance, an activity, a behavior, a relationship, a belief system, etc. Only you know what is being employed to keep you splintered away from your true feelings and only you know why. However, discontinuing the behaviors may call for some assistance. Be sure to get the support you need.

Empath is a person who can sense, understand, respect, and have compassion for what another living being is going through. Traditionally, an empath displays this level of sensitivity by experiencing things from their own perspective and then applying this level of sensitivity to the situation. However, an empath is also described as taking on the feelings of another as their own. For our purposes, an Empath can be empathetic without the loss of the self. The dynamic of getting lost in another's emotional state and experiences is, in regard to our work together, better understood as a Sympath.

Empathic Responses are clear responses in which someone displays that they have heard what someone is feeling, understands why someone may be feeling that way, and has care and concern for this person and their experiences. Agreement about the feelings is not needed for an empathic response, nor is actually sharing the feelings.

Enchantress is one of the four Archetypes of the Divine Feminine. The other three are: Crone, Maiden, and Mother. These expressions of the Feminine work together with the other influential cycles of the Moon, the Seasons, and our Menstrual Cycles. Each Archetype has wisdom, empowerment, and support to share and impart through the experience of womanhood, as well as the larger unified human experience. The Enchantress correlates with the Season of Fall, the Phase of the Waning Moon, and our Luteal, or Premenstrual Phase.

Oftentimes misrepresented as a 'type' of person or storybook character, the energy of the Enchantress offers a deep, dazzling well of understanding for our physical, emotional, mental, and psychic needs. She is mysterious, powerful, and sensual. She creates dynamics for us to enjoy the wild solitude of our own company, sometimes in ways that don't necessarily feel nice, easy, or acceptable. The Enchantress diminishes physical and mental stamina in order for us to meditatively explore the inner recesses of our creativity, eroticism, consciousness, and desires. She can be aggressive, demanding, primal, intimate, and fiery. She prepares us for the death of the Crone, Winter, and Menstruation by teaching that self-care is non-negotiable. The Enchantress doesn't argue, dilly-dally, or put her needs last because she has bought into the toxic belief system that she must caregive at the expense of her own well-being. She howls in outrage when we turn away from directing our energies inward, for she knows that we must continually regenerate in order to fully embody our power. When honoring and validating this aspect of the Feminine, we take ownership of who we are at our very core and channel the gifts of our heightened emotionality for the Greatest and Highest Good.

Endocrine System is the brilliant system of glands which produces our hormones. Once produced, these little sweethearts then secrete the biological juice that regulates our metabolism, growth, development, reproduction, sexual function, mood, sleep, and much more. The glands send out hormones to the tissues of our bodies and the hormones in turn tell our tissues what to do. When this system is not communicating, producing, and secreting in tip-top fashion, dis-ease can occur.

Energetic Body is the body of energetic light that surrounds us, is within us, walks into a room before us, has our back, includes all of our Major and Minor Chakras, carries our ancestrally-held cellular memories, talks to us through our intuition and instinct, and is just a damned cool gift from whoever designed our humanity and humanness. I want to say, "Thank you," right here right now because my Energetic Body rocks! So does yours!

Energetic Field is the field of energy surrounding us. Like the Auric Field, it can be sensed and felt and is typically understood to have four layers above the physical body which are: the Emotional Layer, the Mental Layer, the Personality/Ego Layer, and the Soul Layer.

Energetic Vibration is the vibe we get from everything and *everything* has a vibe… **everything**! We sense this from other people, situations, and experiences. We get different vibes from the things we have in our environments. Our emotions and thoughts have vibrations. So do our belief systems. Literally, everything has an Energetic Vibration and the more we grow and transcend, the more we attune to it and know how to navigate and work with it.

Energetically Sensitive is a state of intuitively sensing energy with detail and specificity. Sometimes this energetic sensitivity can become over-stimulated by too much going on in the energetic field. However, as you work with energy and become efficient at maintaining your own, there is less of a chance of unintentionally taking on unwanted energy.

Energy is everything and everything is energy… you, me, every living thing… and we know every*thing* is living. It is the force of attraction and repulsion, light and dark, expansion and contraction. Our thoughts and feelings are energy. Our intuition and instincts are energy. We feel it, sense it, and know it. Energy is all around us, within us, and between us. It can manifest as desire, disgust, frustration, or release. Our bodies carry energy within every organ, tissue, bone, and cell. It can be witnessed through our movement, awareness, pain, and bliss. Energy keeps us going. Energy stops us in our tracks. It reminds us that, no matter what we are doing, feeling, or experiencing, we are all energetic beings connected through light and love. Our energy, and our dedication to our energy, as individuals and as a collective unites us. It makes us one and it is ours to nurture and share.

Energy Centers are our Chakras. All of them. The Majors, the Minors, and the Nadis. I have been taught that all of the points on our bodies where energy crosses (and there are loads - the Nadis alone comprise of 72,000!) can be thought of as Energetic Centers. Aren't we lucky! We are walking, talking energy!

Energy Exchange is the giving and receiving of energy. Like a currency exchange, we get and give energy all the time. When we are conscious of this, it can be wonderful and empowering. However, as energetic beings, we are very receptive to this type of exchange. If we aren't aware and attuned to ourselves and our environments, this can happen without our knowledge and it can leave us feeling exactly the opposite: disempowered and disenfranchised.

Energy Pollution is just like it sounds. It is the pollution of our Energetic Field. It doesn't feel necessarily good, it changes our vibration, and it can happen with or without our conscious consent. This type of pollution happens in our relationships, and as relational beings, we are 'in relationship' to everything all the time. You can detox this pollution and rebalance your energy, or you can put an end to it altogether by shifting your relationship to the pollutants.

Energy Systems are our Chakras Systems. All of our Chakras correlate to different aspects of our anatomy, physiology, and psychology. These relationships create systems of information exchange, feedback loops, and subsequent responses. We feel, experience, and manifest all of this either as health or dis-ease.

Epigenetics is the biological study of how gene expression can be changed by our environments and experiences without an actual change in the genetic code. This science is now proving that these specific gene expressions are passed down ancestrally and can be witnessed in future generations without those individuals actually having to experience the same or similar circumstances. Think of stress and trauma. If your ancestors experienced either or both enough for it to affect gene expression, you could be biologically experiencing the effects. Epigenetics opens our understanding of the human experience in ways that can be quite overwhelming but also quite mollifying. This science could potentially liberate the shame and blame held around disease, psychopathology, dysfunction, etc. If we can release the construct that somehow symptomology is of our own doing and instead perceive it as a genetic expression passed down from our ancestors' experiences, perhaps we can shift how we treat, support, respect, and comfort one another as well as ourselves.

Epona is the great and important Celtic Goddess of horses, mules, donkeys, and their riders. Beloved by all, she was known to provide special guardianship over mares and foals. Offering abundance, healing, and peace, her cult spread far and wide throughout Europe. Never depicted without a horse, Epona watches over us, riding by our side as we travel through day and night.

Equine Energy is the energy and consciousness of the entire Equine species throughout all time and space. This energy has provided for humanity in generous, altruistic abundance and is also linked to the energy of the Feminine.

Esoteric Energy Healing Session is where Esoteric Healing occurs. Like any healing modality, this work happens within a pre-agreed upon arrangement between practitioner and client. Sessions usually last an hour and can be done individually or in groups. Consent is required for treatment.

Esoteric Healing is an integrative modality of energy work based on the channelings of Djwal Khul by Theosophical writer and teacher, Alice Bailey. Esoteric Healing is subtle, gentle, and powerfully effective as it works to balance our Energetic Centers - also known as Chakras - with the anatomical and physiological systems of the body. Esoteric Healing does not use physical touch. Instead, a Soul-to-Soul connection is made and maintained through an aligning and attuning process. Esoteric Healing can be wonderfully beneficial for individuals, couples, and groups.

Etheric Body is the subtle body, or lowest, densest level of the energetic field which is closest to the physical body. Working with this layer allows us to quickly connect the physical level to the emotional, mental, and spiritual levels of consciousness. The primary role of the Etheric Body is to provide energy to the physical body so that it can do what it needs to do: move, digest, circulate, etc.

Expanded Existence see definition for 'Expansion' below to find out what this is *not*. Just kidding. An expanded existence is living and loving in bliss. When existing this way, you are vibing in the good stuff to bring about the Greatest and Highest Good for all - all. the. time. You are Source experiencing itself. You know nothing and everything simultaneously through both your Inner-Innocence and Inner-Sovereignty. Your heart and your mind are open. You feel awesome. You bring awesome. You are awesome.

Expansion is what we are all working toward whether we know it or not. I mean, what the heck else are we all doing here? Seriously though, expansion is a way of being that is the embodiment of bliss. All of our paths toward expansion are unique. Some of us feel we have to work at it and seek spiritual teachings and enlightenment through various means. Others don't and expansion just 'is' for them. It is so *Hamlet*, right? "To expand or not to expand… that is the question." Maybe there isn't any question at all and *that* **is** the expansion. OK, I'm driving myself crazy here. You doing you with love and light, whatever that is for you… boom - expansion granted.

Explicit/Declarative Memory both refer to one of the two main types of long-term memory storage. Our declarative memories hold facts and events that we can easily and consciously bring up to process and discuss. It is also called our explicit memory because this information can be categorically stored and retrieved. This memory storage is associative and helps us link things together from previous experiences. The other long-term memory storage is the Implicit/Nondeclarative Memory and this memory storage is the exact opposite. Conscious thought is not employed in Implicit Memory and previous experiences cannot be recalled at will. Trauma memories are stored in the Implicit Memory, making them extremely difficult to talk about and process.

Extrasensory can be explained as our sixth, or psychic, sense. This is the part of our knowing and experiencing that moves beyond the other five senses of hearing, smelling, tasting, seeing, and touching. Through our extrasensory perception (also referred to as ESP), we receive information that may or may not fit within the typical boundaries of the physical world in which we live.

~ F ~

Family Cycles are family patterns and traits that play out generationally. These can be functional or dysfunctional. They can be conscious or unconscious. A great way to see these patterns is to do a Genogram. A Genogram is a diagram drawn with specific symbols to clearly depict Family Cycles which tend to repeat themselves through the genetic line. Oftentimes, just identifying these Family Cycles can provide insight and release. Most Mental Health Clinicians are trained to do Genogram work. If this sounds like it might be beneficial, try seeking out some additional support to help you make sense of the patterns and cycles within your family of origin.

Family of Origin is the family that you were raised in. This includes all parental figures, caretakers, siblings, cousins, grandparents, etc. This is not the family you chose, but the people you had around you from the time you were very young onward. The influence of your Family of Origin is pretty huge. The way we were parented nurtures our sense of who we are. It molds our growth and development. These early relationships teach us how to get our needs met, process our feelings, and communicate. Our Family of Origin experiences shape the beliefs we hold about ourselves and give us a foundational understanding of what it means to be human. All of these early influences can affect how we cope and function within our daily lives, how we parent our children, and how we navigate our adult relationships.

Female Spirituality is a Feminine approach to spirituality in which women craft their own customized connection to the Divine. There are no preset rules, no dogma, no standardized practices… only a woman and her relationship to what she defines as spiritual.

Feminine Archetypal Cycle is the influential cycle of the Feminine Archetypes felt through the Lunar Cycle, the Seasonal Cycle, and our Menstrual Cycles. These energies fluctuate and impact us differently depending on external and internal factors. They are understood and embodied as: Crone, Maiden, Mother, and Enchantress, and their wisdom, empowerment, and guidance ebbs and flows throughout our different layers of consciousness akin to the ebbs and flows of the cycles mentioned above. When allowed to be fully expressed, honored, and respected, these cycles inherently work together, allowing us to expertly harness their very generous, needed, and balancing gifts.

Feminine Divinity is the concept of God or Source as female. For thousands of years, our ancestors and ancestresses existed within the cosmology that all life originated from the Feminine. A Great Mother Goddess was venerated, and the incarnate female was the physical representation of this Divine Feminine Energy.

Feminine Energies are the energies attributed to the Feminine, or the Divine Feminine. This energy is receptive, and although complex and dynamic, can be understood as ways of being, personality traits, archetypal qualities, behaviors and mannerisms, and/or elements of cultural and social structures. This energy expresses itself - regardless of gender – through all living things.

Feminine Side is the side of our personalities that is Feminine. Some general qualities of the Feminine that are expressed within the living world regardless of gender are: compassion, mercy, relatability, stillness, intuition, gentleness, patience, nurturing, healing, emotionality and emotional resonance, forgiveness, acceptance, transformation, cyclical wisdom, and interdependence.

Feng Shui is the ancient art and science of creating good fortune through the interactions of human beings and their environments. This philosophy helps people gain balance and harmony in their lives by creating a spatial design that is in alignment with the natural world, the Five Elements, and the energy or 'qi' (pronounced *chee*) that connects all things. By doing this, Feng Shui permits the energy to flow unrestrained throughout the home in order to enhance quality of life. If you are interested in learning more, contact Sister Goddess Jacqui at www.jafengshui.com.

Fetlocks are the name we have given to the metacarpophalangeal and metatarsophalangeal joints (MCPJ and MTPJ) of horses. These joints are kind of like the human ankle. They are below the '*knee*' and above the hoof and bear a tuft of hair.

Flesh it Out is a theatrical process in which an artist gets into the specifics of a character or piece of theatre in order to make that character or piece whole and ultimately more realistic for the stage. Traditionally, a play or musical is only a few hours. Much deep production work has to be done by the actors and creative and technical staff to produce a world for the audience that feels deep, tangible, accurate, natural, and authentic. Fleshing it out is the general directive given to make that happen and can include dramaturgy work, character development, rehearsal, and incorporating the technical aspects of the production.

Full Moon is the third and most well-known phase of the Lunar Cycle. Completely full in the sky, this phase correlates to the Archetype of the Mother, the season of Summer, and the time of Ovulation in the Menstrual Cycle. The bright and complete light of the Full Moon reminds us of our radiant fertility, our abilities to nourish and sustain, and our deep, strong, soul-based desires to connect intimately with our inner and outer worlds. During the Full Moon, we may feel the need to collaborate, co-create, and care for our communities. Our self-confidence can be very high and our self-worth is a protective blanket for the new life we are nimbly birthing into existence. Sexuality is deep and loving, and the expression of femininity is ripe.

~ G ~

Generational Patterns are the repeated cycles that we witness playing out generationally within families. This can be either functional or dysfunctional, conscious or unconscious. Typically, we are most familiar with the generational patterns that present negatively such as divorce, addiction, infidelity, suicide, abuse, etc. However, we can repeat functional generational patterns as well! Think of strong matrilineal and patrilineal bonds, family rituals and routines, entrepreneurship, and empowering life philosophies.

Genetic Coding is the term used to describe the set of rules by which information is encoded into genetic material and then translated by the cells of the body. Spiritually, it can also mean the Celestial or Divine information within the genetic material that informs all layers of consciousness.

Gift Economy is the transitive economy of *giving* in order to create, nourish, and sustain *relationships*. This is the economy of Motherhood, Mother Earth, and the Feminine. We all experience this kind of Economy and regardless of whether we are a Mother, Father, Man, or Woman, are all created to give and receive in this way. The Gift Economy is the opposite of our current monetized economy which is debt and calculation based. This accepted strategy, which has become the archetype for human interactions, is known as the Exchange Economy. The Gift Economy is different in that no payback is required for the initial gift. The satisfaction is gained in fulfilling a need for someone or something else's well-being. This type of relating to the world promotes collaboration, interdependence, and community because there is no need for competition, recognition, or sacrifice.

Gift Economy Paradigm is a model of distinct concepts, philosophies, thought patterns, and standards for living within a Gift Economy. In this type of paradigm, a path is created for qualitative goods like caregiving and relationships to be valued equally or more so than quantitative goods, which can be bought and sold. This promotes a fundamental sense of and desire for communal well-being versus a status of quid pro quo where the individual is primarily focused on the needs of the self. This paradigm also encourages secure attachments and healthy neural development through the mutually beneficial templates of kindness, compassion, and emotional security. Gifts such as goods, services, and care are given without the expectation of receiving something in return of equal or greater value. These happy interactions foster additional incentives for continued 'gifting,' which encourage the transitive resources of trust, connection, holistic health, and unification.

God is the Divine in Male form, the Masculine expression of Divinity, Source, the Universe, and You. You possess all of this within and so does every living thing. Own it, Sis!

Goddess is the Divine in Female form, the Feminine expression of Divinity, Source, the Universe, and You. You possess all of this within and so does every living thing. Own it, Sis!

~ H ~

Habituated is to become so used to doing something that the pattern, choice, reaction, thought, feeling, or response becomes habit-like. This can be conscious; however, like a habit, it is mostly done with little or no conscious effort or awareness. When you consistently do this, either as a conscious or unconscious choice, or without attempting to change the automatic behavior, you act Habitually.

Hag is a word that has been totally misappropriated. The word actually means *'holy woman'* or *'sacred grove'* and is meant to encompass a woman boldly declaring her own self in her own world while creatively and wildly birthing what she needs for her holistic well-being. She is empowered, unapologetic, and untethered to the conventions of what the world would have her believe she needs in order to be good, faithful, successful, or *feminine*. A Hag lives her life in *her* way, always questing for inner truth and authenticity, making the most of every moment, and fully honoring the gift of her human life.

Heart Chakra, Heart Energy Center is the Major Energy Center located anatomically at the center of the chest. Associated with the color green, the Heart Chakra is also referred to as the fourth Chakra. Not visible to the eye, this Energy Center can be sensed, felt, and *known*. The Heart Chakra connects us to our abilities to fully give and receive love. Its energy is affected by our ability to express our lovingness to ourselves and others, the use of will or the forcing of our will onto other people, places, and things, and our involvement in group consciousness as it relates to group needs and group love. Balancing with the Solar Plexus Chakra, the Heart Center can help us to stabilize our emotional energies in order to realign with the consciousness of pure love. When out of balance, our Heart Chakra offers information pertaining to self-love, meeting our own needs, and authentically communicating our needs to others. This Chakra gives us a deep sense of our inner self, and its maintenance is closely related to the energy and balance of the Solar Plexus.

Hecate (pronounced he-***kah***-tay or he-kah-***tee***) is the Greek triple Goddess of the past, present, and future. She is oftentimes associated with the Crone and is known to be a formidable and mysterious force. Always at the crossroads where decisions must be made, Hecate offers us her well of life experience to make them wisely. It was she that came to Demeter's side to help rescue Persephone from Hades, and Hecate's loyalty persisted through many dark trips to the Underworld. Hecate is the Goddess of witches and is a well-known lover of solitude. At a young age, she chose her independence over marriage, and because of that has been misrepresented in modern times as a lonely old woman. However, nothing could be further from the truth.

Hecate claimed her destiny and lived luminously as a sovereign being. Able to see and communicate with both the living and the dead, she reminds us to look closer at that which we turn away from out of fear or misunderstanding. Viewing life through the lenses of past, present, and future, Hecate supports us in releasing what no longer serves us so that we may welcome change and step firmly into our potential.

Hedonism is a way of life that avoids all suffering in order to wholly embody pleasure. For a hedonist, this type of existence is considered the only proper way of living to ensure complete well-being. Ethical hedonism grounds this philosophy in the consideration that pleasure is sought with the welfare of all individuals in mind.

Hero is one of the four main archetypes of the Immature Masculine - or "boyhood psychology" - presented in the book, *King, Warrior, Magician, and Lover: Discovering the Archetypes of the Mature Masculine* by Robert Moore and Douglas Gillette. My understanding of their work is what follows. The Hero is the youthful expression of its mature counterpart, the Warrior. This younger aspect is recognizable as the adolescent stage and is responsible for the child's individuation away from the family of origin in order to be able to survive independently. His desire to quest and dream represents the emerging identity which can be an indicator of the potential his mature self carries. The Hero attempts to access his courage by continually testing his competence to overcome challenges. This shining, brave, and capable aspect of the boy is often misunderstood. Although glorified in movies and other modern narratives, this archetype is also made fun of and attacked. For the Hero to mature into the Warrior, we must all support the very humbling process of facing limitations, honoring our dark side, and learning how to ask for help. If not acknowledged in a balanced way, the Hero can be expressed as a Shadow Pole which represents either an over - or an under - identification with the archetype.

Herstorians are the researchers, scientists, academics, authors, artists, and seekers devoted to respectfully and reverently uncovering the truth of the ancient and not so ancient past as it relates to Matriarchal Societies, Female Empowerment, Feminism, Goddess Worship, Matrilineal Cultures, and Female-Centric perspectives. This is a step away from the Male-Centric, Patriarchal lens that so much of our past has been viewed through due to common cultural and social constructs that - for millennia - have created and supported the narrative of an all-powerful Male God, creator, or figurehead. Herstorians give us additional options for understanding where we came from so that we can create a future that is more balanced, sustainable, and peaceful.

Higher Celestial Chakras are the Energy Centers which are *of* our bodies, but unlike the first through the seventh Chakras, are not *on* the body. These Chakras are the Celestial Chakra, the Solar Chakra, and the Galactic Chakra and are said to connect our Human energy or Matrix through their Cosmic Coordinates to the Galactic Core of Source, or the Merkabah field of oneness. The Celestial Chakra is at the level of the stars and is recognized as a silver ray. The Solar Chakra is at the level of the Earth's sun and is recognized as a golden ray. The Galactic Chakra is at the level of the Grand Central Sun - or center of the galaxy - and is recognized as a platinum ray with a diamond core.

Higher Self is our Soul. This is the aspect of our consciousness that is connected to Source, our Greatest and Highest Good, and unconditional love. Intuition and guidance comes in from our Higher Self, and this part of our being has no doubts, questions, criticisms, or judgments about us at all. Our Higher Self knows without a doubt how pure hearted we are. Our Higher Self is our BFF, big Sis, therapist, partner, and twin flame energy all in one. This part of us can be accessed at any time and is always, always available. Sometimes listening to our Higher Self can seem difficult at first, but like any skill, can get easier and more fluid with continued practice and dedication. We can talk to our Higher Selves and others can, too. The opposite side of that coin is also available to us as we can connect in and talk to other beings' Higher Selves as well. Everything has the Soul energy of a Higher Self. Lucky us!

Highest Conscious Expression is the absolute highest vibratory way of being for all living things. This is experienced and embodied through our responses and reactions and affects all communication, thought, feeling, and *knowing*. Each of us has our own unique way of connecting to this high vibration energy and each of us has our own unique way of expressing it. While in this place, we are conduits of pure love and light. Body, mind, and spirit - throughout all time and space - we are perfection.

Hindu is a culture, ethnicity, and religion traditionally known to be based in India, but observed and practiced worldwide. Although difficult to trace its origins, it is said to be the world's third largest religion and one of the oldest. Hinduism embraces many different beliefs and is sometimes referred to as a 'way of life' or a 'family of religions' versus a specific, structured belief system. With rich traditions, cosmologies, and sacred texts, this way of life is one of respecting the continuous cycles of life, death, and renewal - known as Samsara - as well as the Universal Law of cause and effect, which is known as Karma.

Ho'oponopono is the Hawaiian practice of forgiveness. The word translates from Hawaiian into English as "correction" and its meaning offers the perspective of carefully and mindfully 'making something right.' The Ho'oponopono mantra, "I'm sorry. Please forgive me. Thank you. I love you." is known to be very purifying, cleansing, and cathartic.

Hocks are the joints on a horse's hind legs that are critical in carrying weight, running, jumping, turning, and playing. Oftentimes described like an ankle, being higher up on the leg than the fetlock, they can seem more like an elbow or knee to our human sensibilities. When you look at the back of a horse, the hock is the mid-joint of the leg between the rump and the hoof.

Honorable Harvest is an ancient practice of relating to our worlds. This principle offers a respectful and noble code for the taking of a life in order to sustain a life. In her book, *Braiding Sweetgrass: Indigenous Wisdom, Scientific Knowledge and the Teachings of Plants,* Robin Wall Kimmerer shares about this beautiful tradition as a way of nurturing our Mother Earth to ensure that her generous gifts of food, beauty, and natural riches are available for many generations to come.

Hook is the part of a song that provides the meaning for why the song was written. Usually part of the chorus, you typically hear the hook repeated several times during the tune. It is usually catchy and easy to remember.

Humanarchy is a made-up word that combines the best characteristics and principles of both Matriarchal and Patriarchal societies. This projected structure for humanity is one where all humans are regarded as equals.

Hyperarousal is a specific set of Post-Traumatic Stress Disorder (PTSD), or post-trauma symptoms and is the state of sudden high-alert and anxiety brought on by sensations reminiscent of previously experienced trauma. When hyper-aroused, danger does not need to be present for the physiological and psychological reactions to create a dynamic where it feels like one is experiencing the original traumatic situation again.

Hypervigilance is a way of behaving that involves an elevated state of alertness as a means of preventing oneself from being in a dangerous situation. This is not paranoia, but a chronic anticipation of danger usually brought on by past trauma. Although not responding to an actual threat, a person's brain is overanalyzing sensory information and reacting based on their perception of what needs to occur to prevent reexperiencing trauma which can be either physical or emotional danger (as felt within a relationship when there is conflict or strife).

~ I ~

Idea Children is a term I first learned about while studying Miranda Gray's work. It implies that, as women, we give *birth* to new ideas all the time. Regardless of being a Mother to human children, we are all Mothers to Idea Children. These Idea Children can be new understandings, relationships, levels of compassion, forgiveness, hopes, dreams, insights, visions, etc. They can also be new ideas that we birth for a business or organization. This book is my Idea Child. Idea Children, just like other children, take their time to gestate. There is a labor and delivery process. They must be cared for and loved, honored and valued. Most important, as their Mothers, when conceiving, creating, birthing, and caring for our Idea Children, we, too, deserve support, comfort, rest, replenishment, and love. This is hard work! These Idea Children come in from our Souls and we must honor ourselves for their existence.

Imbue is to permeate something with a feeling. This can be an object, idea, relationship, activity, etc. When you imbue something, you are putting your energy into it and that energy is intentional. Almost like a little force field of love and inspiration, this activation energy holds tight to the vibration of what it is that you are imbuing. Try it. Jewelry is great for this. Imbue a bracelet or necklace with love and wear it for a day. Every time you notice your jewelry, consciously remind yourself of the love energy it possesses. You might never want to take it off!

Immature Masculine is a way of understanding the aspects of the youthful or chronologically younger Masculine as described by Robert Moore and Douglas Gillette in their wonderful book, *King, Warrior, Magician, Lover: Rediscovering the Archetypes of the Mature Masculine.* My understanding of their work is that the four Immature Archetypes of "The Divine Child," "The Precocious Child," "The Oedipal Child," and "The Hero," - when allowed to be fully actualized and enriched by life experiences - transform into the four Mature, or chronologically older Archetypes of "The King," "The Magician," "The Lover," and "The Warrior." These eight main Archetypes can be felt and experienced regardless of gender. They can also be expressed as a Shadow side when there is either an over - or under - identification. Moore's and Gillette's work is elaborate; with all of these potentials, there are 24 Archetypal expressions of the Masculine that can potentially manifest. Although complex, understanding Masculine energies in this way can offer insight, compassion, and empowerment for the very recognizable traits that we may possess and display within our relationships.

Implicit/Procedural Memory both refer to one of the two main types of long-term memory storage. Our Procedural Memories hold on to experiences and are reinforced when the experiences are repeated. These memories are automatically employed without conscious thought and then applied to our behaviors and thoughts. It is also called our Implicit Memory because these memories aren't purposeful. They don't get stored and then categorically recalled later to help us remember things because these memories cannot be consciously brought up in the moment. They don't come forward to be talked about and processed. This can make things extremely difficult for a person who has experienced trauma because trauma memories get stored here. When something traumatic happens, the event gets pinged by the brain to go into the Implicit Memory. Going forward, every time the brain senses anything similar to the original trauma, the 'procedure' of how to survive is unconsciously employed without cognitive awareness. We are totally back in the space of trauma, we may not understand why, and due to the Implicit Memory storage system, it can be extremely difficult to bring these things up, process, make sense of, and hopefully transform them. However, it doesn't always have to be this way. Neuroscience has revealed that if a traumatic experience is processed and made sense of within 72 hours, the memories may be stored in the Declarative/Explicit memory which reduces the likelihood of automatic survival responses. The knowledge of how trauma works with our memories can offer much compassion and support for how we deal with what we've been through. Understanding trauma in this way can alleviate the supposed belief systems that something is unfixable within us when these inexplicable and seemingly uncontrollable reactions to our lives perpetuate.

Imprinting is a process whereby a newborn of a species comes to recognize another individual or thing as the parent. This amazing occurrence is a rapid way of learning habitual behaviors to ensure survival, bonding, mating, and quality of life, and can have lasting effects.

Improvisation is a type of theatre, dance, or song where there is no pre-written or pre-rehearsed script, music, or choreography. The artists jump in and perform, creating tangible and transient art in the moment. Experiencing and participating in this type of art is exciting and exhilarating.

Infant Mental Health is a somewhat new field of Mental Health that focuses on the emotional and social development and well-being of infants and children aged birth to six years.

Inner Child is the younger you that lives within the current you. She is always there, bringing love, wisdom, and innocence to our adult sensibilities. When we listen to her and actively seek to engage with her, our playful natures can come forward unafraid and unencumbered. She can retain the wounds of the past and it is our gift to actively and intentionally comfort, support, heal, and protect her. We are in charge now. This is a different dynamic than what she was used to when other adults were in control and responsible for her well-being and happiness. She can trust you now to create a safe, secure, and happy life for you both.

Inner Knowing is our intuition, instinct, Higher Self Guidance, and bullshit detector all wrapped into one. Our guts communicate it. Our hearts beat with it. Our minds pulse with it. Our Souls sing with it. Every part of our consciousness vibrates with our Inner Knowing. When we follow it, although sometimes it may feel like the hardest option, we are walking in Soul's Guidance and that will always end up being the *best* option.

Inner World is our bottomless recess of dreams, fantasies, truths, hopes, and desires. Our creativity roots here. Our inspirations are born here. When connected to this resource, our supply of 'self' - of what makes us **us** - not only feels infinite, it ***is*** infinite.

Insecurely Attached is a way of understanding our relationships, specifically how secure they may or may not be. Attachment theory is the science of looking at the deep and enduring emotional bonds that living things create to one another across time and space. Insecure Attachments are characterized by that bond being contaminated by fear. This contamination can be expressed within the relational dynamic as a lack of trust, over - or under - dependence, hesitation, and a disinclination toward emotional intimacy and authenticity. It is believed that this style of Attachment is formed in early childhood and is created through the interactions of infants and young children with their caregivers. When a child's needs are not met on a consistent basis, an unconscious belief system can be created within the child which asserts that their needs will never be met, that they ultimately will suffer abandonment or harm in some way, as well as the general feeling that the world is not a good place. There are three types of Insecure Attachment: Disorganized, Ambivalent, and Avoidant. Disorganized Attachment is characterized by confusion, disorientation, and lack of consistency in behavior by both child and parent. Ambivalent Attachment is characterized by extreme distress and separation anxiety. This style is not very common and is the result of poor caregiver availability. Avoidant Attachment is characterized by children showing little to no affect around parent or caregiver due to abuse or neglect. These children typically show no preference for a parent versus a stranger and have learned that asking for their needs to be met will result in punishment. An Insecure Attachment in childhood does not automatically assume that there will be an Insecure Style of Attachment present in adult relationships; however, these early Attachments are very important. Those who have Secure Attachments in childhood tend to experience higher self-esteem and self-reliance.

Instinct has gotten sort of a bad rap. Typically explained as hard-wired genetic behaviors that increase our chances of survival, human instincts can fall under the subheadings of mating and claiming our territory - both by whatever means necessary. Yet our Feminine instincts are much more than that. For our work together, yes, our instincts are rooted in survival. But this is a much different approach. This instinctual survival is focused on the health and sustainability of our relationships. We instinctually do this with compassion, mercy, and softness. We channel our psychic abilities. We harness our blood and birth magick. We listen to our intuition. We follow our hearts and turn toward one another, creating the mutual reciprocity of caregiving and caretaking. We know where to go to get what we need. We trust our body and follow its wisdom. Our instinctual nature cannot be reduced to the mere banality of fighting for the right to dominate and procreate. *That* is the fairy tale… and not the good kind. The real story is that our instinct to love will always be more powerful than our instinct to hate. The Feminine Energy within every living thing must be revalued and revered. When this happens, our true inner-natures, our true inner-instincts, will reign.

Intention is the energy we put into things. We can put intentional energy into our daily living, ceremonies and rituals, relationships, items and objects, and situations. A therapist once told me, "The road to hell is paved with good intentions." That got me thinking. How often do we do things with the best of intentions and yet nothing goes according to plan? Well, the 'good' part of good intentions is pretty subjective… especially when we have expectations. What is good for me may not be good for you. When it comes to intentions, trust in your own goodness and set intentions for yourself, your day, your stuff, your half of any relationship, your experience of the ceremony, etc. Then trust that everyone else's Higher Self is doing the same. You can still hold intentions for others. For instance, in the introduction, I make my intentions for this book very clear. My intentions are for this book to be a source of support and comfort for falling in love with ourselves. What I can't do is try to control your experience because of those intentions. I have to put them out there and trust. What can help keep our sides of the street clean (and help keep our minds from running away with us) is to set intentions, trust them, release, and repeat.

Inter-Species Contract is a Sacred Contract between species that is played out within the physical realm of the Earth Plane. This is completely different than what we have been taught about 'man's dominion over animals' as some kind of human birthright. This concept takes us away from that belief system and posits that all of life is sentient and that there are no hierarchies of importance or value. In this space, an Inter-Species Contract is one whereby a certain species contracts with another for the benefit of the whole living world. Think of dogs and humans. That Inter-Species Contract is one of service and devotion. Horses and humans are similar. The domesticity of our current world has been built on the backs of the Equine Species. They agreed to come in and be 'of service' to us and look at all they have provided! Transportation, brute strength, plowing fields, entertainment, financial success, support during war, therapy, food, medicine, etc. When we can think of these Inter-Species acts of service not just as something we deserve because we believe we are the highest on the food chain, but as loving gifts to be received with the utmost respect, humility, and gratitude, the whole dynamic shifts.

Interconnection is defined as a mutual connection between two or more things. That is a pretty profound statement. We are connected to all kinds of things… but *mutually* connected, that is a different story. The concept of Interconnectedness resonates with me most when I think of the ancient Matriarchal Societies who embodied the aspects of the Feminine in order to peacefully survive. Their tribal connection was mutual. Taking care of others so that they took care of you was just a way of being. Today we can think of Interconnection and Interconnectedness as oneness: a way of being that accepts we are all one, connected, mutually giving and receiving energy, effort, respect, time, love, and value. When we open our consciousness to exist in this way, we also open ourselves to receive in this way.

Interdependence is a way of being in relationship to the world around us where there is a functional exchange of energy whereby parties are responsible to themselves and each other for the good of the *whole*. This empowered connection offers freedom from the perceptions that we must compromise or diminish our gifts, talents, energy, and abilities to make someone or something else content or happy. Interdependent relationships have healthy boundaries, mutual respect, and complete maturity. There is no desire to control situations or to control others because to do that would bring detriment to the group and therefore to the self. This type of relating is clear, secure, open, and in alignment with our Greatest and Highest Good.

Interdependent Leadership is a style of leadership that does not compromise leadership efficacy in order to meet the perceived needs of individuals within the organization or group. Leading in this way is connective, clear, open, flexible, and functional. Within this type of leadership dynamic, all are aware of their responsibilities and able to meet them either on their own or by asking for support. This level of communication and authenticity keeps groups, organizations, and businesses working toward mutually beneficial success for all. Sacrifice of the self is not part of Interdependent Leadership, but a dedication to everyone's well-being is.

Interpersonal are the relationships and ways you have of relating to others.

Intrapersonal is the relationship and way you have of relating to yourself.

Intrapsychic is the internal awareness that we possess signifying the psychic connection to our thoughts, feelings, and senses. When someone is Intra-psychically inclined, they are aware of their sensitivities and their relationship to them is valued and appreciated.

Intuition is the guidance which comes from every aspect of our being to inform our awareness. Our Intuition is our best friend. It is the collaborative voice speaking to us from our Higher Self. Our Intuition combines the energies of Inner Source, Inner Wisdom, Creativity, Instincts, and Divinely Feminine empowerment to speak to us so that we *know* what we **know**. It guides us to explore, to hold back, to dream, or to get grounded. Our Intuition loves us unconditionally and it is always there, helping us uncover what will bring about the Greatest and Highest Good. Sometimes loud and clear, other times soft and faint, our intuition is a high vibration communication from the Soul.

Ishtar is the Babylonian descendant of Sumerian Goddess, Inanna, and she is the one to turn to when you need some support around the cycles of birth, death, and rebirth. As a guardian of fertility and love, she can offer much encouragement for exploring and experiencing passion, sexuality, and sacred sexuality. She is very powerful and although associated with many different names - Esther the Biblical Heroine, Astarte, Lilith, Aphrodite, and others - her myth of descending to the Underworld has been known throughout time. While imprisoned there by Queen Erishkigal (ey-*resh*-kee-gahl), lovemaking upon the surface of the Earth stopped and, without pleasure, the people lost their ability to create new life. Devastated, a manservant pleaded to rescue her and was able to do so. Inanna/Ishtar was brought back into the living world, restoring the people's ability to blissfully create through the holy union of ecstasy. Her regeneration offers a significant lesson regarding creation and destruction for the highest good. It also offers the needed perspective of allowing the whole self to be seen and valued. Ishtar is sometimes called 'The Queen of Heaven,' and is connected to the Feminine Archetype of the Mother. As a Great Mother, she reminds us that through the embrace of our sensuality and strength, we can alternately give and receive, creating and sustaining new life while also nourishing and regenerating the self.

Isis is my homegirl. It was at her temple on the Isle of Philae that I received a message loud and clear to change my life from 'service to self' to 'service to others.' That was 2006. When I got home from Egypt, I started. Within two years I was in graduate school. I had a baby in 2011. I got licensed as a therapist in 2014. I started Divine Mommy in 2016. And I started this book in 2018. Isis can be your homegirl, too. She is a powerhouse of Divinely Feminine magick. Strong, sensual, creative, and compassionate, Isis can support us through absolutely anything. This is the woman that - when her hubby, Osiris, was cut up into pieces by his pain in the neck brother, Set - turned herself into a bird, flew all around Upper and Lower Egypt collecting him, put him together, and hovered over him to impregnate herself with their son, Horus. Talk about determination! This Great Mother Goddess has long been beloved throughout the world and rightfully so. In her winged form, she flies with us through life and death, supporting us as we create our destinies. A brilliantly trained Priestess in the Hathor lineage, through her human incarnation and subsequent Divine embodiment, Isis loves us unconditionally. She is completely sovereign and by the illumination of the bright sun at her Crown, lights the way for all of us to welcome, love, and value every aspect of our beings. Isis teaches us to shine our lights as brightly as we can, never apologizing for or questioning our talents and gifts. She works with us to release the wounding of the past so that we may grow to our full potential within every human lifetime. She has unlimited belief in all of us and can see our true natures of goodness, lovingness, and connectedness. Isis will gently hold our hands, not pushing or forcing us to the next level of ascension but opening our consciousness with the love of the Mother so that we can see our own brilliance and fly unafraid as well. She is *ah-**may**-zing*! She loves you! So do I!

Jungian is someone who is a follower of Swiss psychologist, Carl Jung, and his work. There are many resources out there to learn more about Carl Jung and a number of brilliant artists, writers, researchers, and clinicians who have been inspired by Jung's work to create their own interpretations of his philosophies, theories, and methods of intervention so that we may enrich and better understand this human experience called 'life.' Who knows, you just may be a Jungian, too! It is definitely worth checking out.

~ K ~

Kapalabhati is an important breathing and purification process for the body and mind. Sometimes called 'Skull Shining Breath' because of its ability to supply the brain with fresh, oxygen-rich blood, this ancient hatha yoga technique is taught for internal cleansing. Kapalabhati breathing is done with repetitious, forceful exhalations of breath followed by slower, more relaxed inhalations. This type of breathwork's emphasis is on moving air through the nose and is accomplished by a powerful drawing up of the navel into the body and subsequently contracting the belly. It can reenergize the body, clear the mind, and connect us deeper into the well of our spiritual selves and spiritual being. This way of breathing is also referred to as 'The Breath of Fire.' Depending on which style of yoga you are practicing, the interpretation, technique, and terminology may vary slightly. Different schools of thought feel these are two distinctly different types of breathing, some feel they are similar, and others use them interchangeably. The most important aspect is that you find what works for you regardless of styles, techniques, and designations. The release of rigidity can be a welcome invitation to the Goddess within, knowing what you know rather than what someone else has told you to know. For more great support around breath work and for any yoga questions, contact our Sister Goddess, Kery at: www.keryhelmer.com

Karma is the active and educational information offered through the experience of living life. This set of laws governing our existence can be thought of like a series of interlocking chain links, joined together by the energies of cause and effect. The chain never changes or ends until our Souls are completely liberated; however, the results - or what we *feel* as a result of the cause-and-effect loop – **can**. Karma is not about the things that happen to us. The simplified notion that when we do something negative, we will be repaid in-kind by a malevolent Universal force is not true. Karma is about the internal consciousness and habitual tendencies that stimulate thoughts, feelings, and behaviors. What we hold inside karmically manifests what we experience outside. These established mental, emotional, and behavioral patterns serve as the *causes* for which our present circumstances are the *effects*. Whether the *effects* are pleasant or unpleasant is totally up to us. How we perceive, understand, and experience our worlds dictates how we experience, understand, and perceive the infinite loop of karma. We shift these things by shifting our consciousness. It is said by many that karmic freedom can come to us from our own embodiment of forgiveness, compassion, and service. Self-love is high on that list, too. If your consciousness is one of dedicated self-love, your karma will reflect it. That is why it is wholly imperative that we unabashedly love ourselves and each other. We can karmically create a big old love fest together, alternately offering comfort and compassion when the lessons are challenging and celebrating when the lessons are easy.

King is one of the four main archetypes of the Mature Masculine presented in the book, *King, Warrior, Magician, and Lover: Discovering the Archetypes of the Mature Masculine* by Robert Moore and Douglas Gillette and my interpretation of their work is what follows. The King is born from the full actualization and expression of its Immature counterpart, the Divine Child, and includes all of the other Archetypes. When in balance, it mutually supports them in that a noble King is also a wise Warrior, dedicated Magician, and excellent Lover. With his calm and integrated centeredness, a King embodies a healed and balanced Father energy so that he may create and organize a world which is peaceful, kind, and compassionate. The Land is his primary Queen and their reciprocal love generates a fertile, content, and bountiful way of life for all. When authentically embodying the Archetype, a human King understands that they are only a servant to the larger, more complex energies of these ordering principles.

Kintsugi is the ancient Japanese artform of 'golden joinery' and is a way of repairing pottery by mending the areas between the broken pieces with a special tree sap lacquer that has been dusted with precious metals. This process emphasizes the breakage as a unique opportunity to honor each piece's history. Oftentimes, Kintsugi makes a piece even more beautiful, giving it a second life and allowing one to see perfection through the flaws.

Kundalini is a Sanskrit word that refers to the powerful form of Divine Feminine energy which originates at the base of the spine. This energy is with us from conception and is the source of our life force. Oftentimes visualized as a serpent either coiled or rising through the Chakra Centers, our Kundalini energy can stimulate an empowered awakening of consciousness. Referred to as Kundalini rising, this awakening can be felt on all levels of our physical, emotional, mental, personality, Soul, and spiritual selves. When we activate Kundalini through yogic practices, life events, spiritual ascension, etc., the energy flows up through our bodies, into the belly, juicing all of our Energy Centers as it spirals onward into the heart and the head. As this energy travels, we expand, transform, and ultimately head toward enlightenment; therefore, Kundalini can be thought of as both a goal and the path to reach the goal.

~ L ~

Labradorescence is an iridescent optical experience of seeing light shimmer across a piece of Labradorite.

Lapis is the nickname for Lapis Lazuli, a beautiful deep blue Crystal. This is a traveler's stone and can assist in inter-dimensional voyaging so that we may read and understand sacred texts and high vibration states of consciousness. Because of its likeness to our night sky, Lapis can also assist us in connecting our physical awareness to the celestial realms. Connected to the Throat Chakra, this stone links together the energy of our entire Chakra System in order to support the intrinsically held belief of purity, goodness, and perfection. Use Lapis over the Ajna to fine-tune intuition and Higher Self guidance. Place it on the Heart Chakra to evolve and expand into a visceral experience of oneness. Radiant and powerful, this stone has many possibilities for healing and expansion.

Layers (Levels) of Consciousness are the layers of awareness through which we experience life as taught in Esoteric Healing Practices. The **Physical Layer** is our body. Here we experience the health, dis-ease, pain, and ecstasy typically associated with the human body. This is the densest layer of our consciousness. Next is the **Emotional Layer**, where we experience all of our feelings. This is the second layer of our consciousness and is lighter in vibration than the Physical Layer. Following that is the third level - our **Mental Layer** of Consciousness - where all of our cognitive processes happen. Thoughts and thinking reign supreme in this level and it is energetically lighter than the first two. Next is the **Personality/Ego Layer**, which is where our psyches or sense-of-self resides. All inactivated behavioral responses originate here, and although the Ego gets a bad rap, this layer is still lighter in vibration than the preceding three. The **Soul Layer** rests upon the Personality Layer and this is our Higher Self energy. Continuing the upward swing of a lighter density and vibration, this level of our consciousness works to love the other layers into being. Finally, the last Layer around us is our **Spiritual Layer**, which is our connection to Source, the Zero Point Field, God, Goddess, etc. These layers can be visualized as a multi-level force field surrounding us. They can all hold blockages, which we experience as dis-ease, and they can all be balanced in order to manifest their highest conscious expression, which we experience as optimal health or bliss. Different facets of our anatomical, physiological, energetic, and etheric bodies hold the unique identities of these six layers as well.

Lightlove is an expression that I first encountered while reading *Divine Architecture and the Starseed Template,* a book which has been channeled by Magenta Pixie from a Divine Entity called 'The White Winged Collective Consciousness of Nine.' As they explain Source Energy, "Lightlove is the imploding, contracting force of receptivity and light of the Mother/Father energy within the Feminine." Alternatively, "Lovelight is the expanding, exploding force of momentum and light of the Father/Mother energy within the Masculine." This book is the follow up to the first book channeled in from the Collective, *Masters of the Matrix*.

Life Force is the energy that keeps us alive. It is our sense of vitality and animation and exists within all living things. Light, love, and laughter are all examples of Life Force. This presence gives us strength, determination, magick, and power. It is always there for us but can get compromised, syphoned, and leaked either with or without our conscious participation or permission. Our Life Force is ours to protect, nourish, and hold precious. It makes us *us*. It is important, unique, and very valuable. We can give it away. We can replenish our stash. When we become keenly aware of our individual Life Force energy, we become more empowered, balanced, and grounded. When our Life Force is high, full, and juicy, we are blissful beings. When it is low, dark, or depleted, we can feel exhausted, overwhelmed, crabby, and ready to give up. Ladies, our Life Force is crucial. That is why it is up to us to take care of it. This energy is not to be spent like a credit card with no limit. We know that pesky plastic has to be paid for some time, somehow. Same thing with Life Force. We can give and give and give, but without refilling our own cups, the credit score of our vitality, strength, and general amazingness will tank.

Light Bearer is one who literally '*bears*' or brings the light to others. You are a Light Bearer. You are! We are walking toward self-love and that is a path of enlightenment. We are also seeking to share what we learn while on this path with our Sisters, families, friends, communities, etc. We are the healers and helpers. We *bring the light*.

Litmus Test is a way of testing for alkalinity or acidity that uses litmus, a dye made from lichens that shows red under acidic conditions and blue under alkaline conditions. However, this term has been generalized to mean a decisive test for authenticity.

Lovelight is an expression that I first encountered while reading *Divine Architecture and the Starseed Template,* a book that has been channeled by Magenta Pixie from a Divine Entity called 'The White Winged Collective Consciousness of Nine.' As they explain Source Energy, "Lovelight is the expanding, exploding force of momentum and light of the Father/Mother energy within the Masculine." Alternatively, "Lightlove is the imploding, contracting force of receptivity and light of the Mother/Father energy within the Feminine." This book is the follow up to the first book channeled in from the Collective, *Masters of the Matrix*.

Lover is one of the four main archetypes of the Mature Masculine presented in the book, *King, Warrior, Magician, and Lover: Discovering the Archetypes of the Mature Masculine* by Robert Moore and Douglas Gillette and my interpretation of their work is what follows. The Lover is born from the full actualization and expression of its Immature counterpart, the Oedipal Child. The energy of the Lover encompasses romantic, platonic, erotic, brotherly, sisterly, and every other-ly kind of love. The Lover has a libido for life, living, and the ecstasy experienced not just through sexual appetites, but through the true sacred union of oneness. This energy is primal, vivid, and alert. By asking us to release the shame blocking our conscious connections, our Inner Lovers show us the sincerity and sensitivity needed to compassionately *feel* our worlds. This Archetype is deeply mystical, spiritual, and creative. Oftentimes unconventional, the Lover will fall in and out of love to access the profound and sensuous cycles experienced through the expressive artistry of merely being alive.

Lower Self refers to the Ego Self and is a denser energy than that of our Higher Self. This aspect is sometimes viewed in a negative light because we can automatically categorize something 'higher' as a positive and 'lower' as a negative. However, it is all energy. As we become more aware, we can honor the Lower Self while still consciously deciding how and from where we want to respond. Created for very good reasons, the coping mechanisms of the Lower Self can offer continued life-lessons, growth, and opportunities for transformation.

Lucid sometimes refers to being bright and clear or rational and sane. Although, when it comes to our nighttime dreaming, it can mean something a bit different. When we engage in Lucid Dreaming, yes, we are asleep, but we are also consciously aware of what is going on around us, within us, and sometimes even able to control the environment and narrative of the dream.

Lunar Cycle is the Phases of Mother Moon. We see her differently night by night due to the directly sunlit portion which can be seen from Mother Earth. This is usually observed from Dark Moon to Dark Moon over the period a synodic month which is approximately 29.53 days. In this book, we focus on the four most familiar phases: Dark Moon, Waxing Moon, Full Moon, and Waning Moon. However, she actually goes through eight! They are: Dark (or New) Moon, Waxing Crescent (or Crescent) Moon, First Quarter (or Waxing) Moon, Waxing Gibbous (or Gibbous) Moon, Full Moon, Waning Gibbous (or Disseminating) Moon, Last Quarter (or Waning) Moon, and Waning Crescent (or Balsamic) Moon.

Lunar Phase is a particular part of the Lunar Cycle of which the four main phases are Dark, Waxing, Full, and Waning. These cyclical components correlate to the four Seasons, the four phases of our Menstrual Cycles, and the four Archetypes of the Divine Feminine. As women, we are closely linked with the consciousness of Mother Moon and as she cycles through these four distinct energies, we are dynamically influenced.

Lunar Wisdom is the way in which we harness and utilize the energy of the Lunar Phases within the larger Lunar Cycle. As we learn how best to engage with these dynamics, we can bring about empowerment, ease, and perspective. Each phase correlates with a Season, a phase of our Menstrual Cycle, and an Archetype of the Divine Feminine. The more familiar we are with how these various components work together within our lives, the more we can benefit from this wisdom and use it to understand, normalize, and generate compassion for our physical, emotional, mental, and spiritual energies each month.

Lymphatic System is the body's network of tissues and systems that helps rid us of toxins. The Lymphatic System is part of our Immune System and consists primarily of the tonsils and adenoids, spleen, thymus, bone marrow, appendix, lymph nodes, and Peyer's patches in the small intestines. This amazing system protects our bodies, keeps our fluids level, absorbs fats in the digestive tract, and removes cellular waste. According to Esoteric Healing, the Lymphatic System energetically connects to the Throat Chakra.

~ M ~

Macrocosm is a way of conceptualizing our Great World as a whole. This is the all-expansive, all-inclusive perspective. It can also represent the totality of something. Paradigms, ways of being, belief systems, and other complex structures such as education, spirituality, creation, or government can be thought of in these terms. Macro means large and micro means small, so when thinking on the Macro level you are thinking *big picture*.

Maiden is one of the four Archetypes of the Divine Feminine. The other three are: Crone, Mother, and Enchantress. These expressions of the Feminine work together with the other influential cycles of the Moon, the Seasons, and our Menstrual Cycles. Each Archetype has wisdom, empowerment, and support to share and impart through the experience of womanhood, as well as the larger unified human experience. The Maiden correlates with the Season of Spring, the Phase of the Waxing Moon, and our Follicular or Pre-Ovulatory Phase. Oftentimes misrepresented as just a character in fairy tales, the Maiden is a powerful and energizing sovereign force. Playful, upbeat, and focused on the Physical Plane, she tells us the time is ripe for planting the seeds of new beginnings. She offers renewed strength and confidence so that we may boldly and independently communicate our needs, pursue our truths, and seek out social collaborations. The Maiden awakens our inner activists, enthusiastically flirting with determined ambition to clearly and freshly birth change. She is fertile, sensual, and completely unto herself - reminding us that age, young or old, has nothing to do with beauty, wisdom, empowerment, or knowledge. She does not apologize for lack of experience, she does not try to be who or what she is not, and she does not need contrivances. The Maiden, and our embodiment of her, is a way of being that doesn't wait for anyone's permission to explore and enjoy the world.

Magician is one of the four main archetypes of the Mature Masculine presented in the book, *King, Warrior, Magician, and Lover: Discovering the Archetypes of the Mature Masculine* by Robert Moore and Douglas Gillette and my interpretation of their work is what follows. The Magician is born from the full actualization and expression of its Immature counterpart, the Precocious Child. The energy of the Magician is wise, dedicated, and steadfastly on the path toward enlightenment. What makes the Magician so unique is that the devotion for knowledge is done only with the intention of sharing and teaching what has been learned. This Archetype is a holder of great power and great energy. It is connected to the spiritual and psychic realms. Although perceived as a master, the Magician is an eternal student, tirelessly pursuing wisdom in order to teach others for the benefit of all. This Archetype keeps no secrets, is very thoughtful and reflective, and continually seeks to transform both the inner and outer worlds.

Magick is a way of expressing the heightened intuitive and psychic powers of the Feminine. This spelling is intentionally used as an act of reverence for our bodies, minds, hearts, and spirits. It is a way of honoring menstruation, conception, gestation, birth, and the sustenance of new life - all distinct processes of the female. Magic with a *k* can also describe the powerful connection we feel to the natural world, Mother Earth, and Mother Moon. It is the unknown *knowing* of instinct, the mama gut, and the power of a woman standing in her truth. Magick is Sisterhood, showing up, walking the talk, and knowing how pure and good our hearts are. All of this would be poorly served by a word that is used to define card tricks, disappearing acts, and the entertainment of illusion.

Major Chakra Centers are the seven major centers of the Chakra System: Basic, Sacral, Solar Plexus, Heart, Throat, Ajna, and Crown. These Major Energy Centers rest on the midline of the body where 23 lines of concentric energy cross. Chakras, which translates to *wheel* or *circle* in the ancient language of Sanskrit, are the energetic portals through which we give and receive energy. Each Major Chakra Center relates to a Physiological System, an Endocrine System, and has a correlating Psychological Contribution. For the Centers on the body, the energy flows in from the back and out of the front. For the Ajna, the energy flows into the forehead and out the top of the head behind the Crown. Chakras cannot be seen, but they can be energetically felt, sensed, and *known*. According to the Esoteric Teachings, in addition to the 12 Major Chakras, there are also 70 Minor Chakras where 14 lines of concentric energy cross. Of these 70 Minors, 21 are considered Major Minors and 49 are considered Lesser Minors. It is understood that when in balance and allowed to flow unencumbered, the energy of our Chakras supports us in creating optimal levels of mind, body, spirit health that is free from dis-ease.

Mala Beads are Sacred Prayer Beads with 108 beads and a 'guru' bead used for meditation, prayer, and other spiritual practices. Many traditions incorporate chanting around the Mala and oftentimes use specific Mantras. The practice I learned from teacher, Vicki Noble, is one of beginning and ending at the guru bead and chanting 108 times around the Mala, bead by bead. When you get to the other side of the guru bead, if you want to keep chanting, turn back and go the way you came without 'crossing' the guru bead. Really though, however you decide to work with your Mala is up to you. They make great intentional jewelry. Hang them in your car for protection. Sleep with them under your pillow for powerful dreams. Your Mala will work with you in whatever way you choose. The sacred meaning of the 108 chants symbolizes: 1 = your relationship to Source, 0 = the open, circular characteristics of that relationship ebbing and flowing throughout time and space, and 8 = the infinite nature of the relationship.

Mandala is a sacred geometric pattern of symbols used in different spiritual modalities to focus the mind, create sacred space, meditate, relax, and pursue enlightenment. Mandala is a Sanskrit word that translates to *circle* or *disc*.

Mantra is a spoken or sung word, phrase, or sound that is meaningful to the singer or speaker.

Mantra Practice is using Mantra for the desired outcomes of focusing the mind, relaxation, meditation, clarity, insight, raising energy, and attaining higher states of consciousness. My education of a Mantra Practice involved chanting Mantras (at least) 108 times around the Mala. However, your Mantra Practice can be whatever it needs to be for you. Traditionally, Mantras were Sanskrit words or phrases melodically sung and repeated. Today, Mantras can include anything that is sacred or meaningful. A friend of mine swears by her Parenting Mantra: "I will not lose my shit today." She says she sings that over and over multiple times a day, sometimes out loud and sometimes to herself. Use whatever works for *you* for a Mantra Practice.

Masculine Divinity is the concept of God or Source as male or Masculine.

Masculine Energies are the energies attributed to the Masculine, or the Divine Masculine. This energy is full of momentum and, although complex and dynamic, can be understood as ways of being, personality traits, archetypal qualities, behaviors and mannerisms, and/or elements of cultural and social structures. This energy expresses itself - regardless of gender – through all living things.

Masculine Side is the side of our personalities that is Masculine. Some general qualities of the Masculine that are expressed within the living world regardless of gender are: strong, protective, enduring, confident, courageous, empowering, supportive, present, regenerating, forward motion, growth, rational and analytic thought, independent, reliable, autonomous, and successful.

Masculine Spirituality is a Masculine approach to spirituality in which men craft their own customized connection to the Divine. There are no preset rules, no dogma, no standardized practices… only a man and his relationship to what he defines as spiritual and Divine.

Matriarchal Gift Economy is the societal paradigm of Matriarchal cultures where goods and services are gifted with the intentions of connection and relationship and the good of the tribe is the main focus. This is in direct contrast to an Exchange Economy where goods and services are exchanged for a currency considered to be of equal value and the good of the individual is principal. Ancient Matriarchal Societies, as well as the few current ones still in existence, operate(d) on more of a Gift Economy paradigm versus an Exchange paradigm. The Gift Economy is said to be the economy of Motherhood. It is Feminine in nature and promotes a more interdependent, egalitarian, and peaceful existence. Patriarchal Societies, which dominate most of the world today and have for several thousand years, promote independence, hierarchies, and ultimately - through the insatiable drive for claiming land and territory - warfare.

Matriarchy is when a group is led by women. This can equate to the way a family, an organization, or government is structured. Other terms relating to Matriarchy are: Matrifocal, which is a familial configuration where the women are in charge of the household and little to no input on childrearing is given to the biological father; Matrilineal, in which property, goods, and identity are passed down through the Mother; Matristic, a female-led society; Matricentric, in which societal concepts and ideologies of life are created through the lens of the Mother and of womanhood; Matriarchal, a family structure in which women are the head of the household.

Matrilineal Ancestors are those ancestors from your Mother's line.

Mature Masculine is a way of understanding the aspects of the chronologically older or fully developed Masculine as described by Robert Moore and Douglas Gillette in their wonderful book, *King, Warrior, Magician, Lover: Rediscovering the Archetypes of the Mature Masculine*. My understanding of their work is that the four Immature or chronologically younger Archetypes of "The Divine Child," "The Precocious Child," "The Oedipal Child," and "The Hero," when allowed to be fully actualized and enriched by life experiences, transform into the four Mature Archetypes of "The King," "The Magician," "The Lover," and "The Warrior." These eight main Archetypes can be felt and experienced regardless of gender. They can also be expressed as a Shadow side when there is either an over - or under - identification. Moore's and Gillette's work is elaborate; with all of these potentials, there are 24 Archetypal expressions of the Masculine which can manifest. Although complex, understanding Masculine energy in this way can offer insight, compassion, and empowerment for the very recognizable traits that we may possess and display within our relationships.

Medical Intuitive is a practitioner that uses the powers of intuition to energetically identify the root causes of illness and dis-ease. This is a gentle and holistic approach for detecting issues related to our physical, emotional, and mental well-being.

Menarche is an ancient word that translates to '*beginning month.*' It is also used to describe a girl's first menstrual cycle.

Mental Channels are the pathways that our thoughts and ideas flow through. Many factors such as stress, trauma, exhaustion, and overwhelm can affect how open and clear these channels are. Alternatively, practices employed for increased relaxation, inner peace, and pleasure can provide clarity and improved functioning.

Mental Sobriety is a process of becoming really clear about what we think and believe. Many things in our lives influence us. Other people's opinions, stress, low self-confidence, etc., can confuse, divert, and unsettle our connection to authentic thought. Mental sobriety is where that agitation stops. Discontinuing the use of a particular substance, an activity, a behavior, a relationship, or a belief system can be a great place to begin. Only you know what is keeping you splintered away from your thoughts, and only you know why. Abstaining from the behaviors may call for some assistance, so be sure to get support if you need it.

Mercurial is a way of describing something that is unpredictable or in a constant state of flux and change. Like the heavy metal mercury, being Mercurial is to be in continual motion, always reflecting the perpetual ebbs and flows of life.

Metaphysical is a way of understanding and relating to life that takes into consideration things which are not easily and objectively proven in the physical world. Many Spiritual traditions incorporate Metaphysical concepts and approaches. When we relate Metaphysically, we are attempting to connect to that which is outside of quantifiable reality.

Microcosm is something small, or miniature, that relates to a greater *whole*. Just a piece of the pie, it is a *small picture* perspective representing only a part of a much larger entity. Philosophers often refer to humanity as a Microcosm of the much larger Macrocosm, or Universe. Macro means large and micro means small, so when thinking on the Micro level you are thinking of your own specific little world.

Minor Centers are the Minor Energy Centers of the Energetic Body where 14 lines of concentric energy cross. According to the Esoteric Teachings, there are 70 Minor Centers. Twenty-one are considered Major Minors, and forty-nine are considered Lesser Minors. When in balance and allowed to flow unencumbered, it is understood that the energy of our Major and Minor Centers supports us in creating optimal levels of mind, body, spirit health that is free from dis-ease.

Mirror Neurons are the neurons in the brain that *mirror* what we see. They fire up, sending and receiving information when we perform an action and when we observe someone else doing the same. Mirror Neurons help us reflect feelings, body language, and facial expressions. As you can imagine, they are pretty important for our development and social interactions.

Mirroring is the conscious or unconscious act of imitating the behaviors we observe in others. Mirroring usually creates a feeling of comfort and can be seen quite often in social situations because we use this skill when trying to relate. Some of the behaviors of mirroring - emulating gestures, expressions, and verbal rhythms - help us to feel validated and more meaningfully connected.

Mission Statement encapsulates the overall goals for an organization or business and is typically comprised of three parts: 1.) the specific audience 2.) the contribution and 3.) the unique qualities of the organization or business that will make it stand apart from others.

Missive is an especially long written letter.

Moldavite is a high vibration Crystal of extraterrestrial origins. A form of Tektite, Moldavite was created when a giant meteorite hit Mother Earth some 15 million years ago. Considered to be 'The Holy Grail' of stones because of its abilities to synthesize great change, Moldavite has been used for thousands of years as an amulet for healing, transformation, good fortune, and fertility. A great enhancer of other Crystals, this stone has wonderful powers for communication through the different Realms of consciousness. If you need to talk to Angels, Ascended Masters, or your Starseed family, use Moldavite as a celestial walkie-talkie. It can also cleanse your energetic fields, align your Chakras, and open you up to the next level of transcendence. If traveling through space and time for healing and learning is what you are up to, let Moldavite assist you in this process. Whether it be past lives, future lives, or the conscious and empowered transition into this present life, Moldavite will be a great assistant for the journey. This stone is very powerful! Be sure to ground yourself while working with it or you could experience feeling dizzy, confused, or a little nauseous. This is one of the rarest and most unique Crystals out there. If you feel called to work with Moldavite, play with creating your own relationship to the stone and see what happens. You just might get a return transmission. ☺

Moniker is a name and is sometimes used to signify a *real* or official name versus a nickname.

Monologue is a lengthy speech given by one actor in a play, movie, or other performance piece. However, the term can be applied more generally. For instance, during a conversation when one person is going on a bit, the other participant could say, "Hey, this is a dialogue, ***not*** a monologue."

Moon-Bathing is a practice of bathing our skin in the silvery light of Mother Moon. If you've got an outside bathtub to do this, what is your address? I'm coming over. Seriously though, no water is needed and you can keep your clothes on. Just get yourself where you can see Mother Moon and feel her light (or her *energy* if she is in the Dark Moon Phase) shining on your body and seeping into the layers of your consciousness.

Mortal Coil is a quippy term which refers to the continual hardships of being alive. When one 'pops the Mortal Coil,' they have died.

Mother is one of the four Archetypes of the Divine Feminine. The other three are: Crone, Maiden, and Enchantress. These expressions of the Feminine work together with the other influential cycles of the Moon, the Seasons, and our Menstrual Cycles. Each Archetype has wisdom, empowerment, and support to share and impart through the experience of womanhood, as well as the larger unified human experience. The Mother correlates with the Season of Summer, the Phase of the Full Moon, and Ovulation. The Mother is also the most recognized of the four Feminine Archetypes. Every living thing on Earth has come from a *Mother* and - depending on what type of living *thing* you are - you probably have some pretty deep ideas and expectations regarding this role. Since this is the Highest Conscious Expression of 'The Mother,' this archetypal energy is fertile, nurturing, compassionate, and comforting. In her full, pregnant bellied state, we can safely dance our truth under her protective light. She roots us to our creative power and leads the way for birthing new life into existence. When connected to her, we can experience contentment, peace, and a sense of 'being one' with all life. The Mother energy increases our abilities for collaboration, co-creation, and communication. During her fullness, things can also feel overly intense, like they do when giving birth. Understanding how to utilize this energy for the Greatest and Highest Good is beneficial so that instead of becoming overwhelmed, we remain grounded. When we can do this, the newly created insights, relationships, boundaries, ideas, etc., can be lovingly sustained and totally cared for. Continually Mothering this life cycle into being offers a renewed sense of self-worth and self-confidence. When embodying these Mother energies, you may find yourself as a point of connection for your family and your community.

Motivation as in "What's my motivation?" You hear that joke a lot as an actor. In acting, the entire scene can have a Motivation, the individual characters can have motivations, and each line in the script can work to accomplish a motivation. This is how the character gets what they want. Motivation is *why* a character says *what* they say in the *way* that they say it. Motivation underneath the acting work creates the opportunity for an actor to achieve the objective or the whole goal of why the character exists in the first place. Off the page and stage, we do this quite a bit in real life. So, I ask you, "What is your motivation?"

Mudra is an ancient and symbolic way of holding the hands and fingers to invoke a particular feeling or to assist in healing and meditation. Mudras have been used for thousands of years, and in Sanskrit the word translates to *'closure'* or *'seal.'* Using Mudras creates an additional flow of energy in the body-mind-spirit connection and they are a wonderful addition to any yoga or spiritual practice. When only using the hands, these Mudras are called Hand Yoga, or Hasta Mudra. However, in advanced yoga, there are Mudras that are done with other parts of the body as well.

Multi-Dimensional is a way of holding awareness for different or other dimensions within the Human, or Third Dimensional, experience.

Multi-Dimensional Points of View refers to being able to hold the points of view and perspectives of others in addition to your own. This is a great skill for conflict resolution and functional relationships.

Multi-Sensory is a way of teaching, being aware of, and assimilating Multi-Sensory input and information. Traditionally used as an educational philosophy, a Multi-Sensory approach to learning is done by connecting the learner to the material through visual, kinesthetic, auditory, and/or tactile engagement. However, a Multi-Sensory approach can also include incorporating senses other than sight, sound, taste, smell, and touch. These additional senses can manifest as intuition and instinct, or they can be understood as non-physical senses such as: clairsentience (knowing through *feeling*), clairaudience (knowing through *hearing*), clairvoyant (knowing through *seeing*), and claircognizant (knowing through *knowing*).

Murray Bowen was a medical doctor, scholar, clinician, teacher, researcher, and writer. He was and is a beloved pioneer of human behavioral science. During his career, he developed an incredible new theory of human behavior called Family Systems Theory. This theory was a drastic change from the more traditionally accepted Freudian theories of the time and is responsible for changing psychiatric and medical treatment. Up until that point, when a person presented with symptoms only these were treated. Bowen started to think something big was missing in this approach and began looking at the family unit. His premise was based on the concept that any change in one member of the family unit would be felt and compensated for by other members of the family. Because of that, the family was the focus rather than just the individual. Take for instance if a teenager came in for treatment and his presenting symptoms were depression and anxiety. If the clinical intervention was to put him on medication, how effective would this be at treating the symptoms if no one took a look at the family unit to discover that mom and dad were fighting all the time? This systemic approach of addressing the entire family was profoundly different from the psychoanalytic models of the day. It took into consideration that the functioning of the unit as a *whole* - which included the way every member in the unit functioned - was responsible for either directly or indirectly participating in the presenting *dys*function, or *symptoms*, of another member. Bowen also suggested that treatment need not be solely targeted toward the individual presenting with symptoms, but could be done with other members of the family as well. His work focused on the observable systems of multi-generational patterns with limited reliance on clinical assumptions and guesswork.

~ N ~

Narrative Therapy is a wonderful form of Family Therapy created in the 1980s by David White and Michael Epston. This model of psychotherapy is very positive in that it seeks to alleviate self-blame by guiding clients to externalize their issues and problems. A process of clinical excavation thus begins and the internalization of shame and negative labels is reduced in order to highlight a client's strengths and other positive attributes. Narrative Therapy is very respectful, honoring the bravery of each client engaging in the therapeutic work, while also maintaining that the client - not the clinician - is the expert of their own lives. Additionally, this model is sensitive to social constructs and boundaries and asserts that there is no such thing as 'absolute truth.'

Negative Feedback Loops for Soul-to-Sisterhood are not in alignment with the typically understood biological or psychological definitions. For us, a **Negative Feedback Loop** is when we continually put negative input into our systems and that input creates its own output of: *the new norm*. We get so used to the self-judgment, self-blame, self-recrimination, etc., that it becomes familiar and almost undetectable. It also gets hungry for more. So, what do we do to keep the monster fed? We oblige and engage in further negative behaviors that sabotage self-love. Why? Because it feels *normal* and, if you can believe it… *comfortable*! It is a loop because this way of relating to ourselves can run on and on and on until we put in the conscious effort to stop it and replace the negative feedback with positive feedback. That involves dedication, consistency, and a loving mental script that is compassionate, forgiving, and understanding. Once another *'new norm'* is established, the positive feedback loop can become just as habitual as the negative one. It is up to you which one gets your mental and emotional real estate.

Negative Narratives are the junky stories we tell ourselves. When we are negatively narrating, we tend to only focus on what isn't going right. Like the feedback loops above, this can become habitual as well. However, there is always a way to find a silver lining. Nothing is ever all one way or the other, but it can definitely *feel* like it is. When in this space of running the negative script, if you can identify that it is happening, try moving your physical body to shift the energy. Take some deep breaths and check in with yourself. My Mantra for times like this is: Be honest. Be grateful. Be here. What this translates to is: 1.) Own what is going on by honoring your thoughts and feelings. 2.) Breathe into some gratitude for something – anything - whatever you can muster to be thankful for. 3.) Drop the story that is running in your head and focus on exactly where you are in this given moment by seeing what you see, smelling what you smell, hearing what you hear, tasting what you taste, and feeling what you feel (on your body). Repeat this as many times as necessary and, when you sense some relief and release, try telling a positive story to yourself. One positive story will lead to another and so on. When the *'negs'* come back, reset with the Mantra, and go through the steps again. Remember, you are worth it!

Neolithic is the time period sometimes referred to as 'The New Stone Age,' which spanned 10,000 to about 5,000 years ago with the last Neolithic Society existing in Crete until about 3,500 years ago. It is often speculated that because it was an island off the coast, the Minoan culture somehow remained safe for almost 1,500 years after most others were destroyed. It is important to note that these societies were highly civilized with culturally developed Social and Economic systems. They were matrilineal, partnership-based, and considered to be very egalitarian. This is evidenced by research that indicates very few signs of war or warfare-like activity, minimal indications of inter-familial hierarchy (neither man nor woman was head of household and sex did not define social roles), and no art depicting brutalization and battles. These were agrarian people who worked the land for food and sustainability. There has also been an abundance of Goddess and other Female images and imagery found from the different Neolithic sites suggesting a deep reverence and value for Mother Earth, the Feminine, the female, Feminine traits, and the Great Mother Goddess - Creatress of all life. In Crete, the Minoans had extremely high standards of living. There was advanced architecture, a deep love of nature, and male and female relationships were highly prized because the qualities of both the Masculine and the Feminine were so genuinely valued. The art from Minoa featured empowered, erotic, and ordained women. The sensuality and sexuality of woman was cherished and heralded as a needed contribution toward the sustainability and longevity for all people. This was a social organization of equality, empowerment, and peace. Who is ready to build a time machine and go with me back to Minoan Crete? Take a look at some of this Art for yourself and see what sensations flood to the surface. When we open ourselves to this historical information of our ancestors and ancestresses, the old story of a cave man dragging his cavewoman by the hair across the dirt path is beyond ridiculous. We come from Divine, Oracular Stock. Neolithic women were Priestesses… and so are we!

Neural Hardwiring is the way our brains are wired. Although similar in many, many ways, brains and brain functioning can be as individual as a snowflake. This hardwired circuitry is influenced by both our genetics and our environments. It affects our responses and reactions, relationships and relatability, and can even influence our mental and emotional well-being. If this hardwiring isn't working for us, we can consciously re-train it. Usually, the first step is awareness. From there, with the right support and interventions, new pathways can be created, rewiring the brain.

Neural Pathways are the interlinking synapses in our brains that create ways for information to be sent and received. Every time we learn something, a new pathway is either created or an existing pathway is affected.

Neuroplasticity is the ability of our brains to learn new things - no matter what! For a long time, the belief 'you can't teach an old dog new tricks' was accepted hook, line, and sinker. Not anymore. Even after injury or dis-ease, it is now proven that our brains can reorganize and form new neural connections to compensate. That means our brains can literally create a bypass around what is no longer functioning. So, if you've ever thought you were too old or too set in your ways… think again!

Neutrality is an unbiased approach to living. There is no side to take, no argument to defend, and no hierarchies to uphold. In this place exists a peaceful acceptance that all is what it is, all is connected, all is valuable, all is equal, all is energy, and all is valid. There is no motivation to distinguish good versus bad, worthy versus unworthy, or important versus unimportant.

New Narrative is a story created *by* us *for* us. This isn't an old loop of what we have been told to think and believe about ourselves and the world. This is a fresh, empowered vision for what we want to see and design for the future.

Noble Sacrifice is sacrifice done not out of force but out of a spiritual conviction that in this particular instance, it *is* for the Greatest and Highest Good for all… and that '*all*' includes the person doing the sacrificing. This type of sacrifice is only allowed if you've already got a full week of intense self-love activities booked and paid for with childcare (if applicable) sorted and scheduled. Seriously, there are always going to be times where we can choose to sacrifice ourselves solely for the good of someone or something else. This ain't that time. Doing that cuts you out of the equation and leaves you exhausted, overwhelmed, and pissed off. This is a conscious choice that centers around a defining event. It isn't chronic, static, or expected. It is *noble*. Big difference.

Numerology is an ancient philosophy that uses the universal language of numbers to better understand our human experiences. In working with Numerology, everything holds meaning because everything can be equated to numbers and number combinations. Think of birthdays, anniversaries, dates, times, addresses, ages, etc. Utilizing this powerful way of discovering the deeper significances within our lives can offer support, guidance, and comfort. It can also provide insightful interpretations regarding the cosmic connections of relationships, personality traits, life choices, and our purpose in life.

Objective is the overall goal for either a scene within a play, an entire piece of theatre, or oftentimes the purpose for both. The objective is: *what is wanted*. It can be what the playwright wants *from* or *for* the audience, or it can be what the characters want from each other. The motivation - or actions played as subtext underneath the lines - is *how* we do *what* we do to reach the objective. If motivation is the canoe, the stream it floats on is the objective. It is the *why* of why we are doing this in the first place. We do this in real life all the time whether we are aware of it or not. Think about it, when you engage with another person, what is your objective? What do you want? Why are you engaging? Get clear on that first and then think about the motivations you are using to obtain your objective. I love the phrase "Life is not a dress rehearsal," because it is true. Life is not a rehearsal. But that doesn't mean we don't get another try. Be honest with yourself about your motivations and objectives in regard to the way in which you relate to the people in your life. Check yourself. Ask: are you doing this for the Greatest and Highest Good for all? If you are in complete alignment with your Higher Self, rock on! If not, make some shifts and give it another go. Rewrite your objectives and revise your motivations. It is that easy!

Oedipal Child is one of the four main archetypes of the Immature Masculine - or "boyhood psychology" - presented in the book, *King, Warrior, Magician, and Lover: Discovering the Archetypes of the Mature Masculine* by Robert Moore and Douglas Gillette. My understanding of their work is what follows. The Oedipal Child is the youthful expression of its mature counterpart, the Lover. This young aspect is very passionate, warm, and affectionate. He is also carrying a deep yearning for connection *to* and understanding *of* Divine Feminine energy. This desire to access his own nurturing, beautiful, and profoundly *good* nature represents an emerging identity which can be an indicator of the potential his mature self carries. The Oedipal Child possesses a deep sense of wonder for the world and this influences his feelings of oneness with all of life. Due to this connection and sensitivity, he must witness fair and respectful exchanges between the Masculine and Feminine in order to feel safe and secure. If not acknowledged in a balanced way, the Oedipal Child can be expressed as a Shadow Pole which represents either an over - or an under - identification with the archetype.

Old Belief Systems are the former principles that we used to employ to conceptualize, categorize, and understand our lives. They are *old* because they are no longer valid. They don't fit with our current levels of awareness, and we don't use them anymore because we don't believe in them.

Oneness is the connection we have to all living things throughout all time and space. It is the philosophy that all of life is inextricably connected. It is non-dualistic in the sense that there is no '*other*.' Therefore, no duality exists because we are not separate. Oneness is a very powerful concept. When you really buy into it, hate and prejudice cannot exist because everything and everyone you experience is part of you. How different would our relationship to Mother Earth be if all humans felt intrinsically connected to her, not just out of love or loyalty, but because of the conviction that we are her and she is us? The possibilities are endless when you begin to think about how Oneness can heal, transform, and connect all of life. Makes me a little teary to think about it… and hopeful!

Oracular Visioning is our ability to see and *vision* prophecy through our Divinely Feminine Powers. Sure, these talents may need some polishing up. But honey, you are an Oracle. Your intuition, instincts, and blood and birth magick all come together to give you these gifts. Does that mean you are a Guru, or more special than other people? No. In the grand scheme of things, nobody is more important than anybody else, no matter what. It just means that, for millennia, the Divine Power of the Feminine was recognized and utilized for the Good of **All**. That wisdom has been hidden from us for the last several thousand years, but it doesn't mean that it's not true. It may feel like a fairy tale, but if you go through all of the SPS activities in this book, you will get a sense of your ability to step outside of the physical world to see, hear, sense – or *vision,* if you will – that which cannot be seen and touched but can be *known*. Receiving this information is one thing. Trusting and believing in yourself and your wisdom… now *that* is Oracular!

Oxytocin is the hormone secreted by our brains to help us bond. Some call it the love hormone because it is released when we snuggle and connect socially. This hormone is also well-known for the part it plays in the birthing and subsequent bonding process with our babies. Oxytocin causes uterine contractions to aid with both the delivery of the baby and the shrinkage of the uterus afterward. If nursing, Oxytocin is released when a baby suckles at the breast and in turn stimulates the milk 'let-down.' When a Mother or Father sits to feed their baby, Oxytocin is released to facilitate the deep bonding and connection between parent and child. However, no matter how old we are, Oxytocin can hit us with a dose of the feel-good-feels, but we need to be somewhat relaxed for it to make an appearance. When we are stressed or uptight, the opportunity for authentic bonding and connection can get really difficult. It is such a catch-22, because when we are stressed and uptight is when we need connection the most, right? Yet, if we can relax our systems enough for Oxytocin to be released, we can take a much-needed breather and begin bonding with others in order to offer our hearts and souls a little comfort. How do we do it? We play! That is why there are 180 Sacred **PLAY** Suggestions in this book. Play is not overrated! And it doesn't have to be a game of tag or sitting on the floor with toys for it to count. Play is pleasure. It is whimsy. It is getting to know yourself. It is offering hugs and smiles. It can be deep work that transforms you. You decide what your play is and do that for yourself. Relax so that you can bond. Isolation can make us brittle and unhappy. It can also perpetuate a cycle of not engaging in play. We are social creatures. Our survival has been dependent on our abilities to turn toward one another, to offer care, and to receive love. Go play. Seriously. See what happens. Worst case, nothing. Best case, you just might fall in love with yourself and the world around you a little bit more. And, Oxytocin feels good. Wanna snuggle? ☺

~ P ~

Paleolithic is the time period from about 500,000 years ago to about 10,000 years ago and is broken up into three categories: Lower Paleolithic (500,000 + years ago), Middle Paleolithic (100,000 – 40,000 years ago), and Upper Paleolithic (40,000 – 10,000 years ago). Upper Paleolithic artwork gives us beautiful insight into these early cultures. The cave paintings of male and female animals, Goddess carvings and statues, and drawings and carvings of vaginas and vulvas all indicate a peaceful, nurturing, egalitarian, and Feminine-focused existence. Very different from the 'cave man' characterizations that have been perpetuated via cartoons, Halloween Costumes, etc. the Paleolithic culture was one of deep reverence for all of life. These people sustained a profound connection to the Divine Feminine as a Great Mother Goddess responsible for every living thing. This translated to a way of life that respected and honored the Feminine in all aspects. Most of this was missed upon modern discovery. Male archeologists conceptualizing Paleolithic Art have been doing so through the lens of a Patriarchal, male-dominated society. To them - with their lack of reference for a culture that worshipped a Great Mother - the Goddess imagery was interpreted as mere fertility symbols… or even worse, sex-toy-like objectifications. Because of that, the dedication these early societies held for all of life, Mother Earth, and the very nurturing Feminine qualities needed to sustain life, was missed and subsequently dismissed. Check out Marija Gimbutas' work in her book, *The Language of the Goddess* to flip that old cave-man script into something new, female-centric, and completely empowering.

Paradigms are schools of thought which create the theoretical and philosophical framework that dictates a 'way of being' for individuals living within the context of that Paradigm. These systems of belief can be both beneficial and harmful. They can be large or small, and they can be shifted, amended, or eradicated.

Past Lives, or the concept of having a Past Life, is one in which we believe that our consciousness, or our Soul, has been in existence within other lives and lifetimes. This can be understood and interpreted as a life or lives that have happened in the past. It can also relate to the concept of another life happening simultaneously within the Multi-Dimensional Universe. From this perspective, there are infinite iterations of our world existing congruently with no absolute truth of a timeline. Without a past or future, everything is occurring within the present, even the lifetimes which - to our linear minds – may seem like a past or future lifetime. It's a lot to think about, I know. When you delve into Past Lives and the different philosophies around the concept, it can feel overwhelming. However, much work, writing, and research has been done around Past Lives. If you are interested, you can definitely find an approach that works for you to better understand this phenomenal phenomenon.

Patriarchal is a way of governing or creating a society where men are in the predominant leadership roles and hold primary power as it relates to social privilege, economic control, the family unit, and moral authority. Due to many contributing factors, most of the world today is structured as a Patriarchy.

Patriarchal War Economy is an economy focused on control, ownership, and power over anything considered as '*other*.' This results in war and warfare-like interactions designed to dominate, rule, and take over the chosen lands, cultures, peoples, and other resources deemed attractive or advantageous.

Patriarchy is a way structuring power within a family, culture, community, or government whereby descent is traced through the male line, the father or the oldest male is the head of the household, and men largely hold the economic, moral, and social power while the women are excluded from it.

Patrilineal Ancestors are the ancestors from your Father's line.

Persephone (pronounced pur-*sef*-o-nee) is one formidable Goddess. Associated with the Feminine archetype of the Maiden, Persephone's story is one that inspires, galvanizes, and ignites female empowerment. Yet, we mostly hear about her as just a poor, abducted little lady who can't fend for herself against the powerful God of the Underworld, who also happens to be her hubby, Hades. Just writing that makes me want to roll my eyes. Can't fend for herself? Please! Try this on for size: Persephone is a Virgin Goddess. Now, to us, the word virgin has been misappropriated to mean someone who has not engaged in the act of sex. That really isn't what the word means. Virgin is a way of understanding a woman who is complete unto herself. She is large and in charge and nobody is telling her what to do. Thinking of Persephone in that way, we can view her in a new light. Yes, she can be gentle, passive, and unassuming, but when needed, she transforms into a powerful Queen of the Underworld, offering strength and acceptance to those facing challenges. She is also known to provide support for the never-ending cycles of birth, death, and renewal. I mean, look where she lives half of the year. The girl has experience with death. We can also look to Persephone for guidance around our menstrual wisdom. When Hades took her to the Underworld, she ate a few pomegranate seeds. Sister was hungry! Yet, it is said that because of that snack, Hades kept her prisoner half of the year and refused to let her come back to the Upperworld, which is what her momma, Demeter, wanted. But think of this: maybe those red, plump, and juicy seeds offered her a ticket to descend into the depths of her consciousness in order to psychically vision, replenish, and 'go dark' while bleeding. All things that Blood Magick wisdom teaches us are essential for our continued well-being. With this way of thinking, Persephone offers us a model for self-care around our Menstrual Cycles. I bet she and Hades snuggled up together during those moments and had loads of 'mommy-daddy' time, too. ☺

Pet Peeves are the things that get on your nerves. They are usually particular to an individual and can be anything from general annoyances to specific behaviors. For example, some general Pet Peeves often talked about are: the sound of nails scratching on a chalkboard, chomping gum or eating with your mouth open, friends who are always late, people who eat off of your plate without asking, or people who aren't aware of personal space.

Physical Portals are the places on your body where you feel there is an energetic connection to something else. This could be another level of consciousness, a specific feeling or sensation, a certain memory, or even a spot that holds wisdom.

Plant Consciousness is the awareness of plants. So much of the wisdom of our Plant Family has gone undetected and disrespected. However, it has long been known by certain wise ones - and now is being scientifically supported - that Plants indeed communicate with one another. This consciousness is vast, and although we know very little, most can agree that plants have long been talking to us through their timeless and continual offerings of beauty, food, medicine, and shelter.

Plant Realm is the Realm of Plants. Like the Human Realm which is ours and includes all things 'human,' the Plant Realm is the entirety of Plant Consciousness. It is their communication, connection, dedication, and divinity.

Prayerful Intentions are intentions that are also prayers.

Precocious Child is one of the four main archetypes of the Immature Masculine - or "boyhood psychology" - presented in the book, *King, Warrior, Magician, and Lover: Discovering the Archetypes of the Mature Masculine* by Robert Moore and Douglas Gillette. My understanding of their work is what follows. The Precocious Child is the youthful expression of its mature counterpart, the Magician. This young aspect is very curious, intelligent, and eager. He is also extremely driven to understand why things are the way they are and will adventurously explore the unknown to find out the answers. The Precocious Child is also dedicated to sharing what he learns with whoever will listen as this satisfies his natural urge to help others. For his optimal maturity, he must be shown to value himself and his creativity as beautiful reflections equivalent to the world he so desperately seeks to understand. If this exceptional side of him is not acknowledged in a balanced way, the Precocious Child can be expressed as a Shadow Pole which represents either an over - or an under - identification with the archetype.

Prerequisites are requirements of something that has to happen in order for something else to follow suit. Think of college classes. You have to take Literature 101 in order to take Literature 201. 101 is the prerequisite.

Prophetic relates to the words: Prophecy and Prophet. All three words have been hijacked from the Feminine and reattributed to a Masculine system of monotheistic male deification. The meaning of Prophecy is to correctly foresee something that is going to happen in the future. Well, how many times a day do you do that? Probably a zillion. Go Prophesize, Sister. It's instinct and intuition 101. The only prerequisite is that you don't project your Prophecy all over anyone or anything else.

Psychic Ability is the gift of being able to sense and know things that can't be actually seen, touched, or proven in the physical world. This ability is extrasensory and goes beyond the boundaries of what is typically understood as the five senses. Psychic talents can come in many different forms and are very unique.

Psychic Awareness is our ability to understand, work with, and utilize the talents of our Psychic Abilities in order to bring about the Greatest and Highest Good for all living things. Because we don't live in a world where this type of talent is widely recognized or respected, many turn away from their Psychic talents and hide them in order to fit in.

Psychic Birthright is ours, Sister! As women, it is our birthright to claim our Psychic abilities.

Psychic Purging is releasing all of the old gunk and sludge clogging up our Psychic channels. This jammed up energy can be present for many different reasons. Maybe we were scared of our powers. Maybe we were punished for them. Maybe they weren't cultivated by those who raised us, while more acceptable talents were. As a protective measure, we can attempt to turn this birthright off. But we can turn it back on, too. Purging starts with awareness and acceptance. Sculpting and polishing come next.

Psychic Visioning is the act of opening our awareness in order to channel in guidance and information. As this extrasensory level of processing is happening, both concrete and ethereal material is funneled through the highly sensitive layers of Physical, Emotional, Mental, and Spiritual consciousness.

Psychic Visualizations are the pictures, images, stories, and other information given to us through our Psychic Awareness. The unique ways of accessing and interpreting this guidance is individual to each being. No matter how the information comes forward, your distinct understanding of the extrasensory wisdom – and what to do with it to make this world a better place - is yours. *That* is a beautiful visualization!

Psychodrama blends Psychotherapy and Drama Therapy. Created by Austrian-American psychiatrist, psychosociologist, and educator, Dr. Joseph Levy Moreno, this experiential and creative therapeutic approach uses guided role-play to bring new insights to situations, practice life-skills and behaviors, and resolve issues. With the guidance of a trained professional, a Psychodrama participant will engage in warm-up exercises, enact and re-enact autobiographic and other specific scenes, and then process and share about the scene work in detailed and precise ways. This highly effective and powerful form of therapy offers real-time opportunities to actively express and experience feelings, thoughts, and ideas in order to improve communication, relationships, and overall quality of life.

Psychological Contributions are the sustainable developments and benefits which work toward the psychological health and well-being of all.

Psychotherapy is a form of talk therapy that includes many different models of intervention. It can be beneficial for emotional distress, grief, anxiety, depression, family issues, and assistance around other life situations. While in graduate school to become a Licensed Marriage and Family Therapist, which is also called Psychotherapy, I was taught that this approach to clinical work was systemic, non-directive, and very empowering. As a Psychotherapist, I am never the 'expert' of a client's life… they are. I am there to offer support for exploration, co-creation of solution strategies, and perspectives on how everything came together to create a particular situation. Psychotherapy takes a deep look at relationships and then collaborates with clients to determine what is going to work best for transformation, encouragement, and support.

~ Q ~

Queen is not a glossary word, but the letter Q didn't have any love… so, I had to put it in here. Queen is YOU. You are a Queen. No questions. Nope. None. Queen = You.

~ R ~

Re-storying is an empowering way of retelling a story where you choose the narrative. Pick a different ending, give yourself a magick wand, create a new character… whatever you need to feel a transformation from victim to victorious. When you re-story, you've got all of the power to shift anything you want to shift. Self-censoring, reality checks, and limitations are not invited to this party. This is you - with your imagination - creating a *new* possibility around an experience, hope, or dream that is the full embodiment of what you want and need to happen for your Greatest and Highest Good to come forward.

Red Coral is a stone of myth and mystery. Not really a stone at all but a piece of coral from the sea, this oceanic gem is truly noble, transformative, and said to bring peace and protection to those who wear it. With connections to the blood of Medusa, Red Coral offers an unconditional opportunity for giving and receiving beauty, even when at first glance nothing appears beautiful. This opportunity extends to you, too! How often do you look in a mirror and begin to scrutinize? The next time you find yourself doing this, get a piece of Red Coral nearby to refocus on the stunning beauty of your Soul. Also said to ward off negative energy, Red Coral can reconnect us to our sacred self by assisting us in shedding the patterns of self-punishment, self-hatred, and self-censorship. Through this release we can more fully trust in our purity and goodness. Finally, use Red Coral to dispel fear and disillusion around Psychic Abilities.

Reframing is a way of looking at things from a different and usually more positive perspective. As a clinical intervention, when a therapist posits a Reframe, they are initially seeking to identify how a situation is perceived and then looking to shift the feelings, thoughts, and experiences around that situation to highlight any potential silver linings.

Regenerative relates to a force or energy that seeks to renew and recreate.

Relational Patterns are the positive, negative, and neutral cycles of repeated events experienced in relationships. Sometimes easy to identify and other times not… once revealed, these patterns can be shifted to become more in alignment with our needs and the needs of the relationship as a whole.

Roles are the '*characters*' of our lives that we step into based on what we are doing at any given moment. They can be conscious or unconscious, helpful or unhelpful, expansive or constrictive. Many of our roles – mother, wife, employee, friend, daughter, caregiver, etc., – come with social and cultural limitations, expectations, and boundaries. It is up to us to define whether or not these roles are functional and, if not, how we can shift them so that they are. Our Roles can also be more nuanced and subtle. Think of the different versions of you that you embody as the Role of 'friend.' You can be the *fun* friend, *supportive* friend, *flaky* friend, *tough-love* friend, *frenemy* friend, etc. The Roles we play and the ways in which we play them can provide infinite opportunities for self-reflection and self-awareness. When we can authentically observe *what* we are doing and *why* through the Roles that we play and how we play them, we can determine what is or isn't working and by what means to create new Roles which are more in alignment with our needs.

~ S ~

Sacral Chakra is the Major Energy Center located anatomically between the navel and the base of the spine. Associated with the color orange, the Sacral Chakra is also referred to as the second Chakra. Not visible to the eye, this Energy Center can be sensed, felt, and *known*. The Sacral Chakra connects us to our creativity, stamina, fertility, sexuality, and relationships… especially the relationship we have with ourselves. Because it connects anatomically to our ovaries, womb, fallopian tubes, birth canal, and vagina, I like to call the Sacral Chakra our 'Woman's Chakra.' Our birth and blood magick originate here. This is where the power of orgasm and the creation of new life dance together, taking us on a shamanic journey from life to death and back again. The seeds of self-esteem and self-acceptance are planted here and either fertilized to grow strong or left to shrink under the weight of life. The Sacral Chakra is our place to connect into the womb of our Great Mother Earth. This Center, when open and clear, can take us to the highest heights of manifestation and receptivity. It balances with the Throat Chakra, which is the seat of the Mental Body and our belief systems. When working together in tandem, these two powerful Energy Centers can move mountains, create a life, work miracles, and produce bliss of the highest order.

Sacred is anything that meaningfully connects us to our Divinity. This can include objects, rituals, beliefs, personal practices, places, structures, books, relationships, Crystals, images, art, etc. What is Sacred to you is Sacred to *you*. Maybe it brings you peace or relaxation. Perhaps it helps you listen to your intuition. Or possibly your sovereignty is reflected back to you through your Sacred understandings. This is subjective and it is yours to define, craft, create, and claim. Don't forget, *you* are Sacred, too!

Sacred Boundaries are the physical, emotional, mental, and spiritual borders that we create within our relationships to maintain optimal balance, bliss, and well-being.

Sacred Contracts are the predestined agreements and arrangements made by our Higher Selves for our physical incarnations (a.k.a. *us*) to experience during our lifetimes. Made before we are born, these Sacred Contracts can include relationships, situations, experiences, personality traits, family of origin dynamics, traumas, triumphs, and anything and everything else that comes together during our lives to create our consciousness. It is a lot to process, I know! Think of these contracts as life lessons. They are not here to punish. Like Karma, these Sacred Contracts have been chosen to create growth and awareness. They are filled with information and education. The part about our Higher Selves choosing them before we are born is a lot to digest, too. I get it. However, think about this: we are infinite beings experiencing infinite life and lifetimes. Through that infinite interconnectedness, or Oneness, everything really does affect everything else. And, don't forget to add in there that we *are* Source. Source is within and Source seeks to know itself through unconditional innocence and unconditional knowing. How do we humans learn? How do we get to know ourselves? Through our relationships! It is said that humans crave relationships as much as we crave oxygen. As babies, we need relationships to survive. As adults, we create them to validate our existence. Thinking about Sacred Contracts from the context of relationships might help us to make sense of the inexplicable, nonsensical stuff that happens in life. When the perspective shifts occur through new ways of understanding *what* is happening to us and *why*, perhaps more empowerment and mastery over life can come forward. Instead of feeling put upon – as if life is happening **to** us – how can we shift that in order to view life as happening **for** us? In this light, the Sacred Contracts of life are a Divine Education… preparing us for another leap toward ascension, transcendence, connection, and bliss.

Sacred Pubic Triangle is the triangle of our female reproductive anatomy. Looking at pictures or drawings of our wombs, fallopian tubes, ovaries, and vaginas, they create the shape of a pointed-side-down (or upside-down) triangle. This shape has become a Sacred Symbol of the Feminine. It also represents an egalitarian and interdependent way of organizing a Matricentric society or culture in which the many – who have equal empowerment - care for the few.

Sacred Sexuality relates to honoring our sexuality and sensuality for the Sacred, life-giving, life-creating, life-sustaining, and shamanic processes that they are. Sacred Sexuality allows us to engage with all of life, across all time and space, through the interconnective energy of forward motion, receptivity, and bliss. This is the magick of creation and we can open our consciousness to feel it, witness it, and participate in it through the expression of love, connection, respect, and pleasure. This is the joy of making love, the remarkable sight of an open rose, the humbling sound of delicious music, the incredible taste of perfectly ripe cherries, and the wonderful feeling of hugging someone you love. This awe-inspiring power gifts us the passion to live life fully, to cherish ourselves and others, and to pray each day for peace. Sexuality *is* Sacred in this space and it is truly for the Greatest and Highest Good. Ideas, art, discoveries, miracles, Souls, and more are born here.

Sacred Union of Souls is my hope for balancing, transforming, revaluing, and marrying the Feminine and the Masculine within every living thing. From this perspective, we are all one and we are all Divine. We are our own Twin Flame and simultaneously so is everyone else.

Sacred Womb is our uterus. It is Sacred because a Soul is conceived, developed, and grown into a human being in there! That is some damn fine magickal magick! Put your hands on your belly over the area above your womb right now. It doesn't matter if you still have your uterus organ or if you are still menstruating. The energy of your Sacred Womb is present. Feel it. Connect into it. What wisdom does she have for you right now? You may get a color, a feeling, a sensation. She may talk so much that you have to write a book! Your Womb is Sacred! YOU are Sacred! Women are Sacred. So are men, but in a different way… and it's us who have been denigrated and punished for our Womanhood for thousands of years… so freaking own it, OK? You are amazing! Awe-some! Awe-inspiring! Your body is beautiful and breathtaking. Every piece of you is Divine! No arguments. Are we cool? Good. Love you!

Sanskrit is an Ancient and Sacred language. Initially an oral tradition (known as Vedic Sanskrit), the language was refined into a written form of standardized grammar around 500 BCE and became what is now recognized as 'Classical Sanskrit.' For many years and to this day, Sanskrit has been a rich form of communication used by Hinduism, Buddhism, Jainism, and Sikhism. Said to translate to mean '*perfectly*' or '*entirely done,*' this beautiful and meaningful language has meant many different things to many different people throughout its 3,500 plus year history. For many, the actual sounds of Sanskrit hold beauty and vibration. Try saying a few words out loud and see if you notice anything unique. Om, Chakra, Nadi, Mantra, Mudra, Yantra, Mandala, Karma, Kundalini, and Shakti are some of the Sanskrit words used in this book. Say them a few times and see what happens. The energy of the language is said to relate directly to the energy of what it is describing. What do *you* think?

Secure Attachment is a way of understanding our relationships, specifically how stable they are. Attachment theory is the science of looking at the deep and enduring emotional bonds that living things create to one another across time and space. Secure Attachments are characterized by those bonds being built on the reliable give and take of shared comfort, compassion, safety, and pleasure. It is believed that Attachment is formed in infancy and early childhood and is created through the interactions of children with their caregivers. When Securely Attached, the *security* of the relationship is characterized by the quality of non-verbal communication between child and caregiver. In this style of caregiving, a child trusts that their needs will consistently be met regardless of the child's ability for clear verbal communication. The child also trusts that the caregiver will offer soothing comfort if they are distressed in any way. This sensitivity to a child's needs becomes a crucial building block for social, emotional, mental, and intellectual development. Adults who have experienced Secure Attachment during childhood tend to display relationship skills suited toward problem solving and solutions, emotional intimacy, functional coping strategies for environmental stressors, high self-esteem, and overall long-term enjoyment. However, a secure parental relationship is not always needed for these types of adult relatability to be present. Because our brains are always capable of learning new things, as adults we can choose our own strategies for Attachment and therefore positive interactions. Although this can be challenging for individuals who were not securely attached as young children, it *is* possible. In seeking to understand ourselves better, we can cultivate our own security by finding ways to calm our Nervous Systems enough in order for *us* to meet our own needs for safety, comfort, compassion, and pleasure.

Sexual Security is an authentic feeling of empowerment and trust in one's own sexuality and sensuality. Many of us have received the toxic message that the objectification of physical beauty for someone else's idea of pleasure should equate to the fulfillment of our own. That by itself is confusing and potentially damaging. However, this message comes with an addendum. The oversexualization of our bodies and appearances also comes with the warning not to engage in 'too' much sexual behavior… as if to say, "Look sexy, build your self-worth based on the amount of sexual attention you receive from others, but don't engage in sexual activity *too* much." That last part, the '*too* much' part, is where things get even stickier when it comes to our Sexual Security. The decision-making power of what '*too* much' *is* seems to be subjectively offered to whomever is bestowed with moral authority at the time. And what happens when we break these invisible and ever-changing rules? Whether we feel the punishment as judgement from our peers, a news story of a woman being murdered halfway around the world, or a social media slut-shaming… we certainly know what happens when we step over the line. For me, navigating this absurdity has come through my understandings of Sacred Sexuality, the Divine Feminine, and blood and birth magick. However, find your own balance in your own way. The more we do this, the more we release the ridiculous social and cultural constraints around female sexuality. When we can boldly craft our own respectful, loving, devoted, and empowered relationships to our bodies, desires, wants, and needs, we can begin reclaiming the Divinity of our sexuality and sensuality. We become secure, *not* apologetic, for how we choose to look and dress. We command our sensuality, *not* with explanations, but with ease. We demand that our boundaries, whatever they may be (!), around our sexuality be fully respected… *not* just tolerated, *not* just agreed upon in the moment with the intention to plow through them later, and *not* merely accepted with a side order of vitriol, blame, or humiliation. This is our Sexuality, Ladies! This is the creation force that births real, live human beings! This is our psychic opportunity to heal, transform, and prophesize for the good of *all* through orgasmic bliss! This must be honored and cherished by every living thing. Are we there yet, no. Can we get there? In my lifetime, who knows. But, as we heal this within ourselves, we heal the bloodline of every woman who has come before us, who is here with us, and who will walk after us. What a golden responsibility, right? I'm down. You?

Sexual Sovereignty is the unequivocal respect, wisdom, and knowing that we possess in regard to our bodies, minds, emotions, and souls… especially as it relates to the empowerment, expression, and embodiment of our sexuality and sensuality. Read the above definition for Sexual Security and then ground it, celebrate it, and multiply it by ten. No, a thousand! A million! Wait, more! Think of this as maximum awesomeness. This *is* the energy of the Greatest and Highest Good. It is the high-vibe feeling of "hell yesses", fantastic orgasms, phenomenal make-out sessions, and unconditional love. This is you unto yourself, complete, replete, and with your cup-*runneth*-over because you have no more questions, intimidations, fears, or shame. You are a Sexual Priestess. A Goddess of love, light, and creation. A Medicine Woman who knows how to heal all. An Oracle that visions and makes manifest the highest expressions of consciousness. Every act of your existence is a creation dance to honor the sensuality of the natural world climaxing within and of itself to birth new life into being. Breathe into that. That is my idea of Sexual Sovereignty. What is yours?

Shadow Self is the somewhat mysterious and oftentimes unconscious part of our psyche. Described as a dark or even wounded side of ourselves that we attempt to keep hidden, the Shadow Self and its rich value can be understood from many different perspectives. It is the darkness that balances and anchors the light. Without it, there is no counterpoint for us to identify the various spectrums of emotions, sensations, drives, and desires experienced within a lifetime. It is the Yin to the Yang of consciousness, always ebbing and flowing in and out of itself. It drives authenticity and fuels thoughts and emotions while alternatively grounding and disarming our senses and sensibilities. Just like the Light Self, it is worthy, powerful, transformative, and needed. When we feel we must make our Shadow Self secret - tramping it down to become more acceptable and amenable, easier to deal with, or just simply trying to be more palatable for the world at large - that is when it can rot and rage. Yes, the big thoughts, feelings, ideas, and interpretations of our Shadows are intense. But the common misnomer of considering the Shadow Self to be unhelpful or harmful only perpetuates the misleading messages which assert that certain parts of us are not OK. To integrate the whole self, and that means *everything*, our Shadow Selves ask to be honored, respected, allowed, and loved. Bringing light to the Shadow supports us in knowing the unknown. When we feel the call to cry, rant, stomp, and scream, we release and regenerate. It is part of the process of being human. And, just like a well-done smoky eyeshadow palette, the very beauty lies within the darkness.

Shamanic relates to the work and activities of a Shaman or someone dedicated to experiencing other realms of consciousness which transcend our physical reality. This type of journeying can take us to the Upper World, Lower World, Middle World, Inner World, or *any* world that offers insight, information, wisdom, guidance, and healing. Shamanic work is an 'of-service' vocation. Functioning in this way, we use our Shamanic gifts as transformative tools for the Greatest and Highest Good for All. Communicating with animals, plants, spirits, and other entities to seek answers for the well-being of individuals and communities is often associated with Shamanism. However, in her book, *Shakti Woman: Feeling Our Fire, Healing our World – The New Female Shamanism*, Vicki Noble talks about a different kind of Shaman. The Female Shaman is one who connects to and works with her Blood and Birth Magick, Intuition and Instinct, Lunar and Earthly Wisdom, and the *Her*story of our Matriarchal ancestors. Thinking of Shamanism and Female Shamanism in this way, it can be understood as a codified set of processes with lengthy apprenticeships, or it can also be used to describe a woman in touch with her inner and outer wilderness. Regardless of how one comes to recognize Shamanism, the authenticity of the work is always based in a high-vibration, Soul-led devotion towards health, healing, balance, and bliss for all living things.

Shamanic Experience is what happens to us as we go on a Shamanic journey. Perhaps we experience a different level of consciousness or a different world other than our own. Maybe we are given information or guidance to share and implement. Or it could be such a unique incident that words can't truly do it justice. Whatever your experience, interpreting it can be just as interesting and unique as the original Shamanic event. The calling of Shamanism is one of deep dedication for all of life. No matter where these experiences take you, they are profound gifts of love.

Shamanic Talisman is an object found or given to you through Shamanic Journeying. This object or item can be of the physical world or not. Sometimes while on a guided journey, you will be verbally instructed to pick something up or a being on your journey will share something with you. These can be considered Shamanic Talismans. I have been given pages with words and mantras on them while journeying and written them down after the Shamanic Experience was complete. These pieces of paper are now my Shamanic Talismans. Another friend was gifted information about an herbal remedy. This herb is now a Shamanic Talisman for her. This process and how you choose to use and interpret the information given during your Shamanic Experiences for additional support, assistance, and well-being is truly up to you.

Sixth Plane of Existence is one of the Planes of Existence as outlined by Vianna Stibal in her book, *Seven Planes of Existence: The Philosophy of the ThetaHealing Technique*. My interpretation of her work is as follows: the First Plane of Existence is inorganic material, the Second Plane is organic material, the Third

Plane is our physical human world, the Fourth Plane is the 'spirit world' where spirits exist after death, the Fifth Plane is where the Masters and other Divine Beings reside, the Sixth Plane contains the Laws which govern our worlds, and the Seventh Plane is where Source, or the Creation Energy of All That Is, exists. The governing Laws of the Sixth Plane are the fundamental fabric of our reality and include the Laws of Time, Gravity, Light, Attraction, Karma, Compassion, Justice, and many others.

Social Boundaries are the ways of being and behaving that most of us follow in order to be socially accepted. These are rules that create our culture and manage potential chaos. Regardless of how big or small, clear or unclear, they are typically considered to be the 'rights' and 'wrongs' of a group based upon the agreements that the particular group has created in order to co-exist.

Social Change is the big change we seek to see in the world. This type of change affects the lives, well-being, and sustainability of the *many* versus the *few*.

Social Context is the broader understanding regarding the social implications of something versus just our personal perspectives. For instance, we may feel passionately about the protection of spiders. However, in the broader Social Context, spiders are not commonly protected creatures. This doesn't change the way we feel; it just gives a richer understanding for the level of energy, support, and solidarity we may experience around our values, attitudes, and philosophies.

Social Justice Theatre is a mission focused artform that uses theatre to educate, inform, and inspire. This type of playwriting, production, and performance is crafted to engage the audience toward more cognizant and effective empathic responses for those dealing with and suffering from social and/or political injustice.

Social Paradigm is a socially recognizable framework for dictating behavior based on either the positive or negative consequences experienced as a result of that behavior. Our justice system and the punitive response of potential incarceration is a recognizable Social Paradigm. The oversimplified version of this framework is: you break the law, you go to jail. There are also encouraging Social Paradigms. Think of the Nobel Peace Prize. The oversimplified version of this framework is: do amazing things and get acknowledged with an award. These are larger examples, but there is a unique 'society' or 'culture' contained within the smaller nucleus of every family. What were the Social Paradigms of your family of origin? They may or may not be in alignment with the bigger Social Paradigms of the society or culture at large. These alternating forces can create much compression and confusion for us as we navigate our development and maturity.

Socially Acceptable Paradigms are the schools of thought that determine what is acceptable for a particular social group. These are the paradigms that are not only recognizable but understood as being 'good' or 'right'… sometimes regardless of their benefit or impact. Think about our Socially Acceptable Paradigm of anti-aging practices. Billions of dollars are spent annually on creams, procedures, surgeries, supplements, and other measures to stop our bodies and faces from looking and feeling old. This is totally culturally and socially accepted. However, can you imagine what a wise elder from 200 years ago would say to us about this? Would they find it socially acceptable? Probably not. No judging here, please; I love buying face creams and finding out about what's new for overall health and youthful energy levels. My point is that we have to view these Socially Acceptable Paradigms not as doctrine, but as malleable trends that change with the times.

Societal Messages are the significant constructs, beliefs, preferences, and rules that bombard us from the media (entertainment, news, politics, etc.) and other common entities and organizations. Organized religion, socio-economic policies, hierarchies of power, educational institutions, and other bodies of thought - given the power to govern moral authority, the value of life, and the attribution of wealth and success - can all fall under this influential category. Sometimes these messages can be helpful, and at other times harmful. When identified as not beneficial, even if we don't agree with these conventions, they can still deeply affect us. Awareness is key to providing protection from the potentially negative side effects, as is having the fortitude to choose our own values to live by.

Soft Belly is the concept of softening the tissues and structures around the stomach area so that the Heart can fully expand. Many different modalities work with softening the muscles, tendons, organs, and bones of the belly through massage, meditation, breathwork, and visualization. In doing this, the tightness of the tummy is released. This allows the tension and the reasons for the tension (fear, grief, pain, trauma, unresolved emotions, etc.) to be processed and transformed into overall well-being, balance, peace, and softness. The idea is: when the belly is soft, the heart is open.

Solar Energies can be thought of as the energy that we receive from the Sun. It can also refer to the connection we have with our Solar Chakra, the higher Celestial Chakra which correlates with the color gold. It can also equate to the Masculine Energy we feel from the linear trajectory of the Sun as it predictably travels through the sky, rising and setting with each full rotation of Mother Earth. In this way, the two Divine Energies flow together as a Mother-Father presence. We need and value both, and it is their continued dedication and partnership that nurtures and sustains all of life.

Solar Plexus is the Major Energy Center located anatomically at the navel. Associated with the color yellow, the Solar Plexus Chakra is also referred to as the third Chakra. Not visible to the eye, this Energy Center can be sensed, felt, and *known*. The Solar Plexus Chakra connects us to our feelings and is sometimes called 'The Seat of the Emotional Body.' Also referred to as a 'Power Center,' when this Chakra is balanced we feel sturdy, grounded, and empowered because our emotional body is solid, anchored, and power*ful*! This Chakra is connected to the digestive tract and all of the big stuff like feelings, experiences, and situations get chewed up, processed, and released here… or not. If the Solar Plexus is in balance, the pain of emotional processing can be present without the additional side order of suffering. This Major Center can also bring aspects of the unconscious to the surface. All of the c-r-a-p that hasn't been digested is still in there. Having a well-cared-for Solar Plexus helps us to more efficiently find our centers in response to these big emotional reactions. When overly stimulated, we can feel exhausted and triggered by our own feelings and the feelings of others. Because they are a given (I have yet to meet a human who doesn't have feelings) having a healthy Solar Plexus is a win-win! It also connects to the Heart Chakra. When our emotional bodies are calm and clear, we can more purely feel the unconditional love available to us.

Soul since before recorded history, we've been trying to give words to what exactly this is. Songs have been sung about it, masterpieces have been created to honor it, sacred texts have been written to connect us to it… I say, your Soul is **You**. The *pure* you. The version of you that doesn't question, judge, or criticize. This is the part of you that knows. It has seen it all and still loves unconditionally, has depths of compassion and understanding which defy logic, and never, never gives up. This is the power center for your intuition and instinct. Your ability to love, see, hear, and believe. Your Soul is there, always right next to you, even though it feels the pain every time you turn away from your truth. Like the most unassuming, supportive best friend, your Soul knows what you need and how to make that happen. It will listen with patience and understanding while answering with the sweetest and kindest certainty. You may have forgotten the language of your Soul, but that is only a temporary illusion. A small kernel of energy, a tiny spark of seeking, a minuscule amount of attention is all that is needed to reconnect yourself to it... to *her*. Your Soul knows you, wants you, and will take anything that you can offer. Your only responsibility is to breathe and allow her into your consciousness. With your Soul, you *know*. You are *You*. You are enough. You are the I AM.

Soul vs Ego is a way of conceptualizing the struggle we can feel between these two aspects of our consciousness. However, it doesn't have to be an acrimonious relationship. With awareness and respect, our Souls and Egos can harmoniously co-exist. Both are equally valuable to our Earth School experience and both are deserving of our time, attention, and love.

Soul-Based is when a perspective or outlook is influenced by the Higher Self or Soul. Looking at our lives and experiences through this lens takes both emotional and spiritual maturity. When making sense of something from a Soul-Based point of view, the energies of surrender and acceptance can help us to find the Greatest and Highest Good in any situation... even when it feels nearly impossible.

Soul's Guidance is the information gifted to us from our Higher Self. These messages can come through intuition, thoughts, feelings, the senses, or any other ways we may have of perceiving and receiving this high vibration energy and support.

Source is the Highest Expression of Consciousness. All of creation, life, and awareness originates from Source. God, Goddess, the Universe, Allah, Sophia, Yahweh, Jehovah, and Elohim are just a few of the more common names for this energy. Both all-innocent and all-knowing, this Divine presence is within each of us.

Sovereign is to be complete unto the self. Traditionally used to describe a state of supreme power by a governing body, the Sovereignty we possess in relation to ourselves is not much different. When we are Sovereign, we are our own authority on everything. Sovereignty is our deep inner knowing that we are Source and that Source is us. In this dynamic, there is never a need to question the self. The purity of our hearts is unconditional, and we wholly trust in our wisdom on all things. For this state to truly exist, there is no longer room for self-judgement, self-punishment, or self-criticism. Love, compassion, forgiveness, and service are the foundations for this way of being. When we are Sovereign, does that mean we are a walking, talking encyclopedia filled with the answers to every question? Nope. It means that we trust ourselves even more in our 'not knowing.' When we can 'not-know' from a place of Sovereignty, we can wisely identify that we need assistance. We can then confidently source the information that we seek. With faith in our discernment, we can take what parts of the information works for us and then, without any self-judgement or self-questioning, we can depend on our integration of the new material. It isn't a state of all-knowing; it is a state of unshakeable trust. When we are Sovereign, we are our own best counsel.

Sovereign Loyalty is a state of devotion which comes from a complete and unconditional trust in the self. This is not the loyalty of expectation or force. This is faith for someone or something else born from the absolute faith we have in ourselves.

Spectrogram is an active method of determining how we feel about things. Created as a tool for Psychodrama, this type of group measurement can be applied to many situations. With an invisible line on the floor, participants are asked to stand at different places on the line which represent different values. The line is usually valued from 0-100%. Participants are then asked a series of questions and directed to answer by standing at a place on the line which best reflects how they feel. The goal of this type of physical involvement is to integrate the body in order for more authentic responses to come forward.

Spirit Guides are the beings or entities from the Spirit World that come forward to offer information, support, guidance, and love to the Human Realm. We may or may not be aware of these Guides, and how we receive what they offer is unique to each individual.

Spirit World is the realm of Spirits. This level of consciousness is available to all and many are able to see, hear, know, and translate the vibrations of this world. Interactions with this realm may feel different than those of our physical dimension; however, when dedicated to the Greatest and Highest Good for All, we can become very adept at connecting to and communicating with the Spirit World.

Spiritual Activist is someone who actively utilizes their Divinity in order to inspire change. This can look and feel very different from traditional activism. A Spiritual Activist may dedicate their energies to prayer-work, healing, sacred ceremonies, leading by example, and other ways of engaging the Soul. This is activism as a spiritually dedicated practice. It involves raising awareness through deep and profound love and is never violent or aggressive to the self or any other.

Spiritual Ascension is the process of raising our vibration in order to live in pure, unconditional love and bliss. There are many different paths to Spiritual Ascension, and it is up to us to find the best fit. The path is also a very unique experience and there is no prescribed or 'right' way to follow it. We create the path as it simultaneously creates itself.

Spiritual Awakening is a process of opening our awareness. Usually defined by an initial event or a series of events, this process can take a moment, a lifetime, or many lifetimes. The phases or stages of this awakening are unique, as are our interpretations. Often described as more of a journey than a destination, once *awake* there is little chance of going back to sleep… you can't *unknow* what you *know*.

Spiritual Consciousness is the layer of our awareness that connects us to Source, Center, and all of life throughout all time and space. This 'oneness consciousness' reminds us that we are Divine, holographic replicas of the highest vibratory energy. We can connect into this level of consciousness at will and allow our pure Spiritual energy to come forward. As energy follows thought, an intentional connection is all that is needed to channel this consciousness into our lives and relationships for guidance, wisdom, healing, support, and love.

Spiritual Integration is the blending process that our bodies, hearts, and minds ask for when incorporating all that we are learning, re-remembering, and integrating as a result of our Spiritual education. Downloading, activating, and turning on all of this information can be overwhelming to our human systems. Just like any big event, taking time for everything to settle in can be really beneficial. Even though it can be hard not to, rushing or forcing this can be counterintuitive. Not only for the integration process but for the entire experience. The seeking, the guidance, the work, the shifts, the trust, the work, the faith, the surrender, the work (have I mentioned work yet?) can all become compromised if we don't give ourselves the time and space we need.

Spiritual Journey encompasses our travels as we walk the path toward enlightenment. We may not even know we are on a journey, or we could be consciously seeking for a lifetime. No matter how we walk the path or where our travels take us, everyone's Spiritual Journey is unique and valid.

Spiritual Maturity is the level of authentic maturity we apply to all aspects of our lives and relationships while we learn, grow, transform, and up-level our consciousness through ascension. This is an unconditional choice to walk the high road every moment of every day. Does it mean you have to be perfect? Not at all! We are human, remember…. What it *does* mean is that every situation is an opportunity for growth. Judgement, hate, exclusion, disingenuous behavior, jealousy, miserliness, and anything else that keeps us attached to suffering has to be owned, honored, and dealt with when you are working toward Spiritual Maturity. What then comes in to take their place are purer states of love, acceptance, surrender, honoring and transforming feelings, generosity, compassion, and bliss. These shifts begin in the inner landscape of our relationship to ourselves and then flow out into the outer realms of our daily exchanges and interactions.

Spiritual Realm is the Realm of Spirit. Described by many teachers as Dimensions above our own Third Dimension, these higher vibratory Realms are host to myriad beings and entities devoted to humanity. The Highest of the Realms, which is described in a linear way so that our human minds can better understand, is Source. This is the energy of Mother-Father God, the Creator/Creatrix of all of life throughout all time and space. As we open our awareness to communicate and interact with this Realm, we also open to receive the love, guidance, and wisdom available.

Spiritual Resonance is when you connect deeply to someone or something and feel a sense of spiritual kinship. This kinship can inspire you toward Spiritual Activism or toward meditative prayer as all sorts of dynamics can be born out of this resonance. What can make this type of resonance different than others is that it is *spiritual*, which means it is based in Spiritual Maturity. Instead of agendas or expectations, these types of resonant relationships only vibe with gratitude, appreciation, and love.

Spiritual Self is the part of you that is dedicated and open to your enlightenment. There are many different parts that go into making each one of us our beautiful and unique selves. This is the part that keeps us focused on our path of ascension and transcendence.

Spiritual Sobriety is the sober perspective we have regarding our true spiritual natures. We are human beings having spiritual experiences, and we are also spiritual beings having human experiences. There are going to be hiccups! Where Spiritual Sobriety comes in handy is in the awareness and grace that we afford ourselves when we create the bumps in our own roads. No one is perfect; that isn't what this is about. But with a sobering up of our spiritual outlook, we allow no distractions to cloud our vision when it comes to a genuine assessment of ourselves and our Spirituality. When we are in alignment, we know. When we are out of alignment, we know. However, we can become unclear – almost intoxicated – with the illusion of our Spirituality when we distract ourselves from the truth. Becoming Spiritually Sober can illuminate those distractions, recalibrate us back to our path, and offer the softness and compassion needed for gentle redirection.

Spiritual Wisdom is the knowledge we have regarding our Spirituality and is unique to each of us because we are unique beings. This is the wisdom that pours forth when we put our hands on our hearts and ask to *know*. Some of us may study for a lifetime to have this Spiritual Wisdom. Some of us may never even crack a book. There is no gauge or hierarchy here… only an unconditional devotion to walk the walk and talk the talk of Soul's Guidance in everything we do.

Subconscious is the part of us that lies in the periphery of our conscious awareness. Not hidden like the Unconscious, the Subconscious is sort of like the program running on your computer that you forgot about. It's like, "Oh yeah! I forgot I started that update… *that* is why my computer is running like this!" Influencing everything from our actions and feelings to our beliefs and how we remember the specifics of what has happened to us, this part of our awareness is powerful! And from what I have learned, the more we love it into being, the more in alignment we feel. So… here is the thing… although we aren't really aware of it, the subconscious mind is *always* aware of us and is *always* listening to everything we say. Negative self-talk… guess what? The Subconscious doesn't understand that you are just having a moment. It believes you when you say mean things to yourself. It doesn't really understand time either. When you are constantly running the script of, "I'll be happy when….," it gets programmed to believe that you aren't capable of being happy *now*. Here is another doozy to think about: it doesn't process the negative. What that can mean is that when your words are rooted with lots of won'ts, can'ts, and don'ts… instead of hearing, "I won't eat that chocolate cake," "I can't go out tonight," or "I don't believe in self-sacrifice," your subconscious hears, "I eat that chocolate cake," "I go out tonight," and "I believe in self-sacrifice." Lastly, it doesn't know how to separate daydreams from real life. So, dream BIG, Sister! And watch out for those punishment fantasies where you get mired in the mental muck of 'everybody hates me, think I'm gonna eat worms.' When you tell your subconscious that life sucks, it will believe you. It will also influence those things that I mentioned above - actions, feelings, beliefs, and memories – to create a reality that supports what you tell it. Have I mentioned how powerful it is? Tell your subconscious that life is glorious and that you are a phenomenally beautiful creature - inside and out - deserving of the highest levels of abundance and bliss. Do it. It will believe you and act accordingly to manifest those beliefs. Pretty soon, you won't be able to help yourself. You will believe it, too!

Subconscious Belief Systems are the beliefs running just below the lines of our conscious awareness. They can direct behaviors, choices, and overall ways of being and because they lie just under the radar, we typically don't know they are there or how powerful they can be. With some support and dedication, we can uncover these subconscious or 'core' beliefs and work to recalibrate them so that our lives are more in alignment with what we want. Hidden biases, fears, perceived limitations, and ideas around our self-worth are usually what's kicking around in this space. If we become aware of these things, we can work to discover their roots. With much gentleness and compassion we can then begin to rewrite these belief systems, moving them from the unseen to the seen.

Subtext is what we *really* mean when we say the things we say. It is the emotion underneath the words. In acting, the subtext - not the lines - is authentic. It fuels the motivation so that we can attain the objective of the scene. In our daily lives, subtext can equal authenticity as well. For instance, think of the phrase *I don't know*. You can say it with genuine concern, frustration, disgust, terror, etc. Subtext creates disingenuous dialogue when we aren't genuine about *what* we've just said and *how* we've said it. For example, you say "I don't know" with the subtext of frustration, and the person you are talking with questions it by saying "Why are you so mad?" You can honor your authentic feelings – the subtext – and admit your frustration, or you can hide your authenticity underneath the surface of the words and claim, "I'm not mad. I just said, *I don't know!*" Like many things, Subtext can be beneficial or not depending on how it is used and implemented.

Sympath is someone who feels the feelings of another so deeply that they become connected to the situations and outcomes related to the other person's experiences in ways that prove to be dysfunctional to their own well-being.

Sufi is someone who practices Sufism, a mystical aspect of the Islamic religion. Through a variety of ways, Sufis seek the truth of Divine love through the direct experience of God.

Suspension of Disbelief is a theatrical term which asks that the audience suspend what is not believable in order to have an entertaining and hopefully cathartic experience.

Symbiotic is the long-term, interdependent biological interaction between two dissimilar organisms. When optimal, this type of relationship is mutually advantageous and cooperative. Symbiosis was taught to me from the context of an infant in utero. Within the mother's body there exists a Symbiotic relationship between her and her unborn child.

Symbol Key is a legend or a key for a map that uses small pictures to represent the different features. Oftentimes grouped together in a corner, the smaller symbols are drawn to look like what they represent. For instance, a triangle may be used to represent a mountain or wavy lines may be used to represent a body of water.

Symbolism is a way that we attribute additional meaning to things. Through objects, interactions, art, literature, locations etc., we create invisible connections so that the things in our lives symbolize deeper sentiments and feelings.

Systemic is a way of viewing things which takes into consideration the fact that everything affects everything else. When thinking systemically, we take into account that nothing happens as an isolated event. Situations, interactions, family dynamics, and even feelings are all part of a larger *system*. Like the cogs in a machine, each individual piece comes together to create the whole. When a piece becomes compromised or begins acting differently, it affects the total functioning or outcome.

~ T ~

Talisman is a meaningful object believed to possess certain beneficial energies. These objects need only be important to the person in possession of them for their powers to be felt and appreciated. Throughout time, human beings have sought to imbue physical items with this energy of good fortune. This is evidenced by our devotion to certain mystical and sacred objects and antiquities.

Talking Stick is an ancient and indigenous tool for support around effective and authentic communication. A stick is not necessary as it can be any type of hand-held object that is easy to pass and share among participants. This object, imbued with the intentions of the group, creates a code of conduct in that only the person holding the object is talking while the others respectfully and quietly listen. Traditionally used in large council meetings and sacred circles and ceremonies, Talking Sticks are used today for all sorts of exchanges. Schools use them for teaching classroom etiquette. Therapists use them with clients. Parents use them for family discussions. Passing the stick back and forth in order to respectfully give and receive can create a dynamic of sustained impulse control, reduced emotionality, and strengthened connection. It is no surprise that Talking Sticks are believed to possess magickal powers for peace.

Teachable Moments are the large and small moment-to-moment interactions which happen continuously throughout our day. They become teaching tools when we open ourselves to the offered lessons that these moments present. Hard, easy, euphoric, or devastating… we experience situations that provoke these feelings all the time. Is it realistic to think we will stop and learn from them all? No. But, it can be really advantageous to identify and learn from some of them. One of my teachers says, "Life is a modern-day Mystery School." What I think she means by this is that every moment of every day has the potential to teach us something: to make us better, to show us the way, to calibrate us toward growth. It's just up to us to notice and make these moments *teachable*.

Tele is a concept created by Jacob Moreno and is implemented in his experiential method of group psychotherapy called Psychodrama. It translates to mean the *"unknown knowing."* I say it's our intuition. Sometimes we can't really know *how* we know *what* we know. Yet, it is the faith in our own inner wisdom, our *Tele*, that supports us to continue on our quest of self-discovery; in essence, it is what we are all doing here. Earth School *is* a process of discovery. Once we trust in our Tele, it can touch every aspect of our existence. It can juice our imaginations, energize our relationships, recalibrate our belief systems, and ground our Divine Purpose. We *know* what we *know*. Full stop.

The Physical, Emotional, Mental, Personality/Ego, Soul and Spiritual Bodies are our layers of consciousness. We filter information and express ourselves through these levels of our human awareness, and each has a unique energetic vibration and specialized brand of wisdom. You can connect into them, feel them, and ask them to come to balance. I was taught that each of our Chakras also have these layers. When I do an Esoteric Healing Treatment, part of the initial Aligning and Attuning process is to connect into each Energy Center and allow them to come into their Highest Conscious Expression for each of the levels. For instance, I connect to the Ajna and ask it to come into balance on the Physical, Emotional, Mental, Personality/Ego, Soul, and Spiritual Levels. For me, each level *feels* different and each possesses its own consciousness.

Theatre of the Oppressed is a form of socially and politically active theatre created by Brazilian visionary, Augusto Boal. This powerful form of community-based art uses theatre as a tool for education, activism, conflict resolution, transformation, awareness, and social change. Practiced widely by community organizers, teachers, cultural leaders, and others dedicated to enriching the lives of all, this wonderful artform is both entertaining and inspiring.

Theta Healing is a beautiful modality of transformative healing created by Viana Stibal. According to her official website, "This method is a technique of meditation and a spiritual philosophy that is not specific to one religion, but recognizes all of them with the aim to become closer with the Creator. This training is meant for the body, mind, and spirit and gives one the ability to get rid of limiting beliefs and live a life full of positive thoughts through prayer and meditation." I have been reading her work and it is phenomenal! Check it out for yourself: www.thetahealing.com Maybe we should ask for a special Soul-to-Sisterhood cohort? Who is interested? I'll check it out for us.

Third Dimension is the realm of the physical, our Human Realm. This is the tangible, quantifiable world where things can be materially proven. The Third Dimension can also refer to our visceral senses of what can be seen, heard, smelled, tasted, and felt.

Third Eye is the Ajna Chakra. My teacher taught me that our Ajna is actually the physical manifestation, or external point, of our Third Eye. That's kind of a groovy concept: an invisible, external, energetic manifestation of an invisible, internal, energetic body... both which happen to be complete powerhouses of intuition, high vibration consciousness, and connection to the Divine within. Hmmmmm... can you say "Faith?" We have to have faith - and a lot of it - to open these energy portals and let the love flow through. Perhaps that's what all the *fabulous* fuss is about. When we are grounded in faith and peacefully rooted in our inner knowing, we feel spacious, connected, and free. We can intuit guidance from the Higher Realms. We can walk in Soul's Guidance without fear or judgement. We are interconnected to all of life. There are no questions regarding importance, for every living thing is an essential thread in the fabric of our Universe. When this happens, our Third Eye is *open*! Some schools of thought believe that the biological spot of the Third Eye is the Pineal Gland. I have been taught that the Hypothalamus and Pituitary Gland also correlate to the Ajna. When the Ajna and Third Eye are open and the etheric body is grounded, tethered, calm, and loving, all layers of our consciousness – the Physical, Emotional, Mental, Ego/Personality, Soul, and Spiritual – can work together in harmony.

Throat Chakra is the Major Energy Center located anatomically at the throat. Associated with the color blue, the Throat Chakra is also referred to as the fifth Chakra. Not visible to the eye, this Energy Center can be sensed, felt, and *known*. The Throat Chakra is the seat of our 'Mental Body.' This means that all of our belief systems - *especially* the ones we have about ourselves - reside here. If you believe deep down that you don't deserve love or happiness, the address for those belief systems is going to be: 1234 Throat Chakra Boulevard. When we hold those deep-seated beliefs, it compromises our truth and our ability to communicate that truth. My Esoteric Healing teacher used to describe these higher elemental truths as, "The truth with a capital T!" If the *'truth with a capital T'* is that you are a Divine Being and you are running a contradictory belief system that you don't deserve love, what is going to happen? Are you going to effectively communicate the message to yourself and others that you are Divine and unconditionally deserving of love, bliss, and transcendence? Probably not. The Throat Energy Center also allows us to express another Divine Birthright: our creativity. Do you see how all of these are connected? Our Belief Systems, authentic communication, and creative expression interlink together and the hub for this is the Throat Center. When you believe that you are worthy, you communicate this through your words and actions and others believe it, too. From this empowered place, your creativity can flow unencumbered. Why would you question it? You are in the flow, baby, and you are a Creatrix of the first order! However, think about the other side of this equation. You don't believe that you are worthy. You communicate this message, which is not *really* your 'truth with a Capital T,' but you believe it and so does everyone else because your actions and words are so convincing. Therefore, everyone acts accordingly and supports the belief system both consciously and unconsciously. Before you know it, life becomes a mirror reflecting the message back to you. In this scenario, how authentically creative do you feel? Chances are, not much. The Throat Chakra is really important! Believe in yourself, speak your truth, and express your creativity. Start small and see what happens.

Thymus is a gland in our body that plays a large part in both the Endocrine and Lymphatic Systems. Anatomically located just above the Heart Chakra, this gland is a powerhouse of Immune System support. Large in infancy and decreasing in size as we age, the Thymus produces T-cells that protect the body from certain threats such as viruses and infections. Optimal Thymus health and functioning can equate to long-term health and functioning.

Toxicity relates to something that is poisonous for our bodies, hearts, minds, and Souls. It is easy to figure out if something is toxic for our bodies. We can read labels and research the ingredients of foods, cleansers, products, etc. However, when it comes to the toxicity of our relationships, that is a different story. Someone or something may be toxic for *you* and it may have nothing to do with *them*. I have a few people in my life who I genuinely love… but being around them is not good for me. I fret and worry. I read into what they do. I judge myself for what I did or didn't say. It is exhausting! I know these relationships - as they are right now – are toxic for me because I have growth to do around what is causing me to fall out of alignment. However, when I heal or transform what is going on, that doesn't necessarily mean I jump back in the saddle. At that point, I can decide what is best for my highest good and stick to it! No more questioning and waffling. No more energy leakage. Nada. It is what it is, and the neutrality lets me know that I have shifted whatever it is that needs to be shifted. That is one example, but toxicity can stem from a whole host of other things. The way you talk to yourself, what you put in your body, belief systems, behavioral patterns, environments, the information you digest from media or other sources of entertainment, and basically any other way in which you relate to your world that *isn't* in alignment with your Greatest and Highest Good and the Greatest and Highest Good for All – *that* is toxic.

Transitive is energy that creates more energy and is basically the fancy word for 'pay it forward.' When something becomes transitive, we share it… not because we are going to make money or experience personal gain, but because it is in our hearts to share for the greater good. Writing this book, I have lit thousands of candles with the intention that Soul-to-Sisterhood becomes a transitive tool for healing, transformation, self-love, and Sisterhood. What are you creating today that can be transitive? It can be a smile, a hug, a compassionate ear, or an open heart. From this perspective, everything is big and important, because - once it becomes transitive - it becomes cumulative.

Transmitters are things that carry, generate, and send out energy. We are transmitters. We transmit guidance from our Higher Selves into decipherable messages that our human minds can understand. We transmit the larger Divine Feminine energies of compassion, understanding, mercy, stillness, and caregiving into our lives and relationships. We transmit large amounts of stamina and endurance - even when bone tired - so that we can have at least a few precious moments with ourselves.

Transmute is to change or alter in form, appearance, or nature the original of something into something else which is usually considered to be of a higher form, appearance, or nature. Many ancient alchemical tales spoke of Transmuting base metals into gold. In the context of the Divine Feminine, Transmutation is something regularly carried out by all levels of Feminine Consciousness. The Great Mother Goddess or Source transmutes antimatter into matter to create life. The Feminine Archetypes transmute our psychic, emotional, physical, mental, and spiritual abilities into the creative cycles of birth, life, death, and renewal. Our Mother Earth transmutes everything into everything else, sustaining all of life - her children – so that we may continue to be nurtured, loved, and cared for. The incarnate Female transmutes a fertilized egg into an embryo, water into breast milk, pain into tears, plasma into amniotic fluid, and pleasure into sexual lubrication. Forget gold… what we've got going on is way more valuable!

Trauma is anything that compromises our physical, emotional, mental, and/or spiritual safety. Because we process and perceive our environments and experiences differently, what is Traumatic for one person may not be Traumatic for another. Additionally, an experience may be traumatic at age five but not at age fifteen because we have a greater capacity to make sense of our experiences. All of this can become very influential in our lives due to our unique psychological, physiological, and emotional responses to Traumatic events. The overwhelming stress of Trauma can make us feel scared and isolated while leaving us to regularly question our safety and security. Trauma pushes us to the limits of our coping abilities. When this happens, interpreting, processing, and integrating the events, feelings, and consequences of a Traumatic situation can be very difficult.

Triangulation is a psychotherapeutic concept created by Dr. Murray Bowen. This is a way of conceptualizing our relationships and looking at their functionality based upon how the information and energy flows between the parties. Typically in a Triangulation we look at relational dynamics in terms of threes because this gives us the image of a triangle. We triangulate people and things to avoid feeling our authentic feelings, to avoid directly addressing what is going on, and to avoid making the needed shifts to accommodate what it is that we *do* want, need, and desire. When we triangulate, we stay in a haze of 'status quo.' Take infidelity for example. Things happen within our intimate relationships that are not in alignment. It can be for a million different reasons, but suffice it to say that in this scenario our needs are not being met. Instead of addressing this with our partners (and with ourselves), we pull somebody else in to help us stabilize the situation. The pain of our unmet needs seems insurmountable, so we instigate another relationship – the affair - to help us bear the load. The rub is… it never really works because we never truly address the issue. Triangulation can occur in all sorts of other scenarios, too. Somehow when hurt or upset, we've been convinced that it is much easier to talk to someone else rather than the person who has caused the upset or hurt in the first place… as if that is going to solve the problem. (It won't.) Take this for instance: a friend hurts your feelings by being late for lunch. Instead of being vulnerable with her and telling her how you feel, you call another friend and trash talk your late lunch date. You've now triangulated the friend you called and used her to alleviate your upset. Triangulation can create deceptive bonds of intimacy between you and either what or whom you have triangulated. It is also deceptive in that you aren't being authentic about your feelings and discussing them with the person directly involved. Perhaps the ultimate deception of Triangulation is that we believe that the triangles will last forever. They might last for a while, but they do so at a cost. Think of Triangulation with a substance. Or how a parent might triangulate a child in the attempts of fulfilling a void within the parental dynamic. These concepts are wonderfully helpful to know about and understand… but when it comes to the practical application of implementing these concepts in your life? If you need it - and be honest with yourself about this - get some assistance to help you navigate the triangles. There are so many great clinicians out there. Maybe even find a Marriage and Family Therapist. We are trained in this kind of stuff and having neutral support from a professional can be really beneficial.

Trigger is a stimulus from our environment that somehow mimics a piece of a previous traumatic event. It can be tangible like a sound, smell, or image. It can also be a feeling or thought brought on by a situation that *feels* familiar. Or it can be the actual *type* or *quality* of the feelings or thoughts brought on by a particular situation. With these endless possibilities and the limitless traumatic situations that we may have experienced, Triggers are infinite. When they affect us, depending on our experiences and protective factors, a biological response system can get switched on. In some cases we may be consciously aware of what is triggering us, yet in other cases we may not. Even though the original event is not recurring, because of the Trigger, our brains think that it is, and react accordingly. Then the Nervous System comes online and the responses of fight, flight, or freeze usually follow.

Typecast is a way of categorizing or stereotyping someone or something. In the professional acting world, someone who looks like a certain character might be repeatedly cast in those types of roles. When this happens, one can internalize the characterizations as actual personality traits. This can also be true outside of the professional acting world. When someone is frequently told that they embody certain characteristics, the features of the *role* that they are perceived to be playing can become part of their identity.

Ujjayi is a type of breathing. Often used in yoga practices, Ujjayi breathing is said to calm and relax the mind. This way of breathing has been called by many names and can offer a range of benefits. Perhaps its most defining feature is the sound. If you aren't familiar with it and find yourself in a yoga class with a bunch of Ujjayi breathers, it can take you by surprise. But once you get the hang of it, you can't really help but experience the benefits, no matter how windy your downward dog gets. (Although, that image can lead us into a whole other topic on the potential melodies of a yoga class.) Anyhoo… to try it, keep your mouth closed and take big, deep in-breaths and out-breaths that are equal and controlled while constricting the back of your throat so that your breathing makes a whooshing or a white-noise-like sound. Some people say it sounds like snoring. I prefer the whole water concept, but you do you. Talk to Sister Goddess, Kery, to lean more. She is amazing and one of the most knowledgeable yoginis out there. www.keryhelmer.com

Unconscious is the part of our mind that we are **unaware** of and is different from the conscious mind, of which we are aware. These hidden parts of us influence our lives in majorly bigtime ways. Freud, the original big papa of the Unconscious mind, likened it to the part of an iceberg floating underneath the water. Have you ever seen pictures of icebergs? What lies beneath is about a ga-gillion times bigger than what is seen above the surface. What does that mean? Well, according to him, that huge, unknown underbelly is the primary source of all of our human behavior. Mic drop, right? Basically, what his theory postulates is that all of our feelings, motives, and a lot of the stuff that makes us *us* (including the good, the bad, and the ugly) we aren't even freaking aware of. What?!? OK, let's just say that the *how* and *what* of how we extrapolate and interpolate what we experience in our lives gets stored in a big, mysterious filing cabinet. Tightly sealed, but not impenetrable, this filing cabinet is able to send out smoke signals. How *conscious* we are of that filing cabinet is a direct result of our self-love, self-understanding, and self-awareness. How much dedication we've allocated to figuring ourselves out, and that includes *all* of our processes - functional, dysfunctional, and otherwise - will depend on how significant those smoke signals get to be in our lives and relationships. Will they choke us, fog things up a little, or just add a nice incense-like aroma to the house? Fortunately, we *can* be conscious of this, but it might take some work. There are many great resources out there for exploring the unconscious mind. Books, programs, dreamwork, therapists, etc., are all at our disposal. It is up to us to *consciously* decide how we explore this, why we want to go deeper, and what to do with the rest of that iceberg.

Unconscious Response Systems are the reactive biological, physiological, emotional, and mental processes in place that help us navigate our lives. Sometimes they are awesome! Working away without the need for our conscious input, we can kick back and trust that they will keep the old ship in ship-shape. Other times they aren't awesome at all. Due to the negative experiences and traumas that have been visited upon us in our lives, these response systems can kick start a whole sequence of events that feel anything but optimal. When it comes to the emotional and mental aspects of how these sequences progress, different interventions can be implemented to slow things down and eventually rewire the system all together. Time, attention, and detail can boost this rewiring process, and fantastic resources spanning from trauma informed care and healing trauma wounded neurobiology to habit change science, tapping, yoga, martial arts, psychotherapy, aromatherapy, etc., are available to support us as we go about revamping these response systems.

Universal Energy Field is the energy around and within every living thing, which includes every internal and external interaction, response, thought, and feeling. It can also be understood Multi-Dimensionally as this field applies to the energy and energetic connection throughout all time and space… even beyond that which defies our human capacities for understanding.

Universal Law is the concept that there are Universally accepted principles which govern our lives. These Laws are thought to be ancient and have been applied to the human experience in the hopes of creating more love and joy for all. The number and names of Universal Laws vary, however some of the more well-known Laws are: The Law of Divine Oneness, which emphasizes the interconnectedness of all things; The Law of Attraction, which teaches us that *like* attracts *like*; The Law of Relativity, which posits that there is no good or bad, only neutral; The Law of Cause and Effect, which is better known as Karma; The Law of Rhythm, which is the law of cycles and patterns; The Law of Polarity, which demonstrates that everything has an opposite; and The Law of Perpetual Motion, which tells us that everything is always changing.

Upper Paleolithic is the time period from about 40,000-10,000 years ago. This time in human *her*story was ripe with Goddess Worship, Matriarchy, egalitarianism, stunning works of art, life-sustaining ideologies, and high cultural standards. Relationships were considered sacred during this time period and social roles were not defined by gender. These very wise and ancient people recognized that all life came from the body of the female, therefore Feminine qualities and characteristics were highly respected and valued. Whether it be the body of Mother Earth, the incarnate female, or Feminine characteristics such as caring, non-violence, and nurturing - our early ancestors and ancestresses cherished all aspects of the Feminine from the physical to the spiritual.

Value System is what we believe in. It is our integrity and ethics and the moral ideals which we express through our choices, behaviors, and lifestyles. Values tend to shift and change throughout a lifetime. They also vary from person to person.

Verse is the part of a song written to support the chorus. Typically done with more specific storytelling via the lyrics, the verse of a song is sung multiple times with a consistent melody.

Venerate is to revere something and hold it with great respect and honor.

Vibration Scale is a way of measuring the energy we sense or feel around things like emotions, situations, interactions, people, places, etc. Energy is. Believe it or not, that is a full sentence. Our linear minds want to attribute value to things because that is how we categorize and make sense of our worlds. Yet energy isn't necessarily good or bad (which I know is a huge leap from what we are so used to hearing in that almost everything we experience is now described as either having positive or negative energy). Energy is information. How we experience that information can be used to create a road map for what we want and a Vibration Scale is the symbol key for how to get us there. Take emotions for instance. If we are feeling anger, which is said to be at a number of 150 and we want to get to a feeling of acceptance at 350, how do we make the 200-point jump? Use any numbers that you want. The Vibration Scale values that work for me may or may not work for you. The numbers aren't nearly as important as the awareness that they inspire. Human beings are goal driven creatures. However, sometimes due to all that we have going on, we can't figure out a way of making these goals a reality. By having a scale, it can make things seem more tangible and attainable. Different Mental Health modalities utilize this concept as well. If you are feeling fearful and I ask "What can you do to feel peace?" chances are you are going to say, "I don't know!" Yet if I say, "OK, you are feeling fear and on the Vibration Scale that is 100. What is keeping you from being at a 90 and what will it take to get you to a 110?" Now we have a process in place for identifying the strengths and skills that have gotten you to where you are. We also have a rough idea of what needs to happen for you to make those incremental jumps to get to 600… or, peace. See how it can be really beneficial to view things in this way?

Vices are behaviors that aren't helpful to us and our growth. They can be dysfunctional, toxic, and downright dangerous. These are the things that we keep hidden because on some level they splinter us away from our authenticity and truth. Seldom do we really face the potential or actual fallout of our vices. It is much easier to remain foggy, therefore keeping up the subterfuge of not *really* being responsible. Yet our vices are the rocket fuel that force us away from our true nature: our Divinity. If you are in a relationship with someone and they support these types of behaviors, ask yourself, "What is in it for them?" Yes, the old saying 'misery loves company' applies, but it may be more than that, too.

Virtues are the beneficial traits that we all inherently possess. These are our values and characteristics which make us dedicated to the Greatest and Highest Good for all living things. You are virtuous, just by being you! Add in a nice healthy dose of self-love and you've got it goin' on, Sister. Here is the rub – Virtues, or what generally constitutes being *virtuous* - have been highjacked by those in power and given the right to wield the moral authority stick. If you can, leave that old stuff by the curb and trust your internal Virtue barometer on this. You *know* what is right, just, and good for you. You know what the high road is. You do! Trust your gut, heart, and Higher Self.

Voila' is the French word for 'there it is' or 'done.' Pronounced vwa-*lah*, this whimsical word can be used in all kinds of fun and magickal situations and scenarios.

Waning Moon is the fourth Lunar Phase of Mother Moon's monthly cycle. Diminishing in our night sky, this phase correlates to the Archetype of the Enchantress, the season of Fall, and the Luteal or Pre-Menstrual phase of our Menstrual Cycle. As she slowly and methodically fades, her vanishing light reminds us to begin our human process of pulling-in. This is so that we, too, may slow our output in order to stop and rest. Shadow comes forward during this time and when welcomed, the membrane between the worlds can become thin, allowing our deep psychic talents to be felt and expressed through both our waking and dreamtime states. During the Waning Moon Phase, we may feel irritable and tired or wild and unruly. These wise feelings help us to create the secure solitude and deep quiet needed for replenishment and regeneration. Mother Earth and Mother Moon know the cyclical wisdom of dying (Winter) and going dark (the Dark Moon), so that they may be born again anew. However, this is a process with cycles to be regarded and respected. The season of Fall and the Waning Moon both prepare us - with their beautiful gifts of turning leaves and enclosing darkness – for the lovely death of silence and seclusion. Once we succumb and surrender, our minds, bodies, and spirits are reborn… fresh, energized, and ready to begin again.

Warrior is one of the four main archetypes of the Mature Masculine presented in the book, *King, Warrior, Magician, and Lover: Discovering the Archetypes of the Mature Masculine* by Robert Moore and Douglas Gillette and my interpretation of their work is what follows. The Warrior is born from the full actualization and expression of its Immature counterpart, the Hero. Warrior energy is present within us all and can offer benefits when honored and acknowledged. Unfortunately, due to fear and misunderstanding, hiding or turning away from our Inner Warrior tends to be a more culturally accepted process. Yet the Warrior is clear minded, respectful of death, committed to duty, and wise when it comes to surrendering personal desires in deference to the larger pursuits of loyalty and obligation. Giving us the strength to survive, the nobility to endure, and the courage to defend what is right and just for all, this Archetype is dedicated to causes much greater than mere warfare. Due to equal reverence for both life and death and the fragility which exists between them, the Warrior pours life force energy into all endeavors.

Wasband is the Urban Dictionary term for ex-husband.

Waxing Moon is the second Lunar Phase of Mother Moon's monthly cycle. Growing in our night sky, this phase correlates to the Archetype of the Maiden, the season of Spring, and the Follicular or Pre-Ovulatory Phase of our Menstrual Cycle. Brightly emergent and developing into her full potential, the Maiden Moon reminds us that we, too, are ripe, fresh, and ever-evolving beings. As you notice her bold, productive sensuality, gauge what you are feeling in relation to your own independence, radiance, and ambition. She is active and energetic, and the Waxing Moon Phase may bring out your desire to flirt freely, playfully collaborate, and enthusiastically experience life. Able to increase in intensity and brilliance, this self-confidence and determination is present *due* to the Lunar Wisdom offered through the preceding death of the Dark Crone Mother Moon. She glows *because* of the cycle, not in spite of it. During her phase, birth and rebirth are ours for the taking. Set intentions. Create goals. Conceive ideas. Use the stamina she offers to harness your own wild combustions. Plant your seeds and then settle in to watch them grow.

Way-Shower is a person who leads by example, literally *showing the way* with their actions. This is not the leadership of lip-service, pontification, or condescension. This is a true embodiment of walking the walk and talking the talk. Always seeking how to best be '*of-service*,' a Way-Shower will oftentimes lead silently, looking for no outward titles, accolades, or influence. All of the empowerment, authority, and praise needed for them is derived from within.

White Privilege is the invisible ease and (somewhat) unconscious experience of the safety, security, and societal representation that benefits white people. White privilege is not racism; however, its very existence is a byproduct of the long-term and historical implications perpetuated by racism and prejudice. White Privilege does not mean that white people have not struggled. It means that their struggles are not solely due to or exacerbated by their skin color. This type of privilege cannot be earned or bought, many of the disparities are covert, and the resulting cultural expectations for BIPOC (Black, Indigenous, and People of Color) are systemic, unrealistic, and in the worst cases, criminal. This book could arguably be guilty of White Privilege. I address it in the introduction, and I will again here. Only 14% of the women featured in the chapters of this book are not white. I feel pretty ashamed about that and it's something that I have thought and talked about a lot over the book's creation. I don't have answers or excuses. I only have an open heart. I want to listen. I want to learn. I want to help inspire change and healing. My Divine Purpose is co-creating space for healing within so that we can heal our bloodlines and our relationships. I understand that my reasoning for lack of diversity may seem paltry, lame, and insignificant in the light of all that we have going on in our world right now. How else would I have that perspective without 'white privilege', right? But Sister, you've got to trust me, too. I'm not saying meet me in the middle. I'll walk farther. I'll hold the candle to light our way. Yet, we've got to do this together. I'm a good listener. I'm a good storyteller. Let's create. In Sisterhood, let's birth a new way of being that transcends what we've been doing so far. For me, that spark of life begins with self-love. Once we can do that - really and truly love ourselves - then we can really and truly love others. Let's do these 180 Sacred Play Suggestions as a collective and see what comes next. Most writing on white privilege directs white people to implement their awareness into action. This is my action. My dedicated, Divine action. I am a humble student. I admit, I am going to mess things up and need your guidance. I am also your Sister. We are equal. We need each other. In my vision, we dance around the fire, wildly pounding the injustices of the past into our Great Mother Gaia so that she may take our wounds, transform them, and rejuvenate us all – *every living thing* - with joy, connection, peace, equality, and love.

Withers is the ridge between the shoulder blades on a horse. This is where a horse's height is measured.

Wounded Healer is a concept that the healers among us have been likewise wounded and that is what draws them to the service work of healing. Where the *role* gets restrictive is in the belief that the healer must sacrifice of themselves in order to continue with the noble vocation of offering support and comfort to others.

Wounded Self is the part or parts of us born out of the cyclical response patterns created to survive the recurrent wounds and traumas of life. For instance, you may have a protective side that is very destructive in its attempts to avoid reexperiencing painful situations. In its efforts, this part of your Wounded Self may cause huge dysfunction in your relationships. Perhaps you also have a caretaking side that will support someone or something else to your detriment. This part of your Wounded Self may sacrifice your emotional and physical well-being in order to avoid feeling the deep pain of loss. What about the part of you that says, "Forget it, just give up," when things get intense or difficult? This part of your Wounded Self may find that being the victim is easier than being the *victor* because of the constructed illusion that the victim is not to blame when things don't go as planned. Our Wounded Selves have been created for good reasons. Through them we have been able to find our coping mechanisms. In this way, no matter how toxic, they have kept us alive. Yet sometimes their work is done and we don't realize it is time for them to retire. Shaming and blaming ourselves for their creation is akin to throwing gas on a fire. These aspects of us must be lovingly seen and heard in order to be securely transformed and released. This is deep work, so be sure to get the support you need. Allowing our wounded parts the opportunity for rebirth can be amazing and profound. The healing can take time, but you are worth it!

Wounding Patterns are born from the hurts and traumas that we repeatedly experience in life. To deal with these recurring wounds, response patterns are created. For instance, if you were frequently judged and criticized as a child, a harsh internal critic might be created as part of the Wounding Pattern. This internal critic can provide the illusion of control or power in the present as an attempt to address what used to feel uncontrollable and disempowering in the past. Your own internal critic is familiar because it is what you are used to. However, it can be even more effective in delivering the judgment and criticism that you experienced as a child because now your adult-self is in control. To relieve the pain of the past, a cycle is created whereby we efficiently dish the pain out to ourselves. Within this pattern, we can become even more severe and cruel in the effort to establish control (nobody can hurt us worse than ourselves) and power (we are the punisher; therefore, we are in charge). The sad part is, we aren't in control or powerful at all within these types of patterns. That is only the illusion of the cycle. The real empowerment and release come from consciously working to heal the original wounds in order to transform the Wounding Patterns so that we can choose different options to address our pain. When these different options become integrated into the pattern, the relationship we have to ourselves can become more loving, forgiving, and compassionate. This can ultimately create a new cycle that is more aware, functional, and pleasant.

Xochiquetzal (pronounced cho-chee-ketz-*ahl*) is an Aztec Goddess of Mother Earth, flowers, plants, and love. She isn't mentioned in the text, but she is amazing and we didn't have a word for X. X is a pretty Divinely Feminine letter when you think about it… especially as it relates to the 'X' in the whole 'X meets Y' scenario. In addition to representin', this dynamic powerhouse of Femininity is also a guardian of creativity, Sacred Sexuality, Birth Magick, and fertility. Oh, and get this, she is also besties with Mother Moon. If you often notice butterflies and birds hanging around, that's just Xochiquetzal coming in to offer support and guidance. Her other name is 'Flower Feather.' I. can't. even. *Flower Feather*? Could she get any cooler?

Yantra is the physical expression of a Mantra and represents the Divine in geometrical form. Thought of like a machine, the aspects of a Yantra combine together to create a focused piece of artwork. This art - whether an image hanging on a wall or the actual architecture of a Sacred Temple - is designed with the intention of enhancing our human capacities for enlightenment, peace, and bliss.

Yoni is the Sanskrit word often used to describe our vaginas. The word can translate to mean several different things - womb, vagina, Source, abode, or Sacred Place - and is the external symbol of the Goddess, Shakti Energy, or the Divine Feminine. The imagery and symbolism associated with the word is that of regeneration, divinity, procreation, power, creation, and bliss.

Your Angels are the Angels around you, such as Guardian Angels, Archangels, and Angelic Guides. Always close by to help, they can offer us love, protection, guidance, and spiritual counsel. You may or may not be aware of them, but our Angels are dedicated to our authenticity, integrity, Spiritual Maturity, and living a life that reflects the consciousness of our Highest Selves.

~ Z ~

Zero Point Field is a new(er) scientific paradigm which suggests that the formerly thought to be empty space or vacuum which permeates the Universe is not merely vacant but an immense field of vibration that is not only alive but also conscious. This space is now being explored for its vast energy potentials and connection to what was formerly labeled as paranormal phenomena. Healing, intuition, communication with the unseen world, multi-dimensionality, clairvoyance, telepathy, and lucid dreaming are all getting some street cred thanks to this quantum perspective. The Zero Point can offer explanations as to the way energy is received, exchanged, and processed. It can also connect us deeper into the concepts of oneness and non-duality. It posits that everything is alive, everything is energy, and no place exists where there is not consciousness, therefore we are all aware and we are all connected. My definition is grossly oversimplified. Should you be interested in exploring it further, there are some great resources out there. I just got Lynn McTaggart's book, *The Field: The Quest For The Secret Force Of The Universe.* From my limited understanding, it seems like a great place to begin the quest. At the very least, knowing that there is a limitless supply of conscious energy out there - energy that *we* are a part of - can help us all feel a little less tiny in our very big world.

All proceeds from the Soul-to-Sisterhood Book, Oracle Cards, and other products will go to

Stella's Fund.

Stella's Fund is a benevolent fund created to offer financial assistance to primary custodial parents during the legal proceedings of divorce, child support, and child custody agreements. Those different processes can take years, and if the non-custodial parent chooses not to financially support their children, in most states there is little legal ramification to do so until the proceedings are finalized. Even then, it is challenging to seek financial support or reimbursement from the non-custodial parent. Stella's Fund is inspired by my sister, Stella, and her experiences of being a single mom to three children with little financial support from their father. My hope is that together we can support families and create enough inspiration and awareness around this issue that legal policy follows suit. This Fund is set up to support Moms, Dads, Grandparents, and other family members who are primary caregivers. All proceeds from the *Soul-to-Sisterhood* Book and Oracle Cards will go to support Stella's Fund.

***Soul-to-Sisterhood* Namaste**

From My Highs to My Lows
From My Bliss to My Shame
When I Am in That Place in Me
And You Are in That Place in You
Which is Every Moment of Every Day
We Are One
We are Never Alone

Namaste

I Love You

CPSIA information can be obtained
at www.ICGtesting.com
Printed in the USA
LVHW020150210723
753086LV00016B/842